POWER AND THE BLACK COMMUNITY

CONSULTING EDITOR: **PETER I. ROSE**
Smith College

POWER AND THE BLACK COMMUNITY: A READER ON RACIAL SUBORDINATION IN THE UNITED STATES

EDITED BY **SETHARD FISHER**

University of California, Santa Barbara

RANDOM HOUSE / NEW YORK

Library of Congress Catalog Card Number: 79-92834

Designed by Charles Kaplan

Manufactured in the United States of America by Kingsport Press, Inc., Kingsport, Tenn. First Printing, 98765432.

To Mitsu, Ian, and Gregor
—who, when they are older, I'm sure will agree that it was worth the effort
—and to Myrtha

Contents

Introduction

The needs, interests, and dispositions of the black American community are unmistakably the focus of national attention. The mass media throughout the country increasingly employ black spokesmen and black themes. "Soul" music, "soul" food, and other elements of black culture once confined to the black ghettos now appear to be increasingly infused into the "mass culture" of American society. Natural hairdos are in vogue and are often worn by blacks and whites alike. Colleges and universities throughout the country are faced with demands for "black studies"—courses which will deal more factually and compassionately with the role of nonwhites in American society. Viewed in terms of recent history, these are new developments on the American scene. They suggest some degree of relaxation of the rigid racism that has characterized most of the history of the United States.

Although advancements toward ending racism are readily detectable, symptoms of a formidable resistance to black equality are also evident. A congressional committee is currently "investigating" the Black Panthers, a black youth group with a combination of reformist and revolutionary aims in the interest of black American equality. The National Youth Alliance, a youth group in support of segregationist George Wallace, has, in alliance with the Nazi Party, spawned a national network of local groups with the reported intention of resisting the development of black studies programs on the various college campuses. In addition, this group appears to nurture virulent anti-Semitic and anti-Catholic sentiment and to include in its program resistance to the interests of these groups as well.[1] What has been termed "white backlash" is currently in evidence in city, state, and national politics. In addition to this, abrasive encounters between blacks and whites continue at a high frequency. All of which means that gains achieved by black Americans are thus far fragile tendencies rather than firmly set institutional patterns. These tendencies may prosper and substantially curtail the rampant racism of the country, but not necessarily. The fate of such social tendencies has several alternative possibilities.

One way of characterizing this new emphasis on black culture and prosperity, using the formal language of analytic sociology, is as one major component of an incipient social movement. The issue of black American equality shares this position with other powerful pressures for social change, for example, the "youth movement," the anti-Viet Nam movement, the movement for "women's liberation." The current effort toward black American equality must be seen as part of a more general movement toward patterns of social relations clearly inconsistent with, and abrasive to, the traditional white Anglo-Saxon, Protestant, racist status quo. But the fate of these efforts is not a foregone conclusion. In some instances, as in the case of women's suffrage in the United States, pressures for social change prosper and lead to lasting re-arrangements within a social system. In other instances, as with drug addiction, prostitution, and organized crime, such pressures are chronically frustrated and contained within circumscribed limits. They may remain perennial matters of public debate and controversy. Sometimes, however, pressures for social change are completely destroyed, leaving little, if any, noticeable impact on the status quo; the fate of the Communist party in the United States is a close example. Our knowledge of racism must include ways and means by which the current stirrings in the interest of racial equality can be nurtured and made to lead to enduring change.

Several prominent and influential scholars have propagated the idea that racism is generic to the human condition, and thus that subordination and conflict based upon race are unavoidable. As a loose coalition, the nineteenth century European sociologist Ludwig Gumplowicz and his disciple Gustav Ratzenhofer could be classed with the influential American scholars William Graham Sumner and Franklin Giddings. Common to this group of scholars is the assumption of the inevitability of racial subjugation and, of course, the dominance by whites over other racial groups that were thought to be inferior.[2] These men, and the image of racism they cast, were part of a tradition in social thought known as social Darwinism, a tradition under which racism has flourished. As Hofstadter pointed out, Darwinism "was put in the service of the imperial urge" and the Darwinian mood "sustained the belief in Anglo-Saxon racial superiority which obsessed many American thinkers in the latter half of the nineteenth century."[3] They operated on widely different assumptions from those which have guided the selection and preparation of materials for this volume. I have elected to focus on social systems and social institutions and the means to power within them, rather than on human nature, as an analytic starting point. In doing so there is the underlying assumption that knowledge of the genesis and dynamics of racism within a configuration of social institutions is possible and is a necessary condition for constructive change.

Perhaps brief mention should be made of biases and underlying assumptions. There exists the view that commitment, or partisanship, with reference to a problem under study is improper for disciplined scientific study. Certainly much has been written on both sides of this issue. Opposition to this viewpoint has been expressed with eloquence by such scholars as Bronowski,[4] Polanyi,[5] and Boulding,[6] among others. My own resolution of it is largely in keeping with the following comments by Robert Lynd:

> Nature may be neutral. . . . But culture is not neutral. . . . The social scientist's reason for urging the neutrality of science in such a world of bias is understandable, but it has unfortunate results that curtail heavily the

capacity of social science to do precisely the thing that it is the responsibility of social science to do.

Nobody questions the indispensability of detachment in weighing and appraising one's data. But in other respects, as a matter of fact, current social science is neither as "neutral" nor as "pure" as it pretends to be.[7]

There would be no social sciences if there were not perplexities in living in a culture that call for solution. And it is precisely the role of the social sciences to be troublesome, to disconcert the habitual arrangements by which we manage to live along, and to demonstrate the possibility of change in more adequate directions.[8]

Clearly, racism can be found in several areas of the modern world. This volume, however, deals mainly with the United States, and for a special reason—the movement against racism is perhaps as widespread here as in any other of the major racist countries. Racism in the United States, as Myrdal some time ago characterized it, is a dilemma in the American mind. On the other hand, in Rhodesia and the Republic of South Africa racism is rapidly progressing as a norm of social development. Resolution of the problem in the United States, I believe, will have clear and decisive implications for its demise throughout the civilized world. If the struggle against racism persists with sufficient endurance, intelligence, and humaneness, the necessary institutional and associated attitudinal changes in the interest of racial equality can be achieved. But these cannot be expected without major and perilous confrontation, without relaxation of entrenched beliefs in white superiority, without constructive channeling of the understandable rage within the black community, and without acceleration of political and economic gain by black Americans. It is in the interest of getting on with these developments that the present volume is assembled.

Part I is a brief introduction to the rise of institutionalized racism in the modern world, a background from which its emergence in the United States must be seen. Part II is basically analytic. It is designed to provide a theoretical framework within which the rise of racism historically can be accounted for and its current dynamics in large part explained. Parts III and IV deal with gains and losses historically and more recently among black Americans. Together they show the relative stability of black Americans within the social structure. Part V is a reminder that black subordination has not been quietly accepted. Rather, it has elicited a variety of resistance efforts. One form of black resistance to racist oppression has been a continuous effort to realize political gain. This issue is the subject of Part VI. The final part deals with tactics and strategy for realization of racial equality within the United States.

---

[1] Though this group is newly formed, reports on it have been made by Drew Pearson. See his column in the April 21, 1969 issue of the *San Francisco Chronicle*. In addition see the June 25, 1969 issue, page 21, of the *Berkeley Gazette* for a report

on more recent activities of the National Youth Alliance. A report on an allied group in Cairo, Illinois, called the "White Hats" recently appeared in the June 23, 1969 issue of the *San Francisco Chronicle*, page 1.

[2] This is not suggested as a definitive group. See Richard Hofstadter, *Social Darwinism in American Thought* (Boston: Beacon Press, 1944), pp. 172–173; I. A. Newby, *Jim Crow's Defense* (Baton Rouge: Louisiana State University Press, 1965); Floyd House, *The Development of Sociology* (New York: McGraw-Hill, 1936).

[3] Hofstadter, *op. cit.*, pp. 172–173.

[4] Jacob Bronowski, *Science and Human Values* (New York: Harper & Row, 1965).

[5] Michael Polanyi, *Science, Faith, and Society* (London: Oxford University Press, 1946).

[6] Kenneth E. Boulding, *The Impact of the Social Sciences* (New Brunswick, N.J.: Rutgers University Press, 1966).

[7] Robert Lynd, *Knowledge for What* (Princeton, N.J.: Princeton University Press, 1948), p. 182.

[8] *Ibid.*, p. 181.

I. European Preparations and Legitimations

Often the ideologies and social habits of one's own time are accepted as immutable features of a natural order. Therefore a given set of social arrangements, no matter how inconsistent they may be with declared values, will probably be rationalized as inevitable. A careful consideration of the developmental, or historical, aspect of ideologies and social habits, however, begins to dispel this view. It permits us to see the emergence and development of social institutions as well as their demise and disappearance. This vantage point allows an assessment of conditions instrumental in the development of social institutions, and thus the exercise of some degree of desirable control over them.

The social, economic, and political subordination of black people in North America, all of which constitutes racism, is often thought to be a natural and invariant condition. This view is propagated by various religious groups. It appears in antiquated storybooks of elementary and high school students. It is found in the writings of a variety of determined proponents of white superiority. Yet the institution of black subordination that came to exist in the United States—slavery and its aftermath—did not always exist here, and its form has changed considerably over time. Racism was very much a part of social, political, and economic developments on the European continent. Part I of this volume deals with aspects of the origins of modern racism as a social institution. Certain developmental features of Western European society are presented, followed by a discussion of an individual who played a major role in the historical development of modern racism.

1. The Cultural Residue of European Preparations and Legitimations

Much of the current literature on racism in the United States, with some notable exceptions, fails to place the problem within the context of the developmental history of Western European society. This shortcoming severely limits the range of relevant information about the problem, thus restricting possible means for its resolution. The major social systems of the Western world have been, and continue to be, characterized as capitalistic. This fact has had an important bearing on the development of racism in the modern world. A residue from this European development was carried over into the "New world" and had a most important influence on the subsequent formation of racism and its consequences in the United States.

SETHARD FISHER

The scientific literature of the seventeenth century reflected a rather uniform belief that mankind comprised one species. Although physical differences were known to exist among different peoples, such characteristics were explained as being the result of climatic or geographic factors. Mankind was generally viewed as part of a unitary whole. As Montagu explained:

This was not because the known varieties of man were so few that they suggested no problem requiring solution, but principally, it would seem, because the conception of the "superiority" or "inferiority" of "races" which followed upon the increasing exploitation of other peoples had not yet developed to the point of creating a "race problem" and thus focusing attention upon the significance of the variety presented by mankind. It was not until the economic relations of Europe and the peoples of other remote countries had given rise to the necessity of defining their place in nature that attempts were made to deal with this problem, and such attempts naturally first appeared toward the end of the eighteenth century.[1]

This realization is damning evidence for the many supporters of a racist viewpoint whose justification rests on its presumed naturalness and inevitability. It means that racism as a widely practiced and official doctrine within social systems, that is, as a social institution, has a fairly recent history and that its rise can be seen as related to concomitantly emerging social conditions.

Colonialism as a set of social practices employed by Western European nations to exploit the rest of the world, capitalism as a dominant form of socio-economic organization, and liberal individualism as its accompanying ideological rationale are the main historical sources of modern racism. Brief consideration of these sources will show that racism is not distinctively American in origin, though the United States today is surely one of its major strongholds.[2] Its growth and intensity in the United States cannot be understood without reference to these historical factors, which, of course, are of equal importance as background to the development of racism in its other major citadels, such as Rhodesia and the Republic of South Africa.

The economic relations of Europe with the peoples of remote countries, to which Montagu referred, reflect an exploitative pattern of dominance by European countries over most of the world by force, commonly referred to as colonialism. Countries throughout the world, including North and South Africa, were colonized, and patterns of trade and commerce were established designed to enrich the colonizing countries. Along with the economic exploitation of the subject countries went patterns of association and cultural definitions that placed colonial subjects in an inferior and demeaning status vis-à-vis their dominant white captors. Intellectuals and academicians in the "mother" countries busily elaborated rationalizations and ideologies to justify these patterns of economic exploitation and presumed superiority. Their formulations (for example, the Aryan Myth) today remain highly influential components of the perspective shared by racists in many parts of the world. Heilbroner characterized the effects of colonialism on the subject peoples in the following way:

The result was in many ways a catastrophe for the colonial world. Into its primitive circulation of life a powerful and dangerous virus was ejected with terrible effect. It turned millions of traditionally self-sufficient peasants into rubber-tappers, coffee-growers, tin-miners, tea-pickers—and then subjected this new agricultural and mining proletariat to the incomprehensible vagaries of world commodity fluctuations. It uprooted ancient laws and gave in exchange Western justice, whose ideas disrupted local culture by striking at the roots of time-honored traditions and customs. It brought young men to the universities of Europe to learn the thought of the West, and then placed them in jail when they went home to preach it. Immense strides were made in orderly government, but it was government over and not of the people, and almost invariably concerned with preserving the prerogatives of feudal overlords rather than extending new privileges to the masses beneath them. Colonialism, even in its most missionary moments, never succeeded in seeing the "natives" as equals, and it usually simply took for granted their irremediable inferiority.[3]

In a recent paper on colonialism in Central America, Richard Frucht discussed what he called "internal colonialism." [4] He reminded us that colonialism was accompanied by a distinctive pattern of socio-economic relations, that is, capitalism, which generated the subordination of dark-skinned peoples throughout the world. He aptly pointed out that superiority and inferiority also operated *within* the colonizing countries themselves. So inhumane were the by-products of the capitalistic form of socio-economic organization that, not surprisingly, movements and philosophies of opposition emerged. These arose within the capitalistic countries themselves as well as among the colonial peoples who were also victims of capitalistic domination and exploitation.

The nineteenth and twentieth centuries comprised the period of the greatest growth and influence of capitalism in the West. Most of Europe and North America developed industrial capitalistic systems, each devoted to the leadership of the business world from which were taken their purposes, values, and techniques. Internal opposition to capitalism began to appear with the organization of labor in the various Western countries, though it was not until 1917 that a major government, that of the U.S.S.R., was headed by a labor party. By 1959 France, Germany, the United Kingdom, Norway, Sweden, and Denmark were among the countries which had at least once placed a labor government in power, though they had been strongly committed to capitalism in 1913.

Meanwhile, in the colonial world, the spread of militant nationalist movements increased rapidly. Most of the formerly colonized peoples gained independence after World War II. These events symbolize the growth of a rather formidable challenge to capitalism. Of this growth, Heilbroner said recently:

. . . over the larger part of our history, we have faced a future in which our own form of economic organization, capitalism, was the triumphant and dominant form of economic and social organization in the world. This is no longer true. Today and over the foreseeable future, traditional capitalism throughout most of the world has been thrown on a defensive from which it is doubtful that it can ever recover. As a capitalist nation we are no longer riding with the global tides of economic evolution but against them. [5]

Before the industrial revolution, attitudes about economic activities in most of the Western world were regulated by official doctrine of the Church. Although the Church did defend certain inequalities of social position among men as ordained by God, the Church fathers of the Middle Ages were overwhelmingly opposed to preoccupation with worldly goods. Medieval economics meant a body of moral precepts designed to assure the proper administration of economic activity. Avarice was condemned, and individuals were expected to subordinate their interests in material advancement to their needs for salvation.

Saint Augustine feared that trade obstructed man's search for God. The idea that no Christian should be a merchant was widespread. Nevertheless, the Church had to deal with the issue of trade, though it was essentially considered an evil, for it appeared that it could not be abolished. Thus Christian scholars proposed certain justifications for trade. They advanced the idea of the just price, a price which was seen as inherent in the value of articles of commerce, and a price which, if departed from, resulted in an infringement of the moral code. Condonation of trade, then, depended on whether the exchange that was offered was just, that is, whether that which was given and that which was received were of equal value.

The hold of the Church on economic thought and activity declined with the growth of a money economy, and official Church doctrine gave way to new ideological developments.[6] There arose with the Reformation a new orientation to economic activities and a legitimation of new forms of economic enterprise theretofore prohibited. When Adam Smith wrote his *Wealth of Nations*, three centuries had elapsed since the Middle Ages. During this time a pattern of thought had developed that laid the essential basis for ideas and activities that are today accepted as legitimate in our economic and social life. Trading, commercial, and business activities acquired legitimation in this new view, and individuals involved in such activities attained a new, elevated status and increasing power. Colonialism flourished with the expansion of trade. Profit-making and exploitative patterns of trade and commerce became characteristic of economic life in the Western capitalist world; the new respectability of such activities was provided by a series of intellectual and academic efforts emphasizing individualism and laissez-faire government as proper, natural, and inevitable. These efforts prompted the growth of liberal individualism, which may be seen as the philosophical foundation of contemporary capitalism.

Among the political philosophers of the sixteenth, seventeenth, and eighteenth centuries, such as Machiavelli, Thomas Hobbes, Sir Francis Bacon, and John Locke, there emerged a view of man and society which was at odds with the older theological view. The social-contract theory and the concept of a sovereign authority as elaborated by Hobbes[7] were fundamentally individualistic. Hobbes recognized the individual impelled by self-interest as the basic unit from which to begin his argument. Locke, too, emphasized individual self-interest as the motivating force of conduct. But for Locke:

. . . it was not the medieval Church, nor Bacon's king of divine right, nor yet Hobbes's superhuman Leviathan that was to make an orderly body out of the individual atoms. . . . Its [liberalism's] basis was property, acquired by industry and reason, and entitled to the security which the state could give. Here is a philosophy suited to the new conditions of the economy. It is the embodiment of the victory over the Middle Ages. . . . it is a symptom of the decline of state power which commercial capital had created at an earlier stage of its war against feudalism. . . . It is the first chapter of liberalism, the philosophy of triumphant capitalism.[8]

Liberal individualism also encompassed the belief that social institutions were part of a natural order. Smith saw human conduct as based on six motives: self-interest, sympathy, the desire to be free, a sense of propriety, a habit of labor, and the propensity to truck, barter, and exchange one thing for another.[9] He suggested that each person was the best judge of his own interest and should be able to pursue his goals in his own way. If not interfered with, he would attain his maximum advantage and contribute to the common good in doing so. It was held that self-interested action by the individual conflicted in no way with the good of all.

Smith's view rapidly became influential, because his theory appeared to be in the interest of the industrialists of the time, who wanted to remove restrictions on trade and on labor supply. Industrialists had not as yet acquired widespread respectability, and Smith's theory championed their goals. By glorifying self-interest, analyzing it within a naturalistic framework, and depicting it as inevitably leading to the welfare of all, Smith accorded legitimation to the new industrial capitalists. The pursuit of profit was no longer considered selfish. The belief that trade and commercial activities were sinful and beneath the dignity of man declined.

A century later the social casualties of this liberal individualistic philosophy—the poor, the unemployed, the destitute—were so numerous that the laissez-faire policy to which it gave rise was questioned, challenged, and to some extent counteracted. The rise of the labor movement in Western Europe was a direct response to the new industrial capitalism and the liberal individualism that made it possible.[10] But laissez-faire policy was stoutly defended through new and influential derivative formulations by recurrent waves of intellectual and academic spokesmen. Herbert Spencer in England and William Graham Sumner in the United States vociferously carried on within this tradition now enfolded in a new guise—social Darwinism.

According to Richard Hofstadter:

The most popular catchwords of Darwinism, "struggle for existence" and "survival of the fittest," when applied to the life of man in society, suggested that nature would provide that the best competitors in a competitive situation would win, and that this process would lead to continuing improvement.[11]

The social Darwinist view provided a means for interpreting the social condition of the unfortunate by-products of the new industrial capitalism within the individualistic and naturalistic viewpoint. The condition of the poor, the unemployed, and the destitute was seen as produced by their own inherent imperfections rather than by social conditions resulting from conscious policy decisions. Attempts at social reform in their interest were regarded as efforts to remedy the irremediable and as interferences with the wisdom of nature, which would ultimately lead to social degeneration.

Thus Darwinian ideas, as interpreted by Herbert Spencer, William Graham Sumner, and others, served to reinforce at a later time ideas laid down by Adam Smith and a range of spokesmen whose major purpose had been to prevent governmental interference with the interests and activities of business, industry, and commerce. One main function of this ethic was, and continues to be, to divert attention from social policy and policy makers as the primary sources of social injustice and social inequality.

The historical developments just sketched out have left a cultural residue within the United States of America that renders the country uniquely unsuited to grasp the full meaning of the current race conflict. The human ravages of colonialism, capitalism, and the legitimating ideology of liberal individualism have generated pressure for social change throughout the world, just as did the despotic rule of feudal lords at an earlier time. Formerly colonized African and Asian peoples increasingly demand autonomy from the ravages of the capitalistic world and desire a prominent role in the making of their own destiny and the destiny of the world at large. This attitude has inflamed nonwhite peoples throughout the world, who have long been sensitive to their colonial status. They are no longer content with the colonial image of themselves as inferior, subordinate, and subject people. Yet the historical exploitation of blacks by whites, and especially the abhorrent forms that it took in the United States, has resulted in a lack of understanding by whites of this new motivating force. The generally fearful, punitive, and niggardly response by whites to the current efforts for freedom and equality by black Americans clearly reflects this. This lethargic and malevolent attitude often is perpetuated by intellectual, academic, and scholarly interpretations of the race problem. These treatments suffer from the shortcomings of the liberal individualistic heritage from which, in large measure, they derive.

The varying adaptations of intellectuals and academicians to the system of power within their own society are a constant source of dissension among them. Some scholars develop an ability to view their own period of time from a distance and sometimes provide insight into it not likely to come from more accommodating observers. These voices assess the reality of their time in a way that allows for no dignified peace with it. Thorstein Veblen and C. Wright Mills are representative of this type. On the other hand, there are those who are basically committed to the dominant official values of their society but maintain a watchdog function on the agents and strategems of power. They adopt as a primary concern the incongruence between the stated values of the society and the areas of reality that grossly diverge from these values. They do not, however, question society's values in a fundamental way, and, in fact, generally celebrate their society and its dominant motifs. They are joined in this by another category of intellectual, whose basic adaptation is noncritical. I take Clinton Rossiter and David Cushman Coyle to be representatives of this group. In particular, *Parties and Politics in America*[12] and *The United States Political System and How It Works*[13] reflect this attitude. This does not mean that these individuals fail to use critical judgment and analytic acumen; rather, they largely promote the ends of dominant power interests instead of critically assessing the platitudes and mechanisms of those who rule. In the United States academic and intellectual treatment of the race problem has largely been the product of the latter two varieties of scholarly work. These characteristic approaches to the race problem by American intellectuals and academicians continue to cast it within the liberal individualistic framework, thereby disguising aspects of it which are important to the current crisis.

The first major thrust toward freedom and social equality made by the American people was not intended to include black Americans. Nevertheless, Jefferson's words strike no less a reponsive chord among black men now than they did among white men in 1776:

We hold these truths to be self-evident, That all men are created equal, that they are endowed by their creator with certain unalienable rights; that among these are life, liberty & the pursuit of happiness; that to secure these rights governments are instituted among men, deriving their just powers from the consent of the governed; that whenever any form of government becomes destructive of these ends, it is the right of the people to alter or to abolish it, and to institute new government, laying its foundation on such principles and organizing its powers in such form, as to them shall seem most likely to effect their safety and happiness.[14]

Even as Jefferson wrote the Declaration of Independence, black American men, women, and children were writhing painfully under a slave system which Tannenbaum has characterized as the most cruel system known to the world.[15] In 1774, just two years before this esteemed document was written, we find the following petition to the governor of Massachusetts and the legislative assembly, reflecting a black American reality highly incongruent with it:

. . . That your Petitioners apprehind we have in common with all other men a naturel right to our freedoms without Being depriv'd of them by our fellow men as we are a freeborn Pepel and have never forfeited this Blessing by aney compact or agreement whatever. But we were unjustly dragged by the cruel hand of power from our dearest frinds and sum of us stolen from the bosoms of our tender Parents and from a Populous Pleasant and plentiful country and Brought hither to be made slaves for Life in a Christian land. Thus we are depriv'd of every thing that hath a tendency to make life even tolerable, the endearing ties of husband and wife we are strangers to for we are no longer man and wife than our masters or mistresses thinkes proper marred or onmarred. Our children are also taken from us by force and sent maney miles from us wear we seldom or ever see them again there to be made slaves of for

Life which sumtimes is vere short by Reson of Being dragged from their mothers Breest. Thus our Lives are imbittered to us on these accounts. . . .[16]

This contradiction cannot be understood adequately without an awareness of its connection with the capitalistic and liberal individualistic heritage of the society itself and the colonialist heritage of Europe. This essential point makes understandable many current efforts, by scholars and laymen alike, to view the race problem as caused by black people themselves. Brief attention to this misleading emphasis is important, for a social Darwinist interpretation of the current race problem invites repressive and powerful retaliation by whites, since it suggests that the race problem, in the last analysis, is created by its victims.

Oscar Handlin, a student of ethnic groups, referred to Negroes as "newcomers" to New York City, ignoring evidence which he himself presented regarding their early presence in that city and the subsequent influx of other ethnic groups. Handlin sought to "comprehend the situation of present-day New York ethnic groups," for doing so

. . . may isolate and define the problems involved in the adjustment of immigrants to urban life; it may also supply a basis for assessing the earlier consequences for the community of the presence of groups comparable to those which now trouble it.[17]

Handlin went on to discuss the situation of Negroes and Puerto Ricans, comparing and contrasting it with that of other ethnic groups and describing aspects of the history of each group. He then gave vent to a rather oddly inappropriate, but characteristic, bias:

Giving due regard to what has actually developed, it is still true that the Negroes and Puerto Ricans have not matched the richness and breadth of the communal life of the earlier immigrants.

Poverty alone was not enough to explain the difference. Although these people occupied the lowest level of the occupational hierarchy they were no worse off than the eastern and southern European immigrants of fifty years ago. Indeed, the prosperity of the period since 1940 actually gave the Negroes and Puerto Ricans an earning power superior to that of their predecessors, both in actual and relative terms. The comparative well-being provided them with the means that might have been used to develop a rich associational life had they wished to do so.

They did not. Complex reasons generated among them a sense of apathy toward communal organization that has played an important part in shaping the character of their adjustment.[18]

Handlin suggested that the failure of Negroes and Puerto Ricans to develop a "rich associational life" is a major part of the explanation of why their well-being in the system now is so grossly divergent from that of the earlier immigrants. Yet in considering housing in the suburbs, Handlin appeared to fear the very kind of communal solidarity which at another point he has sought:

In the suburbs they [Negroes] encounter physical and social barriers. There is little good low-cost housing there; and they must seek to penetrate as individuals rather than in a concentrated group. That leads to a clash of ideals between the desire of the whites for homogeneity and the aspiration of Negroes for equality.[19]

The important and revealing implication of Handlin's advice is that the Negro's desire for and right to equality must not challenge the white desire for racial homogeneity. Handlin's former consideration apparently takes priority over the latter. This is, of course, the standard white view of how Negroes might best realize some achievement in American society. It is, however, precisely the movement toward black solidarity (evidence for which Handlin has failed to note) that generates resistance by whites, even among paternalistic spokesmen for dark-skinned minorities.

A more recent discussion of the Negro in New York City by Nathan Glazer and Daniel Moynihan was also heavily weighted with emphasis on the failure of Negroes to develop strong internal structures within the black world, as did earlier immigrant groups. They commented on the failure of the Negro to develop a class of entrepreneurs and the importance of such a class to the welfare of black people. In addition:

Perhaps another way in which Negroes differed from European immigrant groups was that they did not develop the same kind of clannishness, they did not have the same close family ties, that in other groups created little pools for ethnic businessmen and professionals to tap. . . . The Negro family was not strong enough to create those extended clans that elsewhere were most helpful for businessmen and professionals.[20]

Finally:

In the end, the most important factor is probably the failure of Negroes to develop a pattern of saving. The poor may have had nothing to save, but even those better off tend to turn earnings immediately into consumption.[21]

The fact of internal weakness and absence of certain forms of social organization among black Americans is not an issue to be contested. The issue of *why* this condition existed, that is, slavery and the cultural devastation resulting from it, should be the main concern. The implication of the Glazer and Moynihan work is that Negroes really had a margin of freedom for making skillful and rewarding use of their miserable condition, a use which would have made a significant difference in their position within the social structure of New York City. Their failure to utilize this opportunity is viewed as a matter of their own more-or-less willful choice, and thus their current low and degraded social position is largely a matter of their own failure as a social group.

The current direction of the civil rights movement in the United States ought to be highly instructive to students of race and ethnic relations. The move toward black solidarity and prominence is a highly threatening phenomenon to most white Americans—a fact that appears to be under-estimated by these scholars. As pride, social gain, and solidarity accrue in the black American community, fear, envy, and efforts at retaliation develop among many white Americans to restrain and neutralize this movement. And the origin of this interplay is racism, that is, the fear and hatred by whites of blacks deeply ingrained in the American institutional structure.

To stress the structural weaknesses of the Negro world is to misplace emphasis. It causes a mistaken assessment of the nature of social organiza-tion within the black community and puts the main cause for the plight of the black American back in the black community itself. This serves to mitigate and disguise the horror of America's crime against black people and to shield its racism from its own eyes.

Not only is this point of view as presented by its spokesmen harmful to the cause of Negro betterment, but there is also issue to be taken with certain of their presumed facts. It is incorrect to suggest that there has been hardly any development of formal and informal organizations and associa-tions within the Negro world. Such organizations have a long history and include a banking group of which Frederick Douglass was a member, educational associations stimulated and headed by Booker T. Washington, and other groups. Recent studies of community power structure do not report an absence of organization within the Negro community, though they do show important limitations on the amount of power that these communities are able to exercise with reference to the total community, that is, a forceful racism.

In a 1959 study by Barth and Abu-Laban that deals with the power structure of the Negro sub-community, the authors described an identifi-able leadership structure consisting of people engaged in business activity, social work, teaching, etc. In the sub-community of Pacific City they detected twenty-seven organizations in the Negro community and found that the most influential of these have a pronounced political content in their programs. Yet ". . . if power within a community derives in part from high positions in its economic or political structure, it is clear that none of these leaders in Pacific City's Negro sub-community possessed such power." [22]

Floyd Hunter, in his study of Regional City, also found an extensive degree of formal and informal organization within the black community, as well as a corresponding lack of power.[23] A similar finding is reported in Myrdal's voluminous study of the Negro community.[24] It is questionable whether the degree of internal organization of the black community should be given such prominence. Hunter's study of Regional City clearly shows the devastatingly negative response by whites to Negro efforts to achieve social and political equality through black solidarity.

A description of unofficial alliances by white citizens with officials for illegal resistance to black American gain in the South comes from excerpts from a student newspaper. This is further illustration of the mechanics of black repression.

The National Guard Armory was full of 1500 white citizens in their Sunday best eating barbecue chicken at $1.50 a person. By their looks the audience was made up of middle class business people, professionals, and well-to-do farmers, with their wives and children. It could have been a Monday night church dinner anywhere in the United States. But this dinner wasn't just anywhere; it was in Selma, Ala., and the people were there to hear Ross Barnett.

"Thank God that I am an American, a Southerner, a Mississippian and a charter member of the Mississippi White Citizens' Council," yelled Barnett. The former Mississippi governor was the main attraction at the Dallas County White Citizens' Council annual membership dinner and rally.

Barnett told them that, "The secret purpose of our enemies is to diffuse our blood, confuse our minds and degrade our character, that we may not be able to stand against the wiles of the devil.". . .

Barnett's speech called for the maintenance of racial purity and the Anglo-Saxon Protestant heritage, and continuing the fight against the communist conspiracy. He seemed unaware of recent happenings in the county. Barnett talked in generalities. The people were looking for answers to their problems; they wanted specifics; Barnett talked of "Americanism.". . .

In order to "prevent" Negro activity the Council must maintain control over the whole community. This means not only keeping Negroes "in line" but also whites who do not follow its program.

The white group maintains this control through two means: organization and infiltration. It organizes the white leadership of the community to effect its program, because in order to be effective the Council must eliminate all dissent from whites.

Most whites in the community are members, but not all by choice. "There is great social and economic pressure to join. Not to join would be socially lowering and economically damaging," a local white woman said. . . .

The Council most effectively works through individual members who are in important business and government positions. It uses these people to put its program into practice.

Thus the Council's power lies not in the organization but through its individual members who wield an enormous amount of personal power by virtue of their positions in the community.

The Dallas County Council is a prime example of the group's power: its leadership reads like a who's who of the community.

The president of the Dallas Council is former mayor Chris Heinz. Heinz is a member of the board of directors of the Chamber of Commerce and a leading insurance and real estate man. He is also a good friend of Col. Richard Ault, commandant of Craig Air Force Base, one of the major "industries" of Selma. Ault has, on numerous occasions, refused requests by SNCC to declare Selma off limits to air force personnel.

It was Heinz who introduced Barnett at the rally. He told the group, "We can no longer afford the luxury of the attitude of 'Let George (Wallace) do it.'

"We have arrived at a point when all white people must stand up and be counted," the former mayor said. "We must lay aside personal differences and stand united as one unbreakable unit."

The Citizens' Council has its legislative leader in State Senator Walter Givhan of the 30th district which includes Dallas and adjoining Lowndes County. The Senator is past president of the Alabama Association of Citizens' Councils and a member of the executive committee of the Dallas Council.

An even more potentially powerful man than Senator Givhan is Earl Goodwin. Goodwin is owner of two large firms that hire over 300 people. He is former vice-president of the Chamber of Commerce, "Manufacturer of the Year," and a member of the white group's executive committee. Much of his power lies in the fact that he is a member of the State Democratic Executive Committee. Through this office Goodwin controls much of the patronage in the area. "Earl Goodwin is being talked about as the next candidate for governor," a local white reported.

(One of the heads of the Democratic Committee is the infamous Eugene "Bull" Connor of Birmingham. Connor, who is originally from Selma, is Democratic National Committeeman from Alabama. He appeared at the Barnett rally and was heard to comment, "I've belonged to this county (Citizens' Council) since it's been organized.")

The Dallas unit, which might be called a model Council, has an executive committee that includes the president and past president of the Real Estate Association, the past president of the Exchange Club, members of the board of directors of the Chamber of Commerce, the County Engineer, the Clerk in charge of issuing county licenses, a member of the Dallas County Court of Revenues (the governing body of the county), the director of recreation for the city of Selma, and a member of the State Agriculture Department.

The Council must keep control of the white community in order to control the Negro community. And control of the Negro community means holding down registration. Although it was organized in November 1954 as a reaction to the Supreme Court school decision, the Council has concentrated its activities on the prevention of Negro registration.

The Council's method of controlling Negro registration is reported by Hodding Carter in *The South Strikes Back*. The Mississippi editor says,

> During an organizational meeting of the Citizens' Council . . . in Dallas County . . . one speaker said: "We intend to make it difficult, if not impossible for any Negro who advocates desegregation to find and hold a job, get credit, or renew a mortgage."

Economic control is established by having officers of the four major banks on the executive committee. This group is headed by H. P. Hansell, Associate Vice-President of the City National Bank and Treasurer of the Citizens' Council. A SNCC worker reported, "Businessmen who do not support the White Citizens' Council cannot make loans at the local banks."

That the Council has been effective can be seen from a Justice Department report that states: "From June 1954 . . . through 1960, a Board of Registrars of Dallas County, registered more than 200 white persons and only 14 Negroes.". . .

Finally, Negro registration is effectively stifled by an alliance of Council members with law enforcement officials who, if they are not dues-paying members of the organization, work very closely with it.

The sheriff of Dallas County, Jim Clark, is the final link in the conspiracy to restrict Negro citizenship. Clark, who appeared on the podium with Connor and Barnett at the Citizens' Council rally, has a 300-man posse behind him. He is now a defendant in three Justice Department suits charging him with voter intimidation and interference.[25]

The repressive measures against black Americans just described can be seen as typical and deliberately exploitative efforts by whites to maintain their superior social status over blacks in the United States. The basic imperative of black subordination remains built into the structural arrangements of the country, as revealed in figures and trends in employment, income, and occupational status. Significant change in the interest of black American equality requires basic change in these arrangements that would make possible creative new directions in deployment of social resources within the country.[26] Such change, the generation and direction of which must become and remain a major goal of black Americans, will symbolize a needed attention to, and restraint on, the human degradation that capitalism, liberal individualism, and colonialism have given rise to, along with their more praiseworthy contributions.

NOTES

1. Ashley Montagu, *Man's Most Dangerous Myth* (Cleveland: The World Publishing Company, 1964), p. 45.
2. See also Michael Banton, *Race Relations* (London: The Camelot Press, Ltd., 1967), esp. Chapter two.
3. Robert L. Heilbroner, *The Future as History* (New York, N.Y.: Grove Press, Inc., 1961), p. 78.
4. Richard Frucht, "Anthropology of Colonialism in the West Indies," *The Alberta Anthropologist* (February 1967).
5. Heilbroner, *op. cit.*, p. 94.
6. Eric Roll, *A History of Economic Thought* (Englewood Cliffs, N.J.: Prentice-Hall, Inc., 1964), Chapter one.
7. Thomas Hobbes, *Leviathan*, abr. ed., and introduction by Francis B. Randall (New York, N.Y.: Washington Square Press, 1964).
8. Roll, *op. cit.*, p. 91.
9. *Ibid.*, p. 146.
10. Seymour Martin Lipset, *Socialism—Left and Right—East and West* (Berkeley, Calif.: University of California, Institute of Industrial Relations, 1958), Reprint no. 115.
11. Richard Hofstadter, *Social Darwinism in American Thought* (Boston: The Beacon Press, 1959), p. 6.
12. Clinton Rossiter, *Parties and Politics in America* (New York, N.Y.: The New American Library, 1964).
13. David Cushman Coyle, *The United States Political System and How It Works* (New York, N.Y.: The New American Library, 1964).
14. First part of second paragraph of *The Declaration of Independence*.
15. Frank Tannenbaum, *Slave and Citizen* (New York, N.Y.: Vintage Books, 1946).
16. Quoted in *The Negro People in the United States*, ed. Herbert Aptheker (New York, N.Y.: The Citadel Press, 1963), pp. 8–9.
17. Oscar Handlin, *The Newcomers* (Cambridge, Mass.: Harvard University Press, 1959), p. 3.
18. *Ibid.*, p. 108.
19. *Ibid.*, pp. 91–92.
20. Nathan Glazer and Daniel Patrick Moynihan, *Beyond the Melting Pot* (Cambridge, Mass.: The MIT Press, 1965), p. 33.
21. *Ibid.*, pp. 33–34.
22. Ernest A. T. Barth and Baha Abu-Laban, "Power Structure and the Negro Sub-Community," *American Sociological Review*, 24 (February 1959), 72–73.
23. Floyd Hunter, *Community Power Structure* (Chapel Hill: The University of

North Carolina Press, 1953).

24. Gunnar Myrdal, *An American Dilemma*, 2 vols. (New York, N.Y.: McGraw-Hill, 1964).

25. Some more recent works related to this issue are Dan Thompson, *The Negro Leadership Class* (New York, N.Y.: Random House, 1968); Stokely Carmichael and Charles Hamilton, *Black Power* (New York, N.Y.: Random House, 1968).

26. Thomas F. Pettigrew, *A Profile of the Negro American* (Princeton, N.J.: D. Van Nostrand Company, Inc., 1964), see esp. Chapter eight.

2. Gobineau and the Origins of European Racism

Articulate and influential spokesmen for racism have presented their views throughout history. They include well-known persons in a variety of disciplines and places. They include the Englishman Chamberlain and the German sociologists Ludwig Gumplowicz and Gustav Ratzenhoffer. The French, too, contributed substantially to this development, particularly through Gobineau and his influential *Essay on the Inequality of the Human Races.* The discussion of Gobineau which follows serves to remind us of the historical arrogance of many European intellectuals and of their unfortunate practice of regarding other peoples of the world as subordinate and inferior. Many of these antiquated definitions remain central to the stereotypes of nonwhite people today and confound well-intended efforts at amicable and equalitarian association. The reactivation of these definitions as a legitimation of the Nazi tyranny further emphasizes the need to view them as fossils of a specific historical time.

MICHAEL D. BIDDISS

The Nazi and Fascist philosophers owed many debts to the mental aberrations found in previous history. Their debt to Count Arthur de Gobineau was considerable and openly acknowledged. Yet their scant regard for truth ensured that the "gobinism" known to the early twentieth century was a distortion of his theories. It is important not only to describe his ideas accurately but also to relate them to their true social and intellectual context.

Gobineau was born near Paris in 1816, the son of a royalist who had worked for the recently achieved Bourbon restoration. The father had suffered imprisonment under Napoleon, but his hopes for lucrative employment with the restored Bourbons were dashed. The marriage of Arthur's parents was unhappy. Most of his childhood was spent with his mother and he was much influenced by his tutor, one Coindière. The latter gave Gobineau a good knowledge of German, comparatively rare in the France of that day. His formal education was undertaken largely in

From *Race,* Vol. VII, No. 3 (January 1966), pp. 255–270. Published for the Institute of Race Relations, London, by the Oxford University Press, copyright Institute of Race Relations, 1966; reprinted by permission.

German at the College of Bienne. He was captivated by the Orient and its languages and aspired to become a man of letters. His father had wanted him to have a military career but grew convinced that Arthur was unsuitable. In 1835 he was sent to Paris under the care of a royalist uncle. By then the 1830 revolution had enthroned the dull bourgeois figure of the orleanist Louis-Philippe. The middle-class triumph gave little hope for the Gobineau family or for the future of the nobility. Though Gobineau also distrusted the legitimist party his career as a Parisian journalist was marked by the prejudices of his upbringing. Contemporary Parisian society brought home to him the mediocrity of a France that had rejected its Bourbons. Like Stendhal and Balzac he expressed through his writings his dissatisfaction with contemporary society. The symptoms of the mediocrity of orleanist France were the growth of democracy, socialism and bourgeois rule. The 1848 revolution served to confirm his fears. But it was under the new republican government that success came in the form of an appointment to serve as secretary to his friend de Tocqueville at the Foreign Ministry. Thus began the diplomatic career which was to last for thirty years. Yet his disquiet for the future of France and Europe had not abated. By 1850 Gobineau was thirty-four, but the prophet of racism had not yet appeared. This outline of his early years indicates his social pessimism, but it does nothing to explain how it became historical pessimism in racial form.[1]

The solution lies in the more general intellectual complex of the nineteenth century, in thought about such subjects as anthropology, ethnology, prehistory, philology and national history, and also in romanticism and the oriental renaissance.

Gobineau's racism originates with his revulsion against a society which had rejected the virtues of nobility. His social pessimism is a matter of class-consciousness. The writers of French history had for long made such a connection between race and class.[2] The racial interpretation of French history might be traced back to Caesar and Tacitus, but a more conventional origin is to be found in the sixteenth century theory of François Hotman. He described a league between the Gauls and Germans in defence of their common liberty against Roman tyranny. Successors, such as Adrien de Valois, made a distinction between the Gallo-Romans and the Franks. The classic exposition was that of Henri de Boulainviller. He believed that the Franks had conquered the Romans, who were themselves the earlier conquerors of the Gauls. The Franks henceforth formed the French nobility, claiming their position and property by right of conquest. But, like Gobineau, Boulainviller was disturbed by the encroachments of the lower classes since the golden age of Charlemagne. These elements were permutated again by the Abbé Dubos, who described such conquest as illusory and suggested that the Franks came to Gaul as the allies of Rome. Montesquieu and Mably tried to play down the divisive issue of conquest. But at the Revolution the Abbé Sieyès was happy to reverse the idea and justify the supremacy of the Gallic people over the Frankish nobles by the triumph of the third-estate. Not even the national feeling encouraged by the Revolutionary and Napoleonic Wars could silence the argument over race and class in France. Though such writers as Montlosier, Chateaubriand and Augustin Thierry emphasised harmony among the racial elements, the historical fact of conquest remained unshaken and was at hand for the use of a latter-day Boulainviller. Thus for centuries the elements of the French nation and their rivalries had been used to support contemporary polemics. It was not unnatural that Gobineau, with his class assailed by society, should find inspiration in this source of racial historiography.

But the broadening horizons of the nineteenth century revealed material more extensive than that of France alone. Gobineau, like many in the romantic age, was attracted by the renaissance of interest in the Orient.[3] India, in particular, offered the western world the picture of a civilisation which was not only different, but also alive. Inca culture, for instance, had been but a museum-piece. Hindu mysticism and society revealed a past that lived on in the present. The eighteen thirties was the decade when oriental studies most captured the imagination of intelligent youth, and it was then that Gobineau was assiduously reading works on the East, and gaining some linguistic knowledge. The failed seminarists of that decade —and those like Renan in the next—were frequently men who had been led by their Hebrew studies to yet more exotic interests. When Michelet pondered on India he was confirmed in his conviction of the identity of all mankind. Gobineau was to reach opposite conclusions: but they stemmed from the same interests.

It was, more specifically, oriental languages which had the greatest effect on the development of racist thought. In 1788 Sir William Jones argued the connection between the Sanskrit, Greek, Latin, Persian, Celtic and German languages. In 1813 Thomas Young used the term "indo-european" to describe the group. By 1831 J. C. Prichard had introduced the name "indo-germanic," and from 1833 Franz Bopp was publishing his *Comparative Grammar,* which laid the foundations of modern linguistics. It was a short but illogical step from this to the notion that a single race must correspond with this linguistic "family." Thus the Aryan was discovered. Once alive he had to be provided with a birthplace. Bulwer-Lytton and R. G. Latham suggested a European origin. Gobineau was to follow the school of J. G. Rhodes and W. von Schlegel who asserted that the homeland was in central Asia. The word "aryan" was linked to the German *Ehre* (honour) and thus allowed one to stress the nobility and superiority of the Aryan race.

There were other roots to racism independent of linguistic studies. Gobineau appears late in the history of the "biological revolution," which was the prelude to Charles Darwin rather than the result of his work.[4] There was a reaction against the myths of fabulous peoples which had filled, delightfully if not truthfully, the notebooks of many travellers.[5] The revolution showed a new concern with *man*—as studied through anthropology, ethnology and zoology. Scholars wished to classify man in the way that Linnaeus and Buffon had treated other parts of the natural order. Indeed, both naturalists had themselves attempted the task. In 1735 Linnaeus divided the genus *"homo"* into varieties labelled *"monstruosus," "ferus,"* and *"sapiens."* The first included giants, pygmies and cretins, and the last was divided into American, European, Asiatic, and African, largely according to skin colour. Buffon in 1749 distinguished six varieties, and in 1775 Blumenbach described five. The common ground of the debate was the desire to establish some order in the description of mankind. The need had still to be satisfied when Gobineau came to reflect on the problem.

Such studies, together with archaeological and geological investigations, had inevitable religious repercussions. Oriental discoveries too suggested to the more daring minds that the Bible should be seen merely as part of the great primitive poetry of mankind. If scholars could see Genesis, for instance, as poetry they would be liberated from a literal view of its version of human creation.[6] In 1809 Lamarck's *Philosophy of Zoology* argued a theory of progressive evolution wherein all living beings were subject to gradual transformation. Geoffroy Saint-Hilaire adopted his belief in the mutability of species and suggested that a sudden change in the embryo could be caused by cosmic influences, such as variations in the chemical content of the atmosphere. But his own dominant idea was the unity of all organic being. Baron Cuvier, however, stated a theory of fixed and separate organic beings. But by his very work on the paleontology of the vertebrates and the relationship between particular fossils and certain strata he gave unwitting assistance to the transformist school. Lyell's geological work, for instance, benefitted from these researches. Acceptance of Saint-Hilaire's transformism was hindered in religious circles by the general belief in the chronology of Archbishop Usher, which dated the creation of the world at 4,004 B.C. Though Cuvier assumed an original multiplicity of types in the natural order, he continued to see all men as of a single species, and thus supported the literal interpreters of Genesis. Supporters of this "monogenesis" were, in their turn, hindered by the need to explain the rapid changes among men since the creation within Usher's short time-scale. It was difficult to reconcile the traditional chronology with the idea of a single pair of human parents, for it seemed incredible that environmental factors could have worked such great change so quickly.

The form of Gobineau's racist theory was considerably influenced by these debates. And there was obvious stimulation from the growing attention given to the American slavery issue in the years before the Civil War.[7] This tended to divide the loyalties of those who were radical in both politics and religion. The most liberal Christians were beginning to consider Genesis as poetry; but thereby they weakened one of their best arguments against the slaveowner—that according to Genesis, his slaves were men of the same creation as himself.

The amorphous "romantic movement" also had aspects which helped foster racist theorising. It moved away from the rational and led, for instance, to Balzac's concern with insanity in the novels of the thirties and Hugo's fascination with the occult. Romanticism cultivated oriental knowledge, but also revealed the world of the Scandinavian and Celtic north. Rousseau's call for a return to nature encouraged interest in the primitive instinctive barbarism of the north. Thus with Aryanism was combined a Teutonism which found eloquent expression in the poetry and philosophy of the German nationalist romantic movement and which attracted young foreigners who, like Gobineau, were conversant with the native language. Moreover, Rousseau's revulsion against society is precisely the feeling fundamental to an understanding of Gobineau's racism. Significantly it was in his *Discourse on Inequality* that Rousseau himself recognised the fact of natural selection. Both had a vision of a utopian past; in Rousseau it belonged to all humanity, in Gobineau to the Aryans alone.

The foregoing will help us to understand that Gobineau and his racism show much that is typical of an age that has been characterised by the names of Darwin, Marx and Wagner.[8] Racism, with its concern about the physical nature of men, was a natural part of the environment of speculation on natural history which culminated with Darwin. The connection with Marx can be traced through Gobineau's ultimate concern with the attractions, repulsions, and conflicts between classes and races, and—despite his attacks on materialism—through his obsession with a material physical world. Both may be studied to illustrate the connection between conflict and group consciousness. With Wagner there was much later a personal friendship. But, even in 1850, the composer declared that race not climate was the key to artistic creation and already he was becoming inspired by the teutonic past.

Gobineau's great contribution was to attempt to reconcile primitive Aryan unity with its modern diversity. He attempted to use the systematic treatment which was becoming attractive in the positivist age. The result was equally the product of the fertile imagination more typical of the romantics. Yet Gobineau buttressed his work with references to the most reputable scholars of his day: Ewald, Munch, Schaffarick, Keferstein, Ritter and Niebuhr are but a few. The revolution in the scope and depth of historical study, which made Bossuet's *Universal History* seem like a local monograph, was not lost upon Gobineau. But if he was a modern in his scope he was frequently a primitive in his method.

Gobineau began to write his famous *Essay on the Inequality of the Human Races* as a French diplomat in Berne around 1850. He was mindful not merely of the degradation of his class in France but also of the horrors of Swiss democracy. Thus Gobineau, like Gibbon amidst the ruins of the Capitol, begins his vast work with thoughts of decline and fall. The first words are these: "The fall of civilisations is the most striking and, at the same time, the most obscure of historical phenomena." [9] The first part of the work is devoted to a theoretical exposition and the remainder deals with the alleged historical substantiation of the theory. Civilisation is seen as a series of facts, more or less logically connected and produced by the inter-action of complex ideas. He defines it as, "a state of relative stability where the mass of men try to satisfy their wants by peaceful means, and are refined in their intelligence and their behaviour." [10] He suggests that the deaths of civilisations have a common cause. It is not fanaticism, nor indulgence in luxury, corrupt behaviour or irreligion. Aztec society could have survived its excesses had not Cortez appeared. For the Phoenicians the corruption of morals was an instrument of their glory, and the Romans had as many honest men in the fifth century as in the golden age. Gobineau asserts that no nation has experienced discontinuity in religious belief, and he therefore rejects the suggestion that irreligion has destroyed civilisations. Having denounced these well-worn historical explanations he goes on to deny that even the relative merits of governments influence the survival of a people:

If nations were always to die of such sufferings, not one of them would outlast their formative years, for it is precisely then that one finds the worst administration and the most evil and badly observed laws. [11]

What therefore is the cause of the decay of civilisations? It is none other than the physical degeneration of man:

The word "degenerate" means that a people has lost its former intrinsic worth, since it no longer has in its veins the same blood, because continual adulterations have slowly changed it. In other words, though it has the same name as its founders, it no longer represents the same race. [12]

War and conquest are the most active agents of such blood-mixture. But Gobineau denies that institutions influence the creation of ethnic inequalities. Until the most modern times all governments had been forced to adapt themselves to a recognition of natural inequality. Only recently have egalitarian fictions begun to influence institutions. The role of environment, a major topic of the eighteenth century, is also minimised. The world has frequently seen barbarism and civilisation flourishing on the same soil at different periods. The worth of a civilisation is independent of the material conditions of its environment. One notable instance is the achievement of the Jews. Though Palestine was but a miserable corner of the earth, they became:

A people that succeeded in all it undertook, a free people, strong and intelligent, which, before it lost, bravely and with sword in hand, the name of an independent nation, gave to the world almost as many scholars as merchants.[13]

A nation derives nothing from its location; it is the people themselves who give to the land all that it has of moral, economic, and political value.

No Western philosopher of civilisation in the mid-nineteenth century could fail to consider the belief that Christianity was the world's greatest civilising force. Gobineau was sufficiently typical of his age to reject traditional beliefs and yet be embarrassed by his own arguments. He agrees that Christians are found in all climates and latitudes and does not openly deny that all mankind is able to recognise Christian truth. But this is not to say that all men can aspire to civilisation. Christianity is an important social vehicle in achieving, for instance, the reduction of violence or the recognition of the social role of affection. It makes men more reflective and gentle, but only indirectly, because its main concern is not with earthly existence. Gobineau rejects Christianity's civilising potential in this way:

No civilisation whatsoever has aroused its admiration or its contempt; and because of the consequences of this rare impartiality it could rightly be called "catholic" or universal. For it does not belong exclusively to any civilisation. It did not come to recommend any one form of earthly existence. It rejects none and desires to purify them all.[14]

Christian teaching also complicates Gobineau's treatment of the problem of unity and diversity in human origins. The trend of his arguments, as one would expect from an enemy of equality, is towards a number of separate human creations. With Owen he rejected Camper's suggestion of a link between the orang-outang and the human species.[15] Gobineau's partial acceptance of the work of Carus and Morton and his rejection of the monogenist argument that racial differences result from environment would seem to make him an unequivocal supporter of the polygenist case. But religious orthodoxy reared its head at him as at many others. In the face of Genesis the nominal Catholic weakened his argument and seized on the fertility of human hybrids as an indication of man's common origin. He claimed that the Bible undoubtedly made Adam the father of the white race, but admits that this is a weak argument since all races traditionally describe their original ancestor as of their own colour. Gobineau wishes to emphasise the permanence of ethnic differences as they now are:

Whichever side one wants to take in the debate as to the unity or diversity of human origins, today the different families are absolutely separate from one another, since no external influence could cause them to resemble one another or to become assimilated.[16]

Only direct cross-breeding can bring change. With great audacity Gobineau reintroduces the environmental argument he had previously rejected. Relying on Cuvier and Lyell's geological discoveries, he suggests that shortly after the creation climate and environment were forces dynamic enough to achieve the division of races known to later history.[17] Gobineau dates the creation at about 7,000 B.C. and suggests that these changes occurred, "when the earth was still shaken by the recent catastrophes and was totally subjected to the fearful effects of their last death-throes." [18] He believes that no later date can be reconciled with the monogenist claims. Gobineau goes a step further and even claims that the permanence of present racial types is itself the result of the vast amount of climatic energy possessed by the earth when this racial revolution occurred! Original man is equally distinct from each of the new groups. The only signs of common origin among men are a vague resemblance of shape and the facility of hybridisation. Of primal man we have no scientific knowledge; for practical purposes we may ignore him. Thus, having paid lip service to monogenist theory, Gobineau is now free to work out the consequences of his instinctive leaning towards the opposite argument.

The end-product of this cosmic chaos is the production of the White, Black and Yellow races, each permanent in its characteristics and affected only by hybridisation. Gobineau claims that the terms are not strictly related to skin-colouring, but suggests that the latter is a criterion adequate for his purpose. Using the vocabulary of his age, by Whites he means the Caucasian, Semitic and Japhetic races; by Blacks the Hamites; by Yellows the Altaic, Mongol, Finnish and Tartar branches.

The man of Black race is the lowest, marked by animality and limited intellect, but possessing great energy, desire and will. His wild sensuality is the mark of inferiority. He is denoted also by the variability of his moods which make him unaware of the distinctions between vice and virtue. He has little concern for the preservation of his own life, or for that of others, and shows an horrific impassiveness towards suffering.

The Yellow is superior to the negroid and is his antithesis. He tends towards apathy and lacks physical strength. He exhibits none of the moral excesses of the Black, having weak desires and a will which is obstinate rather than extreme. Mediocrity in all things and material enjoyment are favoured by him. He loves utility, respects law, and appreciates moderate liberty. The Yellows prefer theory to practice:

Their desires are limited to living as quietly and as comfortably as they can . . . It is a populace and a bourgeoisie which any founder of civilisation would desire to choose as the basis of his society. Yet it lacks the wherewithal to create that society and give it beauty, energy, and action.[19]

The White is marked by reflective energy or energetic intelligence. He possesses a sense of utility less narrow and more elevated than that of the Yellow. He perseveres in the face of obstacles and has great physical power. His extraordinary instinct for order is a result not of his desire for repose but of his wish for self-preservation. A singular love of life and liberty characterise him. But honour is placed even above life. Though less sensual than the other races, the Whites have superior intelligence. The race is composed of Chamites, Semites, and Japhetides.[20] The true Aryans belong only to the last branch and, having spread from the central Asian plateau, they have formed the Hindu, Iranian, Hellenic, Celtic, Slavonic, and Germanic peoples.

The three races are marked by these permanent intellectual and physio-logical inequalities, and the White race in particular is possessed of an innate idea of its superiority. All men combine the instincts of moral and material satisfaction and in the most elevated race we come nearest to the happy harmonisation of the two. Each race has conflicting feelings of repulsion and attraction for the others. Race-mixture is brought about by the prevailing influence of the latter. Though such mixture is the vehicle of degeneration it is a necessary evil. For Gobineau stresses that civilisa-tion can only be created by the mixture of the White race with an element of alien blood. Unlike the theories of the later "gobinists" this is not a racism of absolute blood-purity. Gobineau the pessimist invents a subtler theory whereby the hybridisation which is the creator of civilisation is also the agent of its decadence, for it is in practice impossible to restrain the alien blood within the bounds where it remains fruitful rather than destructive. Civilisation moves to its inevitable degeneration through a stage of extreme activity, to morbid torpor, and on to death. There is little compensation to be found in the fact that mixture frequently improves the lower race. Gobineau's view of art also shows his ambivalent attitude to blood-mixture. The passion of the artistic temperament is a negroid char-acteristic. The creation of great art needs the combination of reflection and emotion, and is therefore the result of blending the White and the Black.

Robert Ezra Park has described Gobineau's theory of civilisation as being opposed to the "catastrophic" school of Hume or Teggart, where civilisation is alleged, "to flourish at the expense of racial differences rather than to be conserved by them."[21] Though Gobineau denies environ-mental influences this polarisation of attitudes is imperfect. He stresses the important role of conflict, contact and communication, as well as the prominence of war and migration, in encouraging race-mixture. Moreover, the fortunes of states, which are based upon power, are in some degree independent of the fate of civilisations and the cultures deriving therefrom.

The theoretical first volume of the *Essay* precedes the attempt of the remaining three volumes to provide an historical justification.[22] Gobineau's methodology is weak: the theoretical exposition which history is to confirm is itself frequently used to settle doubtful historical points! He also relies heavily on evidence drawn from the exaggerated connection between race and language, which had itself given birth to racial Aryanism. Gobineau, like Toynbee nearly a century later, studied history through the concept of "civilisations." Yet in 1850 it was a much more original venture. Men had more frequently used the term "civilisation" solely to mean a process towards the state of being civilised and not to refer to a particular stage or type of society. But part of the historical revolution was concerned with the idea of organic civilisations with their own histories of rise and fall. Gobineau's historical exposition reveals ten such civilisations:

1. Indian: founded by a branch of the Aryans.
2. Egyptian: created by an Aryan settlement in the upper Nile valley.
3. Assyrian (connected also with the Jews, Phoenicians, and Carthaginians): stemming from descendants of Shem and Ham. The Zoroastrian Iranians (Medes, Persians, and Bactrians) were a part of the Aryan family.
4. Greek: founded by Aryan stock modified by semitic elements.
5. Chinese: originating in Indian colonisation.
6. Roman: produced from a mixture of Celts, Iberians, Aryans and Semites.
7. German: created by the Aryan invaders of western Europe in the fifth century.
8, 9, 10. South American: Alleghanian, Mexican, and Peruvian, inspired by a small element of colonising norsemen.

Gobineau comments that six of the first seven have Aryan foundations and that the other, the Assyrian, owes its climax in the Iranian Renaissance to that family. The historical conclusion is that:

There is no true civilisation among the European nations where the Aryan branch is not predominant. In the ten civilisations no negro race belongs to the initiators. Only when mixed with other blood can it be introduced into one. Similarly there is no spontaneous civilisation among the yellow peoples. And there is stagnation where the Aryan stock is found exhausted.[23]

The framework of racial determinism within which this world history is described minimises the true but maximises the fascinating. But here let us look merely at the final stages—Gobineau's description of the modern western world.

Scandinavia, having given its life-blood to Europe, is now much weakened. Yet it still possesses the strongest physiological and political traces of Aryan influence. Spain is now decadent, though it had once benefitted from a combination of Gothic valour and semitic energy. Though her great Renaissance showed that Italy had preserved some germanic worth in the North, the peninsula is now in the grip of *romanité,* the debasing influence of the semitic Latin which itself brought down the Roman Empire. Russia is treated contemptuously as the home of the degenerate Slavs, and it maintains its empire only through strong French and German administrative and military personnel. But France and Germany are scarcely better treated. Gobineau saw the Frankish nobility crushed beneath the Gallo-Roman plebs in France. Centralisation and the growth of state power had banished feudal and pre-feudal freedom.[24] France is dominated by Paris and it is there that cosmopolitanism has brought the greatest mixture and degeneration. Yet, despite Gobineau's subsequent popularity with them, the modern Germans fare no better. The teutonic warriors of the fifth century are gone; what remains is a people weakened by Celtic and Slavonic influences and a nobility as broken as the French. Prussia itself is less teutonic than the German parts of Austria. England alone receives any credit, and even there the admiration is scant. The Norman Conquest produced a fortunate mixture which encouraged a golden age of chivalry. But the influx of persecuted Huguenots from France, the immigrations fostered by rapid industrialisation, and the Irish migrations of the eighteen forties have hastened decline. Yet it has been comparatively slow and Gobineau can write of England: "It has certainly not been the most brilliant, nor the most human, nor the most noble of European states, but it is still the most vigorous of them all." [25] The only vestiges of vigour left in Europe are found in Britain, Scandinavia, Denmark, Hanover, Alsace, Lorraine, and in the rest of France north of the Seine.

Gobineau keeps his discussion of the United States until the end of the *Essay,* declaring that if hope cannot be found there then civilisation is indeed doomed. And he finds no hope—for the Anglo-Saxon virtues are being swamped by the massive immigrations of mixed stocks. From Ireland, Italy, France, and eastern Europe come men who are incapable of the youth and vigour of a civilising race:

This people which calls itself young is in reality the old European stock, less restricted because of more favourable laws, but no better inspired.[26]

The long voyage to the New World may be a great movement in geographical terms, but it is incapable of achieving a physical transformation.

The original pessimism about France has now become universal despair. The ideas of unity and equality which Gobineau attacked in France are becoming universal physical realities. He prophesies that the final end will come in 5,000 years, yet it is not the conclusion but the interim of decadence which he fears:

The sadness of the future is not death, but the certainty of our reaching it as degraded beings; and perhaps this shame reserved for our descendants would leave us unmoved, if it was not for the fact that we feel with secret horror the rapacious hands of destiny already upon us.[27]

Such a view of human nature, whether in Hobbes or Gobineau, is the stuff from which racism can be made. Gobineau's determinism is summarised thus in the dedication to the work:

I have become convinced that the race question dominates all the other problems of history, that it holds the key to them, and that the inequality of races from whose fusion a people is formed is enough to explain the whole course of its destiny . . . I am at last sure that everything great, noble, and fruitful that man has created on earth in science, art, and civilisation draws the observer back to a single point, issues from a single root, results from a single idea, and belongs to a single family, the different branches of which have reigned in all the civilised countries of the universe.[28]

In this pessimism and determinism lies the essence of Gobineau's historical Aryanism.

Such a racial theory has disastrous ethical consequences. His approval of the Indian caste-system is complemented by an attack on Buddhist egalitarianism. In discussing this aspect of Christianity he had been circumspect, but Buddhism he freely attacks. Its rejection of caste is a crime against Aryan blood-purity and its own degeneration is the inevitable result of a doctrine based solely on morality and reason and not on physical being. For, in Buddhism, "instead of morality stemming from ontology it is, on the contrary, ontology which is derived from the moral law." [29] The logical consequence of his intensely materialistic ethic is a morality based on chemistry. It invites the moral justification by blood which, in the dual ethic of a Nietzsche or Hitler, was to take man beyond all conventional ideas of good and evil. Though one of Gobineau's first critics, Friedrich Pott, saw his treatment of Buddhism as a Catholic attack on this form of Indian "protestantism," Gobineau himself owed much to the protestant tradition. In its extreme predestinarian forms it taught the inefficacy of "works" and cherished the idea of the Chosen People. Arnold Toynbee has given the classic description of the link between this tradition and all racist theories involving predestination by blood.[30]

Views on the nature of government, on intellectual movements, on the role of individuals in history, and other such subjects are fitted, some more credibly than others, into the framework of racial determinism. Urbanisation becomes evil because it encourages excessive race-mixture. Democracy threatens the élite of purer blood and its egalitarian doctrines preach miscegenation. Gobineau is in conflict with other trends of the age. The biological revolution, to which his studies owed much, stressed a vitalism and evolutionism which are negated by his materialistic determinism. Moreover, unlike most future "gobinists," he is no nationalist. Patriotism is "a Canaan monstrosity," [31] an insubstantial fiction of the Greeks, who used it instead of a real person to justify their innate desire to sacrifice themselves entirely to some form of despotism. With the rise of the Gallo-Romans in France the despotism of patriotism has again become evident.

Though a brief summary is somewhat unjust to Gobineau's complex views on patriotism it illustrates how far he was removed from the spirit of the German nationalists who were to use his writings.

Nor was Gobineau an antisemite in the conventional sense. He regarded the semitic peoples as of primarily white stock and, among them, he saw the Jews as vigorous and intelligent. If Gobineau refused to regard them as equals it was only in the same way as he denied equality to all but the Aryan élite. As R. F. Byrnes has shown, French antisemitism of the period is primarily a left-wing phenomenon; but he sees Gobineau as exceptional for the wrong reason.[32] His is an antisemitism which results from ideas not directed primarily against the Jews. It flows more from a general distrust of revolutionary religions, such as Buddhism and including Christianity, than from specific dislike of the Jewish people. Without such distinctions Renan equally could be seen as an antisemite because, as Hannah Aréndt says, "(he) was probably the first to oppose the 'Semites' to the 'Aryans' in a decisive *division du genre humain*.' "[33] Gobineau's elevation of a master-race invited the addition of a particular anti-race. But in his work this was not to be identified with the Jews.

The contemporary reception of the *Essay* was polite but reserved. A work of eighteen-hundred pages could scarcely expect a large readership! Some scholars such as A. von Humboldt corresponded with Gobineau about the book, but behind their courtesies were fundamental disagreements. Though Renan agreed with certain points he was eager to avoid having to publicise the book himself. Max Müller was soon to recant his own earlier view of the identification of race with language. Ewald, like Pott, attacked Gobineau's alleged Catholic extremism. But Schopenhauer found his pessimism attractive. The American South found his arguments convenient, and in 1856 J. C. Nott and H. Hotz published a freely-adapted version of the first book of the *Essay*, dedicated "to the Statesmen of America." Nott dismissed Gobineau's scruples about the multiple origin of man as Catholic equivocation and emphasised the passages convenient to the slaveholders. In 1857 Quatrefages criticised Gobineau's weak anthropological knowledge, but he conceded that the *Essay* had real merit and was a brave attempt at synthesising knowledge about ethnology and kindred subjects.

The most distinguished critic of all, Gobineau's friend Tocqueville, saw the work as full of research and talent, but he attacked the practical consequences of fatalism and materialism. The liberal philosopher claimed that racial determinism would limit, if not abolish, free will and human liberty. Such an idea, whether or not it was false, was practically pernicious:

Do you not see that from your doctrine spring naturally all the evils which permanent inequality begets, pride, violence, the scorn of one's fellow men, tyranny and subjection in all its forms?[34]

Such a work could only weaken still further the troubled spirit which Tocqueville saw among his contemporaries.

Gobineau's intellectual odyssey from the eighteen fifties until his death in 1882 is a fascinating story. But his racism remained much the same. In 1884 there was a second edition of the *Essay*, which included a preface written by Gobineau just before his death. There he wrote,

> Not a line has been changed for the present edition. It is not that considerable works have not marked out progress in detail, but that none of the truths I enunciated has been destroyed.[35]

By that time the progress of ethnology had made inexcusable the defence of his crudities. Prehistorians had helped to undermine his chronology and throw all in doubt. But, since Gobineau had created his own universe of discourse and discord, and as it had a certain amount of inexorable, if arid, logic, he was able to remain deaf to the cries of scientific progress. There is no greater proof that his racial theory was less a body of learning than a political idea, an example of the quality of belief rather than of the power of knowledge, an essay in symbolism rather than in realism. As Ruth Benedict wrote, "Racism is not, like race, a subject the content of which can be scientifically investigated. It is like a religion, a belief that can be studied only historically." [36] Gobineau's racism appealed to the simple-minded with its alleged facts and to the cunning with a symbolism which they could use for their own ends. It was attractive because it was breathtaking in its scope, its pretensions, and in the simplicity of its fundamentals. And it could appeal, in its distorted form, to the egocentric pride of national or racial consciousness.

The subsequent treatment of Gobineau's theory was far from what he intended, and he became the inventor of twentieth century racism rather by accident. Gobineau was a theorist of Aryanism rather than of Germanism, and propounded a great mother-race-idea to which Anglo-Saxonism, Teutonism, and even Celticism were all indebted. But, historically speaking, he was most available for German use. Wagner fêted him at Bayreuth, and from the composer, via Schemann, Nietzsche, H. S. Chamberlain, Spengler and Rosenberg, to Hitler there is a chain of intellectual and personal links. Those relationships are another story, but here is a preview of its climax in the pages of *Mein Kampf*:

> History shows, with a startling clarity, that whenever Aryans have mingled their blood with that of an inferior race the result has been the downfall of the people who were the standard-bearers of a higher culture . . . Every manifestation of human culture, every product of art, science and technical skill, which we see before our eyes today is almost exclusively the product of the Aryan creative power . . . The Aryan neglected to maintain his own racial stock unmixed and therewith lost the right to live in the paradise which he himself had created . . . That is how cultures and empires decline and yield their places to new formations.[37]

Such words could almost be Gobineau's own. But, whereas the Frenchman had despaired of the world and had withdrawn from it while degeneration triumphed, the German continued to hope. Like Wagner and unlike Gobineau, Hitler trusted in regeneration—and erupted into world politics to achieve it. Never was hope more harmful. From much the same "facts" about race Gobineau and Hitler drew very different conclusions. But, then, the facts were unimportant; it was the symbol that was the same.

NOTES

1. A short account of Gobineau's early life by his sister can be found in Ludwig Schemann (ed.), *Quellen und Untersuchungen zum Leben Gobineaus* (Strassburg, 1914), Vol. 1, pp. 107–118. The standard life is Schemann's two-volume adulatory *Gobineau: eine Biographie* (Strassburg, 1913–16). A useful shorter biography is J. N. Faure-Biguet, *Gobineau* (Paris, Plon, 1930). There are interesting critical works by E. Seillière (Paris, Plon, 1903), M. Lange (Strasbourg, 1924), and A. Combris (Paris, Alcan, 1937).

2. Jacques Barzun, *The French Race* (New York, Columbia, 1932), *passim*.

3. Raymond Schwab, *La Renaissance orientale* (Paris, Payot, 1950), *passim*. For the term "oriental renaissance" see Edgar Quinet, *Le Génie des religions* (Paris, 1841).

4. Jacques Barzun, *Romanticism and the Modern Ego* (Boston, Little, Brown & Co., 1944), pp. 76–7.

5. Herbert Collins, "The Fabulous Races" in E. T. Thompson and E. C. Hughes (eds.), *Race: Individual and Collective Behavior* (New York, Free Press of Glencoe, 1965), pp. 238–243.

6. Charles C. Gillispie, *Genesis and Geology* (New York, Harper, 1959), *passim*. Jean Rostand, "The Development of Biology" in G. Métraux and F. Crouzet, *The Nineteenth-Century World* (New York, Mentor, 1963), pp. 177–192.

7. William Stanton, *The Leopard's Spots: Scientific Attitudes Toward Race in America, 1815–59* (Chicago, 1960), *passim*.

8. Jacques Barzun, *Darwin, Marx, Wagner* (London, 1942), *passim*.

9. Arthur de Gobineau, *Essai sur l'inégalité des races humaines* (1st ed., 4 vols., Paris, Firmin Didot, 1853–5), vol. I, p. 1. This translation and those that follow are by the present author. Most of the first volume is available in an English translation by A. Collins (London, 1915). The same portion is available now in the French paperback edition published by Nouvel Office d'Edition (Paris, 1963).

10. *Essai*, vol. I, p. 149.

11. *Ibid.*, pp. 30–1.

12. *Ibid.*, p. 39.

13. *Ibid.*, pp. 96–7.

14. *Ibid.*, p. 109.

15. Among Gobineau's *obiter dicta* is the remark that, "We do not come from the ape, but we are rapidly getting there!"

16. *Ibid.*, p. 225.

17. Gobineau regarded his work as complementary to that of Lyell and saw the *Essay* as a study in "moral geology." (See the Dedication to the book, vol. I, p. x.)

18. *Ibid.*, p. 232.

19. *Ibid.*, p. 353.

20. These names are taken from the sons of Noah. For the fate of his progeny in European history one is referred to Denys Hay's fascinating little book, *Europe: the Emergence of an Idea* (Edinburgh U.P., 1957).

21. Robert E. Park, *Race and Culture* (London, Free Press of Glencoe, 1964), pp. 345–6.

22. More accurately, the work is divided into six Books. The first of these is alone theoretical; but it takes up most of Volume I of the first edition.
23. *Essai*, vol. I, p. 365.
24. Ernest Seillière, *Gobineau et l'aryanisme historique* (Paris, Plon, 1903), pp. 107 *et seq.*, explains some of the complexity of Gobineau's view of French feudalism.
25. *Essai*, vol. IV, p. 201.
26. *Ibid.*, pp. 316–7.
27. *Ibid.*, p. 359.
28. *Ibid.* (Dedication), vol. I, pp. viii–ix.
29. *Ibid.*, vol. II, p. 219.
30. Arnold Toynbee, *A Study of History* (London, O.U.P., 1934), vol. I, pp. 211 *et seq.*
31. Robert F. Byrnes, *Antisemitism in Modern France* (New Brunswick, 1950), vol. I, pp. 112–3, and *passim*.
32. *Ibid.*
33. Hannah Aréndt, *The Origins of Totalitarianism* (London, Allen & Unwin, Revised Edition, 1958), p. 174.
34. Tocqueville to Gobineau, 17 November 1853, in M. Degros (ed.), *Correspondance d'Alexis de Tocqueville et d'Arthur de Gobineau* (Paris, Gallimard, 1959), p. 203.
35. *Essai*, Foreword to the second edition (Paris, Firmin Didot, 2 vols., 1884), vol. I, p. xi.
36. Ruth Benedict, *Race and Racism* (London, 1942), p. 131.
37. Adolf Hitler, *Mein Kampf* (London, Hutchinson's Illustrated Edition, no date), pp. 249, 251, 257.

II. Racism as a Social Institution in the United States of America

Racism in the United States has been characterized by the Swedish sociologist Gunnar Myrdal as a dilemma. This is an apt characterization. Slightly more than one hundred years have passed since slavery was abolished, yet, as several subsequent chapters suggest, there remains a virulent subordination and repression of black Americans in the United States. An understanding of the tenacity of racism requires descriptive and analytical attention, both of which are included in the two chapters in Part II. They deal with selected aspects of black American history within an analytical framework, applicable to Western society generally, of which the historical development of the United States is a significant part. Viewed as part of a larger pattern of social development, that is, capitalism, the persistence of racism in its various forms can be more readily understood. The events, circumstances, and conditions discussed in this part are to be seen both as significant features of black American history, and as phenomena conditioned and fashioned by the dynamics of a social process within which black subordination was, and remains, a functional part.

3. The Dynamics of Unopposed Capitalism

Slavery in the United States of America has been characterized as one of the cruelest and most brutal instances of human bondage known to the world. Many current characteristics of the black American community that are not found in comparable measure among whites are said to be a direct outcome of this inhumane slave system. Differences in level of education, patterns of family life, and so forth are among these characteristics. This selection by Elkins attempts to explain the primary conditions giving rise to this pattern of repression. He goes beyond the simple use of the label "capitalism" to demonstrate the dynamics of its operation in this area.

STANLEY M. ELKINS

How had Negro slavery in the United States come into being? There was nothing "natural" about it; it had no necessary connection with either tropical climate or tropical crops: in Virginia and Maryland, where the institution first appeared and flourished, the climate was hardly tropical, and the staple crop—tobacco—might have been grown as far north as Canada. It had nothing to do with characteristics which might have made the Negro peculiarly suited either to slavery or to the labor of tobacco culture. Slavery in past ages had been limited to no particular race, and the earliest planters of colonial Virginia appear to have preferred a laboring force of white servants from England, Scotland, and Ireland, rather than of blacks from Africa. Nor was it a matter of common-law precedent, for the British colonists who settled the areas eventually to be included in the United States brought with them no legal categories comparable to that of "slave," as the term would be understood by the end of the seventeenth century. "Slavery," considered in the abstract as servile bondage, had existed elsewhere for centuries; indeed, the natives of Africa had known it intimately. Yet nothing was inherent, even in the fact of *Negro* slavery, which should compel it to take the form that it took in North America. Negro slavery flourished in Latin America at that same period, but there the system was strikingly different. In certain altogether crucial respects slavery as we know it was not imported from elsewhere but was created in America—fashioned on the spot by Englishmen in

Reprinted from *Slavery* (1963), pp. 37–52, by permission of the University of Chicago Press.

whose traditions such an institution had no part. American slavery was unique, in the sense that, for symmetry and precision of outline, nothing like it had ever previously been seen.

An important essay by Oscar and Mary Handlin has focused new attention upon these facts.[1] Although the first shipload of twenty Negroes had arrived in Virginia in 1619, it was not until the 1660's that the key item in the definition of their status—term of servitude—was clearly fixed in law. It was apparently possible for the earliest Negroes to fall into the various servant categories long familiar to the common law of England, none of which in a practical sense included perpetual and inherited chattel bondage.[2] The bulk of agricultural laborers coming into the colonies at this period were white servants whose terms, as time went on, were to become more and more definitely fixed by indenture, and the Negroes, so far as the law was concerned, could be regarded as "servants" like the rest; there was no articulated legal structure in the colonies to impede their becoming free after a term of service and entering society as artisans and holders of property. Indeed, it was still assumed that the profession of Christianity should itself make a difference in status.[3] Manumission, moreover, for whatever reason, was a practice common enough to be taken for granted and was attended by no special legal restrictions.[4]

Yet all this began changing drastically with the 1660's. The very need for new colonists to people the country, and the very preference of planters for English-speaking whites rather than African savages as laborers, had already set into motion a trend to define in law the rights of white servants. To encourage the immigration of such servants and to counteract homeward-drifting rumors of indefinite servitude under desperate conditions, it was becoming more and more the practice to fix definite and limited terms of indenture—five or six years—as a guaranty that a clear future awaited the white man who would cast his lot with the colonies. The Negro, as the Handlins put it, "never profited from these enactments. Farthest removed from the English, least desired, he communicated with no friends who might be deterred from following. Since his coming was involuntary, nothing that happened to him would increase or decrease his numbers."[5] In short, every improvement in the status of the white servant, in widening the gulf between his condition and that of the Negro, served to dramatize the deepening significance of color and in effect to depress the black ever closer to a state of perpetual slavery. This tendency was ultimately recognized by the legislatures of Maryland and Virginia, and they were led to embody in law what had already become fact. "All negroes or other slaves within the province [according to a Maryland law of 1663], and all negroes and other slaves to be hereafter imported into the province, shall serve *durante vita;* and all children born of any negro or other slave, shall be slaves as their fathers were for the term of their lives." [6] Such was the first legal step whereby a black skin would itself ultimately be equatable with "slave."

Now there is not much doubt that in actual practice the Negro in Virginia and Maryland had become a slave long before this time. There were precedents in English colonial practice—if not quite in law—that might have been drawn from Barbados any time after the 1630's. [7] In all likelihood the delay in defining Negro status may be ascribed to the fact that their numbers prior to the 1660's were never very great and hardly warranted special legislation. [8] But there is much significance simply in the fact that a state of legal indeterminacy existed for some forty years. During that period there are just enough examples of Negro suits for freedom, Negro ownership of property (with the legal incidents thereof), and so on, to convince one that even so small a margin between automatic lifetime slavery and something else made all the difference—considering what plantation slavery, both in law and in fact, would be a generation later. [9] It meant a precious margin of space, not to be discounted, for the conservation of traditional human rights. However, once the initial step had been taken, and once Negroes began arriving in appreciable numbers —as they did in the years following the Restoration—there was, as it turned out, little to impede the restless inclination of the law to remove ambiguities. A further course of legislation in the colonies—to which by then had been added the Carolinas—was inaugurated in the period roughly centering upon the turn of the seventeenth century; this legislation began suppressing, with a certain methodical insistence, whatever rights of personality still remained to the Negro slave. It was thus that most of the features marking the system of American slavery, as the nineteenth century knew it, had been stamped upon it by about the middle of the eighteenth.

Yet before reviewing in greater detail the legal aspects of this servitude, we should note that the most vital facts about its inception remain quite unaccounted for. The reasons for its delay have been satisfactorily explained—but why did it occur at all? Why should the drive to establish such a status have got under way when it did? What was the force behind it, especially in view of the prior absence of any sort of laws defining slavery? We may on the one hand point out the lack of any legal structure automatically compelling the Negro to become a slave, but it is only fair, on the other, to note that there was equally little in the form of such a structure to prevent him from becoming one. It is not enough to indicate the simple process whereby the interests of white servants and black were systematically driven apart: what was its dynamic? Why should the status of "slave" have been elaborated, in little more than two generations following its initial definition, with such utter logic and completeness to make American slavery unique among all such systems known to civilization? [10]

Was it the "motive of gain"? Yes, but with a difference. The motive of gain, as a psychic "fact," can tell us little about what makes men behave as they do; the medieval peasant himself, with his virtually marketless economy, was hardly free from it. But in the emergent agricultural capitalism of colonial Virginia we may already make out a mode of economic organization which was taking on a purity of form never yet seen, and the difference lay in the fact that here a growing system of large-scale staple production for profit was free to develop in a society where no prior traditional institutions, with competing claims of their own, might interpose at any of a dozen points with sufficient power to retard or modify its progress. What happens when such energy meets no limits? [11]

Here, even in its embryonic stages, it is possible to see the process whereby capitalism would emerge as the principal dynamic force in American society. The New World had been discovered and exploited by a European civilization which had always, in contrast with other world cultures, placed a particularly high premium on personal achievement, and it was to be the special genius of Englishmen, from Elizabeth's time onward, to transform this career concept from its earlier chivalric form into one of economic fulfilment—from "glory" to "success." Virginia was settled during the very key period in which the English middle class forcibly reduced, by revolution, the power of those standing institutions —the church and the crown—which most directly symbolized society's traditional limitations upon personal success and mobility. What the return of the crown betokened in 1660 was not so much "reaction" as the fact that all society had by then somehow made terms with the Puritan Revolution. Virginia had proven a uniquely appropriate theater for the acting-out of this narrower, essentially modern ideal of personal, of *economic,* success. Land in the early days was cheap and plentiful; a ready market for tobacco existed; even the yeoman farmer could rise rapidly if he could make the transition to staple production; and above all there was a quick recognition of accomplishment, by a standard which was not available in England but which was the only one available in Virginia: success in creating a plantation.[12]

The decade of the 1660's, inaugurated by the restoration of the Stuart monarchy, marked something of a turning point in the fortunes of the colony not unrelated to the movement there and in Maryland to fix irrevocably upon the Negro a lifetime of slavery. It was during this decade that certain factors bearing upon the colony's economic future were precipitated. One such factor was a serious drop in tobacco prices, brought on not only by overproduction but also by the Navigation Acts of 1660 and 1661,[13] and the market was not to be fully restored for another twenty years. This meant, with rising costs and a disappearing margin of profit, that commercial production on a small-scale basis was placed under serious disabilities. Another factor was the rise in the slave population.

Whereas there had been only about 300 in 1650, by 1670 there were, according to Governor Berkeley, 2,000 slaves in a servant population of 8,000. This was already 25 per cent of the servants, and the figure was even more significant for the future, since the total white servant population in any given period could never be counted on to exceed their average annual immigration multiplied by five or six (the usual term in years, of their indenture), while the increase of slaves over the same period would be cumulative.[14] Such a development would by now be quite enough to stimulate the leaders of the colony—virtually all planters—to clarify in law once and for all the status of lifetime Negro servitude. The formation in 1662 of a Royal Company of Adventurers for the importation of Negroes symbolized the crown's expectation that a labor force of slaves would be the coming thing in the colonies.[15]

It was thus in a period of relatively hard times that it became clear, if the colony of Virginia were to prosper, that capitalism would be the dynamic force in its economic life. "Success" could no longer be visualized as a rise from small beginnings, as it once could, but must now be conceived as a matter of substantial initial investments in land, equipment, and labor, plus the ability to undertake large annual commitments on credit. With the fall in tobacco prices, and with the tiny margin of profit that remained, the yeoman farmer found it difficult enough to eke out a bare living, let alone think of competing with the large planter or of purchasing slaves' or servants' indentures.[16] Success was still possible, but now its terms were clearer, and those who achieved it would be fewer in numbers. The man who managed it would be the man with the large holdings—the man who could command a substantial force of laborers, white or black—who could afford a sizable yearly investment in the handling of his crop: in short, the capitalist planter.

The period beginning in the 1680's and ending about 1710 marked still a new phase. It saw, now under conditions of comparative prosperity, the full emergence of the plantation as the basic unit of capitalist agriculture. By about 1680 the market for Virginia and Maryland tobacco had been restored, though it is important to note that this was accompanied by no great rise in prices. It was rather a matter of having recaptured the European market by flooding it with cheap tobacco and underselling competitors. Returning prosperity, therefore, meant something far more concrete to the man with resources, who could produce tobacco in large enough amounts to make a slim profit margin worthwhile, than to the one whose productivity was limited by the acreage which he and his family could work. These years also witnessed the initial exploitation of the Carolinas, a process which moved much more directly toward large agricultural units than had been the case in Virginia.[17] The acceleration of this development toward clarifying the terms of commercial production—large plantations and substantial investments—had a direct connection with the widening of the market for slaves during this same period. Hand in hand with large holdings went slaves—an assumption which was now being taken more or less for granted. "A rational man," wrote a South Carolina colonist in 1682, "will certainly inquire, 'when I have Land, what shall I doe with it? What commoditys shall I be able to produce, that will yield me money in other countrys, that I may be inabled to buy Negro-slaves, (without which a planter can never doe any great matter)?' " [18] The point had clearly passed when white servants could realistically, on any long-term appraisal, be considered preferable to Negro slaves. Such appraisals were now being made in terms of capitalized earning power, a concept appropriate to large operations rather than small, to long-term rather than short-term planning.

It was, of course, only the man of means who could afford to think in this way. But then he is the one who most concerns us—the man responsible for Negro slavery. Determined in the sixties and seventies to make money despite hard times and low prices, and willing to undertake the investments which that required, he could now in the eighties reap the fruits of his foresight. His slaves were more valuable than ever—a monument to his patience and planning. What had made them so? For one thing he, unlike the yeoman farmer, had a large establishment for training them and was not pressed by the need, as he would have been with white servants on limited indenture, to exploit their *immediate* labor. The labor was his permanently. And for another thing, the system was by now just old enough to make clear for the first time the full meaning of a second generation of native-born American Negroes. These were the dividends: slaves born to the work and using English as their native tongue.[19] By the 1690's the demand for slaves in the British colonies had become so great, and the Royal African Company so inefficient in supplying them, that in 1698 Parliament revoked the company's monopoly on the African coast and threw open the traffic to independent merchants and traders. The stream of incoming slaves, already of some consequence, now became enormous, and at the same time the annual flow of white servants to Virginia and the Carolinas dropped sharply. By 1710 it had become virtually negligible.[20]

What meaning might all this have had for the legal status of the Negro? The connection was intimate and direct; with the full development of the plantation there was nothing, so far as his interests were concerned, to prevent unmitigated capitalism from becoming unmitigated slavery. The planter was now engaged in capitalistic agriculture with a labor force entirely under his control. The personal relationship between master and slave—in any case less likely to exist on large agricultural units than on smaller ones—now became far less important than the economic necessities which had forced the slave into this "unnatural" organization in the first place. For the plantation to operate efficiently and profitably, and with a force of laborers not all of whom may have been fully broken to plantation discipline, the necessity of training them to work long hours and to give unquestioning obedience to their masters and overseers superseded every other consideration. The master must have absolute power over the slave's body, and the law was developing in such a way as to give it to him at every crucial point. Physical discipline was made virtually unlimited [21] and the slave's chattel status unalterably fixed.[22] It was in such a setting that those rights of personality traditionally regarded between men as private and inherent, quite apart from the matter of lifetime servitude, were left virtually without defense. The integrity of the family was ignored, and slave marriage was deprived of any legal or moral standing.[23] The condition of a bondsman's soul—a matter of much concern to church and civil authority in the Spanish colonies—was here very quickly dropped from consideration. A series of laws enacted between 1667 and 1671 had systematically removed any lingering doubts whether conversion to Christianity should make a difference in status: henceforth it made none.[24] The balance, therefore, involved on the one side the constant pressure of costs, prices, and the problems of management, and on the other the personal interests of the slave. Here, there were no counterweights: those interests were unsupported by any social pressures from the outside; they were cherished by no customary feudal immunities; they were no concern of the government (the king's main interest was in tobacco revenue); they could not be sustained by the church, for the church had little enough power and influence among its own white constituencies, to say nothing of the suspicion its ministers aroused at every proposal to enlarge the church's work among the blacks.[25] The local planter class controlled all those public concerns which most affected the daily life of the colony, and it was thus only in matters of the broadest and most general policy that this planter domination was in any way touched by bureaucratic decisions made in London. The emergent institution of slavery was in effect unchallenged by any other institutions.[26]

The result was that the slave, utterly powerless, would at every critical point see his interests further depressed. At those very points the drive of the law—unembarrassed by the perplexities of competing interests—was to clarify beyond all question, to rationalize, to simplify, and to make more logical and symmetrical the slave's status in society. So little impeded was this pressure to define and clarify that all the major categories in law which bore upon such status were very early established with great thoroughness and completeness.

NOTES

1. See Oscar and Mary F. Handlin, "Origins of the Southern Labor System," *William and Mary Quarterly*, 3d Series, VII (April, 1950), 199–222.
2. The state of villeinage, which had once flourished in England during the

Middle Ages, had many of the attributes which later characterized plantation slavery. Yet one crucial aspect of slavery—the legal suppression of the personality —was never present in villeinage. The status of villein, moreover, had by the seventeenth century become virtually extinct in England.

3. This assumption, having its roots in tradition, was still persistent enough throughout most of the seventeenth century that, as late as the 1690's, colonial assemblies felt the necessity to declare, in legal enactments, that baptism did not confer on the slave the right to be manumitted. See John Codman Hurd, *The Law of Freedom and Bondage in the United States* (Boston: Little, Brown, 1858), I, 232, 250, 297, 300–301.

4. The implications of the Handlin thesis are sufficient for the limited purposes for which it is being used here. To the extent that the Handlins appear to argue that an indentured status was automatically assumed in this period, in the absence of automatic legal guaranties of slavery, to that extent is their essay quite misleading. Insofar as they point, on the other hand, to a condition legally indeterminate—with practice still sufficiently blurred as to allow a number of exceptions, unthinkable a generation later, to automatic slavery—they do no violence to what is known about the period.
   This very indeterminacy has sustained a minor debate going back more than fifty years. James C. Ballagh in 1902 first challenged the accepted notion that slavery in Virginia dated from 1619. The parcel of twenty Negroes sold in that year to the Virginians from a Dutch ship were not held as slaves, Ballagh insisted, but rather as servants, and Virginia law did not recognize out-and-out slavery until more than forty years later. John H. Russell, writing in 1913, accepted Ballagh's position. While admitting that lifetime servitude in Virginia existed long before it was given statutory recognition, he agreed that without a prior system of slavery or a slave code it was "plausible that the Africans became servants who, after a term of service varying from two to eight years, were entitled to freedom." Russell cited examples of Negroes who sued for their freedom or who became independent landowners. The Ballagh-Russell thesis— accepted by Ulrich Phillips—was not questioned until Susie Ames's *Studies of the Virginia Eastern Shore* appeared in 1940. Miss Ames held that there was not enough evidence to support Ballagh and Russell, and that Russell's examples may simply have been of manumitted slaves (in other words, if Negroes were not automatically considered as indentured servants—which she thought doubtful—then they must have been automatically considered as slaves: it had to be one thing or the other). Wesley Frank Craven in 1949 gave further support to Miss Ames's position; in his opinion it was likely that "the trend from the first was toward a sharp distinction between . . . [the Negro] and the white servant." The Handlins, taking issue with Miss Ames, in effect brought the argument back to Ballagh and Russell—not asserting flatly (for Miss Ames and Mr. Craven were at least right about the scarcity of evidence) but calling it "much more logical to assume with Russell that these were servants who had completed their terms." And there the argument rests. See James C. Ballagh, *History of Slavery in Virginia* (Baltimore: Johns Hopkins, 1902), pp. 9–10, 27–31; John H. Russell, *The Free Negro in Virginia, 1619–1865* (Baltimore: Johns Hopkins, 1913), pp. 23–31; Ulrich B. Phillips, *American Negro Slavery* (New York: D. Appleton & Co., 1918), p. 75; Susie M. Ames, *Studies of the Virginia Eastern Shore in the Seventeenth Century* (Richmond, Va.: Dietz, 1940), pp. 100–106; Wesley Frank Craven, *The Southern Colonies in the Seventeenth Century, 1607–1689* (Baton Rouge: Louisiana State University, 1949), pp. 218–19. See also n. 7 below.

5. Handlin and Handlin, "Origins of the Southern Labor System," p. 211.

6. Quoted in Hurd, *Law of Freedom and Bondage*, I, 249. A Virginia act of the year before had assumed and implied lifetime slavery. It provided special punishments for servants who ran away in the company of "negroes who are incapable of making satisfaction by addition of a time." Helen T. Catterall, *Judicial Cases concerning American Slavery and the Negro* (Washington: Carnegie Institution,

1926 ff.), I, 59. The matter was made explicit when in 1670 it was enacted that "all servants not being Christians, imported into this colony by shipping, shall be slaves for their lives. . . ." Hurd, *Law of Freedom and Bondage,* I, 233.

7. It should be noted that the Handlins do rule out rather too hastily the possibility of the Virginians adapting the status of slavery from the West Indies, claiming as they do that Negroes there were still regarded as "servants" as late as 1663. Their assertion is not entirely correct. There were, indeed, few Negroes in the West Indies prior to the 1630's, and there was no slave code there until 1663. But by 1636, Negroes were already coming into Barbados in great enough numbers that the governor's council felt it necessary in that year, law or no law, to issue a regulation declaring that all Negroes or Indians landed on the island would be considered as slaves, bound to work there for the rest of their lives. See Sir Harry Johnston, *The Negro in the New World* (London: Methuen & Co., 1910), p. 211; Vincent Harlow, *A History of Barbados* (Oxford: Clarendon, 1926), pp. 309–10. Even in the Spanish colonies, lifetime servitude had been familiar for nearly a century.

   Some kind of statutory recognition of slavery in the American colonies occurred as follows: Massachusetts, 1641; Connecticut, 1650; Virginia, 1661; Maryland, 1663; New York and New Jersey, 1664; South Carolina, 1684; and Rhode Island, 1700. The apparent significance of this chronology diminishes, however, when it is noted that although enactments in the Northern colonies recognized the legality of lifetime servitude, no effort was made to require all Negroes to be placed in that condition. The number of Negroes, moreover, was so small that in Massachusetts it was not until 1698 that any effort was made to consider the important problem of slave children's status. See Ballagh, *Slavery in Virginia,* pp. 35, 39.

8. See n. 14 below.

9. Russell, *Free Negro in Virginia,* pp. 24–39.

10. The common-law tradition actually worked in more than one direction to help perfect the legal arrangements of slavery. Not only was there little in the common law, simply as law, to prevent the Negro from being compelled into a state of slavery, but the very philosophy of the common law would encourage the colonial courts to develop whatever laws appeared necessary to deal with unprecedented conditions.

11. Ever since the time of Marx and Engels (and indeed, before), the idea of "Capitalism" has been a standard tool in the analysis of social behavior. Up to a point this tool is useful; it can throw light on changes in behavior patterns at the point where capitalistic methods and habits in a society begin to supersede feudal ones. In Europe it made some sense. Here is how Engels argued: "According to this conception," he wrote in *Anti-Dühring,* "the ultimate causes of all social changes and political revolutions are to be sought, not in the minds of men, in their increasing insight into eternal truth and justice, but in changes in the mode of production and exchange; they are to be sought not in the *philosophy* but in the *economics* of the epoch concerned." But then this idea cannot tell us much about the differences between two societies, *both* capitalist, but in one of which the "means of production" have changed into capitalistic ones and in the other of which the means of production were never anything *but* capitalistic and in which no other forces were present to resist their development.

12. Despite the relative mobility of English society since Tudor times, personal achievement and status still inhered in any number of preferable alternatives to trade and production. But the openness of Virginia lay in the fact that purely capitalistic incentives were being used to get people to come there. No nobles, with their retinues of peasants, migrated to the colony; indeed, there was little reason why the ideal of "making good" should in itself hold many attractions for an aristocracy already established. But for others there were rewards for risk-taking which were simply not available in England. True, Virginia did develop its own aristocracy, but it had to be a created one, based on terms peculiar to the new country, and—at least as a basis for aspirations—theoreti-

cally open to everyone. At any rate, the standards for joining it were not primarily chivalric: to be a "gentleman" one must first have been a successful planter.

13. These acts embodied the Puritan mercantilist policy which Cromwell had never been able to enforce but which had been taken over by the Restoration government. Their general purpose was that of redirecting colonial trade (much of which had been engrossed by the Dutch during the Civil War) through the hands of English merchants. Their immediate effects on tobacco, before the market could readjust itself, were, from the viewpoint of colonial planters, most unfavorable. By limiting the sale of Virginia tobacco to England and requiring that it be transported in English ships, the Navigation Acts cut off Virginia's profitable trade with the Dutch and temporarily crippled its profitable foreign markets. This, according to Thomas J. Wertenbaker, was the basic cause for the serious drop in tobacco prices. See *Planters of Colonial Virginia* (Princeton: Princeton University Press, 1922), pp. 85–87, 90.

14. "40,000 persons, men, women, and children, of which 2,000 are black slaves, 6,000 Christian servants for a short time.—Gov. Berkeley." Evarts B. Greene and Virginia D. Harrington, *American Population before the Federal Census of 1790* (New York: Columbia University Press, 1932), p. 36. This figure may be looked at two ways. From the standpoint of *later* populations, one may call attention to its smallness. But consider how it must have appeared to the man looking back to a time only two decades before, when the number of Negroes was negligible. Now, in 1670, with Negroes constituting a full quarter of the servant population (a proportion which gave every promise of increasing), they become a force to be dealt with. By now, men would take them into account as a basis for future calculations in a way which previously they had never needed to do. The very laws demonstrate this. Moreover, Negroes had accumulated in large enough parcels in the hands of the colony's most powerful men to develop in these men deep vested interests in the Negroes' presence and a strong concern with the legal aspects of their future. Among the land patents of the sixties, for example, may already be seen Richard Lee with eighty Negroes, Carter of Corotoman with twenty, the Scarboroughs with thirty-nine, and numerous patents listing fifteen or more. Philip Alexander Bruce, *Economic History of Virginia in the Seventeenth Century* (New York: Macmillan, 1907), II, 78.

15. The subsequent increase of slaves in Virginia was not largely the work of this company. But its formation under royal protection, coming at the time it did, appears to form part of a general pattern of expectations regarding the future state of labor in the plantation colonies. This, taken together with the drop in tobacco prices and coincident with the Navigation Acts and the first general laws on perpetual servitude, all coming at once, seem to add up to something: profitable enterprise, when possible at all, would henceforth as never before have to be conceived in terms of heavily capitalized investment, and more and more men were recognizing this.

16. This had not always been so; the aspirations of a farmer in, say, 1649, with prices at 3 pence a pound, could include a wide range of possibilities. But now, with the price at one-fourth of that figure and costs proportionately much greater than formerly, he could hardly think of the future realistically in terms of becoming a planter. See Lewis Cecil Gray, *History of Agriculture in the Southern States to 1860* (Washington: Carnegie Institution, 1933), I, 263. Now this does not mean that after 1660 the yeoman farmer invariably faced destitution. A great deal depended on how such a farmer conceived his future. The man who made his living from diversified subsistence farming and who planted tobacco as an extra-money crop would undoubtedly suffer less from a drop in prices than the heavily capitalized planter. However if this same farmer hoped to emulate "his predecessors of the earlier period in saving money, purchasing land . . . and becoming a substantial citizen, the task was well nigh impossible of accomplishment." Wertenbaker, *Planters of Colonial Virginia*, p. 97. See also *ibid.*, pp. 96–100, for an extended discussion of the effects of this depression on the yeomanry as a class.

17. The Carolina proprietors had a far clearer notion of the terms on which money was to be made from their colony than had been true of the London Company of sixty years before with regard to Virginia. They appear at the very outset to have fostered the establishment of large estates, and a number of such estates set up in the 1670's and 1680's were organized by Barbados men with first-hand plantation experience. See Gray, *History of Agriculture*, I, 324–25; also J. P. Thomas, "Barbadians in Early South Carolina," *South Carolina Historical Magazine*, XXXI (April, 1930), 89. Although a dominant staple was not to emerge until some time later, with rice and indigo, it seems to have been conceived in terms of large units to a degree never envisaged at a comparable stage in the development of Virginia. One index of this is quickly seen in the composition of the laboring population there; a little over a generation after the first settlements the ratio of Negro slaves to whites in the total population could be safely estimated at about one to one, whereas the same ratio would not be attained in Virginia until late in the eighteenth century. Greene and Harrington, *American Population*, pp. 124, 137.

18. Quoted in Gray, *History of Agriculture*, I, 352.

19. This is another point of view from which to consider the 1671 figure (cited in n. 13 above) on the Virginia slave population. The difference between the 300 Negroes of 1650 and the 2,000 of 1670 is substantial—nearly a sevenfold increase. According to Berkeley's testimony the importations over the previous seven years had not been more than two or three cargoes. If this were true, it would be safe to estimate that a significant number of that 2,000 must already have been native-born American Negroes. As for the period to which the above paragraph has reference—fifteen or twenty years later—the number of native-born must by then have increased considerably.

20. Greene and Harrington, *American Population*, pp. 136–37; Gray, *History of Agriculture*, I, 349–50.

21. As early as 1669 a Virginia law had declared it no felony if a master or overseer killed a slave who resisted punishment. According to the South Carolina code of 1712, the punishment for offering "any violence to any christian or white person, by striking, or the like" was a severe whipping for the first offense, branding for the second, and death for the third. Should the white man attacked be injured or maimed, the punishment was automatically death. The same act provided that a runaway slave be severely whipped for his first offense, branded for his second, his ears cut off for the third, and castrated for the fourth. It is doubtful whether such punishments were often used, but their very existence served to symbolize the relationship of absolute power over the slave's body. Hurd, *Law of Freedom and Bondage*, I, 232; Thomas Cooper and D. J. McCord (eds.), *Statutes at Large of South Carolina* (Columbia, S.C., 1836–41), VII, 357–59.

22. Slaves in seventeenth-century Virginia had become, as a matter of actual practice, classed on the same footing as household goods and other personal property. The code of 1705 made them a qualified form of real estate, but that law was in 1726 amended by another which declared that slaves were "to pass as chattels." Bruce, *Economic History*, II, 99; Hurd, *Law of Freedom and Bondage*, I, 242. The South Carolina code of 1740 made them "chattels personal, in the hands of their owners and possessors and their executors, administrators and assigns, to all intents, constructions and purposes whatsoever. . . ." *Ibid.*, I, 303.

23. Bruce (*Economic History*, II, 108) describes a will, written about 1680, in which a woman "bequeathed to one daughter, . . . a negress and the third child to be born of her; to a second daughter, . . . the first and second child to be born of the same woman."

24. See Handlin and Handlin, "Origins of the Southern Labor System," p. 212. The Maryland law of 1671 could leave no possible doubt in this matter, declaring that any Christianized slave "is, are and shall att all tymes hereafter be adjudged Reputed deemed and taken to be and Remayne in Servitude and Bondage and subject to the same Servitude and Bondage to all intents and purposes as if hee shee they every or any of them was or were in and Subject vnto before such his

her or their Becomeing Christian or Christians or Receiving of the Sacrament of Baptizme any opinion or other matter or thing to the Contrary in any wise Notwithstanding." William Hand Browne (ed.), *Archives of Maryland* (Baltimore, 1884), II, 272. See also n. 3 above.

25. What this meant to the Negro is admirably reflected in a book by Morgan Godwyn, an Anglican minister who served in the 1670's both in Barbados and in Virginia. Godwyn's book, *The Negro's and Indian's Advocate,* was a plea for the care of the Negro's soul. He attacked the planters for keeping religion from the slaves, for "not allowing their children *Baptism;* nor suffering them upon better terms than direct *Fornication,* to live with their Women, (for Wives, I may not call them, being never married). And accounting it Foppish, when Dead, to think of giving them *Christian,* or even decent Burial; that so their pretence for Brutifying them, might find no Contradiction" (p. 37). In Godwyn's eyes the planters were men "who for the most part do know no other God but money, nor Religion but Profit" (Preface). He quotes one Barbadian who "openly maintained . . . that Negroes were beasts, and had no more souls than beasts, and that religion did not concern them. Adding that they [his fellow Barbadians] went *not* to those parts to save souls, or propagate religion, but to get Money" (p. 39). Even the care of white souls in the colonies appears to have occupied a rather low order of concern. The Attorney-General of England in 1693 objected strenuously to the erection of a college in Virginia, though he was reminded of the need to educate young men for the ministry and was begged to consider the souls of the colonists. "Souls! Damn your souls," he replied, "make tobacco." Quoted in Wertenbaker, *Planters of Colonial Virginia,* p. 138. It is doubtful that the planters of Virginia were quite so brutal as the Barbadians in their attitude toward the Negro or in the management of their plantations, but even in Virginia Godwyn found that the idea of teaching religion to the Negro slave was thought "so idle and ridiculous, so utterly needless and unnecessary, that no Man can forfeit his Judgement more, than by any proposal looking or tending that way" (p. 172). That such an attitude had not changed by the eighteenth century is suggested by a piece in the *Athenian Oracle* of Boston in 1707 in which the writer declared, "Talk to a *Planter* of the *Soul* of a *Negro,* and he'll be apt to tell ye (or at least his actions speak it loudly) that the Body of one of them may be worth twenty pounds; but the Souls of an Hundred of them would not yield him one Farthing." Quoted in Marcus W. Jernegan, "Slavery and Conversion in the American Colonies," *American Historical Review,* XXI (April, 1916), 516.

26. For the control exercised over colonial institutional life by this planter elite, see Craven, *Southern Colonies,* pp. 153, 159, 170–72, 274–78; Philip A. Bruce, *Institutional History of Virginia in the Seventeenth Century* (New York: Putnam, 1910), I, 468; and George M. Brydon, *Virginia's Mother Church, and the Political Conditions under Which It Grew* (Richmond: Virginia Historical Society, 1947), I, 94–96, 232.

4. "The Negro Problem": A Case History

The following analysis by McWilliams, while consistent with that of Chapter 3, goes beyond the period of slavery. It deals with the crucial Reconstruction phase of black American history and the shift from slavery to "Jim Crow," as well as with events beyond this period. In this treatment we can see the cyclic process of gain and loss for black Americans which is emphasized in subsequent chapters. In addition, it makes clear the historical change in symptoms and symbols of black subordination, and the relentless continuity of the process itself.

CAREY McWILLIAMS

No domestic social issue has received more attention than "the Negro problem." However the problem is not as old as we think: it dates from the issuance of the Emancipation Proclamation in 1863. Indeed it was this act which created the Negro problem—that is, whether to acknowledge the Negro's emancipation, with all the implications, or to pretend that emancipation had some other meaning. Only in this sense has there ever been a Negro problem in the United States.

As a matter of fact, the attempt to relate prejudice to the specific nature of its object is a cunning projection of the prejudice of the dominant group; "cunning" because it passes as scientific curiosity. As long as the majority can pretend that the source of prejudice inheres in the nature of the victim, social action can be indefinitely postponed; there is always still another investigation which must be made. For example, it can hardly be denied that the Negro has been overstudied and overinvestigated; whereas all too little is known about the circumstances under which we came to have a Negro problem. This chapter, therefore, has been designed to provide a natural history of the Negro problem.

"The Habit Makes the Monk"

Historically, racial discrimination in the United States is an outgrowth of slavery, and slavery, by a strange paradox, was a by-product of the freedom implicit in the discovery of a largely uninhabited New World; slavery "was simply a way of recruiting labor for the purpose of exploiting the great natural resources of America."[1] Indentured servants and bondsmen vanished into the wilderness almost as soon as they arrived and there was no large native population to exploit. Specifically free labor could not be recruited in sufficient volume to meet the requirements in cotton and other plantation crops, nor could free labor be kept on the plantations. On the other hand, the economics of large-scale production on the plantation offset the inefficiency of slave labor. As the plantation system spread, the "poor whites" found themselves at a hopeless competitive disadvantage on their barren hilly acres. Their status, moreover, deteriorated in direct relation to the number of Negro slaves who were used as craftsmen and mechanics as well as field hands. As paradoxical as the fact that slavery stemmed from freedom was the fact that the cessation of the African slave trade, by enhancing the value of slaves, greatly intensified the problem of abolishing slavery.

The dynamic of gain and not any qualities of Negroes as Negroes produced the institution of slavery. Even bondage was not related to "race" as such; indentured white servants were more characteristic of Virginia than Negro slaves in the early eighteenth century. Rights were denied not on the basis of race but on the basis of power. On the eve of the nineteenth century, a tenth of the Negro population lived outside the slave system and these Negroes were recognized as having some of the rights of freedmen. In the United States, slavery was not an antecedent fact; it was a growth or rather an improvisation. Since slavery was not recognized under the common law, the system had to be evolved out of apprenticeship and vagrancy laws and through a gradual accumulation of precedents. The basic paradox and contradiction of racial discrimination in the United States is to be found in the fact that slavery was not a primordial fact but a later acquisition inconsistent with the stated purposes for which the Republic was formed.

"Slavery in America," writes Dr. W. E. B. Du Bois, "is a strange and contradictory story. It cannot be regarded as mainly either a theoretical problem of morals or a scientific problem of race. From either of these points of view, the rise of slavery in America is simply inexplicable. Looking at the facts frankly, slavery evidently was a matter of economics, a question of income and labor, rather than a problem of right and wrong, or of the physical differences in men. Once slavery began to be the source of vast income for men and nations, there followed a frantic search for moral and racial justifications. Such excuses were found and men did not inquire too carefully into either their logic or truth."[2] Myth, as Durkheim once said, imitates society, not nature. The myth of racial inequality did not arise until social institutions, such as slavery, had created unequal relations between men.

Neither a Negro nor a race problem existed under slavery. In the first place, the plantation system did not permit direct competition between Negroes and "poor whites": the large plantation holdings, embracing the best lands, kept the poor whites at a distance. The masters were not in competition with the slaves or the slaves with the masters; the master owned the slave and the slave "belonged to" the master. Ironically the Negro slave was a part, although a subordinate part, of the plantation system; the poor whites were the real minority or subordinate group. "Under slavery," writes Dr. E. Franklin Frazier, "whatever racial antagonisms there might have existed between masters and slaves were reduced to a minimum by the social controls regulating their relations." [3]

Nevertheless in the South, as in Brazil, it was slavery and the one-crop system which most deeply affected "the social plastics" of the region. Out of slavery came the myth of racial superiority and other mischievous self-deceptions and social delusions. Traits which to this day are pointed to as evidence of the Negro's inferiority are clearly not traits of the Negro but characteristics of all slaves. "At times," writes Gilberto Freyre, "what appears to be the influence of race is purely and simply that of the slave, of the social system of slavery, a reflection of the enormous capacity of that system for morally degrading masters and slaves alike. . . ." The Negro unlike the Indian could not escape from slavery; hence "it is . . . an absurdity to hold the Negro responsible for what was not his doing or the Indian's, but that of the social system in which they both functioned." [4] Had it not been for Negro slaves, Indian-white relations might have taken a quite different form; and, conversely, had it not been for the Indian, slavery might not have been enforceable. Slavery, not biological traits or cultural differences, was responsible for the hostility between Negroes, Indians, and whites. The origin of the beliefs upon which racial dominance rests is suggested in the adage quoted by Freyre: "The habit makes the monk." The social form determines the belief; not the belief the social form.

The misidentification of "traits" is illustrated in the matter of sexual morality. As Freyre has pointed out, slavery was opulent in vices since the economic interests of the masters sanctioned depravity. Wherever slavery has prevailed, it has produced the same consequences regardless of the "race" of the slaves. "White slaves" are not slaves because they are white; they are prostitutes because they are slaves. "It was not the Negro," writes Freyre, "who was the libertine, but the slave who was at the service of his idle master's economic interests and voluptuous pleasure. It was not 'the inferior race' that was the source of corruption, but the abuse of one race by another, an abuse that demanded a servile conformity on the part of the Negro to the appetites of the all-powerful lords of the land. Those appetites were stimulated by idleness, by 'a wealth acquired without

labor' . . . by 'idleness' or 'laziness' which means—by the economic structure of the slave-holding regime itself."

Slavery clearly shaped the "social plastics" of the South. For example,
there was a close correlation between the number of Negro slaves and the
degree to which Negroes were completely subordinated and treated as a
form of property. The larger the investment in slaves, and the greater the
economic return from their labor, the more intensely the slave myths were
propagated and the tighter were the social controls. The belief in the
Negro's "inferiority" is today most widely held, and most passionately
affirmed, in those areas where the strongest incentives exist for the exploitation of Negro labor. "Throughout the Cotton Belt," writes Frazier, "race
relations are characterized by the complete social subordination of the
Negro." [5] The degree of the Negro's subordination varies with the acreage
in cotton and in relation to the existence of alternative employment
opportunities.

Slavery, as Oliver Cox has pointed out, is not "a derivative of human
idiosyncrasy or wickedness, but rather . . . a function of a peculiar type of
economic order. . . . The exploitation of native peoples, imperialism, is
not a sin, not essentially a problem of morals or of vice; it is a problem of
production and of competition for markets." [6] In this country, slavery was
an aspect of the relation between Europe and America. Free labor poured
into the United States in quest of free land, and the force of this invasion
would have rapidly undercut slavery had the Industrial Revolution not
created an extraordinary opportunity for the further exploitation of slave
labor in the production of cotton. The more the wealth and power of the
cotton states increased through the shipment of cotton to overseas markets, the more belligerent these states became and the more strenuously
they sought to expand into the free-soil states to the west. From the
beginning, therefore, race relations in the United States have been an
aspect of the relations between Europe and America and between European nations in a competition for world markets.

The means that nations use to exploit other nations are the means by
which one group within a nation exploits another. "For the full profitable
exploitation of a people," writes Cox, "the dominant group must devise
ways and means of limiting that people's cultural assimilation. . . . Assimilation diminishes the exploitative possibilities." [7] Just as a form of cultural
and social parallelism between the dominant and the subordinate group is
an essential aspect of the strategy of dominance, so the industrially
dominant nation seeks to maintain a measure of "social distance" in its
relations with so-called "backward" peoples. This distance may create
prejudice and make for misunderstanding but it does not reflect initial
hostility or aversion. For example, statutes against intermarriage are not
based on racial antipathy; if an attraction did not exist, the statutes would

not be necessary. As a matter of fact the miscegenation statutes were adopted *after* a long history of sexual intimacy between white masters and Negro women held as slaves.

Slave relations are not race relations although they strongly influence the latter. The basic reason why "a Negro problem" did not exist prior to the Civil War is to be found in Chief Justice Taney's remark in the Dred Scott case that the Negro was to be regarded as "having no rights which the white man was bound to respect." This remark explains the basis of the difference between slave relations and race relations. In one sense, "racial conflict" does not arise under a slave system; the conflict is between two types of labor, one free and one slave, and not between free laborers some of whom are white and others colored.

The Discovery of a Dilemma

The discovery of America's racial problem or dilemma dates from the first movement of Union troops into slave territory. "It was only with the advance of the invading armies farther and farther into Southern fields," writes Dr. Paul Skeels Peirce, "that the significance of the Negro as an element in the contest became more exactly defined and more generally apparent." [8] First by the hundreds and later by the thousands, liberated Negro slaves came flocking to the federal army camps for support and protection. Once the Emancipation Proclamation was issued, of course, the problem became at once more urgent and more complicated. A few months later the government established the Bureau of Colored Troops in the War Department and the famous 54th and 55th Massachusetts Negro regiments were formed. These decisions created the Negro problem. "A race problem developed for the first time," writes Dr. Charles S. Johnson, "when the fixed social position of the Negro slave was changed by his emancipation."

As the war continued, various petitions from the Freedmen's Aid Societies finally forced the government to give serious consideration to the problem of what was to be done with 4,100,000 propertyless, largely illiterate former slaves. The administration, Lincoln included, at first toyed with the idea of colonizing the former slaves in Africa or South America —a fantasy which betrays underlying prejudice. Indeed it was only after two years of debate that a bill was finally passed on March 3, 1865, creating the Freedmen's Bureau in the War Department. In freeing the slaves, as Charles Beard observed, the nation had created "a large and anomalous class in the American social order—a mass of emancipated slaves long destined to wander in a hazy realm between bondage and freedom." The haziness of this realm, however, reflected the haziness of the majority's intentions.

For a war-weary nation, the problems thus created were of extraordinary magnitude. Negroes were wandering about in droves: landless, confused, hungry, and full of terrifying uncertainties. The school problem alone was of staggering proportions: of 4,100,000 slaves, some 1,700,000 were of school age. Nor was it a matter of expanding existing institutions to meet new needs: there were no institutions on which to build. In the South, as Dr. Maurice R. Davie has pointed out, "the war had left a stricken upper class possessing nothing but lands and a servile population possessing naught except the labor of their hands." [9] Actually the former slaves were in a worse position than before the war since the basis of their monopoly of certain skilled labor positions had been destroyed and they now faced the competition of the poor whites. Such was the scope of the problem which the Freedmen's Bureau was asked to solve—without adequate funds, precedents, directives, or a clearly formulated policy.

All things considered, the Freedmen's Bureau did a remarkable job in the brief period it was in existence (March 3, 1865, to June 30, 1872). The year the Bureau was abolished it was operating 2677 day and night schools, with 3300 teachers (most of whom it had trained) and 149,581 pupils. In establishing such institutions as Howard and Fisk Universities, Hampton Institute, and St. Augustine Normal School, the Bureau inaugurated a system of professional, normal, and industrial training that was of great value to Negroes. In one year alone, the Bureau trained over 2000 teachers, half of whom were Negroes, and, in many areas of the South, it laid the foundation for what later became a system of tax-supported public schools. The Bureau also provided institutions for the care of the sick and infirm, the insane and the crippled; the aged and the deaf-and-dumb. It established an excellent medical-aid program for Negroes; founded hospitals; and built asylums. Some medical aid was furnished to at least 1,000,000 Negroes. It also aided orphans and the destitute and transported 30,000 "displaced" freedmen to their former homes.

The Bureau also sought to adjust the former slave to a system of free labor. For example, it sought to intervene between the former slave and the plantation owner for the purpose of negotiating an equitable labor contract. Not less than 50,000 such contracts were prepared which contained minimum guarantees as to food, fuel, shelter, and payment of a fixed money wage. In many cases, agents of the Bureau appeared in court on behalf of Negro claimants. In Maryland and Virginia, agents of the Bureau forced the release of hundreds of Negro children who had been "farmed out" to employers as apprentices. While this attempt to provide a shield for the protection of Negroes was not too successful, nevertheless the Bureau "imparted a conception—inadequate and distorted though it may have been—of his [the Negro's] civil rights as a freedman." [10] It encouraged the Negro to vote; protected his right to vote; and, as its enemies charged, probably told him how to vote.

In response to a congressional mandate to provide every freedman with "forty acres and a mule," the Bureau set about the task of distributing abandoned and confiscated lands to former slaves. This, of course, was the crux of the problem; without a measure of economic independence the Negro was certain to be reimprisoned in a system of thinly disguised slavery. But the Bureau never had more than 800,000 acres at its disposal; in fact only two tenths of 1 per cent of the land in the rebel states was ever held by the Bureau. If all these lands had been available, the Bureau could not have given even one acre to every freedman, let alone a mule and the means by which the land might be worked. As a matter of fact, most of the lands were quickly repossessed by the former owners in the wake of wholesale amnesties and the Negroes were promptly dispossessed. With the collapse of this program, the brave venture of the Freedmen's Bureau came to an unhappy end.

In the meantime, of course, the Southern states had boldly enacted the Black Codes which stripped the freed Negro population of all but the barest provision for civil rights—marriage, ownership of property, and the right to appear in court. The Radical Republicans promptly met this aggression by placing ten Southern states under military rule, and by enacting the Civil Rights Act and the 14th Amendment. It now seemed as though Congress intended to carry the "unfinished business" of the Civil War to a conclusion and to end the American dilemma. The determination of Congress was still strong when it passed the Civil Rights Act after the Southern states had rejected the 14th Amendment.

But reconstruction, which appeared to be heroic, was based on a realistic appraisal of a novel aspect of the dilemma which had come with victory. Negroes, of course, were overwhelmingly concentrated in the South. If the Negro was now to be counted as a full person for the purpose of determining representation in Congress, instead of three fifths of a person, the North would have fought the Civil War only to vest political control in the South. This, then, was the real dilemma. To offset the threat of Southern dominance, the Republicans proceeded to disfranchise a large portion of the South's white population through the invocation of military rule. At the same time, federal agents "voted" Negroes in large blocs. The haste with which certain Western states were admitted to the Union in the postwar period shows how desperate were the Republicans and how precarious their control had become. For example, the constitution of Nevada was telegraphed to Washington so that the Republican majority might hastily admit the state, and in similar manner Montana, Idaho, and Washington were invested with statehood to insure the ascendancy of the Republican Party. The political objective of reconstruction, therefore, was to maintain Republican ascendancy by force until such time as a clear Republican majority could be built up in the Western states.

Even so reconstruction might have been carried through to its logical conclusion but for a number of developments of far-reaching importance.

In 1873 came a panic which shook the structure of the national economy from top to bottom and a depression which lasted for five years. The depression made the Northern industrialists ponder the long-range implications of emancipation and reconstruction. "If victory meant full economic freedom for labor in the South, white and black," writes Dr. Du Bois, "if it meant land and education, and eventually votes, then the slave empire was doomed, and the profits of Northern industry built on the Southern slave foundation would also be seriously curtailed. Northern industry had a stake in the cotton kingdom and in the cheap slave labor that supported it. It had expanded war industries during the fighting, encouraged by government subsidy and eventually protected by a huge tariff rampart. When war profits declined there was still prospect of tremendous postwar profits on cotton and other products of Southern agriculture. Therefore, what the North wanted was not freedom and higher wage for black labor, but its control under such forms of law as would keep it cheap. . . . The moral protest of abolitionists must be appeased but profitable industry was determined to control wages and government." [11]

The problem of political control, however, was greatly complicated in the postwar period. There was the usual postwar reaction "against the government"; the depression of 1873 had created wide unrest; a war-expanded American industry was still not in a position to compete for world markets; the Liberal Republicans were appalled by the corruption of the Grant administration; and the Democrats had won important victories in 1874. To build a more or less perpetual Republican majority it was necessary, first of all, to use the revenues from the tariff system to pay Northern veterans a pension; pensions and the tariff were "as inseparable as Gold Dust twins." By 1875 the government was giving Northern veterans $29 million annually and this sum jumped to $60 million in 1879; to $89 million in 1889; and to $159 million in 1893. Pensions helped to provide purchasing power in the North for the products of Northern industry, and Northern industrial production was in turn based on Southern agriculture and cheap Negro labor. At the same time, pensions meant votes. "The Grand Army of the Republic," writes Dr. Walter Prescott Webb, "was powerful at the polls, where it won a far larger percentage of victories than it won against the armies of Lee. No politician dared deny a lifelong subsidy which was paid impartially to the pauper and to the millionaire." [12] Finally there was the West: a new raw-materials empire, rich in mineral wealth, offering an excellent market for the products of Northern industry. The rapid admission of Western territories as states would wed these states to the Republican Party. The presence of many Union veterans in the West, the control of territorial governments by the appointive power, the manipulation of laws governing the public domain, the granting of homesteads to veterans, and liberal appropriations for

Western river-and-harbor and other public improvements, as well as the use of "pork barrel" legislation generally, helped to build up Republican majorities in the West.

Indeed Louis M. Hacker explains "reconstruction" perfectly by suggesting that the real reconstruction was in the North, not the South. By 1875 the Republicans had a firm hold on the key states of Ohio, Indiana, Michigan, and Wisconsin, and the threat of a South-West alliance had been averted. The Civil War, as Dr. Hacker points out, had done its work too well: "it had destroyed a political opposition based upon a class interest"—the kind of opposition to industrial capitalism which the landed aristocracies had presented in Europe.[13] The Republicans, however, could see that a new class opposition might arise; hence they were disposed to strike a bargain with the planter dynasty. Instead of resolving the Emancipation dilemma, they seized upon it as a means by which the appearance of democracy could be used to frustrate the democratic process. This great opportunity arose in 1876—the year in which Congress sent its first committee of inquiry on "the Chinese problem" to California; in which the Reciprocity Treaty with Hawaii went into effect; and in which the first investigation into the new Rockefeller oil monopoly was launched.

Resolution of the Dilemma

"In 1876," writes Dr. Du Bois, "the democratic process of government was crippled throughout the whole nation." [14] Many factors were responsible for this impairment: the emotional letdown after the war; the dispersive effect of the wild rush to the West which drew in its wake the first wholesale European immigration; the confusion produced by the rapid rise of a new social system; and, above all, the vicious counterattack in the South from 1868 to 1871. Reconstruction was a prolonged race riot: over 5000 people were killed and the custom of lynching, which dates from this period, rapidly became institutionalized.[15] The Ku Klux Klan and the "rifle clubs" not only forced Negroes but also many poor whites to "cross Jordan"—that is, to shift to the Democratic Party. By 1876 all the Southern states with the exception of South Carolina, Louisiana, and Florida were under "white rule"; in the latter states federal troops were still stationed.

But to appreciate the precise sense in which democratic processes were impaired in 1876, it must be kept in mind that large masses of disfranchised Negroes and poor whites were used *as the basis* on which the South's representation in Congress was computed. It would have been profoundly undemocratic if the Bourbons had simply excluded Negroes and some poor whites from the polls; but the Bourbons counted these elements for the purpose of determining representation but refused to count their votes. This was more than a denial of democracy; it was a perversion of democratic processes.

The use of force to suppress the rebellion had also weakened democracy. National unity was no longer based on consent. "The Union endured," writes H. J. Eckenrode, "and there was the hope that the stitches by which the almost severed sections had been sewn together would heal in time, though the cicatrices were still raw." In this weakened condition, American democracy was confronted with the rise of an industrial system which posed a host of new social and economic problems. "In 1876," to quote Eckenrode, "the results of war, violence, and unconstitutional rule had become painfully evident. Far more apparent were the consequences of the great and sudden industrial expansion, the conversion of the United States from a primitive, loose-jointed agricultural country into a nation of mills and factories; the rise of modern finance; the beginnings of stock speculation; the creation of an immense railway system, the intoxication and corruption of a novel era, a new page in history. The world has had many deities. The seventies in America witnessed the orgiastic welcome to a new god—Machinery." [16] And with the machine, of course, had come "machine politics."

By 1876 the Bourbons were also ready for a deal. They had largely won the battle of reconstruction by the use of wholesale terror but they were thinking of the future and they greatly feared the possibility of a political coalition between poor whites and Negroes. "To divide the leveling host" it was necessary to separate the underprivileged whites from the Negroes.[17] The way to do this, of course, was *to create* "a race problem." The mind of the poor-white South had been poisoned against the Negro by the competition of slave labor. It was not difficult, therefore, to incite the poor whites against the Negroes by offering them as bait many of the jobs formerly filled by Negroes. For example, there were 100,000 Negro mechanics as compared with 20,000 white mechanics at the close of the war; but between 1865 and 1890 the Negroes were largely driven from these and other jobs. The effect, of course, was to convert the poor whites into a kind of underpaid, unofficial guerrilla constabulary which policed the Negro population and kept it, as a labor force, cheap and docile. Nevertheless the Bourbons had one abiding fear: that the North might intervene, once again, in an effort to protect the civil rights of the Negro.

With the "New South" and the "Reconstructed North" ready to bargain, the election of 1876 provided the last scene in the Civil War drama. The Democrats were odds-on favorites: they had an able candidate in Tilden; they had won important victories in 1874; and resentment against the corruption of the Grant administration was widespread. However, the Republicans still controlled the electoral machinery in South Carolina, Louisiana, and Florida. The returns indicated, of course, that Tilden had won; but the Republicans, knowing that they controlled the three key Southern states, refused to concede the election. After a long deadlock, the famous "Bargain of 1876"—really of 1877—was reached: the Republicans agreed not to interfere with the election of Democrats to state office in South Carolina, Louisiana, and Florida and to withdraw the troops from these states; and the Bourbons agreed to give Hayes the Presidency which Tilden had won. The agreement was even reduced to writing—like a contract. "On the one hand," writes Dr. Eckenrode, "Tilden was sold by the Southerners; on the other, the negro [sic] was sold by Hayes' representatives." Both parties knew that the bargain implied the nullification of the Civil War amendments to the extent that the Negro would thereafter be "eliminated from politics."

There was, indeed, a nice symmetry about the Bargain which resolved the emancipation dilemma. To appease the Abolitionists, the Negro's citizenship was affirmed. Each Negro would now be counted as a full person for the purpose of determining congressional representation but, at the same time, Negroes would simply not be permitted to vote. Thus a large bloc of votes, both in Congress and in the Electoral College, would not be subject to democratic control. In this manner, the Bourbon element would be free to manipulate "the racial problem" and thereby to divide its potential opposition. As Dr. Du Bois points out, the consequences were of far-reaching importance: "the disfranchisement of the American Negro makes the functioning of all democracy in the nation difficult; and as democracy fails to function in the leading democracy in the world, it fails in the world." Out of the racism of this period came the dynamics for the American overseas imperialism of the turn of the century: the dilemma was simply projected on a world-wide basis.

It should be noted, however, that the American people did not make nor did they approve the Bargain of 1876. The majority that had elected Tilden believed that the decision which awarded the Presidency to Hayes was morally wrong.[18] Strange as it may seem, Tilden could probably not have withdrawn the federal troops if only because the Republicans would have been certain to make political capital of the fact.

Dr. Eckenrode's answer to the question of who won the Civil War provides a biased but illuminating answer to the related question of who profited by the Bargain of 1876: "All that had been accomplished was the exchange of one set of masters for another. The industrialists, far more cruel and relentless than the planters had ever been, now ruled the country and ruled it like hereditary lords. The United States had made an immense industrial advance in the Civil War period but the condition of the toilers was little bettered. Great factories, in which herds of 'hands' labored much harder than slaves toiled, had taken the place of the small establishments of primitive America in which the owner worked side by side with his men." Having paid off the native-American element with pensions and homesteads and preferred jobs in industry and government, Northern industrialists could use the South's racism to separate native-born and foreign-born in the North much as poor whites and Negroes were separated in the South.

The real meaning of the Bargain of 1876 was revealed the following year when the railroad workers precipitated the first acute labor crisis in American history. "Class hatred," writes Denis Tilden Lynch, "was a new note in American life where all men were equal before the law." [19] The South was still in the turmoil of reconstruction; anti-Chinese sand-lot rioters ruled in San Francisco; and 100,000 railroad strikers and 4,000,000 unemployed surged in the streets of Northern cities. At a cabinet meeting on July 22, 1877, the administration considered placing several states under martial law. For a moment the nation seemed to hover on the brink of a new civil war—a war of class against class—but the storm subsided.

In the Wake of the Bargain

The Bargain of 1876 did not immediately restore the Bourbons to full power. "The road to reunion" had first to be paved with the sacrifice of the rights which the Civil War amendments had conferred upon Negroes. The first task, therefore, was to convince the Supreme Court to carry out, in judicial terms, the bargain which the legislators had negotiated. Reference to a few Supreme Court decisions will indicate how expeditiously and smoothly the legal phases of "operation reunion" were concluded. In the Cruikshank case (1876), the Civil Rights cases (1883), the Harris case (1889), and *Plessy* v. *Ferguson* (1890), the Supreme Court nullified the Civil War amendments so far as Negroes were concerned and placed the Bill of Rights outside the protection of the 14th Amendment. The effect of these decisions, as Justice Harlan pointed out in a memorable dissenting opinion, was "to permit the seeds of race hate to be planted under the sanction of law."

These decisions made it possible for the South *to legislate* the Negro's subordinate status; that is, to enforce this status by law. Discrimination was not limited to a denial of suffrage: through residential segregation, segregation in institutions and places of public accommodation, in schools, employment, and all walks of life, the Negro was forced into a subordinate world by techniques of dominance which have since been used in other areas, as in South Africa. The notion that this legislation "followed" or "reflected" the mores is far wide of the mark; it *made* the present-day mores of the South. The strategy was perfectly clear: through enforced segregation the Negro was to be denied, so far as possible, the opportunity for assimilating the culture of the dominant group, thereby perpetuating his subordinate status. "Segregation," as Leslie S. Perry has pointed out, "is the vehicle of unrestrained and undisguised white domination." [20] Segregation creates more prejudice than it reflects; it is an artifact, not a natural growth or organism. In the period from 1876 to 1937, about the only area in which the Negro was successful before the Supreme Court was in cases involving criminal trials and procedures and these cases, it will be noted, did not imply an extension of rights to Negroes.

"The year 1876," wrote George S. Merriam, "marked the disappearance of the Negro problem as the central feature of national politics." [21] It also marked the disappearance of all serious concern with the problem of racial discrimination. From 1870 to 1900, the outside assistance furnished by Northern foundations and missionary societies, according to Dr. Charles S. Johnson, constituted "the sole constructive influence from without a south that was itself poor, disorganized, and reactionary." With the exception of a proposal to safeguard federal elections and a proposal to grant federal subsidies for education, no important federal legislation aimed at the Negro problem in the South was even proposed between 1876 and 1906.[22] And congressional inaction, of course, was widely interpreted as equivalent to a declaration that discrimination by states and local communities was permissible.[23] It is quite erroneous, therefore, to believe that the pattern of racial discrimination which developed in this period was never sanctioned by the federal government; on the contrary, it was a direct product of federal policy if not of federal action.

Since the only hope of effective remedial action consisted in the possibility of federal intervention, the national decision to sanction discrimination necessarily led to the dogma of the insolubility of "the Negro problem." The dogma rationalized the decision. "The race question," wrote John Moffatt Mecklin in 1914, "belongs to this class of essentially insoluble problems." "Relations between American Negroes and American whites," wrote Scott Nearing in 1929, "occupy a frontier of conflict which is beyond the pale of organized society." "I have been forcibly impressed," wrote William P. Pickett in 1909, "by the constant repetition of the thought that the problem is in its essential character insoluble." "No matter which way we turn in the north or in the south," wrote André Siegfried in 1927, "there seems to be no solution." There could be no solution since we had decided not to solve the problem. Even the social theory of the period supported this decision with "scientific" rationalizations.[24]

"Constitutional disfranchisement," which began in the 1890's, was intended to place the fruits of the Bargain of 1876 beyond reach of legislative interference. It was not accomplished, however, without significant protest: witness the sharp increase in lynchings and the violence which marked the Populist campaigns in the South. The Wilmington, North Carolina, race riot of 1898, in the opinion of Dr. E. Franklin Frazier, marked the triumph of the constitutional phase of the South's counterrevolution. The riot stemmed directly from the gains which the Populist Party had scored in the 1896 elections by a limited fusion of Populist-Republican, and poor white and Negro votes, in some Southern communities. The triumph of the counterrevolution in 1898 coincided with the beginnings of American overseas expansion. Once the seal of constitutional approval had been placed on the Bargain of 1876, we were ready to extend "white supremacy," which was almost synonymous with "manifest destiny," to the islands of the Pacific. Even before the Wilmington riot, however, Booker T. Washington's famous speech in Atlanta in 1895 had given white America the comforting assurance that Negroes, for the time being at least, would accept a subordinate status.

Despite the fact, however, that discrimination had been given constitutional sanction, Bourbon rule rested on essentially insecure and shifting foundations. For, after all, the Civil War had made some changes. "There *had* been a revolution," wrote Ray Stannard Baker; "society *had* been overturned." On a limited scale, new opportunities had been created for Negroes and the type of leadership which Booker T. Washington symbolized had been quick to take advantage of these openings. As the losses of the war were regained and new industries came to the South, Negroes began to accumulate property and here and there a new Negro middle class began to emerge. But the revolution which had created these opportunities for Negroes had also created new opportunities for the poor whites. Thus in the 1890's the competition for jobs and land between poor whites and Negroes reached a new pitch of intensity and class antagonism developed within the dominant white group. "Wherever the whites divided as Democrats and Populists," writes Dr. Paul Buck, "the rival factions courted the colored vote and some of the turbulence of Reconstruction came back." [25] Noting an upsurge of "racial feeling" half a century after the Civil War, many Americans concluded that "the Negro problem" was really insoluble.

The movement for "constitutional disfranchisement" in the 1890's reflected the Bourbons' concern that the poor whites as well as the Negroes were getting out of hand. The immediate cause, however, was the introduction by Senator Henry Cabot Lodge of legislation aimed at protecting federal elections (as a Republican, Senator Lodge was anxious to stimulate a Democratic-Populist division). Commencing in Mississippi in 1890, the South began systematically to disfranchise the Negro: through grandfather clauses, literacy tests, poll taxes, and other devices. Prior to the appearance of the Populist Party, terror had sufficed to keep the Negro from the polls; but it was now necessary to place his disqualification beyond the reach of federal intervention and at the same time to minimize the political power of the poor whites. For similar reasons, Jim Crowism had to be placed on an official basis: between 1881 and 1907 a system of segregation was enacted in every Southern state. Although these measures were carried into effect by such leaders of the poor whites as Tillman,

Vardaman, and Watson, they actually represented a betrayal of this element; for example, the poll tax probably disfranchised as many "poor whites" as Negroes.

The poor whites, however, were given some concessions—at the expense of the Negroes. The poor whites wanted better social services and more schools and these demands were met, to some extent, by simply diverting funds to segregated white schools. Since states normally appropriate school funds to each county on the basis of the number of children of school age, a large Negro school population could be used as a means of securing an increased state appropriation. Hence, as Leslie S. Perry has pointed out, "the larger the proportion of Negro children in a county, the smaller is the per capita expenditure on their education and the greater the expenditure for the white children." [26]

The new *system of discrimination* that emerged in the South in the 1890's did more than codify existing Jim Crow customs: it greatly increased the scope, variety, and complexity of these customs. As George S. Merriam noted, "there developed a new or a newly apparent aggression upon the weaker race." Not only were devastating inroads made on the new employment opportunities which Negroes had won, but segregation was used to widen the gulf between the races. "The tendency has been," wrote Merriam in 1906, "to a wider separation. Once the inmates of mansion and cabin knew each other's way. Now they are almost unacquainted." "A slow but widespread process of race separation in all parts of the country," wrote Mr. Mecklin in 1914, "is gradually divorcing the Negro from the white man's world." Not only did the gulf seem to be widening but the myths of the Negro's inferiority became increasingly dogmatic. "I am just as much opposed to Booker Washington as a voter," said Senator James K. Vardaman, "with all his Anglo-Saxon re-enforcements, as I am to the cocoanut-headed, chocolate-colored, typical little coon . . . who blacks my shoes every morning." Here the pretense that Negroes were being denied certain rights merely until they had acquired social poise and an education was entirely abandoned.

Dating from the Atlanta race riot of 1906, the new aggression forced many Americans to realize that the Negro problem had grown in magnitude as the old social order had disappeared in the South. "With the passing of the generation of whose life it [slavery] was an accepted fact, both black and white, the relations which it slowly evolved are passing also"—so wrote Dr. A. H. Stone in 1907. "Not only will there be race friction," he continued, "but it will increase as the weaker race increases its demands for the equality which it is denied." This development in American race relations correlated with a somewhat similar world-wide development. About this time, Captain H. A. Wilson, traveling in Africa, noted that the natives in remote areas had somehow heard a vague report that a yellow nation (Japan) had defeated a white nation (Russia).

"There can be no doubt," wrote Dr. Stone, "in the mind of any man who carefully reads American Negro journals that their rejoicing over the Japanese victory sounded a very different note from that of White America. . . . It was a clear cry of exultation over the defeat of a white race by a dark one."

"Up from Slavery"

By forcing the Negro into a separate and segregated world, the whites forced him to form social organizations of his own and to attempt a "national liberation" movement rather similar to that which many colonial peoples have organized; that is, a movement to shake off discrimination. The Negro's struggle to achieve real minority status might be said to date from 1896 when Dr. Du Bois inaugurated the Atlanta University Studies of the Negro: "the first attempt to study in a scientific spirit the problems of the Negro in American life." [27] Previously the Negro's status had been so characterized by various "badges of servitude" that it resembled slave status more than the status of a minority. The difference was indicated by the fact that Dr. Du Bois proposed to study the problems *of* the Negro, not "the Negro problem." The same trend was strikingly apparent in the Niagara Falls conference of 1905—also initiated by Dr. Du Bois—which led to a meeting the next year at the scene of John Brown's raid at Harpers Ferry, and to the ringing declaration: "We shall not be satisfied with less than our full manhood rights." Out of this movement came, of course, the National Association for the Advancement of Colored People.

In the period from 1900 to 1940, such social processes as migration, urbanization, and industrialization worked enormous changes in the structure of "the Negro problem." From 1900 to 1930, some 2,250,000 Negroes left farms and small villages in the South for the cities of the South; and the number of counties in "the black belt" declined from 286 in 1900 to 180 in 1940. In the period from 1910 to 1920, an estimated 500,000 Negroes moved from Southern areas to Northern industrial centers and another 500,000 moved north after the war. In 1900 only 22.7 per cent of American Negroes lived in urban areas but by 1940 the percentage had increased to 48.6. Eighty-nine per cent of the Negroes in the North, two thirds of those in the border states, and 36.4 per cent of those in the South, now live in urban areas. Prior to World War I, Negroes constituted an industrial reserve upon which employers could draw in times of labor shortage, or strikes, but by 1929 they had become an integral part of the labor force in nearly every important industry. In 1930 they made up 22.7 per cent of the building laborers; 16.2 per cent of the unskilled workers in steel; and 25 per cent of the unskilled workers in the meat-packing industry. At the same time, illiteracy dropped from 81.4 per cent in 1870 to 16.3 per cent in 1930. The growth of Negro settlements in urban areas was accompanied, of course, by the establishment of more Negro businesses and the creation of new professional opportunities. With occupational differentiation, socio-economic classes began to emerge in the Negro world and the new Negro middle class began to win political recognition. After 1917 Negroes appeared in the legislatures of such states as Michigan, Illinois, Missouri, New Jersey, California, New York, Pennsylvania, Kansas, Ohio, and West Virginia, and as councilmen and judges in many cities.

The migration of Negroes and the expansion of the activities of the federal government after World War I brought the government into a new relation with Negroes. "Race relations," as T. J. Woofter, Jr., observed in 1925, "have become more national and less sectional because, in its expansion, the federal government has come into contact with the Negro in new ways. The use of Negro troops, aid to the Negro farmer, application of the various funds appropriated for education and public health, the relation of the Negro to the labor problems of the nation, and the influence of the presence of large numbers of Negroes on the immigration policy are all concrete instances of the growth, altogether apart from party politics, of a national attitude to replace the old sectional view of race contacts." [28] The postwar movement of Negroes to the North was, for example, both a cause and an effect of the Exclusionary Immigration Act of 1924.

As much as anything else, perhaps, it was World War I, and the frightful postwar race riots, that changed American race relations by making race relations a national concern. Herbert J. Seligmann, for example, noted that World War I had not so much improved the position of the Negro as it had increased his strategic importance in the national scene. Far from harmonizing the two races, the war had created a situation in which the problem of living together in the same society "was made immensely more urgent and more menacing." [29] The postwar riots indicated that "the south's color psychosis" had spread throughout the nation. The Ku Klux Klan was strong in Western states such as Oregon and Colorado, and in Indiana, and lynchings were reported in Delaware, Pennsylvania, Ohio, Indiana, Illinois, Colorado, and Kansas.

The nationalization of the race problem—striking evidence that Negroes were emerging as a real minority—brought the problem back, once again, to Congress. In 1919 and 1920 resolutions were introduced calling for an investigation of lynchings and in 1918 a Division of Negro Economics was created in the Department of Labor. At about the same time, also, the Supreme Court took cognizance of the new strategic position of the Negro by reinvesting the "due process clause" with some of the original meaning which the court had denied it in the 1870's and 1880's. Beginning with *Moore* v. *Dempsey* in 1923, a new trend was noted in the court's decisions affecting Negroes which has been explained as reflecting "the shifting of the social outlook of some of the justices." But the change also reflected the fact that Negroes now had the resources and the leadership to battle for their rights and the social organization, as in the NAACP, to fight effectively.

Just as the Supreme Court was forced to shift its social outlook, so such racists as Madison Grant, Lothrop Stoddard, and Dr. C. C. Josey began to spin new theories and myths as they correlated the rise of Negroes with "a rising tide of color" in the world. And if one compares two special studies of "the Negro problem" prepared by the American Academy of Political and Social Science, one in 1913, and one in 1928, it can be readily seen that social theorists were also being forced to change their outlook on the problem. The editor of the 1928 volume pointed out that "since that time [1913] students of race as well as laymen have had to discard or even reverse many of their theories concerning 'trends' and 'solutions' of Negro development and 'problems.'" As Negroes verged on minority status, the Negro problem began to give way to various specific problems faced by Negroes. Social theorists also began to see, for the first time, how the myth of *a Negro problem* had confused earlier investigators. "For years the Negro," writes Robert L. Sutherland, "has been a problem in Sunday school quarterlies, textbooks, and public addresses, but an understanding of the full and intricate nature of the problem has seldom been attempted. Typically, these approaches have lumped all twelve million Negroes— black, brown, and light yellow, rich and poor, good and bad—together as a homogeneous group deserving the white man's sympathy, contempt, or assistance." [30]

With World War II, American Negroes emerged into full minority status and their objective became not equal status but complete integration. The Second World War, like the First, greatly enhanced the Negro's strategic significance. Since 1940 it has been perfectly clear that Negroes hold a pivotal position in American politics, in the balance not only between regions and parties but between classes. The tendency of Negroes, during the depression, to turn to left-wing political movements underscored the meaning of this change. The same significance was apparent in the manner in which Franklin D. Roosevelt shifted the Negro vote from the Republican to the Democratic column. The meaning of this new strategic power might be put this way: just as the Bourbons were forced to make concessions to poor whites in the 1890's, so concessions must now be made to Negroes, and for the same reason—to prevent a trend to the left.

By one of the major ironies of American race relations, reaction has found the technique to delay the radicalization of Negro protest in the concept of civil rights. The term "civil rights," by usage dating from the original federal Civil Rights Act, relates to the right of persons to equal accommodation in places of public amusement, entertainment, and convenience.[31] In its origin, therefore, the term is to be distinguished from "civil liberties," which guarantee certain individual rights from encroachment by government. It will be noted that President Truman appointed a Committee on Civil Rights, not on civil liberties.

Since 1947 this distinction has been steadily sharpened so that today "civil rights" has come to mean those civil liberties which a benevolent government grants, more or less as a favor, to racial minorities; while "civil liberties" proper relate to those rights which individuals must assert against government. With subtle but unmistakable emphasis, Negroes have been offered a bargain: civil rights for a repudiation of radical protest. The intent of the bargain, of course, is to keep the racial and economic crises in separate air-tight compartments. Yet, as the Jewish minority has discovered, civil rights do not guarantee full equality when the basis of inequality is to be found in unequal competitive power. For example, it is significant that despite all the gains they have made American Negroes "have failed to develop business enterprises commensurate with their achievements in other phases of American civilization." [32] Studies have shown that while Negro enterprises constitute almost half of all businesses in Negro neighborhoods in Chicago, they receive less than a tenth of all money spent by Negroes in these areas. [33] Certain businesses in which Negroes have generally succeeded, such as mortuaries and certain types of insurance, represent fields which "white" business abandoned and Negro businessmen occupied by default.

The strategic importance of American Negroes has also been greatly enhanced since World War II as part of the changing relation of America to the rest of the world and of the relation of American Negroes to other racial groups. Before the outbreak of World War II, one third of the area and one third of the population of the world were under colonial rule. These 700,000,000 colonial people might be considered as a special minority problem, since they are colored peoples ruled by whites who suffer from various disabilities and discriminations which also affect domestic minorities. As Dr. James G. Leyburn has pointed out, "modern minority problems, with the exception of those in Europe, had their origin in the spreading abroad of Europeans after the discoveries of Columbus" [34] so that there is historical warrant for relating colonialism to the problem of racial minorities. That 5246 Englishmen rule some 22,000,000 natives in Nigeria does not destroy the parallel between the status of Nigerians and a domestic minority; for the essence of minority status is not to be found in the numerical ratio between two groups but in the discrepancy in power. In each case, the test is whether government rests on the consent of the governed.

It is against this background of world colonialism that the enhanced strategic importance of the Negro minority must be measured. For the world colonial problem has passed into a new phase with World War II and the changes which have come in its wake. The number of people under colonial rule has been reduced to perhaps 200,000,000 and the pressure for freedom within these remaining colonial areas has rapidly gathered fresh momentum. Discrimination against racial minorities in the United States is today intimately related to international politics and American foreign policy and one may confidently expect the lot of our domestic racial minorities to improve as colored peoples in other areas emerge from colonial status.

The treatment of American minorities, however, is basically of deepest concern to American citizens and for a reason that has been well stated by Felix S. Cohen. "Here in America," he writes, "the treatment of minorities has always been the best index of liberal civilization. Advances of inventions in our commerce, industry, science, or government begin as unorthodox ideas, and have flourished on this soil because America was par excellence a land where men could differ from their neighbors and find tolerance. American prosperity, not less than American inventiveness and American freedom, are profoundly threatened by an upsurge of intolerance. And of all forms of intolerance that directed against a racial minority is the most terrible, because there is no escape from one's race. . . . And yet, terrible as is the fact of racial oppression to an oppressed minority, it is, in the long run, more terrible to the dominant society of the oppressor. For the fact remains that while racial intolerance has seldom destroyed its intended victim, it has almost always, in the end, destroyed the society in which it flourished. . . . For the rights of each of us in a democracy can be no stronger than the rights of our weakest minority."[35]

NOTES

1. *Caste, Class & Race,* by Oliver C. Cox, 1948, p. 332.
2. Statement presented by the NAACP to the United Nations, October 23, 1947, p. 6.
3. *The Negro in the United States,* by E. Franklin Frazier, 1949, p. 143.
4. *The Masters and the Slaves,* by Gilberto Freyre, 1946, p. 324.
5. Frazier, *op. cit.,* p. 222.
6. Cox, *op. cit.,* p. 336.
7. *Ibid.,* p. 336.
8. *The Freedmen's Bureau,* by Dr. Paul Skeels Peirce, 1904.
9. *Negroes in American Society,* by Maurice R. Davie, 1949, p. 63.
10. Peirce, *op. cit.*
11. See Note 2 above.
12. *Divided We Stand,* by Walter Prescott Webb, 1947, p. 19.
13. *The Triumph of American Capitalism,* by Louis M. Hacker, 1940, p. 383.
14. See Note 2 above.
15. Davie, *op. cit.,* p. 54.
16. *Rutherford B. Hayes: Statesman of Reunion,* by H. J. Eckenrode, 1930, p. 111.
17. Hacker, *op. cit.,* p. 381.
18. Eckenrode, *op. cit.,* p. 230.
19. *The Wild Seventies,* by Denis Tilden Lynch, 1941.
20. See Note 2 above.
21. *The Negro and the Nation,* by George S. Merriam, 1906.
22. *Ibid.*
23. See *The Legal Status of the Negro,* by Charles S. Mangum, Jr., 1940.
24. See "Sociological Theory and Race Relations," by E. Franklin Frazier, *American Sociological Review,* June 1947.

25. *The Road to Reunion,* by Dr. Paul Buck, 1937.
26. See Note 2 above.
27. *The Negro in the United States,* by E. Franklin Frazier, 1949, p. 503.
28. *The Basis of Racial Adjustment,* by T. J. Woofter, Jr., 1925.
29. *The Negro Faces America,* by Herbert J. Seligmann, 1920.
30. *Color, Class and Personality,* by Robert L. Sutherland, 1942, p. xiv.
31. Davie, *op. cit.,* p. 288.
32. Frazier, *op. cit.,* p. 409.
33. *Ibid.,* p. 406.
34. *World Minority Problems,* by James G. Leyburn, 1947, p. 15.
35. *Commentary,* August 1948, p. 143.

III. Historical Gains, Losses, and Patterns of Suppression

The social process characterizing Negro life in the United States may be seen as a periodic acceleration of social, economic, and political gain followed by a halt and deterioration of gains realized. The overall effect of this process has been to stabilize the social position of black Americans at the very bottom of the stratification hierarchy. The selections in Part III deal with the historical operation of this cyclic process. The first two chapters discuss political gains for Negroes after Emancipation and organizational alliances with whites which held political promise. The fact that Negro officeholders were eventually replaced by whites in Georgia, and that black-white alliances did not realize their political potential is significant. These efforts suffered the typical fate of attempts at betterment of the black community. Aspects of the process by which the demise of such efforts has typically come about is reflected in Chapters 7 and 8.

Terror against black people in the United States of America has been commonplace and a major means of maintaining patterns of white supremacy. Much of the terror was the work of a still-thriving organization of white supremacists known as the Ku Klux Klan. The subjects of terror and the Klan are taken up in Chapters 9 and 10.

Chapter 10 deals more generally with the subject of violence in black-white relations. One can clearly see from this study the chronic role of lawlessness and violence as a major means of ensuring black subordination and white supremacy. The fact that illegal violence against black Americans has often been practiced by agents of the law themselves will be specifically dealt with in a subsequent chapter.

5. The Negro Alliance in Alabama

One historical instance of black American gain is reflected in the rather widespread network of alliances on local, state, and national levels, and their potential political relevance. These alliances are estimated to have reached a national strength of 1,200,000 in 1891. The political potential of these alliances—black and white—did not emerge in third-party politics as had been their promise. If black and white alliances are crucial today for the movement toward black equality, a review of these historical efforts may prove instructive.

WILLIAM W. ROGERS

Considerable attention has been devoted to the Negro as an important element in the Populist revolt of the 1890's.[1] Because Populists were pledged to a policy of an unencumbered franchise for all voters and an economic program slanted toward the underprivileged, logic dictated that Negroes would support Populist candidates. In practice, however, Southern Bourbon politicians controlled the election machinery and by manipulating returns, were able to use the Negro vote to win elections. Nowhere was this more in evidence than in Alabama.[2] White Populists overtly sought the Negro vote while Democrats stood steadfast for white supremacy but maintained themselves in power with Negro votes.

Ultimately, Negroes were entirely disfranchised and the Populists discredited for attempting to destroy white supremacy.[3] These political aspects of Populism have tended to obscure the earlier significance and work of the Negro Alliances in the South. Their activities were just being felt when the entire Alliance movement, Negro and white, became entangled in political warfare. For a brief period prior to this, the Negro Alliance in Alabama was an order of great potential.

The first Negro Alliance, known as the Colored Farmers' Alliance, was organized in Houston County, Texas, December 11, 1886. Later that same year a state organization was formed. Other states set up Negro Alliances, and in March 1888, a national convention at Lovelady, Texas, applied for and received a charter as a national organization. Thus, the Colored Farmers' National Alliance and Co-operative Union was born. This Negro

From *Journal of Negro History* (1960), Vol. 45, pp. 38–44; reprinted by permission.

Alliance was represented at various meetings of the major white Alliances, the Southern Alliance (National Farmers' Alliance and Industrial Union) and the Northern Alliance (National Farmers' Alliance).[4] The superintendent of the Negro Alliance was General R. M. Humphrey, a bearded white Baptist missionary, but the other national officers were Negroes.[5]

As white Alliances were being organized throughout Alabama, Negro orders were being formed also. A statewide white Alliance was organized at Beech Grove, Madison County, in March, 1887. After a slow beginning, a second state convention in August, 1887, at Cave Spring in the same county saw the Alliance securely launched.[6] The order grew phenomenally and by May, 1889, had an estimated membership of 125,000 and 3,100 lodges.[7]

By 1891 Humphrey estimated that the Negro Alliance had a national strength of 1,200,000.[8] How the Negroes were organized and the extent of their connection with the white Alliances became increasingly important. Early in 1889 Alabama newspapers mentioned the existence of Negro Alliances.[9] No mention was made of a statewide Negro Alliance similar to that of the whites, although there were various Negro Alliances regional in scope that later consolidated.[10] The big gain in Negro membership appears to have come after the white Alliance meeting in Meridian, Mississippi, in 1888 advocated the organization of a Negro Alliance.[11]

The unity that existed between white and Negro Alliances varied from state to state. On a larger scale, there was no doubt but that national leaders of the white Alliance favored a close relationship between the Negroes and the whites. President Leonidas L. Polk pointed out that while the Negro order was a distinct body, many of its organizers were white.[12] The two orders had similar aspirations. Andrew J. Carothers, a Texas organizer who came to Alabama, remarked, "What we desire is, that the Farmers' Alliance men everywhere will take hold and organize or aid in organizing the colored farmer, and placing him in an attitude to co-operate intelligently and systematically."[13] Similar statements were issued by other white agrarians.[14]

There were, however, serious differences between the orders that militated against complete unity. A recent student of the period has pointed out that the Southern Alliance opposed the Lodge Election Bill but that the Negro Alliance favored it.[15] However, both the Southern Alliance and the Negro Alliance favored the use of oleomargarine without legislative restrictions desired by dairying interests and supported by the Northern Alliance.[16] Further evidence of good will was displayed in 1890 at Ocala, Florida, when various Alliance and labor groups met in convention. Virtual fusion of Negroes and whites was accomplished.[17] Southern Negro Alliancemen, including J. S. Jackson of Alabama, delivered speeches before an open meeting of the Alliance at the Ocala Opera House.[18]

Early Alliances in Alabama were strongly supported by the whites. The order even penetrated the Black Belt, a tier of twenty counties where Negroes constituted more than fifty per cent of the population. In this region any organization of Negroes was automatically suspect. At Union Springs in Bullock County, leaders in the local white Alliance, I. F. Culver and Harry G. McCall, helped organize a Negro Alliance. McCall had been appointed to superintend the introduction of the Negro Alliance into Alabama. One editor reported, "Frank Davis, a solvent and successful negro farmer, is at the head of this colored organization." Congratulating the new order, the journalist was pleased to add, "The Davis organization means business and totally eschews politics." [19]

Throughout the state Alliances were established. In the Black Belt, a Russell County editor noted, "The colored people are organizing Alliances all over the country." [20] There were thirteen Negro Alliances in Butler County.[21] Six more were organized in Montgomery County,[22] and by the summer of 1889 Humphrey estimated that Alabama had 50,000 Negro Alliance members.[23]

Once the Negroes had their county orders organized, they made attempts to carry forward the economic ideas of the Alliance. "The white and colored Alliance are united in their war against trusts," wrote a Black Belt editor, "and in promotion of the doctrine that farmers should establish co-operative stores and manufactures, and publish their own newspapers, conduct their own schools, and have a hand in everything else that concerns them as citizens or affects them personally or collectively." [24]

In Lee County, P. Lawrence, Superintendent of the Negro Alliance, declared that the objectives of the Negro group were identical to those of the whites.[25] It was not unusual, then, for a Monroe County Negro Alliance to make common cause with its white counterpart and pass resolutions boycotting the use of jute and advocating Alliance manufactured cotton bagging.[26] This move was seconded by another Negro Alliance in Clarke County and became a general pattern throughout the state.[27] Several Negro Alliances reported co-operative efforts to obtain higher prices for seed from cottonseed oil mills. They also urged the mills to make earlier purchases.[28]

The most ambitious endeavor was the establishment of a state exchange. The white Alliance located its exchange at Montgomery. This giant purchasing and wholesale house acted as a marketing agency for the farmers and provided bulk purchases of needed items. The Negro Alliance followed this same design. In 1889 Humphrey addressed the Mobile Chamber of Commerce and outlined plans for an exchange. Mobile, he pointed out, could serve as a central point for Negro Alliances in Alabama, Florida, and Georgia.[29] A local paper approved the project since "it doubtless would bring millions of dollars into the commerce of the city." [30] Shortly after Humphrey's visit the exchange was established.

These promising beginnings were short-lived. As the Alliance began to attract both Negro and white adherents, certain Black Belt Democratic papers became alarmed at the political possibilities of the order. The editor of the influential Montgomery *Advertiser* warned, "The white alliances will have no lot or part in the colored alliances." [31] McCall was severely criticized for his role in helping organize the Negro Alliance. He was reminded that the "white people of Alabama don't want any more negro influence in their affairs than they have already had, and they won't have it." [32] McCall replied by stating that a Negro Alliance was needed and declaring that he organized a Negro Alliance at Union Springs "with the assistance of better men and Democrats than anybody connected with THE ADVERTISER." [33]

It should be noted that a number of conservative members of the Alliance were opposed to the Negro order. The Montgomery *Alliance Journal* ran many editorials prophesying the end of the Alliance if the agrarians entered politics. The *Journal* championed the white order but as for the Negroes, "It is hoped that there will be no more of these organizations effected. We are no more in favor of Negro Alliances than we are the so called Negro Masonic Lodges, and would recognize one as quick as the other." [34]

Despite their conservative members, the majority of the white Alliances defended the Negro Alliance. Their relationship became even stronger when the Bourbon attack began to center on the entire Alliance movement. The Birmingham *Alabama Sentinel*, official newspaper of the Knights of Labor in Alabama and an ally of the agrarians, perceived that once the Alliance challenged the Democrats, its Negro members would increase the order's strength and cut into Democratic power. The paper said, "The Bourbon Democracy are trying to down the Alliance with the old cry 'nigger.' It won't work though." The *Sentinel* added, "The Bourbon Democracy have used the negro very successfully in keeping their supremacy over us, and, By—our lady/—we propose to use him in turn to down them for the good of whites and blacks alike." [35] That the labor journal did not overstate the case was seen in the attitude of the Mobile *Register,* whose editor denounced the Negro Alliance in a bitter tirade:

Here is the old Loyal League back upon us again, with its yearning for the lands of the white man, with its ambition that the Federal flag shall float over every school house and over every ballot box. Here is the force bill again with congressional troops and bayonets to decide elections for a free people. Here is the old secret society going in and out with pass word.

This new Loyal League comes to us this time under the wing of the Farmers' Alliance.[36]

Beginning in 1891 the Alliance, white and Negro, became involved in political warfare with the Democrats, and its economic program declined. There were other conditions that held back the Negro Alliance in the years 1889–1891. The movement's vitality was confined to particular counties instead of sections, and there was never an active statewide Negro order. In 1891 the Montgomery *Advertiser* claimed that Alabama had over 1,600 Negro Alliances and contrasted this figure with the Grange, an organization that had no Negroes in it.[37] The *Advertiser* failed to cite the source of its statistics, and there were only a few Granges, white or Negro, in Alabama in 1891.

Negroes were unable to unite on an economic program, and the exchange at Mobile received scant support and was of limited significance. This lack of unity stemmed in part from the fact that Alabama was a rural state with poor communication and transportation facilities. While the white Alliances had any number of state and local newspapers, the Negro Alliance, with a single exception, did not have a journal. This tended to make their orders isolated units.[38]

Negroes did not have the full support of the white Alliance and were actively opposed by the Bourbon Democrats. This latter attitude developed into militant hostility once the Alliance became political in 1892. By this time, however, neither the white nor Negro Alliance placed much emphasis on economic activities.

A Democratic editor summed up a widely held attitude by writing, ". . . the colored Alliance [will make] demands of the white Alliance for a recognition in their political councils. It will come sooner or later, and then the leaders will have to wrestle with it. There can be no compact between the races."[39] Actually, Alabama Negroes had made a strong attempt to work out their economic difficulties through a separate Alliance closely identified with the white order. Only after both groups failed in their economic program did they become political.

NOTES

1. See Joseph H. Taylor, "Populism and Disfranchisement in Alabama," *The Journal of Negro History*, XXXIV (October, 1949), 410–427; Jack Abramowitz, "The Negro in the Agrarian Revolt," *Agricultural History*, XXIV (April, 1950), 88–95; and the same author's "The Negro in the Populist Movement," *The Journal of Negro History*, XXXVIII (July, 1953), 257–289.

2. Discussions of the Populist movement in Alabama may be found in John B. Clark, *Populism in Alabama* (Auburn, Alabama, 1927); and more recently William Warren Rogers, "Agrarianism in Alabama, 1865–1896," Unpublished Doctoral Dissertation, University of North Carolina, 1959.

3. Taylor, "Disfranchisement in Alabama," p. 410, contends that Alabama's disfranchising constitution of 1901 was the "direct result of the threats of Populism." A full account of this point and other issues may be found in Malcolm C. McMillan, *Constitutional Development in Alabama, 1798–1901: A Study in Politics, the Negro, and Sectionalism* (Chapel Hill, 1955), pp. 249–262.

4. N. A. Dunning (Editor), *The Farmers' Alliance History and Agricultural Digest* (Washington, D.C., 1891), pp. 6, 288–289.

5. Abramowitz, "Negro in the Populist Movement," p. 263.

6. Dunning, *Alliance History*, p. 247; Huntsville *Daily Independent*, August 4, 1887. All references to newspapers are to Alabama journals.

7. Opelika *Democrat*, May 23, 1889; Anniston *Evening Watchman*, September 5, 1889.

8. Dunning, *Alliance History*, p. 290.
9. Troy *Enquirer*, January 26, 1889, quoting Montgomery *Advertiser*.
10. Union Springs *Bullock County Reporter*, April 5, 1889, mentions the Planters' National Alliance and the National Union Alliance of America as two regional Alliances. Dunning, *Alliance History*, p. 290, maintains that Alabama did have a state organization.
11. Moulton *Advertiser*, January 31, 1889.
12. C. Vann Woodward, *Origins of the New South 1877–1913* (Baton Rouge, 1951), p. 192.
13. Union Springs *Bullock County Reporter*, April 5, 1889.
14. See remarks of J. H. Turner, National Secretary-Treasurer of the Southern Alliance, in Dunning, *Alliance History*, p. 278.
15. Abramowitz, "Negro in the Populist Movement," p. 258.
16. Herman Clarence Nixon, "The Cleavage Within the Farmers' Alliance Movement," *The Mississippi Valley Historical Review*, XV (June, 1928), 30.
17. Dunning, *Alliance History*, pp. 291–292.
18. Mobile *Daily Register*, December 5, 1890.
19. Union Springs *Herald*, July 10, 1889. A splinter group of Negroes attempted to control the meeting but eventually left, after, so charged the *Herald*, they were unable to make the order political in its objectives.
20. Seale *Russell Register*, February 15, 1890.
21. Union Springs *Bullock County Reporter*, October 18, 1889.
22. Montgomery *Advertiser*, January 17, 1890.
23. *Ibid.*, August 11, 1889.
24. Union Springs *Bullock County Reporter*, October 18, 1889.
25. See letter in Opelika *Democrat*, June 6, 1889.
26. Monroeville *Monroe Journal*, September 6, 1889.
27. Grove Hill *Clarke County Democrat*, October 3, 1889.
28. Prattville *Progress*, July 25, 1890.
29. Montgomery *Advertiser*, August 11, 1889. Dunning, *Alliance History*, p. 290, mentions the establishment of other Negro exchanges at Houston, New Orleans, Norfolk, and Charleston.
30. Mobile *Daily Register*, August 11, 1890.
31. Montgomery *Advertiser*, October 3, 1889.
32. *Ibid.*, December 22, 1889.
33. *Ibid.*, December 31, 1889, quoting Montgomery *Alliance Advocate*.
34. Quoted in Centreville *Bibb Blade*, February 28, 1890. For similar criticism see Talladega *Our Mountain Home*, January 8, 1890.
35. Quoted in Montgomery *Advertiser*, January 8, 1890.
36. Quoted in Anniston *Weekly Times*, July 2, 1891.
37. Montgomery *Advertiser*, August 6, 1891.
38. According to an article quoted from the St. Louis [Missouri] *Globe-Democrat* plans were made to establish at Montgomery a Negro Alliance journal. However, this was never done. See Montgomery *Advertiser*, October 3, 1889. The *Forkland Progress*, November 8, 1890, mentions the Opelika *State Alliance Banner* as being the state's only Negro Alliance newspaper.
39. Centreville *Bibb Blade*, September 1, 1891.

6. Negro Officeholders in Georgia Under President McKinley

Among the current responses to the rapidly rising expectations of equality by black Americans is appointment of Negroes to federal office. An American black man, Robert Weaver, held a Cabinet-level position in the administration of Lyndon B. Johnson for a brief time, though as I will argue subsequently, perhaps not accidentally. Negro officeholders appear less prominent in the administration of Richard Nixon, thus perhaps reflecting a deceleration of the current thrust toward black equality. The dynamics of one instance of the process of black retardation is illustrated by an episode in Georgia political history. The process continues today, involving additional and new strategies of retardation of the black American.

CLARENCE A. BACOTE

The degeneration of the Republican Party in Georgia actually set in after 1872 when it came to be a collection of factions struggling for (1) a seat in the national convention, (2) federal offices as spoils of victory, and (3) race conflict within the party and between the party and Democrats. The Republican Party came to be labeled a "Negro party" led by a few whites and a few Negro office-seekers and some leaders hopeful of enlarged federal protection of the rights of Negroes. It is the purpose of this paper to show how William McKinley, the arch-conservative thirty years removed from the idealism of Charles Sumner and Thaddeus Stevens, will deal with the Negro's aspirations for federal office.

President Cleveland's second administration produced so much internal strife within the Democratic Party that the Republicans in 1896 felt that they could "nominate a rag baby and elect it president." Although a number of candidates sought the Republican nomination at the national convention in St. Louis, it was no surprise when Governor William McKinley of Ohio was named on the first ballot over Speaker of the House Thomas B. Reed by a vote of 661½ to 84½.[1]

McKinley was no stranger to Georgians. Knowing the voting value of

From *Journal of Negro History* (1959), Vol. 44, pp. 217–239; reprinted by permission.

the Southern delegates in the Republican National Convention, Marcus Hanna, his astute political adviser, rented a house in Thomasville in 1895 where he and McKinley met and entertained federal office-holders, white and Negro, from the entire South.[2] Before leaving the state, McKinley and his party visited the Savannah State Industrial College for Negroes where the president, R. R. Wright, a friend of long standing of McKinley's, held a reception and introduced them to fifty of the most prominent Negroes in the city.[3] These gestures on the part of McKinley served to enhance his popularity among the Negro politicians of the state.

Realizing that it was impossible to capture any offices on the state level, party leaders hoped to roll up a large vote or even win the electoral vote of the state in the national election. On August 1, 1896, the Georgia Republicans held their official meeting at Rome for the ratification of McKinley's nomination with Major J. F. Hanson, of Macon, a very wealthy cotton manufacturer and editor and owner of the *Macon Telegraph,* as principal speaker. After blasting the Democrats for their inept leadership, Hanson turned his attention to the race issue. He deemed it unfortunate that the South was a slave to the Democratic Party because of the presence of the Negro. But as for himself, he declared that

"I had rather trust the government of my state and the country . . . to the Negroes of Georgia and the South than to trust them to the forces that Altgeld controls and leads, and for whom the Democratic platform speaks.

"The Negro is not a socialist, he is not an anarchist, he is not an enemy of property, or capital, or money . . . his ambitions point to a fireside that he may call home . . . Where this is the case they plead for the best men for office and for good government.

"Shall I refuse to do my duty to the country because the Negro is true to the country? . . . I do not prophesy, but the time may come when the Negro will constitute the great conservative element in southern politics." [4]

What stronger appeal could be made for Southern whites than by showing that the Negro was a conservative citizen who was contented with the *status quo* and that Southern institutions were safer under a Republican administration than under the Democrats, whose program was replete with radical ideas?

Although it was denied by A. E. Buck,[5] white, and chairman of the Republican State Central Committee since 1882, McKinley clubs composed entirely of white business men were being organized and were working quietly throughout the state.[6] The president of the Atlanta McKinley Club was Thomas H. Martin, editor and publisher of *Dixie,* an organ of the National Manufacturers Association. Associated with him were A. R. Bryan, Edward L. Pratt, John Oliver, and C. W. Hunnicut, all outstanding business men in the community.[7] These men, whose economic philosophy paralleled that of their Eastern associates, were greatly concerned with the future of the American economy if the "radical" monetary policies proposed by William Jennings Bryan and the Democratic Party prevailed.

Since the Democrats had been so successful in using the Negro as a scapegoat in winning state elections, these McKinley clubs borrowed a page from the Democratic campaign handbook. Without mentioning the Negro, these clubs sought to gain support for the Republican Party in Georgia by appealing to the prejudices of the white South against the darker races in general. Thomas P. Ivory, chairman of the Republican State Committee of McKinley Clubs of Georgia, in a letter to the *Atlanta Journal* wrote:

What does the contrast say to the American voter? It stands like a guidepost, pointing to a Republican ballot. To us, who pin our faith to gold it is a consolation to know that our allies are the white races of the world. The mongrel races alone have silver for a standard . . . On the other hand, gold is the money of Christianity . . . What silver nation has a system of free schools . . . Let the silver advocate exchange our country for one of his liking. Let him go to India and bathe in the slimy waters of the Ganges, or to China, where rats are a delicacy, or to Japan, where women have no virtue, or to Mexico where three fourths of the population are practically slaves. Such is the barbarism of the great silver countries.[8]

Thus the Republican Party in Georgia presented a paradox. One segment consisted of the Negroes who, in the Lincoln tradition, supported the party in hopes of gaining their constitutional rights. The other segment was made up of white business men, who put property rights above human rights and were willing to conduct a campaign based indirectly on white supremacy. In this respect, their tactics were no more ethical than those of the race-baiting Democrats of the day.

In the election Bryan had a majority of 34,581 over McKinley in Georgia, the vote being 94,672 to 60,091.[9] This was the largest vote received by the Republicans in a national election since Reconstruction days, and it marked the peak of Republican strength in the state.[10] In Fulton County (Atlanta) the vote was rather close, Bryan receiving 4,503 votes to 3,106 for McKinley. Although the white McKinley clubs claimed the major credit for the large McKinley vote in the state,[11] they disclaimed any desire for political preferment from the administration.[12]

It remained to be seen how the spoils of office were to be distributed. Despite his unprecedented large vote from Georgia whites in 1896, McKinley was in no position to ignore the crucial support of Negro delegates in the national nominating convention. Thus his subsequent policy of appointing Negroes to federal jobs in Georgia is explainable by the dynamics of practical politics. Some of these appointments received the endorsement of Southerners, but others were to produce so much dissatisfaction among local whites that they only strengthened the Democratic Party in the local area.[13]

Much excitement prevailed among the Negro politicians as to the plums that might come their way in view of the apparent rivalry for the same from the white McKinley clubs. William Pledger, long time Republican leader and chairman of the Republican State Central Committee from 1880 to 1882, who conveniently shifted his support from Reed to McKinley at the Republican State Convention, desired the post of consul at Kingston, Jamaica. T. M. Dent of Rome sought the ministership to Haiti. Monroe "Pink" Morton was eager for the postmastership at Athens.[14] Judson W. Lyons, national committeeman, was to fight a losing battle for the postmastership of his home town, Augusta.[15] Henry Rucker, of Atlanta, hoped to be appointed Collector of Internal Revenue for Georgia, while J. H. Deveaux desired the collectorship of the Port of Savannah. C. C. Wimbish of Atlanta expected to be named as Surveyor of Customs in that city, and Jackson McHenry would be satisfied with the chief custodianship at the customs house.[16] These were just a few of the positions sought by Negro Republicans in the state, and they were to cause McKinley much grief before they were settled. The demands for federal jobs by Georgia Negroes were so numerous that McKinley confided to a Republican member of the House that "the Georgia delegation wanted everything in sight, more than they were entitled to." [17]

While Negroes were speculating on their political future, McKinley appointed Buck, long time chairman of the Republican State Central Committee (1882–1897), as minister to Japan.[18] In recognition of his services the Negroes held a reception in Atlanta at the Imperial Theater which was decorated with Japanese lanterns. Tribute was paid Buck by Negro leaders who emphasized his fidelity to the Negro during this crucial period and his devotion to the principles of the Republican Party.[19]

Thus passed from the scene, for he was never to return, the man who guided the destinies of the Republican Party in Georgia since 1882. Although there were times when his leadership was challenged by the Negroes, he was able, through his political acumen, to show himself the master of the situation when the occasion demanded. Despite the severe criticism of some of his policies, it appears that Negroes in general held him in high esteem. Although Buck designated Walter Johnson as leader of the party during his absence, it was expected that Buck would still determine the policies of the party from Tokyo.[20]

White Southerners opposed the appointment of any Negro to a post where he might have frequent contact with whites in general and white women in particular. It was not a question of a Negro's competence, but his color, which was in keeping with the principle of white supremacy, "the central theme" of Southern history.

This usual attitude was demonstrated when Judson W. Lyons, prominent Negro lawyer of Augusta and Republican national committeeman from the state, was proposed by McKinley for the postmastership of

Augusta. Immediately, prominent white citizens of the city registered their protests.[21] They urged Lyons to withdraw his name from consideration for the post, promising him that if he sought some other appointment such as a foreign consulship, he would receive their strongest endorsement. Lyons declined, claiming that he could ill afford to yield for the reasons given and still command the respect of his fellow Republicans. Congressman William H. Fleming, Augusta, called upon McKinley and urged him for the sake of harmony to retain the incumbent, Barney Dunbar, a one-armed Confederate veteran and a Democrat.[22]

Lyons' case was unique in that many of the most prominent white lawyers of Augusta had written letters of endorsement to the Republican administration in Washington, thinking that Lyons would be seeking a foreign post. It was these letters that Lyons was to use to the dismay of the white people of Augusta. These endorsements pointed out that Lyons, unlike Pledger, was a man of integrity and not a strife breeder, and to turn him down would be an insult to the Negro race as a whole, since he was highly respected by all of them. In discussing the case, the *Atlanta Journal* admonished the white people of Augusta not to "endorse a man for one position of trust unless he is worthy and well qualified from every standpoint to fill it. A negro that can serve his government abroad can serve it at home." [23]

The only barrier that stood between Lyons and the Augusta postmastership was Postmaster-General James A. Gary, who told a Georgia congressman:

I believe Lyons is a good negro—that perhaps he deserves this place, but I also known well enough the temper and feelings of the southern people not to inflict upon them unnecessarily. I will oppose his appointment with the idea of giving him something better.[24]

Meanwhile, white opposition to Lyons' appointment was increasing. One Democrat said that if McKinley made the appointment, he would destroy all prospects of building a strong white Republican Party in Georgia, for those Democrats who were inclined to support McKinley would return to their own party. Another declared that this was the reward for those Democrats who helped to elect a Republican president, claiming that if they had supported their own nominees, the question of a Negro postmaster in Augusta would have never arisen.[25] Some business men even had their wives write letters to Washington protesting the appointment.[26] It was even hinted that some Negro school teachers and preachers joined the whites in opposing the appointment.[27]

The vacillating policy of McKinley in connection with the Lyons' appointment aroused the ire of T. Thomas Fortune, militant Negro editor of the *New York Age*. Addressing a large group at the Metropolitan Methodist Episcopal Church in New York City, Fortune blamed Postmaster-General Gary for blocking the appointment. Then he recited a long list of Negroes who had worked faithfully for McKinley's nomination but who had been completely ignored in the matter of federal jobs. He condemned the Republican Party program in general, claiming that the tariff issue did not benefit the Negro. "What chance has any colored man to obtain work through any of the trusts which have been loaded with favors by these tariffs? How much does the tariff help the colored man in the South?" He declared that the entire Negro race was disgusted with the McKinley program and that this resentment would make itself felt in the next campaign.[28]

Yet, Lyons was quick to defend the McKinley administration against Fortune's attack. He stated that the Postmaster-General had never referred to his color while in his presence nor did he express opposition to his appointment as postmaster of Augusta. He expressed the utmost confidence in the administration deciding the issue on its merits and not on the basis of color.[29]

Negroes were very critical of the attitude shown by the white citizens of Augusta toward the Lyons' appointment, claiming that it exposed their hypocrisy and perfidy. Discussing the issue in an editorial, the *Savannah Tribune* declared:

In the heated political contests in Augusta the last six years between the Democrats and Populists, the Democrats hugged the Negro and professed so much friendship for him. In return these same Democrats are showing their friendship by endeavoring to prevent one of the ablest and most respected colored men that can be found from appointment to an honorable position in that city. This is one of the ways in which they show friendship when they have no use for the colored brother.[30]

The Lyons issue placed McKinley in a dilemma. If he appointed him to the Augusta post, strife and discord would be created among the whites. If he did not, then there was the danger of driving the Northern Negro Republicans to the Democrats. Thus in order to ease the tension, Lyons was offered a superintendency in the Post Office Department in Washington at a salary of three thousand dollars a year. Lyons rejected it, claiming that he preferred to continue his law practice in Augusta which netted him an income of between three and four thousand dollars a year. Furthermore, Lyons declared that he considered himself competent to handle the Augusta postmastership.[31]

There were other reasons why McKinley was reluctant to appoint Lyons to the postmastership. A Negro named Lofton had been appointed postmaster at Hogansville, Georgia. The whites were so incensed that they refused to patronize the post office and emphasized their opposition by firing shots at the postmaster. Also, Postmaster-General Gary, who earlier had withdrawn his objections to Lyons, told McKinley that if he insisted on making the appointment, he might as well concede Maryland back to the Democratic Party.[32]

The other post which was offered Lyons was that of Register of the Treasury.[33] When Walter Johnson, Buck's successor as boss of the Republican Party in Georgia, proposed this to McKinley, the latter recognized the merits of the idea but said that he thought that such an important post should go to a state that had gone Republican in the last election.[34] After consulting his Negro friends, Lyons decided to withdraw his name for the postmastership at Augusta and asked the President for an appointment in Washington.[35] Commenting on his withdrawal, the *Savannah Tribune* stated that he showed manhood and dignity during the entire controversy and that under his guidance of the party as national committeeman, "more Georgians have been recognized in more honorable positions than ever before." [36]

As a reward for his services to the party, McKinley told some members of the Iowa congressional delegation that he had decided definitely to appoint Lyons as Register of the Treasury.[37] After he was installed in this post far removed from his native state, the *Atlanta Journal* paid this fine tribute to him:

Lyons is an efficient officer, and one of the most highly respected negroes ever in the public service, demanding respect not merely by virtue of his office, but on account largely of his quiet dignity, modesty and unobtrusive personality.[38]

Once again, color was the only bar which Lyons could not surmount in order to be postmaster of Augusta. White supremacy in no way was to be threatened.

The nomination of Henry A. Rucker of Atlanta for the position of Collector of Internal Revenue for Georgia, the best federal political appointment in the state, was received with much less opposition than that of Lyons. One reason for this was that he had the endorsement of the leading Democrats of the city, including the Mayor, most of the city and county officers, and outstanding business men like James W. English, banker and capitalist, of Atlanta.[39] These strong endorsements deterred the Georgia delegation in Congress from making any bitter protest. Steve Clay, United States Senator from Georgia, stated that he had never heard of Rucker until about a week before the appointment was made but he attributed the action more to Hanna's need for the Negro vote in Ohio than to the endorsement by Southern white Democrats. He claimed that the Negroes in Cincinnati and Cleveland were restless because the McKinley administration had failed to give them any recognition. Thus Hanna insisted on the Rucker appointment to satisfy them.[40]

Some Republicans in Washington, however, regarded the appointment as unfortunate. One prominent senator remarked that "the administration would not think of appointing a white barber to a place of such responsibility. I do not see why it should make an exception in favor of a negro barber." [41] The same opinion was expressed by some Georgians who doubted that McKinley would appoint a Negro barber of Detroit, New York or Chicago to such a place. They concluded that Rucker was appointed solely because he was a Negro since "the ability to hone a razor" certainly did not qualify a person for such an important post.[42]

However, it was alleged that Rucker promised the President that he would not appoint Negroes to positions which would bring them into direct contact with white people.[43] The fact that so many prominent white citizens of Atlanta saw fit to endorse him somewhat substantiates this account. After he had served for over a year, the *Atlanta Constitution* in an editorial captioned "A Courteous Officeholder" praised Rucker as a gentleman, although a member of the African race. If he had been insolent and insulting "to those who are compelled by their business to have dealings with him . . . trouble would ensue, and then we should hear an outcry at the North that he was the victim of race prejudice." [44]

The *Atlanta Constitution* took a realistic view toward Rucker's appointment. It claimed that those Democrats who made the mistake of voting for McKinley in the last election had no reason to complain since they knew that Republican success meant Negro officeholders.[45]

For the post of Collector of Customs at the Port of Savannah, John H. Deveaux, an original McKinley man, was the unanimous choice of Negro Republicans of the state. He had rendered valuable service to the party during its campaigns and had served in various government posts since 1870 when he was appointed clerk in the Savannah Custom House. In 1889, with the endorsement of Savannah white citizens and over the objections of Brunswick whites, President Harrison appointed him as Collector at the Port of Brunswick.[46] Thus by training and experience he was well qualified for the post. The Glynn County (Brunswick) Republican Committee passed resolutions endorsing him for the post not on the basis of color but ability.[47]

Upon hearing of this, the Savannah Cotton Exchange and Board of Trade met on December 17, 1897, and protested Deveaux's appointment to either the postmastership or the collectorship. The resolutions were phrased in such a manner as to make it appear that Negroes in general were inferior beings. This sign of opposition aroused Savannah Negroes to action and a meeting was held on December 22, 1897, with over one thousand in attendance. They drew up resolutions endorsing the appointment and reminded the people of Deveaux's service in the Savannah Custom House for over nineteen years, in addition to the four years he spent as Collector of the Port at Brunswick. The resolutions also pointed out the meritorious service he rendered to the people of the latter city when it was stricken with a yellow fever epidemic by remaining at his post and distributing thousands of dollars for the relief of the citizens without a single penny being unaccounted for. The white citizens of Savannah were asked to set aside their prejudices in order that a man who had demonstrated his ability in the past, might be appointed.[48]

It had been argued by some white citizens that Deveaux's appointment would hurt business at the port as well as drive away immigrants. In answer to this objection, it was stated that foreigners did not care about the color of a man's skin as long as the business was conducted properly, and as far as driving immigrants away, "if the lawless element in the state does not do that, we are sure that a colored man as collector will have no effect." [49]

Negroes found support for Deveaux among some of the white citizens. Alderman Hull, of the Savannah City Council, said that he would oppose the endorsement by Council of the resolutions adopted at the Cotton Exchange. He regarded them as unwise in that they would force the President to take sides with the Negroes rather than with the white Democrats.[50] This stand was appreciated by the Negroes who promised to remember him at election time. Fortunately, however, the City Council refused to adopt the resolutions of the Cotton Exchange.[51]

After Deveaux's appointment was confirmed by the United States Senate, Negroes were advised to stop supporting white office seekers until they had been tested. Special reference was made to white Democrats who at election time were bidding for the Negro vote by making sugar-coated promises, yet opposed a Negro as a federal officeholder.[52]

In Athens, two Negroes sought the postmastership; namely, Madison Davis, who had held the position under President Harrison, and Monroe "Pink" Morton, who had gained some publicity as a result of his picture having been published in the *New York World*.[53] Furthermore, he was a delegate to the Republican national convention in 1896 and had the added distinction of serving on the committee to notify McKinley of his nomination. With these advantages, McKinley appointed him postmaster of Athens on July 24, 1897.[54] Mild opposition was raised by some of the whites, including John S. Cohen, a writer for the *Atlanta Journal*, who regarded the appointment as unfortunate, since the white people of Athens owned twenty-nine-thirtieths of the property and paid practically all of the taxes.[55]

Whereas the appointment of Negroes to the aforementioned offices had created only vocal opposition, that of I. H. Lofton as postmaster of Hogansville, a fourth class postoffice with a population of about five hundred, resulted in violence and bodily harm to the incumbent. His appointment was made over the protests of nearly all of the white citizens of the community.[56] After he was appointed he attempted to establish the postoffice in the business section of the town, but the whites refused to lease any space to him. Consequently, he set up the postoffice in the Negro section, which was quite some distance from the white business center and the railroad station. The white citizens, so as to avoid having direct contact with Lofton, hired a white boy to collect the mail at the postoffice and take it to a store which they had leased. There a white woman was paid from a fund collected from the white businessmen to distribute the mail.[57] To many this arrangement was unsatisfactory. The very thought of a Negro handling their mail even indirectly was more than their prejudices could tolerate. One night, just after Lofton had closed his office and was on his way home, some men emerged from the darkness and shot him three times.[58] The incident produced national repercussions.[59]

In response to a request for his views on the matter by the *New York Herald,* Governor Atkinson stated that the people of Georgia condemned the shooting but on the other hand, he regarded McKinley as an accessory to the crime for appointing Lofton over the protests of the whites who furnished ninety-nine and one-hundredth of the business of the office. He concluded by saying that the people of Ohio would probably react in the same manner if a similar appointment were made against the wishes of the best element of the people. United States Senator A. O. Bacon of Georgia told a reporter for the same paper that if it was necessary to appoint Negroes to office, the appointment should be made in communities where the people approved. "Such communities and such people are not found among the whites of the southern states," concluded Bacon.[60]

The first item of business considered by the legislature in its opening session was the introduction of a resolution by Representative Hall of Coweta County condemning McKinley for appointing Lofton to the Hogansville post office. The resolution stated that such appointments were "exhibitions of petty spite and narrow sectional hate, unworthy of the high office of chief magistrate of the great nation."

When Hall asked that the resolution be adopted without reference to a committee, Representative T. D. Oliver of Burke County stated that it misrepresented the true Southern sentiment by giving the impression that the South endorsed the lawless act. It was finally agreed that the resolution be referred to the Committee on the State of the Republic.[61] This committee, consisting of eleven Populists, two Republicans and four Democrats, reported adversely on its passage. But the House, whose membership was seventy-five per cent Democratic, ignored the recommendations of the committee and adopted the resolution almost unanimously.[62] In discussing this action by the Georgia House, the *Savannah Tribune* said that "The Georgia Democrats, who when they were seeking election as representatives hugged, wined, dined and slept with colored men in order to get their votes, now turn and venomously sting those whose aid they beseeched last year." [63]

Despite bullets, legislative resolutions, and numerous threats, Lofton continued to serve as postmaster. But his problems were becoming more and more acute each day. In an effort to counteract the boycott of the post office by the whites and forestall their practice of mailing their letters on the trains, the Post Office Department ordered the railway mail clerks to lock the mail boxes on the cars. However, to circumvent this order, the whites would give a suitcase full of letters to a salesman or other travellers to mail at the next station, or to mail carriers who left Hogansville daily with mail for country towns. Under these conditions business was very poor. Although a hundred letters were mailed from Hogansville daily, only those of Negroes passed through the post office. As part of his pay was based on stamp cancellations, Lofton averaged about eleven cents a day, whereas his white predecessor earned about sixty dollars a month from this source. The situation became so precarious that Lofton found himself deeply in debt and his creditors were pressing him for payment. Speaking of his dilemma, Lofton said: ". . . it is not pleasant to live in a town where the people do not treat you with respect. If I do not get another position it won't be my fault. I would take another position and be glad to get it." [64]

Finally, the building which was used by Lofton as a post office and which was owned by him, was burned, destroying all of the mail and the post office fixtures.[65] By this time, Lofton realized that the odds were against him. Through the efforts of his friends, he was able to get an appointment in one of the departments in Washington. Without revealing his plans to anyone, not even purchasing a ticket at the railway station, he left secretly for his new post in Washington.[66]

Opposition to Negro officeholders by whites applied not only to post-masterships but to lesser posts. Upon learning that Negroes were to be appointed as census takers in Meriwether County, Congressman Adams of that district sent a wire in protest to Washington.[67] When fourteen Negroes, three of them women, were named for the same position in the Tenth Congressional District (Augusta), the white people expressed their disapproval. When the census supervisor in Washington informed them that he could not remove anyone except for civil service cause, it only increased their resentment.[68]

Thus the attitude of the whites in general toward McKinley's appointments was one of dissatisfaction. In view of the large support given him by white Democrats and his protestations of affection for the Southern people in the last campaign, they felt that he would reverse the Republican policy of the past of appointing Negroes to positions where they would be continually thrown into contact with white people. However, in their opinion, "He has not befriended the black man by this unwise policy and he has lost the confidence and respect of a large majority of the whites." [69]

It is quite clear that the only objection that the whites had to the Negro officeholder was his color, regardless of his competence. Yet, when the facts are examined, even this objection is unfair. Although Negroes represented ninety per cent of the regular Republican strength in the state, their appointments were few in comparison with those given to white Republicans (V. O. Key calls them presidential Republicans), Democrats, and Populists. In fact, so many Democrats and Populists were given political preferment in federal jobs that the Negro Republicans of the Second Congressional District met at Albany, December 30, 1898, and passed resolutions condemning the practice.[70] During McKinley's administration, whites in Georgia received appointments as ministers to Japan and Ecuador, to all of the United States marshalships in the state, in addition to nearly five hundred post-office jobs.[71]

Before the Spanish-American War, the Negroes, in spite of some mistakes, regarded McKinley as the best friend they ever had, pointing out that he had appointed more Negroes to responsible positions in Georgia than all the earlier presidents combined, including posts not held before by the race. Among the appointments cited on the state level were the Internal Revenue Collectorship, Collectorship of the Port of Savannah, postmasterships at Athens and Hogansville, and the superintendency of the stamp division. In addition, a Georgia Negro was appointed as consul at Asuncion, Paraguay [72] and R. R. Wright, president of the Savannah State Industrial College for Negroes, and a graduate of Atlanta University, was appointed paymaster of the United States army with the rank of major.[73]

Thus it appears that the Negroes were satisfied with McKinley as long as he adhered to the policy of giving them recognition as officeholders. However, the Spanish-American War produced a sudden change.[74] The appointment by McKinley of ex-Confederate generals like Fitzhugh Lee and "Fighting Joe" Wheeler to major-generalships in the United States army and the response of Southerners to the call for volunteers helped to alleviate the tension that existed between the sections and enabled the South to resume its position in national affairs. Instead of berating McKinley for his Negro appointments, the South began to express admiration for his forgiving spirit. The net result of this was to alienate from the McKinley standard many Negroes, who felt that he had given support to the Negro hating South "by his conciliatory attitude toward the Spanish-American War." [75]

This changed spirit was much in evidence when McKinley visited Atlanta in December, 1898. Following the signing of the treaty of peace ending the war, Atlanta was the first city to arrange a huge peace jubilee and parade to celebrate the occasion, with President McKinley as the honored guest.[76] Speaking before the joint session of the Georgia Legislature on December 14, McKinley told them, many of whom were ex-Confederate soldiers, that "sectional lines no longer mar the map of the United States."

Every soldier's grave made during our unfortunate Civil War is a tribute to American valor . . . and the time has now come, in the evolution of sentiment and feeling under the providence of God, when in the spirit of fraternity we should share with you in the care of graves of the Confederate soldiers.[77]

These remarks were the occasion for a standing ovation from the solid mass of humanity in the hall. According to McKinley's biographer, "it was the first time that the South had fallen in love with a Republican President."[78]

From Atlanta, after speaking at Tuskegee and Montgomery, Alabama, the President and his party went to Savannah where addresses were made to the Board of Trade and Associated Citizens on December 17 and to the State Industrial College for Negroes the following day. Over one thousand people were present at the College to greet the President. Seated on the platform with him was "Fighting Joe" Wheeler, who had become not only an idol of the South but of the nation.

Dr. J. J. Durham, one of the most eloquent Negro ministers in the city, welcomed the President on behalf of the Negro citizens. He commended McKinley for the achievements of his administration, and then proceeded to narrate the progress made by the Negro race educationally and economically since emancipation. In conclusion, Dr. Durham declared:

If we have not made all the progress and learned all the lessons within the last thirty years that our good white friends think we ought, let them not forget that from the time when the Anglo-Saxon crossed creeks and rivers on logs and rafts, to the time he crossed East River on Brooklyn bridge, was the stretch of more than a thousand years.[79]

The President rose and stated that the eloquent words expressed by the speaker made a profound impression upon him. Concerning the progress of the Negro race, the President asserted "It is better to be a skilled mechanic than a poor orator or an indifferent preacher" and that "nothing in the world commands more respect than skill and industry." He admonished the Negroes to "Be patient, be progressive, be determined, be honest, be God-fearing, and you will win, for no effort fails that has a stout, honest, earnest hand behind it."[80]

While McKinley's southern trip might have increased his popularity among the whites, it definitely produced an unfavorable reaction among the Negroes. The exclusion of Negroes from the reception committees that welcomed the President in the various cities in the South left the Negroes unhappy. Then, too, in all of his speeches, McKinley did not mention or condemn race proscription. When he proposed that the North should share with the South in the care of the graves of the Confederate soldiers, it gave the Negroes the impression that he condoned the Southern policy instead of condemning it.[81] On the other hand, McKinley, in view of the enthusiastic reception accorded him by the South, sincerely believed that the trip had resulted in the nation becoming united once more.[82]

When McKinley was unanimously renominated for President by the Republicans in 1900, there were a few dissenters among Negroes in Georgia, among them being the distinguished prelate, Bishop Henry McNeal Turner of the African Methodist Episcopal Church. Turner had been prominent in Republican politics during the Reconstruction period, having served in the state constitutional convention of 1867–68, and in the Georgia House, 1868–70. During the 1880's he deserted the Republican Party in favor of the Prohibitionists, claiming that the Republican Party had become the party of vested interests. But on September 5, 1900, while still claiming to be a Prohibitionist, Turner announced he would vote for William Jennings Bryan, the Democratic nominee

five times before I would vote for William McKinley once and . . . that between Bryan and McKinley, I am for Bryan . . . because we have tried McKinley for four years and he is of no benefit to the black man, except in giving some of them just a few offices, but the great bulk of my race receive no more recognition at his hands than a man who has been dead for twenty years.[83]

Notwithstanding the stature of Turner and the argument presented by him, it seems that the attachment of Negroes to the Republican Party was so strong that they would not accept his proposal that they become identified with the Democratic Party. For instance, the *Savannah Tribune,* owned by Deveaux, stated that no decent Negro could afford to support the Democratic Party since it was the party of "Jim Crow," disfranchisement, and proscription in general of the Negro.[84] "There is no man in the South," said Judson Lyons, "that the Democrats have so little respect for as the colored man that claims membership in the (Democratic) party." [85]

The election results in Georgia gave Bryan 81,700 votes to 35,832 for McKinley,[86] which was a sharp drop from the sixty thousand received by the latter in the 1896 presidential race. Not only did Negroes rejoice in McKinley's re-election but also prominent white businessmen in Atlanta. J. W. English, president of the Fourth National Bank, Jacob Haas, president of the Capital City Bank, and Frank Hawkins, president of the Third National Bank, all declared that the re-election of McKinley satisfied all businessmen.[87] This is concrete evidence that the Republican Party had become the party of property and big business regardless of its location.

McKinley had little time to consider the Negro question in the South after his re-election. An assassin's bullet ended his career only six months after his second term began. This tragedy at the Buffalo Pan-American Exposition was of especial concern to Negroes of Georgia because of the heroism displayed by a Georgia Negro, J. F. Parker, a waiter, in subduing the assassin after he had fired the fatal shots.[88]

McKinley's death was received as a shock by Negroes. At memorial services held for the chief executive in Savannah, President R. R. Wright of the State Industrial College for Negroes and long-time friend of the deceased president, said that

the most enduring thing is his moral and Christian character . . . Politics and statecraft were forgotten. The mantle of his political life he could drop from his to other shoulders, but the sweet life that he had lived, he carried with him; to us he leaves the memory of it.[89]

It was to be expected that Negroes would be saddened over McKinley's death, since he had appointed more Negroes to federal office than any of his predecessors. However, during his triumphant tour of the South following the Spanish-American War, at which time he endeared himself to white Southerners, he indicated he might have been willing to sacrifice the Negro for North-South rapprochement. From this standpoint, McKinley's death was unfortunate for the South for his successor was Theodore Roosevelt. And Roosevelt, not having any immediate feeling of obligation to the South, would, as McKinley had done in the early part of his administration, continue to appoint Negroes to federal positions in that section.

NOTES

1. Edward Stanwood, *A History of the Presidency* (Boston, 1896), pp. 525, 538.
2. Herbert Croly, *Marcus Hanna—His Life and Work* (New York, 1923), p. 175; Charles S. Olcott, *William McKinley* (Boston, 1916), I, p. 305.
3. *Savannah Tribune*, Apr. 16, 1895.
4. *Ibid.*, August 22, 1896.
5. *Atlanta Journal*, June 26, 1896.
6. *Ibid.*, June 23, 1896.
7. *Ibid.*, November 4, 1896.
8. *Ibid.*
9. Stanwood, *op. cit.*, p. 567.
10. E. Merton Coulter, *Georgia—A Short History* (Chapel Hill, 1947), p. 396.
11. *Atlanta Journal*, November 4, 1896.
12. *Ibid.*, January 20, 1897.
13. Alfred H. Stone, *Studies in the American Race Problem* (New York, 1908), pp. 293–294.
14. *Savannah Tribune*, February 20, 1897; *Atlanta Journal*, March 29, 1897.
15. *Atlanta Journal*, April 22, 1897.
16. *Ibid.*, March 17, 1897.
17. *Ibid.*, April 21, 1897.
18. *Ibid.*, April 5, 1897. Buck was a native of Maine but had lived in Georgia since 1871.
19. *Ibid.*, May 4, 1897.
20. *Ibid.*, May 6, 1897.
21. *Ibid.*, April 22, 1897. Lyons was a graduate with high honors in law from Howard University Law School in the class of 1884. Letter from his widow, Mrs. Mary Lyons, Washington, D.C., April 15, 1951.
22. *Atlanta Journal*, April 22, May 10, 1897.
23. *Ibid.*, May 10, 1897.
24. *Ibid.* Gary was the only Southerner in McKinley's cabinet, having been the Republican national committeeman from Maryland. This was a reward for Maryland giving its electoral vote to McKinley, in the recent election.

25. *Ibid.*, May 15, 1897.
26. *Savannah Tribune,* May 22, 1897. *The Tribune* rejoined that white women of Augusta appreciated the service rendered by the Negro letter carriers in the city and did not object to who was postmaster just so long as they received their mail. Editorial.
27. *Atlanta Journal,* June 12, 1897.
28. *Ibid.*, July 24, 1897.
29. *Ibid.* At the request of McKinley, who told Gary that the party could ill afford to desert Lyons for the post since there was no other position open, Gary withdrew his objections to the appointment. *Ibid.*, July 28, 1897.
30. Editorial, May 1, 1897.
31. *Atlanta Journal,* September 14, 1897.
32. *Ibid.*, September 17, 1897. The Lofton incident is discussed later in the article.
33. *Ibid.*, September 14, 1897.
34. *Ibid.*, September 17, 1897. Already signs of a split in the Republican Party were apparent. Pledger described Johnson as a "spineless" leader and announced his intentions of calling the anti-Buck forces together in the near future for the purpose of reorganizing the party. *Ibid.*, September 14, 1897.
35. *Ibid.*, December 17, 1897.
36. Editorial, February 12, 1898.
37. *Atlanta Journal,* March 22, 1898.
38. Editorial, July 13, 1898.
39. *Atlanta Journal,* July 24, 1887. Rucker received his education in the Atlanta University academy and earned his tuition by teaching during vacation periods. His first experience in politics was when he served as a delegate to the Republican national convention in 1880. After that time he worked in the Internal Revenue office in Atlanta under three different administrations.
40. *Ibid.*, July 26, 1897.
41. *Ibid.*, July 24, 1897.
42. *Ibid.*, September 17, 1897.
43. *Ibid.*, July 28, 1897. After Rucker was in office for over a year, he had over one hundred men under his jurisdiction, of whom about 10 per cent were Negroes. *Savannah Tribune,* December 24, 1898.
44. Quoted in *The Bulletin of Atlanta University,* December, 1898, p. 4.
45. Editorial, quoted in *Savannah Tribune,* July 31, 1897.
46. *Savannah Tribune,* June 12, 1909.
47. *Ibid.*, May 15, 1897.
48. *Ibid.*, December 25, 1897. A Jewish resident of Savannah wrote a personal letter to McKinley protesting the action taken by the Savannah Cotton Exchange and Board of Trade, claiming that his race had been persecuted all over the world and that only in America did they enjoy civil rights. Thus he urged the President to deal justly with the Negro. *Savannah Morning News,* quoted in *Savannah Tribune,* January 1, 1898.
49. Editorial, *Savannah Tribune,* January 1, 1898.
50. *Savannah Tribune,* December 25, 1897.
51. *Ibid.*, January 1, 1898.
52. Editorial, *ibid.*, February 26, 1898. The Port of Savannah was the largest on the South Atlantic coast, and was second only to New Orleans in the South in terms of volume of business. Twelve men served under Deveaux, five of whom were Negroes. *Colored American* (Washington, D.C.), quoted in *ibid.*, December 25, 1898.
53. *Atlanta Journal,* November 21, 1896. Madison Davis was a member of the Georgia House of Representatives from 1868 to 1873.
54. *Ibid.*, July 31, 1897. Morton was born a slave in 1859. By hard work he rose to one of the most prosperous Negroes in the state. He was engaged in the coal and lumber business and acquired a vast amount of real estate. He held several government posts, including route agent in the mail service between Athens and Macon, and as storekeeper and gauger at Lawrenceville. While he himself was denied a college education, he educated two sisters at Atlanta University.

During his five years' tenure as postmaster, he instituted many reforms and improvements. *Ibid., Atlanta Independent,* January 30, 1904.

55. *Atlanta Journal,* September 17, 1897.
56. *Ibid.,* September 6, 1897.
57. *Ibid.,* September 20, 1897.
58. *Ibid.,* September 16, 1897.
59. The *New York Press* in an editorial captioned, "Arms for the Black Civil Servants," said that the only course left was to arm Negroes against the attacks caused by "that high strung southern spirit whose sensitiveness compels it to shoot from ambush rather than see the United States mail or the United States court process sullied by a black hand." Quoted in *Atlanta Journal,* September 18, 1897.
60. *Atlanta Journal,* September 17, 1897.
61. *Ibid.,* October 27, 1897.
62. *Savannah Tribune,* October 30, 1897.
63. Editorial, *ibid.*
64. *Atlanta Journal,* February 4, 1898. In addition to the money earned from collections, Lofton received a salary of two hundred dollars a year.
65. *Ibid.,* November 29, 1899.
66. *Ibid.,* January 26, 1900.
67. *Ibid.,* May 29, 1899.
68. *Ibid.,* May 17, 1900.
69. Editorial, *ibid.,* March 3, 1898.
70. *Savannah Tribune,* February 25, 1899.
71. *Ibid.,* August 7, 1897.
72. *Ibid.,* October 15, 1898.
73. Stone, *op. cit.,* p. 296.
74. Paul Buck, *The Road to Reunion, 1865–1900* (Boston, 1947), p. 306.
75. Stone, *op. cit.,* pp. 299–300.
76. *Atlanta Journal,* December 15, 1898. An interesting sidelight of this parade was the refusal of labor organizations to participate because Negro members were excluded. When the committee in charge of the parade told the Stone Quarryman's Union that their Negro members could not participate, the Atlanta Federation of Trades drafted resolutions condemning this action. They stated that since Negroes were members of the Federation of Trades, the laboring men felt that they should stand together and refuse to parade unless the Negroes were invited. They further asserted that "inasmuch as the color line was not drawn in the mustering of the volunteer or regular army, and . . . it was the colored soldiers who did perhaps the greater part of the heroic fighting that won San Juan from the enemy . . . we affirm that it should not be drawn in The Peace Jubilee." The resolutions were passed. *Ibid., Atlanta Constitution,* December 16, 1898.
77. William McKinley, *Speeches and Addresses of William McKinley from March 1, 1897 to May 30, 1900* (New York, 1900), p. 158. Hereafter cited as *McKinley's Speeches.*
78. Olcott, *op. cit.,* II, p. 301.
79. *Savannah Tribune,* December 24, 1898.
80. *McKinley's Speeches,* pp. 176–178.
81. *Atlanta Journal,* December 22, 1898.
82. Olcott, *op. cit.,* II, p. 301.
83. Letter to the *Atlanta Journal,* September 6, 1900.
84. Editorial, September 8, 1900.
85. *Washington Post,* quoted in *Savannah Tribune,* October 28, 1900.
86. Georgia Comptroller General *Report,* 1901, pp. 232, 238.
87. *Atlanta Journal,* November 7, 1900.
88. *Ibid.,* September 7, 1901. Parker was born in Atlanta in 1857 and received his elementary education at Storr's school and attended the Atlanta University academy for a short time. He was a very large man, being six and a half feet tall, and worked as a waiter in the Kimball House in Atlanta for many years.

Earlier he had taken a minor part in Republican politics in the city. *Ibid.,* September 11, 1901.

89. *The Bulletin of Atlanta University,* November, 1901, p. 4. President Wright had known McKinley since 1880 when they met at the Republican national convention in Chicago. In 1884 Wright served on the platform committee with McKinley at the Republican national convention and claimed that he, with McKinley's consent, wrote the plank in the platform guaranteeing civil and political rights to the Negroes in the South.

7. On Revising Reconstruction History: Negro Suffrage, White Disfranchisement, and Common Sense

During phases of accelerated gain by black Americans, serious distortions of the extent, nature, and relevance of these gains arise within the white racist world. Among the recently emerging racist organizations to counteract recent gains by blacks is SPONGE, or the Society to Prevent Negroes from Getting Everything. The Reconstruction period of American history (like the present) was a time of black American gains. Chapter 7 corrects the misconceptions of racists, scholars, and laymen alike about the extent of Negro gains during Reconstruction, which was the basis of considerable fear, envy, and eventual retaliation by whites.

FORREST G. WOOD

One of the most continuous and pertinacious themes of Reconstruction history is the notion that the Radical control of the South was based on a broad, ill-gotten electorate made up largely of Negroes. While scholars have made some inroads in challenging this interpretation,[1] a great deal of additional research needs to be done before any definitive revision can be made. Compounding the difficulty is the fact that many of the vital statistics are incomplete; thus the historical record may never be conclusive.

In the meantime, the traditional view—a view more compatible with sectional loyalties and romantic myths—lingers. Predicated on the assumption that vast numbers of Negroes were enfranchised while thousands of Southern whites were being denied the ballot, it holds that a Radical Congress overthrew without cause the legitimate state governments established in the immediate post-war period. Negro suffrage and Southern white disfranchisement, the tradition goes, were the twin keys to the success of the carpetbag governments. It was bellowed from both North and South during the Reconstruction, and historians of almost all

From *Journal of Negro History* (1966), Vol. 51, pp. 98–113; reprinted by permission.

persuasions have perpetuated it ever since. One student has asserted that "white majorities were cut down or wiped out entirely," [2] a view repeated so frequently that few have dared to question it. That such universal opinion could be based on such tenuous and fragmentary evidence is one of the enigmas of Reconstruction history.

According to the Eighth Census (1860), two Southern states—South Carolina and Mississippi—had Negro majorities. By 1870, Louisiana probably became the third.[3] The Negro percentages of the populations in the other Southern states in 1870 ranged from 48.8 in Florida to 25.2 in Arkansas. Three of them—Alabama, Georgia, and Virginia—had, like Florida, populations that were over 40 per cent Negro.[4] It was obvious from the outset that any plan to enfranchise the freedmen, unlike suffrage proposals in the North, would involve vast numbers of blacks. In giving the ballot to 800,000 ex-slaves, one northern critic lamented, "Considerations of mere temporary expediency, of mere party advantage, fall paralyzed to the ground." We in the North, refusing to grant impartial suffrage in our own states, force it upon others "by the bushel." "A little retail negro suffrage here, where it can do little harm, is denied," Congressman Samuel Sullivan Cox observed; "wholesale negro suffrage there is enforced where it is supreme." [5]

According to most critics, the freedman's appalling ignorance would destroy the democratic process in the South. Many ex-slaves, they complained, had never heard of the candidates they were asked to support. Others allegedly could not identify their home county or give their exact ages. A few critics went so far as to claim that some freedmen were of such low intelligence that they had trouble remembering their own names. After interviewing an illiterate field hand in Georgia, a Northern traveler regretfully conceded that this man represented the lowest intelligence "among that class on whom it is proposed to confer the right of suffrage." As Tennessee's Governor Brownlow put it: impartial suffrage would "open the ballot-box to the uninformed and exceedingly stupid slaves of the Southern cotton, rice and sugar fields." [6] While the governor was obviously referring to the Negroes of the Black Belt, he was not overlooking the presumed dangers of impartial suffrage in his own state. There was no doubt, of course, that the ignorance of the vast majority of the freedmen was staggering; thus most whites, without considering the causes of or the remedies for that ignorance, concluded that Negro suffrage would lead to the absolute ruin of the South. As a Northern poet put it:

> 'Cause now I'se got de franchise
> Dough I neber goed to school,
> And if Massah Bullock's 'lected,
> I gits forty acres and a mule! [7]

For a variety of reasons, there was an almost ingenuous confidence among white Southerners that Northern public opinion would not permit the Congress to force Negro suffrage on the South. The truculent words of Northern racists were reassuring. "[J]udging by myself, and comparing the limited extent of my prejudice against the colored race with that of the generality of the Northern people," one writer sanctimoniously declared, "I do not believe that the people of the North will allow large armies to be raised for any such unfair and oppressive purpose." [8] More important, the returns from the state elections in the North seemed to justify this optimism. To be sure, the Democratic party's surprising show of strength in such Republican strongholds as Maine, New Hampshire, and Minnesota was especially encouraging. A month after the elections of 1867, white conservatives in Little Rock, Arkansas, pledged to "preserve the principles of the national Constitution by co-operating with the Democratic party of the Union." "In view of the astonishing results of the recent elections in different portions of the Union," they added, "the voices of the Democratic and Conservative masses of the North call upon us to assist in defeating the attempt of radicalism to destroy our old constitutional government and set up in its place one in which others than white men shall have the controlling influence." Democrats in Louisiana met in the following year and, on the basis of the same elections, expressed confidence that Northern Democrats and conservatives would not let them down. [9]

Nevertheless, other Southern whites, less optimistic than their neighbors and refusing to take heart from Northern elections, displayed genuine fear over possible Negro enfranchisement. In fact, there were signs during the early months of Radical Reconstruction that some of them, sensing the inevitable, hoped to capitalize on the black vote and recruit it for their own purposes. While such moves never amounted to much, they did suggest an attempt to make the most of what seemed to be an intolerable but unavoidable development. In 1879, Wade Hampton, a former Confederate general and later governor of South Carolina and a United States Senator, boasted that he had been the first white man in the South to recommend Negro suffrage, and that many "intelligent and reflecting whites" had agreed with him. [10] Hampton was only guessing, of course. In February, 1866, a Texas conservative had offered his state a sweeping plan, including three alternatives, for extending the ballot to the Negro. [11] Seven months later, John H. Reagan, former Postmaster-General of the Confederacy, wrote to Governor Throckmorton of Texas and urged him to consider limited Negro suffrage in order to guarantee white supremacy. Otherwise, he insisted, the Radicals would force mass Negro suffrage on the state. [12] Nonetheless, Hampton's boast that other whites agreed with him, though misleading, was true.

Attempts by Southern conservatives to exploit the Negro vote, of course, were examples of political expediency rather than a genuine concern for the freedman's civil rights. The idea of using the ex-slaves to check the economic encroachments of poor whites and the countermoves of political enemies must have appealed to more than a few former slaveowners. If Negroes are granted the ballot, a Northern writer predicted, "I for one should not at all be surprised to see the great majority of them voting the ticket of their masters." Governor Brownlow recommended the forced removal of all the Negroes in his state to a separate territory because "the great majority of them would be influenced by leading secessionists to vote against the Government, as they would be largely under the influence of this class of men for years to come, having to reside on and cultivate their lands." [13]

Though not always including an endorsement of suffrage, white conservatives did occasionally express sympathy for the freedmen. In December, 1867, delegates to a meeting in Richmond, Virginia, resolved to do all that they could for the Negroes, insisting, however, that the ballot belonged in the hands of the whites only. Conservatives in South Carolina, where Negroes outnumbered whites by three to two, were much more generous and expressed a willingness, "when we have the power," to grant the Negroes, "under proper qualifications as to property and intelligence, the right of suffrage." Even with these ambiguous conditions, the statement was surprising. A short time later, Democrats in Texas announced a desire to see all the freedmen protected by the laws of the state. Pleading for the restoration of white rule, the Democratic State Central Committee of Louisiana even asked the Negro leaders of their state for support.[14]

While predictions of a Negro-supported white conservative oligarchy were certainly exaggerated, they were menacing enough to frighten northern Negro leaders who saw in them a Republican excuse for backing down. In July, 1865, delegates to a convention of colored men in Philadelphia insisted that there was absolutely no basis for the suspicion that former slaveowners would control the southern Negro's vote. The Negro cannot be made to do, "now that he is free, what he could not be forced to do when a slave," the convention proclaimed. As to the charge that the Negro's gross ignorance would corrupt the ballot and make him the tool of a beguiling white Southerner, the delegates pointed to that class of poor whites exploited by the racists and resolved: "That the apparent anxiety to preserve the ballot-box from the influence of the ignorance of the colored man is proved, by the class of [white] men invited and urged to the polls at every election, to be but a hypocritical and malignant subterfuge." In short, those who most feared a white planter oligarchy based on a manipulated uneducated Negro electorate were themselves exploiters of hatred, prejudice, and ignorance.[15]

Since Southern Negroes had majorities in at most three states, impartial suffrage in the South involved more than simply enfranchising the freedmen. According to the traditional interpretation of Reconstruction history, Radical Republicans hoped to disfranchise thousands of southern whites, a move that would easily create black majorities in Alabama, Florida,

Georgia, and Virginia. Theoretically, this would add fourteen men to the United States Senate who, representing Negro majorities, could obstruct any legislation; or voting with the Radical senators from the northern states, pass any bill. To the white Southerner the outlook must have seemed, at best, grim, and, at worst, catastrophic.

Suggestions of mass disfranchisements had first appeared during the war when certain congressmen had proposed test oaths for southern whites as a condition for the reinstatement of civil rights.[16] After Appomattox, what began as a remote suspicion became a genuine fear, at least among the most fanatical opponents of the government. On Saturday morning, April 15, 1865, a few hours after Lincoln's death, a Copperhead extremist savagely denounced an alleged abolitionist plot to secure "Nigger Supremacy" by disfranchising southern whites. It is not just a matter of a few thousand, he complained. On the contrary, Frederick Douglass and Horace Greeley are determined to enfranchise *all* blacks and disfranchise *all* whites. After military reconstruction began in 1867, many whites were certain that their original fears had been justified. The venomous La Crosse *Democrat* attacked the "black niggers from the cotton fields and the white niggers from New England" for stealing the ballot from respectable white Southerners and giving it to illiterate blacks. In a separate pamphlet, *Democrat* editor Marcus Mills "Brick" Pomeroy accused the Radicals of encouraging multiple registration among the freedmen. "[T]he hideous villainy of the reconstruction infamy lies, not in giving the negroes suffrage," the Chicago *Times* lamented in the summer of 1868, "but in disfranchising white men and so legislating as to give the negro party ascendancy." In the South, of course, white conservatives were convinced that mass disfranchisement was an accomplished fact.[17] Thus did the extremist critics of the government propagate a notion that has lingered for a century.

In truth, the fear of white disfranchisements may have been the most exaggerated reaction of the entire Reconstruction era. Since the Radicals *did* overthrow the white conservative state governments that had been set up under the Johnson Reconstruction program, most alarmed observers carelessly concluded that there *must* have been mass disfranchisements. But their conclusions—as well as those of many since—simply do not stand up after a careful examination of the evidence; and, where the evidence is scanty or nonexistent, they do not pass the test of common sense. Known disfranchisement statistics, pertaining only to the preliminary elections held under the Reconstruction Acts of 1867, are available for five states—Virginia, North Carolina, South Carolina, Georgia, and Florida—and in all five, white disfranchisements *did not* give Negro voters a majority![18] South Carolina and Florida were the only states with more registered Negroes than whites. In the former state the whites, with slightly over 40 per cent of the total population, were in the minority to begin with, thus the disfranchisements were hardly necessary to insure a "Negro ascendancy." While it was true that registered Negroes in Florida outnumbered registered whites by a substantial amount, the total number actually disfranchised was so small that, after Negro disfranchisements were subtracted, there was a net loss of only one hundred and fifty white registrations.[19]

In the other three states for which statistics are available, the registered whites retained their majorities in spite of the disfranchisements. Over 16,000 were disfranchised in Virginia, but the whites retained their majority by over 14,000. Registered whites in North Carolina outnumbered registered Negroes by a wide margin: 34,000 out of a total of 179,000 registrations. Oddly, Georgia provided what was probably the best rebuttal to the charge that the Radicals disfranchised whites for the sole purpose of guaranteeing a Negro majority. Though 10,500 were denied the ballot, whites nonetheless retained a narrow margin of slightly over 1,000 voters out of almost 200,000 registrations. If the Radicals had been determined to insure a Negro majority in this state, they could have done so easily by merely disfranchising 1,000 more whites—but they did no such thing. In addition, critics of the government almost always ignored the fact that Negroes were also disfranchised—1,118 in the Carolinas—usually for serious crimes. In short, in at least half of the ten reconstructed states, the disfranchisement of white voters did not create Negro majorities.[20]

The argument does not end here. In the five states where disfranchisements were not recorded, the registrations alone are revealing. Louisiana and Mississippi had registered Negro majorities, but since Mississippi and probably Louisiana had more Negroes than whites to begin with, this should not have been surprising. As in South Carolina, disfranchisements were not "necessary." In Texas and Arkansas the situations were similar to those in Virginia, North Carolina, and Georgia; the white voters retained registered majorities in spite of alleged disfranchisements. Only in Alabama, where the freedmen constituted slightly less than half of the total population (47.7 per cent in 1870), did the figures suggest that disfranchisements could have created a black majority. Here, Negroes had a five to three margin in voter registrations. Yet to get such a result, the Radicals would have had to disfranchise over 60,000 whites. For them to have gone to such lengths is difficult to believe because they could have had the same result—a simple Negro majority—by merely disfranchising a few thousand whites. Thus the traditional complaint loses much of its force for the only state where it made any sense in the first place.[21]

An example of how much guess-work has been involved in the standard view of Reconstruction history can be seen by simply adding the known disfranchisements under the Reconstruction Acts. They total 47,125 for five states; yet many sources, estimating for all ten states, cite a number far higher—some as high as 200,000.[22] A look at the figures makes these guesses seem rather absurd. The five states with recorded disfranchisements accounted for 53 per cent of the total southern white population, including the three largest states. If one merely doubled the known disfranchisements to account for the other five states, the total is considerably less than 100,000. A computation based on the state with the most known disfranchisements would result in an overall estimate of 97,000. Or one based on the state with the highest percentage of known disfranchisements would be about 108,000. In short, no matter how the figures are juggled, they strongly suggest that both the contemporary estimates and the guesses that many have made since were gross exaggerations.

This is not to say that disfranchisements were not significant in the carpetbag control of the South. The difficulty lies in the fact that the statistics are very meager and apply only to the preliminary elections under the Reconstruction Acts. Moreover, there is no guarantee that the existing facts are accurate. After all, the military districts were instruments of the Congress; it may not have been politically expedient to advertise in the North the fact that large numbers of whites were being disfranchised in the South. The fact that five states failed to record any disfranchisements is itself enough to make one suspicious of the figures that do exist. In addition, the figures for Florida and Georgia, since they were so conveniently rounded off, are especially suspect. In other words, the test of "common sense" works both ways.

It also needs to be pointed out that subsequent state and local elections provided many additional opportunities for the Radicals to improve their political positions (or for the conservatives to undermine them); and Congress took it upon itself to deny the ballot to former rebel officials, though certainly not on a massive scale. In any case, the point is not that there were few disfranchisements, but that the critic of the government had so little real evidence on which to base his complaints and thus that much of the contemporary and subsequent criticism of the Radicals is groundless. Indeed, it is far safer to say that there was no widespread, permanent disfranchisement in the South until late in the nineteenth century when white conservative state governments began the mass disfranchisement of Negroes.

A far more credible explanation of both the registration and disfranchisement figures and the subsequent course of southern politics is that the white people of the South lost control of their state governments by refusing to register; or, in some cases, after registering, refusing to vote.[23] They wallowed in self-pity and whined over the odious Radical grip from Congress when they should have been blaming themselves—a reaction that had plenty of eyewitnesses. As arrangements were being made for the various state constitutional conventions under the Reconstruction Acts, the editor of the Charlottesville (Virginia) *Chronicle* bitterly criticized those white Southerners who, "sullen and discontented," had declared they would refuse to register. Their announcement that they "would prefer military government to negro suffrage" was based on a delusion. The only way to guarantee white control, he insisted, was for all eligible white men to register and vote.[24]

The southern boycott was also obvious to Northerners, including some of the same Copperheads who complained of mass disfranchisements. The editor of the Columbus *Crisis,* an avowed opponent of Radical Reconstruction, denounced those Southerners who, "paralyzed by supineness," were just as responsible for the detestable carpetbag governments as the enfranchised blacks. By organizing on Democratic principles, he insisted, the southern whites could easily cast off the Radical-Negro yoke—but they refuse to do so. In Congress, Senator Aaron H. Cragin, Republican from New Hampshire, cited the results of the constitutional referendums in nine of the ten reconstructed states to show that it was the white voters, and not the Negroes, who were responsible for the new state governments. While many southern whites apparently supported the Radical programs, most did nothing. Though it was within their power to control the elections, Cragin concluded, they nevertheless refused to register: "If a man sleep upon his rights shall he complain if he lose them?"[25] Indignation and apathy, not disfranchisements, were major deterrents to white voter registration in the South. Many whites were either defiant or they simply did not care. In either case, they forfeited their right to self-government by keeping their names off the registration rolls or refusing to vote.

There were several reasons for the political abdication of the southern white conservative, some so obvious that critics frequently overlooked them. For example, many whites simply could not accept the idea of standing alongside a Negro—perhaps one of their own former slaves—at the polls. "God save the people of the South," a Northern congressman cried, "from the depredations by which they would be obliged to go to the polls and vote side by side with the negro." In addition, the continuous racist reference to the "savage African" certainly frightened many. One observer conceded that most "white voters deny themselves the franchise, rather than be brought in collision at the polls with a race whose savage fiendishness is well known, and whose weapon of defence is a 'razor.'" Some stayed away from the polls in order to avoid an implied recognition of racial equality; while the refusal to register was, for still others, simply an act of protest. To show their contempt for the Radicals, they decided to disassociate themselves completely from all things related to Reconstruction.[26]

More generally, the feeling of humiliation and disillusionment shared by most white Southerners was extremely important. Surrounded by the ruins of war, disenchanted over the "Lost Cause," stunned by the presence of an army of occupation, and reluctant—after putting their faith in men who had led them into a disastrous war—to become involved in politics and government, many southern whites, like General Lee, decided to refrain from participation in political affairs. A defeated, war-weary population, faced with the monumental task of rebuilding a ravaged countryside, had no time for the luxury of partisan politics and, as Howard K. Beale has observed, "remained politically indifferent through the various turns of political fortune." [27] In short, the southern white man, while complaining of mass disfranchisements, surrendered the right to control his own affairs. It must have been quite obvious from the beginning that the Radicals were going to have things their way; and that the establishment of military districts indicated that they were going to depend on federal bayonets, not Negro voters. Had southern whites turned out in force, it is probable that the Radicals would have resorted to the most obvious expedient: simply secure the disfranchisement of more whites. This probability may have discouraged many from even bothering to make the trek to the registration office. But the existence of such an apprehension, however justified, while it served as a convenient excuse, cannot detract from the fact that many southern whites did not even try and thus were guilty of complicity in their own misery.

One of the reasons for the durability of the traditional version of Reconstruction history is the customary political habit of defining one's terms to suit one's purposes—and the post-war opponent of the government was no exception. Northern and southern critics, despite their obvious sincerity, based their complaints of Negro political domination on some rather illusory arguments. To begin with, they defined "majority" in a peculiar way. As they put it, the freedmen did not need a numerical majority in order to enjoy a political majority. Rather, if the total number of *eligible* Negro voters was greater than the difference in the number cast for each party, the Negroes had a "majority." By selling their votes to the candidate who promised them the most, and by voting as a bloc, the ex-slaves presumably would have the balance of power. Strangely, few defenders of the Radical program challenged this definition.

Though inherently false, such nebulous thinking appeared again and again in complaints against the government's reconstruction policies. Congressman Daniel Voorhees, a staunch Indiana racist, claimed that seventy electoral votes from the Negro-dominated South could decide a presidential election, regardless of the vote in the North. "The negroes of Georgia, in their dense barbarity, are to out vote the freemen of Indiana in the choice of a chief magistrate," he lamented. "The negro on the levees of the Mississippi is to drown the voice of the intelligent farmer of the North. . . . [T]he negro shall make the next President." Speaking before the Jackson Central Association in New York City, Horatio Seymour, disregarding the fact that senators represented states rather than populations, declared that "you cannot give three millions of negroes more Senators than are allowed to fifteen millions of white men living in New York,

Pennsylvania, Ohio, Illinois, Indiana, Wisconsin, Iowa, Kentucky, Missouri, and Michigan." [28] Since the ten southern states would have the *same* number of senators as any ten northern states, Seymour apparently ignored his listeners' ability to multiply ten times two. Speaking strictly in terms of proportion, Seymour was technically correct. But this basis of representation has been true of all senators since the adoption of the Constitution. The Governor's reference to it was obviously little more than a specious attempt to excite and distort.

To the really zealous critic, mathematical deception was an art. With a bewildering display of clamorous histrionics, Francis P. Blair, Jr., tried to show how a few million freedmen would have more congressmen than twenty million whites. On another occasion he attacked the Reconstruction Acts for allegedly making "three millions of ignorant negroes . . . supreme over six million of the white race in the South." The congressmen and electoral votes controlled by the Radical-led ex-slaves are "relied upon to overcome the majority against the Radicals in the North, and enable a minority to control a majority in both sections." [29] In short, Blair contended that two minorities, when added together, would outvote two majorities. Other critics, through speeches, editorials, pamphlets, and articles hammered away at this theme so relentlessly that few dared to challenge them. [30]

The Negroes of the South, of course, "dominated" no state or national election, a fact that has been obvious to anyone who has looked beyond the façade of racist rhetoric. References, both graphic and verbal, to the legislatures of South Carolina and Louisiana have appeared with such regularity that one is left with the impression that all of the reconstructed states were so organized and that black legislators recently freed from slavery controlled them. Yet, even in the five states where Negroes had registered majorities, whites retained virtually all important positions of leadership and made almost all major decisions. Moreover, Negroes who held local or minor offices usually did so at the pleasure of a white official; while the handful who did hold important positions generally served with distinction. As a prominent southern editor admitted, "leaders of the Radical party, with professions of Negro suffrage hot in their mouths, have been sending advice to the Southern Conventions that Negroes should not run for Congress, or aspire to any conspicuous office; that they should be satisfied to fill the lowest seat in political synagogues." [31] Carpetbaggers in South Carolina, a northern traveler observed, were beginning to fear the Negro's desire for public office. As the white supremacist La Crosse *Democrat*'s "De Intelligent Woter" put it: "Dis ijee ob nigro suprimecy is gittin' intirely too much feared an' talked ob and even de Ripublicans was beginning to be scared on it, too." [32]

The critic's "balance of power" definition only made sense in a state where the parties were evenly divided and a substantial number of

Negroes could be counted on to vote together—which was nowhere. A carpetbag congressman from Mississippi complained that the southern Negroes frequently were unpredictable as a political bloc. If the racist's specious definition of majority was valid, he argued, the Negroes of New York could have decided some presidential elections.[33]

In short, there was never any danger that the southern state governments would fall under the control of the Negroes, a fact strikingly underlined by the speed with which white conservatives regained control when they took the initiative. Tennessee, restored to the Union before military reconstruction had begun, became, in October, 1869, the first former Confederate state to return to the control of the white conservatives. Whites in Virginia regained control of their state government in the same month and engineered the state's restoration to the Union in January, 1870; thus the Old Dominion never fell into official carpetbag hands. In the next seven years, the other nine states followed the same course. "Bill Arp's" caustic observation that "slavery for the white foaks and freedom for the nigger runs mity well together now-a-days," was completely groundless; and the traditional interpretation of Negro suffrage and white disfranchisement under the Reconstruction Acts equally indefensible.[34]

NOTES

1. Of the several revisionist studies, two of the best are: John Hope Franklin, *Reconstruction: After the Civil War* (Chicago, 1961); and Kenneth M. Stampp, *The Era of Reconstruction, 1865–1877* (New York, 1965). Both works, while pointing to the accomplishments and failures of these years, suggest that the South was more a victim of its own inertia than any Radical conspiracy.
2. William A. Russ, Jr., "Registration and Disfranchisement under Radical Reconstruction," *Mississippi Valley Historical Review*, XXI, 2 (September, 1934), pp. 163–180. See also, Russ, "The Negro and White Disfranchisement during Radical Reconstruction," *Journal of Negro History*, XIX, 2 (April, 1934), pp. 171–192.
3. The Ninth Census (1870) showed a fractional Negro majority in Louisiana, but an admitted undercount for both races makes a precise determination impossible.
4. United States Bureau of the Census, Department of Commerce, *Negro Population, 1790–1915* (Washington, D.C., 1918), pp. 25–27.
5. Thomas W. Hartley, *Universal Suffrage–Female Suffrage* (New York, 1867), pp. 26–28; Samuel Sullivan Cox, *Speeches of Hon. S. S. Cox, in Maine, Pennsylvania and New York, during the Campaign of 1868* (New York, 1868), p. 7.
6. Whitelaw Reid, *After the War: A Southern Tour, May 1, 1865 to May 1, 1866* (New York, 1866), p. 371; *The American Annual Cyclopedia and Register of Important Events* (84 vols., New York, 1870–1903), 1865, p. 781.
7. La Crosse *Democrat*, May 12, 1868.
8. William Archibald Dunning, *Essays on the Civil War and Reconstruction and Related Topics* (New York, 1898), pp. 189–190; Hartley, *Universal Suffrage–Female Suffrage*, p. 32.
9. New York *Herald*, November 6, 9, 1867; *Ann. Cyc.*: 1867, p. 55; 1868, p. 432.
10. Robert Selph Henry, *The Story of Reconstruction* (New York, 1938), p. 253; C. Vann Woodward, *The Strange Career of Jim Crow* (revised, New York, 1957), p. 34.
11. E. Degener, *The Minority Report in Favor of Extending the Right of Suffrage, with Certain Limitations, to All Men without Distinction of Race or Color Made*

in the Texas Reconstruction Convention (Austin, Tex., February 24, 1866). The three plans were: universal suffrage by the end of 1866; universal suffrage by the end of 1876; and universal suffrage to all "born free" by 1866. The convention refused to consider any of the plans.

12. The letter set off a storm of controversy among several Democratic editors in the North. See especially Columbus *Crisis,* November 21, December 5, 1866; New York *World,* November 19, 20, 1866.

13. Hartley, *Universal Suffrage–Female Suffrage,* p. 35; New York *World,* April 3, 20, 1867; *Ann. Cyc.,* 1865, p. 781.

14. *Ann. Cyc.,* 1867, p. 763; 1868, pp. 696, 731; 1870, p. 457. T. Harry Williams, "An Analysis of Some Reconstruction Attitudes," *Journal of Southern History,* XII, 4 (November, 1946), pp. 474, 476–479, argues that this view has been exaggerated and that the planter class, as a whole, opposed Negro suffrage under any conditions.

15. *Ann. Cyc.,* 1865, p. 694.

16. One student, Harold M. Hyman, *Era of the Oath: Northern Loyalty Tests During the Civil War and Reconstruction* (Philadelphia, 1954), has concluded that the oaths generally were ineffective, thus further deflating the argument that vast numbers of ex-Confederates were excluded from government. Moreover, it must be remembered that it was Andrew Johnson's wholesale distribution of pardons to former rebel officials that triggered a great deal of the congressional resistance.

17. New York *Weekly Day Book,* April 15, 1965; La Crosse *Democrat,* February 25, 1868; Marcus Mills Pomeroy, *Condensed History of the War, Its Causes and Results: Plain Home-Told Facts for the Young Men and Working Men of the United States* (n.p., 1868), p. 11; Chicago *Times,* July 15, 1868; Edward A. Pollard, *The Lost Cause Regained* (New York, 1868), pp. 37–39. A few alarmists even predicted the disfranchisement of northern whites. On July 23, 1868, Congressman S. S. Cox asked a Brooklyn audience: "If Congress can overturn white suffrage South, can it not establish black suffrage North, and withhold it from the whites? If the States South have not the sovereignty power in this regard, have the States North?" A few days later, editor Wilbur Storey of the Chicago *Times* named one Anthony O. Hesing as the leader of a drive, already in progress, to disfranchise Northern whites. See Cox, *Speeches of 1868,* p. 7; and Chicago *Times,* July 29, 1868.

18. Russ, *MVHR,* pp. 178–179, cites *Letter Book,* First Military District, II, pp. 261–262, for the figures on Virginia, and *Senate Executive Document,* 40 Cong., 2 Sess., No. 53, for the statistics on North Carolina, South Carolina, Georgia, and Florida. These are the standard sources and are quoted in several works: see David G. Croly, *Seymour and Blair, Their Lives and Services: with an Appendix Containing a History of Reconstruction* (New York, 1868), p. 277 of appendices; and, Edward McPherson (ed.), *The Political History of the United States of America during the Period of Reconstruction, from April 15, 1865 to July 15, 1870* (Washington, D.C., 1880), p. 374.

19. The exact figures are: South Carolina: white registrations, 46,882; Negro registrations, 80,550; white disfranchisements, 8,244; Negro disfranchisements, 625. Florida: white registrations, 11,914; Negro registrations, 16,089; white disfranchisements, 350; Negro disfranchisements, 200.

20. The exact figures are: Virginia: white registrations, 120,101; Negro registrations, 105,832; white disfranchisements, 16,343; Negro disfranchisements, none recorded. North Carolina: white registrations, 106,721; Negro registrations, 72,932; white disfranchisements, 11,688; Negro disfranchisements, 493. Georgia: white registrations, 96,333; Negro registrations, 95,168; white disfranchisements, 10,500; Negro disfranchisements, none recorded.

21. The exact figures are: Alabama: white registrations, 61,295; Negro registrations, 104,418. Arkansas: white registrations, 43,470; Negro registrations, 23,261. Louisiana: white registrations, 45,218; Negro registrations, 84,436. Mississippi: white registrations, 59,330; Negro registrations, 80,360. Texas: white registrations, 59,633; Negro registrations, 49,497.

22. For example, see: Michael Martin and Leonard Gelber (eds.), *Dictionary of American History* (Paterson, New Jersey, 1959), p. 518.

23. This latter situation was motivated largely by the fact that, under the first Reconstruction Act, it was easier to defeat a proposed Radical state constitution by registering and not voting than by not registering or by registering and voting against it. A supplementary bill quickly changed this practice.

24. Charlottesville *Chronicle*, June 18, 1867.

25. Columbus *Crisis*, April 1, 1868; Congressional *Globe*, 40 Cong., 2 Sess., January 30, 1868, pp. 849–850.

26. Marion Mills Miller (ed.), *Great Debates in American History* (14 vols., New York, 1913), VII, p. 440, quoting Congressman Andrew Jackson Rogers, Democrat of New Jersey; J. R. Hayes, *Negrophobia "On the Brain," in White Men, or an Essay upon the Origin and Progress, both Mental and Physical, of the Negro Race, and the Use to be Made of Him by Politicians in the United States* (Washington, D.C., 1869), pp. 6–7. William A. Russ, Jr., *MVHR*, pp. 178–179, agrees that there were many who, after registering, refused to vote.

27. Howard K. Beale, "On Rewriting Reconstruction History," *American Historical Review*, XLV, 4 (July, 1940), p. 814.

28. Columbus *Crisis*, October 29, 1868; Democratic Party, Indiana, *Proceedings of the Indiana Democratic State Convention, held in Indianapolis, Wednesday, January 8th, 1868* (Indianapolis, 1868), pp. 25–26; James D. McCabe, Jr., *The Life and Public Services of Horatio Seymour: Together with a Complete and Authentic Life of Francis P. Blair, Jr.* (New York, 1868), p. 222.

29. Chicago *Times*, August 8, 1868; McCabe, *Life and Public Services of Horatio Seymour*, pp. 460–461, 487–497.

30. *Ann. Cyc.*, 1868, p. 495; Columbus *Crisis*, October 23, 1867; Philadelphia *Ase:* April 2, May 17, 19, 25, June 13, 20, 1866; March 8, 1867; September 23, 1868; New York *Herald*, September 9, 1867, February 7, 1868; Detroit *Free Press*, August 11, 30, 1867; New York *World*, July 12, 1868; La Crosse *Democrat*, February 26, 1868; S. S. Cox, *Speeches of 1868*, p. 11; Horatio Seymour, *Public Record: Including Speeches, Messages, Proclamations, Official Correspondence, and Other Public Utterances of Horatio Seymour; from the Campaign of 1856 to the Present Time* (New York, 1868), p. 300; McCabe, *Life and Public Services of Horatio Seymour*, pp. 460–461.

31. Edward A. Pollard, "Universal Suffrage in a New Disguise," *The Political Pamphlet*, I, 2 (September 12, 1868), p. 40; Pollard, *Lost Cause Regained*, p. 100.

32. James S. Pike, *The Prostrate State: South Carolina Under Negro Government* (New York, 1935 [1873]), p. 45; La Crosse *Democrat*, March 24, 1868.

33. John R. Lynch, *The Facts of Reconstruction* (New York, 1914), pp. 94–99.

34. Charles Henry Smith, *Bill Arp's Peace Papers* (New York, 1873), p. 184.

8. Atrocities in the Reconstruction Period

White resistance to black American gains during Reconstruction took the form of atrocities. The true extent of atrocities against blacks during this time will probably never be known. We do know, as suggested by Carpenter's article, that the extent of this form of suppression is probably much greater than is generally claimed officially and academically. It is well known that this tactic still flourishes in black-white relations today, especially in the South. It is an instructive note to be kept in mind in the development of modern tactics to counteract racism.

JOHN CARPENTER

One of the most controversial subjects of the history of Reconstruction is that of atrocities against Negroes, carpetbaggers and scalawags. The dispute is over the degree of intensity and seriousness of the atrocities. If they were as bad as the Radical Republicans maintained in the years up to the time that the Ku Klux Klan became active in 1868,[1] then there was greater justification for the refusal to recognize the work of Reconstruction completed under the Johnson plan in the last six months of 1865, for the framing of the Fourteenth Amendment, and for the enactment of the Reconstruction Acts of 1867. For the principal reason advanced to justify these actions was the assertion, in Congress and in the North generally, that Southerners could not be trusted to deal fairly with the freedmen and Unionists and furthermore were actively engaged in a program of oppression and violence against these groups.

On the other hand, if the reports of atrocities were either largely untrue or so grossly exaggerated that they deserved to be ignored, then the Radical Republicans perpetrated a terrible fraud upon the Southern states and the best that can be said for these Radicals is that they were deceived. If the conditions in the South immediately following the war were as bad as has been alleged, it is hard to see how the Congress could have done other than it did; and the argument that Congressional interference only made matters worse is not an indictment of Congress but of the white people of the South who took part in and condoned the atrocities and

From *Journal of Negro History* (1962), Vol. 47, pp. 234–247; reprinted by permission.

outrages. But if the interference was unnecessary, if physical violence was not invoked in the South, to any excessive degree, against freedmen and loyalists then there remained to the Radicals as reason for intervention the argument that the freedman was not accorded civil and political equality, an argument which probably would not have carried enough weight in 1865 and 1866 to have justified the actions which the Congress eventually adopted.

Most accounts of Reconstruction tend to minimize the amount of atrocity and either imply or directly state that the cases were greatly exaggerated or even completely fabricated. Another device frequently used is to attribute what atrocities there were to the poor whites and state that the better element deplored this sort of thing. Throughout these accounts is the intimation that because there was exaggeration then somehow those atrocities that did occur were really not so bad after all. For example, James Ford Rhodes wrote in his *History of the United States from the Compromise of 1850,* "That affairs of the sort ["cruelties practised upon the negroes"] occurred as one of the results of the social revolution was undoubted but on the other hand exaggerated accounts of them were readily believed by those who desired to use them as an argument for a severe policy towards the South." [2] Or take what Robert S. Henry says in *The Story of Reconstruction.* "There can be no doubt," he writes, "that injustices and cruelties were practiced on the freed Negroes, as there have been in all times and all societies on the weak and defenseless. Equally without doubt, there were innumerable instances of kindly and friendly relations between the races. For political purposes, these must be ignored or minimized, which was not difficult to do; the 'atrocities' [note the quotation marks] must be multiplied and exaggerated." [3] After noting that "No atrocity story was too extraordinary to find credence," he goes on to cite examples of trumped up atrocity stories, or at least stories which he intimates are trumped up because no names were ever given by the reporting officer. [4]

One more example will perhaps be enough even though the number could be more or less indefinitely extended. The most recent history of the Freedmen's Bureau, that by George R. Bentley, contains a few passages which intimate that there was not really much to the atrocity reports. For instance, he refers to atrocity "tales." Bentley does admit, though, that "Unfortunately, there was considerable truth in the postwar reports of violence and cruelty." He attributes this to the abnormal times. But, he hastens to add, Bureau agents "were frequently prone to exaggerate the violence they encountered and to report rumors without determining their authenticity." [5] Then for the next four pages he cites examples of unfounded atrocity reports. [6] In one sentence he admits that there was "considerable truth in the . . . reports" and in four pages he shows how such reports were exaggerated!

That there was inadequate reason for interference seems, without much doubt, to be the generally accepted view. The attempted renewal of the Freedmen's Bureau in February 1866 was, it has been maintained, an unnecessary continuation of a temporary institution whose powers were too extensive and whose agents were desperately trying to hold on to their jobs by sending in imaginary or exaggerated atrocity stories.[7] The various provisions of the Fourteenth Amendment, especially the disfranchising section, were merely devices to punish the South unnecessarily.[8] The Reconstruction Acts of 1867 were largely intended to establish, through Negro voting, Republican domination of the South.

In other words, there was little valid excuse for doing all this. The motive was not anything other than desire to punish the South and to enable the Republican Party to remain indefinitely in office. Such is the argument of those who believed that Radical Reconstruction was indefensible.

What of the other side of the argument? Were the Negroes in such danger that only Federal intervention could protect them? Reports coming to the Commissioner of the Freedmen's Bureau, Major General Oliver Otis Howard, from the assistant commissioners and Bureau agents in many parts of the South seemed to indicate that this truly was the case. These reports, the testimony given to the Joint Committee on Reconstruction, and occasional accounts appearing in the Northern press (especially reports of several largescale race riots in Memphis, New Orleans and other places in the South) constituted the bulk of the evidence to support the Radical contention that the Southern state governments as established under President Johnson's plan of reconstruction could not be depended upon to give the Negro protection and fair treatment. To write these off as exaggerations and fabrications is to ignore some rather substantial evidence.

The agents and assistant commissioners of the Freedmen's Bureau submitted reports which indicated that the Negroes were frequently subjected to violent attack, including murder. Other reports simply stated that the freedmen were not receiving equal treatment. These reports, tempered it is true by others which asserted the opposite, came so incessantly and in such volume that the only way one can gain a true appreciation of their impact is by seeing them in their entirety. A fair sampling, however, can convey the impression in part.

One of the earliest complaints was that of Captain D. W. Whittle who had been on General Howard's staff during the Georgia campaign. At the time he wrote, June 8, 1865, he was on garrison duty at Union Springs, Alabama. He stated that the white people found it difficult to grasp the idea that slavery was dead. ". . . there has got to be a constant pressure brought to bear upon the former slave-holders," Whittle continued, "to make them deal fairly with the negroes. . . . they were very well as slaves, but in any other relation they hate them, and will place every possible obstacle in the way of their elevation. . . ." [9]

Howard's assistant adjutant general, Joseph S. Fullerton, on an inspection trip to South Carolina in July 1865 stated that only a few had any hope that slavery would be re-established, but he was of the opinion that "the result of the war [had] not changed the *animus* of the former slave owner." [10]

The assistant commissioner for Tennessee, Clinton B. Fisk, reported in September 1865 that while things in general were progressing favorably, there were, however, too many "who [would] not accept the conclusions of the strife. . . . There is nothing the matter down this way," Fisk said, "but *injustice to the negro*. . . . It is lamentable and astonishing with what tenacity the un-subjugated cling to the old barbarism." [11]

Davis Tillson, assistant commissioner for Georgia, and one of the more conservative men in the Bureau organization, late in November 1865 wrote to Howard urging the retention of a military force in Georgia. "If we really mean to keep sacred the solemn promises made the freed people to protect them in their rights," Tillson said, ". . . the army must not be withdrawn." [12] About three months later Tillson again wrote to Howard reporting the favorable news that plantation owners on the Sea Islands were entering into satisfactory labor arrangements with the freedmen. Yet in another part of the same letter, which was written immediately following receipt of news of President Johnson's veto of the Freedmen's Bureau bill, Tillson expressed fear lest Johnson disturb the system of Bureau courts which he [Tillson] had established. If Johnson should do this, wrote Tillson, ". . . all hope of justice to the freedpeople, for the present, will be lost. I shall decline to act in my present position when no longer able to protect the freedpeople—it would be too mortifying to be endured." [13]

In October of the same year Tillson sent to Bureau headquarters the copy of a letter he had written to the leading citizens of Henry County in Georgia. It seems that these citizens had complained to Tillson of the continued presence of troops in their county. The assistant commissioner replied that it was necessary to retain troops there because the civil authorities had done nothing to protect the Negroes, nothing to investigate crimes against Negroes or to prosecute criminals, nothing to protect the person or the office of the Bureau agent. Tillson went on to explain how ". . . on many . . . occasions the rightful authority of the Government of the United States had been insulted, defied and treated with contempt by the citizens and civil authorities of Henry County." He told them that the Bureau agent had reported to him personally, ". . . that he called upon the Sheriff of Henry County and asked him to arrest certain parties charged with committing outrages on freed people. The sheriff replied that 'it would be unpopular to punish white men for anything done

to a negro—it might be unsafe—that he was not going to obey the orders
of any damned Yankee—and that the rebellion was not over yet in Henry
County.'" It would be his duty, said Tillson, to retain troops in that county
until the conduct of the people there should convince him that the
freedmen would receive protection. "Longer to trust mere profession," he
concluded, "in the presence of facts in my possession, would be to
indulge in criminal credulity." [14]

Other assistant commissioners shared the same views. Major General
Joseph B. Kiddoo in Texas faced a most difficult problem. Distances were
great, the population much dispersed, and the number of troops small. In
August 1866 he reported an increase in the amount of violence and murder
committed against freedmen. He had become, he said, ". . . so powerless
to give proper protection, for want of troops to sustain my agents and
make arrests, that I grow *sick at heart*. . . . The only remedy I can suggest
is Army officers for Agents, and troops to sustain them. If in your judgment it is the *settled policy* of the Executive to leave the Bureau without
adequate military protection, I will desist making these official appeals,
but until I am thus informed, I must continue to plead for such force as
will make my duties here a *reality* instead of a *farce*." [15] In an earlier letter
Kiddoo had complained that he was unable to obtain justice for the
freedmen from the civil courts in criminal cases. Trial of such cases in civil
courts is, he said ". . . *worse than a farce*." [16]

The assistant commissioner for South Carolina, Robert K. Scott, reported at the end of 1866 that whenever garrisons had been removed,
crimes against the freedmen had increased. Included in his letter to
Howard was this expression of concern: ". . . even under the most favorable circumstances that can be anticipated under the present system of
laws the freed people will fail to receive from the civil authorities that
protection to which they are entitled both by right and by law, and
without which they cannot but gradually revert back to a condition differing little from their former slavery—save in name." [17]

Major General E. O. C. Ord, who held the two positions of district
commander and assistant commissioner in Arkansas, was so convinced
that the Negroes could not expect equal treatment from the whites that he
advocated physical separation of the two races. Until this could be done
(and it is doubtful whether he seriously believed his suggestion would be
implemented), he urged the retention of troops in Arkansas.[18]

The district commander and assistant commissioner for North Carolina,
Major General Nelson A. Miles, urged in December 1867 that the Bureau's
life be extended at least another year until the new state government
could have the opportunity of becoming well established. The freedmen,
he noted, were ". . . almost as much within the grasp of their former
owners as in the days of slavery." [19]

Not only the assistant commissioners but lesser officials, the agents of the Bureau, frequently reported the same general conditions. They were really in the best position to know at first hand the true conditions which prevailed in the South.

The agent at Lunenburg Court House in Virginia addressed a letter to the Bureau authorities in Richmond in April 1866 telling of an increase in outrages on Negroes. There was no assurance that the civil courts would aid in punishing the guilty parties and he concluded by saying, "Unless I have power given to give these poor people protection, self respect will compel me to resign." [20]

From Greenville Court House, South Carolina, the Bureau agent, Major A. E. Niles, told of the unfavorable conditions existing in his district. "Toward the Government," Niles wrote, "the feeling is very unfriendly, with no prospect of a change for the better. . . . Toward the Freedmen, there is much bad feeling, and but for the presence of one small garrison I can hardly see how he would manage to live. The men that understand the Freedmen to have, or that they are entitled to any more rights than a horse are exceptions to the general rule." [21]

In his regular report in June 1867, Lieutenant J. C. De Gress, Bureau agent in New Orleans, complained that civil officials were too prejudiced to grant the freedmen equal justice. ". . . whenever they can grind a poor Black man down, they do it to gain popularity, 'as it is nothing but a cursed nigger,' (using their own language)." [22]

Examples such as these could be continued indefinitely. Surely the agents on the local level were aware of a tendency on the part of white southerners to deal unjustly with the freedmen.[23]

Violence has been common to the South throughout its history.[24] Is it any wonder that violence characterized the Reconstruction years? Why should historians assume that stories of violence to Negroes were either fabricated or exaggerated when everyone knows what has been happening to Negroes in the South ever since Negroes first were there? [25] It would have been singularly amazing had there not been an excessive amount of murders (the word lynching seems to belong to a later period) and other atrocities committed against Negroes in the South during the first years after liberation. And what is the evidence? The evidence is that murder and atrocity were as common as one would expect them to be.

In the atmosphere of hostility towards freedmen reported by the assistant commissioners and other agents of the Freedmen's Bureau and described above, specific acts of violence occurred far more frequently than has been generally conceded by the historians of this period. And the extent of this violence made interference by the national government excusable if not justified; in fact interference became obligatory in the light of the responsibility of the national authority toward those whom it had so recently liberated.

In response to an order from Commissioner Howard the various assistant commissioners reported the instances of outrages and murders committed against Negroes in the various Southern states.[26] From these reports which came in during October and November 1866 it is possible to gain some idea of the extent of the problem.

Most of these reports were specific rather than general, naming names, time and place. In some instances the reports did make general charges without details and it is possible that some were fabrications, as is so frequently charged. Yet even these reports came from responsible army officers of high rank and ought not to be airily dismissed. An example of this type of report would be that of Brigadier General John R. Lewis, assistant commissioner for Tennessee, who in October 1866 reported the murder of thirty-three freedmen by white persons since April 1865. It was Lewis' belief that many more unreported murders had occurred.[27]

The assistant commissioners for Arkansas and South Carolina sent in lists of twenty-nine and twenty-four murders respectively.[28] Here in most instances are names, dates and places.[29]

General Joseph B. Kiddoo in Texas not only made an overall report but he also enclosed excerpts from the reports of his subordinates in the various parts of the state who had firsthand acquaintance with the individual murders. There is a genuine frankness about these that makes it highly unlikely that these outrages were dreamed up for any ulterior purpose. One extract is from a letter written by the Bureau agent in Victoria, Victoria County on May 30, 1866. "Again it is my painful duty," wrote the agent, "to report the wilful murder of a freedman, Martin Cromwell, formerly a slave of Mr. Alex. Cromwell, and a man over 50 years of age, was wantonly shot, and killed by Alex. Cromwell Jr. a young man of about 21 years on Sunday evening the 27th inst. on the plantation of his father." In the list of some seventy other cases are with few exceptions the name of the murdered person, the name of the murderer (though some have simply "unknown" in this column), the date, and remarks. Some of the remarks are enlightening as, for example, "Killed because he did not take off his hat to Murphy," or "shot him as he was passing in the street to 'see him kick' as Bullock remarked." [30]

One of the most conservative assistant commissioners was General Jefferson C. Davis whose views frequently were at variance with those of the Bureau. Davis' list of murders should be viewed by the skeptical, then, as being somewhat more authentic than those of some of the other, more radical, assistant commissioners. Davis' territory was Kentucky, a particularly troublesome state. He named nineteen freedmen who had been killed, giving exact dates and the names of the counties where the crimes had been committed. In addition, he said that 233 freedmen had been badly maltreated and in none of these cases of outrage had any action toward punishing the offenders been reported by the state civil authorities.[31]

Major General Joseph A. Mower, Sheridan's successor in Louisiana, in March 1867 sent in a very complete report on outrages in that state from the beginning of the Bureau until February 20, 1867. He gave a detailed account of seventy murders of freedmen by whites and stated that the number might have been twice that. He also told of 210 cases of whipping, beating and stabbing and noted that in almost every instance the persons guilty of these offenses had not been apprehended. Mower's report is thirty pages long and much of it is detailed information concerning the individual murders. One, for instance, tells of the murder of Abraham Allen by Jules Guidry, constable of Donaldsonville, Louisiana. The grand jury several months later failed to find a true bill against Guidry. Another case was that of Martin Day at Lake Providence on May 27, 1866. Day, it seems, answered a white boy "quickly," and was knocked down by a white man by the name of Kingsley. The Bureau agent told how the freedman was "taken thro' the town and across the Levee, and there stripped and terribly beaten, with raw-hides by Kingsley, and some 6 or 8 other men, who put a rope around his neck, nearly choked him, jumped upon him etc." The civil authorities, according to the agent, "took no notice of the affair." [32]

The Bureau agent in Atlanta, Georgia, reported to his immediate superior, Brigadier General Davis Tillson, the murder of a colored soldier on the very day it occurred. He named the murderer, P. Perry, who escaped. "Citizens with whom I have talked," wrote the agent, "seem to justify Berry [sic] in his cowardly act, and with but little reason, other than the soldier was a 'd——d nigger.' " [33]

These examples are only a small fraction of the total to be found in the records of the Freedmen's Bureau. They extend over a considerable span of years and seem to demonstrate beyond a reasonable doubt a high degree of lawlessness in almost all sections of the South. That some of the reports were exaggerated or fabricated does not alter the basic fact: that the freedmen were grossly mistreated by Southern whites during the Reconstruction era. The record of lynchings and other forms of brutality toward the Negro which has disgraced the South in the years since Reconstruction rather puts the burden of proof upon those who question the authenticity of the reports of outrages.

Now it would be quite inaccurate to convey the idea of total lawlessness in the South during the Reconstruction. There is abundant evidence that in some places at some times the treatment of freedmen was at least non-violent. Colonel T. W. Osborn, assistant commissioner for Florida, stated in November 1865 that cases of violence toward freedmen were of "rare occurrence." [34] The assistant commissioner in Mississippi, Colonel Samuel Thomas, admitted that without the Bureau there would be no hesitancy on the part of the white people to oppress and defraud the freedmen but that the "foolish stories of terrible outrages [that] find their way to the press of the North . . . are nearly always greatly exaggerated or entirely without foundation." [35]

That same month General Ord in Arkansas reported "a better feeling prevailing in all the richest cotton counties, to satisfy and protect freedmen. . . ." [36] and soon after General Lewis remarked that there was a general disposition to do what was just by the freedmen in his state of Tennessee.[37]

Obviously the treatment of freedmen varied considerably as is borne out by an inspection report of General Eliphalet Whittlesey, one time assistant commissioner and, at the time of the report, assistant adjutant general of the Bureau. Whittlesey toured Louisiana and Arkansas early in 1867 and observed that treatment of freedmen was spotty. This would, he said, account for the conflicting stories appearing in the Northern press. Yet he passed along to General Howard reports of numerous outrages against freedmen, their inability to gain justice, their being cheated of wages, and the breaking up of Negro schools. Many agents told Whittlesey that they could not carry out their duties without troops.[38]

Over two years later, Howard, in his annual report to the Secretary of War, admitted that atrocity reports seemed to convey the impression that every white person in the South was engaged in a deliberate policy of extermination of the freedmen. But, he went on to say, "careful investigation has proved that the worst outrages were generally committed by small bands of lawless men, organized under various names, whose principal objects were robbery and plunder. There was no civil government with strength enough to arrest them, and they overawed and held in terror the more quiet citizens who were disposed to treat the freedmen with fairness and humanity." It was the Bureau, according to Howard, together with the Federal troops in the South which gave the freedmen, "these victims of cruelty and wrong," some means of protection. "And the evils remedied have probably been far less than the evils prevented. No one can tell what scenes of violence and strife and insurrection the whole South might have presented without the presence of this agency of the government to preserve order and to enforce justice." [39]

Whittlesey's and Howard's admissions serve to correct the false impression which might be conveyed by a simple catalogue of atrocity reports turned in by the Bureau assistant commissioners and agents, and of accounts of race riots in Memphis and other Southern towns reported in the Northern press; they do not, on the other hand, wipe out the record of those reports. The years of Reconstruction in the South were filled with an unusual amount of atrocities, deprivations of rights, and other forms of illegal treatment of Negroes so much so that the Federal Government which had assumed a moral responsibility in its emancipation measures to do more than merely liberate the slaves, had little choice but to intervene. This it did do in successive acts creating and then continuing the Freedmen's Bureau, in the Civil Rights Act, the Fourteenth and Fifteenth Amendments, the Reconstruction Acts, and finally, the Ku Klux Klan Acts of 1870 and 1871. The fate of the freedmen was a decisive factor in the adoption of all this legislation and of the two amendments.[40] The contention of President Johnson and of the Southern whites that the Negro did not need any assistance from the Federal Government flew in the face of the obvious fact that he was receiving anything but equal, fair, and humane treatment. The policy of intervention, unfortunately, led up a blind alley; there was no way out except to abandon the policy, for it could not be continued indefinitely. Instead of the situation which the policy was supposed to produce—a tranquility and a harmonious relationship between the races—there resulted an even greater determination on the part of the Southern whites to end all semblance of Federal control, all vestiges of Carpetbag rule, and any attempt to allow the Negro civil and political equality. That this would be the result might have been anticipated before any intervention began but even if it had been, the obligation to intervene would still have been there.

The failure of intervention meant abandonment of the policy by the Grant administration, and this in turn meant abandonment of the Negro. In the last years of the nineteenth century the growing number of lynchings proved what a hostile white population could do to the Negro when left alone to deal with him as it pleased.[41] In the light of these events and those which have continued to take place in ensuing years, is it being credulous to believe the reports of the assistant commissioners and agents of the Freedmen's Bureau in the first years of transition from slavery to freedom that an unreasonable hostility existed in the South toward the freedmen which made necessary a policy of intervention and control? The solid evidence of these reports seems to lead to but one answer.

NOTES

1. There appears to be little doubt about the fact that the Klan was responsible for numerous outrages against Negroes, carpetbaggers, and scalawags in the Reconstruction period. See e.g. Stanley F. Horn, *Invisible Empire: The Story of the Ku Klux Klan 1866–1871* (Boston, 1939), pp. 361–62.
2. N.Y., 1904, V, 563.
3. N.Y., 1938, pp. 84–85.
4. *Ibid.*, p. 85.
5. George R. Bentley, *A History of the Freedmen's Bureau* (Philadelphia, 1955), p. 110.
6. *Ibid.*, pp. 111–14.
7. E.g., *ibid.*, pp. 110–11.
8. Henry, *Story of Reconstruction*, pp. 167–68.
9. D. W. Whittle to Howard, June 8, 1865, National Archives, hereafter referred to as NA.
10. J. S. Fullerton to Howard, July 28, 1865, NA.
11. C. B. Fisk to Howard, Sept. 2, 1865, NA.
12. D. Tillson to Howard, Nov. 28, 1865, NA.
13. D. Tillson to Howard, Feb. 24, 1866, Howard Papers, Bowdoin College.
14. D. Tillson to Elijah Foster and A. M. Campbell, Oct. 16, 1866, NA.

15. J. B. Kiddoo to Howard, Aug. 8, 1866, NA.
16. J. B. Kiddoo to Howard, June 26, 1866, NA.
17. R. K. Scott to Howard, Dec. 18, 1866, NA.
18. E. O. C. Ord to Howard, Feb. 19, 1867, NA.
19. N. A. Miles to Howard, Dec. 4, 1867, NA.
20. Lt. J. Arnold Yeckley to Capt. James A. Bates, April 19, 1866, NA.
21. A. E. Niles to Major H. W. Smith, May 2, 1866, NA.
22. Report of Lt. J. C. De Gress, June 24, 1867, NA.
23. Not just officials of the Freedmen's Bureau but civilians from the North also reported on the unhappy lot of the Negro in the South. One of these, owner of a plantation near Augusta, Georgia wrote to Secretary of War E. M. Stanton, "The white people about here openly declare that when the Bureau is removed, they will show the Yankees how the Negro should be treated. . . . If the Bureau continues to protect them all will be well, but if it is removed, I tremble for the consequences." C. Stearns to Stanton, Aug. 30, 1866, NA.
24. See e.g. John H. Franklin, *The Militant South* (Cambridge, Mass., 1956); C. Vann Woodward, *Origins of the New South* (Baton Rouge, 1951), pp. 158–60.
25. See e.g. Otis A. Singletary, *Negro Militia and Reconstruction* (Austin, Texas, 1957), pp. 3–6.
26. A. P. Ketchum to Assistant Commissioners, Sept. 24, 1866, NA.
27. J. R. Lewis to Howard, Oct. 3, 1866, NA.
28. R. K. Scott's list from South Carolina covered only the period since he took office, i.e., from January 1866.
29. J. W. Sprague to Howard, Oct. 1, 1866, NA; R. K. Scott to Howard, Oct. 5, 1866, NA.
30. J. B. Kiddoo to Howard, Oct. 25, 1866, NA.
31. J. C. Davis to Howard, Nov. 27, 1866, NA.
32. Joseph A. Mower to Brig. Gen. Samuel Thomas, March 9, 1867, NA.
33. Lt. Col. George Curkendall to Davis Tillson, Dec. 26, 1865, NA.
34. Col. Thomas W. Osborn to Howard, Nov. 1, 1865, NA.
35. Col. Samuel Thomas to Howard, April 12, 1866, NA.
36. E. O. C. Ord to Howard, Nov. 7, 1866, NA.
37. J. R. Lewis to Howard, Dec. 17, 1866, NA.
38. Bvt. Brig. Gen. E. Whittlesey to Howard, Feb. 25, 1867, NA.
39. Report of Gen. O. O. Howard, Oct. 20, 1869, NA.
40. See e.g. Eric L. McKitrick, *Andrew Johnson and Reconstruction* (Chicago, 1960), p. 478.
41. More than 2,500 lynchings occurred in the last sixteen years of the nineteenth century, mostly of Negroes, and mostly in the South. John H. Franklin, *From Slavery to Freedom* (N.Y., 1947), p. 431.

9. The Ku Klux Klan During Reconstruction: The South Carolina Episode

Atrocities against black Americans, during Reconstruction as well as today, were not random acts by individual white racists. Rather they were forms of organized violence with social and political intimidation as primary objectives. The historical operations of a prominent American terrorist organization in South Carolina clearly suggests this. The Ku Klux Klan remains a viable antiblack organization in the American South today, in spite of recent federal inquiry into its activities.

HERBERT SHAPIRO

A focal point of historical controversy about Reconstruction has been the role of the Ku Klux Klan. Racists have pointed to the Klan as an example of the courage with which white Southerners resisted the supposed horrors of Reconstruction while those who resist the racist position, despite differences in their appraisals of Reconstruction, have joined in condemning the Klan for its violence and disregard of lawful government. For both the racist and the supporter of civil rights the Ku Klux Klan stands as a symbol, "either a glamorous or sinister symbol" as Francis Simkins wrote, "for the arousal of issues of race, religion and patriotism in which all Americans . . . are vitally and perennially concerned." [1]

This paper attempts to advance the work of separating the actuality of the Ku Klux Klan from the aura of myth that has surrounded it. Attention is focused on the Klan in South Carolina, a major center of Klan activity and the scene of the Federal Government's most serious effort to curb the organization.

The most thorough study of the Ku Klux Klan in South Carolina has been made by Francis B. Simkins. Simkins sought to dispel some of the romanticism that has enveloped the organization. He wrote that study proved the Klan "was hardly so important, or so definite, or so attractive an organization as popular tradition would have us believe." He set out to "prove how truly indefinite and undramatic, and even unimportant the South Carolina Klan was." He asserted that the Klan was political in

From *Journal of Negro History* (1964), Vol. 49, pp. 34–55; reprinted by permission.

purpose, that the Klan's activities were aimed "against the Negro as a citizen—one attempting to be a voter and at times, the social equal of other men—rather than against the Negro as a violator of law or the infringer upon the rights of other men." Simkins dealt extensively with the violence that was engaged in by the Klan. He believed that on the whole the Klan was a movement of the poorer classes, that although some respectable South Carolinians belonged, the organization was a result of the urge of poor whites to eliminate economic competition. Simkins declared that "one must lose complete faith in Southern chivalry to believe that South Carolinians of standing could have committed the horrible crimes of which the Klan was actually guilty." [2]

How valid are the conclusions reached by Simkins in his study of the South Carolina Klan? What does a re-examination of the evidence with regard to South Carolina indicate about the Klan's general significance? In the present writer's judgment serious modification of some of the conclusions reached in previous studies is called for.

The Klan took its first step toward organization in South Carolina during 1868 when General George Gordon, Grand Dragon of the Tennessee Klan, sent an emissary, R. J. Brunson, to Rock Hill, South Carolina to form an organization in that area. The Klan appeared in the midst of the Grant-Seymour Presidential election campaign, in which control of the national administration, as well as local offices, was at stake. The Klan attempted to create an atmosphere of terror in which Negro voters would be eliminated and victory in a crucial contest thereby assured for the Democrats. The Klan resorted to murder. At least eight Negroes were killed in incidents ranging across three counties. Of particular importance were the slayings by the Klan of James Martin and B. F. Randolph. Martin, who had been a school teacher, was a member of the State House of Representatives from Abbeville County. Randolph, a Presbyterian minister who had previously served as an assistant superintendent of education under the Freedman's Bureau, was a member of the State Senate from Orangeburg County. According to witnesses, Randolph's assassination had been called for by D. Wyatt Aiken, Democratic leader in Abbeville County. Testimony was given that Aiken urged the Democrats of Anderson County "never to suffer this man Randolph to come in your midst; if he does, give him four feet by six." [3] One of Randolph's assassins, William K. Tolbert, later confessed and told of the formation in Abbeville County of a secret committee of the Democratic Party that set out to terrorize Negroes. Tolbert testified that "nearly all Democrats in Abbeville were Klan members." He identified himself and several others of the group that shot Randolph as Klan members.

Activity by the Klan in 1868 was closely associated with the Democratic Party. It is impossible in many places to separate the violence engaged in by groups of Democrats from that of organized Klans. In 1868 the Klan was a new organization in South Carolina. Many raiders engaged in typical Klan activities yet did not use the disguise or other Klan paraphernalia. A representative situation was that of Abbeville County where for any practical purpose there was no distinction between the Klan and the secret committee of the Democratic Party.[4]

The political murders were part of an extensive campaign of intimidation. According to the testimony of John B. Hubbard, chief constable of South Carolina under the Radical government, the Klan by 1868 had achieved a considerable degree of organization in at least ten up-country counties.[5] The objectives of the Klan were clearly political. Confessed members avowed that the Klan aimed at the prevention of Negro voting and the disruption of the Union Leagues.[6] The Klan used various techniques in pursuit of its objectives. In Laurens County, according to one election manager, bands of the Klan rode through the countryside threatening Negroes and firing guns.[7] In other counties as well, similar forays were frequent. In Abbeville, Union, Anderson and Edgefield the Klan rode through the plantations urging Negroes not to vote. One of these disguised bands in Abbeville was estimated to have fifty members. In Abbeville, on the night before the election, the Klan sought to make certain Negroes would not vote by raiding those in possession of Republican election tickets. Several Abbeville Negroes testified that they had been beaten by disguised raiders shortly before Election Day.[8]

Strong economic pressure was another tactic used throughout this election campaign. Several Democratic clubs passed resolutions promising to hire or rent only to Democrats. In Newberry County the Frog Level Democratic Club passed a resolution not to rent land to Radicals. In Abbeville at least two Democratic clubs, those at Donalsville and Calhoun's Mill, resolved on a similar course. A former Democrat testified that the Democrats of Pickens County had voted a resolution threatening with eviction those who would vote Republican. These resolutions were accompanied by numerous threats to Negroes of eviction or dismissal. In Oconee County, according to one Negro witness, it was commonly believed that Negroes would be turned off the land if they voted Republican. One landowner in Oconee tore up the Republican ticket of one of his tenants. In Laurens County, even before the election, a number of Negro laborers were evicted. This tactic of bringing economic pressure to bear upon Negroes was also used extensively in Newberry, Union and York counties.[9]

The violence of the 1868 campaign reached a peak on Election Day. Extensive use was made of force to keep Negroes away from the polls. At White Hall and Greenwood, in Abbeville County, groups of armed whites drove Negroes away from the polls. Two Negroes were killed at White Hall. Testimony was offered that at Santuck in Union County a mob permitted only those with Democratic tickets to vote. In Laurens County

Democrats lined up before the Court House poll and excluded Republican voters. At Rock Hill in York County some fifty Republican voters were forced from the poll. At some places economic pressure, either along with or instead of force, was used. Typical was the poll in Anderson County where the president of the local Democratic club took down the names of Republican voters for the purpose of giving preference in the renting of land to Negro Democrats.[10]

Despite Republican outcries, the intimidation and violence of the 1868 campaign were not without political effect. The number of Negro voters dropped considerably. At White Hall precinct in Abbeville, according to Democratic and Republican witnesses, of 156 votes cast, four were by Negroes.[11] At Due West precinct in the same county, of more than ninety voters, four again were Negroes.[12] In the county as a whole, out of 4200 enrolled Negro voters, only 800 were able to cast their ballots.[13] In Laurens County 1174 Negroes voted although 2500 were registered.[14] In Anderson between seven and eight hundred out of 1400 voted.[15]

The low percentage of Negroes who voted in the fall election helped to produce some sharp changes in the returns. At Rock Hill, York County a majority of 225 had been recorded for the Republicans in the previous April election while in November the Republican majority was reduced to ten or twelve.[16] If the Republican majority was reduced in this locality, in the up-country as a whole it was converted into a Democratic majority. In the April election the Republicans had won all four of South Carolina's Congressional seats. In November the Democrats carried the two up-country Congressional Districts. In the Third District the Democrat Reed defeated the Republican Hoge by 11,774 to 8,776 while in the Fourth District Democrat Simpson received 14,098 votes to 9,807 for Republican Wallace.[17] In what later were called the "KKK counties" Seymour led Grant by 14,186 to 10,379 votes although total South Carolina returns gave Grant 62,916 votes to 45,237 for Seymour.[18] Democratic solicitors were elected in Newberry, Abbeville and Anderson counties.

The 1870 election was the prelude to the major outbreak of terror in South Carolina. In this election Republican Robert K. Scott ran for re-election as Governor against the Union Reform candidate, R. B. Carpenter. The Union Reform Party was formed in 1870 upon the initiative of several Democratic newspapers. By discarding the Democratic label South Carolina's conservatives hoped to attract the additional support needed to defeat the Radicals. As the campaign got underway the conservatives were hopeful that Scott would be defeated. A serious setback, however, was given the hopes of the Carpenter forces by the organization of the Negro militia. During the 1868 campaign Governor Scott had threatened to furnish the Negroes with arms. In 1870 the threat became reality. The Democrats could no longer depend upon intimidation to give them a majority in the up-country. The organization of the militia was carried out under a law passed in 1868 that gave the Governor the power to suspend the writ of habeas corpus and authorized him to call out the militia to deal with "unlawful obstructions, combinations or assemblages of persons, or rebellion against the authority of the government of the state." [19] One historian has stated that it was this organization of the militia that provoked the Klan in 1870. [20] Yet, as stated by Simkins, during the entire turbulent period before and particularly after the October election, virtually nothing in the way of acts of violence could be attributed to the militia.

The results of the election did not come as a complete surprise to political observers. Late in August the *New York Times* gave Carpenter a chance to win only in the Third and Fourth Congressional Districts. [21] Yet the Democrats were embittered by the result. Receiving 85,071 votes to Carpenter's 51,537, Scott was re-elected. [22] *The Charleston Daily News* studied the returns and concluded: "The ingeniously contrived frauds of the Radical Party which have defeated the Reform Candidates in counties where a fair election would have told a different tale, do not, it must be confessed, account satisfactorily for the election of Governor Scott by a majority of thirty or thirty-five thousand votes." In another editorial the *News* analyzed what it thought did account for Scott's election: ". . . the Reform Party was beaten, on the State ticket, by a nearly solid Negro vote, and not by fraud and intimidation . . . we should make no further attempt to pander to the negroes, and should organize thoroughly and systematically, so that we may be prepared for the next political contest." [23]

As the tactic of "conciliation" proved a failure, it became the turn of the Ku Klux Klan to attempt its method of dealing with Radicalism. The disturbances that erupted in the Fall of 1870 were centered in the up-country. The Democrats had carried the up-country in 1868 and were expected to do so again in 1870. The Democrats, however, in twelve up-country counties received only 43% of the votes. In this area Scott was credited with 28,394 votes to 21,365 for Carpenter. Negro militia had become a new factor that interfered with the production of an up-country Democratic majority. The racists set out to put an end to a situation that threatened to leave no part of South Carolina secure for white supremacy.

The first large scale incident took place in Laurens County on the day following the election. Scott had carried Laurens by a vote of 3,022 to 1,967 for Carpenter. [24] The response of the Democrats was forcibly to disarm the Negro militia. Within a few hours of the clash an estimated 2,500 armed whites were assembled in Laurens. As a result of this incident several Republicans were killed, among them Volney Powell, candidate for probate, Bill Riley, custodian of the militia's armory and Wade Perrin, candidate for the Legislature.

The events at Laurens touched off a wave of violence that spread through most of the up-country counties. The Klan was particularly active in three counties, Spartanburg, Union and York. In Spartanburg County the Reverend A. W. Cummings, a Republican, listed 227 residents of the county as beaten or shot. C. L. Casey, deputy U.S. Marshal, estimated that approximately 500 outrages were committed in Spartanburg.[25] Among the crimes committed were the murders of Anthony Johnson, the only Negro magistrate appointed in Spartanburg, and Wallace Fowler, a farmer. Supporters of the Radicals were attacked for a variety of reasons. James Henley was beaten, although he supported Carpenter in the 1870 election, because he accepted a Republican appointment as assessor. Daniel Lipscomb was beaten because it was known he intended to vote Republican and Willis Butler was attacked, although he did not vote, because he was understood to favor the Radical ticket. A white judge, William Champion, was raided because he was supposed to have advocated social equality between the races. Doctor John Winsmith, of a well-established family, was attacked because he was said to be in possession of state militia arms. A Negro farmer, William Moss, was whipped due to the dispossessing of several white farmers from the same plantation on which Moss was a tenant while another Negro farmer was visited because he had accepted employment on a nearby railroad. A white iron foundry owner testified that one of his Negro workers was whipped by the Klan because the Negro had been a replacement for a white worker dismissed for demanding a wage increase.

A similar pattern of activities was unfolded by the Klan in Union County. The Klan in Union, however, did make one addition to the tactics it followed elsewhere. This was the mass lynching carried out by the Klan in two raids, the first on January 4th, and the second on February 12th, allegedly in reprisal for the killing by the Union militia of a whiskey peddler named Stevens. Nothing had been done in Union to punish those who murdered or whipped Republicans. The response to the Stevens killing, in contrast, was swift. Within a day the militia men were disarmed and confined in the Union jail. On January 4, 1871, several of the prisoners were taken from the jail by the Klan and two were killed. Those who managed to escape from the Klan were returned to jail. Testimony was given that three of the Negroes now remaining in jail said that if they were taken away from Union they could identify several of the lynchers. On February 10th a court order arrived in Unionville with instructions that the prisoners be transferred to Columbia, the state capital. The Klan acted to prevent the execution of this order. On February 12th the Klan removed eight Negroes from the jail and murdered them.[26]

This lynching was followed by other Klan activity in Union County. According to a Democratic witness, three Radicals were murdered and several whipped by the Klan at intervals following the February 12th raid. Particularly brutal was the murder of a Negro, Tilman Ward, who was killed because he would not leave the area after his stepdaughter gave birth to a child fathered by a white farmer.[27] In March the Klan posted a notice demanding the resignation of the Legislature members from Union, the school and county commissioners and the school clerk.

In York County, too, lawlessness was widespread. The Army commander stationed in York to investigate the Klan, Colonel Merrill, estimated that in the period from November to July there occurred between three and four hundred incidents of violence in that county. Sixty-eight of these incidents were listed by Merrill, in a partial tally, as whippings.[28] Another estimate came from a Democratic attorney who reported from forty to fifty whippings as occurring in York between October 1870 and July 1871.

As in Spartanburg and Union, a number of murders were committed in York. Merrill listed six, those of Tom Roundtree, Anderson Brown, James Williams, Alexander Leech, Matthew Boyce and Lot Campbell. In York as elsewhere, whippings occurred for a number of reasons. One Negro, Presley Thompson, stated he was beaten because he had said he would be buried in a white cemetery. A Negro preacher, Isaac the Apostle, and his pregnant wife were beaten after being asked by the Klan: "Didn't you say that you would raise your children as good and as nice as anybody's children?" Another Negro was whipped in an effort to compel him to leave the plantation where he was employed.[29] The Klan in York gave particular attention to the schools. A member of the Legislature from York testified that many of the schools in the county were burned by the Klan. According to this witness, one school, that at Green Pond, was burned three times. A white school teacher, Bill Wilson, was beaten for teaching at a Negro school.[30] The Klan also demonstrated its contempt for the Republican government by a raid on February 26, 1871 that succeeded in driving the Republican treasurer of York from the county.[31]

Out of the many incidents of violence a clear pattern of the Klan's major objectives emerges. Perhaps the clearest contemporary summary of the Klan's objectives was provided by President Grant. Grant wrote that the Klan aimed "by force and terror to prevent all political action not in accord with the view of the members; to deprive colored citizens of the right to bear arms and of the right to a free ballot; to suppress schools in which colored children were taught and to reduce the colored people to a condition closely akin to that of slavery." [32] There is little question that Grant was correct in ascribing political objectives to the Klan. The Klan itself avowed its political partisanship. The members of the Klan were informed by the constitution of the secret order that their duty was to "oppose and reject the principles of the radical party." The Klan avowed its respect for the United States Constitution, but only for that version in effect before 1865. The Klan sought to nullify any concept of constitutional liberty that included the extension to Negroes of the right to vote and hold elective office. One former member testified that the order aimed at "putting down radical rule and negro sufferage." [33] According to another ex-member, the order centered its activities on gaining control of the outcome of elections.[34] Suppression of Negro suffrage was essential for this purpose and the spirit with which the Klan entered politics can be read in the statement of a Klan member that the organization intended to "kill all these damned niggers that vote the radical ticket." [35]

The Klan was also, as Grant stated, particularly concerned with disarming the Negroes. "For the past month or two, and since the outrages in Union County began," reported the *New York Herald* from South Carolina during March, 1871, "it seems to have been a determined object on the part of the Ku Klux to wage war on the militia and to destroy their arms whenever and wherever found. Every place where arms of the State were known to have been stored has been visited by this band of midnight marauders . . . and the arms either carried off or destroyed." The Klan sought to make certain that it would be the only armed organization in the up-country.

The response of the state government to the resurgence of the Klan in 1870–71 was largely one of inaction and vacillation. Instead of acting resolutely against the Klan, Scott moved to appease the racists. In February, 1871 Scott's military aide, General Anderson, was sent to York County to disarm the militia. It was after Anderson had collected the arms, testified one Democratic witness, that most of the violence in York occurred.[36] Scott's first reaction to the murders at Chester, according to the correspondent of the *New York Herald,* was to order the disarming of the Chester militia.[37] At a conference with seventeen Democratic leaders, held on March 13, Scott compromised further with the Klan and coupled agreement to disarm the militia with a promise to appoint judges who would be satisfactory to the Democrats. While pursuing his approach of compromise, Scott continued to minimize the seriousness of the situation. On May 26 Scott assured President Grant there was no need to declare martial law in South Carolina.

The weakness of the South Carolina Republican government made it necessary for the Federal Government to act if Klan violence was to be countered. After some delay the Federal Government moved to suppress the Ku Klux Klan. Congress had acted several times to provide Grant with the powers needed to cope with the secret order. In the Enforcement Act of May 31, 1870, Congress made interference with the exercise of the right to vote a criminal offense. In a supplementary act of February 28, 1871, Congress strengthened the Enforcement Act by placing elections for members of Congress under Federal control. United States marshals were empowered to appoint large numbers of deputies to prevent any interference with voting rights. The third and most important piece of legislation was the Ku Klux Klan Act, passed on April 20, 1871. Under this act the

President was given the power to declare any unlawful combination that menaced the public safety of a state to be a rebellion against the United States. To meet such a rebellion the President was empowered to suspend the writ of habeas corpus. On the same day as the Ku Klux Klan Act was passed, a Joint Committee of Congress began an extensive investigation of the organization.[38]

President Grant's first direct action in the South Carolina situation was a proclamation on March 24, 1871 that called on the Klan to disperse within twenty days. On May 3rd Grant urged the state and community governments of the South to enforce the laws. Finally, in the absence of local action to punish those responsible for crimes committed by the Klan, Grant resorted to the full powers of the Ku Klux Klan Act. On October 12, 1871 Grant declared a rebellion against the United States to exist in nine South Carolina counties—Spartanburg, York, Marion, Chester, Laurens, Newberry, Fairfield, Lancaster and Chesterfield. Later, Union County was added to the list and Marion dropped. The suspension of the writ of habeas corpus was ordered by Grant. Federal action struck a staggering blow at the South Carolina Ku Klux Klan. The army investigator, Colonel Merrill, told of hundreds of Klan members and leaders coming in to surrender to Federal officers. Merrill reported that approximately 800 men either fled the state, were taken into custody and paroled, or were jailed. Merrill's aide, Louis F. Post, later wrote that "confessions became quite the fashion as arrests multiplied." [39] The smashing of the Klan organization was followed by attempts to obtain court convictions of those guilty of crime. On November 28, 1871, a series of trials of accused Klan members began in Columbia. The indictments stressed the charge of conspiracy to prevent Negroes from voting for Republican Congressional candidates.

The enthusiasm of the Federal Government for court prosecutions, however, soon waned. After Grant's re-election in 1872 the Federal Government no longer found the imprisonment of Klan members politically useful. Early in 1873 United States Attorney General Williams summed up the results of the South Carolina trials: 831 persons were indicted of whom twenty-seven were convicted, five acquitted; seventy-one pled guilty, three were granted mistrials and fifty-four had their cases discontinued. Charges against the remainder of the 831 were dropped.[40] By the summer of 1873 pardons by President Grant released from prison the last of those sentenced for Klan activities. The released prisoners, however, had no opportunity to rejoin the Klan. The Ku Klux Klan of South Carolina was defunct. The limited steps taken by the Federal Government were adequate to destroy the organization.

Several questions raised by an examination of the Klan in South Carolina should be considered. First of all, what was the extent of Klan activities?

The extent of the Ku Klux Klan's activities in South Carolina can readily be gauged by their impact on the community. Simkins, attempting to minimize the Klan's impact, considered the organization to have been "unimportant" in South Carolina, yet himself provided a good deal of material that refuted his own conclusion. He wrote that the Klan could not be contained by ordinary legal methods, that "the constabulary was forced to flee from the Ku Klux areas; and persons were afraid to make affidavits necessary to bring about convictions in the courts." The Klan, according to Simkins, succeeded in destroying the Negro militia in the up-country. Simkins wrote that the Klan was responsible for the removal of magistrates in the up-country who were unacceptable to the Democrats. He concluded that the activities of the Klan produced a situation where the Radical government in South Carolina was in danger of destruction.[41]

It is clear that the activities of the Klan caused immense suffering to the Negroes in the affected areas. "No one can imagine the sufferings these poor creatures have endured . . ." wrote the *New York Tribune,* "the terrible anxiety, the constant fear of scourging and murder, the sleeping in the woods during the cold winter nights and in the rains of spring, and the actual torture that hundreds endured whose flesh was so horribly mangled by the blows of their brutal assailants that they will never fully recover." The *Tribune* quoted a soldier stationed in Spartanburg as stating of the situation in that county: "It's impossible for me to explain the situation of this county. The KKK's, as they style themselves, have scared the people out of their wits. They are afraid to speak above a whisper." [42]

In addition to statements by Republicans, evidence exists from Democratic sources as to the extent of Klan activity. Democratic Legislature member Robert Smith stated that "there are organizations in this state of considerable extent." Richard B. Carpenter, Union Reform candidate for Governor in 1870, testified that he had "no doubt of the existence in eight or ten counties of some secret organization." Carpenter stated that "there have unquestionably been many cases of violence." The *Nation* reported that Reverdy Johnson and Harry Stanberry, who served as defense counsel for Klan members in the Federal trials, were strongly impressed by the evidence presented. According to the *Nation* Johnson and Stanberry were "quite staggered by the weight of testimony establishing the existence of the Ku Klux order and its political purpose." [43]

Johnson and Stanberry were justified in their reaction. The Klan had, indeed, created a virtual reign of terror in the up-country of South Carolina. Murder was resorted to freely, whippings were numerous and intimidation replaced normal political controversy. The enforcement of the laws in the up-country by the normal machinery of state government was made impossible. Almost every page of the report of the Joint Select Committee is filled with accounts of intimidation, of voters threatened and killed, or of active Republicans forced to sleep in the woods, or of women beaten and raped. If only for the havoc and misery it wrought, the Klan deserves an important place in the history of South Carolina Reconstruction. Any objective appraisal of Reconstruction cannot exclude from consideration the extent of the violence with which, almost from its inception, the Radical government had to contend.

Another question that merits discussion in an examination of the Klan is the nature of the membership the organization attracted and of the support it received. To which of the social classes in South Carolina did the members and leaders belong? Which groups in the community supported the Klan's activities? From the evidence that is available, it is clear that the Klan drew its members and leaders from all classes of the white population in the up-country. This conclusion contrasts with the viewpoint that regards the Ku Klux Klan as an almost exclusively lower-class movement. During questioning by the Congressional Committee Richard B. Carpenter stated that many of the Klan members "were very respectable men in the neighborhood where they lived." Carpenter did not believe that the Klan members "were confined to a low or desperate class of people." According to Democratic testimony in Unionville "every unmarried young man of respectability in the town" belonged to the Klan.[44] A *New York Tribune* report from York County in November, 1871 stressed that the Klan included doctors, lawyers, merchants, teachers and preachers among a membership that embraced almost all of the whites in the county. The *Tribune* stated that both the "landed proprietor and the poor 'crackers' on his estate" belonged to the Klan.[45] This view of the make-up of the Klan's membership was echoed two months later in the charge of the Federal grand jury at Columbia that the order embraced "in its membership a large proportion of the white population of every profession and class." [46] Added to this evidence is the judgment of an Army report that "those arrested and those who have surrendered are of every social grade from the highest to the lowest, including representatives of all the liberal professions, even ministers of the gospel." [47]

The evidence also clearly indicates that a major role in the leadership of the Klan was taken by men from respectable families, by those removed in economic and social position from the poor whites. The Northern press frequently discussed this matter of the Klan's social composition. The *New York Tribune* described the lower-class whites of the up-country, as "ready tools for the designing men who planned the daring scheme to be carried out through the machinery of the Ku-Klux order." The *Tribune* in a later report contended that some of the leading families of the up-country, families who controlled public sentiment "as systematically, and as certainly, as a general commands his army," were responsible for Klan activity. The *Tribune* answered the arguments of those who ascribed the Klan to the white tenant farmers and town laborers:

It has been with too much readiness accepted outside this state that the poor "white trash" committed these outrages when it is now shown that they were planned and executed by men of intelligence, and these men individually and jointly, are responsible for the sentiment and the action of the communities.[48]

A South Carolina correspondent of the *Boston Traveller* also stressed upper class participation in the Klan. The Klan "is not as you suppose composed of 'border-ruffians'" stated this correspondent, "but its members are from what might be called 'respectable families.'"[49]

Upper class complicity in the Klan's activities was charged repeatedly during the Federal trials. The Grand Jury presentment stated that "for all these violations of law and order, and the sacred rights of citizens, many of the leading men of these counties were responsible. It was proven that large numbers of the most prominent citizens were members of the order." The Grand Jury alleged that many of these gentlemen added duplicity to their other crimes, that they pretended opposition to the Klan at the same time they were active in the order "and directing its operations even in detail." The Federal prosecutor, Corbin, echoed this indictment, asserting that the leaders of the Klan were "in many cases men of property who had led and controlled the others." This view of the responsibility of upper-class whites was accepted by Judge Bond who presided at the trials. Said Bond during the sentencing of one defendant, "Men of prominence and education . . . were for the most part participants in the conspiracy, or so much in terror of [it] that you could obtain from them neither protection or advice, had you sought it."[50]

Further study is needed of the specific economic standing of the individuals who belonged to the Klan. However, a study of currently available information points to the substantiation of the charges by newspaper observers and Federal officials as to upper-class involvement in the organization. According to witnesses the chief of the Klan in Spartanburg County was J. Banks Lyle, member of the Legislature and principal of a boys' boarding school at Limestone Springs.[51] Others identified as active Klan members were Doctor J. Rufus Bratton, planter John S. Millar, merchant J. W. Avery, Doctor Thomas Whitesides, and former magistrate Samuel G. Brown.[52] Several prominent citizens were arrested for participation in the Laurens incident. Among them was the intendant of Laurens, Doctor D. A. Richardson, the county sheriff, Colonel Jones, lawyer Colonel Todd, the owner of the town's hotel Colonel Moseley, and minister John A. Leland. Also involved in the Laurens violence was the planter Hugh Farley, described by Leland as a representative of "some of the oldest and most respectable families in the county."[53] The medical profession appears, for some reason, to have contributed more than its share to the Klan. At one time there were six physicians in a group of thirty-five prisoners confined to Newberry jail for Klan activity.

The question of the public support received by the Klan is important in understanding what gave strength to the organization, and what, for a considerable period, provided it with immunity to exposure and prosecution. As with any political organization, the Klan needed the support of nonmembers, but the Klan as a conspiracy was particularly dependent upon the support of those who would not themselves join. What then was the extent of the support received by the Klan from the white community? The evidence appears clear that support for the Klan was voiced repeatedly by individuals prominent in the communities where they lived. Particularly appealing to many property owners were the "benefits" that resulted from Klan violence. One Democratic leader, Robert W. Shand, testified to the aftermath of the Union lynchings:

Since that time the county has been quiet. I know there has been very little stealing since then. The Negroes in the streets have been behaving quietly. The white men and Negroes have been getting on better together. The county is more prosperous, the crops are better worked and everything is better.

With such benefits supposedly accruing to Union County, it is not difficult to understand that there was no excess of concern by Shand with the propriety of lynching.

Shand was not the only conservative leader to welcome the results of the Union violence. Lawyer James B. Steadman testified that Union County, following the murder of ten Negroes, "is in better condition today than I have known it since the war." Joseph F. Gist apparently was prepared to record the lynchings among the major accomplishments of Union County history, commenting that "the fact of the raids upon this jail and the execution of the murderers of Stevens, did more for the peace and quiet of this country than anything that has ever transpired." And if Gist was ready to defend lynching in the name of "peace and quiet," yet another Union leader, physician A. W. Thomson, excused this tactic in the name of civilization. Stated Thomson: "I must believe that it was the shortest road and perhaps the most humane road—for I am speaking in that way—to becoming civilized, as you may say." Thomson did indeed have his qualms—lynching was perhaps a "terrible remedy"—but since he concluded that "ultimate good will follow from it" his doubts were dispelled.[54]

Among the individuals who furthered the activity of the Klan were several of the key leaders of the state Democratic party. These leaders refused to use their influence to suppress the violence and, in effect, used the Klan's activities to blackmail the Republican administration. Matthew Butler, who ran as Union Reform candidate for Lieutenant Governor in 1870, told the Congressional Select Committee that he would not act to stop the terror until Governor Scott appointed trial justices acceptable to the Democrats and disarmed the militia. Another leader who used the activities of the Klan as a lever against the Scott administration was

Benjamin F. Perry, first Provisional Governor after the fall of the Confederacy. Perry wrote to Scott demanding concessions from the Republicans and indicated what might happen if a compromise was not forthcoming. "Permit me to say to you, in candor and sincerity," said Perry, "that the signs of the times indicate, unmistakable to my mind, that we are on the eve of a bloody, tumultuous commotion, unless something is done to quiet public opinion." [55]

With the initiation of Federal prosecution of the Klan, conservative leaders took up the active defense of those arrested. A circular letter was drawn up appealing for a $15,000 defense fund. Among those who signed were Matthew Butler and Wade Hampton, later to play a central role in the overthrow of the Radical government. The conservatives of Charleston responded warmly to this appeal. A meeting to raise funds was called at the Bank of Charleston. The sponsors asked the "assistance of all who sympathize with the good men who have been dragged from their homes and illegally incarcerated." [56]

The process that led members of South Carolina's propertied classes to join or support the Klan was described by the *New York Tribune*. Supposedly respectable citizens were moved to violence when the realization dawned that Reconstruction might not be a merely temporary nuisance. Said the *Tribune:*

> To them the present supremacy of the negro race is a thing unnatural and altogether abominable. At first they looked upon reconstruction as a farce and believed that a Democratic triumph in 1868 would sweep it all away. Now it is a horrible reality. From the state of amazement . . . they passed into a condition of bitterness and rage of which violence and murder was the natural consequence.[57]

Finally to be considered in this paper is an estimate of the degree of success attained by the Klan in South Carolina. Which, if any, of its objectives were achieved? In one major area, of course, the Klan met defeat; it was unable, in the face of government suppression, to maintain its own existence. But the Klan did not pass from the scene without inflicting serious damage on the Republican-Negro coalition. The Klan succeeded, at least in the up-country, in breaking up the Union Leagues that had served to organize popular support for the Radicals at the grass roots level. Destroyed also by the Klan was the Negro militia, the organization that sought to assure the Negro of the free exercise of the voting franchise. No longer were the Negroes, in significant numbers, to be armed by the state government.

The Klan also assisted in the process of undermining the enthusiasm of Northern opinion for the Radical policies. If the Klan's outrages evoked horror they also were utilized to support the views of those who viewed Radicalism as a hopeless failure. A mood of defeatism set in concerning the wisdom of a policy that relied upon the Negroes and their white

Republican allies. Increasingly, consideration was given to a policy that would turn for support to the conservatives of the South, to those who promised peace if only they were not excluded from directing the South's affairs. Representative of this new tendency in Northern opinion was the Republican *Nation*. Following President Grant's declaration of martial law this magazine declared:

> It is useless to proclaim York and Spartanburg . . . as long as the men whose fathers for half a dozen generations have lived and died in South Carolina, and who really love the State, find that while they may not touch its affairs, Northern adventurers are at liberty to make fortunes out of the mismanagement of them.[53]

The solution to Klan violence began to be viewed in terms of amnesty for the former leaders of the Confederacy rather than in terms of further reforms that would eliminate a basis for racism. Such organs as *The Nation* continued to accept the necessity, for the time being, of Federal action to cope with major outbreaks of violence, but there was little heart left for the policy of excluding the aristocracy from political life. The Southern conservatives were economically far stronger than the Negroes and now many in the North were ready to add political power to the conservatives' economic strength.

Perhaps most important the Klan strengthened the morale of the Southern conservatives. The Klan in South Carolina proved that given enough time, money and guns, the use of violence could paralyze the Radical government and overpower resistance by Negroes. The one obstacle that had to be overcome was the threat of Federal intervention. The violence of organized racists was no match for a United States Government that would take seriously its duty to enforce the post-Civil War amendments. But the racists could look forward to a time when they would not need to fear Federal intervention. Then the way would be open for the restoration of political rule based on white supremacy. And when the next opportunity to act would come there would be no need for the disguise and the rituals of a secret order. The Klan members of 1870 needed their masks; the rifle club members who brought Hampton to power in 1876 relied only on their guns and the acquiescence of a passive Federal government.

NOTES

1. Francis B. Simkins, "New Viewpoints of Southern Reconstruction," *Journal of Southern History*, V (February, 1939), 50.
2. Francis B. Simkins, "The Ku Klux Klan in South Carolina, 1868–1871," *Journal of Negro History*, XII (October, 1927), 618.
3. 41st Congress, 1st Session, House Miscellaneous Documents, No. 18, *Contested Election Case of Hoge versus Reed* (Washington: Government Printing Office, 1869), pp. 7, 35, 42; *Charleston Advocate*, October 20, 1868, quotes proclamation by Governor Scott listing murdered; *Report of Evidence Taken by Committee of Investigation of 3rd Congressional District* (Columbia: n. p., 1870), pp. 1169, 1321.

4. 42nd Congress, 2nd Session, *Joint Select Committee Testimony,* IV, 1256–1259, quoting from 41st Congress, 1st Session, House Miscellaneous Documents, No. 18, *op. cit.,* pp. 30–34. Testimony of Klan member W. K. Tolbert.
5. 41st Congress, 2nd Session, House Miscellaneous Documents, No. 17, part 2, *Contested Election Case of Wallace versus Simpson* (Washington: Government Printing Office, 1870), p. 44.
6. 41st Congress, 2nd Session, House Miscellaneous Documents. No. 17, part 2, *op. cit.,* pp. 38, 40; 41st Congress, 1st Session, House Miscellaneous Documents, No. 18, *op. cit.,* p. 34.
7. *Contested Election Case of Wallace versus Simpson,* pp. 44, 45.
8. *Report on Evidence . . . of 3rd Congressional District,* pp. 1033, 1057, 1063, 1129, 1213.
9. *Contested Election Case of Wallace versus Simpson,* pp. 9, 10, 32; *Report on Evidence . . . of 3rd Congressional District; Contested Election Case of Wallace versus Simpson,* pp. 16, 17, 39.
10. *Report on Evidence . . . of 3rd Congressional District,* pp. 1123–26, 1146; *Contested Election Case of Hoge versus Reed,* pp. 5, 6; *Contested Election Case of Wallace versus Simpson,* pp. 3, 6, 29.
11. *Report on Evidence . . . of 3rd Congressional District,* p. 1246; 41st Congress, 1st Session, House Miscellaneous Documents, No. 35, *Papers in Contested Election Case of Reed and Simpson* (Washington, 1869), p. 38.
12. *Report on Evidence . . . 3rd Congressional District,* p. 1284.
13. *Contested Election Case of Hoge versus Reed,* p. 5.
14. *Contested Election Case of Wallace versus Simpson,* p. 19.
15. *Contested Election Case of Hoge versus Reed,* p. 47.
16. *Contested Election Case of Wallace versus Simpson,* pp. 41, 41.
17. *Contested Election Case of Hoge versus Reed,* p. 3; 41st Congress, 1st Session, House Reports No. 7, part 2, *Report on Contested Election Case of Wallace versus Simpson* (Washington, 1869), p. 3.
18. F. P. Blair, *Extension of the Ku Klux Act,* Senate Speech of May 20, 1872 (Washington, 1872), p. 8; *Historical Review of the State of South Carolina* (Charleston, 1884), p. 28.
19. Ellis Oberholtzer, *A History of the United States Since the Civil War,* II (New York, 1922), p. 373, quoting *Statutes At Large of South Carolina* for 1868.
20. Stanley F. Horn, *Invisible Empire* (Boston, 1939), p. 219.
21. *New York Times,* August 25, 1870.
22. *Reports and Resolutions of the General Assembly of South Carolina* (Columbia, 1871), p. 517.
23. *Charleston Daily News,* quoted in Francis B. Simkins and Robert H. Woody, *South Carolina During Reconstruction* (Chapel Hill, 1932), p. 456; *Charleston Daily News,* November 9, 1870.
24. *Reports and Resolutions of the General Assembly of South Carolina,* p. 517.
25. *Joint Select Committee Testimony,* IV, 919–922, 943.
26. *Ibid.,* III, 184, 386, 402, 428, 440, 540, 565; IV, 621, 797, 890.
27. Horn, *op. cit.,* pp. 225–228; See *Joint Select Committee Testimony,* IV, 968–1010, 1121, 1128, 1129.
28. *Ibid.,* V, 1505.
29. *Ibid.,* V, 1702, 1868, 1953.
30. *Trials at Columbia, South Carolina,* record of Federal Ku Klux Klan trials in *Joint Select Committee Testimony,* V, 1704, 1794.
31. *Joint Select Committee Testimony,* IV, 704–707; V, 1362–1402.
32. J. D. Richardson, *Messages and Papers of the Presidents* (Washington, 1898), VII, 164. Grant summed up objectives of Klan in message to House of Representatives, April 19, 1872.
33. *Joint Select Committee Testimony,* V, 1685–86.
34. *Trials at Columbia, South Carolina,* in *Joint Select Committee Testimony,* V. 1708.
35. *Ibid.,* V, 1719.
36. *Ibid.,* III, 226.

37. *New York Herald,* March 13, 1871.
38. Oberholtzer, *op. cit.,* p. 383.
39. Louis F. Post, "A 'Carpetbagger' in South Carolina," *Journal of Negro History,* X (January, 1925), 49.
40. 42nd Congress, 3rd Session, Senate Executive Documents, No. 32, *Report of Attorney General Williams* (Washington, 1873), p. 11.
41. Simkins, and Woody, *op. cit.,* p. 462; Simkins, "The Ku Klux Klan in South Carolina," *op. cit.,* pp. 632, 634.
42. *New York Tribune,* May 31, June 8, November 10, 1871.
43. *Joint Select Committee Testimony,* III, 227.
44. *Ibid.,* III, 244; IV, 984.
45. *New York Tribune,* November 14, 1871.
46. *Joint Select Committee Testimony,* V, 1613.
47. *Ibid.,* V, 1602–1603.
48. *New York Tribune,* November 25, December 28, 1871.
49. *Boston Traveller,* quoted in *New York Times,* June 3, 1871.
50. *Joint Select Committee Testimony,* V, 1613, 1982, 1983.
51. *New York Tribune,* November 24, 1871; *Joint Select Committee Testimony,* V, 1971, 1972.
52. *Joint Select Committee Testimony,* I, 43; *New York Tribune,* November 13, 1871; *Joint Select Committee Testimony,* V, 1363–65, 1386, 1690, 1942.
53. John A. Leland, *A Voice from South Carolina* (Charleston, 1879), pp. 80, 87; *Joint Select Committee Testimony,* III, 336–338.
54. *Joint Select Committee Testimony,* IV, 972, 976, 994, 1030, 1062, 1115, 1116.
55. *Ibid.,* 1191; *Congressional Globe,* 42nd Congress, 1st Session, p. 422.
56. *Charleston Daily News,* November 24, 1871.
57. *New York Tribune,* May 1, 1871.
58. *The Nation,* XIII (December 7, 1871), 364.

10. Lawlessness and Violence in America and Their Special Manifestations in Changing Negro-White Relationships

Violence, whether by individuals or by organized groups, has a long and extensive history in the United States. Past and present patterns of race violence must be viewed within this context. This distinctive form of violence is said to be a product of the breakdown of pre-existing patterns of accommodation between black and white Americans. Grimshaw argues that periods of violence can be specified, each indicating changing patterns of black-white relations as the subordinate black group acquires sufficient strength to challenge racist oppression.

ALLEN D. GRIMSHAW

Ours has been a lawless and violent nation.[1] Indeed, race riots and bombings, although they are particularly dramatic manifestations of conflict, have claimed fewer lives than many other varieties of violence, individual or social. There are more criminal homicides in some American metropolises every year than there have been deaths from all the urban race riots of the 20th Century combined. A few famous feuds, and some important labor disputes have rolled up casualty lists which compare in length with the most spectacular interracial disorders. Social violence,[2] and lawlessness generally, have not been phenomena expressed only in interracial relations in this country. This article reviews briefly two sets of historical data relevant to an understanding of those patterns of race relations in urban areas which have culminated in violence. An introductory section consists of a simple listing of some other varieties of social violence which have characterized inter-group relations in the United States and notes a widespread tradition of lawlessness, a tradition which has been manifested in every area of civic life. The remainder of the article reviews the changing character of interracial relations and their more specific manifestations in social, interracial violence.

From *Journal of Negro History* (1959), Vol. 44, pp. 52–72; reprinted by permission.

A. Our Lawless Heritage [3]

It is possible to make a rough classification of types of lawlessness and violence by reference to the areas of social interaction in which such lawlessness and violence occur. The two categories which emerge from such simple classification overlap, but are nonetheless distinguishable. The first category, that of ethnic violence includes, in addition to Negro-white social violence, conflict and violence focussed on religion and nativity. While the motivation behind much of this violence falls more accurately into the secular area of economic and political violence, the manifest reasons for "punishing" religious and nationality and racial groups have usually referred to religious, cultural and "racial" differences distinguishing these groups from "real Americans."

An anti-Catholic tradition, which has been expressed even in the 20th Century, was responsible for frequent eruptions in the last century, particularly in the period before the Civil War. In the three decades immediately preceding that war, street fights were frequent, sometimes taking on the proportions of major riots, convents and other religious edifices were attacked and sometimes destroyed, and Catholics both within and without the Church hierarchy were subject to constant vilification and occasional physical assault. This anti-Catholicism, particularly as related to an expression of Native-Americanism and the "Know-Nothing" movement, was most frequently directed against Irish Catholics, perhaps because they were resistant to accepting a subservient accommodative status, and had significant economic and political overtones. Jews and Mormons, to mention only two other religious communities, have also been the focus of hostility and violence.

While the Irish Catholics may have received the brunt of the animus and overt violence in Native American riots, they were by no means the only ethnic group attacked. Almost all immigrant groups went through a period of unpopularity, an unpopularity inextricably tied up with their status as perceived economic and political threats to the "older" immigrant groups. Groups distinguishable from the larger population by virtue of physical characteristics were a particular focus of hostility. Assaults upon the indigenous Indian population, commonplace throughout the historical period, were certainly not always necessary for the protection of the white population. A growing resentment toward the Chinese, originally imported as laborers on the transcontinental railroads, culminated in anti-Chinese riots in the closing decades of the 19th Century. Treatment of Mexican-Americans in the American Southwest has been similar to treatment of Negro-Americans in the American South. And the decade of the 1940's saw attacks not only on the civil rights of, but also against the persons and property of Japanese-Americans and Mexican-Americans as well as against Negroes.

The second general category includes a variety of secular types of violence. Most important here are lawlessness and violence growing out of politics and the relations of the populace to the government and out of economic competition. The Republic itself originated in an armed rebellion against the then established government. Like all civil wars and internecine strife, the Revolutionary War was a particularly vicious one, and the treatment accorded Loyalists by "Patriots" was no more gentle than that accorded the central figure in any lynching. The new government hardly found its constituents more tractable. Revolt against the new Republic was manifested in Shay's Rebellion in Massachusetts in 1787, in Pennsylvania's Whiskey Rebellion in 1794, in smuggling and trading with the enemy in the War of 1812 and in the Draft Riots of the Civil War. In the Depression of the 1930's the agrarian population manifested its hostility to the government in the "Penny Bankrupt Sales" and in other rural disturbances. Political hostility has not been limited to direct action against the government. The last century saw spectacular election riots, and elections even today are often characterized by sharp violations of the law.[4]

Economic strife has erupted into violence countless times in the last one hundred years. No major industry accepted unionization without a struggle, but in some, such as the railroads and the mines, the struggle assumed the character of wars. "Bloody Harlan" and the "Herrin Massacre," the Haymarket riot and the Homestead strike, these names conjure up a pageant of lawlessness and violence continuing well into the present century. Assassination and terrorism have been used by both labor and management, and in the "Big Steel" strikes of the 'Thirties the steel companies spent thousands upon thousands of dollars on machine guns and tear gas. Indeed, organizing strikes of today, such as that at Koehler, and similar protracted work stoppages, are still occasionally productive of violence.

America has been, then, a land of lawlessness and violence, ranging from spontaneous brawls between servicemen of different branches and schoolboys from different schools, through the "blood feud" and gangster warfare, to the full-fledged military campaigns which have occurred in struggles between class and class and between adherents of different religious faiths. The tradition of lawlessness includes both a contempt of parking regulations and an admiration of gangster heroes and, on the other hand, an excess zeal in the administration of "vigilante justice," "lynch law," and "six-shooter law" on the frontier. Some areas, such as Harlan County in Kentucky and "Bloody" Williamson in Illinois,[5] have run practically the full gamut of types of social violence suggested above. But there is practically no section of the United States which has not, at one time or another, been a center of lawlessness and violence. If there is less actual participation in violence today, and if Americans must sublimate their propensities to violence by watching television, the potentiality still remains.

The violence and bloodshed which has accompanied adjustments in the accommodative pattern between whites and Negroes in the United States is not unique to interracial relations. It is a thesis of the research on which this article is based that the violence which occurs in interracial relations is an inevitable product of assaults upon the accommodative pattern. Further research on the forms of violence which have been listed in this brief outline will, the writer believes, demonstrate that all social violence results from the interaction of conceptually similar forces in defining patterns of accommodation.

B. The Changing Character of Negro-White Relations and Negro-White Violence in the United States

In this section a rough classification has been made of periods in race relations in this country, the social forces which defined them, and the types of social violence which characterized them. The periods covered are roughly as follows: the period of slave insurrections and resistance (1640–1861); Civil War and Reconstruction (1861–1877); the Second Reconstruction and the beginnings of the Great Migration (1878–1914); World War I and post-War boom and racial readjustment (1915–1929); inter-war and Depression (1930–1941); World War II (1942–1945); and the period since World War II. The suggestion is made that in each of these periods the patterns of race relations and social racial violence were determined more by reaction of the dominant white community to attacks on the accommodative pattern by Negroes than by any conscious determination of policy by the white group. Some major areas in which conflict develops are noted and parallels to other group conflicts pointed out. Thus, it is shown that the Draft Riots of the Civil War were, at least in part, an expression of the hostility of laboring groups to "cheap labor," as had been the case with other immigrant groups, rather than an expression of specifically anti-Negro animus.

1. The Period of Slave Insurrections and Resistance (1640–1861)

While the importation of Negro labor into this country began in 1619, the Negro's status as a member of a racial group was only gradually defined. Frazier has pointed out that the distinction between slavery and servitude was not clear, and that during early years the status of the Negro was similar to that of the white indentured servant.[6] It is only with a clarification of the Negro's status as being a racial one, rather than one of social class, that it becomes legitimate to speak of Negro-white relationships. This clarification was under way by the middle decades of the 17th Century. Even before the beginnings of what has been called the classic period of "antebellum slavery" race relations in this country had begun to emerge as a unique pattern of inter-group relations.

However, while there were slave insurrections and abortive rebellions in the 18th Century, interracial violence was interpreted less in racial terms than in class or social terms, particularly in terms of the master-servant relationship. The racial "threat" concerning white Americans was the American Indian. There are reports of individual interracial assaults and homicides. There were slave plots of considerable scope, interestingly enough in New York, in 1712 and 1741.[7] But while whites were killed in these plots and Negroes slain or transported in retaliation, they were interpreted as uprisings of a servant class or as political plots inspired by "foreign agents" rather than as uprisings of Negroes. Indeed, in the second of these plots, whites were implicated and a white man and his family and a Catholic priest were executed.

With the firm establishment of capitalistic slavery as an American institution, a process catalyzed by well-known developments in agriculture, the black man and his activities, and his racial status, took on a new character and significance. It is after 1800 that apologies for the treatment of the Negro, since that time one of the South's leading literary exports, first began to appear. Approximately the same date marks a burgeoning concern by white Southerners over the control of their Negro slaves in ever broader aspects of their lives ranging from reproduction to religion, but particularly in those areas in which possible crisis lay. A number of authors have shown the near obsession of many Southern whites over the possibilities of slave revolts and have further demonstrated that in many cases this concern and anxiety were well-founded. A number of factors contributed to the failure of slave rebellions. But the plans of Vesey, Gabriel and Turner, to mention only the most well-known insurrectionaries, came alarmingly close to fruition. And, these planned rebellions were not the protest merely of an economically down-trodden and subservient class. That they were racial in character is demonstrated by the fact that whites of all classes were to be exterminated, with the exception of those who had shown good-will toward Negroes. The characteristics of the rebels varied. Some were relatively new arrivals still imbued with the militance of their African tribal heritage, others were longer sojourners in this country who had become literate, acculturated and too familiar with ideas of equality which were meant only for their white masters. But all of them shared, in common with the white group, a conception of a society divided along racial, rather than simply social, lines. They differed from the whites in their refusal to accept the sanctity of the established accommodative pattern.

Other patterns of resistance to slave status are less clearly racial and more frequently individual in nature. There is documentation that suicide, infanticide and self-mutilation were widespread, not only in this country, but also on the boats which brought the slaves and even before that in the slave coffles of Africa itself. Other slaves took an easier pattern of resistance through what we now call the "slow-down" and various forms of "goldbricking." Correspondence of owners and their overseers is replete with complaints about the abuse of working equipment by field hands, the widespread and undiagnosable "miseries," and the unauthorized vacations in the swamps or actual runaways. Rejection of slave status was shown by continual destruction of property; the burnings of barns and hay-ricks, the failure to cinch the master's saddle up tight enough to prevent his being thrown; by the studied insult which is not an insult. In a large number of ways short of physical violence the Negro slave protested his subservient status.[8] It is true that much of this protest was not channeled into social racial protest. But the underlying substratum was one of protest against an accommodative pattern in which the Negro was in a permanently subordinate position.

Many of the activities of whites in the owning class during this period can be viewed as reactions to the various forms of resistance offered by their Negro slaves. It is true that as slavery became an entrenched institution the master had increasing control over the lives of his slaves, until ultimately control over the very life and death of the slave came into the hands of the master. Yet, in spite of the Simon Legree tradition, most Southerners engaged in latifundiary activities had a purely capitalistic orientation. Slaves as instruments of production should have a certain minimum of decent treatment in order to ensure their survival and relative productivity as plantation labor.[9] While there were doubtless many cruel men and women who maltreated their slaves, or in the case of overseers the slaves of their employers, it seems highly probable that much of the brutal treatment was meted out to slaves in an attempt to force non-cooperative workers to produce, to discourage malingering, or to cow potential rebels and insurrectionaries. It is doubtful that many white Southerners enjoyed giving up their evenings to riding on "patrol" enforcing "Black Codes." More likely such activity was interpreted as being necessary for survival. The same may be said of patterns of slave punishment which in retrospect may seem unnecessarily brutal. In this period, as in others, given an initial pattern of superordination-subordination, the attitude and behavior of the Negro determined the pattern of interracial relations.

2. Civil War and Reconstruction (1861–1877)

The period immediately prior to the Civil War was one in which the status of the Negro, and of his relationships to the dominant white group, became increasingly a matter of national concern. While almost all white Americans, from North or South, of Abolitionist or Slavery politics, were agreed on the innate inferiority of the Negro to the white man, there were those who felt that this inferiority did not justify holding the black man in slavery. The War of the Rebellion was an attempt to decide issues in the area of "State's Rights." But lying behind and around all other issues was that of slavery and, more broadly, the relationships between whites and Negroes in all parts of the country.

Even before the War had begun it was apparent that not all Northerners felt toward the Negro as did the abolitionists. Nor was this lack of unanimity confined to areas of Copperhead strength. The domestic situation in the North during the War was marked by numerous civil disturbances.[10] There was violent rioting in Cincinnati in 1862, apparently growing out of competition of Negro and Irish hands on the riverboats. There were lesser riots in Newark, New Jersey and in Buffalo and Troy, New York. These latter riots, like other riots of the War period, combined as their basic causes hostility to the wartime draft and its inequities and a concomitant fear that Negroes would take over the jobs of white labor. The most spectacular of the so-called "Draft Riots," however, was that which took place in New York City in July of 1863.[11]

The draft disturbances in New York remain the most sanguinary case of interracial violence in American history. Estimates of deaths of white rioters alone range as high as 1,500 and while the total number of Negroes slain is unknown, the population of Negroes in the city dropped by 20 per cent, from 12,472 to 9,945, between 1860 and 1865.[12] A major factor in the origin of these riots was a fear of black labor competition which flourished among the contingent of unskilled Irish labor in the city's labor force, a fear nourished and encouraged by anti-Administration politicians and the Democratic press. The Draft Riots in New York had at least two interacting causes, one direct and one indirect, which were related to the status of the Negro. The discriminatory nature of the draft legislation was felt particularly by working-class people who were unable to pay for substitutes. They were being forced to fight in a war about which they had no enthusiasm. In addition, they felt that they were being forced to fight to "free the niggers," whom they perceived as a threat as a source of cheap labor. In some of its aspects the New York riot was similar to earlier riots directed against various foreign-born groups, particularly the Irish themselves, who were considered as undermining the position of native-born white labor.

The Civil War also saw the first large-scale participation of Negroes in military activities in an American war. Negroes were utilized by both Union and Confederate forces, though in the South their participation was largely limited to work in labor battalions. In the Northern armies they fought in several major campaigns, occasionally distinguishing themselves to a minor degree. When captured by Southern troops they could expect no quarter and in at least one case were slaughtered wholesale. Relations with Northern white officers were frequently not much better, a unit of the Corps d'Afrique mutinied against its white officers and other incidents are recorded.[13]

The situation of Negroes in the South during the War period was not uniform. In some cases white owners and other representatives of the dominant racial group thought it expedient to introduce even more rigid controls over their slaves. In other areas Negroes were given added responsibilities and loyal servants stayed at home and protected the "women folk." Even in areas characterized by the latter situation, however, there was a general air of tenseness and the number of slaves who attempted to gain their freedom in the confusion swelled to the point where they hindered the movements of the Northern military forces. The latter, at least in some cases, showed their attitude by returning the runaway slaves to their masters. Some areas were swept with panic as rumors circulated of impending insurrection. The accommodative structure was disintegrating, but no new structure of social relationships was as yet appearing to take its place.

The bitterness of white Southerners at losing the war was hardly assuaged by events of the immediate post-War years. To the injury of shattered pride and economic ruination was added the insult of disfranchisement and "Black Republicanism." The oft-told activities and exploits of "carpetbaggers," "scalawags" and the members of the various "black government" need no re-telling. While not all of those who governed the South in the post-War years were scoundrels and while there was doubtless progressive and intelligent legislation passed in States dominated temporarily by Negroes, the fact remains that there were scoundrels and that illiterate Negroes, unprepared for political responsibility, did put their votes up for sale. There was enough misuse of political power to convince many white Southerners of the venality and incompetence of all Negroes. Motives of revenge did dominate some Negroes and many white Southerners underwent harrowing experiences during this period of continued disorganization. It was in desperation that respectable elements of the white community organized the "Bald Knobbers" of Missouri and other "pre-Klan night-riding" organizations. Only later did these organizations fall into the hands of criminals and outlaws. Repressive activity against Negroes (and some whites) in this period was, again, an attempt to bring some coherence into a disrupted accommodative structure.

By the end of this period the relationship between whites and Negroes had been clearly defined as an interracial relationship and any inter-class aspects were clearly secondary.[14] Henceforward, particularly in the South but with increasing frequency in the North, disputes between whites and Negroes were interpreted as interracial disputes no matter what may have been the initiating incident. Historians may interpret the War as a struggle over "State's Rights." White persons in both the North and the South

have come to regard it as the war to "free the niggers." Any attempt after
this time to resolve differences between the two sections has led to
recriminations by Southerners concerning the crime of the North in un-
loosing the Negro.

3. The Second Reconstruction and the Beginnings of the Great Migration (1878–1914)

Although considerable hostility had been generated by events of the
post-War period, the withdrawal of Federal troops from the South after
the Compromise of 1877 was not followed by an immediate wave of
savage repression against the Negro in the South. Indeed, for a decade it
seemed that the lines of struggle in the new South might be defined along
class lines rather than along racial lines.[15] For a brief period, that of the
acme of Populist power, a tenuous alliance existed between the poor
whites and the Negro populace. White and Negro alike united in a
temporary and doomed attempt to overthrow the "Bourbon aristocracy." It
was after the breakdown of this alliance with the creation of another
coalition including the Bourbons, Northern business interests and the
demagogic leaders of the lower-class whites that the classic period of
repression and lynching began.

During this period of interracial violence the attitude of the white
Southern governments was a "hands off" expression of tacit approval.
Northern liberals were suddenly disinterested, they were tired of breast-
beating about an admittedly inferior race in a remote section, and allowed
themselves to be convinced that the South did, indeed, know the best way
to handle its own problem.[16] It was between the middle 'Eighties and the
early 1900's that most of the increasingly discriminative and repressive
legislation, the "Jim Crow" laws, was passed. During the same period
these laws received support through the courts to the supreme judicial
bench. The Negro was deprived effectively of the franchise, of equality in
compulsory public education [17] and of protection against discrimination in
the use of public facilities. The Negro did not succumb to this attack on
his rights without a struggle. The use of widespread repression and the
high incidence of violence against the Negro populace was, at least in
part, the manifest expression of white reaction to Negro resistance. If
Negroes had "known their place" it would not have been necessary to
lynch Negroes in order to remind them of that "place." There was considerable resistance, though usually unorganized, on the part of the Negro
population. When that resistance failed, a trickle of northward migration
began, a trickle which was to swell into a flood by the end of the First
World War.[18]

The manifest reason for much of the savage repression of this period
was the protection of Southern white womanhood, still a major plank in
the foundation of programs for maintaining white supremacy.[19] However,

while this may have been the public explanation for lynching, rape was not the most frequent alleged cause for the necessity of the primeval justice of lynching, even during the two big lynching decades, the last of the 19th and the first of the 20th Centuries.[20] Failure to show the proper respect to a white man was equally important, and a cause which included a variety of offenses ranging from a demand for an explanation of financial transactions to the more heinous crime of engaging in political activity. Political activity was the underlying cause of the two most savage outbreaks of this period, riots in Wilmington, North Carolina in 1896 and in Atlanta, Georgia in 1906. In the latter case the alleged reason for the outbreak was a series of assaults on white women, but it is clear that the disturbance had as a latent function the exclusion of Negroes from political participation.

Emancipation and military defeat, "Black Republicanism" and the Freedmen's Bureau, the First Reconstruction with its schoolmarms and scalawags, had completely disrupted the "ante-bellum" pattern of accommodation between the two races in the South. The Second Reconstruction, with its Jim Crow legislation, its night-riders and lynching "bees" to enforce racial "etiquette," was an attempt to re-establish that accommodative pattern.

4. World War I and Post-War Boom and Racial Readjustment (1915–1929)

Events of this period made clear the fact that the Negro problem was no longer a regional one, but one shared by North and South alike. Indeed, while lynching continued in the South, major outbreaks of interracial violence increasingly occurred in Northern urban areas with their growing concentrations of Negro population.

There are five patterns of interracial social violence in this period different enough in characteristics to be identifiable. They are (a) lynching, (b) mutiny and insurrection, (c) individual interracial assaults and homicides, racial arson and bombings, (d) "Southern style" race riots,[21] and (e) "Northern style" race riots.

(a) *Lynching.* The first decade of the 20th Century was a peak decade for lynching in the South and during the same decade this pattern of interracial violence spread into Northern States.[22] The most spectacular lynching of this century occurred immediately after World War I in Omaha, Nebraska. The immediate alleged cause was the assault of a Negro upon a white woman. The real cause, however, was at least in part a reflection of the nation-wide reaction of whites to the new militance of the Negro's assault upon the accommodative structure. This new militance was a result partly of the not unsubstantial gains of the Negro in moving North during the War and partly a result of the much publicized treatment of Negro soldiers overseas, particularly in France. Large numbers of whites shared in a determination to "put these uppity niggers back in their place," and violence occurred in widely scattered points throughout the country.

Lynchings continued to occur until the time of World War II and it is only since the War that the Bureau of Records and Research of Tuskegee has stopped publication of data on lynchings on the ground that their occurrence is no longer of major consequence. A common cause continued to be alleged Negro assault upon a white woman, but the actual pattern of precipitating causes remained as varied as it had been in earlier periods. It is probable that here, as in the case of other types of violence, there have been changes in etiology. Attempts, none very successful, have been made to demonstrate that lynchings, particularly during the Depression, were closely related to the fluctuation of various economic indices.[23] While documentation for such relationships has proved insufficient, it is probably true that lynching in later years was founded less frequently on the myth of sexuality and more frequently was a direct expression of reaction against "felt" Negro aggression in the economic sphere.

(b) *Mutiny and Insurrection.* Such aggression, in at least one instance, found expression in the renewal of a pattern which had not occurred since before the Civil War. In October, 1919, there occurred an insurrection of the Negro populace near Elaine, Arkansas. It was claimed that the inspiration for this rebellion came from "Bolshevik" agitation and there is some evidence that the "Progressive Farmer's Household Union" was active in promoting the notion that Negroes were entitled to economic and social equality. Negroes of the area were well organized and were prepared, according to confessions made by several of their number, to follow up demands for fair payment for their cotton with an armed uprising. After a series of brief battles the Negroes were subdued and hunted down, given quick trials, and sentenced, several to death.

In addition to this uprising there were a number of mutinies in the military, the most famous of which developed into the Houston race riot of 1917.[24] In this affair, Negro soldiers, enraged by the shooting of one of their comrades in an affray with the white police over alleged mistreatment of a Negro woman, mutinied against their officers, took weapons and proceeded to storm downtown Houston. Several people were killed, and as a result of the disturbance 65 Negro soldiers received sentences, several of them for life imprisonment.[25]

It is interesting to note that the soldiers involved in the Houston race riot were largely from Northern States. The Elaine uprising and the several mutinies which occurred during the War make up the bulk of cases of direct assaults by Negroes upon the accommodative structure.

(c) *Individual Interracial Assaults and Homicides, Arson and Bombings.* A third pattern of social violence consisted of individual interracial assaults and homicides and other attacks such as arson and bombing. Not all interracial homicides and assaults can be considered to be social violence. In any case where racial membership was important in the interactive pattern and the violence based ultimately on that membership, social violence may be said to have occurred. These manifestations of violence are a part of the riot cycle itself. During the period of increasing tension prior to major riots, during lulls within the riot, and in decreasing tempo after the riot has played itself out or has been quelled, such acts are indicators of the character of interracial relations. In those situations where adequate policing or firm governmental action prevent the actual eruption of hostility into full-fledged riots such behavior patterns may be the sole indication of the high degree of tension.

(*d*) *"Southern Style" Race Riots.* The Atlanta riot of 1906 and the Springfield, Illinois riot of 1908 are examples of Southern style race riots. During the period under discussion, the Washington, D.C. riot of 1919 and the Tulsa, Oklahoma riot of 1921 can be taken as typical examples. In every such riot violence is largely one-sided and consists of attacks, of varying degrees of organization, by whites on Negroes and on the Negro community. In all such riots, whatever may have been the actual background of the riot, there are charges of Negro assaults upon white women.

(*e*) *"Northern Style" Race Riots.* The Chicago riot of 1919 may be taken as the type-case of the Northern style urban race riot.[26] Here the causation, both in background and in actual precipitating incident, is secular in nature and there is no focussing on the alleged violation of the sanctity of white womanhood. Rather there was a long period of constantly increasing tension in other areas, and a series of assaults upon the accommodative pattern by Negroes, indeed, a challenge to the very continued existence of that pattern. The assault was felt particularly in the areas of housing, labor competition and the use of public facilities, especially transportation. The actual precipitating incident was the death, perhaps accidental, of a Negro youth during a dispute over segregated swimming. The riot found organized and unorganized groups of both races engaged in occasional pitched battles and a widespread occurrence of attacks upon isolated individuals of one race by roaming gangs of the other race. While there were claims of police partiality and governmental inefficiency the role of the government was far more neutral than was the case in disturbances in the South, urban or rural.

5. Inter-War and Depression (1930–1941)

In many ways this period is an extension of the immediately preceding one. It has been accorded separate treatment because of the sharp decline of reported violence of an interracial nature during the decade of the 'Thirties. While lynchings continued, particularly in the South, they decreased in number if not in barbarity. Only one major urban disturbance is recorded for the decade, the Harlem riot of 1935. The end of the period was characterized by an increasing incidence of individual interracial violence, presaging the major outbreaks of urban social violence which were to occur in the following period. The period was one in which there was a gradual building up of the strength of organizations on the extreme political left and the extreme political right. These organizations played an as yet incompletely assessed role in the struggles which were coming.

6. World War II (1942–1945)

The most dramatic racial outbreaks of the Second World War were the Detroit and Harlem disturbances of 1943. While there are some similarities between these two outbreaks, there are sharp differences both in background and in the actual course of events in the two cities. The Detroit race riot was, in background, in precipitating incident, and in chronology of violence a "Northern style" riot much like the 1919 Chicago riot. There was little actual interracial violence in the Harlem outbreak, but this lack of overt interracial conflict resulted from differences in ecology and in the application of police controls rather than from differences in general background factors in Detroit and Harlem or from any lower degree of strain in the accommodative relationship in Harlem.

The Harlem and Detroit riots of 1943 were only two of the more spectacular expressions of the resurgence of interracial conflict during World War II. There were riots in other urban centers, both North and South. Nor were riots the only form of conflict and violence occurring during the War. There were difficulties involving Negro service personnel which in at least a few cases came close to ending in old-fashioned lynchings. There was a continuation of the pattern of individual assaults and homicides. Intimately related to all these patterns of actual violence was a much increased militance shown by the Negro press and by a number of Negro organizations. Perhaps most important in terms of long-range consequences was the burgeoning utilization of political, economic and legal coercion in the assault upon the pattern of interracial accommodation. Results of the interaction of all these factors have become obvious in the post-War period.

7. Post-World-War II (1946–the present)

Since the end of World War II there have been large-scale urban disturbances but no real race riots. There have been, however, a number of incidents which, had it not been for the presence of better police controls than existed in the past, might easily have erupted into major urban riots. In the North, these incidents have tended to cluster into two categories; incidents concerning Negro invasion of white residential areas and incidents over the use of public facilities, particularly recreational facilities. In the latter area, St. Louis and Youngstown experienced near riots over the use of swimming facilities by Negroes.[27] Housing incidents have caused near riots in a number of Northern cities. Two which attracted wide attention were those in Cicero [28] and Chicago,[29] Illinois. In some cases, as in Cicero, police partiality toward the white aggressors seems to have been partly responsible for the growth of an initially small disturbance. In Chicago, on the other hand, where a struggle over Negro entrance into Trumbull Park, a formerly all-white public housing project, tied up police for four years; the Negroes remained, and were protected by a well-organized police force which had had special training in interracial problems. In addition to these disturbances there have been bombings in Kansas City, Missouri, and Chicago and demonstrations against the movement of a Negro family into all-white Levittown, Pennsylvania, and scattered incidents in other Northern urban areas.[30]

The sharpest changes in the pattern of interracial relations in the post-War period, however, have been brought about by the renewed and increased vigor of the use of the courts by Negroes.[31] This has been true in the areas already mentioned, housing and access to public facilities and also, and more importantly, in the crucial area of school de-segregation.[32] Eruptions of violence have occurred in Southern communities where court orders to integrate schools have been greeted by organized resistance of the white community. There have been riots in Kentucky, Tennessee and Arkansas and disturbances in other States. At the time of this writing schools have been closed by the Governors of Virginia and Arkansas, ostensibly to prevent further outbreaks of violence. Whether or not the current situation in the South will erupt into violence in the affected Southern communities depends on many factors, including the attitudes of school children and their parents, the actions of State and local governments, decisions of the Federal Executive in enforcing court decrees and, finally, and most importantly, the militance and aggressiveness with which Negroes, through their national organizations such as the National Association for the Advancement of Colored People, press their demands.

Reflecting the new militance of the Negro population in the area of school de-segregation, in attempts to gain the franchise, in bus boycotts, and in other breaches of the accommodative pattern, there have been sporadic outbreaks of violence in the South. The pattern, however, has not been that of the mass lynching or the rural pogrom, but rather one of kidnapping and summary "execution" or of sudden assault in a fashion more reminiscent of Northern gang warfare of the 'Thirties or of post-Civil War Klan activities. The current outbreak of bombings seems to validate this observation.

With the exception of a brief period after the Civil War, the pattern of American Negro-white relationships, especially in the American South, has closely approximated the classic accommodative pattern of superordination-subordination, with the whites a continually dominant group. The most savage oppression, whether expressed in rural lynchings and pogroms or in urban race riots, has taken place when the Negro has refused to accept a subordinate status. The most intense conflict has resulted when the subordinate minority group has attempted to disrupt the accommodative pattern or when the superordinate group has defined the situation as one in which such an attempt is being made. Conflict in Negro-white relationships in the United States has been conflict generated by the breakdown of an essentially unstable accommodative pattern, essentially unstable because the subordinated group has refused to accept its status and has had sufficient power to challenge it.

NOTES

1. The research reported in this article is part of a larger study on urban race riots in the United States as a manifestation of social violence under supporting grants from the Samuel S. Fels Fund and the George Leib Harrison Foundation. Strict limitations on space have necessitated the elimination of completer documentation which will be available in the full study. This fuller documentation is available from the author.
2. Social violence, as the term is here used, refers to assault upon individuals or their property solely or primarily because of their group (ethnic, religious, or racial) affiliations.
3. The title of this section is taken from James Truslow Adams, "Our Lawless Heritage," *Atlantic Monthly*, 142, 6, Dec. 1928: 732–740.
4. E.g., illegal disfranchisement of the Negro electorate in some Southern states.
5. For a journalistic but suggestive account of violence in one such area see Paul M. Angle, *Bloody Williamson*, New York, 1952.
6. E. Franklin Frazier, *The Negro in the United States*, New York, 1957, Part I.
7. Note 18th Century reports from *Gentleman's Magazine* cited in Harvey Wish, "American Slave Insurrections before 1861," in the *Journal of Negro History*, 22, July 1937: 299–320.
8. The ambivalent status of the free Negro produced a wide variety of reactions within that group ranging from militant support of slave resistance, through flight, to complete acceptance and support of white dominance.
9. This may not have been the case with entrepreneurs who contracted for slave labor.
10. See, e.g., Williston H. Lofton, "Northern Labor and the Negro during the Civil War," in the *Journal of Negro History*, 34, July, 1949: 251–273.
11. A dramatic journalistic account of these riots can be found in Irving Werstein, *July, 1863*, New York, 1957.
12. Albon P. Man, "Labor Competition and the New York Draft Riots of 1863," in the *Journal of Negro History*, 36, 4, 1951: 375–405.
13. Fred H. Harrington, "The Fort Jackson Mutiny," in the *Journal of Negro History*, 27, 1942: 420–431.
14. This is not to deny the continued importance of economic factors in defining race relations. Perhaps the strongest statement of the economic interpretation of race relations is Oliver C. Cox, *Caste, Class and Race*, New York, 1948.
15. See E. Franklin Frazier, "Theoretical Structure of Sociology and Sociological Research," *British Journal of Sociology*, 4, 4, Dec. 1953: 293–311 and C. Vann Woodward, *The Strange Career of Jim Crow*, new and rev. ed., New York, 1957.
16. Woodward, *loc. cit.*
17. Compulsory education made law by Negro legislators in some Southern states.
18. "Pull" factors based on the glowing pictures of the North and on recruitment of Southern Negro labor were also important in this migration.

19. Note the importance attached to "mixing" in the current de-segregation dispute.
20. See the mimeographed publications on lynching compiled by the Department of Records and Research of Tuskegee Institute.
21. The Chicago Commission on Race Relations, *The Negro in Chicago*, Chicago, 1922.
22. See note 20.
23. See, e.g., Carl I. Hovland and R. R. Sears, "Correlation of Economic Indices with Lynchings," *Journal of Psychology*, 9, 1940: 301–310 and Alexander Mintz, "Re-examination of Correlations between Lynchings and Economic Indices," *Journal of Abnormal and Social Psychology*, 41, 1946: 154–160.
24. Edgar A. Schuler, "The Houston Race Riot, 1917," in the *Journal of Negro History*, 29, 1944: 300–338, remains the best treatment of this uprising of Negro troops.
25. Many of these sentences were later reduced.
26. Chicago Commission on Race Relations, *op. cit.*, is the best descriptive and analytical study of a race riot yet published.
27. See the mimeographed report by George Schermer on the Fairgrounds Park incident in St. Louis for a careful analysis of one such disturbance.
28. For an excellent account of the Cicero disturbance see William Gremley, "Social Control in Cicero," *Brit. Jnl. of Sociology*, 3, 4, Dec. 1952: 322–338.
29. Chicago Commission on Human Relations, *The Trumbull Park Homes Disturbances*, Chicago, n.d.
30. It is too early yet to assess the meaning of a new wave of bombings, including attacks on synagogues, in Illinois and Georgia which began in the fall of 1958.
31. Activity in this area is covered in detail in the periodical, *Race Relations Law Reporter*.
32. Events in this area are covered in detail in the *Southern School News*.

IV. Modern Gains, Losses, and Patterns of Suppression: The Kerner Commission Report

Although major population shifts among black Americans have occurred since Emancipation, there have been only minor shifts in social position relative to white Americans. Black Americans have moved in large numbers from the rural to the urban South, and from the urban South to the urban North. Yet in the North or South, in rural or urban areas, black Americans are not proportionately represented in all strata of the social system of the United States. They are severely overrepresented at the very bottom of the stratification order and underrepresented in the middle and upper levels. The recent "Report of the National Advisory Commission on Civil Disorders" provides a descriptive account of the current black American condition, including some suggestions for change. Chapters 11 through 15 are drawn entirely from the Kerner Commission Report.

The first selection from this report is a treatment of population shifts among Negroes to the urban North and of the formation of racial ghettos. Chapters 12 and 13 deal with unemployment and family life within the ghetto and with more general ghetto life conditions such as crime, health and sanitation, and exploitation. The final two selections from the report deal with the immigrant and black American experience, and with a program of reform, respectively. Chapter 14 is in noteworthy contrast to black American studies which stress qualitative distinctions between Negroes and immigrant groups. Chapter 15 is noteworthy for its straightforward statement of reform goals and its failure to deal with the issue of means by which these goals are likely to be achieved. Chapter 16 attempts to present a more definitive characterization of black American history as a cyclic social process. It is within this context that the modern gains and losses of black Americans should be seen.

11. The Formation of the Racial Ghettos

One new phenomenon of the black American social situation is the rapid expansion of population concentrations in the urban North. Racist practices by the various agents and agencies of the Northern metropolitan areas have given rise to virtual confinement of blacks in specific areas and to a progressive formation of ghettos in these areas. The hope for a better life, which inspires this migration for many blacks, fades quickly as the life condition of the ghetto is experienced. Yet as the tables suggest, possibilities for change in this situation exist, and these possibilities are explored in subsequent chapters.

KERNER COMMISSION REPORT

Major Trends in Negro Population

Throughout the 20th century, and particularly in the last three decades, the Negro population of the United States has been steadily moving—from rural areas to urban, from South to North and West.

In 1910, 2.7 million Negroes lived in American cities—28 percent of the nation's Negro population of 9.8 million. Today, about 15 million Negro Americans live in metropolitan areas, or 69 percent of the Negro population of 21.5 million. In 1910, 885,000 Negroes—9 percent—lived outside the South. Now, almost 10 million, about 45 percent, live in the North or West.

These shifts in population have resulted from three basic trends:

A rapid increase in the size of the Negro population.

A continuous flow of Negroes from Southern rural areas, partly to large cities in the South, but primarily to large cities in the North and West.

An increasing concentration of Negroes in large metropolitan areas within racially segregated neighborhoods.

Taken together, these trends have produced large and constantly growing concentrations of Negro population within big cities in all parts of the nation. Because most major civil disorders of recent years occurred in

From *Report of the National Advisory Commission on Civil Disorders* (1968), Part II, pp. 115–121.

predominantly Negro neighborhoods, we have examined the causes of this concentration.

The Growth Rate of the Negro Population

During the first half of this century, the white population of the United States grew at a slightly faster rate than the Negro population. Because fertility rates [1] among Negro women were more than offset by death rates among Negroes and large-scale immigration of whites from Europe, the proportion of Negroes in the country declined from 12 percent in 1900 to 10 percent in 1940.

By the end of World War II—and increasingly since then—major advances in medicine and medical care, together with the increasing youth of the Negro population resulting from higher fertility rates, caused death rates among Negroes to fall much faster than among whites. This is shown in Table 1.

TABLE 1. DEATH RATE/1,000 POPULATION

Year	Whites	Nonwhites	Ratio of Nonwhite Rate to White Rate
1900	17.0	25.0	1.47
1940	10.4	13.8	1.33
1965	9.4	9.6	1.02

In addition, white immigration from outside the United States dropped dramatically after stringent restrictions were adopted in the 1920's. [See Table 2.]

TABLE 2.

20-Year Period	Total Immigration (Millions)
1901–20	14.5
1921–40	4.6
1941–60	3.6

Thus, by mid-century, both factors which had previously offset higher fertility rates among Negro women no longer were in effect.

While Negro fertility rates, after rising rapidly to 1957, have declined sharply in the past decade, white fertility rates have dropped even more, leaving Negro rates much higher in comparison. [See Table 3.]

The result is that Negro population is now growing significantly faster

TABLE 3. LIVE BIRTHS PER 1,000 WOMEN AGED 15–44

Year	White	Nonwhite	Ratio of Nonwhite to White
1940	77.1	102.4	1.33
1957	117.4	163.4	1.39
1965	91.4	133.9	1.46

than white population. From 1940 to 1960, the white population rose 34.0 percent, but the Negro population rose 46.6 percent. From 1960 to 1966, the white population grew 7.6 percent, whereas Negro population rose 14.4 percent, almost twice as much.

Consequently, the proportion of Negroes in the total population has risen from 10.0 percent in 1950 to 10.5 percent in 1960, and 11.1 percent in 1966.[2]

In 1950, at least one of every ten Americans was Negro; in 1966, one of nine. If this trend continues, one of every eight Americans will be Negro by 1972.

Another consequence of higher birth rates among Negroes is that the Negro population is considerably younger than the white population. In 1966, the median age among whites was 29.1 years, as compared to 21.1 among Negroes. About 35 percent of the white population was under 18 years of age, compared with 45 percent for Negroes. About one of every six children under five and one of every six new babies are Negro.

Negro-white fertility rates bear an interesting relationship to educational experience. Negro women with low levels of education have more children than white women with similar schooling, while Negro women with four years or more of college education have fewer children than white women similarly educated. Table 4 illustrates this.

TABLE 4.

Education Level Attained	Number of Children Ever Born to All Women (Married or Unmarried) 35–39 Years Old, by Level of Education (Based on 1960 Census)	
	Nonwhite	White
Completed elementary school	3.0	2.8
Four years of high school	2.3	2.3
Four years of college	1.7	2.2
Five years or more of college	1.2	1.6

This suggests that the difference between Negro and white fertility rates may decline in the future if Negro educational attainment compares more closely with that of whites, and if a rising proportion of members of both groups complete college.

The Migration of Negroes from the South

The Magnitude of This Migration

In 1910, 91 percent of the Nation's 9.8 million Negroes lived in the South. Twenty-seven percent of American Negroes lived in cities of 2,500 persons or more, as compared to 49 percent of the Nation's white population.

By 1966, the Negro population had increased to 21.5 million, and two significant geographic shifts had taken place. The proportion of Negroes living in the South had dropped to 55 percent, and about 69 percent of all Negroes lived in metropolitan areas compared to 64 percent for whites. While the total Negro population more than doubled from 1910 to 1966, the number living in cities rose over fivefold (from 2.7 million to 14.8 million) and the number outside the South rose elevenfold (from 885,000 to 9.7 million).

Negro migration from the South began after the Civil War. By the turn of the century, sizable Negro populations lived in many large Northern cities—Philadelphia, for example, had 63,400 Negro residents in 1900. The movement of Negroes out of the rural South accelerated during World War I, when floods and boll weevils hurt farming in the South and the industrial demands of the war created thousands of new jobs for unskilled workers in the North. After the war, the shift to mechanized farming spurred the continuing movement of Negroes from rural Southern areas.

The Depression slowed this migratory flow, but World War II set it in motion again. More recently, continuing mechanization of agriculture and

TABLE 5.

Period	Net Negro Out-migration from the South	Annual Average Rate
1910–20	454,000	45,400
1920–30	749,000	74,900
1930–40	348,000	34,800
1940–50	1,597,000	159,700
1950–60	1,457,000	145,700
1960–66	613,000	102,500

the expansion of industrial employment in Northern and Western cities have served to sustain the movement of Negroes out of the South, although at a slightly lower rate. [See Table 5 on p. 153.]

From 1960 to 1963, annual Negro out-migration actually dropped to 78,000 but then rose to over 125,000 from 1963 to 1966.

Important Characteristics of This Migration

It is useful to recall that even the latest scale of Negro migration is relatively small when compared to the earlier waves of European immigrants. A total of 8.8 million immigrants entered the United States between 1901 and 1911, and another 5.7 million arrived during the following decade. Even during the years from 1960 through 1966, the 1.8 million immigrants from abroad were almost three times the 613,000 Negroes who departed the South. In these same 6 years, California alone gained over 1.5 million new residents from internal shifts of American population.

Three major routes of Negro migration from the South have developed. One runs north along the Atlantic Seaboard toward Boston, another north from Mississippi toward Chicago, and the third west from Texas and Louisiana toward California. Between 1955 and 1960, 50 percent of the nonwhite migrants to the New York metropolitan area came from North Carolina, South Carolina, Virginia, Georgia, and Alabama; North Carolina alone supplied 20 percent of all New York's nonwhite immigrants. During the same period, almost 60 percent of the nonwhite migrants to Chicago came from Mississippi, Tennessee, Arkansas, Alabama, and Louisiana; Mississippi accounted for almost one-third. During these years, three-fourths of the nonwhite migrants to Los Angeles came from Texas, Louisiana, Mississippi, Arkansas, and Alabama.

The flow of Negroes from the South has caused the Negro population to grow more rapidly in the North and West, as indicated [in Table 6].

TABLE 6.

Period	Total Negro Population Gains (Millions)		Percent of Gain in North & West
	North & West	South	
1940–50	1.859	0.321	85.2
1950–60	2.741	1.086	71.6
1960–66	2.119	0.517	80.4

As a result, although a much higher proportion of Negroes still reside in the South, the distribution of Negroes throughout the United States is beginning to approximate that of whites, as Tables 7 and 8 show.

TABLE 7. PERCENT DISTRIBUTION OF THE POPULATION BY RE-GION—1950, 1960, AND 1966

	Negro			White		
	1950	1960	1966	1950	1960 [1]	1966
United States	100	100	100	100	100	100
South	68	60	55	27	27	28
North	28	34	37	59	56	55
Northeast	13	16	17	28	26	26
North Central	15	18	20	31	30	29
West	4	6	8	14	16	17

[1] *Rounds to 99.*

TABLE 8. NEGROES AS A PERCENTAGE OF THE TOTAL POPULATION IN THE UNITED STATES AND EACH REGION 1950, 1960, AND 1966

	1950	1960	1966
United States	10	11	11
South	22	21	20
North	5	7	8
West	3	4	5

Negroes in the North and West are now so numerous that natural increase rather than migration provides the greater part of Negro population gains there. And even though Negro migration has continued at a high level, it comprises a constantly declining proportion of Negro growth in these regions. [See Table 9.]

TABLE 9.

Period	Percentage of Total North and West Negro Gain from Southern In-migration
1940–50	85.9
1950–60	53.1
1960–66	28.9

In other words, we have reached the point where the Negro populations of the North and West will continue to expand significantly even if migration from the South drops substantially.

Future Migration

Despite accelerating Negro migration from the South, the Negro population there has continued to rise. [See Table 10.]

Nor is it likely to halt. Negro birth rates in the South, as elsewhere, have fallen sharply since 1957, but so far this decline has been offset by the rising Negro population base remaining in the South. From 1950 to 1960, Southern Negro births generated an average net increase of 254,000 per year and, from 1960 to 1966, an average of 188,000 per year. Even if Negro birth rates continue to fall they are likely to remain high enough to support significant migration to other regions for some time to come.

TABLE 10.

Date	Negro Population in the South (Millions)	Change from Preceding Date	
		Total	Annual Average
1940	9.9	–	–
1950	10.2	321,000	32,100
1960	11.3	1,086,000	108,600
1966	11.8	517,000	86,200

The Negro population in the South is becoming increasingly urbanized. In 1950, there were 5.4 million Southern rural Negroes; by 1960, 4.8 million. But the decline has been more than offset by increases in the urban population. A rising proportion of interregional migration now consists of persons moving from one city to another. From 1960 to 1966, rural Negro population in the South was far below its peak, but the annual average migration of Negroes from the South was still substantial.

These facts demonstrate that Negro migration from the South, which has maintained a high rate for the past 60 years, will continue unless economic conditions change dramatically in either the South or the North and West. This conclusion is reinforced by the fact that most Southern states in recent decades have also experienced outflows of white population. From 1950 to 1960, 11 of the 17 Southern states (including the District of Columbia) "exported" white population—as compared to 13 which "exported" Negro population. Excluding Florida's net gain by migration of 1.5 million, the other 16 Southern states together had a net loss by migration of 1.46 million whites.

The Concentration of Negro Population in Large Cities

Where Negro Urbanization Has Occurred

Statistically, the Negro population in America has become more urbanized, and more metropolitan, than the white population. According to Census Bureau estimates, almost 70 percent of all Negroes in 1966 lived in metropolitan areas, compared to 64 percent of all whites. In the South, more than half the Negro population now lives in cities. Rural Negroes outnumber urban Negroes in only four states: Arkansas, Mississippi, North Carolina, and South Carolina.

Basic data concerning Negro urbanization trends, presented in tables at the conclusion of this chapter, indicate that:

Almost all Negro population growth is occurring within metropolitan areas, primarily within central cities. From 1950 to 1966, the U.S. Negro population rose 6.5 million. Over 98 percent of that increase took place in metropolitan areas—86 percent within central cities, 12 percent in the urban fringe.

The vast majority of white population growth is occurring in suburban portions of metropolitan areas. From 1950 to 1966, 77.8 percent of the white population increase of 35.6 million took place in the suburbs. Central cities received only 2.5 percent of this total white increase. Since 1960, white central-city population has actually declined by 1.3 million.

As a result, central cities are steadily becoming more heavily Negro, while the urban fringes around them remain almost entirely white. The proportion of Negroes in all central cities rose steadily from 12 percent in 1950, to 17 percent in 1960, to 20 percent in 1966. Meanwhile, metropolitan areas outside of central cities remained 95 percent white from 1956 to 1960 and became 96 percent white by 1966.

The Negro population is growing faster, both absolutely and relatively, in the larger metropolitan areas than in the smaller ones. From 1950 to 1966, the proportion of nonwhites in the central cities of metropolitan areas with 1 million or more persons doubled, reaching 26 percent, as compared with 20 percent in the central cities of metropolitan areas containing from 250,000 to 1 million persons and 12 percent in the central cities of metropolitan areas containing under 250,000 persons.

The 12 largest central cities—New York, Chicago, Los Angeles, Philadelphia, Detroit, Baltimore, Houston, Cleveland, Washington, D.C., St. Louis, Milwaukee, and San Francisco—now contain over two-thirds of the Negro population outside the South and almost one-third of the total in the United States. All these cities have experienced rapid increases in Negro population since 1950. In six—Chicago, Detroit, Cleveland, St. Louis, Milwaukee, and San Francisco—the proportion of Negroes at least doubled. In two others—New York and Los Angeles—it probably doubled. In 1968 seven of these cities are over 30 percent Negro, and one, Washington, D.C., is two-thirds Negro.

Factors Causing Residential Segregation in Metropolitan Areas

The early pattern of Negro settlement within each metropolitan area followed that of immigrant groups. Migrants converged on the older sections of the central city because the lowest cost housing was located there, friends and relatives were likely to be living there, and the older neighborhoods then often had good public transportation.

But the later phases of Negro settlement and expansion in metropolitan areas diverge sharply from those typical of white immigrants. As the whites were absorbed by the larger society, many left their predominantly ethnic neighborhoods and moved to outlying areas to obtain newer housing and better schools. Some scattered randomly over the suburban area. Others established new ethnic clusters in the suburbs, but even these rarely contained solely members of a single ethnic group. As a result, most middle-class neighborhoods—both in the suburbs and within central cities —have no distinctive ethnic character, except that they are white.

Nowhere has the expansion of America's urban Negro population followed this pattern of dispersal. Thousands of Negro families have attained incomes, living standards, and cultural levels matching or surpassing those of whites who have "upgraded" themselves from distinctly ethnic neighborhoods. Yet most Negro families have remained within predominantly Negro neighborhoods, primarily because they have been effectively excluded from white residential areas.

Their exclusion has been accomplished through various discriminatory practices, some obvious and overt, others subtle and hidden. Deliberate efforts are sometimes made to discourage Negro families from purchasing or renting homes in all-white neighborhoods. Intimidation and threats of violence have ranged from throwing garbage on lawns and making threatening phone calls to burning crosses in yards and even dynamiting property. More often, real estate agents simply refuse to show homes to Negro buyers.

Many middle-class Negro families, therefore, cease looking for homes beyond all-Negro areas or nearby "changing" neighborhoods. For them, trying to move into all-white neighborhoods is not worth the psychological efforts and costs required.

Another form of discrimination just as significant is white withdrawal from, or refusal to enter, neighborhoods where large numbers of Negroes are moving or already residing. Normal population turnover causes about 20 percent of the residents of average U.S. neighborhoods to move out every year because of income changes, job transfers, shifts in life-cycle position or deaths. This normal turnover rate is even higher in apartment areas. The refusal of whites to move into changing areas when vacancies occur there from normal turnover means that most of these vacancies are eventually occupied by Negroes. An inexorable shift toward heavy Negro occupancy results.

Once this happens, the remaining whites seek to leave, thus confirming the existing belief among whites that complete transformation of a neighborhood is inevitable once Negroes begin to enter. Since the belief itself is one of the major causes of the transformation, it becomes a self-fulfilling prophecy which inhibits the development of racially integrated neighborhoods.

As a result, Negro settlements expand almost entirely through "massive racial transition" at the edges of existing all-Negro neighborhoods, rather than by a gradual dispersion of population throughout the metropolitan area.

Two points are particularly important:

"Massive transition" requires no panic or flight by the original white residents of a neighborhood into which Negroes begin moving. All it requires is the failure or refusal of other whites to fill the vacancies resulting from normal turnover.

Thus, efforts to stop massive transition by persuading present white residents to remain will ultimately fail unless whites outside the neighborhood can be persuaded to move in.

It is obviously true that some residential separation of whites and Negroes would occur even without discriminatory practices by whites. This would result from the desires of some Negroes to live in predominantly Negro neighborhoods and from differences in meaningful social variables, such as income and educational levels. But these factors alone would not lead to the almost complete segregation of whites and Negroes which has developed in our metropolitan areas.

The Exodus of Whites from Central Cities

The process of racial transition in central-city neighborhoods has been only one factor among many others causing millions of whites to move out of central cities as the Negro populations there expanded. More basic perhaps have been the rising mobility and affluence of middle-class families and the more attractive living conditions—particularly better schools —in the suburbs.

Whatever the reason, the result is clear. In 1950, 45.5 million whites lived in central cities. If this population had grown from 1950 to 1960 at the same rate as the Nation's white population as a whole, it would have increased by 8 million. It actually rose only 2.2 million, indicating an outflow of 5.8 million.[3]

From 1960 to 1966, the white outflow appears to have been even more rapid. White population of central cities declined 1.3 million instead of rising 3.6 million—as it would if it had grown at the same rate as the entire white population. In theory, therefore, 4.9 million whites left central cities during these 6 years.

Statistics for all central cities as a group understate the relationship between Negro population growth and white outflow in individual central cities. The fact is, many cities with relatively few Negroes experienced rapid white-population growth, thereby obscuring the size of white outmigration that took place in cities having large increases in Negro population. For example, from 1950 to 1960, the 10 largest cities in the United States had a total Negro population increase of 1.6 million, or 55 percent, while the white population there declined 1.4 million. If the two cities where the white population increased (Los Angeles and Houston) are excluded, the nonwhite population in the remaining eight rose 1.4 million, whereas their white population declined 2.1 million. If the white population in these cities had increased at only half the rate of the white population in the United States as a whole from 1950 to 1960, it would have risen by 1.4 million. Thus, these eight cities actually experienced a white outmigration of at least 3.5 million, while gaining 1.4 million nonwhites.

The Extent of Residential Segregation

The rapid expansion of all-Negro residential areas and large-scale white withdrawal have continued a pattern of residential segregation that has existed in American cities for decades. A recent study[4] reveals that this pattern is present to a high degree in every large city in America. The authors devised an index to measure the degree of residential segregation. The index indicates for each city the percentage of Negroes who would have to move from the blocks where they now live to other blocks in order to provide a perfectly proportional, unsegregated distribution of population.

According to their findings, the average segregation index for 207 of the largest U.S. cities was 86.2 in 1960. This means that an average of over 86 percent of all Negroes would have had to change blocks to create an unsegregated population distribution. Southern cities had a higher average index (90.9) than cities in the Northeast (79.2), the North Central (87.7), or the West (79.3). Only eight cities had index values below 70, whereas over 50 had values above 91.7.

The degree of residential segregation for all 20 cities has been relatively stable, averaging 85.2 in 1940, 87.3 in 1950, and 86.2 in 1960. Variations within individual regions were only slightly larger. However, a recent Census Bureau study shows that in most of the 12 large cities where special censuses were taken in the mid-1960's, the proportions of Negroes living in neighborhoods of greatest Negro concentration had increased since 1960.

Residential segregation is generally more prevalent with respect to Negroes than for any other minority group, including Puerto Ricans, Orientals, and Mexican-Americans. Moreover, it varies little between central city and suburb. This nearly universal pattern cannot be explained in terms of economic discrimination against all low-income groups. Analysis of 15 representative cities indicates that white upper and middle income households are far more segregated from Negro upper and middle-income households than from white lower income households.

In summary, the concentration of Negroes in central cities results from a combination of forces. Some of these forces, such as migration and initial settlement patterns in older neighborhoods, are similar to those which affected previous ethnic minorities. Others—particularly discrimination in employment and segregation in housing and schools—are a result of white attitudes based on race and color. These forces continue to shape the future of the central city. [See Tables 11 through 15.]

TABLE 11. PROPORTION OF NEGROES IN EACH OF THE 30 LARGEST CITIES, 1950, 1960, AND ESTIMATED 1965

	1950	1960	Estimate [1] 1965
New York, N.Y.	10	14	18
Chicago, Ill.	14	23	28
Los Angeles, Calif.	9	14	17
Philadelphia, Pa.	18	26	31
Detroit, Mich.	16	29	34
Baltimore, Md.	24	35	38
Houston, Tex.	21	23	23
Cleveland, Ohio	16	29	34
Washington, D.C.	35	54	66
St. Louis, Mo.	18	29	36
Milwaukee, Wis.	3	8	11
San Francisco, Calif.	6	10	12
Boston, Mass.	5	9	13
Dallas, Tex.	13	19	21
New Orleans, La.	32	37	41
Pittsburgh, Pa.	12	17	20
San Antonio, Tex.	7	7	8
San Diego, Calif.	5	6	7
Seattle, Wash.	3	5	7
Buffalo, N.Y.	6	13	17
Cincinnati, Ohio	16	22	24
Memphis, Tenn.	37	37	40
Denver, Colo.	4	6	9
Atlanta, Ga.	37	38	44
Minneapolis, Minn.	1	2	4
Indianapolis, Ind.	15	21	23
Kansas City, Mo.	12	18	22
Columbus, Ohio	12	16	18
Phoenix, Ariz.	5	5	5
Newark, N.J.	17	34	47

[1] *Except for Cleveland, Buffalo, Memphis, and Phoenix, for which a special census has been made in recent years, these are very rough estimations computed on the basis of the change in relative proportions of Negro births and deaths since 1960.*
Source: U.S. Department of Commerce, Bureau of the Census, BLS Report No. 332, p. 11.

TABLE 12. PERCENT OF ALL NEGROES IN SELECTED CITIES LIVING IN CENSUS TRACTS GROUPED ACCORDING TO PROPORTION NEGRO IN 1960 AND 1964–66 [1]

	Year	All Census Tracts	75 Percent or More Negro	50 to 74 Percent Negro	25 to 49 Percent Negro	Less Than 25 Percent Negro
Cleveland, Ohio	1960	100	72	16	8	4
	1965	100	80	12	4	4
Phoenix, Ariz.	1960	100	19	36	24	21
	1965	100	18	23	42	17
Buffalo, N.Y.	1960	100	35	47	6	12
	1966	100	69	10	13	8
Louisville, Ky.	1960	100	57	13	17	13
	1964	100	67	13	10	10
Rochester, N.Y.	1960	100	8	43	17	32
	1964	100	16	45	24	15
Sacramento, Calif.	1960	100	9	–	14	77
	1964	100	8	14	28	50
Des Moines, Iowa	1960	100	–	28	31	41
	1966	100	–	42	19	39
Providence, R.I.	1960	100	–	23	2	75
	1965	100	–	16	46	38
Shreveport, La.	1960	100	79	10	7	4
	1966	100	90	–	6	4
Evansville, Ind.	1960	100	34	27	9	30
	1966	100	59	14	–	27
Little Rock, Ark.	1960	100	33	33	19	15
	1964	100	41	18	22	19
Raleigh, N.C.	1960	100	86	–	7	7
	1966	100	88	4	2	6

[1] *Selected cities of 100,000 or more in which a special census was taken in any of the years 1964–66. Ranked according to total population at latest census.*
Source: U.S. Department of Commerce, Bureau of the Census, BLS Report No. 332, p. 12.

TABLE 13. PERCENT DISTRIBUTION OF POPULATION BY LOCATION, INSIDE AND OUTSIDE METROPOLITAN AREAS, 1950, 1960, AND 1966

	Negro			White		
	1950	1960	1966	1950	1960	1966
United States	100	100	100	100	100	100
Metropolitan areas	56	65	69	59	63	64
Central cities	43	51	56	34	30	27
Urban fringe	13	13	13	26	33	37
Smaller cities, towns, and rural	44	35	31	41	37	36

Source: U.S. Department of Commerce, Bureau of the Census, BLS Report No. 332, p. 9.

TABLE 14. NEGROES AS A PERCENTAGE OF TOTAL POPULATION BY LOCATION INSIDE AND OUTSIDE METROPOLITAN AREAS AND BY SIZE OF METROPOLITAN AREAS—1950, 1960 AND 1966

	Percent Negro		
	1950	1960	1966
United States	10	11	11
Metropolitan areas	9	11	12
Central cities	12	17	20
Central cities in metropolitan areas [1] of—			
1,000,000 or more	13	19	26 [2]
250,000 to 1,000,000	12	15	20 [2]
Under 250,000	12	12	12 [2]
Urban fringe	5	5	4
Smaller cities, towns and rural	11	10	10

[1] In metropolitan areas of population shown as of 1960.
[2] Percent nonwhite; data for Negroes are not available. The figures used are estimated to be closely comparable to those for Negroes alone, using a check for Negro and nonwhite percentages in earlier years.
Source: U.S. Department of Commerce, Bureau of the Census, BLS Report No. 332, p. 10.

TABLE 15. POPULATION CHANGE BY LOCATION, INSIDE AND OUTSIDE METROPOLITAN AREAS, 1950–66

[Numbers in Millions]

	Population						Change, 1950–66			
	Negro			White			Negro		White	
	1950	1960	1966	1950	1960	1966	Number	Percent	Number	Percent
United States	15.0	18.8	21.5	135.2	158.8	170.8	6.5	43	35.6	26
Metropolitan areas	8.4	12.2	14.8	80.3	99.7	109.0	6.4	77	28.7	36
Central cities	6.5	9.7	12.1	45.5	47.7	46.4	5.6	87	.9	2
Urban fringe	1.9	2.5	2.7	34.8	52.0	62.5	.8	42	27.7	79
Small cities, towns, and rural	6.7	6.7	6.7	54.8	59.2	61.8	(¹)	1	7.0	13

¹ Rounds to less than 50,000.
Source: U.S. Department of Commerce, Bureau of the Census, BLS Report No. 332, p. 8.

NOTES

1. The "fertility rate" is the number of live births per year per 1,000 women age 15 to 44 in the group concerned.
2. These proportions are undoubtedly too low because the Census Bureau has consistently undercounted the number of Negroes in the U.S. by as much as 10 percent.
3. The outflow of whites may be somewhat smaller than the 5.8 million difference between these figures, because the ages of the whites in many central cities are higher than in the Nation as a whole, and therefore the population would have grown somewhat more slowly.
4. "Negroes in Cities," Karl and Alma Taeuber, Aldine Publishing Co., Chicago (1965).

12. Unemployment, Family Structure, and Social Disorganization

That some degree of economic gain over time took place for black Americans, as for whites, is apparent in Chapter 12. It is important that from 1947 to 1966 the percentage of black families with incomes under $3,000 declined from 65 to 32 percent. Equally important, however, is that in 1966 only 13 percent of white families fell into this income category—a proportion roughly three times smaller than that of black families. Some of the statistics on conditions to which such poverty gives rise among blacks and whites in urban areas are presented in this chapter.

KERNER COMMISSION REPORT

Recent Economic Trends

The Negro population in our country is as diverse in income, occupation, family composition, and other variables as the white community. Nevertheless, for purposes of analysis, three major Negro economic groups can be identified.

The first and smallest group consists of middle and upper income individuals and households whose educational, occupational, and cultural characteristics are similar to those of middle and upper income white groups.

The second and largest group contains Negroes whose incomes are above the "poverty level" but who have not attained the educational, occupational, or income status typical of middle-class Americans.

The third group has very low educational, occupational, and income attainments and lives below the "poverty level."

A recent compilation of data on American Negroes by the Departments of Labor and Commerce shows that although incomes of both Negroes and whites have been rising rapidly,

Negro incomes still remain far below those of whites. Negro median family income was only 58 percent of the white median in 1966.

From *Report of the National Advisory Commission on Civil Disorders* (1968), Part II, pp. 123–131.

Negro family income is not keeping pace with white family income growth. In constant 1965 dollars, median nonwhite income in 1947 was $2,174 lower than median white income. By 1966, the gap had grown to $3,036.

The Negro upper income group is expanding rapidly and achieving sizeable income gains. In 1966, 28 percent of all Negro families received incomes of $7,000 or more, compared with 55 percent of white families. This was 1.6 times the proportion of Negroes receiving comparable incomes in 1960, and four times greater than the proportion receiving such incomes in 1947. Moreover, the proportion of Negroes employed in high-skill, high-status, and well-paying jobs rose faster than comparable proportions among whites from 1960 to 1966.

As Negro incomes have risen, the size of the lowest income group has grown smaller, and the middle and upper groups have grown larger—both relatively and absolutely. [See Table 1.]

About two-thirds of the lowest income group—or 20 percent of all Negro families —are making no significant economic gains despite continued general prosperity. Half of these hard-core disadvantaged—more than 2 million persons—live in central-city neighborhoods. Recent special censuses in Los Angeles and Cleveland indicate that the incomes of persons living in the worst slum areas have not risen at all during this period, unemployment rates have declined only slightly, the proportion of families with female heads has increased, and housing conditions have worsened even though rents have risen.

TABLE 1.

Group	Percentage of Negro Families			Percentage of White Families
	1947	1960	1966	1966
$7,000 and over	7	17	28	55
$3,000 to $6,999	29	40	41	33
Under $3,000	65	44	32	13

Thus, between 2.0 and 2.5 million poor Negroes are living in disadvantaged neighborhoods of central cities in the United States. These persons comprise only slightly more than 1 percent of the Nation's total population, but they make up about 16 to 20 percent of the total Negro population of all central cities, and a much higher proportion in certain cities.

Unemployment and Underemployment

The Critical Significance of Employment

The capacity to obtain and hold a "good job" is the traditional test of participation in American society. Steady employment with adequate compensation provides both purchasing power and social status. It develops the capabilities, confidence, and self-esteem an individual needs to be a responsible citizen, and provides a basis for a stable family life. As Daniel P. Moynihan has written:

The principal measure of progress toward equality will be that of employment. It is the primary source of individual or group identity. In America what you do is what you are: to do nothing is to be nothing; to do little is to be little. The equations are implacable and blunt, and ruthlessly public.

For the Negro American it is already, and will continue to be, the master problem. It is the measure of white bona fides. It is the measure of Negro competence, and also of the competence of American society. Most importantly, the linkage between problems of employment and the range of social pathology that afflicts the Negro community is unmistakable. Employment not only controls the present for the Negro American but, in a most profound way, it is creating the future as well.

For residents of disadvantaged Negro neighborhoods, obtaining good jobs is vastly more difficult than for most workers in society. For decades, social, economic, and psychological disadvantages surrounding the urban Negro poor have impaired their work capacities and opportunities. The result is a cycle of failure—the employment disabilities of one generation breed those of the next.

Negro Unemployment

Unemployment rates among Negroes have declined from a post-Korean War high of 12.6 percent in 1958 to 8.2 percent in 1967. Among married Negro men, the unemployment rate for 1967 was down to 3.2 percent.[1]

Notwithstanding this decline, unemployment rates for Negroes are still double those for whites in every category, including married men, as they have been throughout the postwar period. Moreover, since 1954, even during the current unprecedented period of sustained economic growth, unemployment among Negroes has been continuously above the 6 percent "recession" level widely regarded as a sign of serious economic weakness when prevalent for the entire work force.

While the Negro unemployment rate remains high in relation to the white rate, the number of additional jobs needed to lower this to the level of white unemployment is surprisingly small. In 1967, approximately 3 million persons were unemployed during an average week, of whom about 638,000, or 21 percent, were nonwhites. When corrected for undercounting, total nonwhite unemployment was approximately 712,000 or 8 percent of the nonwhite labor force. To reduce the unemployment rate to 3.4 percent, the rate prevalent among whites, jobs must be found for 57.5 percent of these unemployed persons. This amounts to nearly 409,000 jobs, or about 27 percent of the net number of new jobs added to the economy in the year 1967 alone and only slightly more than one-half of 1 percent of all jobs in the United States in 1967.

The Low-status and Low-paying Nature of Many Negro Jobs

Even more important perhaps than unemployment is the related problem of the undesirable nature of many jobs open to Negroes. Negro workers are concentrated in the lowest skilled and lowest paying occupations. These jobs often involve substandard wages, great instability and

TABLE 2.

Type of Occupation	Percentage of Male Workers in Each Type of Occupation, 1966		Median Earnings of All Male Civilians In Each Occupation, 1965
	White	Nonwhite	
Professional, technical, and managerial	27	9	$7,603 [1]
Clerical and sales	14	9	5,532 [1]
Craftsmen and foremen	20	12	6,270
Operatives	20	27	5,046
Service workers	6	16	3,436
Nonfarm laborers	6	20	2,410
Farmers and farm workers	7	8	1,669 [1]

[1] *Average of two categories from normal Census Bureau categories as combined in data presented in The Social and Economic Conditions of Negroes in the United States (BLS No. 332).*

uncertainty of tenure, extremely low status in the eyes of both employer and employee, little or no chance for meaningful advancement, and unpleasant or exhausting duties. Negro men in particular are more than three times as likely as whites to be in unskilled or service jobs which pay far less than most. [See Table 2.]

This concentration in the least desirable jobs can be viewed another way by calculating the changes which would occur if Negro men were employed in various occupations in the same proportions as the male labor force as a whole (not solely the white labor force). [See Table 3.]

TABLE 3.

Type of Occupation	Number of Male Nonwhite Workers, 1966			
	As actually distributed [1]	If distributed the same as all male workers	Difference	
			Number	*Percent*
Professional, technical, and managerial	415,000	1,173,000	+758,000	+183
Clerical and sales	415,000	628,000	+213,000	+ 51
Craftsmen and foremen	553,000	894,000	+341,000	+ 62
Operatives	1,244,000	964,000	−280,000	− 23
Service workers	737,000	326,000	−411,000	− 56
Nonfarm laborers	922,000	340,000	−582,000	− 63
Farmers and farm workers	369,000	330,000	− 39,000	− 11

[1] *Estimates based upon percentages set forth in BLS No. 332, p. 41.*

Thus, upgrading the employment of Negro men to make their occupational distribution identical with that of the labor force as a whole would have an immense impact upon the nature of their occupations. About 1.3 million nonwhite men—or 28 percent of those employed in 1966—would move up the employment ladder into one of the higher status and higher paying categories. The effect of such a shift upon the incomes of Negro men would be very great. Using the 1966 job distribution, the shift indicated above would produce about $4.8 billion more earned income for nonwhite men alone if they received the 1965 median income in each occupation. This would be a rise of approximately 30 percent in the earnings actually received by all nonwhite men in 1965 (not counting any sources of income other than wages and salaries).

Of course, the kind of "instant upgrading" visualized in these calculations does not represent a practical alternative for national policy. The economy cannot drastically reduce the total number of low-status jobs it now contains, or shift large numbers of people upward in occupation in any short period. Therefore, major upgrading in the employment status of Negro men must come through a faster relative expansion of higher level jobs than lower level jobs (which has been occurring for several decades), an improvement in the skills of nonwhite workers so they can obtain a high proportion of those added better jobs, and a drastic reduction of discriminatory hiring and promotion practices in all enterprises, both private and public.

Nevertheless, this hypothetical example clearly shows that the concentration of male Negro employment at the lowest end of the occupational scale is greatly depressing the incomes of U.S. Negroes in general. In fact, this is the single most important source of poverty among Negroes. It is even more important than unemployment, as can be shown by a second hypothetical calculation. In 1966, there were about 724,000 unemployed nonwhites in the United States on the average, including adults and teenagers, and allowing for the Census Bureau undercount of Negroes. If every one of these persons had been employed and had received the median amount earned by nonwhite males in 1966 ($3,864), this would have added a total of $2.8 billion to nonwhite income as a whole. If only enough of these persons had been employed at that wage to reduce nonwhite unemployment from 7.3 percent to 3.3 percent—the rate among whites in 1966—then the income gain for nonwhites would have totaled about $1.5 billion. But if nonwhite unemployment remained at 7.3 percent, and nonwhite men were upgraded so that they had the same occupational distribution and incomes as all men in the labor force considered together, this would have produced about $4.8 billion in additional income, as noted above (using 1965 earnings for calculation). Thus the potential income gains from upgrading the male nonwhite labor force are much larger than those from reducing nonwhite unemployment.

This conclusion underlines the difficulty of improving the economic status of Negro men. It is far easier to create new jobs than either to create new jobs with relatively high status and earning power, or to upgrade existing employed or partly employed workers into such better quality employment. Yet only such upgrading will eliminate the fundamental basis of poverty and deprivation among Negro families.

Access to good-quality jobs clearly affects the willingness of Negro men actively to seek work. In riot cities surveyed by the Commission with the largest percentage of Negroes in skilled and semiskilled jobs, Negro men participated in the labor force to the same extent as, or greater than, white men. Conversely, where most Negro men were heavily concentrated in menial jobs, they participated less in the labor force than white men.

Even given similar employment, Negro workers with the same education as white workers are paid less. This disparity doubtless results to some extent from inferior training in segregated schools, and also from the fact that large numbers of Negroes are only now entering certain occupations for the first time. However, the differentials are so large and so universal at all educational levels that they clearly reflect the patterns of discrimination which characterize hiring and promotion practices in many segments of the economy. For example, in 1966, among persons who had completed high school, the median income of Negroes was only 73 percent that of whites. Even among persons with an eighth-grade education, Negro median income was only 80 percent of white median income.

At the same time, a higher proportion of Negro women than white women participates in the labor force at nearly all ages except 16 to 19. For instance, in 1966, 55 percent of nonwhite women from 25 to 34 years of age were employed, compared to only 38 percent of white women in the same age group. The fact that almost half of all adult Negro women work reflects the fact that so many Negro males have unsteady and low-paying jobs. Yet even though Negro women are often better able to find work than Negro men, the unemployment rate among adult nonwhite women (20 years old and over) in 1967 was 7.1 percent, compared to the 4.3 percent rate among adult nonwhite men.

Unemployment rates are, of course, much higher among teenagers, both Negro and white, than among adults; in fact about one-third of all unemployed Negroes in 1967 were between 16 and 19 years old. During the first 9 months of 1967, the unemployment rate among nonwhite teenagers was 26.5 percent; for whites, it was 10.6 percent. About 219,300 nonwhite teenagers were unemployed.[2] About 58,300 were still in school but were actively looking for jobs.

Subemployment in Disadvantaged Negro Neighborhoods

In disadvantaged areas, employment conditions for Negroes are in a chronic state of crisis. Surveys in low-income neighborhoods of nine large cities made by the Department of Labor late in 1966 revealed that the rate of unemployment there was 9.3 percent, compared to 7.3 percent for Negroes generally and 3.3 percent for whites. Moreover, a high proportion of the persons living in these areas were "underemployed," that is, they were either part-time workers looking for full-time employment, or full-time workers earning less than $3000 per year, or had dropped out of the labor force. The Department of Labor estimated that this underemployment is 2½ times greater than the number of unemployed in these areas. Therefore, the "subemployment rate," including both the unemployed and the underemployed, was about 32.7 percent in the nine areas surveyed, or 8.8 times greater than the overall unemployment rate for all U.S. workers. Since underemployment also exists outside disadvantaged neighborhoods, comparing the full subemployment rate in these areas with the unemployment rate for the Nation as a whole is not entirely valid. However, it provides some measure of the enormous disparity between employment conditions in most of the Nation and those prevalent in disadvantaged Negro areas in our large cities.

TABLE 4.

Group	Nonwhite Subemployment in Disadvantaged Areas of All Central Cities, 1967		
	Unemploy- ment	Under- employment	Total sub- employment
Adult men	102,000	230,000	332,000
Adult women	118,000	266,000	384,000
Teenagers	98,000	220,000	318,000
Total	318,000	716,000	1,034,000

The critical problem is to determine the actual number of those unemployed and underemployed in central-city Negro ghettos. This involves a process of calculation which is detailed in the note at the end of this chapter. The outcome of this process is summarized in Table 4.

Therefore, in order to bring subemployment in these areas down to a level equal to unemployment alone among whites, enough steady, reasonably paying jobs (and the training and motivation to perform them) must be provided to eliminate all underemployment and reduce unemployment by 65 percent. For all three age groups combined, this deficit amounted to 923,000 jobs in 1967.

The Magnitude of Poverty in Disadvantaged Neighborhoods

The chronic unemployment problems in the central city, aggravated by the constant arrival of new unemployed migrants, is the fundamental cause of the persistent poverty in disadvantaged Negro areas.

"Poverty" in the affluent society is more than absolute deprivation. Many of the poor in the United States would be well off in other societies. Relative deprivation—inequality—is a more useful concept of poverty with respect to the Negro in America because it encompasses social and political exclusions as well as economic inequality. Because of the lack of data of this type, we have had to focus our analysis on a measure of poverty which is both economic and absolute—the Social Security Administration's "poverty level"[3] concept. It is clear, however, that broader measures of poverty would substantiate the conclusions that follow.

In 1966, there were 29.7 million persons in the United States—15.3 percent of the Nation's population—with incomes below the "poverty level," as defined by the Social Security Administration. Of these, 20.3 million were white (68.3 percent), and 9.3 million nonwhite (31.7 percent). Thus, about 11.9 percent of the Nation's whites and 40.6 percent of its nonwhites were poor under the Social Security definition.

The location of the Nation's poor is best shown from 1964 data as indicated by Table 5.

TABLE 5.

| Group | Percentage of Those in Poverty in Each Group Living in Metropolitan Areas | | | |
	In central cities	Outside central cities	Other areas	Total
Whites	23.8	21.8	54.4	100
Nonwhites	41.7	10.8	47.5	100
Total	29.4	18.4	52.2	100

Source: Social Security Administration.

The following facts concerning poverty are relevant to an understanding of the problems faced by people living in disadvantaged neighborhoods.[4]

In central cities 30.7 percent of nonwhite families of two or more persons lived in poverty compared to only 8.8 percent of whites.

Of the 10.1 million poor persons in central cities in 1964, about 4.4 million of these (43.6 percent) were nonwhites, and 5.7 million (56.4 percent) were whites. The poor whites were much older on the average than the poor nonwhites. The proportion of poor persons 65 years old or older was 23.2 percent among whites, but only 6.8 percent among nonwhites.

Poverty was more than twice as prevalent among nonwhite families with female heads than among those with male heads, 57 percent compared to 21 percent. In central cities, 26 percent of all nonwhite families of two or more persons had female heads, as compared to 12 percent of white families.

Among nonwhite families headed by a female, and having children under 6, the incidence of poverty was 81 percent. Moreover, there were 243,000 such families living in poverty in central cities—or over 9 percent of all nonwhite families in those cities.

Among all children living in poverty within central cities, nonwhites outnumbered whites by over 400,000. The number of poor nonwhite children equaled or surpassed the number of white poor children in every age group. [See Table 6.]

TABLE 6. NUMBER OF CHILDREN LIVING IN POVERTY (MILLIONS)

Age Group	White	Nonwhite	Percent of Total Nonwhite
Under 6	0.9	1.0	53
6 to 15	1.0	1.3	57
16 to 21	0.4	0.4	50
Total	2.3	2.7	54

Two stark facts emerge:

54 percent of all poor children in central cities in 1964 were nonwhites.

Of the 4.4 million nonwhites living in poverty within central cities in 1964, 52 percent were children under 16 and 61 percent were under 21.

Since 1964, the number of nonwhite families living in poverty within central cities has remained about the same; hence, these poverty conditions are probably still prevalent in central cities in terms of absolute numbers of persons, although the proportion of persons in poverty may have dropped slightly.[5]

The Social Impact of Employment Problems in Disadvantaged Negro Areas

Unemployment and the Family

The high rates of unemployment and underemployment in racial ghettos are evidence, in part, that many men living in these areas are seeking, but cannot obtain, jobs which will support a family. Perhaps equally important, most jobs they can get are at the low end of the occupational scale, and often lack the necessary status to sustain a worker's self-respect, or the respect of his family and friends. These same men are also constantly confronted with the message of discrimination: "You are inferior because of a trait you did not cause and cannot change." This message reinforces feelings of inadequacy arising from repeated failure to obtain and keep decent jobs.

Wives of these men are forced to work and usually produce more money. If the men stay at home without working, their inadequacies constantly confront them and tensions arise between them and their wives and children. Under these pressures, it is not surprising that many of these men flee their responsibilities as husbands and fathers, leaving home, and drifting from city to city, or adopting the style of "street corner men."

Statistical evidence tends to document this. A close correlation exists between the number of nonwhite married women separated from their husbands each year and the unemployment rate among nonwhite males 20 years old and over. Similarly, from 1948 to 1962, the number of new Aid to Families with Dependent Children cases rose and fell with the nonwhite male unemployment rate. Since 1963, however, the number of new cases —most of them Negro children—has steadily increased even though the unemployment rate among nonwhite males has declined. The impact of marital status on employment among Negroes is shown by the fact that in 1967 the proportion of married men either divorced or separated from their wives was more than twice as high among unemployed nonwhite men as among employed nonwhite men. Moreover, among those participating in the labor force, there was a higher proportion of married men with wives present than with wives absent. [See Table 7.]

TABLE 7. UNEMPLOYMENT RATE AND PARTICIPATION IN TOTAL LABOR FORCE, 25- TO 54-YEAR-OLD NONWHITE MEN, BY MARITAL STATUS, MARCH, 1967

	Unemployment Rate, Nonwhite	Labor Force Participation (Percent), Nonwhite
Married, wife present	3.7	96.7
Other (separated, divorced, widowed)	8.7	77.6

Fatherless Families

The abandonment of the home by many Negro males affects a great many children growing up in the racial ghetto. As previously indicated, most American Negro families are headed by men, just like most other American families. Yet the proportion of families with female heads is much greater among Negroes than among whites at all income levels, and has been rising in recent years. [See Table 8 on p. 176.]

This disparity between white and nonwhite families is far greater among the lowest income families—those most likely to reside in disadvantaged big-city neighborhoods—than among higher income families. Among families with incomes under $3,000 in 1966, the proportion with female heads was 42 percent for Negroes but only 23 percent for whites.

TABLE 8. PROPORTION OF FAMILIES OF VARIOUS TYPES
[In Percent]

	Husband-Wife		Female Head	
Date	White	Nonwhite	[White]	Nonwhite
1950	88.0	77.7	8.5	17.6
1960	88.7	73.6	8.7	22.4
1966	88.8	72.7	8.9	23.7

In contrast, among families with incomes of $7,000 or more, 8 percent of Negro families had female heads compared to 4 percent of whites.

The problems of "fatherlessness" are aggravated by the tendency of the poor to have large families. The average poor, urban, nonwhite family contains 4.8 persons, as compared with 3.7 for the average poor, urban, white family. This is one of the primary factors in the poverty status of nonwhite households in large cities.

The proportion of fatherless families appears to be increasing in the poorest Negro neighborhoods. In the Hough section of Cleveland, the proportion of families with female heads rose from 23 to 32 percent from 1960 to 1965. In the Watts section of Los Angeles it rose from 36 to 39 percent during the same period.

The handicap imposed on children growing up without fathers, in an atmosphere of poverty and deprivation, is increased because many mothers must work to provide support. Table 9 illustrates the disparity between the proportion of nonwhite women in the child-rearing ages who are in the labor force and the comparable proportion of white women:

TABLE 9.

	Percentage of Women in the Labor Force	
Age Group	Nonwhite	White
20 to 24	55	51
25 to 34	55	38
35 to 44	61	45

With the father absent and the mother working, many ghetto children spend the bulk of their time on the streets—the streets of a crime-ridden, violence-prone, and poverty-stricken world. The image of success in this world is not that of the "solid citizen," the responsible husband and father, but rather that of the "hustler" who promotes his own interests by exploiting others. The dope sellers and the numbers runners are the "successful" men because their earnings far outstrip those men who try to climb the economic ladder in honest ways.

Young people in the ghetto are acutely conscious of a system which appears to offer rewards to those who illegally exploit others, and failure to those who struggle under traditional responsibilities. Under these circumstances, many adopt exploitation and the "hustle" as a way of life, disclaiming both work and marriage in favor of casual and temporary liaisons. This pattern reinforces itself from one generation to the next, creating a "culture of poverty" and an ingrained cynicism about society and its institutions.

The "Jungle"

The culture of poverty that results from unemployment and family disorganization generates a system of ruthless, exploitative relationships within the ghetto. Prostitution, dope addiction, casual sexual affairs, and crime create an environmental jungle characterized by personal insecurity and tension. The effects of this development are stark:

> The rate of illegitimate births among nonwhite women has risen sharply in the past two decades. In 1940, 16.8 percent of all nonwhite births were illegitimate. By 1950 this proportion was 18 percent; by 1960, 21.6 percent; by 1966, 26.3 percent. In the ghettos of many large cities, illegitimacy rates exceed 50 percent.

> The rate of illegitimacy among nonwhite women is closely related to low income and high unemployment. In Washington, D.C., for example, an analysis of 1960 census tracts shows that in tracts with unemployment rates of 12 percent or more among nonwhite men, illegitimacy was over 40 percent. But in tracts with unemployment rates of 2.9 percent and below among nonwhite men, reported illegitimacy was under 20 percent. A similar contrast existed between tracts in which median nonwhite income was under $4,000 (where illegitimacy was 38 percent) and those in which it was $8,000 and over (where illegitimacy was 12 percent).

> Narcotics addiction is also heavily concentrated in low-income Negro neighborhoods, particularly in New York City. Of the 59,720 addicts known to the U.S. Bureau of Narcotics at the end of 1966, just over 50 percent were Negroes. Over 52 percent of all known addicts lived within New York State, mostly in Harlem and other Negro neighborhoods. These figures undoubtedly greatly understate the actual number of persons using narcotics regularly—especially those under 21.

> Not surprisingly, at every age from 6 through 19, the proportion of children from homes with both parents present who actually attend school is higher than the proportion of children from homes with only one parent or neither present.

> Rates of juvenile delinquency, venereal disease, dependency upon AFDC support, and use of public assistance in general are much higher in disadvantaged Negro areas than in other parts of large cities. Data taken from New York City contrasting predominantly Negro neighborhoods with the city as a whole clearly illustrate this fact. [See Table 10 on p. 178.]

In conclusion: in 1965, 1.2 million nonwhite children under 16 lived in central city families headed by a woman under 65. The great majority of these children were growing up in poverty under conditions that make them better candidates for crime and civil disorder than for jobs providing an entry into American society. . . .

TABLE 10. SOCIAL DISTRESS—MAJOR PREDOMINANTLY NEGRO NEIGHBOR-
HOODS IN NEW YORK CITY AND THE CITY AS A WHOLE

	Juvenile Delinquency [1]	Venereal Disease [2]	ADC [3]	Public Assistance [4]
Brownsville	125.3	609.9	459.0	265.8
East New York	98.6	207.5	148.6	71.8
Bedford-Stuyvesant	115.2	771.3	337.1	197.2
Harlem	110.8	1,603.5	265.7	138.1
South Bronx	84.4	308.3	278.5	165.5
New York City	52.2	269.1	120.7	60.8

[1] Number of offenses per 1,000 persons 7–20 years (1965).
[2] Number of cases per 100,000 persons under 21 years (1964).
[3] Number of children in aid to dependent children cases per 1,000 under 18 years, using 1960 population as base (1965).
[4] Welfare assistance recipients per 1,000 persons, using 1960 population as base (1965).

Note: Calculations of Nonwhite Subemployment in Disadvantaged Areas of All Central Cities, 1967

In 1967, total unemployment in the United States was distributed by age and color [as seen in Table 11].

TABLE 11.

Group	Nonwhite	White	Total
Adult men (20 and over)	193,000	866,000	1,059,000
Adult women (20 and over)	241,000	837,000	1,078,000
Teenagers (16–19)	204,000	635,000	839,000
Total	638,000	2,338,000	2,976,000

Adjustments for the Census Bureau undercount of nonwhite males in the labor force amounting to 7.5 percent for the teenage group, 18 percent for the adult male group and approximately 10 percent for adult females result in the revised total employment [seen in Table 12].

These figures cover the entire United States. To provide an estimate of

TABLE 12.

Group	Nonwhite	White	Total
Adult men	228,000	866,000	1,094,000
Adult women	265,000	837,000	1,102,000
Teenagers	219,000	635,000	854,000
Total	712,000	2,338,000	3,050,000

the number of unemployed in disadvantaged neighborhoods within central cities, it is necessary to discover what proportion of the nonwhite unemployed are in central cities and what proportion of those in central cities are within the most disadvantaged neighborhoods. The Department of Labor survey in nine large central cities covering the first 9 months of 1967 showed that these cities contained 27.3 percent of the total nonwhite

TABLE 13. NONWHITE UNEMPLOYMENT IN ALL CENTRAL CITIES [Rounded]

Adult men	130,000
Adult women	151,000
Teenagers	125,000
Total	406,000

labor force in the United States, and 26.4 percent of total nonwhite unemployment. Hence, it is reasonable to assume that nonwhite unemployment is concentrated in central cities to about the same degree as the nonwhite labor force. In turn, the nonwhite labor force is located in central cities in about the same proportion as the nonwhite population, or 57.1 percent in 1967. Thus central-city unemployment among nonwhites was presumably about 57.1 percent of the national figures [see Table 13].

Within large central cities, about 62 percent of all nonwhite families lived in certain Census Tracts which have been designated "poverty areas." These tracts ranked lowest in United States cities over 250,000 persons in size, according to an index of "deprivation" based upon family

TABLE 14. NONWHITE UNEMPLOYMENT IN DISADVANTAGED AREAS OF ALL CENTRAL CITIES, 1967

Adult men	102,000
Adult women	118,000
Teenagers	98,000
Total	318,000

income, children in broken homes, persons with low educational attainment, males in unskilled jobs, and substandard housing. On the assumption that conditions in these poverty areas are comparable to those in the nine disadvantaged areas surveyed by the Department of Labor in 1966, the number of unemployed nonwhites in disadvantaged areas of central cities is as [seen in Table 14].[6]

The number of underemployed nonwhites in these areas was about 2.5 times larger than the number of unemployed. But we have already accounted for some underemployment in the adjustment for undercounting —so we will assume nonwhite underemployment was 2.25 times adjusted unemployment for all three age and sex groups. The resulting rough estimates are as [seen in Table 15].

TABLE 15. NONWHITE SUBEMPLOYMENT IN DISADVANTAGED AREAS OF ALL CENTRAL CITIES, 1967

Group	Unemployment	Underemploy-ment	Total Subemployment
Adult men	102,000	230,000	332,000
Adult women	118,000	266,000	384,000
Teenagers	98,000	220,000	318,000
Total	318,000	716,000	1,034,000

NOTES
1. Adjusted for Census Bureau undercounting.
2. After adjusting for Census Bureau undercounting.
3. $3335 per year for an urban family of four.
4. Social Security Administration; based on 1964 data.
5. For the Nation as a whole, the proportion of nonwhite families living in poverty, dropped from 39 percent to 35 percent from 1964 to 1966 (defining "family" somewhat differently from the definition used in the data above). The number of such families declined from 1.9 million to 1.7 million. However, the number and proportion of all nonwhites living in central cities rose in the same period. As a result, the number of nonwhite families living in so-called "poverty areas" of large cities actually rose from 1,561,000 in 1960 to 1,588,000 in 1966.
6. The number of nonwhite unemployed in the more disadvantaged areas was 26 percent higher than it would have been had it been proportional to the total population residing there. Therefore, the proportion of central city nonwhite unemployed in poverty areas is assumed to equal 78.1 percent (62 percent times 1.26).

13. Conditions of Life in the Racial Ghetto

For many in the ghetto, there is no escape. It can be predicted with reasonable accuracy that certain social conditions, clearly incompatible with their own aspirations, hopes, and expectations, will engulf most ghetto residents. Among these conditions are crime, poverty, high mortality rate for infants and mothers, lower life expectancies, and exploitation by retail merchants. It is the growing incompatibility of these conditions with the changing views of what can be legitimately demanded of our society and time that underlies current protest and rebellion in the ghetto and generally among youth keenly sensitive to this dilemma of an affluent society.

KERNER COMMISSION REPORT

The conditions of life in the racial ghetto are strikingly different from those to which most Americans are accustomed—especially white, middle-class Americans. We believe it is important to describe these conditions and their effect on the lives of people who cannot escape from the ghetto.[1]

Crime and Insecurity

Nothing is more fundamental to the quality of life in any area than the sense of personal security of its residents, and nothing affects this more than crime.

In general, crime rates in large cities are much higher than in other areas of our country. Within such cities, crime rates are higher in disadvantaged Negro areas than anywhere else.

The most widely used measure of crime is the number of "index crimes" (homicide, forcible rape, aggravated assault, robbery, burglary, grand larceny, and auto theft) in relation to population. In 1966, 1,754 such crimes were reported to police for every 100,000 Americans. In cities over 250,000, the rate was 3,153, and in cities over 1 million, it was 3,630—or more than double the national average. In suburban areas alone, including

From *Report of the National Advisory Commission on Civil Disorders* (1968), Part II, pp. 133–141.

suburban cities, the rate was only 1,300, or just over one-third the rate in the largest cities.

Within larger cities, personal and property insecurity has consistently been highest in the older neighborhoods encircling the downtown business district. In most cities, crime rates for many decades have been higher in these inner areas than anywhere, except in downtown areas themselves, where they are inflated by the small number of residents.

High crime rates have persisted in these inner areas even though the ethnic character of their residents continually changed. Poor immigrants used these areas as "entry ports," then usually moved on to more desirable neighborhoods as soon as they acquired enough resources. Many "entry port" areas have now become racial ghettos.

TABLE 1. INCIDENCE OF INDEX CRIMES AND PATROLMEN ASSIGNMENTS PER 100,000 RESIDENTS IN 5 CHICAGO POLICE DISTRICTS, 1965

Number	High-Income White District	Low Middle-Income White District	Mixed High- and Low-Income White District	Very Low Income Negro District No. 1	Very Low Income Negro District No. 2
Index crimes against persons	80	440	338	1,615	2,820
Index crimes against property	1,038	1,750	2,080	2,508	2,630
Patrolmen assigned	93	133	115	243	291

The difference between crime rates in these disadvantaged neighborhoods and in other parts of the city is usually startling, as a comparison of crime rates in five police districts in Chicago for 1965 illustrates. These five include one high-income, all-white district at the periphery of the city, two very low-income, virtually all-Negro districts near the city core with numerous public housing projects, and two predominantly white districts, one with mainly lower middle-income families, the other containing a mixture of very high-income and relatively low-income households. The table shows crime rates against persons and against property in these five districts, plus the number of patrolmen assigned to them per 100,000 residents, as [seen in Table 1].

These data indicate that:

Variations in the crime rate against persons within the city are extremely large. One very low income Negro district had 35 times as many serious crimes against persons per 100,000 residents as did the high-income white district.

Variations in the crime rate against property are much smaller. The highest rate was only 2.5 times larger than the lowest.

The lower the income in an area, the higher the crime rate there. Yet low-income Negro areas have significantly higher crime rates than low-income white areas. This reflects the high degree of social disorganization in Negro areas described in the previous chapter, as well as the fact that poor Negroes as a group have lower incomes than poor whites as a group.

The presence of more police patrolmen per 100,000 residents does not necessarily offset high crime in certain parts of the city. Although the Chicago Police Department had assigned over three times as many patrolmen per 100,000 residents to the highest crime areas shown as to the lowest, crime rates in the highest crime area for offenses against both persons and property combined were 4.9 times as high as in the lowest crime area.

Because most middle-class Americans live in neighborhoods similar to the more crime-free district described above, they have little comprehension of the sense of insecurity that characterizes the ghetto resident. Moreover, official statistics normally greatly understate actual crime rates because the vast majority of crimes are not reported to the police. For example, studies conducted for the President's Crime Commission in Washington, D.C., Boston, and Chicago, showed that three to six times as many crimes were actually committed against persons and homes as were reported to the police.

Two facts are crucial to an understanding of the effects of high crime rates in racial ghettos; most of these crimes are committed by a small minority of the residents, and the principal victims are the residents themselves. Throughout the United States, the great majority of crimes committed by Negroes involve other Negroes as victims. A special tabulation made by the Chicago Police Department for the President's Crime Commission indicated that over 85 percent of the crimes committed against persons by Negroes between September, 1965, and March, 1966, involved Negro victims.

As a result, the majority of law-abiding citizens who live in disadvantaged Negro areas face much higher probabilities of being victimized than residents of most higher income areas, including almost all suburbs. For nonwhites, the probability of suffering from any index crime except larceny is 78 percent higher than for whites. The probability of being raped is 3.7 times higher among nonwhite women, and the probability of being robbed is 3.5 times higher for nonwhites in general.

The problems associated with high crime rates generate widespread hostility toward the police in these neighborhoods for reasons described elsewhere in this Report. Thus, crime not only creates an atmosphere of insecurity and fear throughout Negro neighborhoods but also causes continuing attrition of the relationship between Negro residents and police. This bears a direct relationship to civil disorder.

There are reasons to expect the crime situation in these areas to become worse in the future. First, crime rates throughout the United States have been rising rapidly in recent years. The rate of index crimes against persons rose 37 percent from 1960 to 1966, and the rate of index crimes against property rose 50 percent. In the first 9 months of 1967, the number of index crimes was up 16 percent over the same period in 1966, whereas the U.S. population rose about 1 percent. In cities of 250,000 to 1 million, index crime rose by over 20 percent, whereas it increased 4 percent in cities of over 1 million.[2]

Second, the number of police available to combat crime is rising much more slowly than the amount of crime. In 1966, there were about 20 percent more police employees in the United States than in 1960, and per capita expenditures for police rose from $15.29 in 1960 to $20.99 in 1966, a gain of 37 percent. But over the 6-year period, the number of reported index crimes had jumped 62 percent. In spite of significant improvements in police efficiency, it is clear that police will be unable to cope with their expanding workload unless there is a dramatic increase in the resources allocated by society to this task.

Third, in the next decade, the number of young Negroes aged 14 to 24 will increase rapidly, particularly in central cities. This group is responsible for a disproportionately high share of crimes in all parts of the Nation. In 1966, persons under 25 years of age comprised the following proportions of those arrested for various major crimes: murder, 37 percent; forcible rape, 64 percent; robbery, 71 percent; burglary, 81 percent; larceny, about 77 percent; and auto theft, 89 percent. For all index crimes together, the arrest rate for Negroes is about four times higher than that for whites. Yet the number of young Negroes aged 14 to 24 in central cities will rise about 63 percent from 1966 to 1975, as compared to only 32 percent for the total Negro population of central cities.[3]

Health and Sanitation Conditions

The residents of the racial ghetto are significantly less healthy than most other Americans. They suffer from higher mortality rates, higher incidence of major diseases, and lower availability and utilization of medical services. They also experience higher admission rates to mental hospitals.

These conditions result from a number of factors.

Poverty

From the standpoint of health, poverty means deficient diets, lack of medical care, inadequate shelter and clothing and often lack of awareness of potential health needs. As a result, almost 30 percent of all persons with family incomes less than $2,000 per year suffer from chronic health conditions that adversely affect their employment—as compared with less than 8 percent of the families with incomes of $7,000 or more.

Poor families have the greatest need for financial assistance in meeting medical expenses. Only about 34 percent of families with incomes of less than $2,000 per year use health insurance benefits, as compared to nearly 90 percent of those with incomes of $7,000 or more.[4]

These factors are aggravated for Negroes when compared to whites for the simple reason that the proportion of persons in the United States who are poor is 3.5 times as high among Negroes (41 percent in 1966) as among whites (12 percent in 1966).

Maternal Mortality

Mortality rates for nonwhite mothers are four times as high as those for white mothers. There has been a sharp decline in such rates since 1940, when 774 nonwhite and 320 white mothers died for each 100,000 live births. In 1965, only 84 nonwhite and 21 white mothers died per 100,000 live births—but the gap between nonwhites and whites actually increased.

Infant Mortality

Mortality rates among nonwhite babies are 58 percent higher than among whites for those under 1 month old and almost three times as high among those from 1 month to 1 year old. This is true in spite of a large drop in infant mortality rates in both groups since 1940. [See Table 2.]

TABLE 2. NUMBER OF INFANTS WHO DIED PER 1,000 LIVE BIRTHS

	Less than 1 Month Old		1 Month to 1 Year Old	
Year	White	Nonwhite	White	Nonwhite
1940	27.2	39.7	16.0	34.1
1950	19.4	27.5	7.4	17.0
1960	17.2	26.9	5.7	16.4
1965	16.1	25.4	5.4	14.9

Life Expectancy

To some extent because of infant mortality rates, life expectancy at birth was 6.9 years longer for whites (71.0 years) than for nonwhites (64.1 years) in 1965. Even in the prime working ages, life expectancy is significantly lower among nonwhites than among whites. In 1965, white persons 25 years old could expect to live an average of 48.6 more years, whereas nonwhites 25 years old could expect to live another 43.3 years, or 11 percent less. Similar but smaller discrepancies existed at all ages from 25 through 55; some actually increased slightly between 1960 and 1965.

Lower Utilization of Health Services

A fact that also contributes to poorer health conditions in the ghetto is that Negro families with incomes similar to those of whites spend less on medical services and visit medical specialists less often. [See Table 3, p. 186.]

Since the lowest income group contains a much larger proportion of

TABLE 3. PERCENT OF FAMILY EXPENDITURE SPENT FOR MEDICAL CARE, 1960–61

Income Group	White	Nonwhite	Ratio, White to Nonwhite
Under $3,000	9	5	1.8:1
$3,000 to $7,499	7	5	1.4:1
$7,500 and over	6	4	1.5:1

nonwhite families than white families, the overall discrepancy in medical care spending between these two groups is very significant, as shown by Table 4.

These data indicate that nonwhite families in the lower income group spent less than half as much per person on medical services as white families with similar incomes. This discrepancy sharply declines but is still significant in the higher income group, where total nonwhite medical expenditures per person equal, on the average, 74.3 percent of white expenditures.

Negroes spend less on medical care for several reasons. Negro households generally are larger, requiring greater nonmedical expenses for each

TABLE 4. HEALTH EXPENSES PER PERSON PER YEAR FOR THE PERIOD FROM JULY TO DECEMBER 1962

Income by Racial Group	Expenses					
	Total Medical	Hospital	Doctor	Dental	Medicine	Other
Under $2,000 per family per year:						
White	$130	$33	$41	$11	$32	$13
Nonwhite	63	15	23	5	16	5
$10,000 and more per family per year:						
White	179	34	61	37	31	16
Nonwhite	133	34	50	19	23	8

household and leaving less money for meeting medical expenses. Thus, lower expenditures per person would result even if expenditures per household were the same. Negroes also often pay more for other basic necessities such as food and consumer durables, as discussed in the next part of this chapter. In addition, fewer doctors, dentists, and medical facilities are conveniently available to Negroes than to most whites—a result both of geographic concentration of doctors in higher income areas

TABLE 5. PERCENT OF POPULATION MAKING ONE OR MORE VISITS TO IN-DICATED TYPE OF MEDICAL SPECIALIST FROM JULY 1963 TO JUNE 1964

Type of Medical Specialist	Family Incomes of $2,000–$3,999		Family Incomes of $7,000–$9,999	
	White	Nonwhite	White	Nonwhite
Physician	64	56	70	64
Dentist	31	20	52	33

in large cities and of discrimination against Negroes by doctors and hospitals. A survey in Cleveland indicated that there were 0.45 physicians per 1,000 people in poor neighborhoods, compared to 1.13 per 1,000 in nonpoverty areas. The result nationally is fewer visits to physicians and dentists. [See Table 5.]

Although widespread use of health insurance has led many hospitals to adopt nondiscriminatory policies, some private hospitals still refuse to admit Negro patients or to accept doctors with Negro patients. And many individual doctors still discriminate against Negro patients. As a result, Negroes are more likely to be treated in hospital clinics than whites and they are less likely to receive personalized service. This conclusion is confirmed by the data [in Table 6].

TABLE 6. PERCENT OF ALL VISITS TO PHYSICIANS FROM JULY 1963 TO JUNE 1964, MADE IN INDICATED WAYS

Type of Visit to Physician	Family Incomes of $2,000–$3,000		Family Incomes of $7,000–$9,999	
	White	Nonwhite	White	Nonwhite
In physician's office	68	56	73	66
Hospital clinic	17	35	7	16
Other (mainly telephone)	15	9	20	18
Total	100	100	100	100

Environmental Factors

Environmental conditions in disadvantaged Negro neighborhoods create further reasons for poor health conditions there. The level of sanitation is strikingly below that which is prevalent in most higher income areas. One simple reason is that residents often lack proper storage facilities for food—adequate refrigerators, freezers, even garbage cans, which are sometimes stolen as fast as landlords can replace them.

In areas where garbage collection and other sanitation services are grossly inadequate—commonly in the poorer parts of our large cities—rats proliferate. It is estimated that in 1965, there were over 14,000 cases of ratbite in the United States, mostly in such neighborhoods.

The importance of these conditions was outlined for the Commission as follows: [5]

Sanitation Commissioners of New York City and Chicago both feel this [sanitation] to be an important community problem and report themselves as being under substantial pressure to improve conditions. *It must be concluded that slum sanitation is a serious problem in the minds of the urban poor and well merits, at least on that ground, the attention of the Commission.* A related problem, according to one Sanitation Commissioner, is the fact that residents of areas bordering on slums feel that sanitation and neighborhood cleanliness is a crucial issue, relating to the stability of their blocks and constituting an important psychological index of "how far gone" their area is.

. . . There is no known study comparing sanitation services between slum and non-slum areas. The experts agree, however, that there are more services in the slums on a quantitative basis, although perhaps not on a per capita basis. In New York, for example, garbage pickups are supposedly scheduled for about six times a week in slums, compared to three times a week in other areas of the city; the comparable figures in Chicago are two to three times a week versus once a week.

The point, therefore, is not the relative quantitative level of services but the peculiarly intense needs of ghetto areas for sanitation services. This high demand is the product of numerous factors including: (1) higher population density; (2) lack of well managed buildings and adequate garbage services provided by landlords, number of receptacles, carrying to curbside, number of electric garbage disposals; (3) high relocation rates of tenants and businesses, producing heavy volume of bulk refuse left on streets and in buildings; (4) different uses of the streets—as outdoor living rooms in summer, recreation areas—producing high visibility and sensitivity to garbage problems; (5) large numbers of abandoned cars; (6) severe rodent and pest problems; (7) traffic congestion blocking garbage collection; and (8) obstructed street cleaning and snow removal on crowded, car-choked streets. Each of these elements adds to the problem and suggests a different possible line of attack.

Exploitation of Disadvantaged Consumers by Retail Merchants

Much of the violence in recent civil disorders has been directed at stores and other commercial establishments in disadvantaged Negro areas. In some cases, rioters focused on stores operated by white merchants who, they apparently believed, had been charging exorbitant prices or selling inferior goods. Not all the violence against these stores can be attributed to "revenge" for such practices. Yet it is clear that many residents of disadvantaged Negro neighborhoods believe they suffer constant abuses by local merchants.

Significant grievances concerning unfair commercial practices affecting Negro consumers were found in 11 of the 20 cities studied by the Commission. The fact that most of the merchants who operate stores in Negro areas are white undoubtedly contributes to the conclusion among Negroes that they are exploited by white society.

It is difficult to assess the precise degree and extent of exploitation. No systematic and reliable survey comparing consumer pricing and credit practices in all-Negro and other neighborhoods has ever been conducted on a nationwide basis. Differences in prices and credit practices between white middle-income areas and Negro low-income areas to some extent reflect differences in the real costs of serving these two markets (such as differential losses from pilferage in supermarkets), but the exact extent of these cost differences has never been estimated accurately. Finally, an examination of exploitative consumer practices must consider the particular structure and functions of the low-income consumer durables market.

Installment Buying

This complex situation can best be understood by first considering certain basic facts:

Various cultural factors generate constant pressure on low-income families to buy many relatively expensive durable goods and display them in their homes. This pressure comes in part from continuous exposure to commercial advertising, especially on television. In January, 1967, over 88 percent of all Negro households had TV sets. A 1961 study of 464 low-income families in New York City showed that 95 percent of these relatively poor families had TV sets.

Many poor families have extremely low incomes, bad previous credit records, unstable sources of income or other attributes which make it virtually impossible for them to buy merchandise from established large national or local retail firms. These families lack enough savings to pay cash, and they cannot meet the standard credit requirements of established general merchants because they are too likely to fall behind in their payments.

Poor families in urban areas are far less mobile than others. A 1967 Chicago study of low-income Negro households indicated their low automobile ownership compelled them to patronize neighborhood merchants. These merchants typically provided smaller selection, poorer services and higher prices than big national outlets. The 1961 New York study also indicated that families who shopped outside their own neighborhoods were far less likely to pay exorbitant prices.

Most low-income families are uneducated concerning the nature of credit purchase contracts, the legal rights and obligations of both buyers and sellers, sources of advice for consumers who are having difficulties with merchants and the operation of the courts concerned with these matters. In contrast, merchants engaged in selling goods to them are very well informed.

In most states, the laws governing relations between consumers and merchants in effect offer protection only to informed, sophisticated parties with understanding of each other's rights and obligations. Consequently, these laws are little suited to protect the rights of most low-income consumers.

In this situation, exploitative practices flourish. Ghetto residents who want to buy relatively expensive goods cannot do so from standard retail outlets and are thus restricted to local stores. Forced to use credit, they have little understanding of the pitfalls of credit buying. But because they have unstable incomes and frequently fail to make payments, the cost to the merchants of serving them is significantly above that of serving middle-income consumers. Consequently, a special kind of merchant appears to sell them goods on terms designed to cover the high cost of doing business in ghetto neighborhoods.

Whether they actually gain higher profits, these merchants charge higher prices than those in other parts of the city to cover the greater credit risks and other higher operating costs inherent in neighborhood outlets. A recent study conducted by the Federal Trade Commission in Washington, D.C., illustrates this conclusion dramatically. The FTC identified a number of stores specializing in selling furniture and appliances to low-income households. About 92 percent of the sales of these stores were credit sales involving installment purchases, as compared to 27 percent of the sales in general retail outlets handling the same merchandise.

The median income annually of a sample of 486 customers of these stores was about $4,200, but one-third had annual incomes below $3,600, and about 6 percent were receiving welfare payments, and another 76 percent were employed in the lowest paying occupations (service workers, operatives, laborers and domestics), as compared to 36 percent of the total labor force in Washington in those occupations.

Definitely catering to a low-income group, these stores charged significantly higher prices than general merchandise outlets in the Washington area. According to testimony by Paul Rand Dixon, Chairman of the FTC, an item selling wholesale at $100 would retail on the average for $165 in a general merchandise store and for $250 in a low-income specialty store. Thus, the customers of these outlets were paying an average price premium of about 52 percent.

While higher prices are not necessarily exploitative in themselves, many merchants in ghetto neighborhoods take advantage of their superior knowledge of credit buying by engaging in various exploitative tactics—high-pressure salesmanship, "bait advertising," misrepresentation of prices, substitution of used goods for promised new ones, failure to notify consumers of legal actions against them, refusal to repair or replace substandard goods, exorbitant prices or credit charges, and use of shoddy merchandise. Such tactics affect a great many low-income consumers. In the New York study, 60 percent of all households had suffered from consumer problems (some of which were purely their own fault). About 23 percent had experienced serious exploitation. Another 20 percent, many of whom were also exploited, had experienced repossession, garnishment, or threat of garnishment.

Garnishment

Garnishment practices in many states allow creditors to deprive individuals of their wages through court action, without hearing or trial. In about 20 states, the wages of an employee can be diverted to a creditor merely upon the latter's deposition, with no advance hearing where the employee can defend himself. He often receives no prior notice of such action and is usually unaware of the law's operation and too poor to hire legal defense. Moreover, consumers may find themselves still owing money on a sales contract even after the creditor has repossessed the goods. The New York study cited earlier in this chapter indicated that 20 percent of a sample of low-income families had been subjected to legal action regarding consumer purchases. And the Federal Trade Commission study in Washington, D.C., showed that, on the average, retailers specializing in credit sales of furniture and appliances to low-income consumers resorted to court action once for every $2,200 of sales. Since their average sale was for $207, this amounted to using the courts to collect from one of every 11 customers. In contrast, department stores in the same area used court action against approximately one of every 14,500 customers.[6]

Variations in Food Prices

Residents of low-income Negro neighborhoods frequently claim that they pay higher prices for food in local markets than wealthier white suburbanites and receive inferior quality meat and produce. Statistically reliable information comparing prices and quality in these two kinds of areas is generally unavailable. The U.S. Bureau of Labor Statistics, studying food prices in six cities in 1966, compared prices of a standard list of 18 items in low-income areas and higher income areas in each city. In a total of 180 stores, including independent and chain stores, and for items of the same type sold in the same types of stores, there were no significant differences in prices between low-income and high-income areas. However, stores in low-income areas were more likely to be small independents (which had somewhat higher prices), to sell low-quality produce and meat at any given price, and to be patronized by people who typically bought smaller sized packages which are more expensive per unit of measure. In other words, many low-income consumers in fact pay higher prices, although the situation varies greatly from place to place.

Although these findings must be considered inconclusive, there are significant reasons to believe that poor households generally pay higher prices for the food they buy and receive lower quality food. Low-income consumers buy more food at local groceries because they are less mobile. Prices in these small stores are significantly higher than in major supermarkets because they cannot achieve economies of scale and because real operating costs are higher in low-income Negro areas than in outlying suburbs. For instance, inventory "shrinkage" from pilfering and other causes is normally under 2 percent of sales but can run twice as much in high-crime areas. Managers seek to make up for these added costs by charging higher prices for food or by substituting lower grades.

These practices do not necessarily involve exploitation, but they are often perceived as exploitative and unfair by those who are aware of the price and quality differences involved but unaware of operating costs. In addition, it is probable that genuinely exploitative pricing practices exist in some areas. In either case, differential food prices constitute another factor convincing urban Negroes in low-income neighborhoods that whites discriminate against them.

NOTES

1. We have not attempted here to describe conditions relating to the fundamental problems of housing, education, and welfare, which are treated in detail in later chapters.
2. The problem of interpreting and evaluating "rising" crime rates is complicated by the changing age distribution of the population, improvements in reporting methods, and the increasing willingness of victims to report crimes. Despite these complications, there is general agreement on the serious increase in the incidence of crime in the United States.
3. Assuming those cities will experience the same proportion of total United States Negro population growth that they did from 1960 to 1966. The calculations are derived from population projections in Bureau of the Census, *Population Estimates*, Current Population Reports, Series P–25, No. 381, Dec. 18, 1967, p. 63.
4. Public programs of various kinds have been providing significant financial assistance for medical care in recent years. In 1964, over $1.1 billion was paid out by various governments for such aid. About 52 percent of medical vendor payments came from Federal Government agencies, 33 percent from states, and 12 percent from local governments. The biggest contributions were made by the Old Age Assistance Program and the Medical Assistance for the Aged Program. The enactment of Medicare in 1965 has significantly added to this flow of public assistance for medical aid. However, it is too early to evaluate the results upon health conditions among the poor.
5. Memorandum to the Commission dated Nov. 16, 1967, from Robert Patricelli, minority counsel, Subcommittee on Employment, Manpower and Poverty, U.S. Senate.
6. Assuming their sales also averaged $207 per customer.

14. Comparing the Immigrant and Negro Experience

One tactic adopted to neutralize and disqualify the claims of black Americans for equality and justice in the American social system has been to characterize their social condition as of their own making. Many scholars and laymen as well do this by suggesting that white immigrants also started at the bottom in the United States, but through very special efforts and capabilities moved up. The blacks, on the other hand, have failed to move up, these critics often claim, because they failed to make this very special effort, and perhaps because they lacked certain very special qualities. The following chapter is a needed corrective to this vestige of social Darwinism.

KERNER COMMISSION REPORT

In the preceding chapters we have surveyed the historical background of racial discrimination and traced its effects on Negro employment, on the social structure of the ghetto community and on the conditions of life that surround the urban Negro poor. Here we address a fundamental question that many white Americans are asking today: Why has the Negro been unable to escape from poverty and the ghetto like the European immigrants?

The Maturing Economy

The changing nature of the American economy is one major reason. When the European immigrants were arriving in large numbers, America was becoming an urban-industrial society. To build its major cities and industries, America needed great pools of unskilled labor. The immigrants provided the labor, gained an economic foothold and thereby enabled their children and grandchildren to move up to skilled, white-collar and professional employment.

Since World War II especially, America's urban-industrial society has matured; unskilled labor is far less essential than before, and blue-collar jobs of all kinds are decreasing in number and importance as a source of new employment. The Negroes who migrated to the great urban centers

From *Report of the National Advisory Commission on Civil Disorders* (1968), Part II, pp. 143–145.

lacked the skills essential to the new economy, and the schools of the ghetto have been unable to provide the education that can qualify them for decent jobs. The Negro migrant, unlike the immigrant, found little opportunity in the city; he had arrived too late, and the unskilled labor he had to offer was no longer needed.

The Disability of Race

Racial discrimination is undoubtedly the second major reason why the Negro has been unable to escape from poverty. The structure of discrimination has persistently narrowed his opportunities and restricted his prospects. Well before the high tide of immigration from overseas, Negroes were already relegated to the poorly paid, low status occupations. Had it not been for racial discrimination, the North might well have recruited southern Negroes after the Civil War to provide the labor for building the burgeoning urban-industrial economy. Instead, northern employers looked to Europe for their sources of unskilled labor. Upon the arrival of the immigrants, the Negroes were dislodged from the few urban occupations they had dominated. Not until World War II were Negroes generally hired for industrial jobs, and by that time the decline in the need for unskilled labor had already begun. European immigrants, too, suffered from discrimination, but never was it so pervasive. The prejudice against color in America has formed a bar to advancement unlike any other.

Entry into the Political System

Political opportunities also played an important role in enabling the European immigrants to escape from poverty. The immigrants settled for the most part in rapidly growing cities that had powerful and expanding political machines which gave them economic advantages in exchange for political support. The political machines were decentralized, and ward-level grievance machinery as well as personal representation enabled the immigrant to make his voice heard and his power felt. Since the local political organizations exercised considerable influence over public building in the cities, they provided employment in construction jobs for their immigrant voters. Ethnic groups often dominated one or more of the municipal services—police and fire protection, sanitation and even public education.

By the time the Negroes arrived, the situation had altered dramatically. The great wave of public building had virtually come to an end; reform groups were beginning to attack the political machines; the machines were no longer so powerful or so well equipped to provide jobs and other favors.

Although the political machines retained their hold over the areas settled by Negroes, the scarcity of patronage jobs made them unwilling to share with Negroes the political positions they had created in these neighborhoods. For example, Harlem was dominated by white politicians for many years after it had become a Negro ghetto; even today, New York's Lower East Side, which is now predominantly Puerto Rican, is strongly influenced by politicians of the older immigrant groups.

This pattern exists in many other American cities. Negroes are still underrepresented in city councils and in most city agencies.

Segregation played a role here too. The immigrants and their descendants, who felt threatened by the arrival of the Negro, prevented a Negro-immigrant coalition that might have saved the old political machines. Reform groups, nominally more liberal on the race issue, were often dominated by businessmen and middle-class city residents who usually opposed coalition with any low-income group, white or black.

Cultural Factors

Cultural factors also made it easier for the immigrants to escape from poverty. They came to America from much poorer societies, with a low standard of living, and they came at a time when job aspirations were low. When most jobs in the American economy were unskilled, they sensed little deprivation in being forced to take the dirty and poorly paid jobs. Moreover, their families were large, and many breadwinners, some of whom never married, contributed to the total family income. As a result, family units managed to live even from the lowest paid jobs and still put some money aside for savings or investment, for example, to purchase a house or tenement or to open a store or factory. Since the immigrants spoke little English and had their own ethnic culture, they needed stores to supply them with ethnic foods and other services. Since their family structures were patriarchal, men found satisfactions in family life that helped compensate for the bad jobs they had to take and the hard work they had to endure.

Negroes came to the city under quite different circumstances. Generally relegated to jobs that others would not take, they were paid too little to be able to put money in savings for new enterprises. In addition, Negroes lacked the extended family characteristic of certain European groups; each household usually had only one or two breadwinners. Moreover, Negro men had fewer cultural incentives to work in a dirty job for the sake of the family. As a result of slavery and of long periods of male unemployment afterwards, the Negro family structure had become matriarchal; the man played a secondary and marginal role in his family. For many Negro men, then, there were few of the cultural and psychological rewards of family life; they often abandoned their homes because they felt themselves useless to their families.

Although Negro men worked as hard as the immigrants to support their families, their rewards were less. The jobs did not pay enough to enable them to support their families, for prices and living standards had risen since the immigrants had come, and the entrepreneurial opportunities that had allowed some immigrants to become independent, even rich, had vanished. Above all, Negroes suffered from segregation, which denied them access to the good jobs and the right unions and which deprived them of the opportunity to buy real estate or obtain business loans or move out of the ghetto and bring up their children in middle-class neighborhoods. Immigrants were able to leave their ghettos as soon as they had the money; segregation has denied Negroes the opportunity to live elsewhere.

The Vital Element of Time

Finally, nostalgia makes it easy to exaggerate the ease of escape of the white immigrants from the ghettos. When the immigrants were immersed in poverty, they, too, lived in slums, and these neighborhoods exhibited fearfully high rates of alcoholism, desertion, illegitimacy and the other pathologies associated with poverty. Just as some Negro men desert their families when they are unemployed and their wives can get jobs, so did the men of other ethnic groups, even though time and affluence has clouded white memories of the past.

Today, whites tend to contrast their experience with poverty-stricken Negroes. The fact is, among the southern and eastern Europeans who came to America in the last great wave of immigration, those who came already urbanized were the first to escape from poverty. The others who came to America from rural background, as Negroes did, are only now, after three generations, in the final stages of escaping from poverty. Until the last 10 years or so, most of these were employed in blue-collar jobs, and only a small proportion of their children were able or willing to attend college. In other words, only the third, and in many cases only the fourth, generation has been able to achieve the kind of middle-class income and status that allows it to send its children to college. Because of favorable economic and political conditions, these ethnic groups were able to escape from lower class status to working class and lower middle-class status, but it has taken them three generations.

Negroes have been concentrated in the city for only two generations, and they have been there under much less favorable conditions. Moreover, their escape from poverty has been blocked in part by the resistance of the European ethnic groups; they have been unable to enter some unions and to move into some neighborhoods outside the ghetto because descendants of the European immigrants who control these unions and neighborhoods have not yet abandoned them for middle-class occupations and areas.

Even so, some Negroes have escaped poverty, and they have done so in only two generations; their success is less visible than that of the immigrants in many cases, for residential segregation has forced them to remain in the ghetto. Still, the proportion of nonwhites employed in white-collar, technical and professional jobs has risen from 10.2 percent in 1950 to 20.8 percent in 1966 and the proportion attending college has risen an equal amount. Indeed, the development of a small but steadily increasing Negro middle class while a great part of the Negro population is stagnating economically is creating a growing gap between Negro haves and have-nots.

The awareness of this gap by those left behind undoubtedly adds to the feelings of desperation and anger which breed civil disorders. Low-income Negroes realize that segregation and lack of job opportunities have made it possible for only a small proportion of all Negroes to escape poverty, and the summer disorders are at least in part a protest against being left behind and left out.

The immigrant who labored long hours at hard and often menial work had the hope of a better future, if not for himself then for his children. This was the promise of the "American dream"—the society offered to all a future that was open-ended; with hard work and perseverance, a man and his family could in time achieve not only material well-being but "position" and status.

For the Negro family in the urban ghetto, there is a different vision—the future seems to lead only to a dead end.

What the American economy of the late 19th and early 20th century was able to do to help the European immigrants escape from poverty is now largely impossible. New methods of escape must be found for the majority of today's poor.

15. The Community Response

One of the advantages of official reports on social problems is the availability of resources for dealing extensively with them. An important disadvantage is the inability of such documents to suggest unpopular corrective alternatives. Their weakest feature very often is their suggested correction of the ills so extensively described. And so it is with the Kerner Commission Report. This document bravely insists that white racism is the causal element in ghetto violence, thus achieving an unusual level of candor. We are left, however, with such questions as "what is to be done," "how is it to be done," and "who is to do it" after a presumed treatment of these matters in Chapter 15, which follows.

KERNER COMMISSION REPORT

Introduction

The racial disorders of last summer in part reflect the failure of all levels of government—Federal and state as well as local—to come to grips with the problems of our cities. The ghetto symbolizes the dilemma: a widening gap between human needs and public resources and a growing cynicism regarding the commitment of community institutions and leadership to meet these needs.

The problem has many dimensions—financial, political and institutional. Almost all cities—and particularly the central cities of the largest metropolitan regions—are simply unable to meet the growing need for public services and facilities with traditional sources of municipal revenue. Many cities are structured politically so that great numbers of citizens—particularly minority groups—have little or no representation in the processes of government. Finally, some cities lack either the will or the capacity to use effectively the resources that are available to them.

Instrumentalities of Federal and state government often compound the problems. National policy expressed through a very large number of grant programs and institutions rarely exhibits a coherent and consistent perspective when viewed at the local level. State efforts, traditionally focused on rural areas, often fail to tie in effectively with either local or Federal programs in urban areas.

From *Report of the National Advisory Commission on Civil Disorders* (1968), Part II, pp. 147–155.

Meanwhile, the decay of the central city continues—its revenue base eroded by the retreat of industry and white middle-class families to the suburbs, its budget and tax rate inflated by rising costs and increasing numbers of dependent citizens and its public plant—schools, hospitals, and correctional institutions deteriorated by age and long-deferred maintenance.

Yet to most citizens, the decay remains largely invisible. Only their tax bills and the headlines about crime or "riots" suggest that something may be seriously wrong in the city.

There are, however, two groups of people that live constantly with the problem of the city: the public officials and the poor, particularly the residents of the racial ghetto. Their relationship is a key factor in the development of conditions underlying civil disorders.

Our investigations of the 1967 riot cities establish that:

> Virtually every major episode of urban violence in the summer of 1967 was foreshadowed by an accumulation of unresolved grievances by ghetto residents against local authorities (often, but not always, the police). So high was the resulting underlying tension that routine and random events, tolerated or ignored under most circumstances (such as the raid on the "blind pig" in Detroit and the arrest of the cab driver in Newark), became the triggers of sudden violence.
>
> Coinciding with this high level of dissatisfaction, confidence in the willingness and ability of local government to respond to Negro grievances was low. Evidence presented to this Commission in hearings, field reports and research analyses of the 1967 riot cities establishes that a substantial number of Negroes were disturbed and angry about local governments' failures to solve their problems.

Several developments have converged to produce this volatile situation.

First, there is a widening gulf in communications between local government and the residents of the erupting ghettos of the city. As a result, many Negro citizens develop a profound sense of isolation and alienation from the processes and programs of government. This lack of communication exists for all residents in our larger cities; it is, however, far more difficult to overcome for low-income, less educated citizens who are disproportionately supported by and dependent upon programs administered by agencies of local government. Consequently, they are more often subject to real or imagined official misconduct ranging from abrasive contacts with public officials to arbitrary administrative actions.

Further, as a result of the long history of racial discrimination, grievances experienced by Negroes often take on personal and symbolic significance transcending the immediate consequences of the event. For example, inadequate sanitation services are viewed by many ghetto residents not merely as instances of poor public service but as manifestations of racial discrimination. This perception reinforces existing feelings of alienation and contributes to a heightened level of frustration and dissatisfaction, not only with the administrators of the sanitation department but with all the representatives of local government. This is particularly true with respect to the police, who are the only public agents on duty in the ghetto 24 hours a day and who bear this burden of hostility for the less visible elements of the system.

The lack of communication and the absence of regular contacts with ghetto residents prevent city leaders from learning about problems and grievances as they develop. As a result, tensions, which could have been dissipated if responded to promptly, mount unnecessarily, and the potential for explosion grows inevitably. Once disorder erupts, public officials are frequently unable to fashion an effective response; they lack adequate information about the nature of the trouble and its causes, and they lack rapport with local leaders who might be able to influence the community.

Second, many city governments are poorly organized to respond effectively to the needs of ghetto residents, even when those needs are made known to appropriate public officials. Most middle-class city dwellers have limited contacts with local government. When contacts do occur, they tend to concern relatively narrow and specific problems. Furthermore, middle-class citizens, although subject to many of the same frustrations and resentments as ghetto residents in dealing with the public bureaucracy, find it relatively easy to locate the appropriate agency for help and redress. If they fail to get satisfaction, they can call on a variety of remedies—assistance of elected representatives, friends in government, a lawyer. In short, the middle-class city dweller has relatively fewer needs for public services and is reasonably well positioned to move the system to his benefit.

On the other hand, the typical ghetto resident has interrelated social and economic problems which require the services of several government and private agencies. At the same time, he may be unable to identify his problems to fit the complicated structure of government. Moreover, he may be unaware of his rights and opportunities under public programs and unable to obtain the necessary guidance from either public or private sources.

Current trends in municipal administration have had the effect of reducing the capacity of local government to respond effectively to these needs. The pressures for administrative efficiency and cost cutting have brought about the withdrawal of many operations of city government from direct contact with neighborhood and citizen. Red tape and administrative complexity have filled the vacuum created by the centralization of local government. The introduction of a merit system and a professionalized civil service has made management of the cities more businesslike, but it has also tended to depersonalize and isolate government. The rigid patterns of segregation prevalent within the central city have widened the distance between Negro citizens and city hall.

In most of the riot cities surveyed by the Commission, we found little or no meaningful coordination among city agencies, either in responding to the needs of ghetto residents on an ongoing basis or in planning to head off disturbances. The consequences of this lack of coordination were particularly severe for the police. Despite the fact that they were being called upon increasingly to deal with tensions and citizen complaints often having little, if anything, to do with police services, the police departments of many large cities were isolated from other city agencies, sometimes including the mayor and his staff. In these cities, the police were compelled to deal with ghetto residents angered over dirty streets, dilapidated housing, unfair commercial practices or inferior schools—grievances which they had neither the responsibility for creating nor the authority to redress.

Third, ghetto residents increasingly believe that they are excluded from the decision-making process which affects their lives and community. This feeling of exclusion, intensified by the bitter legacy of racial discrimination, has engendered a deep seated hostility toward the institutions of government. It has severely compromised the effectiveness of programs intended to provide improved services to ghetto residents.

In part, this is the lesson of Detroit and New Haven where well intentioned programs designed to respond to the needs of ghetto residents were not worked out and implemented sufficiently in cooperation with the intended beneficiaries. A report prepared for the Senate Subcommittee on Employment, Manpower and Poverty, presented just prior to the riot in Detroit, found that:

Area residents . . . complain almost continually that . . . their demands for program changes are not heeded, that they have little voice in what goes on. . . . As much as the area residents are involved, listened to, and even heeded, . . . it becomes fairly clear that the relationship is still one of superordinate-subordinate, rather than one of equals. . . . The procedures by which HRD (the Mayor's Committee for Human Resources Development, the Detroit Community Action Agency) operates by and large admit the contributions of area residents only after programs have been written, after policies have already operated for a time or already been formulated and to a large degree, only in formal and infrequent meetings rather than in day-to-day operations. . . . The meaningfulness of resident involvement is reduced by its after-the-fact nature and by relatively limited resources they have at their disposal.[1]

Mayor Alfonso J. Cervantes of St. Louis was even more explicit. In testimony before this Commission, he stated:

We have found that ghetto neighborhoods cannot be operated on from outside alone. The people within them should have a voice, and our experience has shown that it is often a voice that speaks with good sense, since the practical aspects of the needs of the ghetto people are so much clearer to the people there than they are to anyone else.

The political system, traditionally an important vehicle of minorities to participate effectively in decisions affecting the distribution of public resources, has not worked for the Negro as it has for other groups. The reasons are fairly obvious.

We have found that the number of Negro officials in elected and appointed positions in the riot cities is minimal in proportion to the Negro population. The alienation of the Negro from the political process has been exacerbated by his racial and economic isolation.

Specifically, the needs of ghetto residents for social welfare and other public services have swelled dramatically at a time when increased affluence has diminished the need for such services by the rest of the urban population. By reducing disproportionately the economic disability of other portions of the population, particularly other ethnic urban minorities, this affluence has left the urban Negro few potential local allies with whom to make common cause for shared objectives. The development of political alliances, essential to effective participation of minority groups in the political process, has been further impaired by the polarization of the races, which on both sides has transformed economic considerations into racial issues.

Finally, these developments have coincided with the demise of the historic urban political machines and the growth of the city manager concept of government. While this tendency has produced major benefits in terms of honest and efficient administration, it has eliminated an important political link between city government and low-income residents.

These conditions have produced a vast and threatening disparity in perceptions of the intensity and validity of Negro dissatisfaction. Viewed from the perspective of the ghetto resident, city government appears distant and unconcerned, the possibility of effective change remote. As a result, tension rises perceptibly; the explosion comes as the climax to a progression of tension-generating incidents. To the city administration, unaware of this growing tension or unable to respond effectively to it, the outbreak of disorder comes as a shock.

No democratic society can long endure the existence within its major urban centers of a substantial number of citizens who feel deeply aggrieved as a group, yet lack confidence in the government to rectify perceived injustice and in their ability to bring about needed change.

We are aware that reforms in existing instruments of local government and their relationship to the ghetto population will mean little unless joined with sincere and comprehensive response to the severe social and economic needs of ghetto residents. Elsewhere in this report, we make specific recommendations with respect to employment, education, welfare, and housing which we hope will meet some of these needs.

We believe, however, that there are measures which can and should be taken now; that they can be put to work without great cost and without delay; that they can be built upon in the future and that they will effectively reduce the level of grievance and tension as well as improve the responsiveness of local government to the needs of ghetto residents.

Basic Strategy and Goals

To meet the needs identified above, we recommend pursuit of a comprehensive strategy which would accomplish the following goals:

Effective communication between ghetto residents and local government.

Improved ability of local government to respond to the needs and problems of ghetto residents.

Expanded opportunities for citizen leadership to participate in shaping decisions and policies which affect their community.

Increased accountability of public officials.

We recognize that not all of the programs proposed below to implement the foregoing goals can be instituted with the immediacy required by the problem. Because the need for action at the local level, where government impinges directly upon the ghetto resident, is particularly urgent, we propose that our suggested programs be implemented in two phases. It is vital, however, that the first phase programs not be regarded or perceived as short term, and anti-riot efforts calculated to cool already inflamed situations. These programs will have little chance of succeeding unless they are part of a long-range commitment to action designed to eliminate the fundamental sources of grievance and tension.

Programs: First Phase Actions

Establishment of Neighborhood Action Task Forces

To open channels of communication between government and ghetto residents, improve the capacity of the city administration to respond effectively to community needs and provide opportunity for meaningful citizen participation in decision-making, we recommend establishment of joint government-community Neighborhood Action Task Forces covering each neighborhood within the city which has a high proportion of low-income minority citizens. While the exact form of these groups will depend upon the size and needs of each municipality, the following basic features should be incorporated:

Composition. Each task force should include a key official in the mayor's office with direct and immediate access to the mayor, ranking city officials from the operating agencies servicing the ghetto community, elected leaders, representatives from the local business, labor, professional, and church communities, and neighborhood leaders, including representatives of community organizations of all orientations, as well as youth leaders. Each task force would be headed by the mayor's representative. In the larger cities, each of these chairmen would sit as a member of a city-wide task force.

Functions. The Neighborhood Action Task Forces should meet on a regular basis at a location accessible to ghetto residents. These meetings will afford an opportunity for ghetto leaders to communicate directly with the municipal administrators for their area to discuss problems and programs which affect the community. In effect, this device furnishes an interagency coordinating mechanism on the one hand and a "community cabinet" on the other.

Ghetto residents should be able to rely on the capacity of the task force to cut through the maze of red tape and to overcome bureaucratic barriers in order to make things—collection of garbage, removal of abandoned cars, installation of lights in the park, establishment of playstreets—happen. To accomplish this purpose, the participating city officials should have operational decision-making authority. Lower-level staff or public relations personnel will be unable to provide the confrontation and interaction with the community representatives which is essential to the effective functioning of the task force. Moreover, there is grave danger that opening channels of communication without providing opportunities for obtaining relief will further estrange ghetto residents. If this is not to happen, the task force should have a meaningful and realistic capacity for securing redress of grievances. For the same reason, it is essential that the task force have the full and energetic support of the mayor and the city council.

The potential for responding effectively to community needs is not limited to available public resources. Acting through business, labor, and church members, and local Urban Coalitions which have already been formed, the task force will have a capacity to involve the resources of the private sector in meeting needs within the ghetto. Possibilities range from support of special summer youth programs (weekend trips, recreation events, camping programs) to provision of cultural and employment opportunities on a year-round basis.

The Neighborhood Action Task Force can play a significant role with respect to youth activities. One approach which has worked in several cities involves the establishment of youth councils to employ young streetleaders (regardless of previous police records) to develop community programs for other alienated youth. These activities might include organizing and operating libraries, neighborhood cleanup campaigns, policecommunity dialogues, and sports competitions in their own neighborhoods.

Finally, such an organization can make a major contribution to the prevention of civil disorders. If the task force has been successful in achieving the objectives stressed above, its members will have gained the confidence of a wide spectrum of ghetto residents. This will enable them to identify potentially explosive conditions and, working with police, to defuse them.

Similarly, the task force could have considerable effectiveness in handling threatening incidents identified by the police. To accomplish this objective, an early warning system could be instituted during the critical summer months. Operating on a 24-hour basis, such a system should have the capacity to receive and evaluate police reports of potentially serious incidents and to initiate an appropriate nonpolice response, utilizing community contacts and task force personnel. Any such operation must have the cooperation of the police, who will be in control of the overall disorder response. To avoid confusion and duplication of effort, the task force should have responsibility for coordinating the efforts of all agencies, other than police and fire, once a disturbance has occurred. An example will serve to illustrate how the system might operate.

Following the slaying last summer of a Negro teenager by a Negro detective in the Bedford-Stuyvesant section of Brooklyn, N.Y., a rumor that the youth had been shot by a white policeman and that the police were trying to suppress this information began to circulate through an already tense neighborhood. The situation became threatening. Yet, within an hour, three white members of the mayor's summer task force group were able to convince a group of black militants that the police version was true. Walking the streets that night and the next two evenings, they worked to dispel the rumor and to restore community stability.

In the larger cities, the city-wide task force could have responsibility for coordinating the programs of various municipal agencies, concentrating their impact on poverty areas, and planning for the more effective implementation of existing public efforts.

The Commission believes that the task force approach can do precisely what other forms of neighborhood organizations have not been able to do. It can connect the real needs and priorities of low-income residents with the energies and resources of both city government and the private sector. It can substantially improve the quality and timeliness of city services to these areas. It will fail unless all of the groups involved are prepared to deal fairly and openly with the problems of the community. But if it succeeds, it will not only produce improved services; it will go far to generate a new sense of community.

Establishment of Effective Grievance-Response Mechanisms

Effective implementation of the Neighborhood Action Task Forces will depend upon the continuing commitment of the city administration to their success. To ensure attention to many of the sources of tension identified above, we recommend that formal mechanisms for the processing of grievances, many of which will relate to the performance of the city government, be established independent of the local administration.

We are convinced, on the record before this Commission, that the frustration reflected in the recent disorders results, in part at least, from the lack of accessible and visible means of establishing the merits of grievances against the agencies of local and state government, including but not limited to, the police. Cities and states throughout the country now have under consideration various forms of grievance-response devices. While we are not prepared to specify the form which such a mechanism should take in any particular community, there are certain criteria which should be met. These include:

Independence: This can be achieved by long-term appointment of the administrator, subject to City Council removal. The grievance agency should be separate from operating municipal agencies.

Adequate staff and funding: Exact costs will vary depending on the size and needs of the city's population. It is most important that the agency have adequate funds and staff to discharge its responsibilities.

Comprehensive coverage of grievances against public agencies and authorities: General jurisdiction will facilitate access by grievants. Moreover, unlike specialized complaint agencies, such as civilian review boards, all agencies would be brought equally under public scrutiny. This should facilitate its acceptance by public officials.

Power to receive complaints, hold hearings, subpoena witnesses, make public recommendations for remedial action to local authorities and, in cases involving violation of law, bring suit: These powers are the minimum necessary for the effective operation of the grievance mechanism. As we envision it, the agency's principal power derives from its authority to investigate and make public findings and recommendations. It should, of course, have a conciliation process whereby complaints could be resolved without full investigation and processing.

Accessibility: In large cities, ready access to grievants may require setting up neighborhood offices in ghetto areas. In others, local resident aides could be empowered to receive complaints. It should be possible to file a grievance orally or in writing. If forms are used, they should be easily understood and widely available.

Participation in grievance process: Grievants should be given full opportunity to take part in all proceedings and to be represented by counsel. They should receive prompt advice of action taken; results of investigations should be made public.

Expanded Legal Services

Among the most intense grievances underlying the riots of the summer of 1967 were those which derived from conflicts between ghetto residents and private parties, principally white landlords and merchants. Though the legal obstacles are considerable, resourceful and imaginative use of available legal processes could contribute significantly to the alleviation of resulting tensions. Through the adversary process which is at the heart of our judicial system, litigants are afforded a meaningful opportunity to influence events which affect them and their community. However, effective utilization of the courts requires legal assistance, a resource seldom available to the poor.

Litigation is not the only need which ghetto residents have for legal service. Participation in the grievance procedures suggested above may well require legal assistance. More importantly, ghetto residents have need of effective advocacy of their interests and concerns in a variety of other contexts, from representation before welfare agencies and other institutions of government to advocacy before planning boards and commissions concerned with the formulation of development plans. Again, professional representation can provide substantial benefits in terms of overcoming the ghetto resident's alienation from the institutions of government by implicating him in its processes. Although lawyers function in precisely this fashion for the middle-class clients, they are too often not available to the impoverished ghetto resident.

The Legal Services Program administered by the Office of Economic Opportunity has made a good beginning in providing legal assistance to the poor. Its present level of effort should be substantially expanded through increased private and public funding. In addition, the participation of law schools should be increased through development of programs whereby advanced students can provide legal assistance as a regular part of their professional training. In all of these efforts, the local bar bears major responsibility for leadership and support.

Assistance for Mayors and City Councils

In [other chapters, we will be directing] attention to broad strategies and programs of national action. Yet the capacity of the Federal Government to affect local problems depends to a great extent on the capacity of city government to respond competently to Federal program initiatives.

In the face of the bewildering proliferation of both community demands and local, state, and Federal programs, mayors and city councils need to create new mechanisms to aid in decision-making, program planning, and coordination. At this time, however, no assistance is available to develop these new and critically necessary institutional capabilities or to support the required research, consultants, staff, or other vital components of administrative or legislative competence.

The Commission recommends, therefore, that both the state and Federal governments provide financial assistance to cities for these purposes as a regular part of all urban program funding.

Hearings on Ghetto Problems and Enactment of Appropriate Local Legislation

Many of the grievances identified in our study of the conditions underlying civil disorders can be redressed only through legislative action. Accordingly, we recommend that the legislative body of each city with a substantial minority population hold, as soon as possible, a series of hearings on ghetto problems. In large cities, these hearings could well be held in the ghetto itself to facilitate full citizen participation.

In addition to establishing a foundation for needed legislative measures, these hearings would constitute a visible demonstration of governmental concern for the problems of ghetto residents. They would also provide a most useful means of bridging the communications gap, contributing to an improved understanding in the white community about the conditions of ghetto life.

Expanded Employment by City Government of Ghetto Residents

We strongly recommend that local government undertake a concerted effort to provide substantial employment opportunities for ghetto residents. Local governments now employ 6.4 million people full time, most of whom live in urban areas; they comprise one of the fastest growing segments of the economy. This offers an opportunity of the greatest significance for local government to respond to one of the most critical needs of ghetto residents and, at the same time, to decrease the distance between city hall and the ghetto by deliberate employment, training, and upgrading of Negroes.

To accomplish this goal, we recommend that municipal authorities review applicable civil service policies and job standards and take prompt action to remove arbitrary barriers to employment of ghetto residents. Reevaluation is particularly necessary with respect to requirements relating to employment qualification tests and police records. Leadership by city government in this vital area is of urgent priority, not only because of the important public employment potential but also to stimulate private employers to take similar action.

Second Phase Actions

Establishment of Neighborhood City Halls

The Neighborhood Action Task Force concept provides a basis on which lasting structures can be erected. The principal change required in order to transform the official component of the task force into a permanent instrument of local government involves the establishment of offices in the neighborhoods served. Depending on the size and composition of the neighborhood, the permanent staff should include an assistant mayor, representatives of the municipal agencies, the city councilman's staff and other institutions and groups included in the task force. This facility would function, in effect, as a "Neighborhood City Hall."

The neighborhood city hall would accomplish several interrelated objectives. It would contribute to the improvement of public services by providing an effective channel for low-income citizens to communicate their needs and problems to the appropriate public officials and by increasing the ability of local government to respond in a coordinated and timely fashion. It would serve as the eyes and ears of the mayor and council and furnish an informal forum for complaints and grievances. It would make information about government programs and services available to ghetto residents, enabling them to make more effective use of such programs and services while making clear the limitations on the availability of all such programs and services. It would expand opportunities for meaningful community access to and involvement in the planning and implementation of policy affecting the neighborhood. Most important, the neighborhood city hall, building on the task force approach, affords a significant opportunity to accomplish the democratic goal of making government closer and more accountable to the citizen.

Development of Multi-Service Centers

Frequently, services vital to the ghetto resident—job placement and location, health care, legal assistance—are inaccessible because they are located at considerable distance from the ghetto, a distance often made greater by the lack of efficient public transportation. This problem is compounded by the fact that many key service institutions are fragmented, requiring those seeking assistance to pursue it at various locations scattered throughout a large urban area.

To meet this need, the Office of Economic Opportunity has funded over 700 neighborhood centers in ghetto areas throughout the country since 1964. Many of these have been small store-front operations housing OEO-funded services. Some, as in Detroit, have had a fairly wide range of services and have served a large number of families.

The principal problem has been that most centers have not been comprehensive enough. They rarely include traditional city and state agency services. Many relevant Federal programs are seldom located in the same center. Manpower and education programs from HEW and the Labor Department, for example, have been housed in separate centers without adequate consolidation or coordination either geographically or programmatically.

The resulting proliferation led the President to call upon the Department of Housing and Urban Development to establish comprehensive one-stop service centers. The experience thus far indicates the need for more effective coordination of Federal programs at the national and regional levels. Legislation may be required to simplify grant procedures and assure such coordination.

Each center should have enough neighborhood workers to reach out into the homes of needy people who are not able to seek help. To assure that the service centers are relevant to the needs and styles of the neighborhood, ghetto residents should be trained and employed at all levels. This purpose can well be served through establishment and involvement of Community Service Center Councils to establish overall policy.

We recommend increased Federal funding for comprehensive centers and implementation of the policy guidelines proposed above.

Improved Political Representation

It is beyond the scope of this Report to consider in detail the many problems presented by the existing distribution of political power within city governments. But it is plain that the Negro ghetto resident feels deeply that he is not represented fairly and adequately under the arrangements which prevail in many cities. This condition strikes at major democratic values.

To meet this problem, city government and the majority community should revitalize the political system to encourage fuller participation by all segments of the community. Whether this requires adoption of any one system of representation, we are not prepared to say. But it is clear that at-large representation, currently the practice in many American cities, does not give members of the minority community a feeling of involvement or stake in city government. Further, this form of representation dilutes the normal political impact of pressures generated by a particular neighborhood or district.

Negro representation and participation in the formal structure of government can also be furthered by a concerted effort to appoint Negroes to significant policy positions in city government.

More Effective Community Participation

One of the most difficult and controversial problems we have encountered relates to ghetto demands for "self-determination" or "community control." To a limited extent, this concept was made a matter of national policy in the Economic Opportunity Act of 1964, which specified that community action programs should be developed, conducted and administered with "maximum feasible participation" of the residents of the areas and members of the groups served.

In the 3 years since the beginning of the War on Poverty, the effort to put maximum feasible participation into effect has met with both success and failure. One measure of its success can be seen in the extent to which the demand for participation, even control, over a variety of programs affecting the ghetto has spilled over into the most traditional areas, such as public school administration.

But the demands made often seem intransigent and the time required for negotiation with residents extravagant. The pulling and hauling of different factions competing for control within the ghetto community sometimes makes it difficult to mount any program. Moreover, it is often easier to organize groups to oppose, complain, demonstrate and boycott than to develop and run programs.

Yet the demand for a community voice represents a marked and desirable gain over the apathy that existed before. Despite its problems, we believe that meaningful community participation and a substantial measure of involvement in program development is an essential strategy for city government. The democratic values which it advances—providing a stake in the social system, improving the accountability of public officials —as well as the pragmatic benefits which it provides far outweigh these costs.

The essential question which city leadership must face is the ultimate goal of community participation. In this sense, community involvement is directly related to the strategy of decentralization, for with the support of the city, neighborhood groups may become an effective force for carrying on a variety of functions—such as physical renewal and redevelopment— which can be highly disruptive when imposed by outside authority.

If these principles are accomplished, then the choice of mechanisms will depend upon the needs of the particular community and the structure of the local government. We have described earlier in this section opportuni- ties for meaningful community participation in the processes of govern- ment. Additional and diverse instrumentalities such as community neigh- borhood school boards, community planning boards, tenants' councils, youth councils, advisory committees and consumer trade organizations offer further ways of providing institutional channels for effective citizen participation in public decision making. The crucial issue, however, is whether city government is willing to legitimize these organizations by dealing with them on a regular basis with respect to matters within their competence. We believe that such an approach offers substantial promise of improving the relationship between local government and ghetto resi- dents.

The involvement of the ghetto community in the planning and opera- tion of development programs need not be confined to the public arena. There is great potential in private community development corporations which can emerge from a combined public-private sponsorship and per- form mixed functions for the community, including sponsorship of locally owned businesses.

A most promising approach is the neighborhood membership corpora- tion, the first of which was established in Columbus, Ohio, in 1965—the East Central Citizens Organization (ECCO), under an OEO grant. Func- tioning as a town meeting, its members include all of the residents of a defined ghetto neighborhood (8,150 people). Its activities encompass day-care centers, credit unions, legal and medical services, newspapers, restaurants and business enterprises.

Both money and manpower will be needed from government, founda- tions and private business to create and assist these corporations and other new community institutions. Technical and professional support will be required. The opportunity that they offer to develop stable community leadership structures and constructive involvement should not be allowed to fail for lack of such support.

Conclusion

Finally, there remains the issue of leadership. Now, as never before, the American city has need for the personal qualities of strong democratic leadership. Given the difficulties and delays involved in administrative reorganization or institutional change, the best hope for the city in the short run lies in this powerful instrument. In most cities, the mayor will have the prime responsibility.

It is in large part his role now to create a sense of commitment and concern for the problems of the ghetto community and to set the tone for the entire relationship between the institutions of city government and all the citizenry.

Part of the task is to interpret the problems of the ghetto community to the citizenry at large and to generate channels of communication between Negro and white leadership outside of government. Only if all the institutions of the community—those outside of government as well as those inside the structure—are implicated in the problems of the ghetto can the alienation and distrust of disadvantaged citizens be overcome.

This is now the decisive role for the urban mayor. As leader and mediator, he must involve all those groups—employers, news media, unions, financial institutions and others—which only together can bridge the chasm now separating the racial ghetto from the community. His goal, in effect, must be to develop a new working concept of democracy within the city.

In this effort, state government has a vital role to play. It must equip city leadership with the jurisdictional tools to deal with its problems. It must provide a fuller measure of financial and other resources to urban areas. Most importantly, state leadership is in a unique position to focus the interests and growing resources, political as well as financial, of the suburbs on the physical, social and cultural environment of the central cities. The crisis confronting city government today cannot be met without regional cooperation. This cooperation can take many forms—metropolitan government, regional planning, joint endeavors. It must be a principal goal, perhaps the overriding concern, of leadership at the state level to fashion a lasting and mutually productive relationship between city and suburban areas.

NOTE

1. Examination of the War on Poverty, Staff and Consultants Reports, prepared by Center for Urban Studies, University of Chicago, for the Subcommittee on Employment, Manpower and Poverty, Senate Committee on Labor and Public Welfare, 90th Cong. 1st Sess. (Sept. 1967), vol. VI, pp. 1721 ff.

16. Essay Review—Negro Life and Social Process

This chapter, the final one in Part IV, attempts to characterize the overall social process that has regulated black American adaptation to society. This process differs from that operative among immigrant groups in important ways. Suggestions are made by which the process of social retardation may be changed, and the progressive movement of black Americans to social, political, and economic equality with whites realized.

SETHARD FISHER

Once again, cries for social justice, equality, and dignity for American Negroes have gained momentum and intensity. Once again, national policy is favorable to the "cause." Yet Negroes have been appointed to high office in earlier times. They gained the franchise many years ago and have been before the cause for massive upsurges of moral indignation. The awesome tale of exploitation, cruelty, and injustice which recounts the history of Negroes in American society has not reached the happy end which some current events may suggest. Ethnicity remains a decided hindrance rather than help to Negroes; a shameful rather than prideful matter. Blackness and dignity remain incompatible in American culture.

How strangely incongruent the Negro experience of today with the image of what it would be like held by two former slaves who became prominent advocates of the Negro cause, Frederick Douglass[1] and Booker T. Washington.[2] Following emancipation and the end of the Civil War, Douglass' work with the Anti-Slavery Society was over and his fight for the cause of free Negroes began. Seeing freedom without power as empty, he undertook the cause of enfranchisement of Negroes. The movement for Negro suffrage grew rapidly; by 1870 the Fourteenth and Fifteenth Amendments had been adopted. With passage, Douglass said: "Negro men are today invested with complete citizenship—the right to vote and be voted for in the American Republic."[3] Yet the following account appears in the recently published *Mississippi Black Paper:*

From *Social Problems* (Winter 1966), Vol. 13, No. 3, pp. 343–353; reprinted by permission of The Society for the Study of Social Problems. I want to acknowledge my debt to Sheldon L. Messinger for helpful editorial assistance and stimulating conversations about the Negro problem. I have also benefited from critical readings of the paper by Myrtha Chabran.

On Feb. 28, 1963, I attended a voter registration meeting in the office of the Student Nonviolent Coordinating Committee in Greenwood, Mississippi. . . . As we were going onto the highway [after the meeting], we noticed a white 1962 Buick that had been driving around the office coming off the highway. There were three white men in the car. . . . They followed us for about seven miles. . . . [Soon] there were no other cars in sight. They speeded up and pulled even with us. When they were right beside us, one of the men in the car opened fire with a submachine gun. He fired for about three or four seconds and then the car sped away. I felt something hit me in the neck. I said "I'm hit." Bob Moses, who was sitting beside me, grabbed the wheel from me and then I slumped in his lap. . . . I had been shot once in the neck and once in the shoulder. When our car was later examined, eleven to thirteen bullet holes were found in it. . . . At the time I was shot I was twenty years old and field secretary for SNCC.[4]

And "The New Abolitionists" have this experience in 1964:

[A twenty-three year old Negro, native of Mississippi named Guyot] . . . was questioned by a state trooper, who became enraged when Guyot refused to say "yes sir" and "no sir." The trooper slapped Guyot repeatedly, then turned him over to a group of Citizens Council members. They beat him until he couldn't lift his arms, hit him again and again in his face until his eyes were so swollen he couldn't open them.

Another SNCC worker . . . managed to get into the jail to see Annelle Ponder. She reported on her visit when she got back to Greenwood: "Annelle's face was swollen. . . . She could barely talk. She looked at me and was able to whisper only one word: FREEDOM." [5]

Booker T. Washington characterized Douglass' career as "almost wholly within the first period of the struggle in which the race problem has involved the people of this country, the period of revolution and liberation." He added, ". . . that period is now closed, we are in the period of construction and readjustment." For Washington, "construction" and "readjustment" were optimistic terms:

. . . there was never a time when I felt more hopeful for the race than I do at the present. The great human law that in the end recognizes and rewards merit is everlasting and universal. The outside world does not know, neither can it appreciate, the struggle that is constantly going on in the hearts of both the Southern White people and their former slaves to free themselves from racial prejudice. . . .[6]

His optimism included the presumption of a dying KKK. It seems a cruel miscalculation considered in the light of reports such as the *Mississippi Black Paper*, Zinn's, or William McCord's[7] on the South today. These recent accounts suggest that Douglass and Washington were themselves part of a social process which they saw only imperfectly if at all.

These accounts also suggest that the social process which has characterized the relation of Negroes to the total society is essentially different from that which characterized the relation of the Irish, Italian, German, and other ethnic groups.[8] Progressive access to the centers of economic, political and social power in American Society, and progressive accumulation of rewards, cannot be substantiated for Negroes. Negro gains in employment, education, and income have been relative rather than absolute; they have been periodically reversed, sometimes to be made again. The social process characteristic of the relation of the Negro to the wider society has been circular and repetitive; it has not taken the progressive and unilinear course characterizing the relation of other ethnic groups to the society. Broom and Glenn cite 1880 through 1915, the depression of the 1930's and the late 1950's as periods of deterioration of gains made by Negroes.[9]

The majority of Negroes during the time of Douglass and Washington spent their lives in the fields, gutters, and ghettoes of America. They continue to do so today. Two recently published autobiographies clearly indicate that Negro degradation and deprivation are confined neither to the South nor to earlier times.[10] Claude Brown and Henry Williamson provide dramatic accounts of life in urban Negro slums. Both are highly readable, although Williamson's seems less complete and less authentic.

Brown tells the story of "Sonny," a Harlem "corner boy" who went to college. His childhood and adolescence included chronic truancy, prolonged friction with his parents, gang fighting and assorted delinquencies. Sonny was intimate with personal danger and suffered severe bodily harm. He was well known to the courts and the youth correctional houses. Although Sonny's childhood and adolescence appear to have been those of many Harlem youth, he was spared the fate of many of his friends: violent death, permanent body injury, demoralization, and fanaticism.

The life of Henry Williamson in a Negro ghetto on Chicago's south side resembled Claude Brown's life in a Harlem slum in many ways. Yet, there were essential differences. Both men lived the street life of urban Negro slums and were engaged in the violence, excitement, and illegality which characterize that life. But Henry's adolescence was in the 40's and Sonny's in the 50's. The antagonism between Henry and the agents and institutions of reform remained constant and unabated; Sonny formed meaningful, though temporary, relations with officials. Both men were deeply immersed in the underworld life of the street but they were attached in different ways. Although both were "cool studs," Henry showed little loyalty to close associates. As he puts it: "There wasn't no honor amongst us. If we stole somethin' at night, didn't sell it that night, and hid it until next morning, any one of us was likely to go out there and take it. They call it gettin' burnt." [11]

Henry, further, tells of the time he accidentally knocked his girlfriend down the stairs during an argument. Her mother located him and, at gun point, brought him back to the scene where "Callie" was aborting a child. Henry was sent to buy medicine for Callie but didn't return for two weeks.

Both Sonny and Henry quit school and became known to law enforcement officers at an early age. Both were sent by their parents to the South as a reform measure and both returned and continued their former activities. Both were wounded by bullets, although it was Henry rather than Sonny who himself nearly killed. Henry's illegal activities led progressively from delinquency to adult crime, and included robbery and theft as major means of gaining a livelihood. Fear of getting a record played a role in curtailing Sonny's illegal behavior beyond his sixteenth year. This appears to be the point at which he began his departure from the world of institutionalized illegality, a departure Henry never made.

Henry's story ends in Federal prison serving sentences of three to twenty and three to fourteen years. Caught in a robbery by a policeman, shot, and paralyzed by a bullet lodged near his spine, it was three and a half years, he says, before he could get out of bed "for any length of time. It was five and a half years before I got back on the streets." Henry learned later that the policeman who shot him had been killed "by some stud in a robbery." He comments, "I wish I coulda pissed on his grave."

Henry's language is that of the insulated northern Negro ghetto, heavily infused with a "down home" flavor. Sonny, on the other hand, is a new breed of cat. His is more the language and style of the hipster, a world so far removed from "down home" as probably to be unrecognizable there. The existence of these differences, which are probably generational, does not obscure the telling testimony of devastation, deprivation, and human misery which both volumes abundantly provide. The overwhelming majority of Negroes today continue to inhabit the bottomless pits of devastation in American society.

The career of Adam Clayton Powell is a forerunner of the now somewhat more widespread tendency for Negroes to occupy a few positions of political and economic prominence. Powell represents a deviant instance of careers among Negroes. In addition, he symbolizes that phase in the cyclic process of Negro history during which cracks in the repressive social mold appear and some gains are made.

A biographical account of Powell has recently appeared which recounts a rather illustrious career.[12] Adam Clayton Powell, Jr. was born in New Haven in 1908. He grew up in Harlem and was well acquainted with the misery of ghetto life, although, being the son of a successful minister of the world's largest Baptist church, he himself was to some extent protected from its ravages. Powell graduated from Colgate University and returned to Harlem to succeed his father at Abyssinian Baptist Church in 1937.

From his power base in Harlem, Powell took up the fight for Negro equality and dignity with militancy. In 1938 he became co-chairman of the Greater New York Coordinating Committee for Unemployment, a highly successful Harlem protest group. In 1941 he was elected to the New York City Council, becoming the first Negro ever elected to that body. During World War II Powell was actively engaged in "Civil War II." He protested segregation in the Armed Forces, job discrimination against Negroes in defense plants, and continually confronted Americans with the paradox of Negroes fighting for democracy abroad and for protection of the "color-caste system" at home. He attacked the federal government for interning Japanese-Americans while not interfering with German and Italian Americans. In addition, Powell maintained a column in the *Amsterdam News,* an influential Harlem newspaper, through which he advocated the cause of Negroes for jobs, for dignity, and for mobilization in self-help activities.

Powell's protests progressively endeared him to the citizens of Harlem. In 1943 he took office as Representative to the 79th Congress, along with Franklin D. Roosevelt and Harry S. Truman. His career as Congressman has been characterized by ongoing fights with Southern legislators and an unrelenting attack on the patterns of segregation and discrimination in the nation's Capitol. In Harlem his stature continued to grow. In the 1946 elections he attained an easy victory due to the solid support of the people of Harlem.

As a new Negro leadership grew and the parade of "marching blacks" picked up momentum, Powell became somewhat antagonistic toward them as he did not have a fixed place in the Movement. "History was moving too swiftly now, and Powell stood in terrible danger of being left in its backwater." The failure of the "Big Six" (Roy Wilkins, NAACP; Whitney Young, Urban League; James Farmer, CORE; A. Philip Randolph, Brotherhood of Sleeping Car Porters; Martin Luther King, SCLC; and John Lewis, SNCC) to accord Powell a place of prominence is said to be responsible for his periodic criticism of them and for his affinity for the Black Muslims. Chairmanship of the powerful Education and Labor Committee has thrust Powell into a position of national influence. His breach with Negro leaders in the Civil Rights movement remains, his resistance to party line politics remains, as does his tenure as the most politically influential American Negro. This atypical career line deserves further and more systematic study for it may suggest important lines of development for the Negro Movement.

The history of Negroes in American society suggests social process of acceleration of gains, followed by a gradual grinding halt and retardation. Certainly the human events which reflect this condition and are caused by it are several, and many are forever lost. The stories of Horace Cayton [13] and of Gideon Jackson,[14] however, illustrate how this process sets in, confounds, halts, and decimates the progressive development theretofore underway. Though covering different historical periods, they reflect essentially the same social process and its repetitive or circular character.

Horace R. Cayton's parents had college degrees at a time when most Negroes were illiterate. They resided in a wealthy white community at the turn of the century when few Negroes lived in the Pacific Northwest. Cayton's mother, a writer and school teacher with a cultivated interest in the arts, was from a "prominent family of the Negro elite." Her father, Hiram Revels (1827–1901), was elected United States Senator from Mississippi after the Civil War in 1870. Cayton's father finished college and eventually settled in Seattle where he became a prosperous newspaper owner, publisher, and real estate speculator. As Cayton suggests: "We, unlike most Negroes, lived in a tradition of success, achievement, and hope for Negro liberation." The development of this proud and successful family seems to have been progressively favorable up to Cayton's generation. The volume provides dramatic testimony to its demise, and to the consequent pain and suffering of a sensitive man.

The population of Seattle was 42,000 in 1890; it grew to 237,000 by 1910. A large influx of Negroes accompanied this population growth. With increased immigration, patterns of race relation in Seattle changed. As Cayton expresses it:

There was no longer a place for an in-between group, and everyone became identified as either Negro or white. We were, to my knowledge, the only Negro family to feel so dramatically the impact of these social forces, and our fall from our unique position was swift and, for us, painful.[15]

With this change in social arrangements in the city as a whole, the station of the Cayton family in the community declined drastically. The *Seattle Republican,* his father's paper, failed. The horses and carriage of the family were sold, and the services of their Japanese servant discontinued. The family moved to a less wealthy area of the city and at one point his mother took a part-time job as a housekeeper. His mother's preoccupation with cultural "uplift" activities among Negroes gave way to "the hard grind of making a home for the family." His father's previous role as leader among Negroes was challenged. Cayton suggests the ensuing changes in the outlook of members of the family toward one another as the most dramatic of all:

Early I had sensed that there was some latent conflict between my parents. Now, under the stress of adversity, these differences began to come out into the open. My mother had never quite forgotten that she was the daughter of a United States Senator and that her family belonged to the aristocracy of free Negroes, nor had she ever completely accepted the fact that Dad was not only the son of a slave but had even been a slave himself. This could be glossed over at the time when Dad had been a successful businessman and a leader in the community. But when a precarious living for the family was possible only if he worked as a janitor and she as a domestic, it was a different matter entirely.[16]

The subsequent career of Horace Cayton has been largely a frustrating suspension between a Negro world in which he felt uncomfortable and alienated, and a white world whose values he shares but satisfaction in which he could not achieve. What he says of his life at sixteen seems to hold for his later years as well:

At sixteen, my life seemed to add up to very little. I was lonesome, having neither school companions nor many Negro friends. I made several futile efforts to gain entrance to the Negro group, including an unsuccessful attempt to become a member of the Mt. Zion Baptist Church. But the services seemed to me loud and vulgar, when I contrasted them with those in the church down-town where I had always gone. . . . I was an outsider, partly because I could not give friendship and partly because I simply didn't know how to act—what to say, how to dress, what language to employ. I could find no acceptance among Negroes, and the white world had rejected me, cruelly frustrating my every attempt to belong.[17]

For a while Cayton "moved with the rising, well-to-do Negro upper class" and university intellectuals. He had several brief involvements with women. He gradually became aware of an "overpowering loneliness," and became frightened about himself, wondering "had I lost love forever?" He found his way to a psychoanalyst and continued this relationship for several years. As his description progresses one is aware of a constant and malignant intrusion of the race issue in every aspect of his life. His torment grew to such heights of intensity that gradually he withdrew from his former associates, began to drink excessively, found himself penniless, and ultimately had what he refers to as a "crack-up" five years following World War II. During these same years his mother and favorite sister died, and he had an angry confrontation with his brother who disowned him. As he expresses it, "my world collapsed; events piled up in a disorderly fashion, shaking my confidence and leaving me stripped of the will to continue."

Cayton himself recovered somewhat from the tragedy which beset his family. However, the social process to which the Cayton family became victim did not end when the family's demise was complete, nor did it originate in Seattle. *Freedom Road* tells the story of Gideon Jackson and is another reflection of the same social process operating at a different historical juncture and in a different social context.

Gideon Jackson's was one of the many families of former slaves which, after the Civil War, remained on the plantations of their former masters. Jackson, who lived on the Carwell Place, was an ignorant and unlearned man goaded on by the demand for leadership among his people. He educated himself and rose to great political heights.

As the Carwell community prospered, it came increasingly under attack by the Klan, especially when Federal troops were removed from the South. At the end, Carwell was surrounded, bombarded, and demolished by "the men who hid their faces from the sun with white hoods." Gideon Jackson's explanation of the demise of Carwell, and of this faltering, hopeful time for Negro betterment does not accord with the Social Darwinist stereotypes which later generations of interpreters have applied to it.

I want to tell you the truth now, I want you to understand why Fred McHugh lies in my house, his arms twisted from their sockets and useless to him, his wife dead, his mind gone. I want to tell you why, when my son and I came down here from Washington, we were forced to ride in a separate car marked "colored." I want to tell you why all over the South, from Texas to Virginia, cries of suffering fill the air. And most of all, I want you to know why from here on, the white man will be set against the black like a dog against a sheep; why, if they succeed, it will be a dream that there had ever been such a place as Carwell.[18]

. . . More than eight years ago, the Klan raided our people at Carwell. That was a clumsy thing, a frightened thing. They burned the barns and killed one little boy. But they were beginning then, as far back as that. From the very first, they planned to destroy us. The war was hardly over before the same people who made it set about planning for the next war, a different one this time, armies that ride in the night, underground organization, intimidation, threats, terror. Now their preparation has been completed; they're ready.[19]

And the curious part is . . . that even those things which you cling to will be forgotten. The black men who sat in the House, in the Senate; they will be forgotten, the black men who built schools and justice—all of it, my friends. We will not be men anymore. They will grind us down until we lose our humanity, until we hate the white men as truly as they hate us. They will make of us a tortured, debased people, unlike any other people on earth. And how long, my friends, before we see a little sunlight again? How long? Ask yourselves that.[20]

Southern white politicians did not simply displace Negro politicians at the end of Reconstruction. The displacement was accompanied by legal restraints and restrictions which barred Negroes from the competitive process. These events point to a more general social process, sometimes more subtly accomplished.

One of the most widely proclaimed virtues of the American political system has been its supposed responsiveness to individuals who band together to exercise pressure for self-advantageous policy formation. Rhetoric depicts this process as a free and equal scramble, regulated by "the rules of the game," and as a fundamental source of creativity and social stability. Current advocates of a pluralist society adhere to this view, sometimes explicitly and sometimes by implication.[21] One important error of this view is its failure to recognize the extent to which gains made through interest groups frequently become accelerated by virtue of the power realized at each point of victory: *as given interest groups achieve specific goals they frequently so alter the "rules" that further achievements are facilitated. Potential competitors are increasingly encumbered as the successful ones maneuver and manipulate from a vantage point of power.* While it may be argued that American society as a whole has prospered under this arrangement, it may also be stressed that this very process has been fundamental in retarding the progress of the American Negro. The point is that gains made through interest groups carry with them a certain degree of leverage, and if such gains are sufficiently cumulative the

resulting leverage permits alteration of the rules of the game in a fundamental way.[22] This subtle process, a generic ingredient of pluralism, in
combination with laissez faire economic arrangements, kept the developmental course of the American Negro circular and relative rather than
unilinear and absolute. A significant portion of the so-called psychological
difficulty which currently corrodes the Negro world stems from the distinctive cultural definitions which emerged as part of this process.

Elkins [23] attributes the uniquely inhumane character of U.S. slavery to
the lack of influence of the church and state on a rampant capitalism.
Negro subordination came to be a necessary ingredient in the long range
plans of influential plantation owners, for economic gain and power. Social
definitions which accompanied and grew out of this total devastation
depicted the Negro as an inhuman thing; a being without a soul, outside
the moral community. His image became the very anti-thesis of an American, both physically and morally. An important self-destructive strain
among Negroes today, noted by E. Franklin Frazier [24] and others, is the
desire or wish to meet the impossible demands of a white Anglo-Saxon
Protestant culture which has crystallized and institutionalized images of
virtue which by definition cannot be met by those with dark skins, kinky
hair, or other negroid features. If blackness and dignity are ever to
become compatible in American culture an assault must be made on this
pathogenic white Anglo-Saxon Protestant cultural syndrome which has
been reinforced by the Western colonialist heritage. But this calls for basic
change in patterns of dominance among major institutions in American
society.

Having the Negro as victim of this debilitating social process in American society has forestalled the kind of societal reaction which might
restrain and delimit it. The most humanly damaging consequences of
American acquisitiveness and competition have been absorbed by the
Negro. In an ethnically homogeneous United States, equal quantities of
devastation would have contributed to separating the social classes and
would have called forth more drastic demands for social change than have
thus far appeared as a result of the Negro movement. The Negro may be
seen as the inadvertent tool who in some measure blocks a more direct and
straightforward corrective social response to a debilitating social process
that claims Negroes as its major victims.

Within the Negro group a major consequence of built-in social retardation and subordination has been a significant degree of defection from
white Anglo-Saxon Protestant culture.[25] The defection is not totally a
matter of voluntary detachment but of traditional social barriers which
circumscribe the degree and kind of participation Negroes are able to
achieve. There is now in the Negro world, particularly among Northern
Negro youth, a growing perspective of futility.[26] Negro youth, and lower

class Negroes in general, are in important measure discarding conventional American society as a social sphere within which to seek acceptance. This both reflects and causes a decline in influence of the other worldly, or religious, outlook among Negroes and an increase in a secular view. This perspective of futility is reflected in a recent poem by a young Negro college student entitled "Burn, Baby, Burn!" [27]

> Sick and Tired,
> Tired of being
> Sick and Tired.
> Lost.
> Lost in the
>   wilderness
> Of white America.
> Are the masses asses?
> Cool.
> Said the master to the slave,
> "No problem. Don't rob an steal,
> I'll be your drivin' wheel."
> Cool.
> And he wheeled us into
>   350 years of black madness,
> To hog guts, conked hair, covadis,
> To bleaching cream and uncle thomas,
> to Watts,
> To the streets,
> To the KILL.
> BOMMMMM . . . . . . 2 honkeys gone.
> MOTHER FUCK the police!
> and parker's siter, too.
> BLACK PEOPLE;
> Tired
> Sick and Tired,
> Tired of being
> Sick and tired—
> Burn, baby, burn. . . . . .
> Don't leave dem bosses rags,
> C'mon, child, don't mind da
>   tags.
> Git all dat motherfucking pluck,
> Git dem guns too, we 'on't give
>   a fuck!
> Burn, baby, burn,
> Cook outta sight—
>   Fineburgs,
>   Whitefront,
>   Wineburgs,
>   Blackfront—
> Burn, baby, burn,
> In time
> He
> will learn.

The aim of social action and change on the part and in behalf of the Negro must be to alter the characteristically circular social process to which Negroes have been subject; it must be hammered into unilinear form, which means continuous, accelerated, and absolute social gain. Pettigrew [28] asserts that the Negro problem at this historical juncture is vulnerable to unprecedented improvement through unrelenting militancy of the civil rights movement. On the other hand, the view of two social scientists from the South is different. Broom and Glenn [29] amass a wealth of data on income, education and employment among Negroes. They conclude that Negroes are not likely to reach achievement levels of whites in these areas. They add that the protest tactics of the civil rights movement must give way to more pacific and, in their view, effective measures to realize the limited possible achievement by Negroes. This surely seems a hazardous suggestion given our limited understanding of the range of alternative avenues by which such achievement could occur. Significant change of course will depend on the resourcefulness, ingenuity, and intelligence of Negroes and their allies. They must provoke and engineer a social response consisting of at least three dimensions.

First, the movement for Negro betterment must involve the development of political skills, leadership, and power among Negroes themselves. This means election and appointment of Negroes to positions of influence in local, state, and national governmental bodies. Negroes would then be better equipped to defend themselves against the efforts of malevolent whites to neutralize their gains by political craft and subtlety—or by whip and gun.

Second, ties between American Negroes and the African and Asian peoples must be developed.[30] The development of bonds of mutual solidarity by Negro Americans with African and Asian peoples could serve the cause of the Negro in America and of America itself, as well as the cause of the industrializing nations of dark-skinned peoples. Such a move would internationalize the condition of the American Negro, a resource which most other ethnic groups in America always had. This achievement would win allies for Negroes and make reversals of their gains and welfare a matter of international importance, and thus less likely to occur. For the industrializing African and Asian countries this move would mean a source of new advocates for their cause who could be highly influential. The cause of skill development, education, and other needs of industrializing nations could be vastly assisted by American Negroes with a militant organization of Civil Rights, religious and other groups with an authentic interest in promoting this kind of liaison. For white America this move could have the effect of promoting an opportunity never yet realized in this country. Whites have not developed ties of friendship and respect with Negroes as social equals. They have not taken seriously the need to dismantle and replace the pathogenic white Anglo-Saxon Protestant cultural syndrome. This is a badly needed experience which could be of great value to this country as more and more it must come to grips with its racist heritage.[31]

A third and final facet of this social response must be to challenge and counteract the rampant acquisitive and competitive tendencies in American society by seeking proscriptions on the power and influence of the dominant economic institutions from which they spring. This means building into American life certain "rules of the game" regarding economic activity which are not vulnerable to the power stratagems of competing interest groups. In this way checks and balances could be built into our economic system which would relax the grip of tenacious economic imperatives and make possible the growth of needed new definitions.

Problem-related social action can only maximize its achievements as it is informed by creative scholarly research. The complex of factors which at different historical periods have reversed the progress of Negroes must be documented in detail so that social policy may be devised which will assure that they do not appear again. Historical and comparative data must be drawn on in pursuit of means by which legitimacy for Negro gains which are absolute, once made, may be achieved.[32] Finally, some research effort must be made to define and characterize more precisely the nature of the social process which has continually worked to stabilize the Negro in an inferior social status. Is this process a necessary component of the system of economic and political arrangements by which American society is defined and defines itself?[33] Does the accumulation of social gain by Negroes automatically mean social loss for other groups? Serious pursuit of these matters could allow new patterns of race relations to appear which promise to curtail the impending violence and destruction which must occur when a mobilized, militant black minority and a defensive, fearful white majority angrily confront one another.

NOTES

1. Frederick Douglass, *The Life and Times of Frederick Douglass* (New York: Pathway Press, 1941); the book was originally published in 1892. A reprint is available: New York: Collier Books, 1963. Citations are to the 1941 edition. See also *A Star Pointed North* (New York: Harper and Row, 1965), by Edmund Fuller; Philip S. Foner, *Frederick Douglass* (New York: The Citadel Press, 1964).
2. Booker T. Washington, *Up From Slavery: An Autobiography* (New York: Doubleday, Page & Co., 1901); reprinted: New York: Bantam Books, 1956. Citation is to the 1941 edition.
3. Douglass, *op. cit.*, p. 438.
4. Statement by James Travis in *Mississippi Black Paper* (New York: Random House, 1965), p. 8.
5. Howard Zinn, *SNCC: The New Abolitionists* (Boston: Beacon Press, 1964), p. 95.
6. Washington, *op. cit.*, p. 319.
7. William McCord, *Mississippi: The Long Hot Summer* (New York: W. W. Norton & Company, 1965).

8. A useful definition and discussion of ethnic groups may be found in a recent publication by Tomatsu Shibutani and Kian M. Kwan. According to the authors "an ethnic group consists of those who conceive of themselves as being alike by virtue of their common ancestry, real or fictitious, and who are so regarded by others." See their *Ethnic Stratification* (New York: Macmillan, 1965), p. 47.
9. Leonard Broom and Norval Glenn, *Transformation of the Negro American* (New York: Harper and Row, 1964), p. 186.
10. Claude Brown, *Manchild in the Promised Land* (New York: Macmillan, 1965), and Henry Williamson, *Hustler!*, edited by R. Lincoln Keiser (New York: Doubleday, 1965).
11. *Ibid.*, pp. 35–36.
12. Neil Hickey and Ed Edwin, *Adam Clayton Powell and the Politics of Race* (New York: Fleet Publishing Corp., 1965).
13. Horace Cayton, *Long Old Road* (New York: Trident Press, 1965).
14. Jackson is the central character in Howard Fast's *Freedom Road* (New York: Pocket Books, Inc., 1962). Although this is a novelistic treatment and suffers some typical weaknesses of such documents, Fast gives the following account of his material: "All the essentials of this story are true. There was not one Carwell in the South at that period but thousands, both larger and smaller." The specific sources of his data are provided on pp. 263–264.
15. Cayton, *op. cit.*, p. 23.
16. *Ibid.*, p. 25.
17. *Ibid.*, p. 34.
18. Fast, *op. cit.*, p. 201.
19. *Ibid.*, p. 175.
20. *Ibid.*, p. 207.
21. See C. Wright Mills' discussion of pluralism in his *The Power Elite* (New York: Oxford University Press, 1959), esp. pp. 242–268; "The Distribution of Power in American Society" by Talcott Parsons, *World Politics*, Vol. 10, October, 1957, pp. 123–143; and, articles by Todd Gitlin and Shin'ya Ona in *Studies on the Left*, Summer, 1965. These sources provide rather extensive discussion of pluralism from diverse viewpoints.
22. This I take to be the essential meaning of what Elkins, Tannenbaum, and others tell us about the Negro situation. See Frank Tannenbaum, *Slave and Citizen* (New York: Vintage Books, A Division of Random House, 1963).
23. Stanley M. Elkins, *Slavery* (New York: Universal Library, 1963).
24. E. Franklin Frazier, *Black Bourgeoisie* (Glencoe: The Free Press, 1957).
25. An insightful and perceptive description of the ethical and moral aberrations occasioned by race prejudice and the manner in which they influence both Negroes and whites is provided by Howard Thurman in his *The Luminous Darkness* (New York: Harper and Row, 1965).
26. The term "futility" is intended to suggest a lack of reorientation from which meaningful goal oriented directions might come.
27. Marvin Jackman, *Soulbook*, Fall, 1965, p. 153.
28. Thomas F. Pettigrew, *Profile of the American Negro* (Princeton: D. Van Nostrand Company, 1964), p. 200.
29. Leonard Broom and Norval Glenn, *op. cit.*, p. 190.
30. For an extensive discussion of this matter in relation to Africa see Charles E. Silberman's *Crisis in Black and White* (New York: Random House, 1964), pp. 162–188.
31. Regarding racism I take the view expressed by Calvin C. Hernton that racism represents "learned behavior and learned emotions . . . that compel one group to conceive of and treat the other on the basis of its physical characteristics alone, as if it did not belong to the human race." See his *Sex and Racism in America* (New York: Doubleday and Company, 1965), p. 175.
32. Attacking the problem of "pluralistic ignorance" is one suggestion offered by L. K. Northwood and Ernest A. T. Barth. See their *Urban Desegregation* (Seattle: University of Washington Press, 1965), esp. pp. 84–86.
33. Pettigrew has answered this question affirmatively. He suggests that ". . . some

basic structural changes in American society will have to occur before viable race relation solutions are possible. These changes include wider employment, a different taxation base, an extension of the minimum wage to cover service workers, and massive retraining. Clearly, the problem we are trying to solve transcends the boundaries of Civil Rights and reaches into the basic structure of American society." See his "White-Negro Confrontations," in *The Negro Challenge to the Business Community,* edited by Eli Ginzberg (McGraw-Hill: New York, 1964). Other essays in this volume which deal with the economic and political aspect of the Negro problem are noteworthy.

V. Black Protest: Past and Present, North and South

Protest among black Americans and those who act on their behalf has taken a variety of forms, ranging from the phenomenon of runaway slaves to current patterns of protest in the ghetto and among black and white college students across the country. Some of these protest efforts have been mercilessly cut down by the force and violence of white resistance, for example, the Nat Turner rebellion and the efforts of John Brown. Other protest attempts, often because they *are* unsuccessful, have achieved a very limited degree of practical gain. Among traditional black American symbols of protest are Rev. Martin Luther King, Jr., Frederick Douglass, W. E. B. Du Bois, and Paul Robeson. Today black and white American youths are in the forefront of protest movements: Stokely Carmichael and H. Rap Brown were recently known as national leaders of the black protest movement. Black Student Union groups are made up largely of college-age youth whose activities, along with those of Malcolm X, have internationalized the black protest movement. Youthful leaders are challenging the older leaders within this movement—such men as Roy Wilkins, who currently heads the NAACP, and Whitney Young, current head of the Urban League.

The current black protest movement has shifted from the South to the North and has become increasingly violent. The tactics and strategy of the late Rev. Martin Luther King, Jr., and his Southern Christian Leadership Conference are decreasingly influential as the new, youthful, and militant black leadership emerges. In many parts of the country black militance has aroused white fear and anxiety, and concerns about white "backlash" have been expressed. Recent Republican political gains may reflect this, as well as the notable absence of black Americans from high positions in the recently elected Republican administration. These matters raise important questions about the kind of protest best suited to achieve black goals. Alternative possibilities are explored in Part V.

17. Rejection and Protest: An Historical Sketch

The current rapid proliferation of black protest groups such as the Black Student Union and the Third World Liberation Front obscures the fact that black groups such as the NAACP were themselves once major symbols of black protest. This growth of new protest groups among blacks is a product of rising expectations within the black community and of an emerging pride and healthy arrogance about being black. The enduring form that black protest will take cannot now be known. One option would be guerrilla warfare in major metropolitan centers should blacks opt to destroy the system which denies their legitimate claims to equality. Another would be a posture of chronic abrasiveness and the build-up of strategic alliances, with the expectation of incremental gain at an accelerated pace. These, among others, are contending possibilities within the overall black protest movement.

The historical emergence of black protest organizations and their cumulative accomplishments can be instructive. Of particular importance is their overall ineffectiveness. As the following article from the Kerner Commission Report points out, as of 1967 the doctrine of white supremacy remains influential, governmental support for blacks is minimal, and only minor gains are the result of monumental effort.

KERNER COMMISSION REPORT

Introduction

The events of the summer of 1967 are in large part the culmination of 300 years of racial prejudice. Most Americans know little of the origins of the racial schism separating our white and Negro citizens. Few appreciate how central the problem of the Negro has been to our social policy. Fewer still understand that today's problems can be solved only if white Americans comprehend the rigid social, economic and educational barriers that have prevented Negroes from participating in the mainstream of American life. Only a handful realize that Negro accommodation to the patterns of prejudice in American culture has been but one side of the coin—for as

From *Report of the National Advisory Commission on Civil Disorders* (1968), Part I, pp. 95–113.

slaves and as free men, Negroes have protested against oppression and have persistently sought equality in American society.

What follows is neither a history of the Negro in the United States nor a full account of Negro protest movements. Rather, it is a brief narrative of a few historical events that illustrate the facts of rejection and the forms of protest.

We call on history not to justify, but to help explain, for black and white Americans, a state of mind.

The Colonial Period

Twenty years after Columbus reached the New World, African Negroes, transported by Spanish, Dutch and Portuguese traders, were arriving in the Caribbean Islands. Almost all came as slaves. By 1600, there were more than half a million slaves in the Western Hemisphere.

In Colonial America, the first Negroes landed at Jamestown in August, 1619. Within 40 years, Negroes had become a group apart, separated from the rest of the population by custom and law. Treated as servants for life, forbidden to intermarry with whites, deprived of their African traditions and dispersed among Southern plantations, American Negroes lost tribal, regional and family ties.

Through massive importation, their numbers increased rapidly. By 1776, some 500,000 Negroes were held in slavery and indentured servitude in the United States. Nearly one of every six persons in the country was a slave.

Americans disapproved a preliminary draft of the Declaration of Independence that indicted the King of England for waging "cruel war against human nature itself, violating its most sacred rights of life and liberty in the persons of a distant people who never offended him, captivating and carrying them into slavery in another hemisphere or to incur miserable death in their transportation thither." Instead, they approved a document that proclaimed "all men are created equal."

The statement was an ideal, a promise. But it excluded the Negroes who were held in bondage, as well as the few who were free men.

The conditions in which Negroes lived had already led to protest. Racial violence was present almost from the beginning of the American experience. Throughout the 18th century, the danger of Negro revolts obsessed many white Americans. Slave plots of considerable scope were uncovered in New York in 1712 and 1714, and they resulted in bloodshed—whites and Negroes were slain.

Negroes were at first barred from serving in the Revolutionary Army, recruiting officers having been ordered in July 1775, to enlist no "stroller, Negro or vagabond." Yet Negroes were already actively involved in the struggle for independence. Crispus Attucks, a Boston Negro, was perhaps the first American to die for freedom, and Negroes had already fought in the battles at Lexington and Concord. They were among the soldiers at Bunker Hill.

Fearing that Negroes would enlist in the British Army, which welcomed them, and facing a manpower shortage, the Continental Army accepted free Negroes. Many slaves did join the British, and, according to an estimate by Thomas Jefferson, more than 30,000 Virginia slaves ran away in 1778 alone, presumably to enlist. The states enrolled both free and slave Negroes, and finally Congress authorized military service for slaves, who were to be emancipated in return for their service. By the end of the war, about 5,000 Negroes had been in the ranks of the Continental Army. Those who had been slaves became free.

The Constitution and the Laws

Massachusetts abolished slavery in 1783, and Connecticut, Rhode Island, New Jersey, Pennsylvania and New York soon provided for gradual liberation. But relatively few Negroes lived in these states. The bulk of the Negro population was in the South, where white Americans had fortunes invested in slaves. Although the Congress banned slavery in the Northwest Territory, delegates at the Constitutional Convention compromised —a slave was counted as three-fifths of a person for determining the number of representatives from a state to Congress; Congress was prohibited from restricting the slave trade until after 1808; and the free states were required to return fugitive slaves to their Southern owners.

Growing numbers of slaves in the South became permanently fastened in bondage, and slavery spread into the new Southern regions. When more slaves were needed for the cotton and sugar plantations in the Southwest, they were ordered from the "Negro-raising" states of the Old South or, despite Congressional prohibition of the slave trade, imported from Africa.

The laws of bondage became even more institutionalized. Masters retained absolute authority over their Negroes, who were unable to leave their masters' properties without written permission. Any white person, even those who owned no slaves—and they outnumbered slaveholders six to one—could challenge a truant slave and turn him over to a public official. Slaves could own no property, could enter into no contract—not even a contract of marriage—and had no right to assemble in public unless a white person was present. They had no standing in the courts.

Discrimination as Doctrine

The situation was hardly better for free Negroes. A few achieved material success, some even owned slaves themselves, but the vast majority knew only poverty. Forbidden to settle in some areas, segregated in others, they were targets of prejudice and discrimination. In the South, they were denied freedom of movement, severely restricted in their choice of occupation and forbidden to associate with whites or with slaves. They lived in constant danger of being enslaved—whites could challenge their freedom and an infraction of the law could put them into bondage. In both North and South, they were regularly victims of mobs. In 1829, for example, white residents invaded Cincinnati's "Little Africa," killed Negroes, burned their property and ultimately drove half the Negro population from the city.

Some Americans, Washington and Jefferson among them, advocated the gradual emancipation of slaves, and in the 19th century, a movement to abolish slavery grew in importance and strength. A few white abolitionist leaders wanted full equality for Negroes, but others sought only to eliminate the institution itself. And some antislavery societies, fearing that Negro members would unnecessarily offend those who were unsympathetic with abolitionist principles, denied entrance to Negroes.

Most Americans were, in fact, against abolishing slavery. They refused to rent their halls for antislavery meetings. They harassed abolitionist leaders who sought to educate white and Negro children together. They attacked those involved in the movement. Mobs sometimes killed abolitionists and destroyed their property.

A large body of literature came into existence to prove that the Negro was imperfectly developed in mind and body, that he belonged to a lower order of man, that slavery was right on ethnic, economic and social grounds—quoting the Scriptures in support.

Spreading rapidly during the first part of the 19th century, slavery held less than one million Negroes in 1800 but almost four million by 1860. Although some few white Americans had freed their slaves, most increased their holdings, for the invention of the cotton gin had made cotton the heart of the Southern economy. By mid-century, slavery in the South had become a systematic and aggressive way of treating a whole race of people.

The despair of Negroes was evident. Malingering and sabotage tormented every slaveholder. The problem of runaway slaves was endemic. Some slaves—Gabriel Prosser in 1800, Denmark Vesey in 1822, Nat Turner in 1831, and others—turned to violence, and the sporadic uprisings that flared demonstrated a deep protest against a demeaning way of life.

Negroes who had material resources expressed their distress in other ways. In 1816, Paul Cuffee, Negro philanthropist and owner of a fleet of ships, transported a group of Negroes to a new home in Sierra Leone. Forty years later, Martin R. Delany, Negro editor and physician, also urged Negroes to settle elsewhere.

Equality of treatment and acceptance by the society at large were myths, and Negro protest during the first half of the 19th century took the form of rhetoric, spoken and written, which combined denunciation of undemocratic oppression together with pleas to the conscience of white Americans for the redress of grievances and the recognition of their constitutional rights.

A few Negroes joined white Americans who believed that only Negro emigration to Africa would solve racial problems. But most Negroes equated that program with banishment and felt themselves "entitled to participate in the blessings" of America. The National Negro Convention Movement, formed in 1830, held conferences to publicize on a national scale the evils of slavery and the indignities heaped on free Negroes.

The American Moral Reform Society, founded by Negroes in 1834, rejected racial separatism and advocated uplifting "the whole human race, without distinction as to . . . complexion." Other Negro reformers pressed for stronger racial consciousness and solidarity as the means to overcome racial barriers. Many took direct action to help slaves escape through the underground railroad. A few resisted discrimination by political action, even though most Negroes were barred from voting.

Frustration, disillusionment, anger, and fantasy marked the Negro's protest against the place in American society assigned to them. "I was free," Harriet Tubman said, "but there was no one to welcome me in the land of freedom. I was a stranger in a strange land."

When Frederick Douglass, the distinguished Negro abolitionist, addressed the citizens of Rochester on Independence Day, 1852, he told them:

The Fourth of July is *yours,* not mine. *You* may rejoice, *I* must mourn. To drag a man into the grand illuminated temple of liberty, and call upon him to join you in joyous anthems, were inhuman mockery and sacrilegious irony. . . . Fellow citizens, above your national tumultuous joy, I hear the mournful wail of millions, whose chains, heavy and grievous yesterday, are today rendered more intolerable by the jubilant shouts that reach them. . . .

The Path Toward Civil War

The 1850's brought Negroes increasing despair, as the problem of slavery was debated by the Nation's leaders. The Compromise of 1850 and the Kansas-Nebraska Act of 1854 settled no basic issues. And the *Dred Scott* case in 1857 confirmed Negroes in their understanding that they were not "citizens" and thus not entitled to the constitutional safeguards enjoyed by other Americans.

But the abolitionist movement was growing. "Uncle Tom's Cabin" appeared in 1852 and sold more than 300,000 copies that year. Soon presented on the stage throughout the North, it dramatized the cruelty of slave masters and overseers and condemned a culture based on human degradation and exploitation. The election of Abraham Lincoln on an antislavery platform gave hope that the end of slavery was near.

But by the time Lincoln took office, seven Southern states had seceded from the Union, and four more soon joined them.

The Civil War and Emancipation renewed Negro faith in the vision of a racially egalitarian and integrated American society. But Americans, having been aroused by wartime crisis, would again fail to destroy what abolitionists had described as the "sins of caste."

Civil War and "Emancipation"

Negroes volunteered for military service during the Civil War—the struggle, as they saw it, between the slave states and the free states. They were rejected.

Not until a shortage of troops plagued the Union Army late in 1862 were segregated units of "United States Colored Troops" formed. Not until 1864 did these men receive the same pay as white soldiers. A total of 186,000 Negroes served.

The Emancipation Proclamation of 1863 freed few slaves at first but had immediate significance as a symbol. Negroes could hope again for equality.

But there were, at the same time, bitter signs of racial unrest. Violent rioting occurred in Cincinnati in 1862 when Negro and Irish hands competed for work on the riverboats. Lesser riots took place in Newark, and in Buffalo and Troy, N.Y., the result of combined hostility to the war and fear that Negroes would take white jobs.

The most violent of the troubles took place in the New York City draft riots in July, 1863, when white workers, mainly Irish-born, embarked on a 3-day rampage.

Desperately poor and lacking real roots in the community, they had the most to lose from the draft. Further, they were bitterly afraid that even cheaper Negro labor would flood the North if slavery ceased to exist.
All the frustrations and prejudices the Irish had suffered were brought to a boiling point. . . . At pitiful wages, they had slaved on the railroads and canals, had been herded into the most menial jobs as carters and stevedores. . . . Their crumbling frame tenements . . . were the worst slums in the city.[1]

Their first target was the office of the provost marshal in charge of conscription, and 700 people quickly ransacked the building and set it on fire. The crowd refused to permit firemen into the area, and the whole block was gutted. Then the mob spilled into the Negro area where many Negroes were slain and thousands forced to flee town. The police were helpless until Federal troops arrived on the 3d day and restored control.

Union victory in the Civil War promised the Negroes freedom but not equality or immunity from white aggression. Scarcely was the war ended when racial violence erupted in New Orleans. Negroes proceeding to an assembly hall to discuss the franchise were charged by police and special

troops who routed the Negroes with guns, bricks, and stones, killed some
at once, and pursued and killed others who were trying to escape.

Federal troops restored order. But 34 Negroes and four whites were
reported dead, and over 200 people were injured. General Sheridan later
said:

At least nine-tenths of the casualties were perpetrated by the police and
citizens by stabbing and smashing in the heads of many who had already been
wounded or killed by policemen . . . it was not just a riot but "an absolute
massacre by the police . . ." a murder which the mayor and police . . .
perpetrated without the shadow of necessity.

Reconstruction

Reconstruction was a time of hope, the period when the 13th, 14th, and
15th Amendments were adopted, giving Negroes the vote and the promise
of equality.

But campaigns of violence and intimidation accompanied these optimistic expressions of a new age. The Ku Klux Klan and other secret organizations sought to suppress the emergence into society of the new Negro
citizens. Major riots occurred in Memphis, Tennessee, where 46 Negroes
were reported killed and 75 wounded, and in the Louisiana centers of
Colfax and Coushatta, where more than 100 Negro and white Republicans were massacred.

Nevertheless, in 1875, Congress enacted the first significant civil rights
law. It gave Negroes the right to equal accommodations, facilities, and
advantages of public transportation, inns, theaters and places of public
amusement, but the law had no effective enforcement provisions and was
in fact poorly enforced. Although bills to provide Federal aid to education
for Negroes were prepared, none passed, and educational opportunities
remained meager. But Negroes were elected to every Southern legislature,
20 served in the U.S. House of Representatives, two represented Mississippi in the U.S. Senate and a prominent Negro politician was Governor of
Louisiana for 40 days.

Opposition to Negroes in state and local government was always open
and bitter. In the press and on the platform, they were described as
ignorant and depraved. Critics made no distinction between Negroes who
had graduated from Dartmouth and those who had graduated from the
cotton fields. Every available means was employed to drive Negroes from
public life. Negroes who voted or held office were refused jobs or punished
by the Ku Klux Klan. One group in Mississippi boasted of having killed
116 Negroes and of having thrown their bodies into the Tallahatchie
River. In a single South Carolina county, six men were murdered and more
than 300 whipped during the first 6 months of 1870.

The Federal Government seemed helpless. Having withdrawn the occupation troops as soon as the Southern states organized governments, the President was reluctant to send them back. In 1870 and 1871, after the 15th Amendment was ratified, Congress enacted several laws to protect the right of citizens to vote. They were seldom enforced, and the Supreme Court struck down most of the important provisions in 1875 and 1876.

As Southern white governments returned to power, beginning with Virginia in 1869 and ending with Louisiana in 1877, the process of relegating the Negro to a subordinate place in American life was accelerated. Disfranchisement was the first step. Negroes who defied the Klan and tried to vote faced an array of deceptions and obstacles: Polling places were changed at the last minute without notice to Negroes, severe time limitations were imposed on marking complicated ballots, votes cast incorrectly in a maze of ballot boxes were nullified. The suffrage provisions of state constitutions were rewritten to disfranchise Negroes who could not read, understand or interpret the Constitution. Some state constitutions permitted those who failed the tests to vote if their ancestors had been eligible to vote on January 1, 1860—a date when no Negro could vote anywhere in the South.

In 1896, there were 130,344 Negroes registered in Louisiana. In 1900, after the state rewrote the suffrage provisions of its constitution, only 5,320 remained on the registration books. Essentially the same thing happened in the other states of the former Confederacy.

Segregation by Law

When the Supreme Court in 1883 declared the Civil Rights Act of 1875 unconstitutional, Southern states began to enact laws to segregate the races. In 1896, the Supreme Court in *Plessy* v. *Ferguson* approved "separate but equal" facilities; it was then that segregation became an established fact, by law as well as by custom. Negroes and whites were separated on public carriers and in all places of public accommodation, including hospitals and churches. In courthouses, whites and Negroes took oaths on separate Bibles. In most communities, whites were separated from Negroes in cemeteries.

Segregation invariably meant discrimination. On trains all Negroes, including those holding first-class tickets, were allotted seats in the baggage car. Negroes in public buildings had to use freight elevators and toilet facilities reserved for janitors. Schools for Negro children were at best a weak imitation of those for whites as states spent 10 times more to educate white youngsters than Negroes. Discrimination in wages became the rule, whether between Negro and white teachers of similar training and experience or between common laborers on the same job.

Some Northern states enacted civil rights laws in the 1880's, but Negroes in fact were treated little differently in the North than in the South. As

Negroes moved north in substantial numbers toward the end of the century, they discovered that equality of treatment did not exist in Massachusetts, New York, or Illinois. They were crowded by local ordinances into sections of the city where housing and public services were generally substandard. Overt discrimination in employment was a general practice and job opportunities apart from menial tasks were few. Most labor unions excluded Negroes from membership—or granted membership in separate and powerless Jim Crow locals. Yet when Negroes secured employment during strikes, labor leaders castigated them for undermining the principles of trade unionism. And when Negroes sought to move into the mainstream of community life by seeking membership in the organizations around them—educational, cultural, and religious—they were invariably rebuffed.

By the 20th century, the Negro was at the bottom of American society. Disfranchised, Negroes throughout the country were excluded by employers and labor unions from white-collar jobs and skilled trades. Jim Crow laws and farm tenancy characterized Negro existence in the South. About 100 lynchings occurred every year in the 1880's and 1890's; there were 161 lynchings in 1892. As increasing numbers of Negroes migrated to Northern cities, race riots became commonplace. Northern whites, even many former abolitionists, began to accept the white South's views on race relations.

That Northern whites would resort to violence was made clear in anti-Negro riots in New York City, 1900; Springfield, Ohio, 1904; Greensburg, Ind., 1906; and Springfield, Ill., 1908.

The Springfield, Ill., riot lasted three days. It was initiated by a white woman's charge of rape by a Negro, inflamed by newspapers, and intensified by crowds of whites gathered around the jail demanding that the Negro, arrested and imprisoned, be lynched. When the sheriff transferred the accused and another Negro to a jail in a nearby town, rioters headed for the Negro section and attacked homes and businesses owned by or catering to Negroes. White owners who showed handkerchiefs in their windows averted harm to their stores. One Negro was summarily lynched, others were dragged from houses and streetcars and beaten. By the time National Guardsmen could reach the scene, six persons were dead—four whites and two Negroes. Property damage was extensive. Many Negroes left Springfield, hoping to find better conditions elsewhere, especially in Chicago.

Protest in the Early 1900's

Between his famous Atlanta Exposition Address in 1895 and his death in 1915, Booker T. Washington, principal of the Tuskegee Normal and Industrial Institute in Alabama and the most prominent Negro in America, privately spent thousands of dollars fighting disfranchisement and segregation laws; publicly he advocated a policy of accommodation, conciliation, and gradualism. Washington believed that by helping themselves, by creating and supporting their own businesses, by proving their usefulness to society through the acquisition of education, wealth, and morality, Negroes would earn the respect of the white man and thus eventually gain their constitutional rights.

Self-help and self-respect appeared a practical and sure, if gradual, way of ultimately achieving racial equality. Washington's doctrines also gained support because they appealed to race pride: If Negroes believed in themselves, stood together, and supported each other, they would be able to shape their destinies.

In the early years of the century, a small group of Negroes led by W. E. B. Du Bois formed the Niagara Movement to oppose Washington's program. Washington had put economic progress before politics, had accepted the separate-but-equal theory and opposed agitation and protest. Du Bois and his followers stressed political activity as the basis of the Negro's future, insisted on the inequity of Jim Crow laws and advocated agitation and protest.

In sharp language, the Niagara group placed responsibility for the race problem squarely on the whites. The aims of the movement were voting rights and "the abolition of all caste distinctions based simply on race and color."

Although Booker T. Washington tried to crush his critics, Du Bois and the Negro "radicals" as they were called, enlisted the support of a small group of influential white liberals and socialists. Together, in 1909–10, they formed the National Association for the Advancement of Colored People.

The NAACP hammered at the walls of prejudice by organizing Negroes and well-disposed whites, by aiming propaganda at the whole Nation, by taking legal action in courts and legislatures. Almost at the outset of its career, the NAACP prevailed upon the Supreme Court to declare unconstitutional two discriminatory statutes. In 1915, the Court struck down the Oklahoma "grandfather clause," a provision in several Southern state constitutions that, together with voting tests, had the effect of excluding from the vote those whose ancestors were ineligible to vote in 1860. Two years later, the Supreme Court outlawed residential segregation ordinances. These NAACP victories were the first legal steps in a long fight against disfranchisement and segregation.

During the first quarter of the 20th century, the Federal Government enacted no new legislation to ensure equal rights or opportunities for Negroes and made little attempt to enforce existing laws despite flagrant violations of Negro civil rights.

In 1913, members of Congress from the South introduced bills to federalize the Southern segregation policy. They wished to ban interracial marriages in the District of Columbia, segregate white and Negro Federal employees and introduce Jim Crow laws in the public carriers of the District. The bills did not pass, but segregation practices were extended in Federal offices, shops, restrooms and lunchrooms. The Nation's Capital became as segregated as any in the former Confederate States.

East St. Louis, 1917

Elsewhere there was violence. In July 1917, in East St. Louis, a riot claimed the lives of 39 Negroes and nine whites. It was the result of fear by white working men that Negro advances in economic, political, and social status were threatening their own security and status.

When the labor force of an aluminum plant went on strike, the company hired Negro workers. A labor union delegation called on the mayor and asked that further migration of Negroes to East St. Louis be stopped. As the men were leaving City Hall, they heard that a Negro had accidentally shot a white man during a holdup. In a few minutes rumor had replaced fact: the shooting was intentional—a white woman had been insulted—two white girls were shot. By this time, 3,000 people had congregated and were crying for vengeance. Mobs roamed the streets beating Negroes. Policemen did little more than take the injured to hospitals and disarm Negroes.

The National Guard restored order. When the Governor withdrew the troops, tensions were still high, and scattered episodes broke the peace. The press continued to emphasize Negro crimes. White pickets and Negro workers at the aluminum company skirmished and, on July 1, some whites drove through the main Negro neighborhood firing into homes. Negro residents armed themselves. When a police car drove down the street, Negroes riddled it with gunshot.

The next day a Negro was shot on the main street, and a new riot was underway. The area became a "bloody half mile" for 3 or 4 hours; streetcars were stopped, and Negroes, without regard to age or sex, were pulled off and stoned, clubbed, and kicked. Mob leaders calmly shot and killed Negroes who were lying in blood in the street. As the victims were placed in an ambulance, the crowds cheered and applauded.

Other rioters set fire to Negro homes, and by midnight the Negro section was in flames, and Negroes were fleeing the city. There were 48 dead, hundreds injured and more than 300 buildings destroyed.

World War I and Postwar Violence

When the United States entered World War I in 1917, the country again faced the question whether American citizens should have the right to serve, on an equal basis, in defense of their country. More than 2 million

Negroes registered under the Selective Service Act, and some 360,000 were called into service.

The Navy rejected Negroes except as menials. The Marine Corps rejected them altogether. The Army formed them into separate units commanded, for the most part, by white officers. Only after great pressure did the Army permit Negro candidates to train as officers in a segregated camp. Mistreated at home and overseas, Negro combat units performed exceptionally well under French commanders who refused to heed American warnings that Negroes were inferior people. Negro soldiers returning home were mobbed for attempting to use facilities open to white soldiers. Of the 70 Negroes lynched during the first year after the war, a substantial number were soldiers. Some were lynched in uniform.

Reorganized in 1915, the Ku Klux Klan was flourishing again by 1919. Its program "for uniting native-born white Christians for concerted action in the preservation of American institutions and the supremacy of the white race," was implemented by flogging, branding with acid, tarring and feathering, hanging, and burning. It destroyed the elemental rights of many Negroes—and of some whites.

Violence took the form of lynchings and riots, and major riots by whites against Negroes took place in 1917 in Chester, Pa., and Philadelphia; in 1919 in Washington, D.C., Omaha, Charleston, Longview, Tex., Chicago, and Knoxville; in 1921 in Tulsa.

The Chicago riot of 1919 flared from the increase in Negro population, which had more than doubled in 10 years. Jobs were plentiful, but housing was not. Black neighborhoods expanded into white sections of the city and trouble developed. Between July 1917, and March 1921, 58 Negro houses were bombed, and recreational areas were sites of racial conflict.

The riot itself started on Sunday, July 27, with stone-throwing and sporadic fighting at adjoining white and Negro beaches. A Negro boy swimming off the Negro beach drifted into water reserved for whites and drowned. Young Negroes claimed he had been struck by stones and demanded the arrest of a white man. Instead, police arrested a Negro. Negroes attacked policemen, and news spread to the city. White and Negro groups clashed in the streets, two persons died and 50 were wounded. On Monday, Negroes coming home from work were attacked; later, when whites drove cars through Negro neighborhoods and fired weapons, Negroes retaliated. Twenty more were killed and hundreds wounded. On Tuesday, a handful more were dead, 129 injured. Rain began to fall; the mayor finally called in the state militia. The city quieted down after nearly a week of violence.

The 1920's and the New Militancy

In the period between the two World Wars, the NAACP dominated the strategy of racial advancement. The NAACP drew its strength from large numbers of Southern Negroes who had migrated to Northern cities and from a small but growing Negro group of professionals and businessmen. It projected the image of the "New Negro," race-proud and self-reliant, believing in racial cooperation and self-help and determined to fight for his constitutional rights. This was reflected in the work of writers and artists known as the "Harlem Renaissance," who drew upon the Negro's own cultural tradition and experience. W. E. B. Du Bois, editor of the *Crisis*, the NAACP publication, symbolized the new mood and exerted great influence.

The NAACP did extraordinary service, giving legal defense to victims of race riots and unjust judicial proceedings. It obtained the release of the soldiers who had received life sentences on charges of rioting against intolerable conditions at Houston in 1917. It successfully defended Negro sharecroppers in Elaine, Ark., who in 1919 had banded together to gain fairer treatment. They had become the objects of a massive armed hunt by whites to put them "in their place," and who were charged with insurrection when they resisted. It secured the acquittal, with the help of Clarence Darrow, of Dr. Ossian Sweet and his family. The Sweets, who had moved into a white neighborhood in Detroit, shot at a mob attacking their home and killed a man. The Sweets were eventually judged to have committed the act in self-defense.

Less successful were attempts to prevent school segregation in Northern cities. Gerrymandering of school boundaries and other devices by boards of education were fought with written petitions, verbal protests to school officials, legal suits, and, in several cities, school boycotts. All proved of no avail.

The thrust of the NAACP was primarily political and legal, but the National Urban League, founded in 1911 by philanthropists and social workers, sought an economic solution to the Negroes' problems. Sympathetic with Booker T. Washington's point of view, believing in conciliation, gradualism, and moral suasion, the Urban League searched out industrial opportunities for Negro migrants to the cities, using arguments that appealed to the white businessman's sense of economic self-interest and also to his conscience.

Another important figure who espoused an economic program to ameliorate the Negro's condition was A. Philip Randolph, an editor of the "Messenger." He regarded the NAACP as a middle-class organization unconcerned about pressing economic problems. Taking a Marxist position on the causes of prejudice and discrimination, Randolph called for a new and radical Negro unafraid to demand his rights as a member of the working class. He advocated physical resistance to white mobs, but he believed that only united action of black and white workers against capitalists would achieve social justice.

Although Randolph addressed himself to the urban working masses, few of them ever read the "Messenger." The one man who reached the masses of frustrated and disillusioned migrants in the Northern ghettos was Marcus Garvey.

Garvey, founder in 1914 of the Universal Negro Improvement Association (UNIA), aimed to liberate both Africans and American Negroes from their oppressors. His utopian method was the wholesale migration of American Negroes to Africa. Contending that whites would always be racist, he stressed racial pride and history, denounced integration, and insisted that the black man develop "a distinct racial type of civilization of his own and . . . work out his salvation in his motherland." On a more practical level, he urged support of Negro businesses, and through the UNIA organized a chain of groceries, restaurants, laundries, a hotel, printing plant, and steamship line. When several prominent Negroes called the attention of the Federal government to irregularities in the management of the steamship line, Garvey was jailed and then deported, for having used the mails to defraud.

But Garvey dramatized, as no one before, the bitterness and alienation of the Negro slumdwellers who, having come North with great expectations, found only overcrowded and deteriorated housing, mass unemployment, and race riots.

The Depression

Negro labor, relatively unorganized and the target of discrimination and hostility, was hardly prepared for the depression of the 1930's. To a disproportionate extent, Negroes lost their jobs in cities and worked for starvation wages in rural areas. Although organizations like the National Urban League tried to improve employment opportunities, 65 percent of Negro employables were in need of public assistance by 1935.

Public assistance was given on a discriminatory basis, especially in the South. For a time, Dallas and Houston gave no relief at all to Negro or Mexican families. In general, Negroes had more difficulty than whites in obtaining assistance, and the relief benefits were smaller. Some religious and charitable organizations excluded Negroes from their soup kitchens.

The New Deal

The New Deal marked a turning point in American race relations. Negroes found much in the New Deal to complain about: discrimination existed in many agencies; Federal housing programs expanded urban ghettos; money from the Agricultural Adjustment Administration went in the South chiefly to white landowners, while crop restrictions forced many Negro sharecroppers off the land. Nevertheless, Negroes shared in relief, jobs and public housing, and Negro leaders, who felt the open sympathy of many highly placed New Dealers, held more prominent political positions than at any time since President Taft's administration. The creation of the Congress of Industrial Organizations (CIO), with its avowed philosophy of nondiscrimination, made the notion of an alliance of black and white workers something more than a visionary's dream.

The depression, the New Deal and the CIO reoriented Negro protest to concern with economic problems. Negroes conducted "Don't-Buy-Where-You-Can't-Work" campaigns in a number of cities, boycotted and picketed commercial establishments owned by whites and sought equality in American society through an alliance with white labor.

The NAACP came under attack from some Negroes. Du Bois resigned as editor of the *Crisis* in 1934 in part because he believed in the value of collective racial economic endeavor and saw little point in protesting disfranchisement and segregation without more actively pursuing economic goals. Younger critics also disagreed with NAACP's gradualism on economic issues.

Undeterred, the NAACP broadened the scope of its legal work, fought a vigorous though unsuccessful campaign to abolish the poll tax, and finally won its attack on the white primaries in 1944 through the Supreme Court. But the heart of its litigation was a long-range campaign against segregation and the most obvious inequities in the Southern school systems: the lack of professional and graduate schools and the low salaries received by Negro teachers. Not until about 1950 would the NAACP make a direct assault against school segregation on the legal ground that separate facilities were inherently unequal.

World War II

During World War II, Negroes learned again that fighting for their country brought them no nearer to full citizenship. Rejected when they tried to enlist, they were accepted into the Army according to the proportion of the Negro population to that of the country as a whole—but only in separate units—and those mostly noncombat. The United States thus fought racism in Europe with a segregated fighting force. The Red Cross, with the government's approval, separated Negro and white blood in banks established for wounded servicemen—even though the blood banks were largely the work of a Negro physician, Charles Drew.

Not until 1949 would the Armed Forces begin to adopt a firm policy against segregation.

Negroes seeking employment in defense industries were embittered by policies like that of a West Coast aviation factory which declared openly that "the Negro will be considered only as janitors and in other similar capacities. . . . Regardless of their training as aircraft workers, we will not employ them."

Two new movements marked Negro protest: the March on Washington and the Congress of Racial Equality (CORE). In 1941, consciously drawing on the power of the Negro vote and concerned with the economic problems of the urban slumdweller, A. Philip Randolph threatened a mass Negro convergence on Washington unless President Roosevelt secured employment for Negroes in the defense industries. The President's Executive Order 8802, establishing a Federal Fair Employment Practices Commission, forestalled the demonstration. Even without enforcement powers, the FEPC set a precedent for treating fair employment practice as a civil right.

CORE was founded in 1942–43, when certain leaders of the Fellowship of Reconciliation, a pacifist organization, became interested in the use of nonviolent direct action to fight racial discrimination. CORE combined Gandhi's techniques with the sit-in, derived from the sit-down strikes of the 1930's. Until about 1959, CORE's main activity was attacking discrimination in places of public accommodation in the cities of the Northern and Border states, and as late as 1961, two-thirds of its membership and most of its national officers were white.

Meanwhile, wartime racial disorders had broken out sporadically—in Mobile, Los Angeles, Beaumont, Tex., and elsewhere. The riot in Detroit in 1943 was the most destructive. The Negro population in the city had risen sharply and more than 50,000 recent arrivals put immense pressures on the housing market. Neighborhood turnover at the edge of the ghetto bred bitterness and sometimes violence, and recreational areas became centers of racial abrasion. The Federal regulations requiring employment standards in defense industries also angered whites, and several unauthorized walkouts had occurred in automobile plants after Negro workers were upgraded. Activities in the city of several leading spokesmen for white supremacy—Gerald L. K. Smith, Frank J. Norris and Father Charles Coughlin—inflamed many white Southerners who had migrated to Detroit during the war.

On Sunday, June 20, rioting broke out on Belle Isle, a recreational spot used by both races but predominantly by Negroes. Fist fights escalated into a major conflict. The first wave of looting and bloodshed began in the Negro ghetto "Paradise Valley" and later spread to other sections of the city. Whites began attacking Negroes as they emerged from the city's all-night movie theatres in the downtown area. White forays into Negro residential areas by car were met by gunfire. By the time Federal troops arrived to halt the racial conflict, 25 Negroes and nine whites were dead, property damage exceeded $2 million and a legacy of fear and hate descended on the city.

Again, in 1943, a riot erupted in Harlem, New York, following the attempt of a white policeman to arrest a Negro woman who was defended by a Negro soldier. Negro rioters assaulted white passersby, overturned parked automobiles, tossed bricks and bottles at policemen. The major emphasis was on destroying property, looting and burning stores. Six persons died, over 500 were injured and more than 100 were jailed.

The Postwar Period

White opinion in some quarters of America had begun to shift to a more sympathetic regard for Negroes during the New Deal, and the war had accelerated that movement. Thoughtful whites had been painfully aware of the contradiction in opposing Nazi racial philosophy with racially segregated military units. In the postwar years, American racial attitudes became more liberal as new nonwhite nations emerged in Asia and Africa and took increasing responsibilities in international councils.

Against this background, the growing size of the Northern Negro vote made civil rights a major issue in national elections and, ultimately, in 1957, led to the establishment of the Federal Civil Rights Commission, which had the power to investigate discriminatory conditions throughout the country and to recommend corrective measures to the President. Northern and Western states outlawed discrimination in employment, housing and public accommodations, while the NAACP, in successive court victories, won judgments against racially restrictive covenants in housing, segregation in interstate transportation and discrimination in publicly-owned recreational facilities. The NAACP helped register voters, and in 1954, *Brown* v. *Board of Education* became the triumphant climax of the NAACP's campaign against educational segregation in the public schools of the South.

CORE, which had been conducting demonstrations in the Border states, its major focus on public accommodations, began experimenting with direct-action techniques to open employment opportunities. In 1947, in conjunction with the Fellowship of Reconciliation, CORE conducted a "Journey of Reconciliation"—what would later be called a "Freedom Ride"—in the states of the upper South to test compliance with the Supreme Court decision outlawing segregation on interstate buses. The resistance met by riders in some areas and the sentencing of 2 of them to 30 days on a North Carolina road gang dramatized the gap between American democratic theory and practice.

The Montgomery, Ala., bus boycott of 1955–56 captured the imagination of the Nation and of the Negro community in particular, and led to the growing use of direct-action techniques. It catapulted into national prominence the Reverend Martin Luther King, Jr., who, like the founders of CORE, held to a Gandhian belief in the principles of pacifism.

Even before a court decision obtained by NAACP attorneys in November, 1956, desegregated the Montgomery buses, a similar movement had started in Tallahassee, Fla. Afterward, another one developed in Birmingham, Ala. In 1957, the Tuskegee Negroes undertook a 3-year boycott of local merchants after the state legislature gerrymandered nearly all of the Negro voters outside of the town's boundaries. In response to a lawsuit filed by the NAACP, the Supreme Court ruled the Tuskegee gerrymander illegal.

These events were widely heralded. The "new Negro" had now emerged in the South—militant, no longer fearful of white hoodlums or mobs and ready to use his collective strength to achieve his ends. In this mood, King established the Southern Christian Leadership Conference in 1957 to coordinate direct-action activities in Southern cities.

Nonviolent direct action attained popularity not only because of the effectiveness of King's leadership, but because the older techniques of legal and legislative action had had limited success. Impressive as the advances in the 15 years after World War II were, in spite of state laws and Supreme Court decisions, something was still clearly wrong. Negroes remained disfranchised in most of the South, though in the 12 years following the outlawing of the white primary in 1944, the number of Negroes registered in Southern states had risen from about 250,000 to nearly a million and a quarter. Supreme Court decisions desegregating transportation facilities were still being largely ignored in the South. Discrimination in employment and housing continued, not only in the South but also in Northern states with model civil rights laws. The Negro unemployment rate steadily moved upward after 1954. The South reacted to the Supreme Court's decision on school desegregation by attempting to outlaw the NAACP, intimidating civil rights leaders, calling for "massive resistance" to the Court's decision, curtailing Negro voter registration and forming White Citizens' Councils.

Revolution of Rising Expectations

At the same time, Negro attitudes were changing. In what has been described as a "revolution in expectations," Negroes were gaining a new sense of self-respect and a new self-image as a result of the civil rights movement and their own advancement. King and others were demonstrating that nonviolent direct action could succeed in the South. New laws and court decisions and the increasing support of white public opinion gave American Negroes a new confidence in the future.

Negroes no longer felt that they had to accept the humiliations of second-class citizenship. Ironically, it was the very successes in the legislatures and the courts that, more perhaps than any other single factor, led to intensified Negro expectations and resulting dissatisfaction with the limitations of legal and legislative programs. Increasing Negro impatience accounted for the rising tempo of nonviolent direct action in the late 1950's, culminating in the student sit-ins of 1960 and the inauguration of what is popularly known as the "Civil Rights Revolution" or the "Negro Revolt."

Many believe that the Montgomery boycott ushered in this Negro Revolt, and there is no doubt that, in its importance, by projecting the image of King and his techniques, it had great importance. But the decisive break with traditional techniques came with the college student sit-ins that swept the South in the winter and spring of 1960. In dozens of communities in the upper South, the Atlantic coastal states and Texas, student demonstrations secured the desegregation of lunch counters in drug and variety stores. Arrests were numbered in the thousands, and brutality was evident in scores of communities. In the Deep South, the campaign ended in failure, even in instances where hundreds had been arrested, as in Montgomery, Orangeburg, South Carolina, and Baton Rouge. But the youth had captured the imagination of the Negro community and to a remarkable extent of the whole Nation.

Student Involvement

The Negro protest movement would never be the same again. The Southern college students shook the power structure of the Negro community, made direct action temporarily preeminent as a civil rights tactic, speeded up the process of social change in race relations, and ultimately turned the Negro protest organizations toward a deep concern with the economic and social problems of the masses.

Involved in this was a gradual shift in both tactics and goals: from legal to direct action, from middle and upper class to mass action, from attempts to guarantee the Negro's constitutional rights to efforts to secure economic policies giving him equality of opportunity, from appeals to the sense of fair play of white Americans to demands based upon power in the black ghetto.

The successes of the student movement threatened existing Negro leadership and precipitated a spirited rivalry among civil rights organizations. The NAACP and SCLC associated themselves with the student movement. The organizing meeting of the Student Nonviolent Coordinating Committee (SNCC) at Raleigh, North Carolina, in April, 1960, was called by Martin Luther King, but within a year the youth considered King too cautious and broke with him.

The NAACP now decided to make direct action a major part of its strategy and organized and reactivated college and youth chapters in the Southern and Border states.

CORE, still unknown to the general public, installed James Farmer as national director in January, 1961, and that spring joined the front rank of civil rights organizations with the famous Freedom Ride to Alabama and Mississippi that dramatized the persistence of segregated public transportation. A bus-burning resulted in Alabama. Hundreds of demonstrators spent a month or more in Mississippi prisons. Finally, a new order from the Interstate Commerce Commission desegregating all interstate transportation facilities received partial compliance.

Organizational Differences

Disagreement over strategy and tactics inevitably became intertwined with personal and organizational rivalries. Each civil rights group felt the need for proper credit in order to obtain the prestige and financial contributions necessary to maintain and expand its own programs. The local and national, individual and organizational clashes stimulated competition and activity that further accelerated the pace of social change.

Yet there were differences in style. CORE was the most interracial. SCLC appeared to be the most deliberate. SNCC staff workers lived on subsistence allowances and seemed to regard going to jail as a way of life. The NAACP continued the most varied programs, retaining a strong emphasis on court litigation, maintaining a highly effective lobby at the national capital and engaging in direct-action campaigns. The National Urban League under the leadership of Whitney M. Young, Jr., appointed executive director in 1961, became more outspoken and talked more firmly to businessmen who had previously been treated with utmost tact and caution.

The role of whites in the protest movement gradually changed. Instead of occupying positions of leadership, they found themselves relegated to the role of followers. Whites were likely to be suspect in the activist organizations. Negroes had come to feel less dependent on whites, more confident of their own power, and they demanded that their leaders be black. The NAACP had long since acquired Negro leadership but continued to welcome white liberal support. SCLC and SNCC were from the start Negro-led and Negro-dominated. CORE became predominantly Negro as it expanded in 1962 and 1963; today all executives are Negro, and a constitutional amendment adopted in 1965 officially limited white leadership in the chapters.

A major factor intensifying the civil rights movement was widespread Negro unemployment and poverty; an important force in awakening Negro protest was the meteoric rise to national prominence of the Black Muslims, established around 1930. The organization reached the peak of its influence when more progress toward equal rights was being made than ever before in American history, while at the same time the poorest groups in the urban ghettos were stagnating.

The Black Muslims preached a vision of the doom of the white "devils" and the coming dominance of the black man, promised a utopian paradise of a separate territory within the United States for a Negro state, and offered a practical program of building Negro business through hard work, thrift and racial unity. To those willing to submit to the rigid discipline of the movement, the Black Muslims organization gave a sense of purpose and dignity.

"Freedom Now!" and Civil Rights Laws

As the direct-action tactics took more dramatic form, as the civil rights groups began to articulate the needs of the masses and draw some of them to their demonstrations, the protest movement in 1963 assumed a new note of urgency, a demand for complete "Freedom Now!" Direct action returned to the Northern cities, taking the form of massive protests against economic, housing and educational inequities, and a fresh wave of demonstrations swept the South from Cambridge, Maryland, to Birmingham, Alabama. Northern Negroes launched street demonstrations against discrimination in the building trade unions, and, the following winter, school boycotts against de facto segregation.

In the North, 1963 and 1964 brought the beginning of the waves of civil disorders in Northern urban centers. In the South, incidents occurred of brutal white resistance to the civil rights movement, beginning with the murders of Mississippi Negro leader Medgar Evers, and of four Negro schoolgirls in a church in Birmingham. These disorders and the events in the South are detailed in [our] introduction to Chapter 1, the *Profiles of Disorder*.

The massive anti-Negro resistance in Birmingham and numerous other Southern cities during the spring of 1963 compelled the nation to face the problem of race prejudice in the South. President Kennedy affirmed that racial discrimination was a moral issue and asked Congress for a major civil rights bill. But a major impetus for what was to be the Civil Rights Act of 1964 was the March on Washington in August, 1963.

Early in the year, A. Philip Randolph issued a call for a March on Washington to dramatize the need for jobs and to press for a Federal commitment to job action. At about the same time, Protestant, Jewish and Catholic churches sought and obtained representation on the March committee. Although the AFL-CIO national council refused to endorse the March, a number of labor leaders and international unions participated.

Reversing an earlier stand, President Kennedy approved the March. A quarter of a million people, about 20 percent of them white, participated. It was more than a summation of the past years of struggle and aspiration. It symbolized certain new directions: a deeper concern for the economic problems of the masses, more involvement of white moderates and new demands from the most militant, who implied that only a revolutionary change in American institutions would permit Negroes to achieve the dignity of citizens.

President Kennedy had set the stage for the Civil Rights Act of 1964. After his death, President Johnson took forceful and effective action to secure its enactment. The law settled the public accommodations issue in the South's major cities. Its voting section, however, promised more than it could accomplish. Martin Luther King and SCLC dramatized the issue locally with demonstrations at Selma, Alabama, in the spring of 1965. Again the national government was forced to intervene, and a new and more effective voting law was passed.

Failures of Direct Action

Birmingham had made direct action respectable; Selma, which drew thousands of white moderates from the North, made direct action fashionable. Yet as early as 1964, it was becoming evident that, like legal action, direct action was of limited usefulness.

In Deep South states like Mississippi and Alabama, direct action had failed to desegregate public accommodation in the sit-ins of 1960–61. A major reason was that Negroes lacked the leverage of the vote. The demonstrations of the early 1960's had been successful principally in places like Atlanta, Nashville, Durham, Winston-Salem, Louisville, Savannah, New Orleans, Charleston, and Dallas—where Negroes voted and could swing elections. Beginning in 1961, Robert Moses, of SNCC, with the cooperation of CORE and NAACP, established voter registration projects in the cities and county seats of Mississippi. He succeeded in registering only a handful of Negroes, but by 1964, he had generated enough support throughout the country to enable the Mississippi Freedom Democratic Party, which he had created, to challenge dramatically the seating of the official white delegates from the state at the Democratic National Convention.

In the black ghettos of the North, direct action also largely failed. Street demonstrations did compel employers, from supermarkets to banks, to add Negroes to their work force in Northern and Western cities, and even in some Southern cities where the Negroes had considerable buying power. However, separate and inferior schools, slum housing, and police hostility proved invulnerable to direct attack.

New Directions

Although Negroes were being hired in increasing numbers, mass unemployment and underemployment remained. As economist Vivian Henderson pointed out in his testimony before the Commission:

No one can deny that all Negroes have benefited from civil rights laws and desegregation in public life in one way or another. The fact is, however, that the masses of Negroes have not experienced tangible benefits in a significant way. This is so in education and housing. It is critically so in the area of jobs and economic security. Expectations of Negro masses for equal job opportunity programs have fallen far short of fulfillment.

Negroes have made gains. . . . There have been important gains. But . . . the masses of Negroes have been virtually untouched by those gains.

Faced with the intransigence of the Deep South and the inadequacy of direct action to solve the problems of the slumdwellers, Negro protest organizations began to diverge. The momentum toward unity, apparent in 1963, was lost. At the very time that white support for the protest movement was rising markedly, militant Negroes felt increasingly isolated from the American scene. On two things, however, all segments of the protest movement agreed: (1) Future civil rights activity would have to focus on economic and social discrimination in the urban ghettos; and (2) while demonstrations would still have a place, the major weapon would have to be the political potential of the black masses.

By the middle of the decade, many militant Negro members of SNCC and CORE began to turn away from American society and the "middle-class way of life." Cynical about the liberals and the leaders of organized labor, they regarded compromise, even as a temporary tactical device, as anathema. They talked more of "revolutionary" changes in the social structure and of retaliatory violence, and increasingly rejected white assistance. They insisted that Negro power alone could compel the white "ruling class" to make concessions. Yet they also spoke of an alliance of Negroes and unorganized lower class whites to overthrow the "power structure" of capitalists, politicians, and bureaucratic labor leaders who exploited the poor of both races by dividing them through an appeal to race prejudice.

At the same time that their activities declined, other issues, particularly Vietnam, diverted the attention of the country, and of some Negro leaders, from the issue of equality. In civil rights organizations, reduced financing made it increasingly difficult to support staff personnel. Most important was the increasing frustration of expectations that affected the direct-action advocates of the early 1960's—the sense of futility growing out of the feeling that progress had turned out to be "tokenism," that the compromises of the white community were sedatives rather than solutions and that the current methods of Negro protest were doing little for the masses of the race.

As frustration grew, the ideology and rhetoric of a number of civil rights activists became angrier. One man more than any other—a black man who grew up believing whites had murdered his father—became a spokesman for this anger: Malcolm X, who perhaps best embodied the belief that racism was so deeply ingrained in white America that appeals to conscience would bring no fundamental change.

"Black Power"

In this setting, the rhetoric of Black Power developed. The precipitating occasion was the Meredith March from Memphis to Jackson in June, 1966, but the slogan expressed tendencies that had been present for a long time and had been gaining strength in the Negro community.

Black Power first articulated a mood rather than a program: disillusionment and alienation from white America and independence, race pride, and self-respect, or "black consciousness." Having become a household phrase, the term generated intense discussion of its real meaning, and a broad spectrum of ideologies and programmatic proposals emerged.

In politics, Black Power meant independent action—Negro control of the political power of the black ghettos and its use to improve economic and social conditions. It could take the form of organizing a black political party or controlling the political machinery within the ghetto without the guidance or support of white politicians. Where predominantly Negro areas lacked Negroes in elective office, whether in the rural Black Belt of the South or in the urban centers, Black Power advocates sought the election of Negroes by voter registration campaigns, by getting out the vote, and by working for redrawing electoral districts. The basic belief was that only a well-organized and cohesive bloc of Negro voters could provide for the needs of the black masses. Even some Negro politicians allied to the major political parties adopted the term "Black Power" to describe their interest in the Negro vote.

In economic terms, Black Power meant creating independent, self-sufficient Negro business enterprise, not only by encouraging Negro entrepreneurs but also by forming Negro cooperatives in the ghettos and in the predominantly black rural counties of the South. In the area of education, Black Power called for local community control of the public schools in the black ghettos.

Throughout, the emphasis was on self-help, racial unity, and, among the most militant, retaliatory violence, the latter ranging from the legal right of self-defense to attempts to justify looting and arson in ghetto riots, guerrilla warfare, and armed rebellion.

Phrases like "Black Power," "Black Consciousness," and "Black is Beautiful," enjoyed an extensive currency in the Negro community, even within the NAACP and among relatively conservative politicians, but particularly among young intellectuals and Afro-American student groups on predominantly white college campuses. Expressed in its most extreme form by small, often local, fringe groups, the Black Power ideology became associated with SNCC and CORE.

Generally regarded today as the most militant among the important Negro protest organizations, they have developed different interpretations of the Black Power doctrine. SNCC calls for totally independent political action outside the established political parties, as with the Black Panther Party in Lowndes County, Ala.; rejects the political alliances with other groups until Negroes have themselves built a substantial base of independent political power; applauds the idea of guerrilla warfare; and regards riots as rebellions.

CORE has been more flexible. Approving the SNCC strategy, it also advocates working within the Democratic Party, forming alliances with other groups and, while seeking to justify riots as the natural explosion of an oppressed people against intolerable conditions, advocates violence only in self-defense. Both groups favor cooperatives, but CORE has seemed more inclined toward job-training programs and developing a Negro entrepreneurial class, based upon the market within the black ghettos.

Old Wine in New Bottles

What is new about Black Power is phraseology rather than substance. Black Consciousness has roots in the organization of Negro churches and mutual benefit societies in the early days of the Republic, the antebellum Negro convention movement, the Negro colonization schemes of the 19th century, Du Bois' concept of Pan-Africanism, Booker T. Washington's advocacy of race pride, self-help, and racial solidarity, the Harlem Renaissance, and the Garvey Movement. The decade after World War I—which saw the militant, race-proud "new Negro," the relatively widespread theory of retaliatory violence and the high tide of the Negro-support-of-Negro-business ideology—exhibits striking parallels with the 1960's.

The theme of retaliatory violence is hardly new for American Negroes. Most racial disorders in American history until recent years were characterized by white attacks on Negroes. But Negroes have retaliated violently in the past.

Black Power rhetoric and ideology actually express a lack of power. The slogan emerged when the Negro protest movement was slowing down, when it was finding increasing resistance to its changing goals, when it discovered that nonviolent direct action was no more a panacea than legal action, when CORE and SNCC were declining in terms of activity, membership, and financial support. This combination of circumstances provoked anger deepened by impotence. Powerless to make any fundamental changes in the life of the masses—powerless, that is, to compel white America to make those changes, many advocates of Black Power have retreated into an unreal world, where they see an outnumbered and poverty-stricken minority organizing itself entirely separately from whites and creating sufficient power to force white America to grant its demands. To date, the evidence suggests that the situation is much like that of the

1840's, when a small group of intellectuals advocated slave insurrections, but stopped short of organizing them.

The Black Power advocates of today consciously feel that they are the most militant group in the Negro protest movement. Yet they have retreated from a direct confrontation with American society on the issue of integration and, by preaching separatism, unconsciously function as an accommodation to white racism. Much of their economic program, as well as their interest in Negro history, self-help, racial solidarity and separation, is reminiscent of Booker T. Washington. The rhetoric is different, but the ideas are remarkably similar.

The Meaning

By 1967, whites could point to the demise of slavery, the decline of illiteracy among Negroes, the legal protection provided by the constitutional amendments and civil rights legislation, and the growing size of the Negro middle class. Whites would call it Negro progress, from slavery to freedom and toward equality.

Negroes could point to the doctrine of white supremacy, its persistence after emancipation and its influence on the definition of the place of Negroes in American life. They could point to their long fight for full citizenship when they had active opposition from most of the white population and little or no support from the Government. They could see progress toward equality accompanied by bitter resistance. Perhaps most of all, they could feel the persistent, pervasive racism that kept them in inferior segregated schools, restricted them to ghettos, barred them from fair employment, provided double standards in courts of justice, inflicted bodily harm on their children and blighted their lives with a sense of hopelessness and despair.

In all of this and in the context of professed ideals, Negroes would find more retrogression than progress, more rejection than acceptance.

NOTE

1. Ladler, *New York's Bloodiest Week*, American Heritage, June, 1959, p. 48.

18. Political Crime and the Negro Revolution

An explanation of the slow and limited achievements of black protest is to be found in the phenomenon of white resistance. White resistance to Negro gains has shown a relentlessness and chronicity. The effectiveness of this retarding social force is often a result of the operation of official offices and agents whose services and efforts are directed in principle to the interest of the total community but in actuality to only that of whites. A systematic assessment of white resistance from this vantage point is provided by Mouledoux.

JOSEPH C. MOULEDOUX

The tactic of nonviolent civil disobedience used in the Negro "revolution" and the nature of the Southern white response have brought into focus the issue of political crime. Two questions arise from this issue: (1) Under what conditions is civil disobedience to be considered criminal? (2) Cannot the legislators and executors of politically divisive ordinances and statutes be judged to be acting criminally? This paper argues for the reintroduction of the two basic dimensions of political crime. It holds that political crime can consist of behavior by agents of government as well as behavior directed against government, and our major emphasis will be on the politically criminal behavior of representatives of Southern political power; a second and far less fully developed concern will be with the question of civil disobedience.

The distinction between crimes against government and crimes by government is not new to criminological literature, and these two facets have been differentially emphasized by various writers. For example, Beccaria emphasized crimes by government while Lombroso's concern was with crimes against government. In the United States Franklin H. Giddings clearly stated that these were the two significant dimensions of political crime. Writing in 1898 an introduction to Louis Proal's study of political crime, Giddings stated:

The term "political crime" has two meanings. Perhaps the more familiar one is that of crimes against governments, such as treason, insurrection, and rebellion.

From *Criminal Behavior Systems* edited by Marshall B. Clinard and Richard Quinney. Copyright © 1967 by Holt, Rinehart and Winston, Inc. Reprinted by permission of Holt, Rinehart and Winston, Inc.

. . . The other meaning is that of crimes perpetrated by governments for alleged reasons of state, and by politicians for alleged reasons of expedience or for political advantage.[1]

The dual aspect of political crime articulated by Giddings has not been the subject of serious discussion in American criminological literature. Rather, the major emphasis has continued to be on crimes against government: both Packer's article entitled "Offenders against the State,"[2] and Elliott's classification of "political offenders"[3] are indicative of this limited perspective.

Although American criminologists have largely dropped "crime by government" out of their picture of political crime, there are indications that they are unhappy with the results and are seeking satisfactory alternatives. For example, Marshall Clinard raises the criterion of "socially injurious"—not politically injurious—behavior in his study *The Black Market*. And furthermore, Clinard attempts to broaden and make more meaningful the concept crime by defining crime as "any act punishable by the state, regardless of whether the penalty is a criminal one *or is administrative or civil in nature*."[4] While this viewpoint recognizes the state's increasing role in reshaping law and in defining the limits of freedom, it fails to perceive that this development may also threaten the political rights of the individual.[5]

To argue, as most criminologists do, that crime is any act punishable by the state is to imply strongly that government and law are one; that is, that all which government punishes is necessarily unlawful. This notion seriously limits the legitimate behavior of political actors, discourages the use of the concept political crime as crime perpetrated by government or its agents, and encourages one to subsume such acts under the concepts white collar crime, occupational crime, or socially injurious behavior.

The fact of the matter is that Americans, by and large, are comfortable with limiting political crime to crime against government. Not only are Americans reluctant to face the possibility that government can act criminally; they avoid the possibility that deliberate political acts against government may be "noncriminal." This is clearly expressed in the punitive sanctions imposed on political criminals. Up to the present civil rights confrontation, American political criminals have seldom received special treatment as political criminals. Rather, they have been defined as "common criminals" and required to serve their sentences along with "common criminals": a condition that is not without unusual difficulties and even dangers to political criminals.

The basis of American attitudes toward political crime and political criminals is deeply rooted. As both Andrew Hacker[6] and Daniel J. Boorstin[7] have indicated, the uniqueness of the American experience is that it has never had a politics. The legitimacy of the political reality that is America has seldom been questioned, partly because of the assumption of human equality and individual dignity which underlie our political order, but also because of the optimism inherent in the Puritanism-turned-pragmatism that has been a predominant orientation of Americans to their environment. It is an optimism colored by a psychology which judges all who, either willingly or because of personal inadequacies, refuse to seek successful participation in the American enterprise and yet who insist on calling into question its legitimacy, to be beyond redemption —to be treated as outcasts rather than as serious questioners and contributors to the American political community. At the same time, this American attitude permits those who participate successfully to judge and question, to select and innovate; in effect, to be politically creative. Such actors as these have often sought to apply the basic presuppositions of liberal democracy: human equality and the political dignity of the individual as distinct and separate from the state. This has produced a theme in our society which stresses the view that government and law are two related yet different orders; government exists as one source of law, but law exists as the superior reality. Government is subsumed under this law, and it is understood that the individual, as a political actor, has not only a right but an obligation to question government in the light of the law.

Within the framework of this paper these presuppositions which are at the root of our American political tradition are used as standards for judging political behavior. It is held that behavior can be judged to be politically legitimate or politically criminal by whether it is oriented toward making law an instrument serving one segment of society through the exclusion of others from the political community, or whether it is directed toward the creative reinterpretation and extension of law consistent with the presuppositions of political dignity and human equality.

A fact of Southern history is the fact of political crime, for the South has denied the Negro entrance into the political community. The Negro has held an integral, if subservient, role in Southern *society*, but he has been cast out of the political community and thereby denied existence under law. Without a legal identity, the Negro as an individual has no existence. His existence is a group existence. As a group the Negro occupies a status within the Southern social order, but as an individual, being denied legal identity, the Negro is truly the invisible man.

Since Southern political power is based on the *exclusion* of the Negro from the political community and inclusion of the Negro in Southern society, it became essential for the South to create a no-man identity for the Negro, to make him without individuality, to keep him "Tom" and "boy." And conversely, the Negro revolt has been a revolt against this state of oblivion, and movement toward carving out an identity, a sense of manhood, an existence as an individual among other individuals within the American political community.

It has been asked, "Where do we date the beginning of the Negro revolt?"[8] With the 1870 "sit-ins" and "ride-ins" occurring in Louisville, Kentucky?[9] With 1909 and the founding of the National Association for the Advancement of Colored People (NAACP)? With the Atlanta Civil and Political League of 1936, founded to stimulate Negroes to register to vote? With 1941 and the threatened march on Washington, D.C., led by A. Philip Randolph, which moved President Roosevelt to create the wartime Fair Employment Practices Commission? With the 1942 Southern Conference on Race Relations at Durham, North Carolina, attended by leading Southern Negroes from educational institutions, trade unions, churches, business and professional associations? With the corresponding conference held by white Southerners, April 8, 1943, at Atlanta, Georgia, under the intellectual leadership of Howard W. Odum, Professor of Sociology at the University of North Carolina and involving leading white Southerners from all walks of life? With the Supreme Court's great white primary ruling of 1944? With President Truman's Executive Order of 1946 and the Supreme Court opinion in *Brown v. Board of Education* which cast out of legal philosophy the apartheid conclusions of *Plessy v. Ferguson* and held that any separation of the races must denote the inferiority of the Negro race? With Rosa Parks and the Montgomery, Alabama, bus boycott of 1955–1956?

There have been many beginnings, but none are more appropriate for an understanding of the present Negro revolt than the attempt made by the Congress of Industrial Organizations (CIO) during the 1930s and 1940s to unionize the South, largely on an interracial basis. As Daniel Bell[10] has noted, labor's situation and the Negro's situation have had many points in common: the "yellow-dog" contracts were a form of segregation; labor was aided in its struggle by the federal government and by favorable court decisions; still labor was ultimately forced to help itself by direct action. Furthermore, in the South the CIO threatened to accomplish many of the ends that are being accomplished today by the civil rights movement, and in so doing, the unions elicited responses similar to those being shown toward the Negro today. Therefore, the struggle to unionize the South provides us with a preview of the present Southern conflict.

The very existence of the CIO in the South was a direct threat to white supremacy. Many union halls were integrated and white Southerners who joined the unions could experience their first contacts, on the basis of equality, with Negroes. Through their educational programs unions attempted to educate their white memberships, to create in them an awareness of mutual political and economic interests with Negro labor. The Political Action Committee of the CIO attempted to initiate political activity that would involve a broad spectrum of Southern communities.

We may take as a single example union activity directed toward encouraging and aiding Negroes to register and to vote. In June 1944 the white primaries were destroyed by a ruling of the Supreme Court which held that Negroes could not be barred from party primaries. Stimulated by this decision, unions began to encourage their Negro members to register and vote, and unions used their funds and resources to agitate the Negro community to so act. In September 1944 editors of *The Southern Patriot* congratulated "the Orleans Parish [Louisiana] Political Action Committee [CIO] for its efforts in adding 1021 new voters to the registration lists." [11] Under union leadership returning Negro GIs in 1946 marched one-hundred strong to the Birmingham Courthouse in a futile attempt to register to vote.[12] Such attempts, for many reasons, were only sporadic, but they did occur, continuing into 1948, when the Progressive party, supported by the left wing-dominated CIO unions, in an attempt to place Henry Wallace on Southern ballots, made their last drive to register Southern Negroes to vote. For example, in September 1948 in St. Bernard Parish, Louisiana, eleven Negroes, accompanied by representatives of the Louisiana Progressive party and the Southern Fur Trappers Union, went to the courthouse to register to vote; they were cursed and turned away by armed deputies.[13]

Labor's attempt to organize the South, under the leadership of left-wing CIO unions, had political as well as social and economic overtones. This fact was clearly understood by most Southern politicians. They knew from the beginning that the CIO's organizational drive, its attempt to initiate a right-to-vote movement, and its struggle to have prolabor legislation passed, could revolutionize the South. As early as January 26, 1938, Senator Richard Russell of Georgia articulated what the Southern power structure most feared—and still fears:

Every Senator on the floor of this body knows that if a measure of this kind were passed, there would be Negro governors and there would be Negro senators. There are many states where two or three or four or five members of the House of Representatives would be Negroes, and no white man would have a chance to be elected. This means that there would be county after county where every officer and every official would be of the Negro race.[14]

This fear, expressed on the floor of the United States Senate, was translated into action in the communities of the South. The police undertook to protect the Southern status quo by direct action against union organizers and members.[15] In the Lumberton, North Carolina, textile strike of 1937, sixty-five union men and Myles Horton, Director of Highlander Folk School and a volunteer organizer, were arrested. In spite of the fact that Horton insisted that the strike be conducted according to principles of nonviolence, the police made it known that "Horton will be arrested regardless of whether he is on the scene should any violence occur on the picket line, or elsewhere, concerning the strike." [16] In Jackson, Mississippi, two representatives of the International Woodworkers of America, and the wife of one of them, were arrested and held for thirty-six hours, without charges being filed against them.[17] In Vicksburg, Mississippi, the vice-president of the International Woodworkers was held for investigation. During the interrogation the police captain informed him that he was "inciting trouble for the police department, and he guessed he [the police] would have to shoot up a bunch of these burr-headed Negroes." The police captain said further that "regardless of what federal laws might be passed, if Negroes get out of place they would probably be lynched and the police department would not interfere." [18] In Port Gibson, Mississippi, the sheriff showed up at the picket line waving his gun and threatening to shoot the women strikers full of lead unless they went back to work.[19]

Not only did the executors of law strike out to protect white Southern political power, but the legislators also contributed their part. In Milledgeville, Georgia, an ordinance was passed which required that union organizers be local residents for one year and pay a $5000 license fee. Although this ordinance was ruled unconstitutional in 1941,[20] the legislators of Cuthbert, Georgia, passed a similar ordinance in 1947. Cuthbert's ordinance required that anyone soliciting members for unions should first secure a city license and pay a fee of $1500 per year for organizing labor.[21] In Arkansas an anti-violence-in-strikes law was passed which permitted the arrest of union officials, members, or pickets on the charge of threatening—not committing—violence against nonunion men while depriving them of their right to work. And in the Arkansas strike against the Southern Cotton Oil Mill a strikebreaker fatally stabbed a Negro striker; yet the Little Rock grand jury failed to indict the strikebreaker. Instead, it indicted five union men, four of whom did not even witness the stabbing, under the antiviolence law.[22]

Southern legislators did not limit the scope of their statutes in support of Southern norms to the activities of union men. Even personnel agents, recruiting Southern labor for Northern industry, were recipients of punitive sanctions. The fact that Northern industry was the backbone of the "war effort" had little import; the South, in an attempt to preserve within its region cheap Negro labor, either passed or dug out of the books dating back to 1870, laws requiring payment of prohibitive license fees for the privilege of soliciting labor for employment outside the state. By 1943 ten Southern states had such emigrant agency laws, and applied them.[23] A New Jersey scrap metal company sent an agent to Georgia in 1943 to recruit and transport workers to New Jersey. The agent successfully secured a number of men, but at Cordele, Georgia, the chief of police boarded the train and took the agent and the prospective jobholders to jail. The company agent was found guilty of enticing, without a license, laborers to be employed beyond the state. He was given a six-month suspended sentence, placed on eighteen months' probation, and given twenty-four hours to leave Georgia; his company was fined $1000.[24]

The unions sought to protect their officials and members by securing aid from the federal government and from the courts. In one surprising instance the city marshal of Walnut Ridge, Arkansas, pleaded *nolo contendere* in federal court on the charge of assaulting and abusing a labor organizer. This case was one of the rare instances in which federal civil rights statutes were used.[25] Aid generally came in the form of behind-the-scenes pressure from the federal government. For example, in Memphis, Tennessee, union organizers were assaulted by a mob. Boss Crump was unavailable to union representatives who sought his assistance. And so a direct appeal was made to President Roosevelt, through Mrs. Roosevelt, resulting in the arrival of a special representative of the Attorney General to investigate charges against the city administration concerning the denial of civil rights to union men.[26] Following this investigation CIO members were not molested, plants were successfully organized, membership grew, and politicians who had previously opposed the unions with vigor showed a remarkable change of heart. In some cases when the FBI investigated charges of unlawful use of police power the behavior ceased.

The legal phase of the Negro revolt was carried on by the lawyers of the National Association for the Advancement of Colored People (NAACP) and other civil rights groups. Because of their activities, the Supreme Court at each of its sessions from 1938 to 1948 decided at least one case involving the rights of minorities.[27] And beginning in 1948 the Supreme Court began to hand down decisions in the area of education.

The results of these legal struggles cannot be overestimated. The *Smith v. Allwright* case of 1944 gave the Negro the right to vote in primary elections, and thus announced him as a potential political power. The 1945 *Screws v. United States* case, in which a Georgia sheriff was, at first, found guilty of blackjacking a Negro prisoner to death, and later acquitted and elected to a state office, made clear the existence of unlawful police conduct in the maintenance of white power in the South. The 1954 *Brown v. Board of Education* decision led to an aftermath which included the Little Rock, Arkansas, and Clinton, Tennessee, riots and the use of federal troops, all of which further crystallized national opinion in favor of the Negro movement and against white supremacy.

Supporters of white supremacy were not lax in responding to these challenges. Negroes who attempted to vote in the primaries were beaten; in Calhoun Falls, South Carolina, August, 1948, Reverend A. Ware, a Negro minister, was stabbed and beaten after he voted in the primary; in Montgomery County, Georgia, D. C. Carter, president of the local branch of the NAACP, was beaten after he voted in the state primary elections. Negroes who attempted to register to vote could seldom find the registrar and were frequently beaten. The NAACP came under increasing attack. Four Southern states passed laws making the NAACP an illegal organization and a fifth state imposed a fine of $1,000,000 on it. In Birmingham, wearers of NAACP buttons had them ripped off by police officers, and police brutality grew to such proportions that in April 1948 the NAACP called an emergency meeting to protest police violence after five Negroes were shot and killed by police officers within a one-month period.[28] The increase of private violence was announced with the resurgence of the Ku Klux Klan (KKK). Three Negro homes were bombed in Birmingham in March 1949 and on June 12, 1949, 126 hooded Klansmen paraded in Tuscaloosa, Alabama.[29] On Christmas, 1951, a bomb was set off in the home of Harry T. Moore, state coordinator of the NAACP in Florida; he died on the way to the hospital and his wife died of her injuries on January 3, 1952. In Virginia the state bar brought charges of unprofessional conduct against NAACP attorney Samuel W. Tucker; these charges grew out of his participation in three NAACP cases in 1949.[30] The basic pattern was set: Negroes pursued their constitutional rights in a legal manner, only to be met by a variety of "criminal" responses on the part of the upholders of white supremacy.

The Montgomery bus boycott of 1955–1956 [31] involved virtually the entire Negro community. The initial response to it was generally limited to police action. Taxicabs and private Negro vehicles were frequently stopped, and motor vehicle violations increased phenomenally. Arrests for hitchhiking, loud talking, walking on lawns, and congregating in white neighborhoods were all part of the attempt to break the boycott. Finally, Martin Luther King and other leaders were arrested, and a crude bomb was thrown against King's home. Four months after the arrest of Rosa Parks, which had started the boycott, the Supreme Court upheld the ruling of a lower court against segregated seating on municipal buses, and this limited victory was complete.

The period between the end of the Montgomery bus boycott and the beginning of the sit-ins in 1960 was essentially limited to court litigation, as exemplified by the *Gomillion v. Lightfoot* case, arising out of the city of Tuskegee, Alabama, redistricting its city boundaries to exclude Negroes, thus making them ineligible to register and vote in municipal elections. In arguing this case before the United States Supreme Court, the legal representatives of Tuskegee and Alabama were asked the following question by Justice Whittaker: *"Could this lawful power you speak of be used to accomplish an unlawful purpose?"* [32] The unanimous decision in favor of the Negro petitioners was affirmation that state power, used as an instrument for circumventing a federally protected right, was unlawful use of such power.[33] In an equally important case in Fayette and Haywood, two counties in Tennessee, landlords were restrained from evicting 48 tenant farmers. In supporting the tenant farmers a United States Court of Appeal concluded:

If sharecropper-tenants in possession of real estate under contract are threatened, intimidated or coerced by their landlords for purposes of interfering with their rights of franchise, certainly the fact that the coercion relates to land or contracts would furnish no excuse or defense.[34]

Thus the courts judged that economic power could be used unlawfully. In a similar manner legislation passed for the purposes of purging voter registration rolls, and of interposing the state constitution between the federal Constitution and the citizen, and thereby avoiding integration of the schools, and all similar legislation, was struck down as unconstitutional. The major thrust against white supremacy during this period was in the hands of the federal courts, backed up by federal power as in Little Rock, Arkansas, and Clinton, Tennessee.

The next development in the Negro revolt was the entrance of middle class Negro students as nonviolent, direct action "sit-iners," protesting against segregation.[35] Originating as a spontaneous protest on February 1, 1960, in Greensboro, North Carolina, this form of protest spread rapidly across the South, and the activists, with some help from the Southern Christian Leadership Conference (SCLC), organized themselves into the Student Nonviolent Coordinating Committee (SNCC), which was to prove to be the most militant of the civil rights groups, instrumental in transforming the Negro revolt as a protest against segregation into a Negro revolution seeking to destroy white political power and to secure political power for Southern Negroes.[36]

The sit-iners elicited vigorous response. As the Southern Regional Council Report noted, "Following the outbreak of the 1960 sit-ins every [Southern] legislature passed laws to regulate—and restrict—sit-in activities." [37] These civil rights activists found themselves being arrested and convicted on such charges as criminal trespassing, blocking fire exits, vagrancy, criminal anarchy (which carried a possible ten-year sentence), criminal mischief, breach of peace, delinquency, and drawing a poster which "libeled the state." [38] Furthermore, sanctions were applied against at least 141 students and 58 faculty members by dismissing them.[39] In spite of such harassment, the sit-ins were relatively successful: Supreme Court rulings overturned the convictions of peaceful, nonviolent protesters and thereby acknowledged the legitimacy of this form of civil disobedience, as well as the illegitimacy of so-called "lawful" power which functions for the purpose of attaining unlawful ends.

Following the spontaneous student protests against segregation, the Congress of Racial Equality (CORE), an essentially Northern-based and highly interracial civil rights organization, invaded the South in a series of "freedom rides." It has been questioned whether this tactic was successful, for as a result CORE was overburdened with excessive legal costs and some pro-civil rights elements were estranged.[40] The reaction included the burning of a Greyhound bus and the beating of its passengers. Violence in Birmingham and later in Montgomery led the federal district court in Alabama to this judgment:

The failure of the defendant law enforcement officers to enforce the law in this case clearly amounts to *unlawful state action* in violation of the Equal Protection Clause of the Fourteenth Amendment.[41]

Out of these "rides" came the unmistakable fact that the refusal of police to protect peaceful demonstrators from violence constituted unlawful police action.[42]

Albany, Georgia, was the site of the next big battle of the civil rights movement.[43] Like Montgomery, it involved a large segment of the community. Beginning as a relatively mild form of protest organized by the NAACP, it was quickly escalated into a more aggressive stage by SNCC activists, who made a direct assault on all forms of segregation. When it became obvious to the Negro leadership that the community supported the SNCC people, the Albany movement, encompassing all civil rights organizations, was born, and Dr. Martin Luther King entered the picture. Protests were made against segregation in train and bus stations, libraries, parks, hospitals, and against police brutality and followed the general pattern of singing and praying marches into the business district, arrests, and then protest marches against these arrests. Violence was not entirely avoided. Some of the marches went through Negro nightspot sections; drinkers entering the marches were not so inclined to nonviolence and on at least one occasion threw objects, rocks and bricks, at the police.

In neighboring Baker County the sheriff was sued by Warren Johnson in the federal district court in Albany, Georgia, on the charge that he had arrested Johnson without a warrant, had handcuffed him, and then in jail had shot him in the neck three times. Following the sheriff's acquittal, civil rights activists picketed the supermarket owned by one of the jurors. The federal government took immediate action against eight members of the Albany movement, charging two with obstructing justice and six with perjury. These indictments and the convictions which followed the verdict of an all-white federal jury, led Martin Luther King to say: "It is tragic that the only instance in which the federal government has moved with vigor has been against Negro leaders who have been working to end the evils of segregation."[44]

On the day of the indictment, street demonstrations held in Americus, a few miles from Albany, resulted in the arrest of three SNCC field workers and a CORE worker; they were charged with unlawful assembly, obstructing lawful arrest, inciting to riot, assault with intent to murder, and attempt to incite insurrection. The latter charge carried the death penalty. The next day, in the demonstrations held to protest these arrests, marchers were clubbed and were burned with cattle prods.

Albany pointed out that mass demonstrations involving the entire community walked on the edge of mob violence. It also demonstrated the vulnerability of civil rights activists to federal sanctions.

In the spring and summer of 1963 [45] conflict between Negro demonstrators and the police occurred in a number of Southern communities, such as Birmingham, Alabama; Danville, Virginia; and Cambridge, Maryland. These confrontations were notable in that they made public the willingness of sizable segments of the Negro population in these communities to violate publicly existing laws in the hope of changing these laws. Even children participated; "one estimate had all but 887 of the 7386 pupils of Birmingham's seven Negro high schools absent during one day at the height of the demonstrations." [46]

While the intent of these demonstrations was clearly nonviolent, they seldom avoided violence. In Birmingham, Martin Luther King's headquarters was bombed, and an outraged Negro mob stoned the police, set fire to a vehicle, and stabbed one policeman. In Danville, Virginia, the police broke down the door of a church where demonstrators were gathered and arrested Negro leaders under an ancient law that made it a felony "to incite the colored population to acts of war and violence." [47]

The summer of 1963 ended with the massive march on Washington, D.C., in which some 200,000 persons participated. Although most of the marchers were Negro, the march represented a broadening of the civil rights movement in that Catholic, Protestant, and Jewish white representatives participated. It is ironic that this broadening of the movement, so much a goal of Negro leadership, was greatly extended and transformed into a firm commitment to act on the part of respectable middle-class whites and especially the Protestant clergy and later the Catholics, by the bombing in September of a Negro church in Birmingham which killed four little girls and injured two more. Following this crime, representatives of white middle class America became actively involved in civil rights protests. The wade-ins and demonstrations at St. Augustine, Florida, March 1964 saw white involvement to the extent that Mrs. Malcolm Peabody, mother of a former governor of Massachusetts, came to St. Augustine to join the demonstrators.

The next development in the civil rights movement began as a controversy within SNCC.[48] As early as the summer of 1961, SNCC workers engaged in a searching dialogue over tactics. Some wished to continue direct action campaigns: sit-ins, pray-ins, stand-ins, demonstrations, boycotts, and so on. Others, with the encouragement of such advisers as Myles Horton of Highlander Folk School, argued for an extensive voter education and registration drive. As Howard Zinn writes: "The result was a compromise. Two arms of SNCC were created." [49] Direct action projects were continued, and a voter registration drive was begun.

Following this decision, SNCC workers began voter registration activities in the very bastion of white supremacy, the Black Belt. In 1959 there were 158 counties in eight states with predominantly Negro populations, and in 51 of these counties less than 3 percent of the nonwhite voting age population were registered to vote.[50] Although SNCC workers became active in all of these states, they concentrated on Mississippi, a state outstanding in that it had the largest nonwhite population, and by far the smallest percentage—less than 1 percent for the state as a whole—of nonwhites of voting age registered. By fall of 1963, SNCC workers had expanded their activities to all five congressional districts in Mississippi and had joined with CORE, SCLC, and NAACP to form the Council of Federated Organizations (COFO), which conducted a "Freedom Vote" campaign in which 80,000 votes were cast for Aaron Henry for governor.[51] One result of this political thrust was the formation of the Mississippi Freedom Democratic party, which presented a slate of delegates to the Democratic Party convention, challenging, with some success, the seating of the regular Democratic party delegates.

Voter registration drives, "freedom schools" to educate the Negro population politically, and community centers to provide a number of services for the impoverished and largely illiterate Negro population, proved to have broad appeal, especially among college students. A Mississippi Summer Project was devised, and, aided by the Committee on Race and Religion of the National Council of Churches, almost one thousand students volunteered to participate in the voter registration drives, freedom schools, and community centers.

Mississippi's legislature moved quickly in response to this invasion of "civil rights agitators" by passing a number of bills concerned solely with civil rights workers. The following are given as examples.[52] House Bill 64 authorized cities to restrict the movements of individuals and groups and to set curfew hours. Senate Bill 1545 outlawed the distribution of boycott literature, and provided a maximum penalty of a $500 fine and/or six months in jail. Senate Bill 1517 increased the maximum fine from $100 to $300 and jail terms from thirty to ninety days for specific traffic violations; such violations were frequently applied against civil rights workers. House Bill 546 prohibited picketing of all public buildings, streets, and sidewalks and other places belonging to the city, county, or state. Senate Bill 1969 made it a misdemeanor to teach in or to conduct an unlicensed school, a measure obviously applicable to the Freedom Schools. House Bill 270 prohibited entry into the state with the intention of violating state laws.

The police, too, were active. Six civil rights workers transferring a trailer of books for the Freedom Schools were arrested on suspicion of carrying materials which advocated the overthrow of the government. The groups of student volunteers for the Mississippi Summer Project began arriving in Mississippi on June 21, 1964, and immediately came in contact with the police: Ruleville, the first carload of volunteers were arrested for questioning; Clarksdale, arriving students were ordered off the streets; Philadelphia, three workers were arrested, released, and then disappeared—until their bodies were unearthed by the FBI; Drew, June 24, 1964, voter registration workers were met by armed whites; Hollandale, June 24,

1964, civil rights workers were ordered out of town by the mayor, who said they needed a permit to do registration work; Itta Bena, June 25, 1964, two white civil rights workers were picked up by two truckloads of white men and taken out of town; Columbus, June 26, 1964, eight voter registration workers were arrested for distributing leaflets.[53] And so forth; the list is seemingly endless.

And then we come to Selma, Alabama.[54] In a significant respect the two major arms of the civil rights movement, direct action and voter registration, united in one massive thrust against white supremacy in Selma, Alabama. In this community in which less than 2 percent of the nonwhites of voting age were registered to vote, action initially started as a SNCC voter registration project in February 1963. By September and October 1963 the community was mobilized behind the registration drive. On October 7, 1964, approximately 300 Negroes stood in line all day seeking entrance into the voter registration office. At this stage the confrontation in Selma was carried primarily by Negroes; according to Zinn, the only local white to show sympathy to civil rights activists was a Catholic priest, Father Maurice Ouillet.[55] And throughout the remainder of 1963 and 1964, the Selma operation was predominantly a SNCC project, which in spite of repeated demonstrations for voter registration, had failed to crack the white power structure symbolized by Sheriff James Clark.

In January 1965 the Selma confrontation entered a new stage, in that SCLC and Dr. Martin Luther King joined SNCC workers in this struggle. Under their joint leadership massive attempts to register were made once again, but without success. King's arrival heightened the struggle; not only did he bring nationwide publicity to the Selma struggle; he brought respectable, middle class whites, especially the clergy, to Selma to participate in the struggle. Following an unsuccessful attempt to march from Selma to the state capitol, Montgomery, in which Negroes were brutally beaten by Alabama state troopers, Dr. King made a nationwide appeal for aid. The response to his appeal gave tangible proof of the fact that the civil rights movement had significantly broadened its base and gained wide support. Rabbis, ministers, priests, nuns, professors, students, and others, came to Selma immediately. There followed mass marches and demonstrations in Selma; the murder of Reverend James Reeb, a white minister from Boston; and the immediate arrest of alleged KKK members who were charged with the murder. The march from Selma to Montgomery, with massive federal protection, ended in a display of strength which saw more than 25,000 civil rights supporters from all over the country marching in Montgomery. Then followed, that evening, the murder of a white female civil rights worker.

What is clear from our survey is that the South has used all dimensions of its power to maintain the existing white supremacist political structure. It has used private power unlawfully; it has misused lawful power and made it criminal; it has used economic power illegally. Legislatures have passed statutes and ordinances that were obviously unconstitutional; police have violated due process of law; judges have demeaned the bench; administrative sanctions have been applied to schoolteachers, students, and professors; lawyers have been harassed in such a way that civil rights activists could have been denied the right to counsel; individuals and groups such as the KKK have struck out with brutal violence against civil rights workers. Some parts of the South have earned the label "the closed society," and may well deserve being called "a totalitarian order." The Catholic lay magazine, *Ramparts,* in describing details of the Goodman, Schwerner, and Chaney murders, used the following quotations from Adolf Hitler:

Make them live in a valley of fear . . . a valley guarded by our men who will be both their only hope and the source of their fear.[56]

Activists in the civil rights movement either have openly and consciously violated laws they have held to be unlawful or have frequently found themselves in the position of having their behavior defined as a violation of local ordinances and statutes.

Thus civil rights activists have forced us to face the question of political crime, first, by their choice of action, and, second, by what they have chosen to confront. If we are to seek a valid assessment of their challenge we must acknowledge that the primary objective of law is to encourage certain kinds of behavior while discouraging others.[57] Regardless of the issue at hand, be it civil rights or international affairs, we must ask whether we wish members of the body politic to confront government, in all its forms, and to demand articulation and clarification of issues, and we must know whether we wish to encourage legal forms of protest against government and its agencies when disapproval of and disagreement with the positions and actions of government exist.

What is critical is that the behaviors which we are encouraging or discouraging should not be determined by existing social norms nor by administrative judgment. Sociologists cannot abdicate the responsibility of judgment and accept the state's criteria of crime. A superior referent must be sought.

Civil rights activists, by openly and consciously violating laws they have held to be unlawful, have stimulated sociologists to explore this complicated problem of man, the state, and the rule of law. And in spite of their numerous arrests and their philosophy of civil disobedience, many writers are not disposed to judge these activists as criminals, political or otherwise, but rather to view their behavior favorably. Robert K. Merton,[58] for example, writes in a tone and style which clearly communicate his favorable attitude toward the civil rights movement. Distinguishing between two types of deviant behavior, nonconforming and aberrant, he holds that the nonconformist, in contrast to the aberrant, (1) announces his dissent publicly, (2) challenges the legitimacy of the norms and laws he violates, (3) aims to change the norms he is denying in practice, (4) is acknowledged by conventional members of society to depart from prevailing norms for disinterested purposes, and not for what he personally can get out of it, and (5) lays claim to a higher morality and to ultimate values, rather than to the particular norms of society. The nonconformist is therefore similar to Max Weber's *saint,* and, of no little importance, he acts, according to Merton, in a social context which acknowledges and respects his other than personal motivations.

Merton's analysis is attractive, but it is doubtful that it can provide us with essential distinguishing criteria. First, in requiring that conventional members of society acknowledge that the nonconformist is behaving "for disinterested purposes," Merton keeps the sociological observer chained to the opinions of these "conventional members of society." Furthermore, simply to state that the nonconformist "lays claim to a higher morality and ultimate values" without specifying a basis for these, makes it extremely doubtful that Merton's classification permits distinguishing between a "radical right-wing" nonconformist and a "civil rights" nonconformist; and, lacking such analytical discrimination, its use is obviously limited.

A more successful attempt to distinguish politically significant forms of behavior is shown in Waskow's article,[59] in which he identifies three types of political action: (1) politics of order, that is, acting within the existing rules of society and making reforms when needed; (2) politics of violence, which is illegal behavior justified in that it is directed either against or toward the destruction of an enemy; and (3) politics of creative disorder, which refuses to do violence, but which seeks to achieve change by a militant attitude but by nonviolent means. And he has concluded:

The new techniques [of civil disobedience] are also likely to revivify the practice of that kind of democracy in which all citizens participate directly, in which each man has an active share in the shaping of his own destiny and that of his society.[60]

Waskow's three types of political action point the way toward a classification which is consistent with the contents of this paper. It is suggested that behavior can be judged to be (1) apolitical behavior, (2) politically obedient behavior, (3) creative political crime, or (4) destructive political crime. *Apolitical behavior* is behavior which seeks to satisfy the needs and interests of an individual or a group outside the political realm. Such behavior seeks either to deny the need for a political order or to subvert it into essentially nonpolitical forms. *Politically obedient behavior* acknowledges the existing political forms as legitimate and necessary and seeks to work within their framework. It understands that existing forms and instant governmental acts have a constitutional basis, but the politically obedient adheres to and accepts the official interpretation of these constitutional presuppositions. The politically obedient, in effect, removes himself from a creative role in the political order; he plays a passive, conformist, obedient role. *Political crime as creative behavior,* in the United States at least, similarly adheres to the constitutional presuppositions of the political order, but insists on the right and responsibility of the individual to impose an other than official interpretation. Thus, basic to the creative political actor are the premises that all men belong to, and should be encouraged to participate in, the body politic, and that this right is basic to political identity and must be protected by law, a law that applies equally to all. The politically creative actor insists that the state tolerate and refrain from seriously punishing politically deviant actions when these are directed toward the maintenance, through creative interpretation, of the existing political order, rather than toward the destruction of that order. The politically creative actor insists on the right to rebel—in Albert Camus' sense of that word—the right to protest nonviolently, by civil disobedience if necessary, against the actions of the political state. Finally, the *politically criminal* seeks power for himself, his party, or his group by violating the constitutional and ethical presuppositions of the political order and interpreting the law in an exclusive and politically divisive manner. The political criminal seeks to maintain or acquire power by excluding class, race, ethnic, religious, or political groups by denying their participation in the political order.

This survey has examined the politically criminal nature of Southern political power. It has shown that the South, by denying political identity to its Negro population, has violated the basic constitutional presuppositions of political community; that is, the right of all to live under law and to participate in the making and executing of that law. By developing this pattern of "exclusive" politics, the South has created a police state rather than a political community; the Negro has been forced to accept his subservient social status by techniques of extralegal violence supported by police power. And thus the South has moved frighteningly close to a totalitarian political order.[61]

In seeking a political identity, by acting in the public sphere in a nonviolent manner, seeking a meaningful application of existing laws, the creative interpretation and extension of laws, and the making of new laws, the Negro has given legitimacy to, and proven the success of, this form of "creative" political activity. This phenomenon may be of great importance for the future, as we move into a "post capitalistic" period,[62] a period characterized by government *largesse* rather than by "free enterprise," and, correspondingly, a shift from a class society with rights grounded in property to a society generally based on privileges arising from status.[63]

As we advance into this government-created status society, individuals will be increasingly faced with the struggle to transform the *privileges* of status into the *rights* of the individual. This will mean direct confrontation with government; it will sometimes mean action directed against government. But it need not mean political crime in the destructive sense of the word. Rather, the civil rights movement and other contemporary nonviolent protests point the way to a form of political creativity open to man in mass society dominated by government *largesse.*

NOTES

1. Louis Proal, *Political Crime,* with an introduction by Franklin H. Giddings, New York: D. Appleton & Company, Inc., 1898, pp. v–vi.
2. Herbert L. Packer, "Offenders against the State," *The Annals,* 339 (January 1962), 77–89.
3. Mabel A. Elliott, *Crime in Modern Society,* New York: Harper & Row, Publishers, 1952, pp. 179–197.
4. Marshall Clinard, *Sociology of Deviant Behavior,* New York: Holt, Rinehart and Winston, Inc., 1963, p. 160.
5. See the excellent paper by Charles A. Reich, entitled "The New Property," *Yale Law Journal,* 73 (April 1964), pp. 733–787.
6. Andrew Hacker, "Liberal Democracy and Social Control," *The Political Imagination,* Edgar Litt (ed.), Chicago: Scott, Foresman and Company, 1966, pp. 267–277.
7. Daniel J. Boorstin, *The Genius of American Politics,* Chicago: University of Chicago Press, 1953.
8. "Direct Action in the South: A Southern Regional Council Report," *New South,* Vol. 18 (October–November 1963). Our discussion of direct action in the South, 1960–1963, is based upon and closely parallels the account in this report.
9. Alan F. Westin, "Ride-in's and Sit-in's of the 1870's," *Freedom Now! The Civil Rights Struggle in America,* Alan F. Westin (ed.), New York: Basic Books, Inc., 1964, Chap. 10, pp. 68–74.
10. In a discussion of Arthur Waskow's "Creative Disorder in the Racial Struggle," *The Correspondent,* No. 33 (Winter 1965), p. 103.
11. *Southern Patriot,* 2 (September 1944), p. 2.
12. *Southern Patriot,* 4 (March 1946), p. 5.
13. *Southern Patriot,* 6 (October 1948), p. 4.
14. As quoted by Pettis Perry, *Negro Representation—A Step towards Negro Freedom,* New York: New Century Publishers, 1952, pp. 22–23.
15. This brief enumeration of instances of police action is not at all exhaustive; it is given only as representative of the type of police behavior which was common with regard to union activists.
16. Lucy Randolph Mason, *To Win These Rights: A Personal Story of the CIO in the South,* New York: Harper & Row, Publishers, 1952, pp. 44–46. The quotation is from the *Charlotte Observer* of July 8, 1937.
17. Mason, pp. 72–73.
18. Mason, p. 76; Miss Mason quotes from a letter from William Botkins, vice-president of the International Woodworkers, CIO, to George Brown, director of organization for the union, April 1944.
19. Mason, p. 78.
20. *Southern Patriot,* 2 (September 1944), p. 2.
21. Mason, pp. 81–83.
22. *Southern Patriot,* 4 (February 1946), p. 4.
23. These laws were strongly condemned as unconstitutional in articles in *Cornell Law Quarterly,* March 1943 and June 1943.
24. *Southern Patriot,* 1 (February–March 1943), p. 6.
25. This alleged assault took place at Walnut Ridge, Arkansas, in 1942; see *Southern Patriot,* 1 (November 1943), p. 3. See also, for a discussion of federal

criminal sanctions against unlawful police power, "Federal Civil Sanctions" in *Justice; 1961 Commission on Civil Rights Report,* Washington, D.C.: Government Printing Office, 1961, Chap. 5, pp. 69–78.

26. Mason, pp. 111–113.
27. Herbert Hill and Jack Greenberg, *Citizen's Guide to Desegregation,* Boston: The Beacon Press, 1955, p. 61.
28. *Southern Patriot,* 6 (April 1948), p. 1.
29. *Southern Patriot,* 7 (June 1949), p. 1.
30. *Southern Patriot,* 18 (February 1960), p. 3.
31. L. D. Reddick, "The Bus Boycott in Montgomery," *Voices of Dissent,* New York: Grove Press, Inc., 1958, pp. 169–179.
32. Bernard Taper, *Gomillion Versus Lightfoot,* New York: McGraw-Hill Book Company, Inc., 1962, p. 103.
33. Taper, p. 113.
34. Wallace Mendelson, *Discrimination,* Englewood Cliffs, N.J.: Prentice-Hall, Inc., 1962, pp. 22–23.
35. "Direct Action in the South," pp. 3–6.
36. Bayard Rustin, "From Protest to Politics," *Commentary,* 39 (February 1965), pp. 25–31.
37. "Direct Action in the South," p. 25.
38. See *Southern Patriot,* Vol. 17 (April 1959), Vol. 18 (October 1960), Vol. 18 (November 1960), Vol. 19 (January 1961), Vol. 19 (February 1961), Vol. 19 (March 1961), and Vol. 19 (April 1961).
39. "Direct Action in the South," p. 4.
40. William Goldsmith, "The Cost of Freedom Rides," *Dissent,* 8 (Autumn 1961), pp. 499–502. See also "Direct Action in the South," pp. 7–9.
41. As quoted in Mendelson, p. 159 (italics added).
42. Howard Zinn has an excellent chapter on the freedom rides in his book, *SNCC: The New Abolitionists,* Boston: Beacon Press, 1964.
43. "Direct Action in the South," pp. 12–16. See also *Upside-Down Justice: The Albany Cases,* Albany, Ga.: National Committee for the Albany Defendants, n.d.; a pamphlet, p. 8. Our material on the Albany situation including the Americus, Georgia, arrests is taken from these two sources.
44. *Upside-Down Justice . . .,* p. 8.
45. "Direct Action in the South," pp. 17–22.
46. "Direct Action in the South," p. 18.
47. "Direct Action in the South," p. 19.
48. Zinn, pp. 57–61.
49. Zinn, p. 59.
50. Quoted by Mendelson, pp. 170–171, from the 1961 Report of the United States Commission on Civil Rights.
51. *Mississippi Freedom Project,* Atlanta: Student Nonviolent Coordinating Committee, n.d.; a pamphlet.
52. See *Student Voice,* 5 (June 9, 1964), pp. 1–2; and 5 (May 26, 1964), p. 2.
53. The account of these arrests and harassments is taken from *Student Voice,* Vol. 5 (June 30, 1964). The murder of the three civil rights workers is described in detail in *Mississippi Eyewitness,* a special issue of *Ramparts* Magazine edited by Maxwell Geismar, Menlo Park, Calif.: The Layman's Press, 1964. For a full account see also Jack Minnis, *Mississippi; A Chronology of Violence and Intimidation in Mississippi Since 1961,* Atlanta: The Student Nonviolent Coordinating Committee, 1964; this material was first published in the *Congressional Record,* April 4, 1963, and subsequently brought up to date for this article.
54. Here we follow Howard Zinn, Chap. 8.
55. Zinn, p. 150.
56. David Welsh, "Valley of Fear," *Mississippi Eyewitness, loc. cit.,* p. 50.
57. H. L. A. Hart, "Prolegomenon to the Principles of Punishment," *Philosophy, Politics and Society,* Peter Laslett and W. G. Runciman (eds.), Oxford: Basil Blackwell, & Mott, Ltd., p. 163.
58. Robert K. Merton, "Social Problems and Sociological Theory," *Contemporary*

Social Problems, edited by Robert K. Merton and Robert A. Nisbet, New York: Harcourt, Brace & Wcrld, Inc., 1961, Chap. 15, pp. 697–737.

59. Arthur Waskow, "Creative Disorder in the Racial Struggle," *Correspondent,* No. 32 (Autumn 1964), pp. 61–73.

60. Waskow, p. 73.

61. While this writer has strong reservations about characterizing the South as totalitarian, it must be noted that such a characterization has recently been made. See Joseph L. Brent III and Perry H. Howard, "Toward a Sociological History of the American South: Implications of Regional Totalitarianism in a Pluralistic Society," unpublished manuscript; paper read at the Montreal meeting of the American Sociological Association, September 1964.

62. Ralf Dahrendorf, *Class and Class Conflict in Industrial Society,* Stanford, Calif.: Stanford University Press, 1959.

63. Reich.

19. Citizenship: Strategies and Techniques

The issues, strategies, and techniques of protest among blacks have changed from time to time, and from one locale to another within the country. Yet certain issues, and certain strategies and techniques for dealing with them, are central to many, if not most, communities. Thompson's report from New Orleans focuses on such common features in black-white relations.

DANIEL C. THOMPSON

In attempts to achieve equal citizenship, Negro leaders and uplift organizations have relied upon five basic strategies: *protest*, which is largely verbal in nature; *negotiation*, which usually emphasizes persuasion; *litigation*, intended primarily to have legal barriers to equal citizenship declared unconstitutional; *political action*, designed to achieve civil rights through bloc voting and other political maneuvers; and *direct action*, calculated to force state and local governments to abandon "Jim Crow" laws.

Protest—Police Brutality

The strongest and most consistent protest the Negro community has voiced has been directed at police brutality. The problem was well summarized in a memorandum sent to Negro leaders by a "Committee to Prevent Police Brutality to Negro Citizens." Dealing with "recent beatings of Negroes by police without justification," it called attention to—

A matter of grave and extreme importance that cries out for our *support*; for the *support* of every key Negro leader in the Parish of Orleans. This matter concerns itself with the increased *wave* of Police beatings of Negroes who have become the subject of arrests.

Because of the fact that numerous persons have contacted various Negro leaders to do something about this dastardly thing, we have found it necessary to call a "SUMMIT CONFERENCE OF NEGRO LEADERS" to discuss the grave issues involved herein and to develop a *program of action* to prevent the recurrence of this violation of human rights.[1]

From Daniel C. Thompson, *The Negro Leadership Class,* © 1963. Reprinted by permission of Prentice-Hall, Inc., Englewood Cliffs, New Jersey.

Protest by Negro leaders of "unequal protection of the law" is designed primarily to inform Negroes of the facts regarding this problem, and to arouse the "conscience of white men of good will" who have the power to intercede in the Negro's behalf. This latter purpose was suggested as early as 1940 in a *Louisiana Weekly* editorial. The writer presented the case against police brutality and concluded with the recommendation that "the most satisfactory solution . . . would be to have a higher selective police force, properly and effectively trained." [2] A year later, the *Louisiana Weekly* again found it necessary to call attention to police brutality. Lamented the editor—

Everytime a Negro is shot to death in such a manner for resisting arrest and allegedly attempting to escape, as was the case of Wilbur Smith, Willie Buggage, and 15-year-old Jesse Walton, it lessens our faith in this so-called "democracy" we are being conscripted to defend and serves to make us less and less willing to put such matters in the hands of the Lord, as we have done for the past 75 years. [3]

Another type of response registered by Negroes is mass protest. During the early 1940's, when there were fewer than 400 Negroes registered to vote in New Orleans, a militant Negro labor leader called mass outdoor meetings to protest repeated instances of police brutality. It was his custom to present to those gathered the actual victims, who would describe their ordeals in their own way. On these occasions representatives of the police department were usually present. After such mass meetings Negro leaders often received verbal pledges from police authorities that "the situation will be promptly investigated and whatever action deemed necessary will be taken."

This labor leader relates an interesting technique of direct protest that had some effectiveness, after the mayor had refused repeatedly to see him on this matter. He finally got several "thuggish-looking" Negro men to accompany him to the mayor's office. He is still amused when he recalls the excitement and frustration of the receptionists "when they looked up and saw all of us rough-looking Negroes waiting to see the mayor." At first they attempted to have the visitors wait outside in the hall until the mayor had concluded a "high level" conference. When they refused, the mayor's secretary rushed into his office and within seconds the mayor was out asking them what he could do. Whereupon, the leader told him that this was a committee from the Third Ward and they wanted to talk with him about police brutality. The mayor agreed to talk, but requested that the other members of the group wait outside. The leader refused, and all of them went into the mayor's private office. This leader reported that the mayor was so anxious to get them out that "he promised us anything we asked for." He interprets this manifest concern of City Hall as a "fear of race riots, not the Negroes' votes, because we had none."

Still another kind of mass response is the "protest funeral" for Negroes who are killed by the police. On such occasions a number of prominent Negro leaders make speeches intended to appeal to "all Negro and white people who believe in the principles of equality and justice that are so fundamental to our Christian and democratic society," as one speaker said at the funeral of an eleven-year-old boy who had been killed by an officer "in the line of duty."

Since speakers at "protest funerals" are often leading citizens, their statements are widely circulated. Knowing this, one leader revealed an important purpose of this technique by remarking that—

This funeral will shake up City Hall quite a bit. I don't think it will arouse any sympathy, but it may eventuate in some definite action. You see the mayor likes to sweep all the dirt in New Orleans under the carpet, so when the tourists come everything will look nice and clean. He knows now we don't plan to keep quiet about continual police cruelty to our people. If we keep on hollering loudly enough he is afraid we will be heard in Washington. He doesn't want that.

A new type of protest in New Orleans is picketing. On August 25, 1961 a group of Negroes, led by a Protestant minister, was arrested for picketing a district police station. Their action was meant as a protest against the police "murder" of Ezell Ward, twenty-one-year-old Negro, who had just been beaten to death by police officers after being arrested for simple burglary. This was the second such protest within a week.

For several years Negroes protested discrimination in the hiring of policemen. At first, Negro leaders gathered information relative to the practices of other southern cities, and endeavored to show that wherever used, Negro police had been instrumental in significantly decreasing the incidence of crime among Negroes. This line of reasoning has been summarized from time to time in the *Louisiana Weekly* as a basis for its protests. Thus, in a 1943 editorial, the editor poses the rhetorical question:

Why a southern city of the size of New Orleans doesn't have Negro police is a fitting question to ask in the light of the high homicide rate among Negroes in this community with apparently nothing being done to halt its apparent upsurge.[4]

In retrospect, protest against police brutality has been focused on these issues: more humane treatment of Negroes suspected of crime, hiring of Negro policemen, and the need to curb crimes among Negroes by "substituting scientific methods of detection for ruthlessness and cruelty."

Equal Justice

Insofar as the courts are concerned, Negro leaders have not voiced quite the same level of continual protest as they have in regard to police brutality. Their criticisms were originally directed at the absence of Negroes on juries. For several years the Negro community protested this periodically, particularly when some Negro was convicted of a crime against a white person that received wide publicity. Therefore, protest against court procedures is almost always linked with what the Negro community regards as differential justice. The thorniest problem is that of Negroes who are sentenced to be executed for the rape of white women. This subject has been the basis of numerous mass meetings and formal resolutions sent to local and federal authorities. Sometimes at mass meetings substantial sums are raised for the appeals of those so convicted.

Interestingly enough, the most effective protest directed at all-white jury convictions has been organized by a group of Negro women who have manifested little concern about other racial issues. This association has been active primarily in seeking justice for Negroes accused of rape. The most celebrated case in which this organization played a major part was that of Edgar Labat and Clifton Alton Poret, sentenced to die for the alleged rape of Helen Rajek in 1950. These two Negroes were given national publicity in *Look Magazine.*[5] In an interview with a Louisiana lawyer the author was told bluntly that "the law says you have to prove a man guilty beyond a reasonable doubt. But, the plain fact down here is that if a white lady accuses a Negro of raping her, *he* has to prove that he is innocent beyond any doubt." Therefore, despite the fact that the federal courts have seen fit to order several stays of execution and the United States Supreme Court remanded the case to the federal district court because of "systematic exclusion" of Negroes from the trial jury, these two men are still awaiting execution for rape, twelve years after the alleged crime.

The conflict over equal justice in this case was summarized by Mars in two quoted statements. One is that of a Louisiana state official who said, "This is just a question of two niggers against the integrity of a white lady." The other is in the comment of an expert on United States Supreme Court actions: "For a capital case, this is one of the shakiest I have ever seen."

Years of protest against "lily white" juries and differential justice was summarized in a *Louisiana Weekly* editorial in March, 1960. It attacked all-white juries which had found—

"Three white ex-cops not guilty in the alleged rape of a 23 year old Negro mother . . . thus upholding an old 'Southern custom' of reserving the death penalty for Negroes only who have been charged with rape involving women of the 'master' race."

The editor pointed out that—

There is no question that there is a double standard of justice for the crime of rape in the South. . . . In other words, according to southern customs rape of a Negro woman is not as vicious and ugly as when a white woman is raped. . . . The Communists do not have to raise a finger. "Southern justice," WCC (White Citizens Council) race haters and demagogues are doing a better job than they could ever hope to do in stirring up unrest. . . . The stench of injustice has become too strong to stomach any longer.[6]

In March 1961, a "Citizens Committee for Concerted Action" urged Negroes to protest segregation in the courts of the city. It called attention to certain of the most objectionable indignities: segregated rest rooms in the civil district court building, and segregated seating in the juvenile court. The committee asserted, "Municipal courts are the most notorious ones. They have segregated everything."

The committee suggested that citizens write letters, draw up petitions, delegate committees to wait on individual judges and the mayor, and threaten wide publicity and political censure for judges who live in wards with large numbers of Negro voters. They feared that racial discrimination in the use of court facilities would lead inevitably to differential justice.

It is not easy to evaluate the effect Negro protest has had in securing equal protection of the law. But one might ask: With relatively little voting strength, what would have been the story of the courts' treatment of Negroes if they had not protested apparent injustices? One thing is clear: protest has been an important strategy used by Negroes to create a national public opinion unfavorable to differential justice. Local court decisions have had to withstand the glare of a critical United States citizenry. This, no doubt, has functioned to make local courts somewhat more careful in their administration of justice. Thus, according to a prominent Negro lawyer, trial judges often "bend over backwards because they fear that Negro criticism might eventually lead to appeals which could result in reversals from federal courts."

The Right to Vote

When it comes to protest against voting restrictions, Negro leaders in New Orleans have joined forces with Negro leaders throughout the South. They have insisted that voting rights are federal, not state prerogatives. Thus, all protests against local or state restrictions have been directed toward the stimulation of federal action. As one Negro leader stated the problem—

White politicians are not fools. They know that if a large number of Negroes are registered to vote, their first show of power would be to vote them out of office, because most of them are known segregationists anyway. Negroes would be wasting time trying to get southern politicians to liberalize voting regulations where they are concerned. All of them boast about their perfect records in fighting civil rights, particularly voting rights. Our position is clear: we must call voting injustices to the attention of the federal government. This is our only hope.

All types of Negro leaders concur on at least one point: the Negro electorate in New Orleans, and throughout Louisiana, must increase to 75 or 80 percent of its potential before Negro citizens can expect to enjoy equal citizenship status. They seldom pass up an opportunity to denounce local and state authorities who are dedicated to keeping the Negro politically powerless, in the "sacred" tradition of the Solid South.

An NAACP field director reported to the Civil Rights Commission on Negro voter purges in Louisiana—

The most potent weapon available to citizens today is the ballot. We believe that the Commission on Civil Rights and others in the Government concerned with human freedom and justice should foster a "Voice of America" program for Americans, so that political leaders and citizens alike, knowing the promises of democracy, might work toward the fulfillment of those promises.

In the meantime our Federal Government must continue to work, in every possible way, to secure for all of its citizens those basic rights which some states and individuals would usurp. We believe this because we believe that America must first guarantee to its own their heritage of freedom before we can be fully worthy of carrying forward the democratic concepts to peoples abroad. . . .

The essence of the Negro leaders' protests against voting restrictions was captured in a *Louisiana Weekly* editorial—

The oft heard expression of the "professional" Southerners "Leave us alone. . . . Let us solve our own problems. . . . We love the Negro and treat him fairly" has worn pretty thin after 80 odd years or more. In fact, it has worn so thin in some Southern areas that the U.S. Justice Department announced last week it will file more court suits where Negroes are denied the right to register and vote.

It is now time for leaders and statesmen of this so-called democracy of ours to move against the "political hoodlums and racketeers" that infest Southern politics and deny Negroes the rights to register and vote.

Said Roy Wilkins [National NAACP Secretary] in a recent speech: "The right to vote is a basic American right. . . . Through trickery and threats and even violence, Negroes have been kept from the polls. . . . If democracy is precious in Hungary, it is precious in the South."

Meager and slow as this action by the Justice Department might be, it gives most Negroes in the South a boost in morale and renews their faith in democracy.[7]

Public Facilities

Negroes in New Orleans have long protested against segregated public accommodations. Their denunciations of segregation have taken several forms. Individuals have protested in public addresses, "letters to the editor," poetry, newspaper articles, scholarly papers, and books. During the early 1940's one teacher expressed his condemnation of segregation on intracity carriers by paying his students small sums to remove "screens" (the signs that partitioned Negro and white passengers) from buses or streetcars.

At one time or another, all Negro organizations in New Orleans find some means of expressing their objections to segregated public facilities. Occasionally, this protest is expressed in their bylaws, constitutions, or formally adopted objectives. Even when this is not the case, Negro organizations denounce segregation indirectly in their public meetings, at which speakers are expected to defend the rights of Negroes to enjoy equal citizenship status. Such speakers, as a rule, will also register strong disapproval of certain white individuals and organizations that attempt to prevent Negroes from attaining civil rights.

Perhaps the most significant protest technique employed by Negroes has been the carnival "blackout" movement. This movement brought to focus practically all of the grievances Negroes have had in regard to racial segregation. It was sponsored by an organization of social clubs. This organization is composed of representatives of the several Mardi Gras clubs and a musicians' union. Just before the 1957 carnival season, leaders of the united clubs appealed to all of its member clubs to cancel their annual balls to indicate sympathy with the Montgomery and Tallahassee bus boycotts. They coined the slogan, "It is immoral for Negroes in New Orleans to dance while Negroes in Montgomery walk." Member clubs were asked to contribute whatever amounts they had budgeted for their balls to uplift organizations that are "in the fight for freedom and first-class citizenship."

Although the request to cancel balls was made rather late in the year, after some clubs had already made cash deposits on bands and ballrooms, the effort did meet with surprising success. Most carnival clubs either canceled their balls altogether or held them on a much more modest scale than was their custom.

For three years after the 1957 carnival blackout, the Negro clubs went back to their traditional practice of having elaborate annual balls. Then came the school desegregation crisis of 1960, which was characterized by punitive legislation and vilification of Negroes by white supremacists. This was done so blatantly and viciously that one Negro leader summarized the attitudes of Negroes thus—

During the last several weeks segregationist forces in this state have left no stone unturned to show how much they despise Negroes. The state legislature, with its obviously unconstitutional anti-Negro laws; newspapers, that sound like the official organs of the White Citizens Council; and television stations, that have broadcasted Negro stereotypes in homes to poison the minds of children; all have made the Negro mad.

This speaker went on to endorse the 1961 blackout movement "as one way we can show white supremacists, and the nation, that we are tired of being segregated."

Not only did Negro leaders ask for a cancellation of balls, but they also called for a total carnival blackout in protest against all forms of segregation in New Orleans. This time they included such activities as attending balls given by others, participation in small parties, and attendance at carnival parades. Some leaders even suggested that Mardi Gras should be set aside as a day of prayer. As a result of the wide publicity given this blackout movement, every major ball was canceled; Negroes were noticeably absent from parades, and some actually attended church on that day of traditional festivities.

Immediately after this Mardi Gras the *Louisiana Weekly* observed—

> For all who were willing to look, the Negro was conspicuous by his absence [at carnival parades]. Negroes, spearheaded by the United Clubs, Inc., are to be congratulated for the manner and spirit in which they shouldered almost to the man, woman and child the burden of protesting against second-class citizenship.[8]

The frustrations often experienced by Negro leaders in their attempts to secure the full rights and privileges of citizenship are summarized in a formal protest adopted by the New Orleans Chapter of the Frontiers' Club at the height of the school desegregation crisis. The state legislature was in the midst of its fourth special session. It had passed scores of Jim Crow laws and numerous resolutions calculated to preserve the rigid pattern of racial segregation throughout the state. The behavior of this legislative body caused Negro leaders grave concern. A special committee of the club drew up the following protest:

> Today Louisiana is controlled by a handful of power-mad segregationists who are determined to keep Negroes relegated to an inferior citizenship status. All efforts to stem the tide of punitive legislation, economic pressures, and character assassination have failed. It has become necessary for Negro leaders to appeal to the conscience of well-meaning people outside the South to come to their aid, because—
> One, Negro citizens cannot depend upon elected officials to uphold their civil rights.
> Two, enlightened white individuals and groups in Louisiana who disagree with these "Black Codes" are subject to many of the same punitive measures as are Negroes.

The above statement indicates that one important focus of Negro protest is to create favorable civil rights opinion in other parts of the nation. It is an expressed hope that when the North is sufficiently disturbed about what is happening to Negroes in the South, their congressional representatives might be encouraged to take a more definite stand in supporting legislation designed to secure equal rights for all American citizens.

Negotiation

Another of the strategies Negro leaders have used in order to get things done is negotiation. Though the techniques have varied somewhat according to the type of leader, negotiation, as such, generally follows a predictable pattern. It is closely related to protest and is usually carried on by selected members of protest movements and uplift organizations.

Groups that espouse some civil rights issue will gather the facts and then attempt to devise methods by which Negroes might receive equal rights in that particular area of community life. The Negro community, thus, is informed of the nature of the problem under consideration. If the investigating group is mass-oriented, the next step will be public protest. If the group is class-oriented, negotiations will follow fact-finding and propaganda.

Therefore, as an adjunct to protest, Negro organizations, notably the NAACP, have engaged in negotiations with white men of power in order to achieve equal citizenship status for Negroes. Negro negotiators generally find themselves playing rather awkward roles, since bona fide negotiation presupposes the equality of the parties involved. With practically all political and economic leaders in New Orleans pledged to maintain racial segregation and inferior citizenship status for Negroes, the racial diplomat and the race man are likely to be maneuvered into playing some version of the Uncle Tom role if they are to get things done. It is primarily this noncomplimentary role-playing that prevents negotiation from being a more successful strategy in the Negro's struggle to become a full participating citizen in New Orleans.

Looking back over the past twenty years, *Negro leaders in New Orleans have accomplished little in the advancement of colored people through negotiation.* The Negro community has felt keenly the need to use negotiation to a much greater extent than has been possible in the past. All civic groups among Negroes have petitioned public officials and civic and business organizations in the white community to find some better way whereby fruitful negotiations between the races might be established. Although mayors, for example, have been petitioned time and again to appoint "human relations" or "race relations" committees, just two aborted attempts have been made to do so. Both ended unsuccessfully because Negroes complained that they had not been properly represented or that the mayor had selected Uncle Toms as Negro representatives. Therefore, nothing concrete has resulted.

As far as we are able to ascertain, Negroes in New Orleans have received only two definite citizenship gains as a result of genuine negotiation (without threat of legal or direct action). These are access to the municipal auditorium, and desegregation of the public libraries.

For many years the municipal auditorium was unavailable for Negro use. Negro leaders protested to no avail. Finally, a highly respected Negro diplomat requested the use of the auditorium for a "cultural program." When it was refused, he secured the services of an influential white lawyer, who assisted him in getting information about the use of city auditoriums in other southern cities. They found that all of the forty cities responding had adopted policies whereby certain "trusted" Negro groups could obtain use of their auditoriums. The white lawyer, armed with this information, went with the Negro leader to see the mayor. After receiving the information they had gathered, the mayor proceeded to establish a policy that would permit selected Negro groups to use the auditorium on a segregated basis.

Even now the city auditorium is not available for equal use: just prior to the school desegregation crisis in New Orleans, the NAACP was denied use of the auditorium for a meeting in which Thurgood Marshall, chief attorney for that organization, was to be the main speaker because they allegedly feared racial disturbances might ensue. Yet Negro leaders point out that only a few weeks later, in the midst of the school crisis, this auditorium was let to the white Citizens' Council to hold a segregation rally on the night of the first day of school desegregation. This rally is generally credited with having abetted the riots that occurred after the first peaceful day of desegregation. Again, in early 1962, the white Citizens' Council was permitted to use the auditorium to present an address by a Protestant minister entitled "Why I Believe in Segregation." This mass rally was picketed by a Negro group protesting the fact that only a few days earlier the auditorium had been denied to Martin Luther King, Jr. on the basis that he was controversial. Furthermore, Negroes who attend concerts or other public programs in the auditorium where white people are in attendance are still segregated in "reserved" seats in the balcony, or "buzzard roost."

The desegregation of the public libraries was carried out in a quiet, even secretive manner. There were no public protests or fanfare preceding it. After a group of Negro and white leaders simply "sat down with the proper authorities and talked sense," certain Negro groups in the community were advised that they might use public library facilities without discrimination.

One thing might be pointed out in regard to the two successes achieved by negotiation: The Negro negotiators were class-oriented diplomats, and the white authorities "were intelligent white people who understood that Negroes could use these facilities with the same kind of care as anyone else," according to a Negro leader who played a prominent part in the limited use of the municipal auditorium and the desegregation of the public libraries. There are still vestiges of the old pattern in the use of these public facilities, however. Drinking fountains and rest rooms are still designated by race, and the staffs continue to be all white.

Litigation

A third strategy Negro leaders have employed in attempts to secure equal protection of the law has been litigation. It is, in fact, their most successful strategy. Thus, when Negro leaders were asked: "Suppose a law is passed by the Louisiana State Legislature or Congress that a large number of people believe to be contrary to their best interests, or even unjust—what do you think they should do about it?" they usually concurred that any such law should be obeyed, regardless of hardships, until that law can be changed or declared unconstitutional.

One leader, commenting on "constitutional" laws, pointed out that "there has never been a time when Negroes were not called upon to obey laws they regarded as unconstitutional." He mentioned such laws as those designed to limit the rights of Negroes to vote, to live wherever they can afford to buy or rent, to use tax-supported facilities indiscriminately, and to participate freely in community affairs. He concluded, "No matter how unjust a law is, we must seek to remain law-abiding citizens. This, I believe, gives moral and spiritual strength to the Negro's continuing struggle for equality and justice."

Police Brutality

Negro leaders have used whatever legal means available to them to curb police brutality. They have filed numerous complaints in the district attorney's office and with the United States Justice Department, naming policemen who had committed crimes against Negroes and acts "unbecoming an officer." In most instances, such cases were either dropped "for lack of evidence," or the accused officers were allowed to plead guilty to some lesser offense.

In one year, 1949, the NAACP handled ten charges of alleged police brutality. An official of this organization confided that this was only a very small proportion of the actual number of complaints his office received regarding the "Gestapo-like" methods police used with Negro suspects. He feels that despite the fact that only a few policemen have been temporarily suspended for criminal action against Negroes, legal action taken by the NAACP has served an important purpose. He contends that—

The mere fact that we bring legal charges against these officers lets them know that if they do not show more humane treatment to Negro people, the police department in New Orleans might eventually be subjected to a federal investigation, which would uncover a whole lot more illegal activities than just police brutality.

According to the above statement, at least one basic logic underlies Negro leaders' use of the courts: This action is a tangible threat to local authorities that "if we do not receive proper consideration from you, we will make our complaints to officials of the federal government." Actually, in almost all legal actions taken by Negroes to achieve equal citizenship status, the local courts become significant only in their relationship to the federal judiciary. As one Negro leader interpreted, "Were it not for the fact that our state courts are a part of the federal system (whether segregationists like it or not) the Negro's fight for justice would be so much wasted energy."

Voting Rights

Most of the litigation regarding unfair registration and voting practices to which Negroes have been subjected has been handled by the NAACP's national office. No local test case has reached the United States Supreme Court, though evidences of such practices in New Orleans have been noted by federal authorities.

Since voting is regarded as a basic constitutional right, any test case anywhere in the United States that leads to validating this right results in improving the citizenship status of Negroes in New Orleans. Thus, Negroes in New Orleans have shared, with Negroes throughout the South, in the citizenship gains provided by the *Classic* case,[9] in which the United States Supreme Court ruled that Congress has the authority to regulate primaries as well as elections when primaries effectively control the choice of congressmen; and by the *Smith* v. *Allwright* decision,[10] which outlawed the "white primary" as a violation of the Fifteenth Amendment. These rulings have been sustained several times, but most importantly in *Elmore* v. *Rice*,[11] in which the district court and the court of appeals ruled that the party and the primary were instruments of the state and functioned to elect public officials, and that as such they were subject to the same regulations as stipulated in the *Allwright* case.

Legally, Negroes in Louisiana have not been forced to fight voter restrictions through the courts. Instead, their main task has been that of insisting that state officials abide by the constitutional "law of the land," as interpreted in decisions involving Negroes in other sections of the country. The litigation, then, involving Negroes in New Orleans (or Louisiana) has stemmed from the constitutional right to vote as set forth in basic federal court decisions.

Public Facilities

Negro leaders in New Orleans are aware of the fact that the most effective strategy available to them in their bid for equal citizenship has been litigation or the threat of it. Most gains made through protests and negotiations fall within the scope of a biracial society. That is, though rights are gained, the system remains segregated. *Whenever segregation is broken down, it is almost always as a result of federal court orders, not the voluntary action of state and local authorities.*

Negroes protested segregated transportation facilities for decades. Also, there was hardly a year when some group did not seek to negotiate with responsible officials in attempts to get unsegregated accommodations for Negroes on public carriers. These efforts were fruitless. Negroes were forced eventually to initiate suits intended to bring about federal action. It was in 1958 that a New Orleans physician and a Protestant minister-politician won their suit in the United States Supreme Court, which ruled that "segregation in local buses and trolleys in New Orleans is unconstitutional and unlawful."

Another suit brought by New Orleans Negroes in 1949 involved the unsegregated use of City Park facilities. After nine years of litigation, the Supreme Court affirmed a lower court ruling barring segregation in golf courses and other public park facilities. On December 21, 1958, the park's general manager announced resignedly that segregation in City Park had come to an end. He said, "We have reached the end of the rope. This means that Negroes are now permitted to use all park facilities—the tennis courts, the baseball fields, the golf courses, the amusement rides . . . all facilities."

Since the Supreme Court decisions cited have reference to the total Negro population, except for the cases involving segregation in education, they mark the most significant gains in the citizenship status of Negroes in New Orleans since the adoption of the Civil War Amendments.

For many years Negro leaders insisted that one of the most estimable ways of securing more equal protection of the law would be the employment of Negro policemen. Hardly a year passed when individual leaders and various organizations in the Negro community did not petition the mayor to appoint Negro policemen.

One of the most frequently offered excuses for not employing Negro policemen was that a Civil Service examination had to be passed in order for the applicant to qualify, and from some quarters it was suggested that Negro applicants could not hope to compete successfully with white applicants on such an examination. Whether this propaganda was intended merely to discourage Negro applicants or its advocates actually believed in the mental inferiority of Negroes, cannot be determined here. In any event, Negro leaders took the challenge seriously. They encouraged a capable young college graduate and war veteran to take the required Civil Service examination. He was officially informed that he had passed with a high score. Some say that his was the highest score made by an applicant at that time. According to some informed leaders this Negro applicant was "given the brush-off." It was done in this way: According to Civil Service regulations, if one appointment is to be made, the administrator in charge may select any one of the three top candidates according to examination scores. And so, despite his high score, the Negro applicant was "picked over."

Sensing the weakness of making demands under such circumstances, Negro leaders encouraged several highly qualified Negroes to apply for the Civil Service examination required by the police department. Six of them passed the examination, also with high scores. None was appointed. This fact gave the sponsoring organizations, particularly the NAACP, legal evidence of discrimination, and a court case ensued. It went through several hearings, and finally in 1950 two Negroes were appointed. Since

1950, after the initial breakthrough, several other Negroes have been appointed to the police force.

Although Negro leaders still insist that "Negroes do not fill anywhere near their deserved quota of policemen," there is now no litigation in progress to increase their number. The main issue since 1950 has been the restricted authority of Negro policemen. For a time, they served mainly on "special assignments," that is, with the juvenile division and at Negro public gatherings. Eventually, they were given uniforms and assigned beats in predominantly Negro neighborhoods. Later, they were occasionally assigned to traffic duty during rush hours. Even now, after eleven years on the police force, Negro policemen are not thought of as regular patrolmen. Only infrequently are they assigned patrol cars, and none is with the motorcycle corps. It is still generally believed that Negro policemen are expected to keep order among Negroes only.

Negro leaders have limited themselves to two primary techniques of litigation to secure equal justice in the courts. They raise money to employ able lawyers to ensure that equal justice in federal courts is received by Negroes, and they remind local court officials, particularly elected judges, that the "Negro people must have fair treatment in the courts." They promise political support to the man who is able to convince them that they will be treated like all other citizens. Thus, a politically ambitious Negro lawyer summarized the attitude many Negroes have regarding court officials when he told a candidate for a judgeship, "We don't want any special sentencing; no special fines; no special courtesies. Give us your promise to be a judge of all of the people according to law, and my people will support you."

Since the Negro vote has always been weak, needless to say, the most trusted of the two techniques has been that of remanding questionable local court action to federal courts. There is no doubt in the minds of Negro lawyers that this technique is the more effective. Most Negro lawyers agree that except in cases involving assaults against white persons by Negroes, "most judges attempt to be fair." They acknowledge, of course, that when there is a minimum and maximum punishment for a crime, Negroes are more likely to get the maximum punishment than are whites. As one lawyer said, "This is not a miscarriage of justice, rather it is the prerogative of the trial judge. In such cases they are not threatened with reversals from federal courts."

Finally, during the twenty or more years in which Negro leaders and organizations have used every strategy and technique at their disposal to guarantee Negroes equal protection of the law in New Orleans, there is no record of white leaders or white "men of power" allying themselves with them in this cause. The vast majority of them apparently ignore the importance of the Negro's efforts to attain equal justice. It may be said, then, that whatever progress has been made in this area has been due entirely to the insistence of Negro leaders and organizations, and to federal intervention. *All evidence indicates that without constant prodding from Negro leaders, and what segregationists call "interference" from the federal government, Negroes cannot hope to achieve equal protection of the law in New Orleans.*

Political Action

In order to make the Negro ballot a potent weapon in their fight for "full freedom" or equal citizenship, Negro leaders use the strategy of political action, along with protest, negotiation, and litigation. Thus, in addition to voter-registration drives and registration schools, sponsored regularly by various uplift organizations, by far the most promising instrument has been political organizations. These organizations have adopted every strategy and technique available to them in attempts to expand and influence the Negro electorate, including programs and slogans which reflect dedication to the highest ideals of Americanism. One such organization founded during World War II has as its central purpose "to promote an interest among its members in civic, social, educational and governmental affairs; to work to improve housing, streets and drainage in all parts of the community."

From time to time these organizations have sponsored voter-registration drives and protest meetings, along with their sporadic political programs. Most of the political activities engaged in by Negro political factions have been designed to get some white segregationist elected to public office. Occasionally, these political factions have sponsored Negro candidates for public office, but their efforts have never been as united behind Negro candidates as might be expected. There were always one or two factions among the eight or so that refused to give unanimous support.

Despite the fact that Negroes have had the legal right to participate more or less freely in the Democratic primary since 1948, and Negro political leaders have given unswerving support to the Democratic party (except for some defection in the 1956 national election), only one Negro political leader has held a public office, that of assistant district attorney. This appointment came as a result of a combination of two factors: strong support given the Negro candidate in the first primary, and the fact that the white candidates going into the second primary had about the same political strength. The Negro candidate thus offered the balance of power that barely ensured the election of the district attorney. For his support the Negro was appointed assistant district attorney, the highest political office held by Negroes since Reconstruction days. Except for this appointee, Negro political leaders and their followers have had no official voice in influencing the policies or practices of the Democratic party in Louisiana. They are excluded from the Democratic Parish Committee and the powerful state executive committee, where the qualifications of Democratic candidates are passed upon.

Unlike the Democratic party, which ignores Negro political leaders in state and national policy-making, the Republican party, with only about 250 Negro members in the city, has consistently included its single Negro leader in its policy-making. Though powerless in local elections, he has served as secretary of the Orleans Parish Republican Executive Committee, and as a delegate to the party's national conventions.

During the last twenty years, Negro political organizations have made at least two important contributions to Negro advancement. First, their leaders, in connection with political campaigns and mass meetings, have been able to create among the Negro masses some definite awareness of the role of politics in our modern industrial society. All segments of the Negro community have been brought to see that directly or indirectly their welfare will be determined in large measure by the type of leaders who are elected to public office. Second, though the Negro electorate is still weak, Negro leaders in New Orleans generally agree that it would be even weaker had there not been political factions upon whom white political aspirants could depend to muster a balance-of-power vote. One of the most successful Negro political figures contends that "the only Negroes who are registered in many sections of the state, New Orleans included, were permitted to do so because I, and a few others like me, promised the governor [who appoints the registrar of voters] that I would register enough Negroes to guarantee him victory in a close election."

Under this permissive system of registration, Negro political leaders have not been able to marshal enough Negro votes to present a serious challenge to the *status quo*, but they have been able to register just enough Negroes to ensure the political security of certain white supremacists who are dedicated to the preservation of the biracial system in Louisiana. Much of the increase in Negro registration is also due directly to Negro political candidates who have run for office during the last decade. It is a well-established fact that in their efforts to win political office, Negro candidates have done a better job of convincing the masses of Negroes to register than is done at any other time. The best example of this is the accomplishment of an independent Negro candidate, who ran for a seat in the state House of Representatives in 1960.[12] After qualifying for the second primary he knew that he needed a substantially larger number of Negro votes from his ward than those already registered. Though repeated voter drives in past years had resulted in a Negro registration of only 7,299, his efforts added 1,000 or more Negroes to the rolls within a five-week period.

The career patterns of Negro political leaders present a study in contradiction. All of them began their leadership in the role of race man. Most were literally pushed into political leadership by hopeful Negro followings. Several of them acknowledged that in the beginning they had no political ambitions. One said,

> When I looked out before me and saw all of those black faces depending upon me to represent them to the white folks, I was struck with the idea that if I could get them to stick with me I might become governor. From that moment I stopped talking so much about how we have been treated and started talking about voting. Man, I had myself a vision.

"Neo-Uncle Tomism"

When we look at the careers of such race men, turned politicians after they have gone through what Max Weber termed "routinization," [13] or a coming to grips with reality, it is sometimes surprising to see the transformation. In some cases they have been conditioned to play roles similar to that of the traditional Uncle Tom. They tend to beg for favors rather than demand rights. They develop this technique because practically all of the powerful white politicians in the state are segregationists. And, as we have already noted, the Uncle Tom is about the only type of Negro leader with whom segregationists will do business.

A sobering fact to be considered by Negro politicians is that legal codes in Louisiana are sufficient to prevent any Negro from voting if the registrar elects to keep him from doing so. Therefore, segregationists have demanded that former race men play Uncle Tom roles as a price for allowing certain Negroes who have been well screened to register. As one Negro politician put it—

> The only way I could persuade the governor to pass the word to the registrar to let my people register, was by pledging him my loyalty and promising him that I would not intercede for any Negro who might vote for . . . candidates.

Another Negro politician revealed his orders covering the support of even Negro candidates. He said that the head of a white political organization—

> . . . expects me to support all of its candidates. The only exception I am allowed is when a Negro is running against them. And, then only when in my best judgment the Negro has a chance of winning.

He went on to explain that officials of this organization realize that he can be valuable to them only if he maintains the good will of the Negro masses, and that the masses expect him to support Negro candidates. To be successful, race relations leaders must have the confidence of two polar-extreme groups: equalitarian-oriented Negroes, and powerful segregationists. Faced with this dilemma, some Negro political leaders behave in very inconsistent ways. For example, there have been occasions when a Negro candidate might have won if he had been able to get the support of certain Negro political leaders. This sets in motion a kind of "self-fulfilling prophecy," because predicting that a Negro candidate cannot win is tantamount to voting against him, thus ensuring his failure. In such a situation, the conduct of Negro leaders is precisely that of the traditional Uncle Tom, who for personal gains identifies with white authorities in opposition to the welfare of his own people. This is what one educator termed "Neo-Uncle Tomism."

Perhaps the greatest single weakness of Negro political leaders in New Orleans is their lack of organizational ability. Though they have been trying sporadically for two decades to establish an effective city-wide organization of Negro voters, none of them has as yet achieved his goal. Instead, their efforts have resulted in numerous rival organizations. The constant bickering among themselves functions to undermine the confidence the Negro masses would probably place in them under other circumstances, and to isolate from them groups that would be necessary to their success. Most of these organizations remain one-man organizations insofar as decision-making is concerned.

Bloc Voting

All Negro leaders interviewed, including those primarily interested in politics, agree that about the only way Negro voters can significantly influence political affairs in the city is by bloc voting. Fear of the Negro bloc has been expressed by most white candidates. Time and again, the NAACP, Communists, and Negro "troublemakers" have been accused of cementing the alleged Negro bloc. It is referred to as something sinister, un-American, and dangerous. Segregationists are apparently unaware of the fact that the most potent weapon the South has used to prevent civil rights has been the use of the bloc vote of its representatives in Congress and its legislators in the several southern states.

Actually, bloc voting among Negroes is widely misunderstood and misinterpreted. In the first place, as we have noticed, Negro political leaders have been far from unified in any political campaign; some of them have refused even to campaign for one another when they have run for public office. During the last gubernatorial campaign some supported candidates who were avowedly "100 per cent" for segregation, others supported a candidate who boasted of his loyalty to sacred southern traditions and estimated that he was "1,000 per cent" for segregation, and another prominent Negro political organization backed a candidate who attempted to prove that he was "1,000,000 per cent" for segregation. One of the candidates who received the unswerving support of a "militant" Negro political leader, assured the Louisiana Association of Registrars of Voters that he was "a billion per cent" for segregation.[14] Such divisions among Negro political leaders, themselves, are hardly conducive to bloc voting.

In the second place, the majority of Negroes who cast their votes for a given city or state politician did not do so because their votes were "controlled" by some organization. They voted the way they did mainly because the candidates had become well known for certain "favors," and they were regarded as the less rabid of the segregationists seeking office.

Perhaps Negro political leaders were responsible for propagandizing what one called the "gentlemanly qualities" of their respective candidates, yet in the end Negroes voted for those they considered the lesser evils. There is reliable evidence that most Negro voters follow their individual wills and vote for the candidates of their own choosing rather than following the dictates of some organization.

Since the beginning of the crisis in public-school education in New Orleans, Negro leaders have been trying to find some means to bring all of the warring political factions in the Negro community together. This is proving to be an extremely difficult task because there are so many forces mitigating against it. The most significant of these factors is that most of the leaders with political ambitions are already "married" to various white factions.

Direct Action

Negro leaders advocate direct action as a strategy in the achievement of equal citizenship only after protest, negotiation, litigation, and political action have proven ineffective.

The Sit-in Movement

One of the most significant and far-reaching results of the 1956 Montgomery bus boycott is that it established the strategy of direct action as an accepted means of obtaining equal citizenship. Previously, the NAACP had handled test cases of individuals who deliberately violated local or state laws as a first step toward having them eventually declared unconstitutional by a federal court. The only objective in the deliberate violation of a law was to get concrete evidence of its unconstitutionality for federal courts.

Such forms of direct action as "sit-ins," "kneel-ins," and "freedom rides" are not calculated as a step toward having "Jim Crow" laws declared unconstitutional, although this might be a result. Instead, the central purpose of this movement is to force state and city officials to abandon such laws. Thus, whereas a Negro sponsored by the NAACP might sit at an "all white" lunch counter for the purpose of getting evidence for a test case, a Negro member of the Congress of Racial Equality (CORE) would sit at the same counter in order to get served.

The essential motivation behind the direct-action strategy was expressed eloquently by Roy Wilkins, Executive Secretary of the NAACP. He said, in part—

American Negroes have been stirred deeply by events in the past few years. They are restless and frustrated. They are tired and snappish. They remember the lynching of Mack Charles Parker . . . defiance of the Supreme Court . . . filibuster in the Senate.

Negro citizens are weary of the old-time promises and excuses. Young Negro students have served unmistakable notice that they are through with the old order of segregation and racial insults.

He predicted that—

The minute Negro young people agree spontaneously that they will go to jail rather than submit to the old practices, those practices are dead. . . . white people can be "tough." . . . It will not affect the final outcome: Segregation in public places must go! [15]

Direct action was officially launched in New Orleans on September 17, 1960 when an interracial group of four CORE members was arrested at a lunch counter of a downtown five-and-ten-cents store. Since then there have been consistent efforts to break down segregation at various types of eating places—restaurants, bus and train stations, and the dining room at the airport. Also, there have been several "kneel-ins," and picketing incidents by members of CORE, the youth chapter of the NAACP, and by individuals acting independently.

This strategy shocked the established leadership in New Orleans—both Negro and white. Individually, Negro leaders at first tended to criticize such methods of direct action and to underestimate their potential effectiveness. After the initial shock passed, most Negro organizations endorsed the strategy as appropriate in the Negro's struggle to break down Jim Crow laws. These organizations contributed funds and provided space for mass meetings, and Negro leaders in all walks of life, particularly ministers, gave moral support by publicly lauding those who participated in direct action. One minister said, in a speech before a large mass rally where freedom riders were honored, that—

There has not been in modern history as true a demonstration of Christian suffering as we see here tonight. Those who were beaten because they dared to act like first-class citizens have set for us an exceptionally high standard of Christian behavior.

Although CORE is interracial in nature and practically all of its direct action has been shared by white participants, its strategy has been unequivocally condemned by all white organizations expressing themselves on the issue. White segregationists have been particularly vituperative of white CORE members. One white youth participating in the first series of sit-in demonstrations received the most abusive treatment, and was the only one of the demonstrators charged with criminal anarchy. The district attorney interpreted his action in refusing to desist from sitting with a Negro companion at a lunch counter "to be a statement against the state of Louisiana." He was placed under a $2,500 bond.

The direct-action strategy to desegregate public places was condemned by white persons in newspapers, editorials, resolutions passed by civic organizations, and from pulpits. The demonstrators were accused of instigating riots, creating racial tension, disrespecting laws, being "headline-seekers" and "invaders," and indulging in "childish and foolish behavior."

After virtually ignoring the problems of race relations in its editorials for a decade or more, on April 3, 1960, the New Orleans *Times-Picayune* took issue with what it termed "sitdowns" by college students:

The tragedy is that all the effort is so grossly misdirected while the tensions growing out of it lead toward hatred, fear and violence. This accomplishes nothing.

Certainly it can gain for the Negro students only the contempt of the majority.

At this time it is not possible thoroughly to evaluate the significance of the direct-action strategy in the Negro's struggle for equal citizenship. However, there have been at least two instances in which it has brought about definite Negro advancement.

First, throughout the South generally, and in New Orleans specifically, there has been some measure of desegregation of public places that can be attributed to direct action. Negroes have received service in eating facilities once reserved for "white only" in bus stations and train stations, and in the coffee shop of the airport.

Secondly, direct-action strategy has done more to facilitate communication between segregated southern Negroes and others outside the South than has any other strategy. This era of positive communication was begun during the Montgomery bus boycott. Action makes better headlines and more interesting reading for the masses than do other strategies Negroes have used. Mass media in other sections of the United States have made the Negro's plight in the South common knowledge to all segments of the American population, and indeed throughout the world. Unlike the protest strategy, which seldom reaches beyond the Negro public[16] and almost never has any publicity in media outside the South, organized direct action on the part of Negroes is usually fully reported with accompanying pictures. As one Negro leader put it—

Negroes in the South have always been persecuted and treated worse than foreign enemies. So called "good people" in the South choose to ignore our situation, and the busy people in the North have no time to concern themselves. What we are doing now [reference here to the freedom riders] is shocking the whole world. Our President pointed out yesterday that our international security may depend upon how we solve this problem. The conscience of the world has been touched.

One of the clearest statements of the motivation, dedication, and strength of the direct-action strategy was enunciated by a college student in answer to the *Times-Picayune* editorial cited. He said—

We have just as much right to this country as any other people.

We fought, toiled and died for this country.

We will strike the moral conscience of the white man and not his physical body.

No longer can we endure the back door of public places; the denial of equal job opportunities, the right to vote, or any privileges granted to a full time citizen.[17]

According to the statement quoted, the sit-in movement is a great deal more complex than what most southern authorities have been willing to acknowledge. For example, one segregationist was "amazed that a person will spend sixty days in jail and pay a stiff fine for a hamburger and a cup of coffee." Actually, lunch counter demonstrations are only means whereby Negro youths have expressed dissatisfaction with the total biracial system.

To summarize, since the end of World War II, Negro leaders in New Orleans have engaged in an intensive drive to achieve equal citizenship. They have employed five basic strategies: Protest, Negotiation, Litigation, Political Action, and Direct Action. They have used practically every technique available to them. These have met with only limited success.

As the goal of Negro leaders has shifted away from the "separate but equal" doctrine toward integrated use of public places, the race man is becoming more and more the spokesman for the Negro "cause." He is essentially an idealist who visualizes a completely integrated society. He enunciates the philosophy of "first-class" citizenship; points up the fallacies and disadvantages in "second-class" citizenship, and sets up what he regards as the ultimate, democratic goals to be attained. The racial diplomat espouses essentially the same social philosophy and goals of the race man, yet he differs from this type in that he is far more realistic on how to "get things done." He is more apt to realize that the process of attaining goals may require certain intermediate steps. Therefore, the racial diplomat brings to the Negro's struggle his skills as negotiator, "peacemaker" and organizer. The Uncle Tom is rapidly passing from the leadership scene.

The shift in Negro leadership is the basic condition underlying the crisis in race relations. Pointedly, Negroes have come to rely upon the race man to set goals to be achieved and upon the racial diplomat to map out ways and means of achieving these goals, while white segregationists continue to rely upon the Uncle Tom who has characteristically demonstrated loyalty to the biracial social system. There is, then, little effective communication between accepted leaders of Negroes and the official leaders of white people in New Orleans. As might be expected, every strategy and technique employed by the "new" Negro leadership is met with stern, often violent resistance from segregationist leaders. Consequently, one fact has become increasingly clear since 1954: *left to itself New Orleans* (indeed all of the deep South) *does not seem to have the will, the courage, the "morality," or the leadership required to voluntarily grant Negroes equal citizenship status.*

NOTES

1. Dated July 7, 1960.
2. February 3, 1940.
3. *Ibid.*, May 31, 1941.
4. *Op. cit.*, June 6, 1943.
5. Peter Mars, "The Man Who May Break Chessman's Death-Cell Record," *Look Magazine*, July 19, 1960, pp. 19 ff.
6. March 1960.
7. November 28, 1959.
8. February 25, 1961.
9. *United States* v. *Classic*, 313 U.S. 299, 318 (1941).
10. *Smith* v. *Allwright*, 321 U.S. 649, 661 (1944).
11. *Elmore* v. *Rice*, 333 U.S. 875 (1948).
12. Local white Democrats have never endorsed Negro candidates. However, a few Negro candidates have placed certain white candidates on their ballots.
13. See H. H. Gerth and C. Wright Mills, *From Max Weber* (New York: Oxford University Press, 1958), pp. 53, 54, 262–264, and 297.
14. These statements were actually used repeatedly by the candidates to describe their racial views.
15. *Louisiana Weekly*, April 16, 1960.
16. In most instances, Negro mass rallies are attended by Negroes only. On occasions, when outstanding Negro personages such as Martin Luther King and Thurgood Marshall have spoken, just a few white people may attend. White newspapers usually give only the briefest summaries of such meetings.
17. *Louisiana Weekly*, April 9, 1960.

VI. Black Politics: South and North

There is no doubt that black protest activities will become increasingly political. This means that they must lead to an increased national political consciousness and heightened levels of political participation among Negroes. In some areas of the deep South this means organization and action to guarantee the franchise. Elsewhere it may mean the intensification of voter registration efforts, the preparation of black political candidates, the development of white alliances, or any or all of these efforts. The relevance of this development in the black community is perhaps best revealed by the chronic efforts by white racists on local levels to resist it through various techniques of intimidation and violence, and through various legislative and administrative maneuvers. The most outstanding of these tactics of political repression, short of total disfranchisement, has been the development of the white primary. This development, now illegal by Supreme Court mandate, for a long time effectively prevented the development of local political strength by blacks. Gerrymandering and the strategic deployment of scarce resources by whites among blacks have also been used for the same purpose.

The destruction of resistance to full political participation by black Americans will mean their widespread participation on state and national bodies of major political groups, as well as substantial participation in the realm of "new politics." Significant black involvement across the political spectrum will give greater leverage to the movement for black equality. Such involvement, in conjunction with allied white groups, will give an urgency to black demands for equality. This will mean that the political process can neglect the black community and its interests only at the risk of introducing fundamental change in that process itself. For should conventional politics close ranks on blacks, alliances in the interest of basic change would be readily possible. An important requirement for adoption of this strategy is sufficient awareness of the relevance of politics, and sufficient skill in political action among blacks to make possible this degree of internal flexibility.

20. Negro Registration in Louisiana

The South, even today, remains well fortified against full political participation by black Americans. The heritage of a slave system and of "Jim Crow" have left a recalcitrant residue of racism that dissolves only too slowly, and even then only with substantial, sustained, and determined effort. Much of this effort has been, and must continue to be, a deployment of the resources of the federal government itself. Yet within this apparent white monolith there are important variations in political possibility and achievement by blacks. The following study by Fenton and Vines shows the relationship between the religious base of voting districts and the extent of Negro registration. Findings of this kind are essential for the articulate development of effective political strategy among black Americans.

JOHN FENTON AND KENNETH VINES

The 1944 action of the Supreme Court voiding the white primary ended the last effective legal block to Negro voter registration in the South. After that, resort to legal steps to block Negro registration was either outlawed by the courts or else could only be a delaying device. In the state of Louisiana, however, the decision in *Smith* v. *Allwright* did not result in Negro registration comparable to white registration. In 1956, twelve years later, 30 percent of the potential Negro voting population was registered, compared to 73 percent of the whites. This study is an investigation of some factors in that discrepancy, and in particular, of the differences in registration between Catholic and Protestant areas.

An important characteristic of Negro registration in Louisiana is the extreme range of variation to be found among the several parishes. Table 1 shows 17 parishes with fewer than 20 percent of the eligible Negroes registered, and 11 parishes with 70 percent or more of the potential Negro vote registered. Therefore, the statewide "average" percentage of Negro registration[1] has little meaning without more detailed interpretation.

Among the factors responsible for these differences is the religio-cultural variable. Louisiana offers a unique opportunity to study the influence of this variable on the registration aspect of race relations. Catholicism is dominant in southern Louisiana and Protestantism in northern Louisiana.

From *American Political Science Review* (1957), Vol. 51, pp. 704–713; reprinted by permission.

TABLE 1. LOUISIANA PARISHES BY PERCENTAGE OF NEGROES 21 AND OVER REGISTERED, 1956

Registration Percentage	Number of Parishes
0–9	7
10–19	10
20–29	9
30–39	6
40–49	5
50–59	13
60–69	3
70–79	6
80–89	3
90–100	2

The two regions are very nearly separate worlds. Other variables enter, but this one is the focus of this paper.

The material for this study was gathered from Census Reports and from specialized and local sources on the cultural characteristics of Louisiana. Sixteen parishes were visited throughout the state, chosen to represent different degrees of Negro registration, different socio-economic areas, and different religio-cultural areas. Interviews were conducted with state and parish officials and local political leaders, both white and Negro.[2]

I. The Religio-Cultural Variable

Every Louisianian is aware of the religious complications of his state's politics. It has usually been thought, though experience provides exceptions, that only Protestants can be elected to state-wide offices or as congressmen from the north Louisiana districts; and only Catholics can be elected to major offices in south Louisiana. The Catholicism of Louisiana is predominantly French, and it is said that a French name is worth 50,000 votes in south Louisiana in a statewide election.

Roughly the southern 25 parishes form French Catholic Louisiana while the remaining parishes in the north are predominantly Protestant and Anglo-Saxon. The French parishes remain French-Catholic because of their assimilation of extraneous cultural elements entering the area.

As Table 2 indicates, Negro registration, in percentages of potential eligibles, is more than twice as great in Louisiana's French-Catholic parishes as in its non-French parishes. In only two of the 25 French-Catholic parishes are less than 20 percent of the eligible Negroes registered, whereas in 13 of the 39 non-French parishes less than 20 percent of the potential Negro vote is registered. In seven of the French-Catholic par-

TABLE 2. NEGRO REGISTRATION BY RELIGIO-CULTURAL SECTIONS OF LOUISIANA, 1956

	French-Catholic Parishes [1]	Non-French Parishes [2]
Number of Negroes registered	70,488	90,922
Potential Negro vote	138,000	390,000
Percentage of Negroes registered	51	23
Mean of parishes—percentage of Negroes in total population	32	38
Mean of parishes—percentage of urbanism	30	26
Mean of parishes—percentage of Catholics among all religions [3]	83	12

[1] French parishes: Acadia, Ascension, Assumption, Avoyelles, Calcasieu, Cameron, Evangeline, Iberis, Iberville, Jefferson, Jefferson Davis, Lafayette, LaFourches, Plaquemines, Pointe Coupee, St. Bernard, St. Charles, St. James, St. John the Baptist, St. Landry, St. Martin, St. Mary, Terrebonne, Vermilion, West Baton Rouge. Definition of French parishes taken from T. Lynn Smith and Homer L. Hitt, The People of Louisiana (Baton Rouge, 1952), p. 143.
[2] Predominantly Anglo-Saxon Protestant.
[3] From 1926 Census of Religious Bodies, the most reliable source available. It is recognized that the figures contain a bias because of the difference between Catholic and Protestant practice in counting children as members of the church. However, the purpose of the figures is to show differences in degree of Catholicism.

ishes Negro registration is 70 percent or more, while only four of the non-French-Catholic parishes equal or exceed the 70 percent mark. Yet no significant differences exist between the two groups of parishes with respect to Negro-White population balance or to urbanism.

The reasons for the different reaction of French and non-French population groups to Negro registration seem, in large part, to be due to fundamentally different attitudes of each culture toward the Negro. Both Negro and white leaders agree that social attitudes toward the Negro differ in the two cultures.

Some objective evidence of this difference is to be found in these facts: (1) at political meetings in southern Louisiana crowds are often racially mixed, even at indoor meetings, whereas in northern Louisiana such crowds are always segregated; (2) the Citizens' Council organizations have comparatively little support in French-Catholic Louisiana, while in northern Louisiana, as a Madison Council official put it, "Here the Citizens' Councils are the prominent people"; (3) racially hybrid communities occur more frequently in south Louisiana than in north Louisiana.[3]

It should be emphasized that the people of French-Catholic Louisiana are not in favor of integration. Yet they do evidence, people and leaders alike, a permissive attitude toward Negro participation in political affairs

that is generally lacking in the northern parishes.[4] These permissive attitudes seem to stem in large part from the social and religious practices of
the Catholic Church. The Church looks upon segregation as a sin, and
Archbishop Rummel of New Orleans has led the clergy in an all-out
doctrinal attack on the practice. Catholic clergy cite the "catholic" character of the Church as the reason for its advanced stand on racial issues and
emphasize the fact that the Protestant churches are national in origin and
tend to be exclusive in character, whereas the Catholic Church is more
universal in both its background and orientation. Many Catholics also
point to the effect of the Church on the Negro as a reason for the high
percent of Negro registration in Catholic parishes. According to this
argument, the Catholic Negro enjoys religious and ethical training which
is identical with that received by the white community, and from a
well-educated priest. Therefore, the Catholic Negro's value system more
nearly approaches that of the white community than does that of the
Protestant Negro, and, accordingly, he is more readily accepted by the
greater community.

Since the Catholic Church attempts to build a Catholic culture wherever it exists by providing educational, recreational, and fraternal organizations for its members, the influence of the Church as a social institution
is great. It appears to be the principal, in many areas the only, unsegregated social institution in Louisiana. In the French parishes where Catholicism has been the major formative factor in the culture for many years, it
has been, Catholics say, important in producing the permissive attitudes of
the people toward the political and social activities of the Negro.

In north Louisiana, on the other hand, one finds little or no objective
evidence that the dominant Protestant religion has aided in the creation of
tolerant attitudes toward Negro political activity. Negro leaders in these
areas rarely cited white Protestant ministers as friends of the Negro, and
seldom referred to a Protestant church as an ameliorative factor in the
easing of racial tensions. Although most Protestant national organizations
are opposed to racial prejudice and segregation, their position has not
effected many changes in the attitudes of local congregations. Protestant
churches, in contrast to the authoritative control by the Catholic hierarchy, are dominated by local congregations, and Protestant ministers,
though often mindful of national pronouncements on segregation, must
remain passive on such matters so as not to offend their flocks.

Although the mean percent of Negro registration is low in north Louisiana, there are parishes with large Negro registration. As Table 3 shows,
this usually occurs where Negroes are not an important part of the
population, that is, where there are few Negroes, little economic tenancy,
and no heritage of a plantation society.

When the parishes of northern Louisiana are grouped into areas, this
correspondence of a high rate of tenancy and concentration of Negro

TABLE 3. RELATION BETWEEN PERCENTAGE OF TENANCY, PERCENTAGE OF NEGRO POPULATION, AND PERCENTAGE OF NEGROES REGISTERED IN FRENCH AND NON-FRENCH PARISHES OF LOUISIANA, 1956

Percentage of Tenancy	Number of Parishes		Mean Percentage of Negro Population		Mean Percentage of Negroes Registered	
	French	Non-French	French	Non-French	French	Non-French
50 and over	6	11	34	52	65	11
40–49	0	4	–	43	–	23
30–39	7	6	33	39	48	25
20–29	5	6	23	36	67	36
10–19	7	9	34	25	43	53
0– 9	0	3	–	19	–	59

population to a low Negro registration becomes clearly evident and significant. In the north-central cut-over pine section where the percentage of Negroes in the total population (mean of parishes, 24 percent) and prevalence of tenancy (17 percent) is relatively low, there is a great deal of Negro registration (55 percent). In this area, there has been little fear of the Negro as a political force, and the society tends to be pluralistic.[5]

The Mississippi Delta area, in northeast Louisiana, is the section with the highest rate of tenancy (60 percent), the greatest proportion of Negroes (51 percent), and the lowest Negro registration (11 percent) in the state. It remains a plantation society. There are plantation owners in Tensas and Madison parishes who take pride in the resemblance between the plantations of 1856 and 1956, in terms of the physical appearance of the Negro and his cabin, and of the social and economic relationships between Negro and white.

The survival of this kind of society depends upon excluding the Negro from all political and economic power. Outsiders are assured that the Negro happily accepts the existing power structure, and strenuous efforts are made to demonstrate the mutual advantages which accrue from it.

Thus in non-French Louisiana, Negro registration varies with the number of Negroes present and the nature of the economy. In a plantation economy, a tight power structure exists which makes it possible to exclude Negroes from the polls. In addition the numerical strength of Negroes in such communities arouses real or imagined fears of possible Negro rule if he should obtain the ballot.

As Table 3 indicates, the economic structure of many of the French-Catholic parishes differs from that of the northern portion of the state. In French-Catholic Louisiana the Negro is not typically in a tenant-master relationship to the white community. Rather, his position is that of a free wage-earner. The reason is that much of southern Louisiana is engaged in the production of cane sugar, which does not lend itself to the tenant system of farming.

The free wage-earner is more remote from his master than is the tenant farmer, and thus (at least in prosperous times) enjoys greater social and economic freedom. Therefore, the difference in the economies of the two regions undoubtedly exercises an important conditioning effect on Negro registration.

However, even in those French-Catholic parishes where a plantation economy does exist the percent of Negro registration tends to be considerably above that of the northern plantation parishes. In three French-Catholic parishes (St. Landry, Pointe Coupee, and West Baton Rouge) both the percentage of Negro population and the percentage of tenancy is 45 or more. The percentage of Negro registration exceeds 20 in all three parishes and reaches a level of 87 in St. Landry. This highlights the importance of the French-Catholic religio-culture in producing a permissive attitude toward Negro registration.

II. The Effect of Negro-White Population Balance

Perhaps the most widely accepted belief concerning Negro registration in the South is that the amount will vary inversely to the proportion of Negroes in the local population. According to this theory, areas with large Negro populations, (1) were most passionately attached to the cause of the Confederacy, and (2) because of the greater number of Negroes have more reason to fear Negro voting. The theory concludes that the centers of Negro population will be the last to extend the suffrage to the Negro.

Table 4 shows that there is certainly no uniform correlation between the

TABLE 4. RELATION BETWEEN NEGROES IN TOTAL POPULATION AND NEGRO REGISTRATION IN PARISHES OF LOUISIANA, 1956

Percentage of Negroes in Total Population	Number of Parishes			Mean Percentage of Negroes Registered		
	Total	French	Non-French	Total	French	Non-French
60 and over	4	–	4	0	–	0
50–59	10	4	6	37	44	33
40–49	8	3	5	33	57	19
30–39	19	6	13	32	47	25
20–29	12	6	6	52	51	53
10–19	10	5	5	62	65	59
0– 9	1	1	–	94	94	–

proportion of parish population Negro and the proportion of Negroes registered. However, at the extreme ends of the scale, the relationship is significant. The four Louisiana parishes with no Negro registration—Tensas, Madison, West Feliciana, and East Carroll, neighboring parishes in the Mississippi Delta area—are the only parishes with over 60 percent Negro population. In the parishes with less than 29 percent Negro population there is a significant increase in the percentage of Negro registration. However, in ten parishes with a majority of Negro population (50 to 59 percent) the mean percentage of Negroes registered (37 percent) slightly exceeds that for the two intervals with fewer Negroes (40 to 49 percent and 30 to 39 percent).

Table 4 also shows that the presence or absence of large numbers of Negroes has a similar effect on Negro registration in French and non-French parishes. However, as the table indicates, the range of variation tends to be much narrower in the French than in the non-French parishes. Of course, the degree of economic tenancy is another variable present in this figure, a factor which has already been discussed.

In conclusion, it can be definitely stated that, in Louisiana, the simple fact of the presence of a high proportion of Negroes and a tradition of a plantation economy (such as in St. Landry parish) does not necessarily militate against the registration of Negroes in sizeable numbers, especially where a French-Catholic culture predominates.

III. The Effect of Urbanism

Contrary to the widely held belief that Negro registration in the South is concentrated in urban areas, Table 5 indicates that no clear relationship exists in Louisiana between the degree of urbanism and the extent of Negro registration.

The reason, in all probability, for the stereotype about urbanism and Negro registration is that those few Negroes who were registered to vote prior to 1944 resided in the large urban centers. In addition, the first increases in Negro registration after 1944 largely occurred in urban areas. The urban areas of the state contain the largest concentration of professional and business Negroes, equipped to provide leadership toward registration; and the cities provide, one might imagine, an environment of political competition better suited to encourage Negro political participation.

As Table 5 indicates, however, Negro registration in Louisiana is, if anything, lower in the large urban centers than in the more rural portions of the state. The table also shows that an identical though more pronounced pattern obtains for white registration too. Taking the religio-cultural areas of the state separately, the same relationship between urbanism and registration exists in both regions as in the state as a whole,

**TABLE 5. RELATION BETWEEN URBANISM AND WHITE AND NEGRO REGISTRA-
TION, FOR STATE AND BY RELIGIO-CULTURAL SECTIONS, LOUISIANA, 1956**

| | | | | Mean Percentage Registered of Potential Vote | | | | | |
| | Number of Parishes | | | Negro | | | White | | |
Percentage of Urbanism	Total	Fr.	Non-Fr.	Total	Fr.	Non-Fr.	Total	Fr.	Non-Fr.
70 and over	5	2	3	29	43	20	64	70	60
50–69	4	3	1	45	48	35	75	78	69
40–49	8	2	6	27	67	13	78	79	77
30–39	10	3	7	46	54	42	84	84	84
20–29	14	8	6	49	61	33	90	91	88
10–19	6	3	3	28	43	13	88	89	87
0– 9	17	4	13	43	53	40	92	93	90

but with both Negro and white registration in the French parishes tending to be either equal to or higher than registration in the non-French parishes.

Negro registration tends to be lower in the urban than the rural areas for a variety of reasons. Many an urban Negro is rootless, and tends to feel little identification with his community or his fellow Negroes; his leadership often works at cross purposes, and is particular rather than general. In addition, local interest in registration and voting tends to be more intense in Louisiana's rural areas, where the election of a sheriff is an important event, than in the urban areas. All of these factors tend, also, to operate on the level of white registration.

Even though the urban centers do not provide favorable environments for securing a high proportion of Negro registration, the "pilot" role of activities in urban centers toward launching Negro registration is important. In all parishes studied the registration of Negroes was initiated by business and professional Negroes residing in the major urban center of the parish. In the event resistance to Negro registration made it necessary to resort to legal and political action, the city provided the resources and locus for suits against the registrar, for requests to the F.B.I. to investigate reluctant registrars, and for bargains which might be negotiated with court-house politicians.

IV. The Political Factor

The first concern of every politician is to be elected and reelected to office. Therefore, the existence in any community of a reservoir of untapped voters tends to act as a magnet on politicians in search of votes.

The Negro vote in Louisiana, however, was not exploitable until the Supreme Court declared the white primary laws unconstitutional. After 1944, Louisiana politicians could legally pursue the Negro vote.

In all the Louisiana parishes except those with the very largest cities, political power and interest center in the courthouse of the parish seat. The dominant political figure in the courthouse is the sheriff, whose election occasions the most interest and largest voter turnout in the parish. Where Negro registration has occurred in large numbers, the sheriff has almost invariably been friendly to the idea.

The process by which this political variable helps bring Negroes to the polls works generally as follows. Community attitudes must, first of all, be permissive with respect to Negro registration. If the white community is strongly and unalterably opposed to Negro voting, the sheriff or other politician will rarely venture to seek the Negro vote. Instead, as in the Mississippi parishes with no registration, the sheriff will help keep the Negroes away from the polls. This is true because the politician fears the reaction of his townspeople to Negro registration and because he, too, generally shares the dominant attitude.

Secondly, the sheriff, by the very nature of his office, is subject to manifold temptations relating to law enforcement, particularly, in Louisiana, to the classic "payoff" to permit gambling. When a sheriff permits gambling, he is charged with corruption of his office by the good government, middle-class voters of his community. In this event the sheriff is compelled to turn to lower socio-economic groups or to marginal groups in the community for support.

After Negro leaders have initiated the movement for registration and thus demonstrated their group's potential voter strength, the sheriff or other official can then use to his own profit the power of his office to prevent interference with registration, or else later encourage registration drives and voter turnout campaigns. In many parishes the Negro vote has become a "balance of power" factor.

Finally, the reward of the Negro for his vote is respect from the politicians and attendance at Negro political meetings, cessation of police brutality, and promises made and often kept regarding such matters as street improvements and better school facilities. It is ironical that this advance may thus result from an alliance of shady white and underdog Negro elements against the more "respectable" white segment of the community.

The political factor is also important as an inhibiting influence. For example, in the two French parishes (Terrebonne and Plaquemines) with a rate of Negro registration below 20 percent, the local sheriff has been instrumental in keeping the Negroes from the polls. In these cases, the sheriff is unalterably opposed to Negro voting, primarily out of fear that it will cost him the election, and, consequently, he uses the power of his office to prevent registration. In all probability, a different sheriff could permit Negro registration without suffering a serious reaction from the white community.

V. Conclusions

This paper is concerned with the problem of differences in the political behavior of the South toward the Negro. These differences have been studied, here, through an analysis of Negro registration for voting in Louisiana. Negro registration is basically related to Southern politics not only because it is the fundamental step for the Negro toward the power of the ballot box but also because it appears to be vitally related to the willingness or unwillingness of specific societies to allow the Negro an equal place in the community. The evidence indicates that Southern attitudes and practices toward the Negro are in large part a function of the culture in which the relationships occur.[6] Our inquiry here is whether religio-cultural variables in the South, long celebrated as the "Bible-belt" of the nation, are related to Negro-white political relationships insofar as these can be defined by practices and attitudes toward Negro registration.

The findings of this study emphasize the importance of religio-cultural factors in defining white attitudes and practices toward Negro registration. In the southern French-Catholic parishes the percentage of Negroes registered is more than twice as great as in the northern Anglo-Saxon Protestant parishes. Socio-economic factors, urbanism and Negro-white population balance, account for some of the difference. Yet where non-religious cultural factors are held constant, as in cotton plantation areas with large Negro populations, the religio-cultural variable emerges as a cleary influential factor in Negro registration.

First-hand observations in the parishes of Louisiana support the statistical evidence that Negro registration is related to the type of religio-cultural area involved. Permissive attitudes toward Negro registration in French-Catholic parishes seem expressive of the basic value that the Negro is spiritually equal in a Catholic society. Such a view of man's relation to man, a scheme of elementary justice implicit in a Catholic society, some Catholics maintain, is sustained by traditional Catholic theology and actively promoted by the Church in Louisiana. There is little evidence in the Protestant parishes of cultural values assigning the Negro a spiritually equal place in the community or of activity by the church itself toward these values.

Dr. Frank Tannenbaum has written a brilliant exposition of the comparative treatment of the Negro in North and South America, maintaining that differences are in large part a function of the respective Protestant and Catholic cultures.[7] Curiously, the religio-cultural analysis has been largely neglected in race-relations analysis of the United States, even though the role of the Protestant ethic, for instance in economic behavior and intellectual development, has been well stated.

It is not the intention of the authors to urge religious determinism in this paper but to maintain that, on the evidence, the politics of Negro registration in Louisiana can be understood only by consideration of religio-cultural variables with other relevant factors. In consequence we suggest that religio-cultural analysis may be useful in understanding the whole of Southern politics. Excepting Maryland, possibly, the type of analysis employed here would not be possible in other Southern states due to the lack of distinctive religio-cultural areas. Some attention could be given, however, to the general problem of the Protestant ethic in the South and its involvement with political behavior.

NOTES

1. Current estimates on population figures were obtained as follows: (1) The estimated total population of each parish for 1956 was obtained from *Sales Management Annual Survey of Buying Power,* May 10, 1956. (2) It was assumed that the 1950 ratio of Negroes to the total population in each parish would remain constant. (3) It was assumed that the 1950 ratio of Negroes 21 and over to the total Negro population in each parish would remain constant. (4) Thus by taking percentages of the 1956 total population estimate as derived from the 1950 census, a 1956 estimate was obtained for the potential Negro vote in each parish.
2. The authors wish to acknowledge the aid of the Southern Regional Council in support of this project. The Louisiana project was part of a Southern-wide survey of Negro registration and voting sponsored by the Council.
3. See Alvin L. Bertrand, *The Many Louisianas,* Bulletin No. 46, Louisiana State University, Agricultural Experiment Station, June, 1955, p. 21.
4. The more "permissive" attitude of the French-Catholic parishes may be demonstrated additionally by comparison of its record on race relations with the northern parishes on such matters as rates of lynching, 1900–1941; and the number of racially integrated state colleges. It was also confirmed in interviews with both Negroes and whites from the two areas.
5. It should be noted, however, that resistance to Negro registration is stiffening in north-central Louisiana. Efforts to purge Negroes from the rolls are being vigorously pressed by Citizens Council groups in the section. For a detailed statement of the procedures being used there, see the letter from Assistant Attorney General Olney to Senator Douglas, *Congressional Record,* Vol. 103 (August 1, 1957), pp. 12156–7 (daily ed.); New York *Times,* August 4, 1957, which, however, misplaced the parishes cited as in the southern part of the state.
6. See, for example, V. O. Key, Jr., *Southern Politics* (New York, 1949); and Hugh Douglas Price, *Negro and Southern Politics, A Chapter of Florida History* (New York, 1957).
7. *Slave and Citizen: The Negro in the Americas* (New York, 1947).

21. The Negro and Florida Politics, 1944–1954

Political participation by blacks in Louisiana shows some obvious similarities to the pattern in Florida, as this chapter reveals. Under-registration by blacks is the most prominent of these similarities, in addition to registration increases among blacks in recent times. The author recognizes the extensive political potential which rests in the black community of Florida. This may account for his questionable assessment of past aspirations of blacks in Florida and his projections about their future aspirations. Although it may be true that Florida blacks have had essentially white middle-class aspirations, there is no reason to believe that this will continue to be the case. Whether or not this remains so will doubtless depend upon the flexibility of the white community in Florida. Since this article was published, events concerning black political aspirations have moved swiftly. It predates the rise of campus protest by blacks and the influence of new young black leaders of the Stokely Carmichael and H. Rap Brown variety. This new national development among blacks will undoubtedly influence political aspirations among blacks, even in such well-fortified bastions of racism as Florida.

HUGH DOUGLAS PRICE

In the excitement over the Supreme Court's recent decision against segregation in the public schools another important landmark in the history of the South has been overlooked: 1954 also marked the tenth anniversary of the historic *Smith* v. *Allwright*[1] decision which spelled the beginning of the end for the "white primary." With the current discussion of widespread changes or of violent reaction due to the school decision it is doubly interesting to trace the result of federal court intervention to secure Negro rights in the political sphere.[2] This study seeks to show what effect the 1944 court decision has had in one Southern state, the rôle which the Negroes of that state have assumed as voters, and the consequences of these changes on the use of the Negro as a political issue.

The choice of Florida as a laboratory for the study of Negro voting is not accidental. Although a comprehensive survey of the whole South would obviously be desirable, Florida is the only state in the South which publishes registration figures broken down by race for each party.[3] With-

From *Journal of Politics* (May 1955), Vol. 17, No. 2, pp. 198–220; reprinted by permission.

out the basic information as to how many Negroes register, where they register, and how the precincts composed largely of Negroes actually vote, only fragmentary and impressionistic accounts are possible. Moreover, on the basis of the best available estimates of Negro registration in the South, a higher percentage of Negroes register and vote in Florida than in any other Southern state.[4]

The outstanding fact indicated by the tremendous growth of Negro registration since 1944 is that "a revolution which will rank second only to Reconstruction in the emancipation of the Southern Negro"[5] has occurred. By 1954 a total of 128,329 Negroes were registered in Florida. These Negroes, representing 64 of the state's 67 counties, accounted for over ten percent of the state's total registration.[6] By contrast, in 1944 no Negroes were registered in 36 Florida counties and the remainder had a total of about twenty thousand, all registered as Republicans and hence ineligible to participate in the decisive Democratic primaries.[7] Table 1 indicates the

TABLE 1. NEGRO REGISTRATION AND PARTY AFFILIATION IN FLORIDA: 1944–1954 (AS OF MAY IN EACH YEAR)

Date	Number of Negro Democrats	Number of Negro Republicans	Total Negro Registration
1944	0 [a]	20,000 [a]	20,000 [a]
1946	32,280	15,877	48,157
1948	53,368	8,647	62,015
1950	106,420	9,725	116,145
1952	112,868	8,045	120,913
1954	119,975	8,354	128,329

[a] *In 1944 Negroes were ineligible for registration as Democrats by stipulation of the State Democratic Executive Committee. Since the 1944 registration figures were not published separately by race, the Republican figure is an estimate arrived at on the basis of the earliest 1945 segregated returns and by tracing the drop in total Republican registration from 1944 to 1946.*

tremendous growth of Negro registration, and the rapid shift of party affiliation.

The figures in Table 1[8] are significant in several ways: the rapidity until 1950 of the rise in Negro registration, the decisive Negro "crossing of the Jordan" from Republican to Democratic affiliation, and the marked slowdown in the rate of increase of Negro registration since 1950. The slowdown since 1950 can be accounted for on several grounds. In the early years the most aggressive Negroes and those in counties where there was least white opposition registered; since 1950 the registration drive has had to work with the less aggressive and more apolitical Negroes, and it has had to seek gains in those areas of most intense white opposition. Also, after 1950 a more conservative trend in public affairs set in, both locally with the defeat of Senator Pepper and nationally, so that fewer issues of real concern to the Negro have been raised. Finally, the white organization for Stevenson went to pieces in Florida in the 1952 presidential campaign, and in 1954 none of the gubernatorial candidates made any major drive to register additional Negro voters.

The biggest increase in Negro registration in any of the two-year periods came in 1948–1950. Much of this increase can be attributed to the concerted drive for Negro votes made on behalf of Senator Pepper, but Negro interest in local elections and in the 1948 presidential election are also of importance. The latter factor is emphasized by the fact that a breakdown by race of the registrants for the November, 1948, election showed a total of 85,180 Negroes, thus accounting for 23,165 of the 54,130 increase over the May, 1948, to May, 1950, period. That the bulk of the currently eligible Negroes likely to register have by now enrolled is apparent from the small changes reported in most counties for the most recent two-year period, 1952–1954: most counties showed only tiny increases in Negro registration, and there was even a decline in 19 counties. Nevertheless, total Negro registration for the state continues to mount, slowly but surely. This should continue for a number of years since the present state-wide average of adult Negroes registered, 35.0 in May, 1954, is still only about one half the average of registration for adult whites.

In general, the commonly accepted idea that Negroes participate in politics most heavily in the urban areas is correct; however, the sharp increase in total Negro registration is by no means entirely caused by large-scale registration in the cities. As Table 2, which classifies the

TABLE 2. PERCENTAGE OF ELIGIBLE NEGROES REGISTERED IN FLORIDA, BY COUNTY: 1946–1954

Percent of Adult Negroes Registered	Number of Counties in Each Class, as of May of Each Year				
	1946	1948 [a]	1950	1952	1954
None	4	4	5	4	3
0.1– 9.9	30	15	10	8	5
10.0–19.9	20	16	10	5	8
20.0–29.9	9	11	16	14	14
30.0–39.9	2	6	9	11	11
40.0–49.9	1	5	8	12	11
50.0–59.9	1	7	6	5	8
60.0 and over	0	1	3	8	7

[a] *Two counties unreported by race in 1948. All 67 reported in each of the other years indicated.*

number of counties in each range of Negro registration by years, shows, there has been general state-wide acceptance of Negro registration.[9] In fact, the highest percentages of registration are in relatively small counties where a single particularly able Negro leader [10] can encourage registration in a way that cannot be done in a large city where there are thousands of Negroes. The largest concentration of Negro voters in the state, however, is in Duval County (Jacksonville) where 25,774 were reported registered in 1954. Dade County (Miami) had 20,179 Negro registrants; Escambia (Pensacola) reported 6,545; and Volusia (Daytona Beach), 4,537. In each case this represents between forty and fifty percent of the county's 1950 adult Negro population; however, this relatively high level of registration is not found in all major Florida cities.[11] In 1954 Hillsborough County (Tampa) reported only 4,003 Negro registrants, or 16.0 percent of its adult Negroes; Pinellas (St. Petersburg) reported 3,408, or 28.1 percent; Palm Beach (West Palm Beach) reported only 5,198, or 23.4 percent; and Orange (Orlando) reported only 2,687, or 18.8 percent.[12] Since two-thirds of the adult Negroes in the state live in the twelve most populous counties, the low levels of registration in some of the cities are quantitatively more important in state-wide elections than is the lack of significant numbers of Negro registrants in some of the rural counties with the highest proportion of Negroes in their total population.

Another commonly accepted idea, that Negroes are least active where the proportion of Negro to white population is highest, and the whites consequently most resistant, is not entirely borne out by the facts in Florida. Table 3 indicates the percentage of eligible Negroes registered in 1952 in the seven Florida counties with over forty percent Negro population, and in the six counties with less than ten percent Negro population. Two of the "black belt" counties had levels of Negro registration above that of the state average, and two of the counties with a small percentage of Negro population reported a total Negro registration of ten in one case and none in the other. Thus the extent of Negro participation is not a mechanical reflex of the proportion of Negroes to whites in a county. Sometimes it is a matter of Negro leadership, of white candidates seeking Negro support, or both. The extent of Negro registration in a given area appears to depend upon a cultural complex of mores, folkways, habits, prejudices, and beliefs.

For the South as a whole the correlation between "black-belt" counties and low Negro registration is probably quite high, but the deviations— where counties have recently become concentrations of Negro population, as in parts of South Florida, or where much of the Negro population has drifted away—show that the correlation need not mean causation.[13] . . . The resistance to Negro voting is explicable not as an automatic result of the percentage of current Negro population, but as a manifestation of a

TABLE 3. PERCENTAGE OF NEGRO ADULTS REGISTERED AND PERCENTAGE OF NEGRO POPULATION IN FLORIDA COUNTIES OVER FORTY PERCENT NEGRO AND IN COUNTIES UNDER TEN PERCENT NEGRO

County	Percent of Negroes in County Population as of 1950	Percent of Adult Negroes Registered as of 1952
Florida counties over forty percent Negro		
Flagler	45.6	0.2
Gadsden	56.1	0.1
Glades	40.8	44.9 [a]
Hamilton	42.2	8.6
Jefferson	62.5	3.8
Madison	45.6	0.0
Seminole	44.4	47.2 [a]
Florida counties under ten percent Negro		
Gilchrist	9.9	0.1 [b]
Hardee	7.4	69.3
Holmes	4.4	47.8
Lafayette	9.4	0.0 [b]
Okaloosa	8.0	26.0
Santa Rosa	8.5	55.6
State Average	21.8	33.0

[a] *These two deviations from the expected "black belt" pattern are both located outside the Suwannee-Apalachicola River "Old South" region.*
[b] *These two deviations from the expected pattern in counties with small Negro populations are both located within the Suwannee-Apalachicola River region.*

whole culture and way of life which, a century ago, rested upon large numbers of Negro laborers.

Three of the four counties which had no Negro registrants from 1944 through 1952 [14] are located within the Suwannee-Apalachicola region, and 15 of the 18 counties in the area have a smaller proportion of registered Negroes in 1954 than does the state as a whole. These counties have in common a high proportion of rural population, low income level, static or declining total population, a virtual absence of registered Republicans, and intense devotion to "white supremacy." [15] Where migration of the rural Negro population to the North or to Southern cities has left a lower percentage of Negro population, in such counties the intense opposition to Negro "pretensions" has continued; but in the new centers of Negro population outside this area there has been relatively little opposition to Negro voting. The remarkable thing, however, about the political revolution taking place in the South since 1944 is not the white resistance to

Negro voting in a few areas, but the widespread acceptance of Negro voting by Southern whites. Although many regard it as a "necessary evil," they see it as an inevitable fact and accept it.[16]

The registration of large numbers of Negro Democrats has raised delicate problems for both the white candidates and for Negro leaders. Although the Negroes are in the Democratic Party of the South, they are not of it; to date they have been successfully "Jim-Crowed" within the party. In Florida this has helped to preclude any mass exodus of white voters from the Democratic Party. Despite the fact that Eisenhower carried the state in 1952, the Republican Party in 1954 still could claim only somewhat less than ten percent of the registered voters in the state. What increases there have been in Republican registration can be accounted for by the gradual drift of economic conservatives to the Republican Party and by the continuing Northern migration into the state. In the rural "white supremacy" counties, where resentment over Negro political activity is strongest, the increase in Republican registration has been least.[17] Moreover, the fact that most local and state contests are still settled in the Democratic primaries operates powerfully to prevent voters.

Negroes are generally excluded from participation in the organization of the Democratic Party. A few Negroes have been elected to the Democratic county committees in Florida, but predominantly Negro precincts usually elect whites to the Democratic county committee or go unrepresented. The shift of Negro voters from the Republican to the Democratic ranks has been so complete that the old Negro Republican leaders can no longer exercise a real voice in the state Republican organization, and yet the state Democratic organization is controlled by those who oppose extension of Negro influence or the mixing of the races in any sort of relation. And to date Negro voters themselves have shown an almost total indifference to party primary elections for county, state, and national committee members and—what is more significant—to elections for delegates to the national convention.[18]

Segregated rallies have become a common practice. Frequently the county Democratic committee will schedule Negro rallies for the Negro neighborhood. All the Democratic candidates are invited to appear, and most usually do so. Negroes regard the segregated rallies as a definite gain even in areas where they freely attend mixed rallies. Facing an all-Negro audience the candidates have to speak on some matters of genuine concern to Negroes. Also, present political mores allow the candidates to take stands at such rallies on many local issues of concern to the Negro, although to give a proportionate amount of time to such questions at a general rally would alienate many white voters. Under such circumstances the candidates are tempted to make, and often do make, promises they would not make before a mixed audience.

In addition, Florida Negroes have developed a large number of local voters' organizations and political leagues to work within the Democratic Party and to designate the candidates deserving of Negro support in the Democratic primaries. With the rise of these political organizations the Negro ministers, church organizations, fraternal orders, and community morticians have declined in political influence, especially in the cities. The new leaders are more ideological, less in the "accommodating" tradition, and more conscious of the critical attention with which many Southern whites view Negro voting. Besides endorsing a slate and holding rallies, the local political leagues distribute literature, facilitate Negro registration, personally solicit the voters, and get out the Negro vote on election day. On paper the Florida Progressive Voters' League, organized by NAACP leaders in 1944, speaks for all the state's Negro voters, but actually its influence is largely limited to a few counties where the state officers are also the local Negro leaders. The really effective Negro organizations are local, and in the larger cities—Jacksonville, Miami, and Tampa, for instance—there are several competing Negro political leagues.

Since the essential function of the Negro political league is to endorse a slate of candidates, the key position in the organization is that of chairman of the endorsing committee. This group meets with the various candidates, studies their past records, asks their position on pending issues, and sometimes even submits a written list of questions on specific issues. The subject of money may or may not become important. Some groups are so sensitive on this point that they refuse any contribution from candidates even for expenses; others frankly operate on a fee basis with endorsements going to the candidates they believe best, provided that these pay the minimum assessments.[19] A few groups apparently have endorsements "for sale" to the highest bidder, but such organizations quickly lose their position in the Negro community and are seldom able to swing many Negro voters. The recommendations of the endorsing committee are generally accepted by the league. The final slate is usually kept secret as long as possible up to the last minute before the election since Negro endorsements have repeatedly been reprinted in various forms by the unendorsed candidates for use in gaining white support by picturing the endorsed candidates as "nigger-lovers." The most effective method seems to be that of personally delivering endorsement cards with the names and voting machine lever numbers of the endorsed candidates to Negro homes the night before the election—the more powerful leagues have regularly organized groups of ward, precinct, and block workers for this purpose.[20]

The importance of the Negro political leagues can be seen in the voting patterns of Florida Negroes. Although the percentage of registered Negroes who actually vote is generally from ten to twenty percent below that of the white registrants, the leagues play an important part in getting out the vote. For another thing, the league endorsements are an additional factor contributing to the much-discussed "block voting" in which eighty-five, ninety, or even ninety-five percent of the Negro vote goes to one candidate. Finally, Negroes display a much greater inclination to "single shot" or "double shot" the key contests and to fail to indicate a choice in the others than do white voters. And where they do vote in only one or two races, they tend to vote for the candidates heading the locally endorsed slate and not necessarily for the candidates appearing first on the ballot.[21]

Negro participation has been highest and "block voting" most marked in opposition to avowed "white supremacy" candidates, in support of municipal and county officials such as mayor, sheriff, or school superintendent who are regarded as favorable in their treatment of Negroes, and in national races where integrated liberalism or Negro rights were an issue. In such races Negro political league endorsements have occasionally been made for the "wrong" candidate—in such cases the Negro voters have overwhelmingly repudiated the league endorsements and have voted in terms of their own self-interest. In more routine elections the league endorsements generally prove decisive, although the multiplicity of competing groups in the larger cities has sometimes resulted in differing slates and a factionalized Negro vote.

That Negroes vote as much as twenty to one against "white supremacy" candidates is hardly surprising. What is often overlooked in discussions of "block voting" is that the die-hard opponents of Negro rights in the "Old South" rural counties often vote *for* "white supremacy" candidates by even heavier margins than the Negroes turn in for their opponents. Table 4, for example, shows the percentage of votes cast in Jacksonville Negro precincts for Senator Kefauver and three local candidates strongly supported by Negroes in the 1952 first primary. None of the four carried the county, but their majorities in the Negro precincts are impressive. But, while Kefauver was winning 80–85 percent of the Negro vote in the presidential preference primary, his opponent, Senator Russell, won 93.2 percent of the Madison County vote and outran Kefauver by better than three to one in 17 of the 18 counties of the Suwannee-Apalachicola area! Incidentally, the candidate receiving the lowest Negro support of the four listed in Table 4 (Mr. Taylor) was a Negro.[22]

Analysis of the returns from the state's predominantly Negro precincts indicates that Truman in 1948, Pepper in the senatorial race of 1950, and Stevenson in 1952 each received Negro support of ninety percent or more. Due to the confused pattern of residential segregation very few counties have precincts composed solely of Negro voters;[23] however, there were four such precincts in Palm Beach County. Although Smathers carried the county by almost two to one, the four Negro precincts turned in from 90.4 to 95.7 percent of their votes for Pepper. The percentage of registrants voting for the county as a whole was 70.1, but for the four Negro precincts it ranged from 33.4 to 64.8. By 1952 most of the urban counties had a

TABLE 4. DEGREE OF NEGRO SUPPORT FOR SELECTED CANDIDATES IN DUVAL COUNTY (JACKSONVILLE) FIRST DEMOCRATIC PRIMARY, MAY 6, 1952

Precinct Number	Percentage of Negroes in Precinct Democratic Registration	Percentage of Precinct Vote Cast for Each Candidate [a]			
		Kefauver for President	Sweat for Sheriff	Boyd for School Superintendent	Taylor for Justice of Peace, in District 2
2-G	95.6	82.3	78.4	83.9	79.6
2-H	98.2	84.9	79.3	87.2	– [b]
3-A	99.9	86.5	79.4	87.4	75.4
3-B	99.8	88.2	89.4	88.3	83.2
3-F	99.2	87.0	80.4	86.2	79.6
5-A	99.9	81.0	77.9	87.5	76.7
5-C	99.9	85.4	77.8	84.2	70.1
5-D	98.9	79.9	80.8	82.1	78.1
5-F	99.7	81.4	81.8	85.9	– [b]

[a] *All four candidates listed failed to win a majority in the first primary in the county as a whole.*
[b] *Taylor's district did not include these two precincts.*

number of precincts composed almost wholly of Negroes. Table 5 shows the mean percentage of Negro registrants in the predominantly Negro precincts of six Florida counties in 1952. Comparison of the percentage vote for Stevenson in those precincts and in the counties as a whole shows that, although Eisenhower was the choice of a majority of the white voters in each of the counties except Escambia, the Negroes voted overwhelmingly for Stevenson. Considering that most of the predominantly Negro precincts still contained some white voters, the differences between white and Negro performance were even greater than the figures of Table 5 indicate. Also noticeable is the markedly lower percent of registrants voting in the predominantly Negro precincts in each county except Escambia. Again the actual difference in participation rate between white and Negro registrants is greater than the figures indicate, not only because of the effect of the whites in the predominantly Negro precincts but because the county-at-large figure is influenced by the performance of the Negro precincts within the county.[24]

Negro voters as a whole have been least interested in the gubernatorial and other state races. For one thing there have been no strongly anti-Negro candidates for governor nor any candidates raising issues of vital concern to the Negro. Other factors which have tended to a lower level of Negro interest in state politics than in national and local races include: the blandness of one-party politics, the meaningless factionalism, the failure to raise basic issues, the weakness of the Florida governor as popular and

TABLE 5. COMPARISON OF SUPPORT FOR STEVENSON AND PERCENTAGE OF REGISTRANTS VOTING IN NOVEMBER, 1952, IN SIX FLORIDA COUNTIES AT LARGE AND IN THE PREDOMINANTLY NEGRO PRECINCTS IN THOSE COUNTIES

County (and City)	Electoral Constituency	Percent Negro Registrants [a]	Percent for Stevenson	Percent of Registrants Voting
Dade	4 precincts	79.6	71.6	46.0
(Miami)	county-at-large	6.4	43.2	74.7
Duval	9 precincts	99.1	89.5	72.1
(Jacksonville)	county-at-large	19.7	51.8	81.1
Escambia	6 precincts	68.1	78.5	71.6
(Pensacola)	county-at-large	13.0	62.7	69.1
Orange	2 precincts	57.3	63.3	68.6
(Orlando)	county-at-large	5.8	28.9	81.8
Pinellas	2 precincts	75.0	68.2	70.5
(St. Petersburg)	county-at-large	4.8	28.6	79.6
Volusia	5 precincts	71.8	72.0	55.8
(Daytona Beach)	county-at-large	15.0	37.5	79.9

[a] *Mean percentage of Negro precincts; percent of total for the county-at-large.*

legislative leader, and the seeming lack of relevance of most state issues to the concrete problems of the Negro. Thus in 1948 there were fewer votes cast in the predominantly Negro precincts in the hotly contested governor's race than in the largely unorganized presidential election; the reverse was true in most white precincts. In the absence of basic issues the Negro voter tends to be influenced in state elections by local white voting trends and by the endorsements made by the local Negro leagues.

In several Southern states Negro candidates for public office have been elected in recent years, but this has not yet happened in Florida. Negroes have qualified as candidates in the Democratic primaries, carried on active campaigns, and even succeeded in getting into the second primary run-off, but none has yet been elected, at least not since around the turn of the century. This is caused in part by the fact that most local officials—even city councilmen—are now elected at large rather than from districts and wards. Also, the Negro candidates who have run in Florida have not been the outstanding leaders of the Negro communities. Several have been "promoters" or newspapermen apparently interested in the publicity, and a few have had suspicious encouragement from the extreme left. Several of these factors combined to prevent the election of a Negro city councilman in Jacksonville in 1947, when councilmen were still elected from districts.[25]

The political weaknesses of the Negro in the South are remarkably similar to those of organized labor, another relatively new major factor in

American politics, on the national scene. By substituting "Negro" for the word "labor" one can paraphrase most of the outstanding weaknesses of organized labor, as they have been summarized by Samuel Lubell,[26] and apply them to the Southern Negro. (1) An overly militant campaign to register Negro voters or to gain Negro support provokes so much fear and opposition that it produces an anti-Negro reaction. (2) The Negro and the Democratic Party are still uneasy allies; in fact, in many Florida counties the formal Democratic Party organization and the local Negro voters are political opponents. (3) Negro leaders have been unable to deliver the Negro vote as a block except in the direction it was already inclined to go.

The Southern Negro is also under some handicaps which do not plague labor. There is the continued general prejudice against Negro voting, and the tremendously important and generally under-estimated factor of the existence of the one-party system. Although Florida has the makings of both a liberal and a conservative group within the Democratic Party,[27] the issues are rarely raised or are so blurred and blended with personalities and factionalism that the power of a cohesive minority group such as the Negro is minimized.[28] Finally, the context of primary contests is wholly different from that of general elections: there can be no appeal to party loyalty and consequently no effective restraint on demagogic use of the race issue.

The various factors inhibiting the political influence of the Negro in the South make it imperative to consider not only the behavior of the Negro as a voter, but the rôle of the Negro as a political issue. Can the strength which a candidate gains from Negro voters be offset or turned into a net loss by reducing his support among race-conscious whites? Florida experience over the past ten years indicates that such can but need not necessarily be the result in a Democratic primary contest, but that it will generally not be the case in a general election. The most striking illustration of the differing importance of the racial issue in a primary as compared to a general election is provided by the Kefauver and Stevenson votes in May and November of 1952. In the presidential preference primary, where Kefauver was saddled with the stigma of FEPC and deprived of the protecting mantle of traditional party loyalty, he lost every one of the 25 counties bordering or west of the Suwannee River. In the general election just six months later Stevenson, also under fire because of FEPC, won every single one of these same 25 counties, and by almost as heavy margins as had Russell.[29]

The impact which the development of a two-party system, where the real decisions are made in general elections, would have on the rôle of the Negro voter can hardly be overestimated. Within a statewide Democratic primary, when the Negro question is raised, the Negro precincts vote ten to one for the liberal candidate (Pepper in 1950; Kefauver in 1952), but many of the "Old South" counties are alienated or closely divided. However, in a national election between the Democratic and Republican parties, the predominantly Negro precincts will go ten to one for a Truman or a Stevenson; and the "Old South" rural counties, true to their Democratic Party tradition and favoring high federal crop supports, will at the same election likewise pile up heavy majorities for the Democratic presidential nominee, at least under broad conditions similar to those existing in 1952. Thus in a primary contest *within* the party the Negro urban precincts and the "white supremacy" rural counties are apt to be enemies; but in a general election contest *between* the two parties the Negro precincts and the "Old South" counties tend to be allies, each piling up large majorities for the Democratic Party.[30] So long as the Negro voters and the poor whites of the rural counties tend to neutralize each other in the primaries, the way is made clear for victory for the candidates supported by the conservative counties and more prosperous urban classes. Since the chief beneficiaries of the present one-party system are the economic conservatives who would have to pull out of the Democratic Party to establish a two-party system—there being no place for the liberals to go—it is doubtful that anything short of a liberal victory, both in the state and nation, will greatly hasten the rise of a two-party system in the state.

The classic example, to date, of the genuine appeal for Negro support and wide-spread use of the Negro as an issue in Florida was the Pepper-Smathers campaign of 1950. Samuel Lubell has written that "the defeats of both Pepper and Graham [in North Carolina] can be credited largely to heavy Negro voting, which spurred an even heavier anti-Negro outpouring." [31] While this seems to have been the case with Senator Graham, it is not the sole or even the main explanation for the defeat of Pepper. Unlike Graham—who had polled within one percent of a clear majority in the first primary, before the race issue became dominant—Pepper was defeated in the first primary by 67,561 votes out of approximately seven hundred thousand. Pepper's greatest loss of strength, in comparison to his successful 1944 campaign, was not in the racially sensitive Suwannee-Apalachicola region, but in the towns and small cities of central Florida and the East Coast.[32] As another writer has pointed out, the Smathers pattern of victory over Pepper "is much the same as the Hoover-Dewey-McCarty [1948] pattern, only more extensive." [33] This pattern, which the Eisenhower victory also followed, is primarily one of economic conservatism, not—as in the 1952 Russell pattern—one of "white supremacy."

The combined effect of heavy Negro Democratic registration and of the potentially explosive race issue has been to cause a certain ambivalence on the part of the candidates. The Negro vote is too large for conservative candidates to risk indulging in undiluted Negro-baiting, but neither do liberal candidates dare expose a too pro-Negro program or make too open a bid for Negro support. Even in the Pepper-Smathers campaign both candidates faced both ways: Pepper denounced compulsory FEPC, and Smathers emphasized that his own record was not that of a Negro-baiter. In the gubernatorial campaign of 1952, Dan McCarty, in the absence of any overt raising of the Negro question and with the aid of most of the urban Negro political leagues, was able to pile up heavy majorities in most Negro precincts and also carried 15 of the 18 counties in the "Old South" region. The special gubernatorial primary of 1954, occasioned by the death of Governor McCarty in office, posed a dilemma to Negro voters. Acting Governor Charley Johns had been one of the five state senators supporting a private "white primary" bill in 1947,[34] but was regarded as pro-labor and promised more generous old-age pensions. Johns' opponent in the run-off, LeRoy Collins, who ultimately won the nomination, was a middle-of-the-road candidate who made few popular promises, but Collins had fought in the state senate against the "white primary" and in support of a bill to unmask the Klan. Under this cross pressure the Negro vote split, with an unusually large number of Negroes staying away from the polls.

The long-run effects of the one-party system on Negro voting and on the Negro as an issue can be traced through a number of stages. By its tendency toward meaningless factionalism it makes effective Negro "balance of power" politics most difficult. By its transfer of most real political contests from the general election to the party primary it removes the restraining factor of party loyalty and makes Negro-baiting much more tempting. By increasing the likelihood of use of the Negro as an issue it makes it much more difficult for a candidate to make a public appeal to the Negro as a voter; the difficulty of appealing to the Negro as a voter frequently makes it necessary that appeals for Negro support be made privately to Negro leaders. This, in turn, opens the possibility of "deals" and actual buying of support rather than giving more incentive to the Negro voters to make a rational choice on issues.

Despite all the handicaps, the lack of experience, white opposition, the one-party system, and a shortage of middle-class leaders, Negroes in Florida have won impressive gains from their re-entry into politics. At the local level the Negro community in many places is getting better police protection,[35] and Negroes accused of offenses against white people seem to be receiving more just treatment. Street lights, side walks, and paved streets are more common in communities where Negroes vote in substantial numbers. Such things as Negro civic centers, bandshells, playgrounds, libraries, hospital annexes, and even swimming pools are found in increasing numbers of Florida cities. To date these developments have been within the context of "separate but equal" facilities. Thus special "reserve days" for Negro use of municipal golf courses and auditoriums have also been within this pattern. The importance of federal aid in providing low-rent housing projects for Negroes, and the impetus of federal court decisions in the education field in providing more Negro schools and better pay for Negro teachers cannot be overlooked. All these developments are farthest advanced in those communities where Negroes register and vote in large numbers.

At the state level the Florida legislature has steadily refused to enact measures designed to circumvent the *Smith* v. *Allwright* decision. In 1953 a proposal to cut off all state funds for public schools in the event of a Supreme Court decision abolishing segregation in the Florida public schools was dropped. An expensive state detention home for Negro girls, the Forrest Hills Correctional Institute, has recently been opened. Also, for the first time in history, the Florida Farm Colony for the feeble-minded recently opened several wards for Negroes.

The possible influence of the Southern Negro on national politics is hard to gauge, particularly because of the conservative trend in the past several years. But the overwhelming vote in the Negro precincts for Truman in 1948, for Kefauver in the preferential primary of 1952, and for Stevenson in the presidential election of 1952 shows that Southern Negroes think politically along the same lines as do Negroes in Detroit, Chicago, Pittsburgh, and New York. Of all the Florida groups responsible for Truman's victory in the state in 1948 and for Stevenson's large vote in 1952, the Negroes were the most solid in their support.

A review of the rôle which Negroes have played in Florida politics during the past ten years indicates that they, like Americans everywhere, are interested in tangible benefits for themselves, a high standard of living, and a greater share of the good things which American society has to offer. Very few Florida Negroes have shown any interest at all in a separate political party, extreme left-wing movements, or selling their votes. To date they have relied largely on Negro middle-class leadership and have participated in local, state, and national politics with traditional American aims and values in mind and within the framework of traditional American party and political institutions. The real revolution in the South during the past decade has been not the quadrennial histrionics of the Dixiecrats, but the successful entry into politics of that long-excluded American—the Southern Negro. The increasing participation of Negro voters in the South, already estimated to be over a million strong,[36] should be watched for its effects both upon political behavior within the one-party system and for its rôle in producing conditions which will hasten the development of a two-party system.

NOTES

1. 321 U.S. 649 (1944). The possibility of large-scale evasion was largely precluded by *Rice* v. *Elmore*, 165 F 2d 387 (1947), certiorari denied. The various schemes for disfranchisement are described in V. O. Key, Jr., *Southern Politics in State and Nation* (New York: Alfred A. Knopf, 1949), chapters 25–31. In the 1953

case involving the "Democratic Jaybird Club" in Texas, *Terry* v. *Adams,* 345 U.S. 461 (1953), the Supreme Court held that the Fifteenth Amendment applies even to a pre-primary election if it is the controlling step in the election process.

2. Although the public school and primary voting situations are not completely parallel, there has been the same loose talk of "blood in the streets" in connection with both. Thus, in regard to Negro voting, one South Carolina legislator was quoted in *The Southern Frontier,* VI, No. 11 (November, 1945) as saying that "we'll fight him at the precinct meeting, we'll fight him at the county convention, we'll fight him at the enrollment books, and, by God, we'll fight him at the polls if I have to bite the dust as did my ancestors." In 1952, however, the Southern Regional Council estimated that there were 115,000 Negroes registered in South Carolina, and some observers credited Stevenson's narrow margin in the state to the Negro vote.

3. Louisiana publishes state and parish registration totals by race, but does not break the party registration down by race. For Virginia some information can be drawn from local poll tax records, and in all Southern states rough estimates can be made on the basis of total registration in precincts predominantly inhabited by Negroes.

4. Official registration figures of May, 1952, indicated that 33 percent of Florida's adult Negroes, as reported in the 1950 census, were registered. The Southern Regional Council's estimates of Negro registration for November, 1952, work out to the following percentages of adult Negroes: Florida, 34.1; Texas, 30.0; South Carolina, 29.5; Arkansas, 28.0; Tennessee, 26.7; Georgia, 25.6; Louisiana, 20.8; North Carolina, 18.2; Virginia, 16.6; Alabama, 9.6; and Mississippi, 4.0. Except for the low percentages of Alabama and Mississippi this rank order shows little connection with increasing percentage of Negro population in the individual states.

5. William G. Carleton, "The Fate of Our Fourth Party," *The Yale Review,* XXXVIII, No. 3 (March, 1949), 451.

6. The three counties with no Negro registrants—Lafayette, Liberty, and Union—are sparsely populated rural counties with less than one half of one percent of the state's adult Negro population.

7. In 1944 Negroes made up about one half of the Republican registration in the state, and much more in some counties. Thus the 1944 total Republican registration in Duval County (Jacksonville) was 6,089, but the 1946 figures—broken down by race—indicated only 654 white Republicans. In Jackson County the corresponding figures were 600 in 1944 and 12 in 1946. As might be expected, Negro leaders had played an important rôle in the state Republican Party's leadership with Negroes from Jacksonville and Miami serving as delegates and alternates to Republican national conventions. Prior to 1944 the actual Negro voters had been of importance only in municipal politics in a few cities, such as Gainesville and Daytona Beach.

8. Unless otherwise noted all state-wide and county registration election returns for Florida are based on the *Biennial Report of the Secretary of State* for the appropriate year. Precinct data was personally obtained by the author from supervisors of registration in numerous counties.

9. Detailed comparison of the percentage of adult Negroes registered as compared with whites is impossible for many of the smaller counties, where laxity of the supervisors of registration has resulted in rolls with more registrants than there were adults reported in the 1950 census. In 1952, for example, there were 28 Florida counties reporting more white registrants than there were white adults in 1950. This distortion, which results from failure to purge the rolls, pads white Democratic totals, but probably has relatively little effect on the Republican and Negro figures since they represent mostly recent additions to the rolls. A check of total votes cast in the counties concerned gave no indication of "graveyard voting"—the turn-out was about what would be expected on the basis of the census figures.

10. Thus Brevard County, home of the late Harry T. Moore—the leading NAACP

worker in the state after the war—had over fifty percent of its total adult Negro population registered by 1950. The importance of such personal and organizational factors lessens the possibility of finding clear-cut social or economic correlates to Negro political participation.

11. Of the 14 counties in Florida with cities of 25,000 or greater population in 1950 there are 8 above the state average in percentage of Negroes registered (as of 1954) and 6 below. The considerable differences are quite clearly *not* due to differences in percentage of Negro population: of the 7 such counties with a higher percentage of Negroes than the state as a whole 5 have a higher proportion of Negroes registered than does the state as a whole; for the 7 such counties with a lower percentage of Negroes than the state 4 have a lower percentage of Negroes registered than does the state as a whole.

12. In most of these cities the Negro middle class is smaller and local white politicians have made less effort to win Negro votes than in the previously mentioned cities.

13. Such areas are particularly evident in Florida, and the inverse correlation between percentage Negro population and percentage of adult Negroes registered is consequently rather low:—.35 on the basis of the most recent registration and census figures. Of the 42 counties with a higher percentage of Negroes than the state as a whole 22 have a higher percentage of Negroes registered than the state as a whole and 20 are below the state average. Of the 25 counties with a smaller share of Negro population than the state average 13 are above the state average for percentage of adult Negroes registered and the remaining 12 are below. The importance of cultural-historical factors is shown by a comparison between the non-urban Suwannee-Apalachicola counties (excluding only Leon County, which has a city of over 25,000) and the remaining counties with no city of over 25,000. About two-thirds of the counties in each category are above the state average in percentage Negro population, but the non-urban Suwannee-Apalachicola counties divided 14 below and 3 (plus urbanized Leon) above the state average for percentage of Negroes registered; the other non-urban counties divided 12 below and 24 above the state average for Negro registration. Thus in the "Old South" area there are approximately five counties *below* the state average in percentage of Negroes registered for every one above the average. In the remaining non-urban counties the ratio is two counties *above* the average for every one below.

14. Liberty, Lafayette, and Madison are the three counties within the area; Union County is an isolated cultural holdover of the "Old South" way of life still remaining in the north-central part of the state, most of which has been transformed by migration and urbanization. Within the Suwannee-Apalachicola region proper only Leon County, site of the state capitol at Tallahassee, has been greatly changed by recent trends.

15. This is the area where the Ku Klux Klan may also be a factor in preventing Negro registration. When Bill Hendrix resigned as Grand Dragon of the Florida Klan and ran for governor in the 1952 Democratic primary, this was the region giving him the most support. Hendrix, who polled only 1.52 percent of the state-wide vote, received 18.00 percent in Wakulla County, 15.03 in Liberty, 10.80 in Jefferson, 9.26 in Madison, 7.61 in Suwannee, 6.40 in Lafayette, 6.16 in Franklin, 4.10 in Gadsden, and 3.65 in Taylor. All nine of these counties are in the area bordering or between the Suwannee and Apalachicola Rivers, and Liberty, Lafayette, and Madison were three of the four counties with no Negro registrants from 1944 through 1952. Before the 1954 primaries, 586 Negroes went *en masse* to the Madison County courthouse and were registered (558 as Democrats and 28 as Republicans). All previous attempts to register by individual Negroes had been successfully "discouraged" by Klan parades, threats of intimidation, or persuasion. It is not strange that Negroes are somewhat slow to press their rights in an area where one out of every ten whites will throw away his vote on behalf of a Klan candidate.

16. Here again the Dixiecrat movement, which can be regarded as the counterrevolution to check not only Negro civil rights but the social and economic

implications of Negro voting, failed. The reasons behind the Dixiecrat failure are analyzed by Emile B. Ader, in "Why the Dixiecrats Failed," *The Journal of Politics,* 15, No. 3 (August, 1953), 356–69.

17. Leon was the only county of the 18 in the Suwannee-Apalachicola region where the 1952 Republican registration accounted for over one percent of the county total. Only three counties in the whole West Florida "panhandle" had over one percent Republican registration, and none of these reached the five percent level.

18. Despite the tremendous Negro support for Kefauver in the 1952 presidential preference primary only a fraction of those Negroes voting in the second primary (when the actual delegates were elected) indicated choices for the Democratic convention delegates.

19. The money collected from candidates is not so much an additional source of income for Negro political leaders as it is a means of meeting the inevitable operating overhead of an effective organization. The more effective groups have purchased voting machine mock-ups, maintain card files listing the Negro voters in each district, print their own literature, and hire additional workers for election eve and election day. All this costs money. As a matter of fact, a candidate regarded as particularly desirable but with limited funds may receive a "free ride" endorsement.

20. An alternate method frequently used in smaller communities is for the Negro voters' league to hold a rally the night before the election. At the rally only the endorsed candidates are invited. Obviously this is a much less democratic method than having a segregated party rally at which all candidates appear.

21. In the April, 1951, Jacksonville municipal election, for example, the precinct organization of the largest Negro precinct in the city (with over 2,000 Negro voters) endorsed candidates in each of the five races for the city council. The candidate in the contest appearing first on the ballot was also first on the endorsed list, and 1,913 votes were cast in the race. The second highest number of votes, 1,398, was cast in the race which was fourth on the ballot but second on the league endorsement cards. The race which was second on the ballot but third on the endorsement cards involved only 1,222 votes. Here again, however, the correlation need not indicate causation. It is usually a case of the Negro leaders anticipating the reactions of the Negro voters, and not of the voters blindly following the league endorsements.

22. He was defeated in the first primary. The candidates for sheriff and school superintendent listed in Table 4 had both built up favorable reputations with Jacksonville Negroes and, in the second primary, each received over ninety percent of the vote in each of the precincts listed. Mr. Sweat, the candidate for renomination as sheriff, won his run-off, but Mr. Boyd was defeated in the school superintendent's race despite his heavy Negro support.

23. During 1946 and 1947 some counties experimented with the use of separate voting machines for whites and for Negroes. Although the practice had been upheld by the state attorney-general, it was quickly abandoned because of the needless delay in having whites wait while the Negro machines were empty and vice versa. For elections where the practice did prevail, exact information on the Negro turn-out and vote could be obtained by checking the vote for the machines used by the Negroes. Since abandonment of the attempt to use segregated voting machines, the only way to check on Negro voting is by studying the returns for those precincts where Negroes make up most of the registration.

24. The lower rate of voter turn-out among Negro registrants is also apparent in the estimates of Negro voting in the 1954 primaries which have been compiled by the Attorney-General of Florida (see appendix to Florida's *amicus curiae* brief filed pursuant to discussion of implementation of the May 17, 1954, segregation decision). For whatever they may be worth (and such estimates of aggregates must be treated with caution) estimates of the number of Negroes voting in the first primary were received from supervisors of registration in 59 of the 67 counties. These 59 counties reported 98,833 Negro registrants, but estimated

that only 44,531 Negroes (45.1 percent of those registered) voted in the first primary. Remarkably, the brief suggests, page 179, that either the estimates are "poor guesses," or that "any Negro who dares register is determined to exercise his right to vote." This evaluation is made since—according to the brief—"the percentage of registered Negroes who vote is much higher than one would estimate on the basis of the socio-economic levels which correlate with voting interest." This is the exact opposite of what the estimates—and other data—clearly indicate.

25. The candidate was a thirty-five dollar a week mortar mixer, who was taken to the city office to qualify by a white merchant seaman alleged to have been the executive-secretary of the Florida Community Party. Most of the qualifying fee was said to have been paid by the left-wing National Negro Congress. The long-standing Negro community leaders, most of middle class background, did not appreciate the intrusion. In the run-off between the Negro and a white candidate the Negro leaders "went fishing" and only about thirteen percent of the Negro registrants, who outnumbered whites in the district, voted. The Negro was defeated, and the next session of the legislature amended the Jacksonville city charter to make councilmen elected at large. A sequel to the incident, which is instructive of the sort of horse-trading common in politics, was the construction of a municipal swimming pool for Negroes in the district where the leaders had failed to rally behind the self-appointed Negro candidate.

26. *The Future of American Politics* (New York: Harper and Brothers, 1951), p. 190.

27. See Herbert J. Doherty, Jr., "Liberal and Conservative Voting Patterns in Florida," *The Journal of Politics*, 14, No. 3 (August, 1952), 403–17.

28. Talk of "balance of power" politics is obviously inappropriate when, as in most primary races, there are no fixed centers of power to be balanced.

29. Prejudice designed to work against a Democratic *candidate* may actually result in an increased vote for the Democratic *party* in a general election. Thus in 1928 Al Smith, an economic liberal, should have had appeal to the entire West Florida "panhandle," but he lost six of the seven counties in the extreme western half. He might well have done as poorly, because of the religious issue, in the eastern half but for the long-standing identification of "white supremacy" with the Democratic Party. As it happened, however, Smith carried 17 of the 18 counties in the Suwannee-Apalachicola region, but only 9 in the rest of the state. Truman in 1948 and Stevenson in 1952 also carried every county in the Suwannee-Apalachicola region. The outcome in a Democratic primary, as evidenced by the 1952 Kefauver-Russell contest, is apt to be the reverse with the liberal candidate losing this area.

30. Thus Samuel Lubell's suggestion, *op. cit.*, p. 122, that "in state politics in the South the Negro's interests parallel more closely those of the urban Republicans in their struggle against the anti-Negro rural areas" has proved partially correct in Florida. It applies to Democratic primary contests when Negro rights become the dominant factor; it does not apply to general elections or to primary contests where the basic division is economic rather than racial.

31. Lubell, *op. cit.*, p. 120.

32. Of the 18 counties in the Suwannee-Apalachicola region Pepper and Smathers each carried nine, with Pepper losing four of the eleven he had carried in 1944, but winning two which he had lost in 1944. Pepper carried 13 of the 21 counties west of the Suwannee River; he won in only 7 of the remaining 46 in the state.

33. Doherty, *op. cit.*, p. 414.

34. Although the bill was sponsored by a senator from Jacksonville, each of the other four voting or paired in favor of the measure had one of the four counties with no Negro registrants in his district. Of the eleven counties which the five senators collectively represented, eight are in the Suwannee-Apalachicola River region. The sponsor of the measure, incidentally, was defeated in the 1948 Democratic primary.

35. Much of the Negro dissatisfaction on this score has been due to the extreme laxity of Southern white police, juries, and judges in regard to Negroes accused

of committing crimes against other Negroes. "Rough stuff" and unnecessary severity in dealing with Negro suspects has also caused dissatisfaction. See Gunnar Myrdal, *An American Dilemma* (New York: Harper and Brothers, 1944), chapters 25–26. The rapid rise in the number of Negro policemen in Florida cities, from 5 in 1940 to 30 in 1946 to 96 in 1952, has done much to alleviate both these situations.

36. As of the end of 1952 the Southern Regional Council estimated total Negro registration for the eleven ex-Confederate states to be 1,040,000. *Pittsburgh Courier,* February 21, 1953.

22. Tuskegee, Alabama: The Politics of Deference

In contrast to the emergence of the "politics of deference" among black Americans, Carmichael and Hamilton suggest politics of "black power." Their study of Tuskegee illustrates very well the dynamics of white resistance once substantial gains by blacks become imminent. The idea of "black power" represents an alternative course of political development in areas with large black populations. This alternative, they suggest, should be fully and consciously developed by blacks. It is implied that by this means major and stable increments of needed power by blacks, power less susceptible to traditional tactics of white resistance, could be achieved. Although this article does not deal with the question of the politics of black minorities, it clearly has relevance for many areas of the South where blacks remain today large dispossessed majorities.

STOKELY CARMICHAEL AND CHARLES V. HAMILTON

The town of Tuskegee, in Macon County, Alabama, is undoubtedly one of the most significant areas in the history of the black man in this country. People throughout the world know Tuskegee as the home base of Booker T. Washington, from 1881 to his death in 1915. He founded Tuskegee Institute in 1881 and he was widely acclaimed as *the* leader of black people during that period. Dr. George Washington Carver, the scientist, became a second great name; his accomplishments in the Tuskegee Institute science laboratory with peanuts and sweet potatoes made him internationally known and respected at a time when most whites and many blacks knew nothing of Dr. W. E. B. Du Bois, William Monroe Trotter and other black intellectuals of that day. In 1924, the nation's first, all-black-staffed Veterans' Administration Hospital was established at Tuskegee, bringing to the county a wealth of educational and medical talent. During World War II, Tuskegee was the site of the first training base for black Air Force pilots. Then, in 1958, it became the first community to be investigated by the United States Commission on Civil Rights, set up under the 1957 Civil Rights Act.

From *Black Power* (1967), pp. 122–145; reprinted by permission of Vintage Books.

Since the nineteenth century black people have constituted the main population of Macon County—then, and now, roughly eighty-four percent. In the post-Civil War period, blacks voted and made their vote felt at times, as we will illustrate. But in 1901, the white racist state legislature amended the state constitution and effectively disfranchised most of the black citizens. Booker T. Washington protested mildly, but subsequently acquiesced.

This chapter will describe the long, hard, successful fight waged by some in the county to regain the ballot—to regain the previous status of broadened participation in politics—and the manner in which this regained participation has been exercised. It has been exercised with "restraint," that is, the black leaders have not utilized their new position to exercise effective political power. The black leaders have pursued what we call a "politics of deference." [1] Many people there, and throughout the country, have looked on Tuskegee as a "model" of "bi-racial" government —blacks and whites working and governing together. We reject that conclusion. We see the present-day Tuskegee situation as perpetuating a racially deferential society, and we suggest that a politics of Black Power, as defined in this book, would be far healthier for the community. We suggest that Tuskegee could become a better model—North and South— for those numerous electoral districts where black people have a commanding majority.

First, let us discuss the political history of this community.

An entire philosophy of race relations developed around Booker T. Washington's leadership in the late nineteenth century. This philosophy encouraged black people to concentrate their time and energy on developing their educational and economic potential. It de-emphasized political activity; Washington was not noted for advocating that blacks run for public office. The good white folks would take care of the political business and as black people proved themselves "worthy," they would slowly be "accepted" by their white neighbors. Always embedded in Washington's philosophy was the notion that black people had to prove themselves to white people. Lerone Bennet, Jr., has described Washington's leadership as follows in *Before the Mayflower*:

Almost everything Washington said or did was shot through with a certain irony. He bowed before the prejudices of the meanest Southerner, but he moved in circles in the North which were closed to all but a few white men. He told Negroes that Jim Crow was irrelevant, but he himself violated the law by riding first class in Pullman cars with Southern white men and women. And irony of ironies: he who advised Negroes to forget about politics wielded more political power than any other Negro in American history [p. 277].

A most ironic aspect of Booker T. Washington's career is the context in which that career started. Tuskegee Institute itself was established precisely because, in 1880, the black people of Macon County possessed political power. As we have already stated, blacks then constituted the great majority of the county population. A former Confederate Colonel, W. F. Foster, was running for the Alabama legislature on the Democratic ticket. Obviously needing black votes, he went to the local black leader, a Republican named Lewis Adams, and made a deal: if Adams would persuade the blacks to vote for him, he would—once elected—push for a state appropriation to establish a school for black people in the county. Adams delivered; Foster was elected and a sum of $2,000 per year was appropriated to pay teachers' salaries for a school. Adams wrote to Hampton Institute in Virginia for a person to come and set up the school. The head of Hampton recommended one of his best teachers, Booker T. Washington.

Thus the black people of Tuskegee used the ballot effectively to gain their goals. They were not begging, relying on sentiment or morality; they traded their votes for a specific and meaningful reward. If Foster had not kept his part of the bargain, they could have "punished" him with their political power at the next election. This kind of strength could come only from organization and recognition of *their* interests. Foster respected their Black Power. This historical fact seems to have been forgotten by many people today who counsel black people to follow the teachings of Washington in regard to mitigating political activity. If Mr. Adams and the black people had not acted politically, Washington might never have acquired the influence he did.

Another frequently overlooked lesson of Washington's career concerns that aspect of his position which called upon whites to "reward" blacks with "ultimate" inclusion in the political process. Washington believed strongly that once black people acquired skills useful to the southern environment (blacksmithing, carpentry, cooking, farming, etc.), once they acquired a sound economic base, once they bought homes and became law-abiding citizens of the community, the whites should and would "accept" them as "first-class citizens." This meant, to Washington, ultimately including them as voters and public office-holders. With this goal in mind, Washington addressed letters to the state constitutional conventions of Louisiana (1898) and Alabama (1901), urging them not to revise their constitutions to deny the vote to black people. He felt that any revisions should apply equally to whites as well as blacks, that it might be wise to exclude *all* illiterate, uneducated people.

Southern whites did not heed his counsel. The fact is that Washington overestimated the "good will" and "good faith" of white America. The blacks of Tuskegee, for the most part, did follow the teachings of the Institute's founder. They did not concentrate on politics; they did concentrate on acquiring skills, on building an economically secure life. But they were not "rewarded" with political participation. The Institute and later the Veterans' Administration Hospital—both of which were black-staffed —had attracted to the community a black population with higher educational and economic status than in any other county of the state. These black people built fine homes and went about their business at the college or the hospital without challenging the political control of the sixteen percent white population.

A modus operandi had been reached between the Tuskegee blacks and whites: the blacks would run Tuskegee Institute and the V.A. Hospital while the whites would provide commercial services (banks and stores) and hold all political offices—thus overseeing law-enforcement, the assessing and collecting of taxes, the public school system and so forth. The accommodation was perfect, and many people throughout the country pointed to Tuskegee as a showplace of harmonious race relations. So the sizeable black middle-class society had its debutante balls and social clubs, made no great demand to take part in political decision-making, and seemed to have forgotten—or perhaps they never knew—the earlier political history of the county when black people voted and gained political benefits.

We [previously] noted that in 1890 Mississippi had been the first state of the old Confederacy to rewrite its laws so as to exclude blacks from voting—a procedure eventually adopted by virtually all of those states. In 1901, it was Alabama's turn. The state revised its constitution, purging all voters—black and white—from its rolls. It then adopted new rules for registration; these provided for a "literacy" test in which an applicant had to read, write *and interpret* a section of the U.S. or the state constitution. Local boards of registration were set up in each county and controlled, of course, by whites; they could reject an applicant if he did not "interpret" the constitution to their satisfaction. A "voucher" system was also set up whereby two registered voters had to "vouch for" or identify the applicant. The registrars required black applicants to get white vouchers. Thus, a network of devices—ostensibly not racial, because the Fifteenth Amendment to the U.S. Constitution prohibited voting discrimination based on race—were established; this meant that black people would have a most difficult time getting back on the registration books. Needless to say, whites registered without delay or dilatory tactics on the part of the registrars. And, again needless to say, the whites soon had a majority of registered voters; White Power was firmly entrenched.

But there was always a handful of black people in the community who did not accept the politically subordinate position assigned to them. They knew they were colonial subjects in their own land. Early in the 1930's, a black sociologist joined the faculty of Tuskegee Institute; he later stated: "Booker T. Washington came to teach the Negroes how to make a living. I came to teach them how to live." [2] By this he meant that black people should become more active in civic affairs. A small group began to organize in the late 1930's to get more blacks registered. The leadership came from some thirty black men who formed the Tuskegee Men's Club. This group reorganized as the Tuskegee Civic Association (TCA) in 1941. The TCA confronted a comfortable black middle class that was satisfied to let the status quo remain and the town whites who were all too pleased with the good manners of these blacks who "knew their place." Professor Charles G. Gomillion, one of the leaders of the TCA, has quoted a statement by a white public official in 1940 which sums up the nature of race relations in the county: "Sometimes some of the rural Negroes and some of the colored professors at the Institute think that we don't treat them fairly, but in general we manage to keep them pacified." [3]

Slowly, however, black names increased on the voting rolls: in 1940, there were approximately 29 registered black voters, 115 in 1946, 514 in 1950, and 855 in 1954. The figure rose against the most incredible obstacles: registrars would resign and not be replaced; black Ph.D.'s were rejected for not being able to state the precise length of time—down to the days—they had been residents. On one occasion, the Board of Registrars met in the vault of the local bank, in an attempt to avoid having to take registration applications from black applicants. This occurred on April 19, 1948, and a very light-skinned person (who could "pass" for white) had to locate the meeting place of the board after several black people were refused the information.

Many educated black people chose not to become involved in this sham process. Rather than submit to constant indignities, they simply withdrew. "We just don't bother with those white folks downtown," became a common response. This was, of course, precisely what the white power structure wanted: such an attitude would never challenge their control.

Unlike other areas in the black belt, Macon County remained relatively free of overt acts of violence and intimidation during the forties and fifties. This, again, contributed to the facade of "good race relations" in the county. Only infrequently did the Ku Klux Klan march across the black campus or into the black community. Only infrequently did one hear of the white sheriff mistreating blacks—and then it was the "rural blacks," out on the plantations. Seldom, if ever, were "the Institute or hospital Negroes" mistreated. This, too, was part of the bargain.

Unlike other areas, also, the blacks in Tuskegee were not economically dependent upon the whites. There was no discernible way the local whites could invoke economic reprisals against black individuals as they could in Lowndes County, since many of the blacks were employed by the federal hospital and the private college. It was among these blacks that the leadership of the black community centered. Let us take a closer look at the structure of Tuskegee's "Negro Establishment."

The people in the top echelons of the college and the hospital were powerful in the black community because they could exact certain very limited benefits from the white power structure (a traffic light at a certain corner, a paved road) here and there. They were also influential in the black community because the middle-class blacks identified with them. The rural black people either did not matter or they looked up to the "Institute colored folks"—a logical carry-over from the days when Booker T. Washington and his assistants maintained a close, paternalistic relationship with the black people in the outlying areas. The distinctions between power and influence which existed in Lowndes County did not exist in Macon. The black ministry was not nearly as influential in Tuskegee as in, say, Lowndes. In later years—the late fifties and sixties—ministers held a few leadership positions in the TCA (one was elected to the City Council and another to the county Board of Revenue in 1964), but positions of power or influence, or both, were generally held by the hospital staff and by Institute faculty members. As Professors Lewis Jones and Stanley Smith, two black sociologists on the Institute faculty in the late fifties, commented:

. . . the Negro ministers are not accorded the status and recognition which they usually experience in other Deep South communities. This may be explained, partially, by the fact that they are lost in "a sea of professionals." [4]

No one in the black community challenged the established black leadership. Even the small group of people who formed and developed the Tuskegee Civic Association did not see themselves as striving to replace the traditional leadership. The TCA was heavily oriented toward education: toward a program of careful patient study of such things as the duties of local county officers, the duties of citizenship, etc. In a sense, they were simply extending the curriculum outlined by Booker T. Washington to include civic concern. Professor Gomillion has written:

The officers of the TCA have considered their major responsibility to be that of the civic education of all citizens in the community, Negro and white, and the facilitation of intelligent civic action on the part of an increasing number of Negro citizens. [5]

The black leadership of the TCA never envisioned a future which might include the formation of a separate political party; they wanted, ultimately, to get within the local Democratic party. That leadership did not perceive itself as out to overthrow, replace or supplement established structures, much less alter the system. That leadership was never alienated from the established values of the society; they believed it was possible to work within the existing structures to bring about change. Thus, the TCA could gain the allegiance of many blacks in the community without those blacks seeing themselves as turning their backs on their philosophical leader, Booker T. Washington. Again in the spirit of Washington, the black people of Tuskegee told themselves that they could convert their white neighbors, that they could "work with" the whites in town—at first, economically, and then, hopefully, politically.

The TCA held a peculiar position in the black community. Not many people openly supported it (and many wished it would just quiet down), but they recognized that something was wrong with the one-way deferential relationship existing between the races in the community. They knew that it was incongruous for them to have economic and educational achievements and to remain at the political mercy of a white minority. It was, to say the least, embarrassing, and for this reason many black people never talked about it. They withdrew and let the TCA fight their political battles. So the Institute administration affirmed its position on academic freedom, that it would not censure the civic acts of its professors (this affirmation went only so far, however), while the federal hospital kept one eye on its employees and the other on the Hatch Act, which prohibited "partisan political" activity by governmental workers.

Naturally the middle-class blacks of Tuskegee would have preferred to vote and be a part of political decision-making, but they needed a potent catalyst to spring them into action. Apparently, they still believed that they had not proven themselves enough in the Washington sense; indeed, they were—and in many respects, remain—like little children constantly looking for love from their parents—an approving pat on the head, a condescending smile—despite the fact that those parents are derelict, neglectful, even vicious to them.

One jolt came in 1957.

It had become clear by then that blacks in Macon County would soon have more votes than the whites. Although the TCA leadership had been making conciliatory statements for years to the effect that "We do not intend to take over complete power," the whites of the county and the state were not reassured. They did not believe them because it was unnatural *not* to vote against those who had kept you in political subordination for decades. The whites assumed that the blacks would recognize that their political interest required them—in the context of twentieth-century Macon County history—to vote for black people. What white person had not participated in the racist past, and whose sincerity would be trusted now? The whites therefore persuaded the state legislature to pass a law gerrymandering the city of Tuskegee. On July 13, 1957, the city boundaries were changed to make a four-sided municipality into a 28-sided one. Some 420 black voters were thereby excluded from the city; ten black voters were left; no whites were touched. The growing black vote could not take control of the city. This was Alabama's answer to the teachings of "political patience" of Booker T. Washington.

As Professor Lewis Jones has said, the whites breached the contract between Booker T. and the white community. Washington had understood that "eventually" the blacks would be permitted entrance into the political arena, but the whites had "never" in their minds. The middle-class blacks were shocked and hurt; they could not believe that their good white neighbors would do this to them! The TCA called for a selective-buying campaign (boycotts were illegal under the state law) against the white merchants in the town. They assumed that the law would not have been passed without the consent—tacit or overt—of the city. (This, again, points to the black community's strongly held view, nationwide, that a monolithic white power structure exists.)

The "boycott" lasted for about four years at a high level of effectiveness. During a period of two years, twenty-six businesses operated by whites closed down. But even then, the whites did not give in politically. The black people of Tuskegee had economic independence from local whites and they used it. But their *political* power did not increase. Apparently, the whites were willing to suffer economic disaster rather than concede political power to the blacks. (The city boundaries were not restored until 1961, and then as a result of legal action culminating in a federal court decision of 1961 which ruled that the gerrymander had been racially motivated in violation of the Fifteenth Amendment and that a state may not gerrymander municipal boundaries on the basis of race. The former boundaries were restored.) [6]

Writing in 1958, Jones and Smith declared:

The application of economic pressure by Negroes in withholding trade from white merchants has seriously endangered the business community and has created an economic crisis for the entire area. However, since the application of such pressure was designed to influence and change the political attitude of merchants and other white groups toward Negro voting rights, it is necessary to observe that the goal of the Negro campaign has not been achieved. . . . Historically, it is significant that in this major test, the dominant white group has been economically affected to a very serious degree by Negro action, though its political power remains intact.[7]

The blacks had achieved education and economic security—both of which are still projected throughout the nation as cure-alls—but the whites continued to lay and collect taxes, rule over the school system, determine law enforcement practices. The reason is obvious enough: blacks did not have *political* power. Economic security or the promise of it may, as we noted [earlier], be vital to the building of a strong political force. But in a vacuum it is of no use to black people working for meaningful change.

During the same period as the gerrymander dispute, the United States Commission on Civil Rights conducted investigations in Macon County, which highlighted the long-term denial of voting rights. TCA officials testified before the Commission and were able to show that during the seven-year period from 1951 to 1958, 1,585 applications for voter certificates were made by blacks. Only 510 certificates were issued. The TCA documented that, for a twelve and one-half year period prior to December

1, 1958, Macon County was without a Board of Registrars for a total of three years and four months as a result of resignations and the refusal of the Governor and other members of the state appointing board to fill vacancies. Of course, the Governor refused to appoint any black people to the Board of Registrars. The picture presented to the Commission was one of continuous political frustration of black efforts.

The TCA demonstrated great skill in administration and data-collecting —a skill which defies the claim of some whites and blacks in the community that black people would not be able to run the county and city governmental machinery. The TCA produced a complete record of every black person who applied for a voter certificate since 1951, the number admitted into the registration office and the length of time needed for each to complete the application process. A TCA representative was stationed at the courthouse day after day, year after year—how patient can black folks be?—to record this information; that person also noted the time the Board of Registrars started work, the length of time it remained in session, and the days it was supposed to meet but did not do so.

As if to add further white insult to black injury, the TCA had documented that it could not receive a hearing from the person allegedly representing Macon County in the state legislature. In February, 1959, the TCA sent him a certified letter; it was *returned, unopened, marked "Refused"!* And all this in a county where black people had a majority, were economically independent and were educated. Yet the country never seemed to get too upset about White Power.

In 1959, Macon County became one of the first counties against which the Department of Justice filed a suit charging voting denials. Slowly, tediously, with one judicial decree after another handed down by federal Judge Frank M. Johnson, sitting in Montgomery, black people were added to the rolls. Soon the number of blacks exceeded whites as voters by a substantial margin. In 1964, there were approximately 7,212 voters in the county: 3,733 blacks, 3,479 whites. In 1966, these figures had increased substantially: 6,803 blacks, 4,495 whites. The white fears which had instigated the attempted gerrymander came true.

Now the big question was: would black people run for office and attempt to take and use political power? New groups and individuals in the community began to urge that blacks vote for blacks. But the TCA was true to its word: it decided in 1964 not to contest all five seats on the City Council; to run no black person for the powerful position of probate judge; to endorse only one black person for the county Board of Revenue.

These decisions were made on the premises that (1) it was wiser to seek only a few offices in order to show the local whites that they had nothing to fear from the growing black vote; (2) it was best to gain "experience" in public office before even thinking about assuming full control; (3) if the blacks elected all black candidates, the whites—in addition to pulling up stakes and leaving the county—might, during the lame-duck period, so disrupt the financial status of the county as to render the incoming blacks incapable of governing effectively.

A new group of black people in the community, the Non-Partisan Voters' League, took strong exception to this position. They felt that the least the black people should do was to control a majority of the seats on the City Council and on the county Board of Revenue, in addition to electing a black probate judge.

The TCA leadership counseled black people to vote a straight Democratic party ticket: a slate of black and white candidates, who were endorsed by the Macon County Democratic Club, the political arm of the TCA. They counseled black people *not* to vote for the independent black candidates endorsed by the Non-Partisan Voters' League. In a statement to the black leaders of the county precincts, dated October 28, 1964, Gomillion said:

Dear Leaders in the Precincts:

Following is a statement which might be used as a guide for your thinking and for the information which you give to voters on Monday evening, November 2, when you meet with them.

1. The Macon County Democratic Club officers believe:
   a. The Negro voters can demonstrate political strength and power most effectively by affiliation with, and participation in, a political party.
   b. That such political power by Macon County Negroes can best be expressed through the Democratic Party, at least at the present time.
   c. That the best way to reveal or express that power in the election of November 3 is by casting the largest possible number of votes for the *Democratic nominees.*
   d. That the best way to cast the largest number of votes is by voting the *straight Democratic ticket.* [. . .]
   h. That voting the straight Democratic ticket on November 3 might give the impression that we *know* what we want, and we know *how* to get it. [. . .]
   j. That voting the straight Democratic ticket for *all* Democratic nominees on state and county levels will reveal to us the kind of strength available for possible use in electing other Negroes to positions in the County, such as tax collector, members of the County Democratic Committee, members of the Lower House of the Alabama Legislature.

. . . The important issue here is whether or not we want to continue to act and be treated as Negroes, or to move into the larger area of politics and act as Democrats, who *happen* to be Negroes. . . . The Club did *not* refrain from endorsing the Independents because they are Negroes, but because they are Independents. . . . Let's show Alabama and the Democratic National Committee that Macon County Negro voters are loyal Democrats.

The TCA/MCDC position carried the day. The white press around the country praised the black people of Tuskegee for their decision not to take over all the offices, for not pre-empting all the public offices, for not establishing a "black oligarchy" to replace a "white oligarchy." Tuskegee blacks were showing "good sense," "forbearance." The country began to look upon Tuskegee once again as a "model" for other racially tense areas; it was pointing the way for other black people. Tuskegee was thus launched on a new political experiment—"bi-racial" government in the black-belt South. A novel thing indeed!

The two black people elected to the Tuskegee City Council immediately came in for severe criticism from a portion of the black community. The councilmen were criticized for not speaking out more for the black race, for not raising the issue of segregation in some white-owned places. The important and curious thing about these complaints was that since ultimate power still remained with the whites, the *only* thing the two token councilmen could do was "speak out." This did not, of course, mean that the grievances would be alleviated. With the existing ratio of 3–2 on the Council, the blacks could still be out-voted. The pitiful thing is that the black community had not needed to settle for representatives who could only "speak out"; it could have had political control.

Complaints were also heard against the white mayor for not appointing a black person to serve as clerk in the city office; political threats had to be made before he relented. Two black people were elected as justices of the peace, but the white sheriff did not take business to them.

In 1966, Tuskegee got a second jolt.

During the summer of the previous year, a number of Tuskegee Institute students had challenged various forms of overt discrimination which existed in the town. They had tried to enter "white" restaurants (and had been refused), held rallies, picketed stores for not hiring black people. Several times they tried to attend the segregated white churches, and were brutally beaten twice. Then, in January of 1966, one of the student leaders —Sammy Younge, Jr.—was shot to death by a white man when he sought to use the "white" rest-room at a gas station. (The man was later acquitted by an all-white jury in another county.) Younge himself was a member of a respected middle-class family in the town; his murder (not to mention the beatings at the churches) should have made clear to the black middle-class the folly and hopelessness of their previous approach. For some, it did; others went their comfortable way, unchanged.

Later that year, with no encouragement or aid from the TCA, a black citizen, Lucius Amerson, decided to run for sheriff of the county. One officer of the TCA—himself a member of the City Council—came out publicly in favor of the incumbent white sheriff as "the better man." Amerson waged a campaign throughout the county, especially among the rural black people. It was not a "racist" campaign; time and again he reiterated that he would conduct his office equitably and without favoritism to race. Amerson was elected in November, 1966, despite the lack of TCA support.

But the White Power of the community lingered on. Amerson was immediately faced with efforts by the whites to undercut his power. The white-controlled Board of Revenue reappointed the outgoing sheriff as Beer License Inspector, a position Amerson stated he wanted inasmuch as his duties included such matters. The Board denied him extra funds needed to operate his office. White constables were appointed by the local white justices of the peace in an attempt to circumvent the new sheriff's law enforcement power.

In other areas of Tuskegee life, whites retained ultimate control in 1967. The City Council remains controlled by whites; so does the county Board of Revenue, the school board, the offices of probate judge, tax assessor, county solicitor and several local planning boards.

There are several conclusions one could draw about this county in black-belt Alabama.

The middle-class black community is clinging to a set of values and a rhetoric which never applied in that area or any other of this country: a language of Christian love, charity, good will. When Sammy Younge, Jr. was killed, a frustrated student group held protest demonstrations in the town, and there was some damage to property as a result of the demonstrators being harassed and intimidated by local police. Vocal black people condemned the students rather than the conditions which permitted Younge to die. One Negro woman, prominent in civic affairs in Tuskegee, said:

> Anyone who knows me understands that I yield to no one in dedication to equal citizenship rights. I have long worked for elimination of injustices and discrimination. I believe in the American dream—the Christian principle—of democracy for all regardless of race, color or creed. I have stood by this conviction.
>
> In recent days, especially last Saturday, the events connected with the equal rights movement did nothing for progress but only damaged the cause of responsible citizenship. I refer, of course, to the display of undisciplined and irresponsible behavior by a few young persons which was marked by rock and bottle throwing. I am ashamed of every person who set off this ugly incident or who had any part in it.
>
> . . . the vast majority of mature, Christian, right-thinking Negro citizens regret what happened.
>
> There are many needs in the present situation. The first is responsible action and the exercise of calm judgment by every citizen. Those of us who live here and love this community have much at stake. The SNCC-type from outside and the handful who are persuaded to act outside the law do not seem to understand this. We want a type of relationship, built on solid ground, which will endure through the years—a relationship depending upon mutual trust and respect. This does not derive from rowdyism and lawlessness. . . . There was an article in last week's *Time* magazine which referred to the recent inexcusable murder as having removed the facade which had covered up lack of progress in equal rights. Anyone who knew the voter situation here several years ago and who knows the facts today could not agree with that statement. . . . Sure, we have not realized all our ambitions. Certainly, we have a long way to go. But the important thing is that we were on the way—that we had made remarkable progress, and that this progress had been made without violence of any type.
>
> . . . Tuskegee is our home, we are proud of its institutions. We insist on equality of opportunity—under law and under God—but we are not radical

street demonstrators, losing control of our good instincts. Nor will we endorse or support those who work without purpose or concern for law and order.

Let all of us—white and colored—join hands in securing justice, obedience to law and good will which will bring progress in every area of our common life.[8]

This letter represents the thinking of a vast number of middle-class black people in Tuskegee. These people do, in fact, "believe in the American dream." But that dream, as already noted, was not originally intended to include them and it does not include the black masses today.

Nor is the lady realistic about white attitudes. Black people must stop deluding themselves that the basic intentions of *most* white people are good. White America, in many ways, has been telling black people that the hopes and language of the letter reproduced above are nothing more than naïve lamentations. Note the warnings of the "respectable" editorial writers of *The Saturday Evening Post:*

We are all, let us face it, Mississippians. We all fervently wish that the Negro problem did not exist, or that, if it must exist, it could be ignored. Confronted with the howling need for decent schools, jobs, housing, and all the other minimum rights of the American system, we will do our best, in a halfhearted way, to correct old wrongs. The hand may be extended grudgingly and patronizingly, but anyone who rejects that hand rejects his own best interests. *For minimum rights are the only rights that we are willing to guarantee, and above those minimum rights there is and will continue to be a vast area of discrimination and inequity and unfairness,* the area in which we claim the most basic right of all—the right to be stupid and prejudiced, the right to make mistakes, the right to be less and worse than we pretend, the right to be ourselves.[9] (Authors' italics).

These clear indications of feelings make the language of Tuskegee's middle-class black people seem ludicrous—and also rather shameful. Such blacks are pleased that certain changes have occurred without violence. But had there been a more sincere confrontation with whites by those blacks so intent on avoiding violence for avoidance's sake, Sammy Younge and many other black people would not be dead today. Those who look to Tuskegee for progress should ponder the following statement of a professor on the faculty at the Institute:

If one considers Tuskegee to be a model community that has made steady progress toward racial reconciliation rooted in mutual respect and acceptance, it is difficult to explain the intense reaction to Younge's death—an intensity that is only weakly suggested by the four civil rights marches that have already occurred. In point of fact, the events of the past year make it abundantly clear that Tuskegee has been living a lie—a lie made all the more dangerous by the apparent control that Negroes have secured over the political agencies of the community. . . . The fault lies in the self-deceptive nature of the vision that guides both groups, and in the external pressure that constrains that vision from moving from status to contract.[10]

The black people of Tuskegee—the largely middle-class blacks—soothe themselves into thinking that they are describing what is or can be. They are simply deceiving themselves. Their grand language—applauded by many whites—may make them feel morally superior but it does nothing to gain political power, the power necessary to stop killings and discrimination. Black people of Tuskegee do not need to show whites that they can talk a good rhetoric. White people know that power is not love, Christian charity, etc. If these things come, let them develop out of a respect for mutual power. The whites will stop killing blacks and kidding blacks when the blacks make it no longer worthwhile for them to do so.

The black people of Tuskegee are perpetuating a deferential society wherein the blacks must always prove something to the whites. First, they had to prove that they could wash up, clean up, get an education and be nice little black people before the whites would "accept" them. Then, when they got the ballot—with absolutely no help from the local whites —they had to prove their patience and good will by not making effective use of it. Supposedly, they had to learn how to govern from the white man. No more succinct rejection of this view has been articulated than that of Dr. Paul L. Puryear, formerly of the Tuskegee faculty: "How can we learn from those who have demonstrated their incompetence?"

The whites of Tuskegee have ruled for decades and that rule has been despotic. The only lesson the whites of Tuskegee could teach the black people was how to exclude blacks from positions of power. Black people must not indulge the fanciful notion that whites, because they are white, have a priority on leadership talent. The only sure talent that Tuskegee whites have demonstrated is the ability to suppress and oppress black people. To cater to this despicable history in the name of "love" and "bi-racialism" is absurd. The black people should create rather than imitate—create new forms which are politically inclusive rather than imitate old racist forms which are politically exclusive. The black people have nothing to prove to the whites; the burden is on the whites to prove that they are civilized enough to live in the community and to share in its governance.

Tuskegee, Alabama, could be the model of Black Power. It could be the place where black people have amassed political power and used that power effectively. The black people of Tuskegee could play a major role in building an independent county political organization which would address itself to the needs of black residents along lines we have already indicated. Such an independent force would give greater meaning to the election of Amerson by creating a genuine, organized base of power—not merely putting one black man, however valuable, into office. In addition, despite the special circumstances prevailing in Macon County—the high educational level, economic security—Tuskegee Institute could serve as a training center for potential indigenous community leaders from other areas.

It would be naïve to expect that the operation of Black Power in Tuskegee could transform Alabama state politics. But it could establish in that one area a viable government based on a new and different set of values—on humaneness—and serve as an example of what civilized government *could* be in this society.

Black people need not be apologetic or defensive about controlling their communities in this manner. We have seen that this is the one sure way to end racism in this country. The Tuskegee model *could* be applicable to black areas in other parts of the country, including the northern ghettos. Although no widespread possibility of governing whole counties exists in the North at this time, we are aware that, in the very near future, many of the northern urban cities will be predominantly black. Pockets of Black Power could develop and become illustrations of what *legitimate* government really is—a phenomenon we have not experienced to date in this society. . . .

NOTES

1. This phrase is attributed to Dr. Paul L. Puryear, former political science professor at Tuskegee, now at Fisk University.
2. Charles V. Hamilton, *Minority Politics in Black Belt Alabama*, Eagleton Institute, Cases in Practical Politics. New York: McGraw-Hill, 1962, p. 1.
3. Charles G. Gomillion, "The Tuskegee Voting Story," *Freedomways*, Vol. 2, No. 3 (Summer, 1962), p. 232.
4. Lewis Jones and Stanley Smith, *Voting Rights and Economic Pressure*, Anti-Defamation League, 1958, p. x.
5. Gomillion, *op. cit.*, p. 233.
6. The gerrymander case went up to the Supreme Court, which made the crucial procedural ruling that a federal court could hear the case. The whites had argued that the issue was political, not juridical. Once referred to a federal court, Judge Frank M. Johnson ruled in favor of the black appellants.
7. Jones and Smith, *op. cit.*, p. 43.
8. Letter to the Editor, *The Tuskegee News* (January 20, 1966), p. 2.
9. "A New White Backlash?" *The Saturday Evening Post* (September 10, 1966), p. 88.
10. Arnold S. Kaufman, "Murder in Tuskegee: Day of Wrath in the Model Town," *The Nation* (January 31, 1966), p. 119.

23. The Making of
the Negro Mayors 1967

Considering the nature of black politics in the urban North, the recent rise of Negro mayors in major metropolitan areas must be seen as a spectacular development. This development has occurred in such places as Richmond, California, Gary, Indiana, and Washington, D.C. This timely analysis by Hadden, Masotti, and Thiessen explores some of the essential ingredients of this achievement in Cleveland, Ohio. The election of Carl Stokes to the highest political office of this city can be instructive for the planners of black political strategy in the urban North. Can this accomplishment be seen as a consequence of the "politics of deference" as described by Carmichael and Hamilton, or is it a phenomenon of "black power"? What is the relevance of this achievement to black pride and "black power"? Is it simply tokenism or will it be of substantial benefit to blacks in Cleveland and throughout the country? Such questions are important to blacks and whites alike, for answers to them have an important bearing on the direction black protest should take.

JEFFREY K. HADDEN, LOUIS H. MASOTTI, AND VICTOR THIESSEN

Throughout most of 1967, black power and Vietnam kept this nation in an almost continual state of crisis. The summer months were the longest and hottest in modern U.S. history—many political analysts even felt that the nation was entering its most serious domestic conflict since the Civil War. Over a hundred cities were rocked with violence.

As the summer gave way to autumn, the interest of the nation shifted a little from the summer's riots to the elections on the first Tuesday of November. An unprecedented number of Negroes were running for office, but public attention focused on three elections. In Cleveland, Carl B. Stokes, a lawyer who in 1962 had become the first Democratic Negro legislator in Ohio, was now seeking to become the first Negro mayor of a large American city. In Gary, Ind., another young Negro lawyer, Richard D. Hatcher, was battling the Republican Party's candidate—as well as his own Democratic Party—to become the first Negro mayor of a "medium-sized" city. And in Boston, Louise Day Hicks, a symbol of white backlash, was conducting a "You know where I stand" campaign to capture the mayorality.

Normally, the nation couldn't care less about who would become the next mayors of Cleveland, Gary, and Boston. But the tenseness of the summer months gave these elections enormous significance. If Stokes and Hatcher lost and Hicks won, could Negroes be persuaded to use the power of the ballot box rather than the power of fire bombs?

Fortunately, November 7 proved to be a triumphant day for racial peace. Stokes and Hatcher won squeaker victories, both by margins of only about 1500 votes; in Boston, Kevin H. White defeated Mrs. Hicks by a 12,000 plurality. Labor leader George Meany was exultant—"American voters have rejected racism as a political issue." Negroes in the three cities were also jubilant. In Gary, the most tense of the cities, Richard Hatcher urged the mostly Negro crowd at his headquarters to "cool it. I urge that the outcome of this election be unmarred by any incident of any kind. . . . If we spoil this victory with any kind of occurrence here tonight, or anywhere in the city, it will be a hollow victory." The evening *was* cool: Joyous Negroes danced and sang in the streets.

But beyond the exultation of victory remain many hard questions. Now that Cleveland and Gary have Negro mayors, just how much difference will it make in solving the many grave problems that these cities face? Will these victories cool militancy in urban ghettos next summer, or will the momentum of frustration prove too great to put on the brakes? A careful analysis of *how* these candidates won office may help provide the answers.

The focus of this report is on Cleveland because:

As residents of Cleveland, we are more familiar with the campaign and the election.

Cleveland is unique because, in 1965, it had a special census. By matching voting wards with census tracts, we can draw a clearer picture of voting behavior than we could in the other cities, where rapid neighborhood transitions have made 1960 census data quite unreliable in assessing voting patterns. Having examined Cleveland in some detail, we will draw some comparisons with the Gary and Boston elections, then speculate about their significance and implications.

Cleveland—City in Decline

Cleveland has something less than 2,000,000 residents. Among metropolitan areas in America, it ranks eleventh in size. Like many other American cities, the central city of Cleveland is experiencing an absolute decline in population—residents are fleeing from the decaying core to the surrounding suburbs. The city certainly ranks high both in terms of absolute and proportional decline in the central-city population.

Between 1950 and 1960, the population of the central city declined from 914,808 to 876,050, a loss of almost 39,000. By 1965 the population had sunk to 810,858, an additional loss of 65,000. But these figures are only a partial reflection of the changing composition of the population, since new Negro residents coming into the central city helped offset the white exodus. *Between 1950 and 1960, nearly 142,000 white residents left the central city, and an additional 94,000 left between 1960 and 1965—nearly a quarter of a million in just 15 years.*

During the same period the number of Negro residents of Cleveland rose from 147,847 to 279,352—an increase from 16.1 percent to 34.4 percent of the city's population. There is no evidence that this dramatic population redistribution has changed since the special 1965 census. Some suburbanization of Negroes is beginning on the east and southeast side of the city, but the pace is not nearly so dramatic as for whites. In 1960, approximately 97 percent of the Negroes in the metropolitan area lived in the central city. This percentage has probably declined somewhat since then—16,000 Negro residents have moved to East Cleveland. But the basic pattern of segregation in the metropolitan area remains. The development in East Cleveland is little more than an eastward extension of the ghetto, and the older, decaying residential units the Negroes have moved to are hardly "suburban" in character.

While the population composition of Cleveland is changing rapidly, whites are still a significant majority—about 62 percent. Again like many other central cities, a significant percentage of the white population comprises nationality groups that live in segregated sections, with a strong sense of ethnic identity and a deep fear of Negro encroachment. (In 1964, the bussing of Negro students into Murray Hill, an Italian neighborhood, resulted in rioting.)

In 1960, the census classified 43 percent of the central city's white residents as "foreign stock." In that year, five groups—Germans, Poles, Czechs, Hungarians, and Italians—had populations of 25,000 or greater; at least 20 other nationality groups were large enough to have to be contended with in the political arena. But today these ethnic groups—although unwilling to admit it—have become less than the controlling majority they constituted before 1960.

The Cuyahoga River divides Cleveland, physically as well as socially. When Negroes first began to move into the city, during World War I, they occupied the decaying section to the south and east of the central business district. As their numbers grew, they continued pushing in this direction and now occupy the larger part of the east side (except for some ethnic strongholds). There are no stable, integrated neighborhoods in the central city—only areas in transition from white to black. To the west, the Cuyahoga River constitutes a barrier to Negro penetration.

Ever since 1941, when Frank Lausche was elected, Cleveland has had a succession of basically honest but unimaginative Democratic mayors. These mayors have kept their hold on City Hall by means of a relatively weak coalition of nationality groups. At no point in this 26-year Lausche dynasty did a mayor gather enough power to seriously confront the long-range needs and problems of the city.

By early 1967, the city had seemingly hit rock bottom. A long procession of reporters began arriving to write about its many problems. The racial unrest of the past several years had, during the summer of 1966, culminated in the worst rioting in Cleveland's history. This unrest was continuing to grow as several militant groups were organizing. Urban renewal was a dismal failure; in January, the Department of Housing and Urban Development even cut off the city's urban-renewal funds, the first such action by the Federal Government. The exodus of whites, along with business, shoved the city to the brink of financial disaster. In February, the Moody Bond Survey reduced the city's credit rating. In May, the Federal Government cut off several million dollars of construction funds—because the construction industry had failed to assure equal job opportunities for minority groups. In short, the city was, and remains, in deep trouble. And while most ethnic groups probably continued to believe that Cleveland was the "Best Location in the Nation," the Negro community—and a growing number of whites—were beginning to feel that Cleveland was the "Mistake on the Lake," and that it was time for a change.

Carl Stokes's campaign for mayor was his second try. In 1965, while serving in the state House of Representatives, he came within 2100 votes of defeating Mayor Ralph S. Locher. Stokes had taken advantage of a city-charter provision that lets a candidate file as an independent, and bypass the partisan primaries. Ralph McAllister, then president of the Cleveland School Board, did the same. For his hard line on *de facto* school segregation, however, McAllister had earned the enmity of the Negro community. The Republican candidate was Ralph Perk, the first Republican elected to a county-wide position (auditor) in many years. A second generation Czech-Bohemian, Perk hoped to win by combining his ethnic appeal with his program for the city (Perk's Plan). He had no opposition for his party's nomination. The fourth candidate was Mayor Locher, who had defeated Mark McElroy, county recorder and perennial candidate for something, in the Democratic primary.

It was in the 1965 Democratic primary that the first signs of a "black bloc" vote emerged. The Negroes, who had previously supported incumbent Democratic mayoral candidates, if not enthusiastically at least consistently, made a concerted effort to dump Locher in favor of McElroy. There were two reasons.

Locher had supported his police chief after the latter had made some tactless remarks about Negroes. Incensed Negro leaders demanded an audience with the mayor, and when he refused, his office was the scene of demonstrations, sit-ins, and arrests. At that point, as one of the local reporters put it, "Ralph Locher became a dirty name in the ghetto."

Stokes, as an independent, and his supporters hoped that the Democratic primary would eliminate the *stronger* candidate, Locher. For then a black bloc would have a good chance of deciding the general election because of an even split in the white vote.

Despite the Negro community's efforts, Locher won the primary and went on to narrowly defeat Stokes. Locher received 37 percent of the vote, Stokes 36 percent, Perk 17 percent, and McAllister 9 percent. Some observers reported that a last-minute whispering campaign in Republican precincts—to the effect that "A vote for Perk is a vote for Stokes"—may have given Locher enough Republican votes to win. The evidence: The popular Perk received only a 17 percent vote in a city where a Republican could be expected something closer to 25 percent. Had Perk gotten anything close to 25 percent, Stokes would have probably been elected two years earlier.

Although he made a strong showing in defeat, Carl Stokes's political future looked bleak. No one expected the Democratic leaders to give Stokes another opportunity to win by means of a split vote. Nor were there other desirable elected offices Stokes could seek. Cleveland has no Negro Congressman—largely because the heavy Negro concentration in the city has been "conveniently" gerrymandered. The only district where Stokes might have had a chance has been represented by Charles Vanik, a popular and liberal white, and as long as Vanik remained in Congress Stokes was locked out. Stokes's state Senate district was predominantly white; and a county or state office seemed politically unrealistic because of his race. So, in 1966, Stokes sought re-election to the state House unopposed.

Between 1965 and 1967, Cleveland went from bad to worse, physically, socially, and financially. With no other immediate possibilities, Stokes began to think about running for mayor again. The big question was whether to risk taking on Locher in the primary—or to file as an independent again.

The Primary Race

In effect, Stokes's decision was made for him. Seth Taft, slated to be the Republican candidate, told Stokes he would withdraw from the election entirely if Stokes filed as an independent in order to gain the advantage of a three-man general election. Taft had concluded that his best strategy was to face a Negro, *alone,* or a faltering incumbent, *alone,* in the general election. But not both. In a three-man race with Locher and Stokes, Taft correctly assumed that he would be the man in the middle with no chance for victory. (Taft would have preferred to run as an independent—to gain

Democratic votes—but the county Republican leader threatened to file *another* Republican candidate unless Taft ran as a Republican.)

Meanwhile, Locher committed blunder after blunder—and Democratic party leaders began to question whether he could actually win another election. In the weeks before filing for the primary, Democratic leaders even pressured Locher to accept a Federal judgeship and clear the way for the president of the city council to run. But the Democratic leaders in Cleveland are not noted for their strength or effectiveness, as is evidenced by the fact that none of the Democratic mayors since 1941 were endorsed by the party when they were first elected. When Locher refused to withdraw, the party reluctantly rallied behind him.

Another Democratic candidate was Frank P. Celeste, former mayor of the Republican westside suburb of Lakewood. Celeste established residency in the city, announced his candidacy early, and—despite pressure from the Democratic Party—remained in the primary race.

There was always the possibility that Celeste would withdraw from the primary, which would leave Stokes facing Locher alone. But the threat of Taft's withdrawal from the general election left Stokes with little choice but to face Locher head-on in the primary. A primary race against Locher and a strong Democrat was more appealing than a general election against Locher and a weak Republican.

Now, in 1965 Stokes had received only about 6000 white votes in the city in a 239,000 voter turnout. To win in the primary, he had to enlarge and consolidate the Negro vote—and increase his white support on the westside and in the eastside ethnic wards.

The first part of his strategy was a massive voter-registration drive in the Negro wards—to reinstate the potential Stokes voters dropped from the rolls for failing to vote since the 1964 Presidential election. The Stokes organization—aided by Martin Luther King, Jr. and the Southern Christian Leadership Conference, as well as by a grant (in part earmarked for voter registration) from the Ford Foundation to the Cleveland chapter of CORE—did succeed in registering many Negroes. But there was a similar drive mounted by the Democratic Party on behalf of Locher. (Registration figures are not available by race.)

The second part of the Stokes strategy took him across the polluted Cuyahoga River into the white wards that had given him a mere 3 percent of the vote in 1965. He spoke wherever he would be received—to small groups in private homes, in churches, and in public and private halls. While he was not always received enthusiastically, he did not confront many hostile crowds. He faced the race issue squarely and encouraged his audience to judge him on his ability.

Stokes's campaign received a big boost when the *Plain Dealer,* the largest daily in Ohio, endorsed him. Next, the *Cleveland Press* called for a change in City Hall, but declined to endorse either Stokes or Celeste. But since the polls indicated that Celeste was doing very badly, this amounted to an endorsement of Stokes.

More people voted in this primary than in any other in Cleveland's history. When the ballots were counted, Stokes had 52.5 percent of the votes—he had defeated Locher by a plurality of 18,000 votes. Celeste was the man in the middle, getting only 4 percent of the votes, the lowest of any mayoral candidate in recent Cleveland history.

What produced Stokes's clear victory? Table 1 reveals the answer. The decisive factor was the size of the Negro turnout. While Negroes constituted only about 40 percent of the voters, 73.4 percent of them turned out, compared with only 58.4 percent of the whites. Predominantly Negro wards cast 96.2 percent of their votes for Stokes. (Actually this figure underrepresents the Negro vote for Stokes, since some of the non-Stokes votes in these wards were cast by whites. Similarly, the 15.4 percent vote for Stokes in the predominantly white wards slightly overestimates the white vote because of the Negro minority.)

Newspaper and magazine reports of the primary election proclaimed that Stokes could not have won without the white vote. Our own estimate —based on matching wards with census tracts, and allowing for only slight shifts in racial composition in some wards since the 1965 special census—is that Stokes received 16,000 white votes. His margin of victory was 18,000. How would the voting have gone if the third man, Celeste, had not been in the race? Many white voters, feeling that Stokes could not win in a two-man race, might not have bothered to vote at all, so perhaps Stokes would have won by an even larger margin. Thus Stokes's inroad into the white vote was not the decisive factor in his primary victory, although it was important.

Stokes emerged from the primary as the odds-on favorite to win—five weeks later—in the general election. And in the first few days of the campaign, it seemed that Stokes had everything going for him.

Stokes was bright, handsome, and articulate. His opponent, Seth Taft, while bright, had never won an election, and his family name, associated with the Taft-Hartley Act, could hardly be an advantage among union members. In addition, he was shy and seemingly uncomfortable in a crowd.

Both the *Plain Dealer* and the *Cleveland Press* endorsed Stokes in the general election.

The wounds of the primary were quickly (if perhaps superficially) healed, and the Democratic candidate was endorsed by both the Democratic Party and Mayor Locher.

Labor—both the A.F.L.-C.I.O. and the Teamsters—also endorsed Stokes.

He had a partisan advantage. Of the 326,003 registered voters, only 34,000 (10 percent) were Republican. The closest any Republican mayoral candidate had come to winning was in 1951, when—in a small

TABLE 1.

	City Totals			Negro Wards			White Wards			Mixed Wards		
	1965 General	1967 Primary	1967 General	1965 General	1967 Primary	1967 General	1965 General	1967 Primary	1967 General	1965 General	1967 Primary	1967 General
Registered voters	337,803	326,003	326,003	103,123	99,885	99,885	159,419	152,737	152,737	75,261	73,421	73,421
Turnout	239,479	210,926	257,157	74,396	73,360	79,591	111,129	88,525	119,883	53,962	49,105	57,113
Percent turnout	70.9	64.7	78.9	72.1	73.4	79.7	69.7	58.0	78.5	71.7	66.9	77.8
Stokes votes	85,716	110,769	129,829	63,550	70,575	75,586	3,300	13,495	23,158	18,866	26,699	30,872
Percent Stokes votes	35.8	52.5	50.5	85.4	96.2	95.0	3.0	15.2	19.3	35.0	54.4	54.1

turnout—William J. McDermott received 45 percent of the vote.

Stokes had 90,000 or more Negro votes virtually assured, with little possibility that Taft would make more than slight inroads.

Perhaps most important, voting-behavior studies over the years have demonstrated that voters who are confronted by a dilemma react by staying home from the polls. Large numbers of life-long Democrats, faced with voting for a Negro or a Republican by the name of Taft, were likely to stay home.

Had this been a normal election, Democrat Carl Stokes would have won handily. But this was not destined to be a normal election. During the final days of the campaign, Stokes knew he was in a fight for his political life. Those who predicted that the cross-pressures would keep many voters away from the polls forgot that the variable "Negro" had never been involved in an election of this importance.

On Election Day, an estimated 90 percent of those who voted for Locher or Celeste in the Democratic primary shifted to Taft—many pulling a Republican lever for the first time in their life. Was this clearly and unequivocally bigoted backlash? To be sure, bigotry *did* play a major role in the election. But to dismiss the campaign and the election as pure overt bigotry is to miss the significance of what happened in Cleveland and the emerging subtle nature of prejudice in American society.

The Non-Issue of Race

A closer look at the personal characteristics and campaign strategy of Seth Taft, the Republican candidate, reveals the complexity and subtlety of the race issue.

In the final days of the Democratic primary campaign, Taft repeatedly told reporters that he would rather run against Locher and his record than against Carl Stokes. On the evening of the primary, Taft appeared at Stokes's headquarters to congratulate him. As far as he was concerned, Taft said, the campaign issue was, "Who could present the most constructive program for change in Cleveland?" Further, he said he didn't want people voting for him simply because he was white. A few days later, Taft even presented a strongly-worded statement to his campaign workers:

The Cuyahoga Democratic party has issued a number of vicious statements concerning the candidacy of Carl Stokes, and others have conducted whisper campaigns. We cannot tolerate injection of race into this campaign. . . . Many people will vote for Carl Stokes because he is a Negro. Many people will vote for me because I am white. I regret this fact. I will work hard to convince people they should not vote on a racial basis.

Seth Taft's programs to solve racial tensions may have been paternalistic, not really perceptive of emerging moods of the ghetto. But one thing is clear—he was not a bigot. Every indication is that he remained uncomfortable about being in a race in which his chances to win depended, in large part, upon a backlash vote.

Whether Taft's attempt to silence the race issue was a deliberate strategy or a reflection of deep personal feelings, it probably enhanced his chances of winning. He knew that he had the hard-core bigot vote. His task was to convince those in the middle that they could vote for him and *not* be bigots.

Stokes, on the other hand, had another kind of problem. While he had to draw more white votes, he also had to retain and, if possible, increase the 73 percent Negro turnout that had delivered him 96 percent of the Negro votes in the primary. Stokes's campaign leaders feared a fall-off in the voter turnout from Negro wards—with good reason. The entire primary campaign had pushed the October 3 date so hard that some Negroes could not understand why Carl Stokes was not mayor on October 4. Full-page newspaper ads paid for by CORE had stated, *"If you don't vote Oct. 3rd, forget it. The man who wins will be the next mayor of Cleveland!"* So Stokes felt he had to remobilize the Negro vote.

The moment came during the question-and-answer period of the second of four debates with Taft in the all-white west side. Stokes said:

The personal analysis of Seth Taft—and the analysis of many competent political analysts—is that Seth Taft may win the November 7 election, but for only one reason. That reason is that his skin happens to be white.

The predominantly white crowd booed loudly and angrily for several minutes, and throughout the rest of the evening repeatedly interrupted him. Later, Stokes's campaign manager revealed that his candidate's remark was a calculated risk to arouse Negro interest. Stokes probably succeeded, but he also gave Taft supporters an excuse to bring the race issue into the open. And they could claim that it was *Stokes,* not Taft, who was trying to exploit the race issue.

To be sure, *both* candidates exploited the race issue. But, for the most part, it was done rather subtly. Stokes's campaign posters stated, "Let's do Cleveland Proud"—another way of saying, "Let's show the world that Cleveland is capable of rising above racial bigotry." A full-page ad for Stokes stated in bold print, "Vote for Seth Taft. It Would Be Easy, Wouldn't It?" After the debate, Taft was free to accuse Stokes of using the race issue—itself a subtle way of exploiting the issue. Then there was the letter, signed by the leaders of 22 nationality clubs, that was mailed to 40,000 members in the city. It didn't mention race, but comments such as "protecting our way of life," "safeguard our liberty," and "false charges of police brutality" were blatant in their implications. Taft sidestepped comment on the letter.

No matter how much the candidates may have wanted to keep race out of the picture, race turned out to be the most important issue. Both Taft and Stokes could benefit from the issue if they played it right, and both did use it. And although the Stokes's remark at the second debate gave white voters an excuse to vote for Taft without feeling that they were bigots, many whites probably would have found another excuse.

Taft as a Strategist

The fact is that Taft, for all his lackluster qualities, emerged as a strong candidate. He was able to turn many of his liabilities into assets.

Taft was able to insulate himself against his Republican identity. He successfully dissociated himself from his uncle's position on labor by pointing to his own active role, as a student, against "right to work" laws. At the same time, he hit hard at Stokes's record as an off again–on again Democrat. This strategy neutralized, at least in part, Taft's first political disadvantage—running as a Republican in a Democratic city.

A second liability was that he came from a wealthy family. Taft was an Ivy League intellectual, cast in the role of a "do-gooder." He lived in an exclusive suburb, Pepper Pike, and had bought a modest home in Cleveland only a few weeks before declaring his candidacy. How, it was frequently asked, could such a man understand the problems of the inner-city and of the poor? Almost invariably the answer was: "Did John F. Kennedy, Franklin D. Roosevelt, and Nelson Rockefeller have to be poor in order to understand and respond to the problems of the poor?" Taft's campaign posters were a side profile that bore a striking resemblance to President Kennedy. Whether he was consciously exploiting the Kennedy image is an open question. But there can be little doubt that when Taft mentioned his Republican heritage, he tried to project an image of the new breed of Republican—John Lindsay and Charles Percy. This image didn't come across very well at first, but as he became a seasoned campaigner it became clearer.

Another liability was that Taft had never held an elected office. His opponent tried to exploit this—unsuccessfully. Taft could point to 20 years of active civic service, including the fact that he was one of the authors of the Ohio fair-housing law. Then too, the charge gave Taft an opportunity to point out that Stokes had the worst absentee record of anyone in the state legislature. Stokes never successfully answered this charge until the last of their four debates, when he produced a pre-campaign letter from Taft commending him on his legislative service. But this came moments *after* the TV cameras had gone off the air.

Still another liability emerged during the campaign. Taft's strategy of discussing programs, not personalities, was seemingly getting him nowhere. He presented specific proposals; Stokes, a skilled debater, succeeded in picking them apart. Stokes himself discussed programs only at a general level and contended that he was best-qualified to "cut the red tape" in Washington. His frequent trips to Washington to confer with top Government officials, before and during the campaign, indicated that he had the inside track.

Taft, realizing at this point that his campaign was not gaining much momentum, suddenly switched gears and began attacking Stokes's record (not Stokes personally). Stokes had claimed he would crack-down on slumlords. Taft discovered that Stokes owned a piece of rental property with several code violations—and that it had not been repaired despite an order from the city. He hit hard at Stokes's absenteeism and his record as a "good" Democrat. He put a "bird-dog" on Stokes and, if Stokes told one group one thing and another group something else, the public heard about it.

The upshot was that in the final days of the campaign Taft captured the momentum. Stokes was easily the more flashy debater and projected a superior image; but Taft emerged as the better strategist.

Should Taft Have Withdrawn?

One may ask whether all of this discussion is really relevant, since the final vote was sharply divided along racial lines. In one sense it *is* irrelevant, since it is possible that a weaker candidate than Taft might have run just as well. It is also possible that a white racist might actually have won. Still, this discussion has buttressed two important points.

Taft was not all black, and Stokes was not all white. Taft proved a strong candidate, and—had he been running against Locher instead of Stokes—he might have amassed strong support from Negroes and defeated Locher.

By being a strong candidate, Taft made it much easier for many white Democrats, who might otherwise [have] been cross-pressured into staying home, to come out and vote for him.

Some people felt that Taft should have withdrawn and let Stokes run uncontested. But many of the same people also decried white liberals who, at recent conferences to form coalitions between black-power advocates and the New Left, let black militants castrate them. It is not traditional in American politics that candidates enter a race to lose. Taft was in to win, and he fought a hard and relatively clean campaign—as high a compliment as can be paid to any candidate.

Yet all of this doesn't change the basic nature of the voting. This is clear from the evidence in Table 2. Stokes won by holding his black bloc, and increasing his white vote from 15 percent in the primary to almost 20 percent in the general. An enormous amount of the white vote was, whether covert or overt, anti-Negro. It is hard to believe that Catholics, ethnic groups, and laborers who never voted for anyone but a Democrat should suddenly decide to evaluate candidates on their qualifications and

TABLE 2. PERCENT STOKES VOTE BY WARD

White Wards	% Negro	1965 General	1967 Primary	1967 General
1	.6	3.2	17.2	20.5
2	.3	1.9	12.8	17.4
3	.9	2.5	13.6	22.1
4	.3	3.0	18.2	20.9
5	.6	1.7	11.8	17.8
6	.8	2.3	15.1	16.7
7	.6	3.4	16.5	23.7
8	3.0	6.1	24.7	29.3
9	.2	1.9	12.4	16.4
14	1.4	1.1	12.7	13.0
15	1.4	1.2	9.2	14.1
22	5.7	8.1	22.5	26.3
26	1.1	2.8	16.3	19.9
32	2.4	2.9	10.0	15.3
33	.3	2.5	17.7	21.4
Average		3.0	15.2	19.3
Negro Wards				
10	91.3	88.7	97.3	96.7
11	91.8	86.3	95.9	96.0
12	82.7	76.9	90.4	90.5
13	75.2	75.8	90.7	88.4
17	99.0	86.6	98.1	97.9
18	89.3	84.0	96.0	95.7
20	91.0	83.0	95.0	92.8
24	92.6	90.6	98.1	98.1
25	90.9	91.3	98.4	98.2
27	85.7	85.2	95.6	94.0
Average		85.4	96.2	95.0
Mixed Wards				
16	56.6	50.7	69.9	70.1
19	25.3	29.2	48.0	39.9
21	61.1	55.2	66.3	68.9
23	20.3	9.8	18.2	23.2
28	28.5	26.5	54.8	57.3
29	24.4	26.8	43.2	42.3
30	51.7	51.5	75.3	71.4
31	21.8	16.9	31.8	39.0
Average		35.0	54.4	54.1

programs, and—in overwhelming numbers—decide that the Republican candidate was better qualified. The implication is that they were prejudiced. But to assume that such people perceive themselves as bigots is to oversimplify the nature of prejudice. And to call such people bigots is to make their responses even more rigid—as Carl Stokes discovered after his remark in the second debate with Taft.

This, then, is perhaps an important lesson of the Cleveland election: Bigotry cannot be defeated directly, by telling bigots that they are bigoted. For the most part Stokes learned this lesson well, accumulating as many as 30,000 white votes, nearly five times the number he received in 1965. But another slip like the one in the second debate might have cost him the election.

A few words on the voting for Stokes ward by ward, as shown in Table 2. Wards 9, 14, and 15—which gave Stokes a comparatively low vote— have the highest concentration of ethnic groups in the city. Not only is there the historical element of prejudice in these areas, but there is the ever-present fear among the residents that Negroes will invade their neighborhoods. (This fear is less a factor in ward 9, which is across the river.)

Wards 26 and 32 also gave Stokes a low percentage of votes, and these wards are also the ones most likely to have Negro migration. They are just to the north of East Cleveland, which is currently undergoing heavy transition, and to the east of ward 27, which in the past few years has changed from white to black. In these two wards, then, high ethnic composition and a fear of Negro migration would seem to account for Stokes's 19.9 and 15.3 percentages.

The highest percentage *for* Stokes in predominantly white areas was in wards 8 and 22. Ward 8 has a growing concentration of Puerto Ricans, and—according to newspaper polls—they voted heavily for Stokes. Ward 22 has a very large automobile-assembly plant that employs many Negroes. Now, in 1965 the ward was 5.7 percent Negro—a large increase from 1960. Since 1965, this percentage has probably grown another 2 or 3 percent. Therefore, if one subtracts the Negro vote that Stokes received in this ward, the size of the white vote is about the same as in other wards.

"Imminent Danger" in Gary

The race for mayor in Gary, Ind., was not overtly racist. Still, the racial issue was much less subtle than it was in Cleveland. When Democratic chairman John G. Krupa refused to support Richard D. Hatcher, the Democratic candidate, it was clear that the reason was race. When the Gary newspaper failed to give similar coverage to both candidates and sometimes failed to print news releases from Hatcher headquarters (ostensibly because press deadlines had not been met), it was clear that race was a factor.

Even though race was rarely mentioned openly, the city polarized. While Stokes had the support of the white-owned newspapers and many white campaign workers, many of Hatcher's white supporters preferred to remain in the background—in part, at least, because they feared reprisals from white racists. Hatcher didn't use the black-power slogan, but to the community the election was a contest between black and white. And when the Justice Department supported Hatcher's claim that the election board had illegally removed some 5000 Negro voters from the registration lists and added nonexistent whites, the tension in the city became so great that the governor, feeling that there was "imminent danger" of violence on election night, called up 4000 National Guardsmen.

Negroes constitute an estimated 55 percent of Gary's 180,000 residents, but white voter registration outnumbers Negroes by 2000 or 3000. Like Stokes, Hatcher—in order to win—had to pull some white votes, or have a significantly higher Negro turnout.

The voter turnout and voting patterns in Cleveland and Gary were very similar. In both cities, almost 80 percent of the registered voters turned out at the polls. In the Glen Park and Miller areas, predominantly white neighborhoods, Joseph B. Radigan—Hatcher's opponent—received more than 90 percent of the votes. In the predominantly Negro areas, Hatcher received an estimated 93 percent of the votes. In all, Hatcher received about 4000 white votes, while losing probably 1000 Negro votes, at most, to Radigan. This relatively small white vote was enough to give him victory. If Stokes's miscalculation in bringing race into the Cleveland campaign gave prejudiced whites an excuse to vote for Taft, the glaring way the Democratic Party in Gary tried to defeat Hatcher probably tipped the scales and gave Hatcher some white votes he wouldn't have received otherwise.

The School Issue in Boston

The Boston election, unlike the Cleveland and Gary elections, didn't pose a Negro against a white, but a lackluster candidate—Kevin White—against a 48-year-old grandmother who had gained national attention over the past several years for her stand against school integration. On the surface, Mrs. Hicks seems to be an obvious racial bigot. But she herself has repeatedly denied charges that she is a racist, and many who have followed her closely claim that this description is too simple.

Mrs. Hicks, perhaps more than any other public figure to emerge in recent years, reflects the complex and subtle nature of prejudice in America. Her public denial of bigotry is, in all probability, an honest expression of her self-image. But she is basically unaware of, and unwilling to become informed about, the way her views maintain the barriers of segregation and discrimination in American society. In 1963, when the N.A.A.C.P. asked the Boston School Committee to acknowledge the *de facto* segregation in the schools, she refused to review the evidence. Meeting with the N.A.A.C.P., she abruptly ended the discussion by proclaiming: "There is no *de facto* segregation in Boston's schools. Kindly proceed to educational matters." Later, when the State Board of Education presented a 132-page report on racial imbalance in Massachusetts schools, she lashed out at the report's recommendations without bothering to read it.

Mrs. Hicks, like millions of Americans, holds views on race that are born out of and perpetuated by ignorance. John Spiegel, director of Brandeis University's Lemberg Center for the Study of Violence, has summed up the preliminary report of its study of six cities:

> . . . the attitude of whites seems to be based on ignorance of or indifference to the factual basis of Negro resentment and bitterness. . . . If white populations generally had a fuller appreciation of the just grievances and overwhelming problems of Negroes in the ghetto, they would give stronger support to their city governments to promote change and to correct the circumstances which give rise to strong feelings of resentment now characteristic of ghetto populations.

Prejudice is born not only out of ignorance, but also out of fear. There is much about the Negro ghettos of poverty that causes whites, lacking objective knowledge, to be afraid, and their fear in turn reinforces their prejudice and their inability to hear out and understand the plight of the Negro in America.

In Boston, the voter turnout was heavy (71 percent) but below the turnouts in Cleveland and Gary. White accumulated 53 percent of the vote and a 12,000 plurality. Compared with Stokes and Hatcher, he had an easy victory. But considering Mrs. Hicks's lack of qualifications and the racial overtones of her campaign, Boston also experienced a massive backlash vote. Had it not been for the final days of the campaign—when she pledged, unrealistically, to raise police and firemen's salaries to $10,000 without raising taxes, and came back from Washington with "positive assurance" that nonexistent Federal monies would cover the raises—she might even have won. But throughout the campaign Mrs. Hicks repeatedly revealed her ignorance of fiscal and political matters. Mrs. Hicks had another handicap: She is a woman. The incredible fact that she ran a close race demonstrated again the hard core of prejudice and ignorance in American society.

Now let us consider the broader implications these elections will have on the racial crisis in America. To be sure, the immediate implications are quite different from what they would have been if Stokes and Hatcher had lost and Mrs. Hicks had won. If the elections had gone the other way,

Summer '68 might well have begun November 8. As Thomas Pettigrew of Harvard put it a few days before the election, "If Stokes and Hatcher lose and Mrs. Hicks wins, then I just wonder how a white man in this country could ever look a Negro in the eye and say, 'Why don't you make it the way we did, through the political system, rather than burning us down?'"

The Meaning of the Elections

But do these victories really alter the basic nature of the racial crisis? There is, true, some reason for hope. But to assume that anything has been fundamentally altered would be disastrous. First of all, it is by no means clear that these elections will pacify militant Negroes—including those in Cleveland, Gary, and Boston. In Boston, some militants were even encouraging people to vote for Mrs. Hicks—because they felt that her victory would help unify the Negro community against a well-defined foe. In Cleveland, most militants remained less than enthusiastic about the possibility of a Stokes victory. Of the militant groups, only CORE worked hard for him. In Gary alone did the candidate have the solid support of militants—probably because Hatcher refused to explicitly rebuke Stokely Carmichael and H. Rap Brown, and because his opponents repeatedly claimed that Hatcher was a black-power advocate.

If the Stokes and Hatcher victories are to represent a turning point in the racial crisis, they must deliver results. Unfortunately, Hatcher faces an unsympathetic Democratic Party and city council. Stokes has gone a long way toward healing the wounds of the bitter primary, but it remains to be seen whether he will receive eager support for his programs. Some councilmen from ethnic wards will almost certainly buck his programs for fear of alienating their constituencies.

Stokes and Hatcher themselves face a difficult and delicate situation.

Their margins of victory were so narrow that they, like Kennedy in 1960, must proceed with great caution.

Enthusiasm and promises of change are not the same as the power to implement change. And the two mayors must share power with whites.

They must demonstrate to Negroes that their presence in City Hall has made a difference. But if their programs seem too preferential toward Negroes, they run the risk of massive white resistance.

This delicate situation was clearly seen in the early days of the Stokes administration. Of his first ten appointments, only two were Negroes. Although relations with the police have been one of the most sensitive issues in the Negro ghetto, Stokes's choice for a new police chief was Michael Blackwell, a 67-year-old "hardliner." This appointment was intended to ease anxieties in the ethnic neighborhoods, but it was not popular in the Negro ghetto. Blackwell, in his first public address after being sworn in, lashed out at the Supreme Court, state laws, and "publicity-seeking clergy and beatniks" for "crippling law enforcement." Cleveland's Negroes are already beginning to wonder whether a Negro in City Hall is going to make any difference.

Some observers believe that Stokes' is basically quite conservative, and point to his sponsorship of anti-riot legislation. To be sure, Stokes's position on many issues remains uncertain, but what does seem fairly clear from his early days in office is that his efforts to gain support in white communities is going to lead to disaffection among Negroes. How much and how quickly is a difficult question.

Race relations is only one of many problems that these two new mayors must face. Stokes has inherited all of the problems that brought national attention to Cleveland last spring—poverty, urban renewal, finance, transportation, air and water pollution, and so on. Hatcher faces similar problems in Gary, and must also cope with one of the nation's worst strongholds of organized crime. If they fail, the responsibility will fall heavier on them than had a white man failed. Some whites will generalize the failures to all Negro politicians, and some Negroes will generalize the failures to the "bankruptcy" of the American political system.

Almost certainly, Washington will be a key factor in determining if these two men succeed. The national Democratic Party has a strong interest in making Stokes and Hatcher look good, for it desperately needs to recapture the disaffected Negro voters before the 1968 national election. But how much can the party deliver? The war in Vietnam is draining enormous national resources and Congress is threatening to slash poverty programs. Even if Federal monies were no problem, there is the question whether *any* of Washington's existing programs are directed at the roots of ghetto unrest. Many informed administrators, scientists, and political analysts feel they are not. And the chances for creative Federal programs seem, at this moment, fairly dim.

Another clear implication of these elections is that white resistance to change remains large and widespread. More than 90 percent of the Democrats in Cleveland who voted for a Democrat in the primary switched, in the general election, to the Republican candidate. Now, not many American cities are currently composed of as many as 35 percent Negroes; the possibility of coalitions to elect other Negro candidates appears, except in a handful of cities, remote. Additional Negro mayoral candidates are almost certain to arise, and many will go down to bitter defeat.

Stokes and Hatcher won because black-voter power coalesced with a relatively small minority of liberal whites. It was not a victory of acceptance or even tolerance of Negroes, but a numerical failure of the powers of discrimination, a failure that resulted in large part because of the massive exodus of whites from the central city. The election of Stokes and Hatcher may break down white resistance to voting for a Negro, but this is, at best, problematical. Also problematical is how bigoted whites will react to the election of a Negro mayor. Their organized efforts to resist change may intensify. As we have already indicated, the pace of white exodus from the central city of Cleveland is already alarming. And an acceleration of this pace could push the city into financial bankruptcy.

America Has Bought a Little Time

In short, while the implications of the November 7 elections are ambiguous, it does seem that the victories of Stokes and Hatcher, and the defeat of Mrs. Hicks, have kept the door open on the growing racial crisis. America has, at best, bought a little time.

On the other hand, we do not find much cause for optimism in those elections—unlike George Meany, and unlike the *New York Times*, which, five days after the election, published a glowing editorial about "the willingness of most voters today to choose men solely on personal quality and impersonal issues." To us, it would seem that the elections have only accelerated the pace of ever-rising expectations among Negroes. And if results don't follow, and rather rapidly, then we believe that the Negro community's frustration with the American political system will almost certainly heighten.

The hard task of demonstrating that Negroes can actually achieve justice and equality in America still lies ahead.

24. Mayor Stokes: The First Hundred Days

Some of the issues associated with black politics and power can be best understood by a close acquaintance with the everyday conduct and feelings of black people in office. Such familiarity tells of the special problems of black people assuming the unfamiliar roles of holders of political power and prestige. In many ways, no doubt, such problems are the same for whites occupying similar positions. On the other hand, they have a special and instructive meaning for blacks as a means of becoming acquainted with the unfamiliar, and for influencing black aspirations and expectations along one possible political course. Since this article was written, Stokes has been re-elected and is rather widely acclaimed as successfully fulfilling his mandate to blacks and whites alike.

JAMES M. NAUGHTON

It is tough to look like a national archetype when you are sitting on the edge of a white brocade sofa wearing your yellow-red-white-and-blue-striped pajamas under your red-black-and-gray-checked robe.

Carl Burton Stokes didn't. He didn't look like the cocksure, articulate Negro who, a little more than 100 days ago, became the first of his race to take possession of a big-city mayor's chair.

He could have been just another middle-class Negro lawyer, aged 40, fidgeting with a cigar and worrying about how much damage the two kids were doing to the linoleum on the basement floor with their roller skates.

He wasn't. He was the guy with the burden, the first of his kind. That meant almost more to people he had never seen and never would see—other Negroes searching more prosaically for equal opportunity—than it would ever mean to him. He had to be good.

The Carl Stokes who sat in his living room on a Sunday evening and talked about his attempt to be good at government was indeed not the same Carl Stokes who won that burden by 1,644 votes at 3:10 A.M. on Nov. 8, 1967. He was not the man with the dazzling white smile who raised his arms to quiet the crowd on that morning so recent and yet so long ago and said: "This vindicates my faith in the people . . . this is an American dream."

Dreams have a way of fading. Reality persistently bulls its way into life. It has bulled its way into the life of Mayor Stokes, and the change it has worked on him is dramatic.

From the New York Times Magazine, Feb. 25, 1968. © 1968 by The New York Times Company. Reprinted by permission.

Carl Stokes had bristled with energy. Mayor Stokes was tired. Carl Stokes had delighted in lancing opponents with spears of wit. Mayor Stokes was grave. Carl Stokes had amazed newsmen with his candor. Mayor Stokes was evasive. Carl Stokes had been supremely confident. Mayor Stokes was optimistic.

And the Carl Stokes whose inauguration was hailed around the world as a step down glory road for America's eighth largest city was faced in his home town with dwindling faith in his ability to live up to his campaign slogan: "Let's do Cleveland proud."

Cleveland wants to be proud. Yet the urgency of this desire leads it to make harsh judgments. Stokes is being judged not as just another new Democratic mayor. He is being judged as a new Negro mayor. He is under more intense scrutiny than any of his predecessors. It matters little in Cleveland that any new mayor faces problems that have crunched atop one another for much of this century without having been solved. Carl Stokes now has the responsibility of trying to solve them. Perhaps unfairly so soon in the game, black Cleveland wants and white Cleveland demands proof of progress. In 100 days, there has not been much; it is questionable whether anyone could have done much so soon.

Ask most Clevelanders and they tell it like this: less than three and a half months into his two-year term, Mayor Stokes is in trouble. He has lost two front-office aides amid scandal-bred headlines. William H. Stein, a white suburban professional who was to be the link between City Hall and the state and national administrations, was quietly persuaded to resign after having been shot in the shoulder on Christmas Eve in the home of another man's wife. Geraldine Williams, a Negro whose organizational ability helped put Stokes in office, was dropped from the staff when *The Cleveland Press* disclosed her somewhat hazy connection with a club charged with violating the liquor laws.

The cabinet that Stokes vowed would be chockablock with the most talented people around is instead a mixed bag of old and new political types, confused neophytes and a couple of outstanding professionals. The Community Development Department, which was going to unsnarl the nation's worst urban renewal maze, is just now getting a director. A holdover from the regime of former Mayor Ralph S. Locher has been staying on as Port Director until Stokes can find someone to take the job. There is nobody in charge of the Health and Welfare Department.

Stokes himself is on the receiving end of the barbs, especially for having spent 13 days out of the city—most of them in the Virgin Islands—resting from his grueling campaign and first two trying months on the job. "Jack Kennedy never took 13 days off," said a college professor. And a downtown restaurateur feigned excitement to crack: "Did you hear who's in town today? The Mayor of Cleveland!"

It was while Stokes rested in St. Thomas last month that the Geraldine

Williams case erupted. At the same time, Cleveland streets were clogged by a major snowstorm. In the midst of the furor back home, Stokes flew to New York to analyze the President's State of the Union speech on National Educational Television. Hopeful supporters figured that maybe the Mayor would come home to handle the flak. Instead, he flew back to the sun.

One young member of the Stokes administration, a political purist who worked hard to get the Mayor elected, was crushed. "The ship of state is sinking," he moaned, "and the captain isn't even here to go down with it."

A merchant telephoned *The Plain Dealer* (which endorsed Stokes even before the Democratic primary, a bold act in a race-conscious city a year after a riot) and threatened to sue if the newspaper printed one more article saying that Stokes "knows what the city's problems are." "How can he know what the problems are?" the merchant shouted into his phone. "He isn't even here!" The merchant was here, along with a $2,000 bill from a contractor for removing snow piled on the street in front of his business.

All over Cleveland the talk turned to the black man in City Hall. There were a lot of "I told you so's" from the whites who had predicted that no good would come of a Negro mayor. Worse yet, the Stokes stalwarts—housewives who had packed the kids off to a neighbor's to become volunteer envelope lickers during the campaign and lawyers who had stood amid stares from voting officials making sure that the count was honest—suffered an epidemic of infectious dismay. "The man hasn't firmed up any policy," grumbled a supporter who gave more time to the Stokes campaign for four months than he did to his job.

Negroes said they were incensed because the Mayor had fired Geraldine Williams without even talking to her first—"just like a white man would do it," said one. A social worker turned to a civic leader, a fellow Stokes campaigner, during their squash game at the Y.M.C.A. and said: "We got taken." He wasn't talking squash scores.

One of the Mayor's earliest backers said: "I'm awfully disappointed. I believed all that stuff about 'Get the city moving' and so on. I'm still convinced that Carl meant it and that he knows he's a national symbol and his success means more than just personal triumph. I don't understand what's happening."

What's happening is reality. Cleveland is a city that seldom has something to get excited about. National Football League titles are getting more elusive for the Browns. The Indians haven't come up with a winner since about the same time they beat General Custer. You can become an awful bore bragging about George Szell and the Cleveland Orchestra, and idle conversation does not often provide an opportunity to proclaim: "We're No. 1 in production of auto parts."

But—joy of life!—what a wondrous attraction you were when, after Carl Stokes took over City Hall, you popped into a bar in San Diego or Minneapolis and let it be known that you were from Cleveland. "No kiddin'?" they'd say in Cincinnati. "Howzat colored guy doin'?"

In the city itself, instant euphoria. Once again Cleveland, the town that took pride in its progressive thinking during the twenties, had something to stand for. It was first in political brotherhood. Even the bigots lay low at first. Ah, well, they said, we'll give the man a chance to show what he can do.

But Cleveland is also a town that sticks only with winners. Along came Bill Stein and a bullet, Geraldine Williams and a bar. The team's heavy hitter was on the bench in the sun. "It's the end of the inning," said a City Hall bleacherite. "No runs. No hits. Three errors."

There had been a widespread impression that, in the toughest league going, Carl Stokes was Lou Gehrig, Ted Williams, Joe DiMaggio, Babe Ruth and Bob Feller all in the same uniform. Suddenly it wasn't enough to be just Jackie Robinson in a slump.

Now Carl Stokes, that Jackie Robinson of urban politics, clad in his pajamas and robe, turns out to be human, too. "No miracles have occurred, but some progress has," he says, trying to get the fans back in the ballpark. "Anyone who expected overnight solutions has already been disappointed. But the responsible citizens—those who recognize that the entrenched, ingrained problems of 25 years of neglect are of such depth, scope and magnitude as to require months and months, years and years of attention and treatment—those responsible people are excited at the base we are building and the evidences of forward progress."

Swell. To a city thirsting for achievement it is like being lost in the Alps and coming upon a St. Bernard with a keg of Pepsi.

But, in truth, Stokes is right about the problems. For a quarter-century they have been piling up on a community that moved toward the future on tiptoe, keeping taxes down and turning its back on trouble. A dynasty of status quo mayors, begun in 1941 by Frank J. Lausche, now Ohio's senior Senator, and ended in November by the defeat of Locher, blithely ignored the danger signals noted by more progressive leaders in other cities. By the time Stokes took over, Cleveland had suffered a Negro riot in 1966; it was the lone big city to lose its Federal renewal funds for lack of progress; whites were skittering to the suburbs, choking off the development of the central city; municipal checks were in danger of coming back from the bank marked "not sufficient funds," and, for a clincher, somebody noted that Cleveland's Cuyahoga River is so polluted it may be the only body of water in the world that's a fire hazard.

With that kind of backdrop, it was foolish to expect any substantial progress in the new Mayor's first 100 days. But Stokes himself contributed to the rising expectations with campaign statements like this one on urban renewal:

"We don't need a lot of expensive new surveys, studies, reports and committees. What we need is action. Immediate action!"

Campaigner Stokes repeatedly vowed to "slash the red tape, knock down the barriers, flash the green light" for urban renewal.

Instead of producing immediate action and green lights, Stokes has named a five-man task force to try to straighten out the Community Development Department and win back Washington's confidence . . . and money. It may make political waves. For 15 years, the urban-renewal bureaucracy in Cleveland has been a dumping ground for political hacks. Councilmen and others who owed patronage would pay off with a spot in urban renewal. After all, Uncle Sam was helping provide the paychecks there.

How quickly can Stokes hope to clean out the hacks? Within a few more weeks, he says, the task force will have some progress to report, and he adds: "Is four months too long to wait, compared with 15 years of inaction?"

Stokes feels that there has been some forward movement in downtown development, though he notes that it is not the sort of "sexy stuff you fellows like to write about." The sexless accomplishments include the groundbreaking for a downtown bank's new building (this required getting Federal approval, which the Locher Administration had been unable to secure, for a renewal-plan change) and the settlement of a Locher regime feud with a developer. The peace treaty opens the way for another new office structure and may lead to the city's first new luxury hotel in 50 years.

A more critical shortage in Cleveland's renewal plan has been low-income and middle-income housing. By working quietly, "not on the front pages," Stokes thinks he's getting some momentum built up there, too. But so far it is limited to getting Ernest Bohn, the grandfather of American public housing, to retire from his longtime post as Executive Director of the Cleveland Metropolitan Housing Authority and putting on the authority's board some members who'll be more inclined than Bohn and his colleagues were to accelerate housing programs.

The Mayor set himself up for other falls. He said so often on the campaign trail that he would rush to Washington to see the President and to Columbus to meet Gov. James A. Rhodes, a Republican, that there was a widespread impression that he'd be coming back with loaded Brink's vans. So far, Stokes has received little visible aid from either capital.

And, in another sense, capital is what Stokes sorely needs right now. It will have to be raised locally; in the process Stokes is breaking a campaign pledge. The Mayor told the electorate that he would hike neither property nor income taxes during his two-year term. The way it turned out, property, no; income, yes. A Little Hoover Commission named by Stokes recommended meeting the threat of fiscal doom and a $95,000 budget deficit inherited from Locher with a rise in the rate of the one-half of 1 percent city income tax. Coming at a time when, nationally, guns are more plentiful than butter (indeed, the latter seems more like oleo), when inflation is sure to be 1968 campaign fodder, and when people are tinkering with Form 1040, higher taxes are not going to be too popular.

City employees are demanding more pay, and every new cop puts an added strain on the budget. Stokes wants to beef up his force of housing inspectors to help halt residential decay; they, too, will cost money. And money, it turns out, is in short supply. Fifteen percent of Cleveland's $76.9-million operating budget comes from income taxes and 53 percent from property taxes. The rest of the revenue comes from such sources as estate taxes and a split of the Cuyahoga County Local Government Fund, which are either unpredictable or unlikely to grow. With nearly 77 percent of the city's expenses tied up in wages and wages sure to go up, Stokes must turn to either property or income taxes for help. He has turned to the income tax.

All Stokes can do is blame his predecessor, whose Finance Director was noted for padding the budget with a million bucks here or there. Stokes figured to find at least a few hundred thousand stashed in the 1967 budget. It wasn't there. Now Stokes is dealing in semantics to explain the higher taxes, saying that it was the Little Hoover Commission, not the Mayor, that wanted the increase. "They're an independent commission," he says. But it is up to the Mayor to put their recommendations into effect. As Stokes has finally conceded: "I'm not going to permit a campaign promise—based on information which proved to be inaccurate—to stand in the way of the needs of the city."

Another sour post-election note is the Mayor's inability to settle a protracted strike at privately owned St. Luke's Hospital. Nonprofessional workers—most of them Negroes—hit the bricks in April in a demand for union recognition. Hospital trustees refused to meet with the union to talk terms, and Stokes pledged to use the Mayor's prestige to bring the two sides together. He hasn't been able to do so. Now the Mayor is seeking unprecedented municipal labor legislation to force the hospital to recognize the union. Even if it is enacted, chances are that it will be tied up in court for a long while.

Then there was the matter of the defense procurement contract. Stokes told a Puerto Rican audience during the campaign that he would announce, within days of his inauguration, a Federal contract to an unnamed Cleveland industry. It would mean defense jobs and a Federal grant to underwrite schooling to provide the unemployed with skills to man the assembly lines. Stokes said the Cleveland project had been cleared by authority as high as Vice President Humphrey. Perhaps that wasn't high enough. The project hasn't been announced.

Stokes promised during the campaign to put more policemen on the streets to combat mounting crime, and he has. By rearranging some sections of his police department, the Mayor has added 225 men to basic patrol duty. In the process, though, morale in the department has plummeted. There is resentment because of shifts in assignments. Worse, there is a simmering feud between Safety Director Joseph McManamon and Police Chief Michael J. Blackwell, both of whom are Stokes appointees. The new Safety Director wants to make even more wholesale changes in departmental structure. Blackwell is resisting. He leaks tidbits to newsmen about disgruntled police executives, telling reporters to attribute them to "authoritative sources." He says privately that he has threatened several times to resign. It is questionable how much good even the added cops have done. Bookies still operate on Short Vincent Avenue, three blocks from the Mayor's office. Prostitutes are still in business despite an announced crackdown and complaints from ghetto clergymen. Booze still is poured after hours and on supposedly dry Sundays. A relative of a man who is reputed to be one of Cleveland's biggest numbers game operators is a Stokes appointee on a city commission.

Other areas offer more hope. A city-county port authority, long urged by newspapers and businessmen, has been established under the leadership of Stokes, though he was in the Virgin Islands when City Council enacted the enabling legislation. Councilmen were distressed, in fact, that nobody dickered for their votes. They're used to trading support on key legislation for municipal green stamps—promises of street repaving here, playground improvement there. Stokes should remember, after five years as a state representative, how political horse trading works. If he doesn't, he is in for trouble.

Council leaders want to cooperate with Stokes. If he tries, the Mayor can get along with the 33 legislators, 11 of whom are Negroes. But Stokes partisans keep whispering that Council President James V. Stanton, who would give a case of 86 proof Tullamore Dew on St. Patrick's Day to be Mayor, is masterminding a plot to make Stokes look bad.

Actually, Stanton has confessed privately that he no longer has any hope of making it to the Mayor's chair. If Stokes sets a pattern for progress in the next two years he will be unbeatable. If the Mayor falls on his political face, Stanton will share the blame. Either way, he can't get elected. So he is running now for Congress. And Stanton bluntly told Democratic colleagues at a Council caucus: "We've got to go as far as we can, short of political suicide, to cooperate with the administration." He advised white councilmen that their cooperation would wring more out of the Stokes administration than that of their Negro counterparts because "Stokes has the Negro vote, but he has to build for the future with your constituents."

One area in which Stokes clearly has built for the future is improved relations between City Hall and the Cleveland power élite. Mayor Locher regarded businessmen, especially those in private utilities, as wolves huffing and puffing to blow down the municipal house. Expansion-minded industry got little cooperation in trimming bureaucratic red tape. Conservative for starters, the business types hedged on investing in Cleveland. Now they are welcome in the Mayor's office and are talking of projects that long were in limbo.

If Stokes swings with the moneyed men, he may not with those at the opposite end of the social scale. Not yet, at least. To be sure, he has named a blue-ribbon commission to inquire into the welfare situation, and he raised $130,000 to clothe poor kids by charging admission to his inaugural ball. But life in the Cleveland ghetto is every bit as depressing as it was when Stokes grew up there.

Militant Negroes are not overly impressed with the reply Stokes gives to inquiries about any debt he might owe them: "Of course I owe them a debt—good government and equal opportunity."

The attitude is typical of Stokes. His civil rights associations have been with the moderate organizations, the Urban League, the N.A.A.C.P., even the white-dominated Cleveland Welfare Federation. Says one black firebrand: "Hunh. The whites just let him have the job. Now they're going to cut him up."

The same firebrands lay low last summer, when Stokes was on the ballot. This lent credence to the theory that a Negro mayor would help Cleveland avoid the long hot summers plaguing white mayors all over the nation. Now not everyone is so sure of that. "It won't make a damn bit of difference whether the Mayor is Locher or Stokes," says a Negro working to cool off ghetto hotheads. "If the city blows up, it won't be because of the militants. It'll be because conditions in the ghetto are the same now as they always have been."

Stokes plans to establish a new cabinet-level Department of Human Resources. But another Negro working in the ghetto complains: "We can't get the administration to do even some of the little visible things—cleaning the streets, leveling the lots where houses have been torn down, putting trash containers on the street corners. They say these are superficial things. But, hell, they're things the people can see."

Ironically, Stokes seems to be headed for an embarrassing year politically because Cleveland Negroes finally have something Stokes long has advocated, a chance to elect a Negro Congressman. When the Ohio Legislature completed Congressional redistricting in January, the 21st District in Cleveland ended up about 65 percent Negro. A scramble is on among Negro politicians for the job, and it is tearing the Stokes political machine to pieces.

Councilman George L. Forbes, a Democrat who thought he had a promise of support from Stokes in the district, now finds that one of those seeking the party nomination is the Mayor's brother, Louis Stokes, a leading Cleveland defense lawyer. Forbes appears to have been written off; he is not happy about it. And who else has popped into the crowded primary field? Geraldine Williams, complete with much of the campaign organization that put Mayor Stokes where he is. So far, the Mayor has tried to stay out of the Congressional situation.

Indeed, Stokes may have little more direct contact at present with the Negro community than driving through it on his way home at night. For that matter, he does little of the socializing and ribbon-cutting that many people, white and black, expect of a mayor.

"You have to make a choice," he says. "If you take up the social aspect of the position you're not going to be able to meet the requirements of the job. As pleasing as it may be to be the center of attraction at a social gathering, you have to establish the priorities, I think, of getting about the job."

For Stokes, the priorities have meant closeting himself in his office. Except for his junket to the Virgin Islands, he has spent 14 and 16 hours a day at his desk, seeming almost afraid that someone else might take over if he left to make a speech.

He sits in the majestic, wood-paneled office, hunched over papers on the massive desk or, when someone is with him, leaning back in the leather-bound swivel chair trying to keep a conversation going. It is not easy. An aide comes in with a routine query. Stokes wrinkles his brow, shoots back an answer and asks his guest what it was they were talking about. The telephone rings. Stokes handles the business involved on the phone and gets stuck exchanging pleasantries. He shrugs his shoulders, a sign to the guest that he wishes the phone conversation could end. It drags on. Stokes squeezes his forehead between his thumb and middle finger. He sighs when, finally, he hangs up the phone, out of sight beneath his desktop. It is a constant battle to focus on one thing at a time, and most of the focusing is done in secluded Room 221 of City Hall.

When Stokes does get out of the office for a civic luncheon or the dedication of a ghetto housing project started by his predecessor, he travels alone in the city's 1966 black Lincoln, escorted only by his city detective-driver. His wife, Shirley, a pretty and charming woman, stays at home with their son, Carl, Jr., and daughter, Cordi. She has no desire to be a public personality.

The risks Stokes takes in not getting out more are great. Clevelanders have grown accustomed to having their mayors among them—chatting in Hungarian at a Sunday-afternoon picnic, eating Polish sausage at a church social or sucking at a schooner of beer during a political rally. Stokes thrived on such confrontations during the campaign, saying that in meeting people he got the kind of emotional boost necessary to carry him through a grinding quest for their approval.

Stokes has that rare ability to stand before a hostile audience and charm it. But he has not used it much as Mayor. And he must. A Negro mayor in a city two-thirds white has got to mingle with the white masses from time to time, bolster their belief in his impartiality and give them a few examples of his engaging wit. He feels that he has little enough time for reviving the city; he can't go parading about telling jokes.

The underlying cause of much of Stokes's early difficulties may well be a do-gooder who revamped the city's charter in the nineteen-thirties. At that time it was considered essential to avoid the pitfalls of a lame-duck mayor. So the charter revisionists gave the outgoing mayor six days to pack his bags. Stokes had to assume office Nov. 13, allowing him barely enough time to catch his breath after the campaign that ended Nov. 7.

"The greatest problem I personally have had to face," he says, "is having to take office the Monday following election and be immediately beset by the accumulated problems, about which little or nothing had been done, while at the same time reorganizing the government."

Leaping immediately into the maelstrom of municipal madness, Stokes had no time to assemble a cabinet, no time to reflect about priorities, no time to set about making alliances.

Neither did the staff he was able to come up with. It is an obvious drawback. No mayor can function effectively unless he has around him competent and streetwise people who can assume much of his responsibility: handing out patronage; touching bases with City Council; deciding who ought to see the Mayor and who should deal with the administrative assistants; following up orders to department heads. Stokes had in his front office only two people with backgrounds suiting them to those tasks —Bill Stein and Geraldine Williams. Now he is left with a lackluster collection of governmental novices.

Finance Director Dorward C. Witzke, a management consultant who was the full-time staff man for Mayor Locher's Little Hoover Commission, has offended councilmen with his standoffish manner. Others feel he was a poor choice because of what they see as his erroneous impression that all government needs to be successful is to adopt corporate management techniques. Indeed, Witzke's final report to the Little Hoover Commission recommended that the city create a deputy mayor. Among his reasons: "One of the major elements of administration is decision-making. A lawyer in practice does not make decisions. He gives opinions." Stokes, like most mayors before him, is a lawyer.

Because Polish-Americans make up the city's biggest ethnic bloc, Stokes picked as his Utilities Director 29-year-old Ben S. Stefanski II, whose father is president of the Polish community's biggest savings and loan association. Aside from paying his utility bills, Stefanski has no technical preparation for the job.

To make political hay with another major ethnic community, Stokes promoted Locher's Commissioner of Printing, Andy Dono, to staff assistant. Now Dono draws close to $300 a week for little more than representing the Mayor at Hungarian meetings and translating daily editions of the Hungarian-language newspaper *Szabadsag,* which endorsed Stokes after he won the primary.

Meanwhile, at least two hotshots from Locher's staff who were willing to work for Stokes have given up and quit. Airports Commissioner John A. Doyle resigned in anger after learning that negotiations with airlines for new rates to pay for airport expansion were going on without him. It was an apparent snub, and another one followed. When 600 community leaders took part in a luncheon honoring Doyle for his contribution to Cleveland aviation, Stokes was scheduled to sit at the speakers' table. He did not appear, nor did he send a substitute.

Howard Bruce, a budget analyst who compiled for Stokes a list of the Locher departmental heads who are protected by civil service and a memorandum on why some were and others weren't working hard, became disillusioned with the lack of change under Stokes. He left for a job in Washington, telling a friend: "I don't think the Stokes people really want to do a job. The hell with it."

Stokes has learned that it is not easy to get or keep the people who have the capacity to do the job. For one thing, the city's anachronistic salary scale is not very inviting to someone who would have to leave a corporate hierarchy, perhaps never to return. The mayor himself gets only $25,000 a year, and there are few jobs under him that rate $15,000.

Stokes confided to one newsman that he was stymied by salary limitations in his search for a director of human relations. Checks with assistant administrators in similar departments elsewhere indicated that the going rate for an assistant was about $22,000. Even for the top man in Cleveland the Mayor had only $20,000 to offer.

It has been demoralizing, too, for Stokes to discover that all those talented people who got him where he is are content now to sit back and read the newspapers to find out how he's doing. "People not only thought that once they elected Carl Stokes the problems would be solved," says Carl Stokes. "They also went home. The many good, concerned people who provided the needed thrust, advice and aid and assistance during the campaign—many or most of whom had never been involved in a political campaign—then went back to their normal pursuits. They didn't recognize the need was as great, if not greater, for them to remain to help implement that which they had managed to win in the election."

Much of Stokes's time so far seems to have been spent trying to talk people into joining him. Even those whose commitment during the campaign was like that of a college kid to his guru have failed to accept the challenge to help Stokes make a go of government. After 10 days of trying to persuade one of them to take Stein's place in the administration, Stokes asked: "Why is it all those people who encouraged me to run are content now to sit on the sidelines? Why can't they make the same personal sacrifice I have?" Maybe, he muses, they would not be so reluctant if he had a four-year term.

Despite their reluctance to join Stokes in the obscure thickets of City Hall, most Clevelanders—even those griping about the way things have gone thus far—truly hope that the first Negro mayor of a major American city will be a success. Negroes especially are praying for better days. As one Negro leader put it: "Every Negro sees himself in Stokes. If Stokes fails, every Negro fails." When the snow was piled up on Cleveland streets, Negro councilmen were besieged by constituents, but not one of them stood up to protest at their next meeting. "Do you think I would get up there and give our Mayor hell?" asked one.

The newspapers have been cozier with Stokes than with any previous administrator. Locher's foibles were blasted regularly, in some cases in full-page editorials in *The Plain Dealer*. But editorially *The Plain Dealer* and *The Press* have refrained from sniping at Stokes in the hope that he will set his house in order.

Most of those in positions to criticize seem to realize that Stokes means as much to the nation as to Cleveland. He is a symbol, just like apple pie and mom. "You don't see many editorials against apple pie and mom," said one newsman.

Stokes recognizes this, too. He admits that the case against Geraldine Williams is flimsy. She contends that she severed her association with the 32d Cedar Club, which was cited by Ohio liquor enforcement agents for serving drinks to nonmembers and after hours. Her position is backed up by a notary who said she did not sign an application for renewal of the liquor license and by her ex-husband, the licensee, although a handwriting expert says her signature is on the application.

Stokes, a former police prosecutor and defense lawyer, was asked why he did not stand up for Miss Williams if he believed she had a defense. His answer: "This administration is one that has ramifications far beyond Carl Stokes personally. I am not permitted to react just from what I would personally want to do or, were it not for the uniqueness of my own election, would have to do. After all, we know in Boston they had Irish mayors elected in jail. The facts of life are this is one of the burdens I must carry."

There is no more dramatic illustration of Cleveland's craving for Stokes's success than the reticence of the man who would have most to gain from a Stokes failure. Seth Chase Taft, the patrician grandson of President William Howard Taft and the man who came closer to winning the mayoralty than any other Republican in a quarter-century, is unswerving in his determination to give Stokes an equal opportunity to produce. Short of noting that the "general level of cabinet appointments is disappointing," Taft's public remarks have been limited to a suggestion that the

Mayor take a look at Taft's plan to restructure city government. Recognizing that government and business both want Stokes to succeed, Taft states simply: "I, too, have participated in this. After all, I have a stake in this city."

So, it seems, has the nation.

"Carl means so much, so much," said a friend of the Mayor, shaking his head. "I still feel there's time to save the ship from going on the reef, but I don't know how the hell it can be done."

One hundred days. A benchmark of sorts. A starting point. A taste of the total. Now, for Stokes, for Cleveland and perhaps for many people whose hopes for the future are riding on the man in the striped pajamas and checked robe, there is only one answer. Stokes knows what it is:

"To the extent that I do produce, faith will be restored.

"But the importance of it is that I cannot do this alone."

25. The Search for New Forms

Carmichael and Hamilton remind us that the election and appointment of a few blacks to high political office does not resolve the problem of adequate and meaningful political representation by blacks. There remain the questions of raising unpopular issues and making unpopular policy choices, that is, issues and choices which are in the interest of the black community but which have been alien to white officeholders. Black control of the economic, educational, and political life of black communities is one such set of issues. This is the directional course which relevant black politics must take, according to the authors. This passage raises crucial questions which must be answered by black strategists—questions of integration and separation of the races. It challenges the assumption that integration and black equality are possible at this time.

STOKELY CARMICHAEL AND CHARLES V. HAMILTON

We are aware that it has become commonplace to pinpoint and describe the ills of our urban ghettos. The social, political and economic problems are so acute that even a casual observer cannot fail to see that something is wrong. While description is plentiful, however, there remains a blatant timidity about what to *do* to solve the problems.

Neither rain nor endless "definitive," costly reports nor stop-gap measures will even approach a solution to the explosive situation in the nation's ghettos. This country cannot begin to solve the problems of the ghettos as long as it continues to hang on to outmoded structures and institutions. A political party system that seeks only to "manage conflict" and hope for the best will not be able to serve a growing body of alienated black people. An educational system which, year after year, continues to cripple hundreds of thousands of black children must be replaced by wholly new mechanisms of control and management. We must begin to think and operate in terms of entirely new and substantially different forms of expression.

It is crystal clear that the initiative for such changes will have to come from the black community. We cannot expect white America to begin to move forcefully on these problems unless and until black America begins

From *Black Power* (1967), pp. 164–177; reprinted by permission of Vintage Books.

to move. This means that black people must organize themselves without regard for what is traditionally acceptable, precisely because the traditional approaches have failed. It means that black people must make demands without regard to their initial "respectability," precisely because "respectable" demands have not been sufficient.

The northern urban ghettos are in many ways different from the black-belt South, but in neither area will substantial change come about until black people organize independently to exert power. As noted in earlier chapters, black people already have the voting potential to control the politics of entire southern counties. Given maximum registration of blacks, there are more than 110 counties where black people could outvote the white racists. These people should concentrate on forming independent political parties and not waste time trying to reform or convert the racist parties. In the North, it is no less important that independent groups be formed. It has been clearly shown that when black people attempt to get within one of the two major parties in the cities, they become co-opted and their interests are shunted to the background. They become expendable.

We must begin to think of the black community as a base of organization to control institutions in that community. Control of the ghetto schools must be taken out of the hands of "professionals," most of whom have long since demonstrated their insensitivity to the needs and problems of the black child. These "experts" bring with them middle-class biases, unsuitable techniques and materials; these are, at best, dysfunctional and at worst destructive. A recent study of New York schools reveals that the New York school system is run by thirty people—school supervisors, deputy and assistant superintendents and examiners. The study concluded: "Public education policy has become the province of the professional bureaucrat, with the tragic result that the status quo, suffering from many difficulties, is the order of the day." [1] Virtually no attention is paid to the wishes and demands of the parents, especially the black parents. This is totally unacceptable.

Black parents should seek as their goal the actual control of the public schools in their community: hiring and firing of teachers, selection of teaching materials, determination of standards, etc. This can be done with a committee of teachers. The traditional, irrelevant "See Dick, See Jane, Run Dick, Run Jane, White House, Nice Farm" nonsense must be ended. The principals and as many teachers as possible of the ghetto schools should be black. The children will be able to see their kind in positions of leadership and authority. It should never occur to anyone that a brand new school can be built in the heart of the black community and then given a white person to head it. The fact is that in this day and time, it is crucial that race be taken into account in determining policy of this sort. Some people will, again, view this as "reverse segregation" or as "racism."

It is not. It is emphasizing race in a positive way: not to subordinate or rule over others but to overcome the effects of centuries in which race has been used to the detriment of the black man.

The story of I.S. 201 in New York City is a case in point. In 1958, the city's Board of Education announced that it would build a special $5-million school in District 4, whose pupils are ninety percent black, eight percent Puerto Rican, with the remaining two percent white. The concept was that students from elementary schools in that district would feed into the new school at the fifth grade and after the eighth grade would move on to high school. This concept, at least according to official policy, was supposed to speed integration.

The parents of children who might be attending the school mobilized in an attempt, once and for all, to have a school adequate for the needs of Harlem. The Board had picked the site for I.S. 201: between 127th and 128th Streets, from Madison Avenue to Park Avenue—in the heart of Central Harlem. The parents argued against this location because they wanted an integrated school, which would be impossible unless it was located on the fringes, not in the heart, of Central Harlem. Their desire clearly points up the colonial relationship of blacks and whites in the city; they knew the only way to get quality education was to have white pupils in the school.

The Board of Education indicated that the school would be integrated, but the parents knew it could not be done and they demonstrated against the site during construction. When they saw that the school would have no windows, they also raised the question of whether this was merely a stylistic or practical innovation, or a means of closing out the reality of the community from the pupils for the hours they would be inside.

During the spring and summer of 1966, some six hundred pupils registered at I.S. 201—all of them black or Puerto Rican. Their parents then threatened that if the school wasn't integrated by fall, they would boycott it. The Board of Education, giving lip service to the parents, passed out and mailed 10,000 leaflets to the white community—in June!

Needless to say, few people go to a school on the basis of a leaflet received while getting off the subway or wherever, and even fewer (white) people want to send their children to school in Harlem. The request for "volunteers" had no effect, and on September 7, the Board of Education finally admitted its "apparent inability to integrate the school." It was the inability of that class . . . "whose primary interest is to secure objects for service, management, and control," the objects in this case being the mothers of I.S. 201. Threatened by a boycott, the school was not opened as scheduled on September 12, 1966.

At this point, the parents—who were picketing—moved in the only way they could: to demand some form of control which would enable them to break out of the old colonial pattern. In view of the fact that whites would not send their children to the school, one parent stated, "we decided we would have to have a voice to ensure that we got quality education segregated-style. We wanted built-in assurances." The parents knew that within a few years, given that pattern, this new school would be like all others which started with fine facilities and deteriorated under an indifferent bureaucracy. The parents' demands thus shifted from integration to control.

On September 16, Superintendent Bernard E. Donovan offered them a voice in screening and recommending candidates for supervisory and teaching positions at the school. An East Harlem community council would be set up with a strong voice in school affairs. The parents also wanted some control over the curriculum, the career guidance system, and financial matters, which the Board deemed legally impossible. Shortly afterward, the white principal—Stanley Lisser—voluntarily requested transfer. A black principal had been one of the parents' key demands. With these two developments, the parents announced that they would send their children to school.

At this point (September 19), however, the United Federation of Teachers bolted. The teachers at I.S. 201 threatened to boycott if Lisser did not stay. Within twenty-four hours, the Board had rescinded its agreement and restored Lisser. (It is contended by many that this was the result of planned collusion between the Board and the U.F.T.) Nine days late, the school opened. The parents became divided; some gladly began sending their children to school while others did the same because they were unaware that the agreement had been rescinded.

The parents' negotiating committee had moved to get outside help, while the city's top administrators, including Mayor Lindsay, entered the picture. A Harlem committee representing parents and community leaders proposed on September 29 that I.S. 201 be put under a special "operations board" composed of four parents and four university educators with another member selected by those eight. This board would pass on the selection of teachers and supervisors, and evaluate the curriculum at I.S. 201 as well as three elementary or "feeder" schools. But the U.F.T. attacked this proposal. As the struggle dragged on, it became clear that once again efforts by the community to deal with its problems had been laid waste.

Later, in October, the Board of Education offered the parents a take-it-or-leave-it proposal. It proposed a council of parents and teachers that would be purely advisory. The parents flatly rejected this. Father Vincent Resta, a Catholic priest and chairman of the local school board which covered I.S. 201, stated, "In theory the Board's proposal is something that could work. But an advisory role implies trust. And this community has absolutely no reason to trust the Board of Education." The local board later resigned en masse.

But the issue of community control did not end there. It had become clear to the parents that their problems were not restricted to School District 4. When the Board of Education met to discuss its proposed budget in December, 1966, I.S. 201 parents and others came to protest the allocation of resources. Unable to get any response, at the end of one session they simply moved from the gallery into the chairs of those meeting and elected a People's Board of Education. After forty-eight hours, they were arrested and removed but continued to meet in another location, with the Rev. Milton A. Galamison—who had led school boycotts previously in New York City—as President.

At one of its executive sessions on January 8, 1967, the People's Board adopted a motion which stated its goals as:

1) To seek to alter the structure of the school system . . . so it is responsible to our individual community needs, in order to achieve real community control. This may require legislative or state constitutional convention action. This means, of course, decentralization, accountability, meaningful citizen participation, etc.

2) To develop a program which will get grassroots awareness for, understanding of, and support for the goal stated above. It is suggested that we give top priority to organizing and educating parents and citizens in the poverty areas (approximately 14).

3) That we recognize that power should not rest in any central board, including our own, and that by every means possible we should encourage the development and initiative of local people's groups.

The parents at I.S. 201 failed because they are still powerless. But they succeeded in heating up the situation to the point where the dominant society will have to make certain choices. It is clear that black people are concerned about the type of education their children receive; many more people can be activated by a demonstrated ability to achieve results. One result has already been achieved by the I.S. 201 struggle: the concept of community control has now rooted itself in the consciousness of many black people. Such control has long been accepted in smaller communities, particularly white suburban areas. No longer is it "white folks' business" only. Ultimately, community-controlled schools could organize an independent school board (like the "People's Board of Education") for the total black community. Such an innovation would permit the parents and the school to develop a much closer relationship and to begin attacking the problems of the ghetto in a communal, realistic way.

The tenements of the ghetto represent another target of high priority. Tenants in buildings should form cohesive organizations—unions—to act in their common interest vis-à-vis the absentee slumlord. Obviously, rents should be withheld if the owner does not provide adequate services and decent facilities. But more importantly, the black community should set as a prime goal the policy of having the owner's rights forfeited if he does not make repairs: forfeited and turned over to the black organization, which would not only manage the property but own it outright. The absentee slumlord is perpetuating a socially detrimental condition, and he should not be allowed to hide behind the rubric of property rights. The black community must insist that the goal of human rights take precedent over property rights, and back up that insistence in ways which will make it in the self-interest of the white society to act morally. Behavior—in this case, the misuse of property—can be regulated to any extent the power structure wishes. No one should be naïve enough to think that an owner will give up his property easily, but the black community, properly organized and mobilized, could apply pressure that would make him choose between the alternatives of forfeiture or compliance. Thousands of black people refusing to pay rents month after month in the ghettos could have more than a salutary effect on public policy.

. . . Virtually all of the money earned by merchants and exploiters of the black ghetto leaves those communities. Properly organized black groups should seek to establish a community rebate plan. The black people in a given community would organize and refuse to do business with any merchant who did not agree to "reinvest," say, forty to fifty percent of his net profit in the indigenous community. This contribution could take many forms: providing additional jobs for black people, donating scholarship funds for students, supporting certain types of community organizations. An agreement would be reached between the merchants and the black consumers. If a merchant wants customers from a black community, he must be made to understand that he has to contribute to that community. If he chooses not to do so, he will not be patronized, and the end result will be *no* profits from that community. Contractors who seek to do business in the black community would also be made to understand that they face a boycott if they do not donate to the black community.

Such a community rebate plan will require careful organization and tight discipline on the part of the black people. But it is possible, and has in fact already been put into effect by some ethnic communities. White America realizes the market in the black community; black America must begin to realize the potential of that market.

Under the present institutional arrangements, no one should think that the mere election of a few black people to local or national office will solve the problem of political representation. There are now ten black people on the City Council in Chicago, but there are not more than two or three (out of the total of fifty) who will speak out forcefully. The fact is that the present political institutions are not geared to giving the black minority an effective voice. Two needs arise from this.

First, it is important that the black communities in these northern ghettos form independent party groups to elect their own choices to office when and where they can. It should not be assumed that "you cannot beat City Hall." It has been done, as evidenced by the 1967 aldermanic elections in one of the tightest machine cities in the country: Chicago. In the Sixth Ward, an independent black candidate, Sammy Rayner, defeated an incumbent, machine-backed black alderman. Rayner first ran in 1963 and missed a run-off by a mere 177 votes. He then challenged Congressman William L. Dawson in 1964 and lost, but he was building an image in the black community as one who could and would speak out. The black people were getting the message. In 1967, when he ran against the machine incumbent for the City Council, he won handily. Precincts in the East Woodlawn area that he had failed to carry in 1963 (23 out of 26), he now carried (19 out of 26). The difference was continuous, hard, day-to-day, door-to-door campaigning. His campaign manager, Philip Smith, stated: "Another key to Sammy's victory was the fact that he began to methodically get himself around the Sixth Ward. Making the black club functions, attending youth meetings and all the functions that were dear to the hearts of Sixth Ward people became the order of the day." [2]

The cynics will say that Rayner will be just one voice, unable to accomplish anything unless he buckles under to the Daley machine. Let us be very clear: we do not endorse Rayner nor are we blind to the problems he faces. It is the job of the machine to crush such men or to co-opt them before they grow in numbers and power. At the same time, men like Rayner are useful only so long as they speak to the community's broad needs; . . . black visibility is not Black Power. If Rayner does not remain true to his constituents, then they should dislodge him as decisively as they did his predecessor. This establishes the principle that the black politician must first be responsive to his constituents, not to the white machine. The problem then is to resist the forces which would crush or co-opt while building community strength so that more of such men can be elected and compelled to act in the community's interest.

(It should be noted that Rayner is one of numerous black leaders who have rejected the term Black Power although their own statements, attitudes and programs suggest that they endorse what we mean by Black Power. The reason for this, by and large, is a fear of offending the powers-that-be which may go by the name of "tactics." This again exemplifies the need to raise the level of consciousness, to create a new consciousness among black people.)

The very least which Sammy Rayner can give the black community is a new political dignity. His victory will begin to establish the *habit* of saying "No" to the downtown bosses. In the same way that the black Southerner had to assert himself and say "No" to those who did not want him to register to vote, now the northern black voter must begin to defy those who would control his vote. This very act of defiance threatens the status quo, because there is no predicting its ultimate outcome. Those black voters, then *accustomed* to acting independently, could eventually swing their votes one way or the other—but always for *their* benefit. Smith signaled this when he said: "The disbelievers who felt that you could not beat City Hall are now whistling a different tune. The victory of Sammy Rayner in the Sixth Ward should serve as a beacon light for all who believe in independent politics in this city. . . . Rayner is going to be responsible for the aldermanic position taking on a new line of dignity. Black people are going to be able to point with pride to this man, who firmly believes that we need statesmanlike leadership instead of the goats-manship we have been exposed to." [3]

Let no one protest that this type of politics is naïve or childish or fails to understand the "rules of the game." The price of going along with the "regulars" is too high to pay for the so-called benefits received. The rewards of independence can be considerable. It is too soon to say precisely where this new spirit of independence could take us. New forms may lead to a new political force. Hopefully, this force might move to create new national and local political parties—or, more accurately, the first *legitimate* political parties. Some have spoken of a "third party" or "third political force." But from the viewpoint of community needs and popular participation, no existing force or party in this country has ever been relevant. A force which is relevant would therefore be a first—something truly new.

The second implication of the political dilemma facing black people is that ultimately they may have to spearhead a drive to revamp completely the present institutions of representation. If the Rayners are continually outvoted, if the grievances of the black community continue to be overlooked, then it will become necessary to devise wholly new forms of local political representation. There is nothing sacred about the system of electing candidates to serve as aldermen, councilmen, etc., by wards or districts. Geographical representation is not inherently right. Perhaps political interests have to be represented in some entirely different manner —such as community-parent control of schools, unions of tenants, unions of welfare recipients actually taking an official role in running the welfare departments. If political institutions do not meet the needs of the people, if the people finally believe that those institutions do not express their own values, then those institutions must be discarded. It is wasteful and inefficient, not to mention unjust, to continue imposing old forms and ways of doing things on a people who no longer view those forms and ways as functional.

We see independent politics (after the fashion of a Rayner candidacy) as the first step toward implementing something new. Voting year after year for the traditional party and its silent representatives gets the black community nowhere; voters then get their own candidates, but these may become frustrated by the power and organization of the machines. The next logical step is to demand more meaningful structures, forms and ways of dealing with longstanding problems.

We see this as the potential power of the ghettos. In a real sense, it is similar to what is taking place in the South: the move in the direction of independent politics—and from there, the move toward the development of wholly new political institutions. If these proposals also sound impractical, utopian, then we ask: what other real alternatives exist? There are none; the choice lies between a genuinely new approach and maintaining the brutalizing, destructive, violence-breeding life of the ghettos as they exist today. From the viewpoint of black people, that is no choice.

NOTES

1. Marilyn Gittell, "Participants and Participation: A Study of School Policy in New York City," New York: The Center for Urban Education. As quoted in the *New York Times,* April 30, 1967, p. E90.
2. Philip Smith, "Politics as I See It," *The Citizen,* Chicago (March 22, 1967).
3. *Ibid.*

26. The Negro in Politics

Wilson questions a black political strategy that would solidify white political opposition. He emphasizes the need for "coalition" politics rather than for an all-black political party such as the Freedom Democratic Party in Mississippi. Furthermore, he presents a sober cautionary note. The structure of American politics and the nature of the Negro community, he suggests, may severely limit the possibility of accomplishing the goals of the Negro community. This raises the serious question of whether or not black politics should be addressed to inherently limited gains through coalitions or to longer-range basic change in American political structure and in the Negro community itself. In either case black-white alliances would be necessary; however, these two alternative developmental options require radically different priorities among white groups with which alliances would be made. But this issue goes beyond Wilson's very thoughtful article.

JAMES Q. WILSON

Perhaps the best way to understand the political position of the American Negro today is to compare what some Negroes are asking of politics with what politics seems capable of providing. I mean here politics in the narrower sense—the competitive struggle for elective office and deliberate attempts to influence the substance of government decisions—and not, in the broadest sense, as any activity by which conflict over goals is carried on. Although something is sacrificed by limiting the definition (rent strikes, boycotts, and sit-ins may have consequences for office-holders and legislation), the sacrifice is necessary if we are to understand what is meant by the statement that the civil rights movement, and Negro protest generally, ought to become a *political* movement. Bayard Rustin, in a recent issue of *Commentary*, has put the argument in its most succinct and lucid form in an article significantly entitled, "From Protest to Politics: The Future of the Civil Rights Movement." [1] Briefly, Rustin argues that the problems of the Negro cannot be solved by granting him even the fullest civil rights, for it is his fundamental social and economic conditions, more than his legal privileges, which must be changed. Such changes, in the magnitudes necessary, require radical—indeed, revolution-

From Lawrence H. Fuchs, ed., *American Ethnic Politics* (1968), pp. 217–246; reprinted by permission of Harper & Row.

ary—programs in education, housing, and income redistribution; these programs, in turn, will be attained only by an organized radical political coalition of Negroes, trade unions, church groups, and white liberals.

Those who remember the political currents of the 1930's may smile wanly at the call today for a Negro-labor alliance. When the call was issued thirty years ago, few responded. In the South, the Negro was almost entirely disfranchised; in the North, he was politically unorganized except by a few (largely Republican) big-city machines. Everywhere, Negroes —including the miniscule leadership class—were effectively excluded from almost all the institutions of American life. Negroes had nothing and attempted little. It was probably fortunate for A. Philip Randolph that he was not required to deliver on his threat of a massive march on Washington in 1941. In their most charitable mood, even the more radical trade union leaders saw Negroes as a group which could produce (perhaps worthy) demands but not votes or money or influence; less generously, they viewed Negroes as scabs and strike-breakers.

Apparently, enough has changed since to suggest that a reappraisal may be in order. The Negro electorate has grown greatly in both North and South. It is estimated (no one knows) that as many as six million Negroes were registered in 1964, about a third of whom were in the South. In most of the large cities where these voters are to be found, there is no political machine; in the typical case, leadership is competitive, uncontrolled, sometimes demagogic but just as often responsible, and to an increasing extent aggressive. A massive and impressive march on Washington has occurred. The proliferation and vigor of civil rights organizations suggest that expectations are rising more rapidly than achievements; the national leaders of these groups have become the spokesmen of the American Negro, virtually eclipsing elective officials. Among these men, all shades of radical (as well as moderate) opinion can be found, accompanied, as one might expect, by a passionate concern for distinguishing subtle (and sometimes vague) sectarian differences. And in 1964, the Negroes gave President Johnson an unprecedented 94 percent of their vote (according to an estimate by the Gallup Poll). Perhaps these changes are sufficient to make the Negroes ready for an effective and liberal coalition.

While there is little doubt that Negro voters will continue to exert a liberalizing influence on American politics, the possibility of a stable, organized liberal—to say nothing of radical—coalition is, I believe, slight. Furthermore, attempts to fashion one may be dangerous unless it is a very loose and *ad hoc* arrangement. The Negro is already a partner in a set of tacit, though unorganized, coalitions; they are probably the only viable ones but they are certainly not radical ones. To break existing alliances, tenuous though they are, in favor of a new alliance which may be impossible of realization may be a costly experiment. This is particularly true in the South; it is to a lesser extent true in the North.

I. The Negro Voter in the South

A useful oversimplification is that, in the South, the enemy of the Negro is the lower- and lower-middle-class, particularly rural, white; and the ally of the Negro is the upper-middle-class, particularly urban, white. Since Reconstruction, the Bourbons and the Populists have engaged in intermittent political warfare; occasionally the Negro has been used—particularly in the last two decades of the nineteenth century—as an ally of one white class against the other, while at other times—particularly in the first half of the twentieth century—he has been disfranchised in order to prevent him from being allied with either class. The political suppression of the Negro did not, as C. Vann Woodward makes clear, occur immediately after the withdrawal of Union troops but only after the white community, divided along class lines, discovered that the competitive wooing of Negro votes created a politically unstable situation best resolved by eliminating the Negro vote—and thus the Republican party—and bringing the white majority into the dominant Democratic party.[2]

But the Negro is no longer disfranchised, except in Black Belt counties; probably one-third of the potential Negro vote has been registered, and more gains can be anticipated. Negroes of voting age constitute one-fifth of the adult population of the eleven Southern states but less than one-twelfth of the registered Southern voters. If another 570,000 Negroes can be added to registration rolls now estimated to contain nearly two million Negroes, half the potential Negro voters will be eligible. In those areas where the Negro vote is already significant, the politics of a "Second Reconstruction" seem to be emerging—with the important difference that the Negro may no longer be disfranchised if competition for his vote proves unsettling.

Negroes, when they vote, can cause a startling change in the style, if not the substance, of Southern politics. Segregationists will have to choose between abandoning race-baiting as a political tactic or getting out of politics. (The prospect of large numbers of politicians quitting politics—especially in the South, where politicians are shrewd and politics is a way of life—seems, to say the least, remote.) And politicians who are by nature inclined to entertain sympathetically legitimate Negro demands will be encouraged to entertain them publicly. For example, Rep. Charles L. Weltner, Democrat of Georgia, voted against the 1964 Civil Rights Act when it first came before the House in February, 1964. By July, however, when the bill came back from the conference committee for final passage, he had changed his mind and voted in favor of it. It does not detract from the moral quality of Weltner's bold action to note that between the two crucial votes the governor of Georgia signed into law a bill to redistrict the state's congressional seats in a manner that substantially increased the proportion of enfranchised Negroes and decreased the proportion of lower middle-class whites in Weltner's district.[3]

In the past, at least, neither political party could take the Southern Negro vote for granted. A majority of their votes twice went to Dwight Eisenhower and frequently were cast for Republican candidates in such cities as Atlanta and Louisville. In 1960, many—though not all—Southern Negro precincts voted for President Kennedy; in 1964, almost all of them supported President Johnson.

The independence—which, to the politician, can mean only uncertainty —of the Southern Negro vote has various causes. One, of course, is that the Southern Democratic party has so conspicuously been the enemy, its candidates in all but a few cases outbidding each other in defending segregation. Another is that the issue confronting the Southern Negro in many elections is clear and dramatic: which white candidate scores lowest on the segregation scale, this being, for the Negro, the only important scale. Unstable politics is here the result of single-issue politics. A third reason is that potential Negro political leaders, being largely excluded from an active role in both the majority party and the increasingly "lily-white" Republican minority party, have not been co-opted by the system. Negro politicians, without permanent organizational commitments to white leaders, have been free to deliver Negro votes to whichever candidate or party seemed most attractive in each election. Where the Negro leader was corrupt, he delivered the vote in exchange for tangible considerations; [4] where honest, in exchange for intangible concessions. [5] Negro politics in the South has yet to be professionalized, and thus the distinction—commonplace in the North—between the (usually moderate) party hierarchy and the (often militant) civic and "race" leadership has not become widespread.

To say that the Southern Negro political leadership is unprofessional does not mean that it is either unskillful or unsuccessful. In those cities or counties where the Negro voter is neither terrorized nor apathetic, he is capable of voting with almost incredible unanimity and precision, at least for the most visible offices. When Ivan Allen, Jr., ran against Lester Maddox in 1961 for mayor of Atlanta, Negro Precinct Seven-D gave Allen 2,003 votes, or 99.9 percent of the total, and Maddox 4 votes. Since there were five white voters living in the precinct, it is quite likely that Allen got *all* of the Negro votes—an almost unbelievable feat of organization and communication, especially when one recalls that Allen was a wealthy white businessman who was scarcely an all-out integrationist. [6] The single-issue politics of the South has produced a form of political behavior among Negroes and whites which is highly rationalistic and extraordinarily sophisticated. [7] Voters become exceptionally sensitive to almost imperceptible differences in the positions candidates take, publicly or privately, on "The Issue" and go to considerable lengths to conceal group preferences lest premature revelation prove counterproductive.

In the South, more than anywhere else, a deliberate balance of power politics may be practiced in which viable coalitions may be formed. The most important and most successful example of this is what might be called the Atlanta Coalition. Formed in the 1950's by Mayor (now "Mayor Emeritus") William B. Hartsfield and continued by Mayor Ivan Allen, Jr., it is, stripped to its essentials, a tacit alliance between upper-middle-class whites and Negroes against lower-middle-class whites. In even blunter terms, the Bourbons and the Negroes have voted together to exclude the rednecks from power in the city. There are, of course, strains in the alliance. The more militant Negroes are restless with the leadership of the Atlanta Negro Voters' League and with what they regard as the insufficient progress in race relations under Hartsfield and Allen. White businessmen, in turn, often feel the mayor has gone too far, as when Allen testified before Congress in favor of the elimination of segregation in public accommodations. Furthermore, it is not clear that every Southern city could put together such a coalition even if it wanted to do so. Some cities have lost their Bourbons to the suburbs (Atlanta carefully annexes all upper-income suburbs and avoids annexing any working-class suburbs) while others have a business leadership that is composed of small shopkeepers rather than a commercial and industrial elite concerned with establishing the city as a great regional center.[8] And in some cities, such as New Orleans, the Negroes themselves have been unable to create a stable and effective political organization representative of all elements of the community.[9]

Whatever the limitations or difficulties, however, there can be little doubt that the natural ally of the Southern Negro, for the foreseeable future, is the cosmopolitan white bourgeoisie.[10] In part, this reflects self-interest: race conflict is bad for business, destructive of property, and productive of unfavorable national publicity. In part, it reflects an enlarged conception of the common interest: Negroes have a moral right to vote, to be free from arbitrary arrest, and to be protected from official abuse, even if century-old prejudices require that the Negro not live next door to whites. The issues now being pressed by the Negro in the South make the most fundamental claims of elementary justice; when the claims of simple justice are reinforced by self-interest, the potential for effective action is great. But this white ally has little interest in a massive redistribution of income, the nationalization of political authority, or the re-ordering of society.

In the Black Belt, where Negroes outnumber whites, such alliances are hard to create. In Mississippi there seem to be no allies whatsoever. It is precisely in such areas that a more radical Negro politics is emerging, though it is still so apocalyptic in its vision and unrealistic in its methods that it can point to little progress. The Freedom Democratic party won a great victory at the Democratic National Convention in Atlantic City, but the radical leadership which now appears to influence it not only rejected that convention's seating compromise but seems intent on rejecting all compromises with what, to it, is an essentially corrupt and hypocritical society. Given the massive, unyielding, and violent nature of white resistance to Negro demands in many Black Belt counties, it is not hard to understand some of the attitudes of the increasingly radical Negro political leadership. Early and measured accommodation to Negro political demands has, in many Southern cities, led to the emergence of relatively moderate Negro leaders and of a Negro strategy emphasizing limited objectives. But the Black Belt has not, except in a few cases, made concessions—in part because Negroes there are in the majority and in part because such largely rural or small-town areas lack a white upper class of sufficient size and strength to challenge white extremists.

There are some Black Belt counties where Negroes can and do vote, but ironically the gains that have accrued to them from politics in these areas are less than the gains from politics in areas where Negroes are a minority but where social and economic conditions are more favorable to political organization, articulation of demands, and bargaining over changes in the welfare or status of Negroes. Where Negro voting has occurred in the Black Belt, it has meant (in general) the cessation of police abuse and administrative discrimination, the appointment of Negroes to certain government positions, and higher expenditures on public facilities in Negro neighborhoods.[11] It has rarely meant general integration of schools or public accommodations or new public works programs to improve Negro living conditions. The financial resources and community tolerance for such efforts simply do not exist. White voters do not even approve such projects for themselves. By contrast, in some of the highly urbanized areas where Negroes vote but are in a distinct minority, a combination of factors —the availability of tax resources, a well-organized white political structure with which bargains can be struck, and a large and self-sufficient Negro leadership class—makes it easier to translate votes into substantive gains.

All this suggests that the substantive, rather than psychological, consequences of Negro voting in Black Belt counties are not likely to be so great as the diehard white resistance might imply. The resistance itself, however, should it continue for long, may change this significantly. When the social, economic, and political demands of a group are linked with a protracted and bitter struggle for the franchise, the members of that group are more likely to acquire a permanent sense of political identity and a more intense commitment to the goals of the group than would be the case if substantive goals were asserted long after the franchise had been won. (One of the reasons—there are many—that no socialist or labor party developed among American workers may be that their major economic demands were made long after the franchise had been acquired without a struggle.)[12] The campaign for the vote now developing among Southern

Negroes is likely to have profound effects on subsequent Negro political organization and tactics, for the campaign can generate morale, a sense of unity (the vote is a wholly instrumental objective that permits otherwise competing leaders to submerge their differences), and an independence from traditional party loyalties.

Discussion, in such states as Mississippi, of the possibility of a Negro political party suggests one alternative—in my judgment, a disastrous one —to the pattern of coalition politics now being practiced outside the Black Belt. For the Negro vote to be (potentially) the marginal vote, it is not enough that it be an uncommitted vote. Since Negroes in every Southern state are a minority (although in some states a very large one), it is also necessary that the white vote be divided. In such states as Georgia and North Carolina, the Negro vote can be the marginal vote—both because white votes are divided along party or factional lines and because the Negro vote is not an automatic expression of traditional party loyalties. Within the Black Belt, not only must the franchise be won for the Negro, but some way must be found of dividing the white vote. This is not the case in Mississippi, where in a clear choice Barry Goldwater defeated Lyndon Johnson by winning an incredible 87 percent of the vote. In Table 1, the present and potential Negro vote is shown for each Southern state. In the first column is the percentage of registered voters who, in 1964, were estimated (by the Voter Education Project) to be Negro; in the second column is the percentage of all voting-age persons who in 1960 were Negro. If *all* adults, Negro and white, voted, this last figure would be the "Negro vote." If every Negro in Mississippi had voted in 1964, Goldwater would still have won; in other states, the Negro's need for allies is even greater.

Dividing the white vote will not be easy under the best of circumstances, but it is not likely to be easier if Negro political strategists either elect to form a separate party or emphasize objectives which draw closer the white cosmopolitan elite and white lower-middle-class extremists. Continued Negro pressure, with federal assistance, for the franchise and for the observance of constitutional and legislative guarantees will ultimately divide the opposition; broadening Negro demands at this time to include more radical objectives may unite it. This may be an expression of the willingness on the part of the bourgeoisie to support demands for *liberty* (the franchise, legal justice, and equal access to public facilities) but to oppose demands for *equality* (the elimination of intergroup differences in income, occupation, and place of residence). Negro-white coalitions in the South, where they exist at all, are by and large libertarian rather than egalitarian in purpose.

The history of one such coalition—or rather sequence of coalitions—is illuminating. Described by Donald Matthews and James Prothro in their forthcoming book on Southern Negro politics, the events took place in a city which the authors call "Urbania." [13] A thriving commercial center in the Piedmont region, the city has a cosmopolitan white business elite as well as a strong Negro middle class and a unionized industrial labor force. As early as 1935, a Negro political organization was formed (at a meeting held at the Negro Tennis Club!); by the 1940's, a coalition of Negroes with white liberals and union leaders had been formed that was strong enough to capture the county Democratic organization. The alliance, never a firm one, was successful as long as it had limited political objectives. After the 1954 Supreme Court school desegregation decision, however, strains developed. Because of the defection of white workers, the

TABLE 1. THE SOUTHERN NEGRO VOTE, PRESENT AND POTENTIAL

State	Percentage of All Registered Voters Who Are Negro (April, 1964)	Percentage of All Voting-Age Persons Who Are Negro (1960)
Alabama	5.7%	26.2%
Arkansas	7.7	18.5
Florida	7.8	15.2
Georgia	9.9	25.4
Louisiana	9.0	28.5
Mississippi	2.4	36.0
North Carolina	9.7	21.5
South Carolina	10.5	30.6
Tennessee	10.1	15.0
Texas	6.8	11.7
Virginia	5.2	18.9
The South	7.7	20.0

coalition lost control of the party by 1958; nonetheless—and this may be suggestive of the emerging pattern of Southern politics—the mayor remained sympathetic to the Negro demands and he and other city officials worked openly, before and after the tense months of the 1963–1964 protest demonstrations, to integrate public facilities and private businesses. This policy of accommodation apparently was in part the result of the attitude of the white business elite, part (but not all) of which was sufficiently cosmopolitan to favor whatever degree of integration was necessary to avoid a "bad business climate" or unfavorable national repercussions. It was not, on the other hand, in favor of the liberal economic policies of the early labor-Negro coalition. In Urbania, the Negroes found unionized white workers the appropriate allies when political power was the object; when progress on certain libertarian issues (here, school desegregation) was at stake, the labor alliance collapsed and the support of white businessmen became important.

Coalition politics is important not only because of the need for allies, but also because of the problem of motivating Negro voters. As a result of their low socioeconomic position, getting Negroes to register and vote even after all administrative barriers have collapsed can be very difficult. (In 1959, Southern urban Negroes had a median income less than *half* that of Southern urban whites.) Surprisingly high voter participation can be obtained, however, when the contest is important *and the Negro vote may decide the outcome.* In the Allen-Maddox election in Atlanta, for example, 80 percent of the registered voters in nine predominantly Negro precincts turned out to vote; by comparison, only 69 percent of the registered voters in ten predominantly lower-income white precincts voted.[14] (Negroes participate less than whites in elections for offices less visible than mayor; they also register in slightly smaller proportions.) Although there is no direct evidence on this, it seems likely that the remarkably high Negro voter turnout in cities like Atlanta might be much lower if the candidate supported by Negroes had no chance of winning— as would be the case if he did not have the backing of a substantial bloc of white voters.

II. The Negro Voter in the North

It is in the North that politics as conventionally practiced seems less relevant to the needs of the Negro. This may appear paradoxical, given the great importance attached to the Northern urban Negro vote in influencing contests for President, governor, and senator. It is of course true that the Negro is concentrated in areas of high strategic significance for statewide or national political candidates. The Negro vote for President Kennedy was, in several Northern industrial states, greater than the margin by which Kennedy carried those states. The same, however, can be said for the Jewish vote, the Catholic vote, and the labor vote. With so many apparently marginal votes cast, a President might be forgiven if he allowed himself to be paralyzed by the competing demands of their spokesmen. (For some time it appeared that President Kennedy was in exactly this position, but he responded to Negro protests which began in the spring of 1963 with a vigorous affirmation of the moral rights of Negroes—becoming not only the first President to have said this, but perhaps the first to have believed it.) In Congress, the Negro vote is likely to have a much greater long-run effect in the South than in the North. Over *half* of all Southern congressional districts in 1963 had a population that was one-fifth or more Negro. In the North and West, by contrast, fewer than one-twelfth of the districts had so high a proportion of Negroes.

Furthermore, the civil rights legislation so far enacted has been directed primarily at remedying discrimination against the Negro in the South—in voting, public accommodations, and the like. To the extent that Negro political influence in the North contributed to the passage of these bills, it was influence wielded on behalf of Southern Negroes and as part of a much larger liberal coalition in which religious organizations played an exceptionally important role.[15] Further legislative progress on behalf of Southern Negroes is still possible; the question, however, is what progress can be made on behalf of Northern Negroes and what political tactics should be used.

The utility of politics to the Northern Negro is limited for a variety of reasons. First, his traditional party loyalties are strong and thus his vote, particularly in general elections, is less likely to be uncertain. There are some obvious exceptions to this pattern, of course. In cities such as Boston, where party organization is almost nonexistent and where an attractive Negro candidate can be found in the Republican party, Negroes will cross party lines in very large numbers. (Edward Brooke, the Negro Republican Attorney General of Massachusetts, carried Negro precincts by margins of ten to one at the same time that Democrat Lyndon Johnson was carrying these precincts by margins of fifty to one.) In most of the largest Northern cities, however, the only question surrounding the Negro vote in partisan elections is its size rather than its direction.

Second, the major issues confronting the mass of Northern Negroes are economic and cultural rather than political or legal. Rustin is entirely correct in saying that "at issue, after all, is not *civil rights*, strictly speaking, but social and economic conditions." [16] The paradox is two-fold. On the one hand, American political institutions provide no way for the organized political pressure of a particular disadvantaged group to re-shape in any fundamental sense social and economic conditions. Whereas the identity and political obligations of a sheriff or a governor can pro-foundly affect the lives of Negroes in the South by determining whether or how they will be intimidated or harassed, the election of a public official in the North rarely has any direct or obvious consequences for the average Negro voter. (It is *because* it makes so little difference, of course, that Northern party leaders have found it relatively easy to instill traditional party commitments in Negroes. A simple decision rule—such as "vote Democratic"—is more economical, for both the party and the voter, than the kind of elaborate and subtle group interest calculations that occur where, as in the South, the outcome *is* important.)

That is not to say that it makes no difference which party or faction controls the White House or Congress. The probability of there being certain kinds of redistributionist and welfare programs enacted does de-pend on election outcomes, but not in a way that makes it possible for any particular voting bloc to hold any particular public official responsible for such programs. Such considerations ought to be borne in mind when one evaluates assertions about the "alienation" of the urban voter, particularly the low-income Negro. That politics seems irrelevant to their daily preoccupations is not necessarily an expression of neurotic withdrawal or separateness but may well be the rational conclusion of a reasonably well-informed citizen.

The other paradoxical element is that, when major programs *are* launched to deal with basic social and economic conditions, they are likely to be the product of a political coalition in which the persons whose lives are to be changed play a relatively small role. The recent federal programs to deal with delinquency, poverty, and housing were assembled by bureaucrats, professors, and White House politicians. The most dramatic of these—the "war on poverty"—did not come about, as Daniel Patrick Moynihan makes clear, as the result of any great upsurge of popular demand.[17] Nor were these programs aimed explicitly at the "Negro problem." Indeed, it might have been much harder to get them adopted if they had been defined as "Negro programs." (In fact, some of these programs —particularly the antipoverty program—were in part intended by many of their supporters, probably including the President, to dampen the civil rights "revolution" by improving the material condition of Negroes.) At the local level, public expenditures for the benefit of the poor are often authorized in local referenda elections in which the civic leadership as well as a substantial portion of the votes comes from upper-class whites who join with lower-class Negroes to secure the adoption of measures which, if they were national rather than local matters, these whites would oppose.[18] Rich suburbanites will favor free medical care for the indigent if the issue is stated in terms of building a new county hospital and is voted on locally but not if the issue is called "socialized medicine" and is voted on in Washington.

All this suggests that the Negro is in need not of a single grand alliance, but of many different and often conflicting alliances which take into account the different bases of support available for different kinds of issues. Nationally, organized labor may support civil rights and income-transfer measures but locally it is often likely to support (at least tacitly) segregated housing and economy in government. Religious groups are very effective when the issue is voting rights; they are much less effective in dealing with economic questions where simple morality is not at issue. Upper-class businessmen may support Negro voting claims in Southern cities and Negro-oriented public works programs in Northern cities, but nationally they will oppose large-scale income redistribution. A grand Negro-liberal coalition, if achieved, may so rationalize these inconsistent positions as to deliver the leadership of would-be allies into the hands of those elements who are least in favor of (or least effective on behalf of) Negro causes. Nowhere are these problems better seen than in the relationship between Negro and white workers in our major industrial cities.

While it may be true that Negroes and whites have a common interest in ending unemployment, improving housing and education, and resisting technological displacement, a stable and enduring alliance to attain these objectives will not be easily achieved. The only major political mechanism by which poor whites and Negroes have in the past been brought into alliance—the big-city machine—is collapsing; except for a few large industrial unions, no substitute has yet appeared.

Only Philadelphia and Chicago, of the larger Northern cities, have strong city-wide machines (that is, political parties based on the distribution of material rewards). In these areas, Negro and white political leaders are paid to work together, albeit for very limited objectives; Negro and white voters, in turn, are induced by door-to-door persuasion to vote together, particularly in primaries.[19] Such organizations cannot endure much longer, for the resources at their command are diminishing. When they collapse, Negro political leadership will fall into the hands of men who can find effective substitutes for organization: personal charisma and bellicose militancy (such as that of Adam Clayton Powell in New York or Cecil Moore in Philadelphia), expertise in factional manipulation and strategic alliances (such as that of J. Raymond Jones in New York), or successful appeals to middle-class white voters and white political leaders (such as that of Edward Brooke in Massachusetts or Augustus Hawkins in Los Angeles).[20] Yet to emerge, but certain to come, are Negro political leaders who will obtain their major support from the more militant civil rights organizations. In only a very few cases does there seem to be much likelihood of organized political coalition between white and Negro workers similar to that found from time to time in Detroit. The United Auto Workers, and to a lesser extent the United Steel Workers, have, through the political action of integrated locals, elected carefully balanced tickets of Negro and white politicians.

Even under UAW leadership, the Negro-white workers' coalition has been subject to tensions. The most important of these has been the necessity of emphasizing economic objectives that do not require social reorganization (such as integrated housing) close to home. The UAW cannot deliver votes of white workers for liberal mayors or those of Negro workers for conservative mayors without great difficulty. Furthermore, the coalition was created in a period of rising demand for workers; how it will function when Negroes and whites are competing for a decreasing number of jobs remains to be seen. (The fact that the locals are integrated and that an elaborate code of seniority rules has been devised may help reduce what might otherwise be a starkly racial conflict over jobs.) Finally, no one should allow himself the comfort of believing that President Johnson's massive victory over Barry Goldwater disproves the existence of strong anti-Negro sentiments among many white Northern Democratic voters. At most it suggests that, faced with a complex political decision involving issues of foreign relations, economic policy, and welfare programs as well as civil rights, the white worker decided that peace and security were, under the circumstances, more important than registering a protest against Negro claims.

The area in which this latent conflict between Negro claims and white resistance is most likely to erupt is that of public safety and administration of criminal justice. It is one of the few issues (schools are another) in the North over which a clear political contest can be waged. The police are highly sensitive to the explicit and implicit directives of local elective officials; unlike economic issues, a political victory here can have direct and immediate—although perhaps not drastic—consequences for Negroes. The white concern over "violence in the streets" and unchecked criminality is not (as critics of Goldwater charged) simply a rhetorical mask for opposition to civil rights demonstrations or even for anti-Negro sentiment (though it involves a significant element of this). Polls taken by both parties during the campaign suggest that Johnson was never able to meet this issue effectively; perhaps a majority of voters thought Goldwater was best able to handle this problem.[21] For the Negroes, the issue of "police brutality" and police corruption is probably the single most effective appeal for the mobilization of mass Negro protest activity, particularly among rank-and-file lower-income Negroes. Many middle-class Negroes will, of course, admit privately that they, too, would like to see the police check criminal behavior among lower-class Negroes, but it is becoming increasingly difficult for them to say this publicly.

What is remarkable is that so few candidates for mayor or governor are openly exploiting white fears of crime, particularly Negro crime. In part this is because too many of them must face Negro voters who would immediately interpret such views as anti-Negro prejudice even if, in fact, prejudice had nothing to do with it. And in part this is because there is a deep and general distrust of the police among upper-middle-class whites, particularly white liberals, such that it is often better politics to be "anti-cop" than "anti-Negro." On this issue, even more than on the issue of income redistribution, the natural Northern ally of the Negro is the white liberal.

It is, of course, fashionable today to attack the "white liberal" as hypocritical on civil rights issues. After all, he is likely to live in a "lily-white" suburb, attend a "lily-white" church, and perhaps teach in a university with no Negroes on its faculty. And the white liberal, in the eyes of Negro radicals, makes the fatal error of believing that meaningful change can be accomplished within the present political, social, and economic system. By accepting the system, he accepts the necessity of compromise, and compromise is seen as both morally wrong and practically unworkable.

All this misses the point, which is that the white liberal is, in the North, one of the Negro's *only* significant allies in a situation in which allies are essential. He is not and cannot be an all-purpose ally, however. The upper-class business or professional man is a more useful ally in the South where, by halting and nervous steps, his support is being mobilized to achieve voting rights and end police abuse; he is also a more useful ally in the North when the issue is legitimating a local public welfare program. The principal value of the white liberal, on the other hand, is to supply the votes and the political pressures (increasingly mobilized through religious organizations) that make it almost suicidal for an important Northern politician openly to court anti-Negro sentiment.

The alliance, however, is as much tacit as explicit. If Negroes increasingly distrust liberals (because they are both ideologically suspect and rivals for power), liberals have had difficulty finding Negroes who have both a genuine mass following and a commitment to what the liberals regard as appropriate means and ends. The hoped-for alliance in Manhattan between liberal Democratic reform clubs and Harlem political leaders has not materialized to any degree.[22] The most popular Negro leader in Philadelphia, Cecil Moore, is regarded with incredulous disdain by white liberals. Negro machine politicians, such as William Dawson of Chicago, are rejected by both those middle-class Negroes and those middle-class whites whose commitment to social change exceeds their faith in the Democratic party leadership.[23] Negroes, such as Edward Brooke, whom white liberals find attractive are usually prevented by their position (that is, being responsive to a largely white constituency) from being in the visible forefront of civil rights campaigns. The cause of most of this unrequited love is that the Negro has come of age politically at a time when not only machines are collapsing, but the whole lower-class style of politics—the politics of friendships, trades, patronage, and neighborhood localism—is falling into disrepute. Negroes are expected to climb a political ladder which, as a result of several decades of successful reform efforts, is now missing most of its rungs. For whites, vaulting to the top is easy—television is one way; converting an established business or civic reputation into appointive and elective office is another. But the Negro community lacks the business and civic infrastructure which is necessary to convert private success into public office. Enough money has yet to be earned by enough Negroes to produce a significant precipitate of Negro civic statesmen.

Negroes know this and therefore are demanding that economic differences between Negroes and whites be eliminated. If the white liberal reformer is to be allowed to abolish the system by which political and economic progress was once made, then he must (many Negroes argue) replace it with something better. The Negro demand for economic equality is no longer, as Nathan Glazer points out, simply a demand for equal opportunity; it is a demand for equality of economic *results*.[24] American politics has for long been accustomed to dealing with ethnic demands for recognition, power, and opportunity; it has never had to face a serious demand for equal economic shares. Thus, in the North as well as the South the principal race issue may become a conflict between liberty and equality. This may be the issue which will distinguish the white liberal from the white radical: the former will work for liberty and equal opportunity, the latter for equal shares. This distinction adds yet another complication to the uneasy liberal-Negro alliance.

If the alliance is hard to sustain today, it will be subject to even greater strains in the future. The Northern Negro community, lacking a single clear objective and a well-organized and unified leadership, will continue to be volatile. Protest demonstrations will reveal less discipline than those in the South, and the likelihood of violence will be greater. The church simply does not have the importance to the Northern Negro that it does to the Southern, nor are the targets in the North so visible as those in the South. The Negro riots of the summers of 1964 and 1965 in Harlem, Rochester, Chicago, Brooklyn, Los Angeles, and elsewhere were not in any obvious sense "race" riots (that is, riots of Negroes against whites in protest against claimed injustices) or the outgrowth of civil rights demonstrations. But whatever their cause (simple hooliganism was an important element), their lesson for genuine civil rights demonstrations is clear: there is always a potential for violence, particularly when the demonstration is as much against indifference as against injustice.

That the movement is badly organized, understaffed, and threatened by violence does not mean it is ineffective. As other sources of power decline in strength, the power of the civil rights organizations increases. It is not yet possible for them to *elect* candidates, even in all-Negro districts, to many significant offices, but it is entirely possible for them to *prevent* someone else from being elected, even in heavily white districts. In most Northern cities, there are now a small number of Negro civil rights leaders whose reputation is such that their concerted opposition to a Negro candidate would prevent his election. They are often strong enough to hurt the chances of white candidates by casting on them (rightly or wrongly) an "anti-civil-rights" label which will be the kiss of death for white liberal (and even not-so-liberal) voters. As one Negro leader in Boston, a hopelessly unorganized city, told me recently, "We are entering a new political era of guerrilla warfare in which the lack of organization and discipline will not be nearly so important as the possibility of well-placed sniping at the enemy."

Competition to get the pro-civil-rights label (or, more accurately, to avoid getting the anti-civil-rights label) will become more intense. The 1964 presidential campaign may well have facilitated this process by involving Negroes in unprecedented numbers both as voters and as campaigners. The intense opposition to Goldwater resulted in Negroes registering as Democrats in overwhelming proportions in both North and South. The Democratic National Committee mobilized ministers, barbers, beauticians, and other strategically placed Negroes as volunteer campaigners. Nationally known civil rights leaders, particularly Martin Luther King, toured the country giving ostensibly "nonpartisan" speeches, urging Negroes to vote but not telling them whom to vote for (that was hardly necessary). Only time will tell what effect Goldwater will have on Negro political loyalties (particularly in the South, where they have been in doubt) and on the number and style of Negro political activists. It is possible, though far from certain, that 1964 will have fixed Negro political loyalties in the same way that Al Smith in 1928 and Franklin D. Roosevelt in 1936 fixed white loyalties and will bring into politics a new cadre of Negro leaders just as 1952 and 1956 brought in new white cadres. Regardless of whom the Republicans nominate, the Democrats will be running against Goldwater for the next twenty years.

Apart from building fires under politicians, there remains the question of what Negro (or Negro-white liberal) politics can accomplish. Simply electing more Negroes to public office will make some difference, for politics depends as much as anything on communication. Groups not in a position to know in time cannot act in time; protest as a strategy is better suited to *blocking* change than to initiating it, and this requires a good intelligence network. There are already an estimated 280 Negroes holding elective offices, including 6 congressmen and 90 state legislators.[25] And as Negroes rise in seniority in various legislative systems, they will acquire power with which to bargain. (For better or worse, Representative Adam Clayton Powell, as chairman of the House Committee on Education and Labor, is an astute bargainer perfectly prepared to trade a concession on a bill favoring organized labor for a concession by labor on a matter of interest to Negroes.) Furthermore, the greater and more direct involvement of the federal government in the affairs of cities and metropolitan areas under circumstances which require that federal authorities not visibly deny the precept of equal justice for all means that Negroes, through injunctive procedures as well as political pressure, will be able to compel changes in the administration of local programs in schools, housing, and the like as a precondition to receiving the growing volume of federal aid.[26]

In those areas where elective officials administer and are directly responsible for programs affecting the lives of Negroes, Negro voting strength will, of course, be important. One such area is the administration of justice. In the South, the impact of Negro enfranchisement on these practices could be revolutionary; even in the North, Negro political power can significantly constrain mayors and police chiefs. (The mayor of Detroit, Jerome Cavanaugh, attracted widespread—and possibly decisive—Negro electoral support because of Negro discontent with Detroit police practices under the previous administration; immediately upon assuming office, Cavanaugh replaced the police commissioner and supported efforts to alter police behavior in Negro neighborhoods.) Education is another area where elected officials can sometimes be held accountable to the voters. But here the Negro voters face a paradox: in cities (such as New York) where Negroes are sufficiently numerous to be taken seriously by politicians, they are also so numerous as to make a solution to the problems of racial imbalance or low standards in the public schools very hard to find. Where (as in Boston) Negroes are sufficiently few in number to make solutions possible (at least in principle), they are also so few as to be a relatively inconsequential political force.

Negroes, in short, will increasingly be able to play marginalist politics. But this approach rarely produces wholesale or fundamental changes in the life chances of large numbers of people. Some Negro (and white) leaders, recognizing the limitations of conventional politics, are suggesting new forms of organization. One of these is the power-oriented neighborhood association, exemplified by The Woodlawn Organization (TWO) in Chicago.[27] Such groups mobilize Negroes (or lower-income voters generally) by defining and dramatizing adverse local conditions which are the result of the indifference or hostility of outside forces, such as the city administration or nonresident white businessmen. Relying on indigenous leadership, the organization mounts a neighborhood protest against the outside "enemies"; by blocking proposed changes or by effectively challenging current programs, the group acquires the power to bargain with outsiders, especially city politicians and administrators. Demands are made and enforced concerning the appropriate kinds and levels of city services to be provided in the area.

The key to this strategy is the effort to build an indigenous political organization which is not part of the city-wide political apparatus and thus is not subject to its constraints. The plan is to fill the vacuum created by the decay of the ward organization of city-wide machines by substituting a nonpartisan but power-oriented civic association which seeks to provide collective rather than divisible benefits (such as patronage) for its members and followers. Since it trades in general rather than individual benefits, the civic association must find new ways to motivate its members; it does so by relying on a combative ideology. There are at least two major problems with this strategy, however. First, the resources with which to sustain such an organization are very scarce. It obviously cannot rely on government or business support (although the recent history of New York's Mobilization for Youth, patterned in many ways on the TWO model, suggests that at least in the immediate future it may be possible to use government funds—such as federal antipoverty or antidelinquency money—to launch organizations aimed at challenging government policies). Foundation and philanthropic support is available (TWO was begun in this way), but such support depends on the programs of the action groups being consistent with what middle-class white liberals who operate foundations will tolerate. In short, it depends on a Negro-liberal white alliance.

The second problem is that it may prove difficult to generalize such a strategy. Building a coalition of several neighborhood combat organizations necessitates finding the terms on which groups with essentially local interests can work together. This is difficult even for a traditional political party which can control patronage and nominations for office. A nonpartisan neighborhood association, on the other hand, which attempts to maximize benefits for its area often must do so at the expense of other areas; this potentially competitive situation may make collaboration difficult. A coalition might, of course, be formed out of a common allegiance to a candidate for major political office, but this means accepting the constraints (principally, moderation) that inevitably accompany electoral contest.

III. The Negro Voter in the Future

In short, the possibility for an effective radical Negro political strategy seems remote and the effort to achieve it costly. In the South, the potential supporters of at least current Negro objectives are the members of the commercial and industrial elite. Although they are everywhere slow to emerge and in some places wholly absent, there is at present no reasonable alternative. Atlanta is an example of both the strengths and weaknesses of such an alliance; even there, of course, it rests on a delicate population equilibrium which could be upset should either the Negroes become too numerous or the upper-class whites too few. What will happen after federal intervention has opened the ballot box to Negroes in the Black Belt counties remains to be seen. There are very few precedents from which one might infer predictions about political behavior when Negroes are in the majority in a city or county and vote. (In Washington, D.C., Negroes are the voting majority, but there are few issues of substance to decide.) There are some Southern communities which are over 50 percent Negro and in which many (though not all) Negroes vote. Little is known about them except that, while the franchise has ended harassment by public officials and law enforcement officers, it has not revolutionized the living conditions of the Negroes. Perhaps the safest prediction is that the vote will have very different effects in different places. In some communities, patronage-based Negro political machines will emerge; in others, non-ideological Negro-white alliances will develop; in still others, militant and even radical Negro movements will appear (particularly, perhaps, in parts of Mississippi where the young cadres of SNCC and the Freedom Democratic party have begun to instill a radical ideology, though not yet to build a serious organization). In general, the type of Negro political organization which emerges will depend crucially on the type of white political organization already in existence.

In the North, the Negro, facing goals more complex and less clearly moral than those faced in the South, will continue to require white liberal, business, and union support for slow progress toward programs productive of income, education, and wider opportunities. The urban vote already greatly influences the presidential election; how much more it will influence state and congressional elections now that reapportionment is upon us is uncertain. It will clearly be on state legislatures that the Supreme Court's edict will fall most heavily. Congress is not likely to be revolutionized; indeed, there is some evidence that an absolutely equal apportionment system might *strengthen* the "conservative" vote.[28] In any case, the role of Congress is more the product of our localistic political structure than of the apportionment system, and this is not likely to change significantly for a very long time.

Negro-labor alliances will still be possible, but like all such alliances in American politics they will be *ad hoc*, imperfectly organized, and difficult to sustain. From the point of view of the Negro, one of the chief advantages of the American political system is surely that the "undemocratic" convention and caucus system by which political parties are governed makes possible *leadership* coalitions that, while not based on a perfect fusion of interests and aims, are not without influence in the choice of candidates and even the outcome of elections. Indeed, to the extent political parties are made internally more "democratic"—by abolishing conventions in favor of primaries, by reforming the governance of local political organizations, and by flooding the deliberations of party leaders with the merciless light of publicity—these coalitions may become more difficult to assemble and sustain, for an informed rank and file requires leaders who emphasize rather than compromise the very great differences which now separate, for example, white and Negro working-class voters.

The fact that many different alliances must be maintained will not only call for a high degree of tactical flexibility; it will probably also mean that the civil rights movement will remain divided and even at war with itself. The divisions among Negro leaders are the result not simply of personal rivalry or organized ideology, but of the effort to adapt a movement to the necessity of simultaneously occupying incompatible positions in order to draw strength from others.

The various white partners in these alliances will themselves be changed by civil rights activity. The nonpolitical strategies developed by the Negro for bargaining power—the sit-in, the protest march, and passive resistance—have already been adopted by whites concerned with everything from American foreign policy to university administration.[29] Physically obstructing the operation of an organization—often illegally—has, in the 1960's, become a commonplace method for attempting to change the behavior of that organization. This "spill-over" of civil rights tactics into other areas of social conflict has probably been one of the most important consequences of increased Negro militancy.

Because of the structure of American politics as well as the nature of the Negro community, Negro politics will accomplish only limited objectives. This does not mean that Negroes will be content with those accomplishments or resigned to that political style. If Negroes do not make radical gains, radical sentiments may grow. How these sentiments will find expression is perhaps the most perplexing and troubling question of all.

NOTES

1. *Commentary* (February, 1965), 25–31.
2. C. Vann Woodward, *The Strange Career of Jim Crow* (New York, 1957), pp. 38–47, 60–8.
3. Rep. Weltner voted against final passage of HR 7152 on February 10, 1964. On February 17, the United States Supreme Court ordered redistricting in Georgia (Wesberry v. Sanders, 376 U.S. 1 [1964]). The Georgia Senate, anticipating the ruling, had already passed a redistricting bill on February 12; the House followed suit on February 21. The governor signed the bill into law on March 10; it divided Weltner's old district into two new districts—Weltner's (the Fifth), consisting of Fulton County (Atlanta); the other (the Fourth) consisting of suburban DeKalb County. As a result of this change, the percentage of Weltner's district which was Negro rose from 26.5 to 33.3. Weltner voted for House acceptance of the Senate-amended Civil Rights Act in July. An interesting analysis of Weltner's relationship to the Negro vote is M. Kent Jennings and L. Harmon Zeigler, "A Moderate's Victory in a Southern Congressional District," *Public Opinion Quarterly*, XXVIII (Winter 1964), 595–603.
4. Alfred B. Clubok, John M. Degrove, and Charles D. Farris, "The Manipulated Negro Vote; Some Pre-Conditions and Consequences," *Journal of Politics*, XXVI (February 1964), 112–29. This is not confined to the South. In 1964, certain Negro precincts in Harrisburg, Pennsylvania, voted for Senator Goldwater while Northern Negroes elsewhere were voting ten-to-one for President Johnson. One can only speculate on the ways by which that extraordinary result was achieved.
5. Cf. H. Douglas Price, *The Negro and Southern Politics: A Chapter of Florida History* (New York, 1957); Bradbury Seasholes and Frederic N. Cleveland, "Negro Political Participation in Two Piedmont Crescent Cities," in F. Stuart Chapin and Shirley F. Weiss (eds.), *Urban Growth Dynamics* (New York, 1962), pp. 265–70; Henry Holloway, "The Negro and the Vote: The Case of Texas," *Journal of Politics*, XXIII (August, 1961), 526–56. These Negro voters' leagues are effective only if they operate within the consensual framework of the Negro community. Price (on page 72) notes that a "league endorsement of a wrong candidate in a contest where a clear difference in attitude toward the Negro exists does not swing many Negro votes; rather it raises the question, 'who sold out?'" Holloway (on pages 539–40) observes that "Negro leaders don't have the power to deliver a bloc vote at will. . . . The Negro voter has his own fairly constant voting propensities which leaders disregard at risk to themselves."
6. Jack Walker, "Negro Voting in Atlanta: 1953–1961," *Phylon*, XXIV (Winter 1963), 379–87.
7. Negro voting in many Southern cities is an empirical case of the rationality model suggested in Anthony Downs, *An Economic Theory of Democracy* (New York, 1957).
8. The Atlanta Coalition is described in Edward C. Banfield, "Atlanta: Strange Bedfellows," in *Big City Politics* (New York: Random House, 1965).

9. Daniel C. Thompson, *The Negro Leadership Class* (Englewood Cliffs, N.J., 1963), pp. 112–14.
10. Survey data on the importance of education (and class position) for the racial attitudes of Southern whites can be found in Herbert B. Hyman and Paul B. Sheatsley, "Attitudes Toward Desegregation," *Scientific American* (July 1964), 16–23, and Melvin M. Tumin, *Desegregation* (Princeton, N.J., 1958). But Matthews and Prothro, using ecological correlations, show that the level of education among Southern whites must be very high before it affects Negro voter registration rates. Donald R. Matthews and James W. Prothro, "Social and Economic Factors and Negro Voter Registration in the South," *American Political Science Review*, LVII (March, 1963), 36–8.
11. United States Commission on Civil Rights, *1961 Report* (Book 1, Part 3).
12. Seymour Martin Lipset, *Political Man* (Garden City, N.Y., 1960), pp. 84–85.
13. Donald R. Matthews and James W. Prothro, *Negro Political Participation in the South* (New York, forthcoming).
14. Walker, *op. cit.*, p. 384.
15. The importance of political factors other than the Negro vote in obtaining civil rights legislation is illustrated by the state adoption of "open occupancy" laws barring discrimination in the private housing market. The first states to pass such laws were typically states with a very small Negro population. See James Q. Wilson, "The Negro in American Politics" in John P. Davis (ed.), *American Negro Reference Book* (Englewood Cliffs, N.J.: Prentice-Hall, 1965).
16. *Commentary* (February 1965), 26.
17. Daniel Patrick Moynihan, "Three Problems," an address given before the Conference on Poverty in America at the University of California at Berkeley, February 26–28, 1965 (mimeo).
18. James Q. Wilson and Edward C. Banfield, "Public-Regardingness as a Value Premise in Voting," *American Political Science Review*, LVIII (December 1964), 876–87.
19. James Q. Wilson, *Negro Politics* (New York, 1960), Chs. ii, iii, iv; and James Reichley, *The Art of Government: Reform and Organization Politics in Philadelphia* (New York, 1959).
20. Edward C. Banfield and James Q. Wilson, *City Politics* (Cambridge, Mass., 1963), chap. xx, discusses alternative Negro political styles.
21. See *Election '64*, a report of the Ripon Society (Cambridge, Mass., 1965), p. 29.
22. James Q. Wilson, *The Amateur Democrat* (Chicago, 1962), Ch. ix, discusses reform-Negro relations.
23. In Chicago, certain white and Negro civil rights groups ran a Negro candidate (A. A. Rayner, Jr.) against Rep. William L. Dawson in the 1962 Democratic primary. Dawson won, easily carrying the lower-income Negro precincts but losing (by as much as two to one) many middle-class Negro precincts. The Dawson organization is very strong among lower-income Negroes, particularly those in public housing projects.
24. Nathan Glazer, "Negroes and Jews: The New Challenge to Pluralism," *Commentary* (December, 1964), 34.
25. *The New York Times*, December 23, 1964, quoting the Democratic National Committee.
26. Title VI of the Civil Rights Act of 1964 will facilitate challenges.
27. Charles Silberman, *The Crisis in Black and White* (New York, 1964), Ch. x, describes TWO.
28. Andrew Hacker, *Congressional Districting* (Washington, D.C., 1963), pp. 87–91.
29. Recently, interns protesting the pay policies of a California county hospital practiced a "heal-in." They flooded the hospital with patients, many not in need of hospitalization, in order to overload the organization and thus acquire bargaining power vis-à-vis the administration.

VII. Strategies for Freedom and Reform

Having presented aspects of black American history and current social conditions reflecting the cyclic nature of social, political, and economic gain, and having given some attention to the factors that tend to undermine these gains, this volume now focuses upon the question of how to alter this historical tendency effectively.

Chapter 27 reinforces one of the main points of emphasis in this volume, and stresses the primary historical and current means, that is, white resistance, for reversing gains made by black Americans. Simultaneously, this chapter suggests important aspects of strategy—forceful black-white alliances—as a means of stabilizing and continuing gains already made. This suggestion, it should be recognized, is contradictory to a trend now growing among black Americans, and supported by many whites, toward militant black racism.

In Chapter 28 recapitulation of the basic argument of this volume is presented in essay form. Chapter 29 attempts to assess more systematically and intensively some current tendencies in the overall effort for acceleration of gains by black Americans. Such an assessment is necessary because a major objective of current activity on behalf of, and on the part of, American Negroes must be to force a departure from the cyclic social process that historically has served to undermine their social, economic, and political gains. Only as this effort is realized will racism disappear as a social institution in the United States—a reality desired by increasing numbers of Americans.

27. When Will America's Negroes Catch Up?

The current affluence of American society, affecting both blacks and whites, combined with at least a rhetorical emphasis on improving the conditions of ghetto life, have obscured the reality that the present rate of gain by blacks is entirely insufficient to assure income, job, and educational equality within a reasonable time. Based upon the rate of gain in these areas during the ten-year period from 1950 to 1960, educational equality would be achieved in the year 2022, and this is estimated to be considerably before the date when equality in jobs and income would be realized. Only by an acceleration of the rate of gain can the rather enormous racial inequalities be eliminated.

LEONARD BROOM AND NORVAL D. GLENN

In recent years a great deal of publicity has been given to educational, occupational, and economic gains of Negroes in the United States. Viewed in absolute terms, these gains since the beginning of the Second World War have been impressive. For example, the median years of school completed by non-whites 25 years old and older (more than 90 percent of whom were Negroes) rose from 5.8 in 1940 to 8.2 in 1960. In 1940 only 7.6 percent of non-white adults had completed high school, whereas 21.7 percent had done so in 1960. The quality of Negro education also improved substantially during this period. In 1940 only 8.5 percent of employed Negro workers were in white collar or skilled manual occupations, whereas by 1960 almost 20 percent were employed in such work. The median wage and salary income of gainfully employed non-white males increased threefold in constant (1962) dollars, from $995 in 1939 to $3,023 in 1962. Yet these substantial gains have not been sufficient to forestall the almost explosive increase in Negro protest activity since 1963. The discontent which prompted this protest grew in large measure out of such conditions as segregation of public facilities, housing discrimination and inequitable treatment of Negroes by police; but it also grew in large measure out of Negro dissatisfaction with progress in the basic spheres of education, occupation, and income.

A major reason for Negro dissatisfaction with recent gains, large though

From *New Society* (March 25, 1965); reprinted by permission. This article is condensed from chapters 5 and 6 of *The Transformation of the Negro American* (Harper and Row, 1965).

they have been, is that white gains have also been large, and therefore the gap between Negroes and whites has not closed rapidly. Skilled and white collar occupations and good education have given many Negroes a better vantage point from which to judge their relative condition. And Negroes who have moved from all-Negro to interracial social circles have often experienced a decline in relative status and a heightened sense of deprivation. More casual and stylised contacts, such as in the classroom and on the job, have had a similar but lesser effect on the experiencing of relative deprivation. Increased travel and greater exposure to the mass media of communication have also given Negroes greater knowledge of the life styles and consumption patterns of middle class white Americans and have widened the disparity between Negro aspirations and attainments.

If, therefore, Negro aspirations are to be satisfied and Negro discontent stilled, there must be a marked closing of the gap between Negroes and whites as well as large absolute Negro gains. The prospects for such a closing in the near future are not good. At the 1950 to 1960 rates of change in the relative standing of Negroes, they would attain equality with whites in education long before they would attain equality in occupation and income. But even the education gap, as indicated by the ratio of the non-white to the white median years of school completed, would not close until the year 2022. And the income gap, as measured by the ratio of non-white to white median family income, would not close until 2410!

Negro males would become proportionally represented in most intermediate level occupations within a few decades but would not attain equality in some upper level occupations for centuries. In a few occupations—including physicians and surgeons, and managers, officials, and proprietors —Negro representation did not increase during the 1950s, and therefore equality cannot be projected at any date. The projected dates for proportional representation in a few selected occupations are as follows:

clerical workers	1973
craftsmen and foremen	2023
dentists	2072
civil engineers	2140
school teachers	2190
lawyers and judges	2253
sales workers	2365

These extrapolations of recent rates of convergence are not, however, predictions and are given only to show that Negroes have not been gaining on whites rapidly. Negro income and occupational gains are likely to accelerate so that virtual income equality will be attained in less than four and a half centuries and proportional representation in the upper level occupations will be attained in less than the time indicated. On the other hand,

Negroes almost certainly will not attain educational equality with whites as soon as the above projection would indicate—a conclusion we reach from an analysis of data on educational attainment by age.

Since most people do not receive further formal education after about 25 but will live and influence the educational data for many more years, virtual educational equality in the total population will not likely be attained until four or five decades after equality is attained among young adults. And the educational gap between Negroes and whites in the age range from 25 to 29 was substantial in 1960, and at the recent rate of closure will not disappear for three or four decades. Nearly a century probably will pass before there is virtual equality in the total population.

In addition to the gap in the quantity of Negro and white education, there is a vast gap in quality. The average year of Negro schooling represents far less than the average white year, in terms of the skills and knowledge which result from it. In many localities, Negro pupils average only as well on scholastic achievement tests as whites two or three grade levels below them. But this gap in quality, we can be fairly certain, is slowly closing. There has been appreciable desegregation of schools and colleges in the border states during the past decade, and the southern states have at least improved the physical facilities of their Negro schools in an attempt to lessen pressure for desegregation.

De facto segregation, however, based upon residential segregation, has increased recently in some northern and western cities, and the predominantly Negro schools, pervaded with a lower class slum culture and usually poorly staffed and equipped, almost invariably offer inferior opportunities to learn and stimulate less incentive to do so. Although there is virtually no discrimination against Negroes by northern and western colleges and universities, Negro college students, handicapped by poor backgrounds and limited financial resources, are highly concentrated in institutions with low academic standards. Even so, a large percentage of them do not fare well in competition with their white classmates, and almost 60 percent of the non-white males who complete one year of college never complete four. The comparable percentage for white males is somewhat less than 50.

It seems, therefore, that some difference in the average quality of Negro and white education is likely to remain for some time after the gap in years of school completed is virtually closed. True educational equality is probably more than a century away, even if recent favourable trends accelerate.

There is still considerable discrimination against Negroes in employment and in rates of pay, but such discrimination has declined sharply in recent years. Since no overall measure of discrimination is available, one cannot determine the exact rate of decline, but it seems that if the recent and present rate continues, discrimination may virtually disappear within only a few years, except in isolated "Black Belt" areas of the south. If this is the case, the occupational and income gaps will close as soon as educational equality is attained. Employment opportunities are already opening more rapidly than Negroes can become qualified to take advantage of them—especially in many professional and technical occupations in which a scarcity of qualified personnel of any race makes it impractical for employers to discriminate, and in which "conspicuous employment" of Negroes is considered good public relations. The low average Negro occupational qualifications—the result of centuries of past subordination —are now a greater hindrance than current discrimination.

Widening Income Gap

The slow but steady closing of the educational gap and the more rapid decline in discrimination have not produced a convergence of Negro and white incomes. The reason is a growing gap between the incomes of well educated and poorly educated workers. For instance, in 1949 males with only one to four years of formal schooling had a median income 31 percent of that of males with four or more years of college, whereas by 1959 this percentage had declined to 24. Underlying this change was a widening of the income gap between unskilled workers and professional, technical, and managerial workers—a change which in turn resulted from automation and other technological developments which increased the demand for the highly trained and decreased the demand for the unskilled and untrained. A much larger percentage of Negroes than of whites are still poorly educated and unskilled, and the decline in the relative status of these Negroes almost completely offsets the economic advancement of the minority of Negroes who became well educated.

The widening of the chasm between the opportunities and economic conditions of poorly educated and well educated workers is continuing and perhaps accelerating. As a consequence, Negroes are on a treadmill; they must gain steadily on whites in education and occupational status merely to stay the same distance behind in income. There is likely to be enough automation during the next decade or so to make it hard for Negroes to keep up, and the income gap could widen appreciably.

Impact of Automation

Any widening of the income gap will necessarily impede Negro efforts to catch up in education, and any slowing of the convergence of Negro and white educational status will in turn tend to widen the income gap further. Consequently, the imminent prospects of widespread automation give great urgency to the drive to improve Negro education and occupational qualifications.

As automation replaces discrimination as the major force keeping Negroes near the bottom of the social heap, Negro efforts to attain equality must necessarily change. The battle against discrimination may soon be won, but Negro attempts to impede or prevent automation are likely to be futile. The most rational future strategy to improve Negro status would be a massive programme of uplift and self-improvement, necessarily with white assistance. The shift away from emphasis upon protest to such a programme will not come easily. Negroes are marshalled to fight discrimination, they increasingly focus their hostility upon whites, and they can release their pent up hostility in protest activities. They are not likely to turn their attention upon themselves readily and to settle down quickly to the arduous and unexciting tasks of uplift. Perhaps even more important, whites, whose consciences are being eased by the elimination of the more flagrant forms of discrimination, may not readily give the support and cooperation needed for a really successful programme of Negro uplift.

In short, neither recent trends in Negro status nor the potentialities of the methods now being used for Negro advance lead us to expect a rapid closing of the gap between Negroes and whites. Only a massive programme of education, job retraining, and occupational upgrading—on a scale far greater than anything now proposed by Negro leaders, the federal government, or any agency or organisation concerned with Negro welfare and status—can save the majority of Negroes from many more decades of inferior status.

28. The Role of White Resistance and Facilitation in the Negro Struggle for Equality

Although the degree and kind of internal mobilization of the black community is an essential element in achieving social gains, the white community, too, can be viewed in terms of its areas of differential amenability to this process. In the following article Glenn discusses the differential amenability of the white community and stresses the importance of strategic and powerful black-white alliances.

NORVAL D. GLENN

The fate of Negro Americans has been and remains largely in the hands of the dominant white population. Since whites are almost 90 percent of the population, are more than 95 percent of the college graduates, and have perhaps 95 percent of the wealth, and since they occupy almost all key positions in the social order and control the armed forces and law enforcement agencies, they could, by acting in unison, prevent any economic, educational, or other gains by Negroes. In fact, Negroes could be pushed much lower in the social heap than they are now. Whites have not only largely controlled the opportunities for Negroes; they have been responsible also for the experiences and circumstances that have conditioned the aspirations and incentive of Negroes to take advantage of available opportunities.[1]

The harshness of the fact that Negroes are largely at the mercy of whites is tempered by the fact that they have had many white benefactors. White abolitionists worked to free them, a white president gave them legal freedom, and the efforts of thousands of white soldiers made that freedom a reality. White people were responsible for the Thirteenth, Fourteenth, and Fifteenth Amendments to the Constitution. They were more numerous than Negroes among the founders and early leaders of the National Association for the Advancement of Colored People, and for many years they provided most of the financial support of that organization and of the National Urban League, until recently the only other major organization devoted solely to the welfare and advancement of Negroes. All Negro

From *Phylon* (Summer 1965), Vol. 26, pp. 105–116; reprinted by permission.

action organizations, including the Congress of Racial Equality, the Southern Christian Leadership Conference, and the Student Non-Violent Coordinating Committee, still depend heavily on white contributions. An all-white Supreme Court rendered a series of decisions favorable to the rights of Negroes, and in 1964, a predominantly white Congress passed, and a white president signed into law, a sweeping civil rights bill designed to give Negroes equal voting rights, equal access to public accommodations, and equal employment opportunities. Many whites who have not worked for the advancement of Negroes have not opposed it or have not resisted it effectively.

The dependence of the advancement of Negroes upon white action and permissiveness is undeniable; the Negro leadership is painfully aware of it, even though some whites apparently are not. More debatable, however, are the reasons for white assistance, permissiveness, and resistance. Why have powerful whites come to the aid of Negroes at times, whereas at other times they have not? Why did white benefactors of Negroes generally forsake them around the turn of the century? Why did white resistance to the advancement of Negroes lessen during the 1940's? What accounts for the variation in resistance among geographic, social, and economic categories of the white population? In general, under what conditions have whites encouraged and permitted gains by Negroes and under what conditions have they resisted? Answers to these moot questions are requisite to an intelligent prediction of Negro-white relations and to selection of effective strategies for the advancement of Negroes.

There are many differing explanations of variations in white action and policy toward Negroes. In order to better explain, compare, and evaluate these explanations, it is useful to subsume the factors that influence white action and policy into three categories: (1) self-interest (perceived and/ or objective), (2) values and morals, and (3) emotion.[2] Self-interest motives include the anticipation of economic, prestige, and power gains and of gratification of biological needs. Values and morals (the normative influences) are embodied in the conscience, which provides internal rewards and penalties for adherence to and deviation from them. They can prompt action, inhibit the following of emotional urges, and restrict the means employed to pursue self-interest. Emotional influences include urges to act that result from love, hate, sympathy, and other emotions. A person has an urge to act positively toward objects of his positive emotions and negatively toward objects of his negative emotions, and therefore emotions may, in the absence of strong deterring influences, be important determinants of behavior.

These distinctions are in a sense arbitrary and are difficult to apply concretely. In a broad sense, all deliberate behavior is self-interested; following the dictates of one's conscience relieves or prevents guilt feelings and gives one a satisfying feeling of self-righteousness, and yielding to emotional urges is gratifying. The distinctions are theoretically useful, however, and in race relations theory the more restricted meaning of self-interest, which excludes the gratification that comes from following conscience or emotional urges, is of considerable utility. Nevertheless, one must keep in mind that a combination of types of influences is likely to prompt the action of one individual, and the motivations of different individuals who engage in collective action are likely to be different. For instance, one white participant in civil rights activities may be prompted by humanitarian (normative and perhaps emotional) considerations, whereas another may be seeking recognition and power (self-interest). The picture is complicated by the fact that when two or more influences lie behind action, one may cause or partly cause one or more of the others. For instance, white action against Negroes may be prompted by hate, which in turn grows directly or indirectly out of frustrated pursuit of self-interest in competition with Negroes. Or, the values and morals that guide behavior may have been devised, modified, or selected to justify and support the pursuit of self-interest, either of the actor or of others, past or present. On the other hand, the different categories of influences frequently oppose one another; for instance, self-interest and morality often conflict. Even the different influences within one category may conflict, as when pursuit of sexual gratification (self-interest) hampers pursuit of economic goals (also self-interest). Or, a person may accept inconsistent values or experience conflicting emotions.

The picture is complicated further by the distinction between perceived and objective self-interest and the fact that the two do not always coincide. Incorrect perception of the consequences of action may lead a person or group to act in a manner that does not serve his or its interests or that does not do so as well as possible alternative actions would. In such cases, the perception of interest may be influenced by emotion or values, although the influence is likely to be indirect. For instance, values are linked in ideological systems with, and may be at least partially responsible for, beliefs about the nature of reality, and these beliefs can affect perception of what action will best further one's interests. In addition, objective self-interest that is not clearly perceived may influence action. In such cases there may always be some kind of perceptual link between interests and action, but this may be very indirect. If the action is traditional, the link may have been made in earlier generations. If the action is collective, the relationship between interests and action may be perceived by some but not all of the individuals. The actor may perceive the relationship at a low level of consciousness but may tend to repress awareness of it in order to avoid guilt feelings. The immediate spur to action may be normative, and the actor may be unaware that self-interest has molded the values by which he lives. In such a case, values are intervening variables between interest and motivation.

Explanations of white action and policy vis-à-vis Negroes almost always include all these categories of factors, but usually one is emphasized more than others and theorists do not agree on how the factors are interrelated. Some theorists, including Marxists and those strongly influenced by Marxist theory, believe that objective self-interest is the basic force and that values and emotion derive from and support self-interested action.[3] These theorists usually emphasize economic interests and dismiss others as relatively unimportant in determining the treatment by whites of Negroes. Other theorists, while not denying the force of self-interest, believe that morality can be a potent counter-influence. For instance, Gunnar Myrdal believes that the "American creed" of equality is a strong influence for more favorable treatment of Negroes.[4] He thinks that a strain toward value consistency tends to bring actions and other beliefs and values into conformity with the ideal of equality of opportunity. Still other theorists, mostly psychologists, grant pre-eminence to emotional influences. According to their view, hostility generated by forces other than interracial competition and conflict tends to become focused on Negroes. A "need to hate" is regarded as an important independent influence, not derived from other forces that influence the action by whites toward Negroes.

Our view is that self-interest is the most basic and important force underlying white policy and action vis-à-vis Negroes. Such action more often than not serves the interests of the actors or is accounted for by incorrect perception of objective interest. Values and morals do under certain conditions prompt and guide the action, but they appear to be powerless to motivate any large segment of whites to act in unison against their perceived interests. Emotion appears to be a more potent influence than values, and emotional action, individual and collective, contrary to self-interest is fairly common, and, more often than not, unfavorable to Negroes. However, the emotions are often, and perhaps, usually, generated in interracial relations, in which cases they are not truly independent influences. We do not agree, however, with the Marxist view that only economic interests are important forces. The pursuit by whites of prestige, power, respectability, and other valued attributes is also of great importance. Furthermore, the Marxists err in attributing racial discrimination only to the interests of high-status whites, since the interests of all classes of whites are in some ways opposed to the interests of Negroes.

We believe that the independent role of values in race relations is less than Myrdal and many other theorists believe. However, we do not deny that values and morals are very important influences on certain other kinds of behavior. They are not always selected, rejected, molded and modified to support self-interested action; under certain conditions they can effectively deter self-interested acts and motivate disinterested behavior. The influence of values and morals tends to vary inversely, and the influence of self-interest tends to vary directly, with the size of the group that engages in concerted action. In other words, the larger the group, the more nearly its actions are likely to conform to its self-interest. The role of self-interest is smaller and the role of conscience and sympathy is greater with individual than with group behavior. Values and standards are implanted and sustained in the conscience through social contacts and are likely to be changed only with the support of other persons. Since the conscience is socially determined, the individual cannot mold it freely and shape it to suit his individual interests. In contrast, the tendencies of different individuals in a group to change their values to conform to their common interests are reinforcing; the individuals give one another the social support needed to realign the dictates of conscience. The larger the group, the greater this mutual reinforcement tends to be. At the upper end of the size scale, the actions of national states vis-à-vis one another are guided very largely (some social scientists would claim almost completely) by considerations of national interest. Individuals often find it difficult to act selfishly; social controls and conscience stand in the way. But selfish action comes easily for large groups of people because the more potent social controls and influences on conscience are in the group itself.

Once accepted by a group, values do tend to have a life of their own and can sustain themselves for some time in the absence of the interests and other forces that led to their acceptance. As the interests of a group change, the values tend to conform to them; but in a period of rapid change, the values may lag considerably so that the fit is far from perfect. Or, values may be diffused to groups whose interests they do not support. For instance, prejudice is prevalent in some small towns and rural areas in West Texas, the Mountain States, and the Midwest where there are few Negroes. The prejudice is perpetuated by social isolation, and the people probably are much more susceptible to conversion to egalitarian racial values than people whose interests are still served by discrimination.

There is widespread agreement among social scientists that important interests of whites are served by subordination of Negroes. Where Negroes are numerous they do most of the lower-level work and whites have an unusually favorable occupational status.[5] Keeping Negroes down in the occupational structure keeps whites up. Both job discrimination and the poor job qualifications of Negroes—the latter having resulted from various kinds of past discrimination—handicap Negroes in the competition for the better jobs and facilitate the occupational advancement of whites. The restriction of Negroes to certain jobs increases the competition for those jobs and reduces labor costs of many employers. Low earnings of Negro males and widespread family disorganization force many Negro females into the labor force, thus increasing the supply and reducing the costs of domestic servants. Moderate income families in the South often can afford a full-time household servant, whereas families with comparable incomes in other parts of the country can afford little or no domestic help.

Because whites gain in these ways from the subordination of Negroes, any appreciable advancement by Negroes in areas of high Negro population concentration ordinarily would cause loss to many whites. If large numbers of Negroes in the South were to move up to skilled and white-collar work, or if the number of Negroes were to decline appreciably, the costs of locally produced goods and services such as laundry and cleaning and restaurant food would increase sharply. Unless the number of skilled and white-collar jobs were to increase proportionately, white workers would be displaced. Also, many genteel middle-class housewives would have to start cooking their own food, scrubbing their own floors, and doing other menial tasks to which they are not accustomed.

To be sure, the low status of Negroes is not in all ways economically beneficial to whites. It increases public welfare costs and keeps down the sales of businesses, mostly owned by whites, that cater to Negroes. Keeping the productivity and buying power of Negroes low keeps down the total productivity of the national economy, perhaps by several billions of dollars per year,[6] and the abundance of unskilled and semiskilled Negro labor depresses the wages of whites at lower occupational levels. However, the economic losses that come from discrimination are more diffuse, less direct, and less obvious than the gains. The losses are so widely distributed that few people are hurt very much and few are likely to be aware of the losses, or greatly concerned if they are aware of them. The Southern white worker may not know that discrimination against Negroes tends to keep his wages low, and if he does, he is likely to know also that it increases his chances of advancing to a higher job level, keeps his cost of living low, and gives him someone to whom he can feel superior. The white man who hears an estimate that discrimination against Negroes reduces the gross national product by several billions annually is not likely to be greatly concerned, especially if he knows that discrimination enhances his relative standing in the economic hierarchy. Discrimination keeps the total economic pie smaller, since it prevents the most efficient utilization of human resources, and it may even keep the whites' share of the economic pie absolutely smaller. However, it keeps the whites' share relatively larger, and from their point of view this may be more important. Above the level at which one's biological needs are more or less met, one's satisfaction depends apparently more upon one's relative than upon one's absolute economic standing, and whites may derive satisfaction simply from ranking above Negroes.

The gains in prestige and self-esteem by whites may be more important than the economic gains in perpetuating discrimination. As long as Negroes are defined as socially inferior, and as long as jim crow practices and the traditional Southern etiquette of race relations continually emphasize social distinctions between Negroes and whites, all whites, regardless of how lowly they may be, gain a feeling of importance and superiority.

Southern Negroes traditionally have showed deference to all whites, regardless of age, occupation, education, or economic standing, so that no white person was without an ever-ready source of ego-enhancement.[7] Deference from Negroes was an important source of ego-enhancement not only to lower-class whites but to those with other strong bases of self-esteem. For instance, Dollard, a well-educated Northerner, reports that it is impossible not to respond with self-satisfaction and exhilaration to the deference of the Southern Negro.[8]

When Negroes no longer grant the traditional deference, when they refuse to sit at the back of buses, demand service at lunch counters and restaurants that serve whites, and demand the right to send their children to the same schools, the prestige gain of whites is threatened or already lost. The sweet satisfaction that comes from looking down on others as categorically inferior, of being able to go where the inferiors cannot go and do things they cannot do, is slipping away. This loss and anticipation of loss is perhaps the main source of the anger and aggression with which whites meet the attempts by Negroes to break down racial barriers. This is an instance of a "zero-sum" situation, that is, the gain of one party necessarily involves loss by another. Negroes cannot gain in prestige and self-esteem without loss by the whites.

It is not surprising that few Southern whites willingly submit to this loss, especially since the change is being forced by Negroes and Northern whites and therefore affords no compensatory feeling of self-righteousness. On the other hand, the reward of a feeling of self-righteousness generally is not great enough to prompt voluntary change. Conscience and morals prompt relatively few Southern whites to give up the gains they receive from discrimination; numerous ready-made justifications for discrimination are provided by the Southern cultural heritage, and new ones can be devised easily as old ones are discredited. Southern whites have been exposed to egalitarian values, and often have accepted them in the abstract, but they see little or no inconsistency in refusing to apply these values to Negro-white relations. They see little or no conflict between egalitarian values and the values supporting segregation and discrimination, which they have also accepted. As is usual when people are exposed to conflicting values, they continue to act in accordance with the values that support their interests.

Whites outside the South are no less inclined to pursue self-interest but traditionally they had little incentive to discriminate because little could be gained from subordination of the small Negro population. As Negro populations have grown in non-Southern cities, the possibility of gains by whites has increased; but a proportionate increase in discrimination has been prevented by a number of influences, including the Negro vote, the buying power of Negroes, and anti-discrimination legislation, which has resulted to a large extent from the Negro vote. Also, it is harder to initiate discriminatory practices than to perpetuate traditional, institutionalized discrimination, and people will not put forth as much effort to obtain an advantage they have never had as they will to preserve a traditional one. For instance, most Northern whites have never experienced for any extended time the ego-satisfaction that comes from the servile deference of the old-fashioned Southern Negro, and therefore they do not feel deprived because they do not receive such deference. Ideological forces also have tended to prevent increased discrimination in the North and West, although these forces could be overcome if opposing white interests were very strong and pervasive. However, the reversal of the drift toward egalitarian values would not be abrupt, since that trend has enough momentum to keep it going without its supporting social forces and in the face of at least some opposition.

When Negroes threaten the traditional advantages of Northern and Western whites, resistance is stiff and often violent. For instance, movement of a Negro family into a previously all-white neighborhood is perceived as a threat to both the economic interests and social standing of white residents, and many who claim to have no anti-Negro prejudice are usually among those who strongly oppose the Negro invasion and/or flee from it. Probably many of these whites are not prejudiced, but they fear that the value of their property will drop and they know that living near Negroes is a mark of low social status. They may sympathize with the need of Negroes for housing and realize that the residential segregation of Negroes creates inferior segregated schools, but they do not want the problems of Negroes to be solved at their expense. As usual, humanitarian motives lose force in the face of threatened self-interest.

Although whites seldom sacrifice strong and important interests to aid Negroes, those who can support the Negro cause without great sacrifice often do so. Values and ideals that do not oppose perceived self-interest can spur action effectively. Thus, the Northern or Western white person is likely to be influenced by the "American creed" to favor extension of Negro rights in the South, since he has no stake in the traditional Southern social order; and he may devote some time, money, and effort to the cause. Typically, however, such a person does not devote enough time and money to the Negro cause to detract greatly from his pursuit of other interests and values. He will help Negroes only if it is convenient and easy to do so.

A few whites, on the other hand, have put forth much effort to further the Negro cause and have made that cause their own: the abolitionists, the Northern missionaries who went south to set up Negro schools after the Civil War, the white founders of the NAACP, the white freedom riders, the students who risked their lives by participating in voter registration drives in Mississippi in the summer of 1964, and others. However, such active supporters of this cause are but a minute proportion of the total white population and also only a minute proportion of those who support verbally the rights of Negroes. Their efforts have been important but not really crucial influences on the status and welfare of Negroes. With the exception of a few philanthropists, the altruistic white benefactors of Negroes lack access to the major sources of power. Prominent among them are students—not yet caught up in the adult struggle for occupational success, money, and social standing—who are, of course, relatively powerless. Others are childless housewives and similar individuals whose more typical and self-interested activities do not absorb all of their time and energy. The influence these people can exert varies greatly but on the average is not great. Still other white activists in the struggle for rights for Negroes are persons who have forsaken the pursuit of self-interest, as we have defined it, and who seek a satisfying self-image through humanitarian activities. The very fact that they have renounced self-interest often grows out of their powerlessness.

Of more consequence than the activities of such altruistic benefactors of Negroes is the support of the Negro cause by groups and individuals whose support in some way serves their own interests. Although historians continue to debate the issue, it seems that humanitarian concern was not the basic Northern motive behind the interregional dispute that culminated in the Civil War; the emancipation of the slaves may have been no more than an incidental by-product of a war fought to further Northern industrial interests. Northern industrialists and the Republican Party protected the newly gained rights of Negroes because they needed the Negro vote, but they forsook Negroes when reconciliation with Southern whites became more important to their interests.[9] The federal government assumed a more beneficent stance toward Negroes when their migration to the North and West gave them a balance of political power in key states with large electoral votes. Likewise, many state and local politicians became friends of Negroes when they became an important segment of the electorate. Industrial unions admitted Negroes and espoused a doctrine of racial equality when management started using Negroes as strikebreakers. Companies adopted more egalitarian employment and promotion policies when Negroes became numerous and affluent enough to provide an important market for their products. White taxpayers in such states as New York, Illinois, Ohio, and Michigan became concerned about Negro education in the South when swarms of semi-literate Negro migrants swelled unemployment rolls and increased public welfare costs in those states. Negroes were admitted to occupations from which they had been excluded previously when an acute labor shortage during World War II created a need for additional workers in those occupations.

We could continue with examples, but these are sufficient to illustrate our point: the most potent forces working for Negroes are self-interested actions of powerful whites that for one reason or another benefit the

Negro cause. These actions are sometimes beneficial because Negroes and their white benefactors have interests in common; for instance, both slaves and Northern industrialists gained from the collapse of the Southern aristocracy, and therefore the industrialists by pursuing their interests aided the Negroes. To give a more recent example, both Negro and white workers have benefited from minimum wage legislation and other direct and indirect consequences of the labor movement. In fact, the labor movement, which was largely controlled by and for whites in its earlier years, has aided indirectly many Negroes excluded from the unions by fostering a general improvement in wages and working conditions. Perhaps a more common type of self-interested action by whites that benefits Negroes is prompted by the knowledge that Negroes will reciprocate favors or withhold detrimental action against their benefactors. Politicians and officeholders befriend Negroes in return for votes, businessmen do so in return for patronage, and so forth. The extent of this latter kind of beneficial action depends largely on how effectively Negroes use their votes, buying power, and other resources to reward their friends and penalize their enemies. In spite of the so-called white backlash to the Negro "revolt," Negroes are receiving more effective support by whites than they did a few years ago, largely because they have more resources for rewarding and penalizing and are making better use of the resources they have.

Even within the South strong white interests can be enlisted to support the advancement of Negroes. For instance, Southern businessmen want to prevent racial disturbances because such breaches of the peace hurt business and discourage industry from locating in the troubled localities. If Negroes make lowering of traditional race barriers the cost of peace, then many businessmen are willing to make concessions, even though yielding to the demands of Negroes goes against their emotional inclinations. When all-out resistance to school desegregation threatens to close schools and seriously disrupt the education of white children, then many whites who do not favor desegregation are willing to accept it rather than pay the price of resistance. Compliance by Southern businessmen to the public accommodations section of the 1964 Civil Rights Act was widespread within two or three days after the bill became law, even though Southern resistance to other federal pressures for desegregation had been adamant. The key factor behind this widespread compliance was that it was not really contrary to the interests of the businessmen. As long as most restaurants, hotels, and similar establishments that catered to whites excluded Negroes, no establishment could individually desegregate without risking loss of much of its white clientele. However, when all were required by law to desegregate, all could do so without fear of loss; their disgruntled white customers had no place to go to avoid Negroes, and the federal government could be blamed.

Several recent social and economic changes in American society have reduced the conflict of Negro and white interests. For instance, an expansion of upper- and intermediate-level jobs has made possible the upward movement of Negroes without displacement of whites.[10] Widespread unemployment of unskilled Negro workers has placed a burden upon middle-class white taxpayers, who may now favor improved education and job opportunities for Negroes so that relief costs will be reduced. A decrease in the relative number of Negroes in some Southern and Border localities has reduced the economic incentive for discrimination and lessened fears of the Negro vote.[11] The cold war and our attempts to woo the nonwhite peoples in the neutral and loosely aligned nations have made democratic race policies in the national interest. These and similar changes underlie the increase in egalitarian race values and practices in recent years.

Although many whites now support the Negro cause out of self-interest, Negro and white interests still are, and will continue to be, opposed in many ways. Furthermore, moral persuasion will not prompt large segments of whites who perceive that their interests are threatened by the advancement of Negroes to accede willingly to the demands of Negroes. Force—legal, economic, and otherwise—not persuasion, will batter down white resistance and clear the way for gains by Negroes, as it has in the past. And this force will be exerted by Negroes with the help of whites whose vital interests are served or at least are not threatened by the advancement of Negroes.

NOTES

1. A minority population can exert considerable pressure upon the majority simply by withdrawing participation in those activities in which their cooperation is essential (see James W. Vander Zanden, "The Non-Violent Resistance Movement Against Segregation," *American Journal of Sociology*, LXVIII (March, 1963, 544). However, even effective "non-cooperation" requires solidarity, organization, and leadership of the minority population that the concerted efforts of the majority could prevent.
2. Some action by whites may be prompted merely by habit or tradition, but in such cases the habit or tradition has been formed by earlier action motivated by self-interest, values, and/or emotion.
3. For instance, see Herbert Aptheker, *The Negro People in America* (New York, 1946).
4. Gunnar Myrdal, *An American Dilemma* (New York, 1944).
5. John Dollard, *Caste and Class in a Southern Town* (3d ed.; New York, 1957), ch. vi; and Norval D. Glenn, "Occupational Benefits to Whites from the Subordination of Negroes," *American Sociological Review*, XXVIII (June, 1963), 443–48.
6. George Eaton Simpson and J. Milton Yinger, *Racial and Cultural Minorities* (rev. ed.; New York, 1958), p. 273.
7. Dollard, *op. cit.*, pp. 173–74.
8. *Ibid.*, p. 173.
9. C. Vann Woodward, *The Strange Career of Jim Crow* (New York, 1957), pp. 49–95.
10. See Norval D. Glenn, "Some Changes in the Relative Status of American Nonwhites, 1940 to 1960," *Phylon*, XXIV (Second Quarter, 1963), 111–13; and

Leonard Broom and Norval D. Glenn, *Transformation of the Negro American* (New York, 1965), chs. vi and ix.

11. For evidence that discrimination against Negroes varies directly with the relative size of the Negro population, see David M. Heer, "The Sentiment of White Supremacy: An Ecological Study," *American Journal of Sociology,* LXIV (May, 1959), 592–98; Thomas F. Pettigrew, "Demographic Correlates of Border-State Desegregation," *American Sociological Review,* XXII (December, 1957), 683–89; and Norval D. Glenn, "The Relative Size of the Negro Population and Negro Occupational Status," *Social Forces,* XLIII (October, 1964), 42–49.

29. New Techniques of Retardation—New Strategies for Freedom and Reform

The historical pattern of mobilization and demobilization within the black community in the interest of black equality, and white facilitation of or resistance to this interest, constitute a social process. I claimed in Chapter 16 that this process can be viewed as cyclic in nature, as opposed to the steady gains made by white ethnic or immigrant groups. One basic objective of reform in the United States, to be assumed by blacks and whites alike, must be to change this cyclic process to a steadily progressive form. This requires constant assessment of those factors which at given points in time tend to retard the movement toward black equality and the development of effective counterstrategy. Chapter 29 is such an assessment.

SETHARD FISHER

In Chapter 16 I emphasized the cyclic, or unsteady, nature of gains and losses by black Americans in the United States. In addition, I have suggested that a knowledge of the heritage of liberal individualism, colonialism, and capitalism is fundamental to understanding the current reluctance and hesitation of Americans to bring about social, political, and economic equality for black Americans. In this, the final chapter of this volume, I shall give special emphasis to the current situation and to certain achievements necessary for a fundamental change in the pattern of cyclic retardation.

Several recent events suggest that the current effort for Negro betterment may have reached a peak in the United States. The emergence of a gradual halt to "the movement" is reflected in several ways. Among these are chronic, illegal, and violent resistance to civil rights activities in the South by Southern racists; the implications of the assassination of President John F. Kennedy; the ejection of Congressman Adam Clayton Powell, a black American, from his seat in Congress, and thus from a most powerful position as head of the influential Health, Education, and Labor committee; removal of Cassius Clay, a black American, as world heavyweight boxing champion and failure to recognize his claim to the status of conscientious objector; the assassination of Reverend Martin Luther King, a black American, the charismatic leader of a most powerful black-white coalition which before his death appeared headed for broad social change in the interest of black Americans and poor Americans; the assassination of Senator Robert F. Kennedy, a widely recognized and politically powerful ally of black Americans; the degree of national popularity of the racist presidential aspirant George Wallace of Alabama; the emergence of white resistance to Negro betterment efforts in the North; the rise of militant black racism; and separatist tendencies among blacks. These are but a few of the symptoms of decline, and it is recognized that they are not of equal importance. Clearly, they must be viewed in light of a series of gains made by black Americans in recent times.[1]

In spite of these considerations, the current rate of social, economic, and political gains by black Americans makes the prospects for equality in these areas appear dim indeed. Thomas Pettigrew made the following assessment:

There were gains of sorts in employment in the 1950–1960 decade, but if the same rate of gain were to continue into the future, Negroes would not be proportionately represented among clerical workers until 1992 and they would not have proportional representation among skilled workers until the fifth year of the next century. They would not have proportional representation among professionals until the seventh year of the next century, or among sales workers until 2114, or among business managers and proprietors until 2730, which is eight centuries away.[2]

Pettigrew added that, although assets of Negro savings banks have increased thirty-two times since 1947 (compared to three times overall), total assets in Negro savings and loans constitute only .3 percent of the total assets of all savings and loans institutions. Also, if one combined the assets of the fifty-five Negro-controlled insurance companies, they would equal better than 320 million dollars, which, however, is a very small fraction of the assets of any one of the larger insurance companies in the United States.[3]

Broom and Glenn, too, provided a sobering assessment:

In 1950, there were about 42,500 self-employed male Negro businessmen in the United States. In 1960, there were only about 32,400—a decrease of 24 percent.[4]

As for black professionals:

The situation of Negro professional and semi-professional workers is similar to that of Negro businessmen, since most serve other Negroes as entrepreneurs or employees of Negro institutions . . . the representation of Negroes in the independent professions, such as medicine, dentistry, and law, was far less than the expected proportion in 1960. And in each of these there was a wide gap in earnings between whites and non-whites.[5]

On occupations they wrote:

The Negro-white occupational gap obviously is still very wide, and it is closing so slowly it will not disappear within the next century unless the rate of Negro gains sharply accelerates.[6]

Income gains for Negroes have been slower than occupational gains:

Negro Americans are on a treadmill. They must keep gaining on whites in education and occupation simply to stay the same distance behind in income.[7]

The inadequacy and the relative nature of Negro gains is clearly stressed in these studies. Negro occupational and income gains seldom, if ever, appear in the absence of more substantial gains in these same areas by whites. This can in no way be considered sufficient for realization of black equality with white Americans within a reasonable time.

Under most conditions of national disaster, of which black deprivation has now become an example, one can look to governmental intervention for major corrective action. Yet the history of governmental action in relation to black Americans has ranged in nature from uncertainly and reluctantly positive to overtly punitive and debilitative. The reason for this vacillation and uncertain assistance is that governmental structures normally reflect the interests and values of the dominant social institutions of a society, which in turn reflect the beliefs and values of major segments of a population. The question then becomes how a social movement with racial equality as a major goal can be built into a basically racist society. An analytical beginning in this direction will be made by bringing into sharper focus the underlying ethos that has neutralized the moral imperatives that one would expect to prohibit a flourishing racism in America.

Largely through the influence of the modern expression of liberal individualism, that is, social Darwinism, we are prone to view the victims of social problems as the originators of their own problems.[8]

As Hofstadter suggested:

Darwinism was one of the great informing insights in a long phase in the history of the conservative mind in America. It won those who wished to defend the status quo, above all the laissez-faire conservatives, who were first to pick up the instruments of social argument that were forged out of the Darwinism concepts.[9]

Thus, in speaking of a social problem, we have tended to refer to what was considered a personal, rather than a social, condition. We have tended to explain and understand the social problem in terms of individual expressions of it. Problems such as crime and delinquency, poverty, minority degradation, and so forth are often viewed in America as manifestations of the personal imperfection of individual representatives of these conditions; their social-problem status is explained as the result of their unsuitability for the competitive processes.

Social scientists have now shown that the stereotype of black Americans and other racial minorities as lazy, unmotivated, and prodigal individuals, as the social Darwinist view suggests, is ill-fitting. Their social condition must then be seen as resulting, not from inadequate personal qualities, but from lack of opportunity to become better situated. This emphasis immediately turns our attention to social policies and social institutions, for it is in this area that corrective efforts must be taken, rather than solely in the realm of the private and personal. Individual destitution must itself be seen as generated by pathogenic social policies and their supporting ideological vocabularies.

The liberal individualistic ethic, and its laissez-faire emphasis, is clearly inadequate as an orienting philosophy regulating the relation of government to the total society. This inadequacy is not only reflected in the manner by which rejects of an unfair competitive process are made to appear personally unfit through the rhetoric of social Darwinism. It is also shown by the kinds of policy responses of government to the periodic waves of social dissatisfaction generated by its favoring private business, commercial, and industrial interests. The increasing incapability of the "private sector" is readily apparent.

Technological innovation is increasingly making high levels of productivity possible with fewer workers. As machines and new productive techniques replace large segments of semi-skilled and unskilled workers, new training and new jobs are called for that cannot be provided by current patterns of economic organization, that is, private industry.

More than one in every three jobs added to the U.S. work force since 1947 has been in government, either at the federal, state, or local level, claimed Moynihan. He added that since 1957 state and local governments have provided 46 percent of the jobs added to the American work force.[10] The 1965 Manpower Report by the U.S. Department of Labor provided the following assessment:

. . . between 1947 and 1957, over three-quarters of the additional jobs created in the non-farm economy were in the private sector, . . . whereas between 1957 and 1962 only one-half of total non-farm job growth was in the private sector. In private non-farm industries employment growth fell from an average of 700,000 additional jobs per year between 1947 and 1957 to a yearly gain of only 270,000 jobs from 1957 to 1962. . . .
Starting in 1961 the Government undertook a number of expansionary fiscal and monetary actions aimed at solving specific manpower problems. . . . Despite what would have been considered by most past standards a healthy increase in output and employment, unemployment actually rose by 150,000 between 1962 and 1963.[11]

The report continued:

It became obvious that further major steps must be taken . . . to stimulate a higher rate of job creation . . .[12]

Finally, on private versus public sector performance, the report stated that:

. . . despite the renewed strength in private industry (particularly the goods industries) the government sector continues to be a major employer of the

Nation's manpower. . . . Consistent growth in the government sector . . . has characterized postwar economic development.[13]

Although government employment appears to be rapidly replacing private industry as a source of new jobs, this development has but a negligible positive effect on the black community:

> Although there appears to be less discrimination by government agencies than by private industry, only a small percent of Negroes can hope to find government work. Like all other work, it increasingly requires higher skills and therefore is not open to the poorly educated and unskilled. Removal of all remaining discrimination against Negroes in government employment, or even considerable reverse discrimination, would effect only a small closing of the occupational and income gaps in the total labor force. Closing of these gaps depends more on removal of racial barriers in private employment, where most jobs are located, and, as we have repeatedly emphasized, an increase in the relative qualifications of Negroes.[14]

The significant fact about job expansion is that the private sector is no longer capable, with new technology and an unrelenting adherence to the profit motive, of meeting the work needs of the country. As this capability of the private sector declines, substitute mechanisms must appear if widespread unemployment is to be averted. The consequences of this crisis will be most devastating for black Americans.

The insufficiency of governmental response to minority needs, however, is no more crucial than the nature of the insufficient responses that are made. These involve a strategy of financing large-scale programs that have broad middle-class appeal and profitability. Although such programs appear to provide some short-range material advantage to the poor and to blacks, they have the additional probable consequence of actually destroying potential in the black community for institutionalized structures, which would make continuous and accelerated gain possible. The case of the Office of Economic Opportunity and the "Model Cities" program is illustrative.

Pettigrew has referred to 1963 as the year of Negro revolt. Stirrings throughout the country were underway among the underprivileged, especially the Negroes, to begin an articulation of their grievances with others similarly aggrieved. Fanny Lou Hamer, Aaron Henry, and Medgar Evers were among the new leaders in the Negro's struggle for equality. The student movement had built several strategic bases among Negroes in the South—stimulating, coercing, helping along the activation of Southern Negroes, and nurturing the development of a new, more militant movement throughout the South for Negro equality. CORE, SNCC, and the Southern Christian Leadership Conference were among the major groups stimulating this new development. A coalition of these diverse forces resulted in a massive demand by a broad spectrum of Americans that elected leaders provide some solution to the plight of Negroes and the underprivileged. The Office of Economic Opportunity may be seen as the official response to the growing public awareness of, and dissatisfaction with, the plight of the black American, and of poor Americans generally.

As stated in the legislation, the Economic Opportunities Act

. . . authorizes assistance . . . for communities conducting campaigns to reduce poverty . . . communities will be encouraged and helped to develop individual programs aimed at the special problems of their own poor families. . . . Each community action program will afford experience in the operation of this program—(a nation-wide action, research, and demonstration program) and will suggest new ways in which communities may attack the problems of poverty.

To be eligible for Federal assistance, there should be a showing that the program—
"(1) will mobilize and utilize public or private resources in an attack on poverty;
"(2) will provide activities of sufficient scope and size to give promise of progress toward the elimination of poverty or a cause or causes of poverty;
"(3) is developed and will be conducted and administered with the maximum feasible participation of the residents of the area, including the poor themselves; and,
"(4) will be conducted, administered, or coordinated by a public or non-profit private agency, with maximum feasible participation of the public agencies and private non-profit organizations primarily concerned with the community's problems of poverty." [15]

The work, which local Economic Opportunity Agencies took as a major goal, was a substantial remedy to a range of problems confronting the poor. There was, and is, wide variation in the kinds of concrete programs implemented locally to achieve this goal, as well as wide variation in effectiveness of operating local programs. Eventually a range of local community action agencies was spawned throughout the country. Much of the energy and enthusiasm that went into these organizations came from the civil rights movement, as this movement suddenly came to view the "anti-poverty" program as a means of correcting some of the substantial ills of American society, especially as these ills related to the poor and to the black minority. In many areas of the United States there occurred during 1965–1966 a rather large-scale transfer of leadership from the civil rights movement to the ranks of the paid staff of the "anti-poverty" program, and thus a gradual demise of the mobilized civil rights effort. For many the major motif for civil rights and protest activity no longer existed. The momentum of the social movement for change was decelerated. This is one important effect of the anti-poverty legislation on the massive civil rights build-up of 1963. As local efforts began to gain strength throughout the country, the development of a somewhat organized sense of advocacy and militancy by the poor, and especially the minority poor, began to occur also. This to some extent appeared to justify the shift in the view of those who sought reform through the civil rights movement into more local and programmatic concerns. "The Mothers" of San Bovar county are perhaps representative of these new stirrings among the poor.

This "club" was made up of a group of low-income women in a valley community of a far-Western state. They were all Negro, with low levels of education, and an extraordinary eye for action on the "establishment" in the interest of their community. This group began with a grievance over failure of the local school system to provide bus service for the children from their community, whereas such service was provided to a "white" community an equal distance from the school. A few articulate women of the community began to meet, at first spontaneously and later on a regular basis, to discuss the issue. Out of these gatherings there grew community-wide meetings wherein the issue was aired and support for "The Mothers" developed throughout this sector of the community. Meetings with school officials and local, state, and federal government officials followed, as "The Mothers" confronted a reluctant, hesitant, and fearful officialdom on the school issue. Among the local organizations in support of this group in its earliest developmental phases was the local community action agency, though this support was not a reflection of uniform approval by the board of the agency. Rather, it was based on the interpretation of his task by a young, capable, idealistic executive director of this agency.[16]

Eventually some concessions were gained by "The Mothers" of San Bovar county, but more noticeable during a six- to ten-month span were their gains in sensitivity to and knowledge about their own community and its relation to the broader community, especially its power structure. Eventually the group took up other issues, and began to criticize and challenge the traditional Negro leadership groups, especially the local NAACP. A bitter public controversy emerged between the two groups, one effect of which was to prod the traditional group into greater use of its influence and resources in the interest of the minority poor.

"The Mothers," for a brief time, were a new force in their community— an organized, militant force in the interest of the minority poor. Their protest activities were a major concern of politicians, especially elected politicians, at all governmental levels. This kind of unprecedented challenge to the established injustices against minority and poverty communities, which "The Mothers" presented, appeared in many communities with the gradual build-up of the community action program. It was undoubtedly recognition of the potential for far-reaching and much-needed change in the interest of the minorities and the poor which led, after two years of operation, to considerable congressional concern about the Office of Economic Opportunity in general, and the community action program in particular. Proposals began to appear in Congress, and within the OEO, for transfer of many of the functions of the community action program to established agencies, a direction that has much support within the federal establishment, especially among the established agencies such as the Labor Department and the Office of Education. Immediately prior to the summer of 1967, before the Negro revolt spread through the major cities in the North, there was the general feeling among regional and central office staff in OEO that the organization would be dissolved as an agency altogether. Another projected version of its fate was that it would be relocated and demoted within the federal bureaucratic structure. As the summer of 1967 approached, widespread rioting in black ghettos occurred. The pressure to do away with OEO abated somewhat, and its continuation at least for an additional year was more or less assured, though not without considerable congressional dissatisfaction.

It became apparent as the fate of OEO was publicly and privately debated that the limit of its innovative and creative potential in the interest of the poor possibly had been reached. The program had developed no widespread, vocal, articulate spokesmen in the general population.[17] It had become something of a perennial target for conservative criticism. The accomplishments of OEO were certainly far less than had been hoped for and expected by its idealistic liberal and radical supporters from the civil rights movement. It had not begun to deal with the crucial issues facing the poor in America. Problems of job creation, job training, medical services, and remedial education were relatively untouched by this new agency, as it was required to struggle for survival on a year-to-year basis. Such a precarious existence made long-range planning impossible.

Recognition of the failure of the OEO to deal with the fundamental problems of the poor and the increasing dissatisfaction with this agency in the eyes of the general public represent a betrayal of the faith in it by those who left the civil rights movement and saw the OEO as a needed replacement for their efforts. At this point the OEO appears to have a rather uncertain life expectancy. Its main accomplishment seems to have been to rather successfully cripple the organized massive protest movement which brought it into being.

It is perhaps because of recognition of the fact that a successful OEO, as originally conceived, necessarily involves widespread political, social, and economic change that great emphasis and support has been given another federal program, the functions of which appear to overlap in many ways those of the OEO. It should be stressed that this new program is far less meaningful to the interests of the poor generally than was the OEO, and it is potentially a significant factor in retarding the progressive movement of minorities in American society. The new program is that of the Housing and Urban Development agency, an agency elevated by President Johnson to cabinet-level status.

In 1966 Congress passed the Demonstration Cities and Metropolitan Development Act, the important feature of which, for this discussion, was Title I, Model Neighborhoods in Demonstration Cities.[18] This title of the legislation

. . . provides for a new program designed to demonstrate how the living environment and the general welfare of people living in slum and blighted neighborhoods can be substantially improved in cities of all sizes and in all parts of the country. It calls for a comprehensive attack on social, economic and physical problems in selected slum and blighted areas through the most effective and economical concentration and coordination of Federal, State, and local public and private efforts. The statute provides financial and technical assistance to enable cities to plan, develop and carry out comprehensive local programs containing new and imaginative proposals to develop "model" neighborhoods.[19]

The neighborhoods selected for rehabilitation in large part overlap the "target areas" of the Office of Economic Opportunity. As the *Guide* states:

The model neighborhood area should be predominantly residential in character. Commercial and industrial areas of the city should not be included except as they are directly and primarily related to the needs of the people of the neighborhood for services or for jobs.

Areas selected for upgrading into model neighborhoods should be at least in part hardcore slums in which low-income families are concentrated. These areas are characterized by social and economic pressures resulting from such factors as overcrowding, poverty, unemployment, dependence on welfare payments, low educational and skill levels, poor health and disease, and crime and delinquency.[20]

This is envisioned as a massive or "comprehensive" effort in urban areas, and, as is true of the OEO effort, it is to be based on a broad consensus in each participating city. To carry out this program each local project

. . . should be truly comprehensive, both in range and completeness of the activities proposed and in the resources brought to bear, with special effort made to enlist the effective support and meaningful participation of private enterprise as well as individual citizens.[21]

And, further, it is explained that

. . . the City Demonstration Agency should not be a special purpose agency with an independent governing board which is not representative of the major agencies and interests involved in the program. . . .

The City Demonstration Agency should be assured of the cooperation of independent public and private agencies whose participation is necessary to program success.[22]

Great stress is placed in this program on utilization of existing agencies, public and private; participation by the poor themselves, although not explicitly ruled out, is in no way stressed to the extent that the OEO both emphasized and mandated such participation. This is clearly a program that will utilize existing agencies and institutions. A special section of the *Guide* re-emphasizes the intention of this project to make use of "private initiative and enterprise" to the maximum extent possible:

The program should make special effort to enlist the support and participation of private enterprise. In achieving the various goals of the program, steps should be taken to create a climate within the model neighborhood area which will encourage business activities resulting in employment opportunities for area residents.

The involvement and encouragement of private enterprise can be achieved in a variety of ways: soliciting the advice and consultation of business leadership within the community; working with employers to develop training and manpower programs; preserving and expanding small business and commercial opportunities within the model neighborhood area; encouraging and assisting builders and contractors in rehabilitation, and new construction and lending institutions in providing financing. Of particular interest would be consideration of special tax and other incentives designed to encourage rehabilitation and new construction and to help attract major commercial or industrial activities to the area.

The program should also be designed to ensure maximum involvement of voluntary non-profit health, welfare and religious organizations in planning and executing the program.[23]

Although this legislation does stress employment of low-income people in the various programs and provision of gainful employment for the community generally, there is no mandate that community residents share in the governing apparatus of the Demonstration Cities Agency. It is stressed that

. . . the program should provide opportunities for the constructive involvement of citizens in the Model neighborhood area and the city as a whole in planning and carrying out program activities. . . . planning should be carried out both *with* as well as *for* the people living in the affected area. . . . Programs should provide mechanisms for a flow of communication and meaningful dialogue between the citizens of the area and the demonstration agency. . . . Existing neighborhood organizations which have already established close ties with the area population, as well as new organizations developed by grass-roots organizational efforts, should be utilized.[24]

The crucial factor here is that residents of the areas of focus have no legislative right to be an official part of the Demonstration Cities program. To the extent that this program replaces the efforts of the Office of Economic Opportunity in low-income areas throughout the country, there will be a loss of leverage by the poor as autonomous advocates for their needs and interests. But the corrosive nature of this program on potential and much-needed political gains for blacks is perhaps its most ominous feature.

Population shifts among Negroes in recent years have led to new possibilities for political gains for black Americans. These shifts have taken several directions, one of which is from rural to urban areas in both the South and the North. Another shift is from the South to the North.

Migration to the North has led to large concentrations of Negroes in the central cities of the major Northern metropolitan areas.

During the decade following 1910, the great migration of Negroes from the rural south began with the pull of new opportunities for industrial employment in the North. . . . All heavily industrialized states now have sizeable Negro populations, and 40 percent of all Negroes live outside of the South. . . . At the same time, the Negro percentage of the population has increased sharply in many localities in the North and West.

Thirty percent of urban Negroes compared with 26 percent of urban whites lived in the twelve largest metropolitan areas in 1960. . . . In the twelve most populous metropolitan areas in 1960, 55 percent of the whites lived outside the central cities, compared with only 19 percent of the Negroes.[25]

Tilly, Jackson, and Kay in their report on Wilmington, Delaware, have described the mechanism within urban areas by which this has come about. They found that segregation in residential areas increased between 1940 and 1950 and has not decreased since 1950, and that housing segregation in Wilmington serves mainly to keep nonwhites out of white areas.

In 1934, about two-thirds of Wilmington's Negro population lived in blocks with white majorities; by 1940, the figure was one-third of the Negro households, by 1950, a quarter, by 1960, less than a fifth. . . . white families . . . moved out and were replaced by Negro families. The eventual effect of many moves of this kind is, of course, the production of new all-Negro neighborhoods.[26]

A more general and inadvertent consequence of this phenomenon in many major metropolitan areas has been the creation of enormous political potential for Negroes. Table 1 by Banfield and Wilson[27] shows this

TABLE 1. PERCENTAGE OF NON-WHITES IN LARGE CITIES, 1950 AND 1960

City	1950	1960
Boston	5.3	9.8
Chicago	14.1	23.6
Cincinnati	15.6	21.8
Cleveland	16.3	28.9
Dallas	13.2	19.3
Detroit	16.4	29.2
Houston	21.1	23.2
Kansas City	12.3	17.7
Los Angeles	10.7	16.8
Milwaukee	3.6	8.9
New York	9.8	14.7
Philadelphia	18.3	26.7
Pittsburgh	12.3	16.8
Richmond	31.7	42.0
San Francisco	10.5	18.4
St. Louis	10.0	28.8
Washington	35.4	54.8

Source: Edward C. Banfield and James Q. Wilson, City Politics (Cambridge, Mass.: Harvard University Press, 1963), p. 13.

potential by pointing up increases in Negro percentages of population over time.

Table 2 by the same authors points to the large gap in nine cities reflecting unused Negro political potential as of 1960.[28]

Recognition of the vast potential increases in political power for Negroes in urban areas is what makes recent federal trends, in the interest of the total community, of dubious value to Negroes. With the decline, or emasculation, of the OEO and the rise of demonstration cities, the breaking up of Negro concentrations in the large cities and the consequent decline of political potential appear a very likely consequence.[29]

TABLE 2. NEGRO REPRESENTATION ON CITY COUNCILS IN SELECTED NON-SOUTHERN LARGE CITIES

City	Total City Council Seats	Seats Held by Negroes in 1961	Percentage of Seats Held by Negroes	Negroes by Percent Population, 1961
Detroit	9	1	11.1	28.9
Cleveland	33	8	24.2	28.6
St. Louis	29	6	20.7	28.6
Philadelphia	17	1	5.9	26.4
Chicago	50	6	12.0	22.9
Cincinnati	9	0	0	21.6
New York	25	2	8.0	14.0
Los Angeles	15	0	0	13.5
Boston	9	0	0	9.1

Source: Edward C. Banfield and James Q. Wilson, City Politics *(Cambridge, Mass.: Harvard University Press, 1963), p. 293.*

Thus, one important technique of retardation may be seen as governmental failure to make strategic use of the public resources at its disposal to promote equality for Negroes. Indeed, this tactic suggests a governmental strategy to subvert the development of black American equality by use of strategically designed programs, ostensibly in the interest of all. The use of public resources must be of major concern to the movement for Negro betterment. This movement must adopt as a first priority the goal of unstinting use of public resources, at the local, state, and federal levels, in the interest of the dispossessed black and of poverty populations. This means, of course, overriding the entrenched and well-fortified business, commercial, and industrial interests whose profits are realized at the expense of the poor and the dispossessed. One specific goal in this direction must be government-sponsored cooperative economic activity in selected commodity and service areas. Such activities should be located in ghetto areas and run primarily by ghetto residents. Special areas of economic life should be designated for ghetto production and/or service, and in other areas federally financed and ghetto-run economic enterprise should compete with private enterprise. The groundwork laid by the Office of Economic Opportunity in setting up community action agencies in local communities could easily become the organizational mechanism through which such developments could take place. This requires, of course, more extensive funding of the OEO, a renewal of the mandate for participation by the poor, and a prohibition against the destruction of black American population concentrations by governmental programs.[30] Because of the trend toward regional government and away from city government, black population concentrations cannot exert much power or have much say in the overall way in which a city is run. They are generally able to influence only decisions affecting their particular regions.

Clearly, the straightforward and unstinting use of public resources in the interest of black Americans and other destitute groups is impossible given the ethic of social Darwinism as a starting point, for it stresses that the condition of blacks is largely brought about by their own personal imperfections. This realization suggests a second strategic focal point of the movement for Negro betterment—the development of a new ethic of American life.

In Chapter 16 I have referred to the white Anglo-Saxon Protestant cultural syndrome and to its pathogenic effect on black Americans.[31] It is important that the historical and international aspect of the ethic of white superiority embodied in this cultural pattern be emphasized, in order that its functional significance in the United States of America today be better understood. Such understanding is a necessary precondition for its effective demise and for the emergence of a new ethic that promotes respect for and pride in blackness by blacks and whites alike. The *negative* and *subordinate* characterization of black people so deeply embedded in the cultural and institutional structure of the United States is a legacy of the widespread exploitation of blacks by the major European powers, which I have referred to as colonialism.[32] Colonialism generated a definition of those who were dehumanized and exploited as inhuman and soulless, thereby neutralizing ethical proscriptions against their dehumanization. The current imagery employed by white Americans in their thought about black Americans, and unfortunately by many black Americans about themselves, is a direct derivative of this colonialist past. It is a chronic, latent source of legitimation for white aggression and violence that periodically has been a typical feature of black-white relations in the United States. As several studies reveal, movements by blacks to mobilize in the interest of changing their subordinate role breed countermovements among whites, who find themselves unequipped to view blacks comfortably as social equals. When solidarity and pride in blackness begin to emerge among Negroes and efforts toward social equality develop, they touch off fear and alarm among white Americans. This, then, sets the climate for white aggression against blacks, legitimated among whites by reactivation of the colonialist and racist imagery of blacks, from which American society has not as yet escaped.[33]

Not all groups in the United States are equally amenable to the kind of change sought by the movement for Negro betterment. Anti-Negro sentiment is highest among those whites for whom the social Darwinist myth yet holds promise. They are those who share the overall goal within the culture of monetary success and accept conventional means for achieving it, but whose opportunities for goal achievement are narrowly restricted.[34] Such persons see the movement for Negro equality as a threat to their own upwardly mobile aspirations. In social-class terms, they are whites in the upper-lower and lower-middle rungs of the class spectrum. These people are most keenly sensitive to social gain by black Americans, largely because of their own very real difficulties in achieving and maintaining their goal of upward mobility. This group is most receptive to antiblack slogans, ideology, and actions. Community groups composed predominantly of these class elements within the white community are likely sources of movements of antiblack resistance, as studies of the Ku Klux Klan and other virulently racist groups show.[35]

Those who would plan and initiate strategy in the interest of black American betterment must seek creative coalitions with amenable elements of the white community in an effort to build a broad base for necessary nonracist social change in the United States. These must be coalitions of equals rather than a restructuring of past patterns of dominance and subordination. This requires an increasing militancy and sense of strategy among black Americans and a growing recognition of the retarding effect of black-separatist tendencies on the overall movement. The black separatist, antiwhite viewpoint leads to isolation of blacks from other forces for social change in the society, thereby allowing their goals to be more readily thwarted by a mobilized white resistance. It is precisely the organization and mobilization of white resistance which historically has been a major element in undermining Negro gains. As Glenn suggests in Chapter 28, white resistance must be overcome by a forceful countermovement with broad social change as its objective. This movement must be unified by a new ethic that encompasses enthusiastically, and takes for granted, pride in blackness and the need for black power. I take Wilensky's and Lebeaux's suggestion of an ethic of social responsibility [36] as including this possibility.

Curiously, traditional radical rhetoric appears insufficient as a guide for the development of black-white alliances in the interest of social change at this point in history.[37] Dominant elements of the working class are least amenable to social change in the interest of black American betterment. Thus, seeking a base for social change in the American working class is at this time an unrealistic move. The influence of the traditional left would likely tend to be more conservative than the influence of other groups unencumbered by allegiances to past political history. As Eldridge Cleaver, Peace and Freedom party presidential candidate in 1968, explained to party members in attempting to pacify those who objected to his choice of Jerry Rubin as running mate:

> The Peace and Freedom party was failing to come to terms with the cultural revolution. . . . The cultural revolution in the white community is to the left of the political left in the white community. Jerry Rubin understands that.[38]

Traditional leftists based their objection to Rubin on his involvement with groups such as "Diggers, Hippies, Yippies, Up-Against-the-Wall-Mother-fuckers, and other street people."[39] The traditional left viewed these groups with the abhorrence and awe of the conventional community. Cleaver favored involvement and recognition of such groups based on their conscious departure from the dominant Anglo-Saxon cultural traditions of the country, an important aspect of the growth of a relevant black movement for social change.

It is among Americans who are sensitive to the need for social change and who are aware of and sympathetic to the peculiar need for pride and power for blacks that alliances must be sought. In nurturing and developing such alliances care must be taken that the needs of the black community remain of the highest priority.

Current trends toward retardation of black American gains reflect essentially the same social process that historically has worked to stabilize blacks in a subordinate status. The rise of white resistance in the form of the Ku Klux Klan and other newer paramilitary groups is but a repetition of the usual societal reaction to Negro gains. It is, in fact, social gain by black Americans that calls such groups into being. They represent the conspiritorial efforts of the white racist community to preserve its prerogatives and to preserve the subordination of blacks by force and violence. Nor is governmental manipulation of the social situation of the black community new, though the impetus now given this tactic at the federal level appears to be an ominous new feature.[40] Traditionally, gerrymandering has been a more locally initiated racist tactic. Thus, to call these tactics new is, in a sense, to mislabel them. Nevertheless, they do call attention to the need for new strategies for freedom and reform. Among these must be continuous and accelerated assertions of black pride, and the growth of black culture. This growth must temper itself by the recognition that pride in blackness does not mean a virulent and indiscriminate antiwhite attitude, but rather an antiracist attitude. This new strategy must also consciously seek new and creative alliances with white groups, such as students, liberals, and others who also seek to promote black equality. Finally, these new tactics must be developed and executed with full realization that the goal of black equality is a generational matter, because the kinds of structural and ideological changes within the country that would make such an achievement possible are fundamental. They require continuity of effort and a few generations of relentless struggle with the racist status quo, and determined detachment from its racist culture. Many who were involved in the initiation of this antiracist reaction are not likely to see it move to a successful conclusion. However, the fact that there are those still willing to play a deliberate part in the drama is testimony to the tenacious survival of the humanistic tradition of the Enlightenment on which the prosperity and continuity of civilized life itself in large part depends.

NOTES

1. This includes the election of a Negro senator from Massachusetts, appointment of several Negroes to high positions in the federal government, and some political gains in both the North and South amid traditional and current rampant black repression:

   > Twenty-three black candidates, seven of them supported by the Freedom Democratic Party (MFDP), now have won political office in Mississippi, following the recent general election. The biggest gain was Robert Clark's Holmes County victory, which made him the first black man elected to the legislature since Reconstruction.

   See "Struggle Changes in Mississippi," *The Southern Patriot* (December 1967), p. 2.
   In Memphis, Negroes won three seats on the ten-member council.
   See also "Election Gains in the South," *The Southern Patriot* (December 1967), p. 2.
2. Thomas Pettigrew, "White-Negro Confrontations," in Eli Ginzberg (ed.), *The Negro Challenge to the Business Community* (New York: McGraw-Hill, 1964), p. 46.
3. *Ibid.*
4. Leonard Broom and Norval Glenn, *Transformation of the Negro American* (New York: Harper & Row, 1965), p. 136.
5. *Ibid.*, p. 143.
6. *Ibid.*, p. 115.
7. *Ibid.*, p. 119. More recent data (1966) from the U.S. Bureau of Labor Statistics suggests some improvement in income, educational, and occupational gains for Negroes, but no alteration of the overall pattern described here. See *Social and Economic Conditions of Negroes in the United States*, BLS, Report No. 22, U.S. Dept. of Commerce, 1967.
8. Albert K. Cohen, following Kingsley Davis, has referred to a more general version of this phenomenon in connection with research on crime and delinquency—the "evil causes evil fallacy." See Albert K. Cohen, "Multiple Factor Approaches" in Marvin E. Wolfgang *et al.* (eds.), *The Sociology of Crime and Delinquency* (New York: Wiley, 1962), pp. 77–80.
9. Richard Hofstadter, *Social Darwinism in American Thought* (Boston: Beacon Press, 1959), p. 5.
10. Daniel P. Moynihan, "Political Perspectives," in Eli Ginzberg (ed.), *The Negro Challenge to the Business Community* (New York: McGraw-Hill, 1964), p. 79.
11. *Manpower Report of the President* United States Department of Labor (Washington, D.C.: Government Printing Office, 1965), p. 10.
12. *Ibid.*
13. *Ibid.*, p. 16.

14. Broom and Glenn, *op. cit.*, p. 156.
15. *Economic Opportunity Act of 1964* (Washington, D.C.: Office of Economic Opportunity, August 20, 1964).
16. Such support, however, encountered intense opposition from conventional elements within the community action agency itself. Very often the alignments of such agencies were against insurgent new developments of this kind.
17. With the exception of the annual conference of mayors, which seemed to be a continuing source of support for an autonomous O. E. O. The mayors' primary concern, of course, was directed toward the additional funds which the O. E. O. brought into their local communities.
18. *Improving the Quality of Urban Life: A Program Guide to Model Neighborhoods in Demonstration Cities,* U.S. Department of Housing and Urban Development (Washington, D.C.: Government Printing Office, 1966).
19. *Ibid.*, p. 1.
20. *Ibid.*, p. 6.
21. *Ibid.*, p. 8.
22. *Ibid.*, pp. 11–12.
23. *Ibid.*, p. 18.
24. *Ibid.*, p. 14.
25. Broom and Glenn, *op. cit.*, pp. 159, 160, 162, 163.
26. Charles Tilly, Wagner D. Jackson, and Barry Kay, *Race and Residence in Wilmington* (New York: Columbia University Press, 1965), pp. 60–61.
27. Edward C. Banfield and James Q. Wilson, *City Politics* (Cambridge, Mass.: Harvard University Press, 1963), p. 13.
28. *Ibid.*, p. 293. Of course, some change in these figures would be required in the light of political events in several of these cities since 1960. Yet it is unlikely that the power vacuums reflected in the table are closed.
29. An additional related tactic is the recent emphasis on regionalization of local government in many parts of the country. The effect of this tactic for black Americans would be to broaden the racial composition of the relevant political territory and thus diminish the likelihood of Negro political rule.
30. An additional related goal in the interest of betterment of the minority and poverty communities must be designation of percentages of public funds on a local, state, and federal level to be used exclusively to provide new jobs and job training for the dispossessed, both black and white. Beginnings in this direction have been made to a limited extent, but such efforts are invariably insufficient. Significant portions of such funds invariably are taken by the already affluent.
31. Sethard Fisher, "Negro Life and Social Process," *Social Problems,* vol. 13 (Winter 1966).
32. See "The Cultural Residue of European Preparations and Legitimations," p. 2 of this volume.
33. Myrdal stresses the ambivalence among white Americans about black subordination, suggesting that substantial anti- or non-colonialist imagery also exists in America. See Gunnar Myrdal, *An American Dilemma,* vol. 1 (New York: McGraw-Hill, 1967), pp. 1–80.
34. A scheme used by Robert Merton to explain differential rates of deviance within a social system. The same phenomenon has often been identified in studies of race relations in the United States, though in somewhat different language. For example, Myrdal writes:

> It has often occurred to me, when reflecting upon the responses I get from white laboring people on this strategic question, that my friends among the younger Negro intellectuals . . . have perhaps . . . not had enough occasion to find out for themselves what a bitter, spiteful, and relentless feeling often prevails against the Negroes among lower class white people in America. . . . The competitive situation is, and is likely to remain, highly unstable. [Myrdal, *op. cit.*, p. 69.]

35. See the Mouledoux article, Chapter 18. Note in this connection the fairly recent reports of infiltration of police forces in Northern metropolitan areas by "right-

wing" elements and the illegal violence, and threats of violence, which they promote. One brief account of this appeared as an Associated Press report from New York. Representatives of The Law Enforcement Group of New York allegedly converged on a group of Black Panthers and their supporters in the sixth-floor corridor of a criminal court building. This report appeared in the September 5, 1968 issue of the *Edmonton Journal*, p. 2.

Another instance comes from a report on Ann Arbor, Michigan. This report describes policemen who are members of an organization called Breakthrough. They were described as illegally pursuing Tom Hayden, founder of Students for a Democratic Society and a participant in several efforts of radical social reform. See the August 23–29 issue of *The Berkeley Barb*, p. 5.

36. Harold L. Wilensky and Charles N. Lebeaux, *Industrial Society and Social Welfare* (New York: Free Press, 1965).
37. Myrdal, *op. cit.*, I, p. 69.
38. "Cleaver Tells How He'll Lead," *The Berkeley Barb*, Aug. 23–29, 1968, p. 5.
39. *Ibid.*
40. The Housing and Urban Development Agency, the federal agency from which the model cities program comes, was first headed by a black American, Robert Weaver.

SUGGESTIONS FOR FURTHER READING

Part I

Du Bois, W. E. B. *Black Folk: Then and Now.* New York: Henry Holt and Company, 1939.

A wide-ranging account of the early history and the cultural and political development of Africa within the context of colonialism. It also treats the topics of slave trade and the social history of black people in the United States. In the final chapter the question of the future relations of black people to the rest of the world is considered.

Fanon, Franz. *The Wretched of the Earth.* New York: Grove Press, 1963.

This volume, written by a black psychiatrist and revolutionary, deals with the human ravages wrought by colonialism and with the strategy by which decolonialization throughout the world may be achieved.

Gobineau, Joseph Arthur, Comte de. *Essay on the Inequality of Human Races.* London: Heinemann, 1915.

An historical expression of the rationale for white superiority over other races by an influential French diplomat-scholar.

Heilbroner, Robert L. *The Limits of American Capitalism.* New York: Harper Torchbooks, 1965.

We are told that the dominant system of economic organization in the Western world, capitalism, will inevitably change. This change will have an important bearing on social development in the rest of the world, especially on the so-called underdeveloped countries that are inhabited largely by black and brown people.

Hitler, Adolph. *Mein Kampf.* Boston: Houghton Mifflin, 1943.

A modern expression of the Aryan Myth and of the need for the use of state power to promote and maintain the superiority of Aryans.

Part II

Cayton, Horace R. *Long Old Road.* New York: Trident Press, 1965.

This autobiography clearly reflects, within one black family, the deterioration of black American social gain that comes with the onset and spread of racist repression.

De Tocqueville, Alexis. *Democracy in America*. New York: Vintage Books, 1945. See especially chap. XVIII.

An account of the blacks, whites, and Indians by an astute French observer whose main concern is with the strengths and weaknesses of democracy and its institutions in America. His prognosis for the three above-mentioned groups is noteworthy.

Du Bois, W. E. B. *Black Reconstruction in America 1860–1880*. Cleveland: World Publishing, 1964.

An account of the resubordination of black Americans after Emancipation within an economic frame of reference. Especially noteworthy is the sixteenth chapter, which clearly sets forth the mechanism of resubordination.

Elkins, Stanley. *Slavery*. 2nd ed. Chicago: University of Chicago Press, 1968.

A detailed examination of slavery as a social institution functional to capitalism. A comparison of slavery in Protestant and Catholic countries is presented. An interesting though less relevant aspect of the volume is a discussion of the psychological consequences of slavery in the United States.

Fast, Howard. *Freedom Road*. New York: Duell, Sloan and Pearce, 1944.

The story of Gideon Jackson, which symbolizes black aspirations and possibilities for social development immediately after the Civil War. The increase in intensity of white resistance to black prosperity is dramatically presented.

Styron, William. *The Confessions of Nat Turner*. New York: Random House, 1967.

A powerful account of an important though abortive episode in the history of racism in the United States. This volume aroused extensive criticism among a group of black American intellectuals. See John Hendrik Clarke *et al. William Styron's Nat Turner: Ten Black Writers Respond*. Boston: Beacon Press. On the other hand, it has been eloquently defended by a white American radical. See Genovese, Eugene D. "The Nat Turner Case," *The New York Review of Books* (September 12, 1968), pp. 34–37.

Tannenbaum, Frank. *Slave and Citizen: The Negro in the Americas*. New York: Vintage Books, 1946.

This short volume deals with the distribution of blacks in the Americas and with the differences between Latin American, British, French, and American slave systems.

Woodward, C. Vann. *The Strange Career of Jim Crow*. New York: Oxford University Press, Inc., 1957.

The second major episode of black subordination in the United States is discussed in detail in this volume. This is the institution of Jim Crow that succeeded slavery after a brief period of prosperity for black Americans after Emancipation.

Part III

Broom, Leonard and Norval D. Glenn. *Transformation of the Negro American*. New York: Harper & Row, 1965.

Drawing on 1960 census data, the authors analyze in detail the educational, occupational, and financial situation of black Americans.

Brown, Claude. *Manchild in the Promised Land*. New York: Macmillan, 1965.

A youthful autobiographical account of modern life in a black ghetto of New York.

Hickey, Neil and Ed Edwin. *Adam Clayton Powell and the Politics of Race*. New York: Fleet Publishing Corporation, 1965.

A biographical account of the most politically influential black in America. This account does not cover his ejection from Congress by his white colleagues, or his recent return to Congress though deprived of his former seniority, by vote of his constituency.

Pettigrew, Thomas. *A Profile of the Negro American*. Princeton, N.J.: Van Nostrand, 1964.

A selective look at the modern black Americans that explodes certain strongly-held myths about them, for example, that of their alleged lower intelligence when compared with whites. The author's recommendations regarding the unique opportunity of the Civil Rights Movement to advance the cause of the black American is, in retrospect, instructive.

Report of the National Advisory Committee on Civil Disorders. Kerner Commission. Washington, D.C.: Government Printing Office, 1968. Vols. I and II.

This new document attempts to discover the causes of ghetto violence and courageously concludes that white racism is a central causal element. As an overview of the current situation of black Americans it is without equal.

Thompson, Daniel C. *The Negro Leadership Class.* Englewood Cliffs, N.J.: Prentice-Hall, 1963.

A study of patterns of political leadership in the black community of New Orleans, Louisiana. Changing styles of leadership are described and analyzed in terms of the current race crisis.

Weinberg, Kenneth. *Black Victory: Carl Stokes and the Winning of Cleveland.* Chicago: Quadrangle Books, 1968.

An account of the rise and subsequent prosperity of a black Mayor in a major metropolitan area of the United States.

Part IV

Aptheker, Herbert. *American Negro Slave Revolts.* New York: Columbia University Press, 1943.

Documentation of black resistance to white oppression under slavery.

Baldwin, James. *The Fire Next Time.* New York: Dial Press, 1963.

An insightful account of aspects of the inner elements of black resentment to white oppression in the United States, written by a black writer-intellectual.

Burns, W. H. *The Voices of Negro Protest in America.* London: Oxford University Press, 1963.

An account of major black protest figures in the United States.

Elinson, Howard. "Radicalism and the Negro Movement," in Raymond J. Murphy and Howard Elinson (eds.), *Problems and Prospects of the Negro Movement.* Belmont, Calif.: Wadsworth Publishing Company, Inc., 1966, pp. 355–375.

An establishment-oriented interpretation of the relationship between black protest and radicalism in the general community.

Killian, Lewis M. *The Impossible Revolution? Black Power and the American Dream.* New York: Random House, Inc., 1968.

A useful recent account of the development of the current black protest effort and of its prospects for basic change in the interest of black equality.

Lincoln, Charles E. *The Black Muslims in America.* Boston: Beacon Press, 1961.

An account of the history, ideology, and prominence of the major black separatists in the United States.

Part V

Cornwell, Elmer E. "Bosses, Machines, and Ethnic Groups," *The Annals,* Vol. CCCLIII (May 1964).

An examination of the rule of machine politics and ethnicity in American political life.

Fuchs, Lawrence (ed.). *American Ethnic Politics.* New York: Harper & Row, 1968.

Several articles on the role of ethnicity in American politics. Chapters 8, 9, and 10 deal with black Americans specifically.

Rustin, Bayard. "From Protest to Politics: The Future of the Civil Rights Movement," *Commentary,* Vol. 39 (February 1965).

The argument that black protest must become political is made here.

————. " 'Black Power' and Coalition Politics," *Commentary,* Vol. 42 (September 1966).

The need for development of strategic black-white alliances is stressed in this article, and suggestions are made regarding the direction which such alliances should take.

Wilson, James Q. *Negro Politics.* Glencoe, Ill.: The Free Press, 1960.

An assessment of the current condition of black politics and of its prospects in light of the aspirations of the black community.

Part VI

Blumer, Herbert. "The Future of the Color Line," in John C. Kenney and Edgar T. Thompson (eds.), *The South in Continuity and Change.* Durham, N.C.: Duke University Press, 1965.

This article contradicts the rather popular and optimistic view that the color line, or racism, in the South will inevitably decline with the rise of industrialism. The decline or prosperity of racism in the South rests on decisions made at particular levels of industrial management.

Carmichael, Stokely, and Charles V. Hamilton. *Black Power: The Politics of Liberation in America.* New York: Random House, 1967.

A suggested strategy to help black communities gain control of the institutions within them. Such control is seen as a basic requirement for realizing power.

Moynihan, Daniel P. *Maximum Feasible Misunderstanding: Community Action and the War on Poverty.* Glencoe, Ill.: The Free Press, 1968.

A critical assessment of the Office of Economic Opportunity by a government official.

Powledge, Fred. *Black Power: White Resistance.* Cleveland: World Publishing, 1967.

A descriptive account of the current black protest movement in the South and the North. Some thoughtful suggestions of techniques for overcoming white resistance to the movement toward black equality are made.

Silberman, Charles. *Crisis in Black and White.* New York: Random House, 1964.

A stimulating account of the current crisis in black-white relations, with provocative remedial suggestions.

Van Den Berghe, Pierre. *Race and Racism: A Comparative Perspective.* New York: Wiley, 1967.

A comparative analysis of racism in four different countries, including a suggested scheme for such comparative study. Racism in the United States is included in the comparison.

Index

Index